REVISED
COMMON
LECTIONARY

EPISCOPAL EDITION

NEW REVISED
STANDARD VERSION

3 YEAR CYCLE

1st Printing 2001

REVISED COMMON LECTIONARY
EPISCOPAL EDITION

NEW REVISED STANDARD VERSION

ISBN 0-9618112-4-2

St. Mark's Press
Good Shepherd Episcopal Church
8021 West 21st Street
Wichita, KS 67205-1743
1-800-365-0439

ACKNOWLEDGEMENTS

"The scripture quotations contained herein are from the New Revised Standard Version of the Bible, copyrighted, 1989 by the Division of Christian Education of the National Council of Churches of Christ in the United States of America, and are used by permission. All rights reserved."

Adapted from The Revised Common Lectionary copyright © 1992 by the Consultation on Common Text (CCT), P.O. Box 340003, Room 381, Nashville TN 37203-0003, USA. Used with permission.

The texts of the contemporary Collects of the Day and Psalms are from *The Book of Common Prayer* 1979.

TO ORDER LECTIONARIES
OR TO SUGGEST IMPROVEMENTS

Please contact:
St. Mark's Publishing
Good Shepherd Episcopal Church
8021 West 21st Street
Wichita, KS 67205-1743
Tel: 1-800-365-0439

REVISED COMMON LECTIONARY
EPISCOPAL EDITION

INTRODUCTION

REVISED COMMON LECTIONARY
EPISCOPAL EDITION

INTRODUCTION

Lectionary

A lectionary is a table or list of readings from scripture for use throughout the year in public worship. The word lectionary is related to such words as lection (the selected Bible reading), lector (the reader), and lectern (the place from which the reading is done).

Possible Uses of this Lectionary

1. So that Lectors may practice in advance
2. As an aid in preparation for clergy and musicians
3. For individuals and groups to study the readings before services
4. For reading the lessons during the liturgy (this lectionary is bound so that after a little use it will lie flat)
5. For persons with impaired hearing to follow readings during services
6. As a basis for programs by study groups

The Revised Common Lectionary

The Revised Common Lectionary (RCL) is an ecumenical lectionary with texts selected by the Consultation on Common Texts (CCT), a group with representatives from the Roman Catholic Church and sixteen Protestant denominations, including the Episcopal Church. The RCL is a revision of the CCT's earlier work, *The Common Lectionary*.

The RCL was authorized for trial use in the Episcopal Church by the 71st General Convention in 1994. Continuation of trial use was approved by the 72nd General Convention in 1997.

The RCL: Episcopal Edition

In 2000, the 73rd General Convention approved continued trial use of the RCL. It authorized a list of fifteen separate adaptations to the RCL, which are included in this Episcopal Edition of the RCL.

This edition includes the texts of the contemporary version of the appropriate Collects of the Day from *The Book of Common Prayer* 1979 (BCP). It also includes Propers for Major Feast days on the Episcopal calendar that are not included in the RCL.

In addition, the texts for the "Response" (the Psalm or Canticle which follows the first reading) are taken, whenever possible, from the text of the BCP.

The New Revised Standard Version (NRSV) is the translation used for the lessons. The numbering of verses may differ from other translations. Additionally, since the Psalter in the BCP follows Hebrew, rather than Latin, versification, there are sometimes differences in numbering between the original citation of a Psalm in the RCL and the same text in the BCP. In this edition, the texts of the Psalms are congruent, even though the verse numbers may differ slightly from the original RCL.

Comparison between the RCL and BCP

Like the Eucharistic Lectionary in the BCP, the RCL is arranged in a three-year cycle, in which the Year A always begins on the First Sunday of Advent in years evenly divisible by three. For example, 2001 divided by three results in the whole number 667. Thus the First Sunday of Advent, December 2, 2001, will be the beginning of Year A. In 2002, Advent 1 will be the beginning of Year B, etc.

For most Episcopalians, the differences between the RCL and the BCP would be difficult to discern without careful study and comparison. The major exception is the two different tracks of Old Testament readings in the RCL for the Sundays after Pentecost, each of which is paired with an appropriate response (usually a Psalm).

One track is similar to the arrangement in the BCP. The lesson from the Old Testament is chosen to complement the themes of the particular Gospel reading for the day. The lessons and responses for this track are marked with the symbol, "☩."

The other track arranges the Old Testament lessons in a semi-continuous narrative, similar to the way the Epistles are read in ordinary time. In Year A, the focus is mostly on the major narratives of Genesis and Exodus. Year B focuses on the Davidic narrative and Wisdom literature. Year C focuses on the Prophets, arranged in chronological order, with a heavy emphasis on Jeremiah.

It is strongly urged and intended that a parish pick one track or the other, and not alternate between the two within a given year.

Apocrypha

In the RCL, alternate canonical readings are always provided wherever there is a reading from the Apocrypha.

Length of Readings

Any reading may be lengthened at discretion, and the responses (Psalms) may be lengthened or shortened at discretion (BCP p. 888). Suggested lengthenings are cited in parentheses ( ) and the texts are placed within brackets [ ].

REVISED COMMON LECTIONARY

EPISCOPAL EDITION

**NEW REVISED
STANDARD VERSION**

3 YEAR CYCLE

FIRST SUNDAY OF ADVENT

The Collect

Almighty God, give us grace to cast away the works of darkness, and put on the armor of light, now in the time of this mortal life in which your Son Jesus Christ came to visit us in great humility; that in the last day, when he shall come again in his glorious majesty to judge both the living and the dead, we may rise to the life immortal; through him who lives and reigns with you and the Holy Spirit, one God, now and for ever. *Amen.*

Year A
Isaiah 2:1-5
Psalm 122
Romans 13:11-14
Matthew 24:36-44

The Lesson   Isaiah 2:1-5

The word that Isaiah son of Amoz saw concerning Judah and Jerusalem. In days to come the mountain of the LORD's house shall be established as the highest of the mountains, and shall be raised above the hills; all the nations shall stream to it. Many peoples shall come and say, "Come, let us go up to the mountain of the LORD, to the house of the God of Jacob; that he may teach us his ways and that we may walk in his paths." For out of Zion shall go forth instruction, and the word of the LORD from Jerusalem. He shall judge between the nations, and shall arbitrate for many peoples; they shall beat their swords into plowshares, and their spears into pruning hooks; nation shall not lift up sword against nation, neither shall they learn war any more. O house of Jacob, come, let us walk in the light of the LORD!

The Response   Psalm 122

Psalm 122   *Laetatus sum*

1   I was glad when they said to me, *
    "Let us go to the house of the LORD."
2   Now our feet are standing *
    within your gates, O Jerusalem.
3   Jerusalem is built as a city *
    that is at unity with itself;
4   To which the tribes go up,
  the tribes of the LORD, *
    the assembly of Israel,
    to praise the Name of the LORD.

5 For there are the thrones of judgment, *
    the thrones of the house of David.
6 Pray for the peace of Jerusalem: *
    "May they prosper who love you.
7 Peace be within your walls *
    and quietness within your towers.
8 For my brethren and companions' sake, *
    I pray for your prosperity.
9 Because of the house of the LORD our God, *
    I will seek to do you good."

The Epistle   Romans 13:11-14

You know what time it is, how it is now the moment for you to wake from
sleep. For salvation is nearer to us now than when we became believers; the
night is far gone, the day is near. Let us then lay aside the works of darkness
and put on the armor of light; let us live honorably as in the day, not in
reveling and drunkenness, not in debauchery and licentiousness, not in quarreling and jealousy. Instead, put on the Lord Jesus Christ, and make no
provision for the flesh, to gratify its desires.

The Gospel   Matthew 24:36-44

On the Mount of Olives, Jesus said to his disciples privately about his coming,
"But about that day and hour no one knows, neither the angels of heaven, nor
the Son, but only the Father. For as the days of Noah were, so will be the
coming of the Son of Man. For as in those days before the flood they were
eating and drinking, marrying and giving in marriage, until the day Noah
entered the ark, and they knew nothing until the flood came and swept them all
away, so too will be the coming of the Son of Man. Then two will be in the
field; one will be taken and one will be left. Two women will be grinding meal
together; one will be taken and one will be left. Keep awake therefore, for you
do not know on what day your Lord is coming. But understand this: if the
owner of the house had known in what part of the night the thief was coming,
he would have stayed awake and would not have let his house be broken into.
Therefore you also must be ready, for the Son of Man is coming at an unexpected hour."

Year B
Isaiah 64:1-9
Psalm 80:1-7, 16-18
1 Corinthians 1:3-9
Mark 13:24-37

The Lesson   **Isaiah 64:1-9**

O that you would tear open the heavens and come down, so that the mountains would quake at your presence — as when fire kindles brushwood and the fire causes water to boil — to make your name known to your adversaries, so that the nations might tremble at your presence! When you did awesome deeds that we did not expect, you came down, the mountains quaked at your presence. From ages past no one has heard, no ear has perceived, no eye has seen any God besides you, who works for those who wait for him. You meet those who gladly do right, those who remember you in your ways. But you were angry, and we sinned; because you hid yourself we transgressed. We have all become like one who is unclean, and all our righteous deeds are like a filthy cloth. We all fade like a leaf, and our iniquities, like the wind, take us away. There is no one who calls on your name, or attempts to take hold of you; for you have hidden your face from us, and have delivered us into the hand of our iniquity. Yet, O LORD, you are our Father; we are the clay, and you are our potter; we are all the work of your hand. Do not be exceedingly angry, O LORD, and do not remember iniquity forever. Now consider, we are all your people.

The Response   **Psalm 80:1-7, 16-18**

Psalm 80:1-7, 16-18   *Qui regis Israel*

1   Hear, O Shepherd of Israel, leading Joseph like a flock; *
        shine forth, you that are enthroned upon the cherubim.
2   In the presence of Ephraim, Benjamin, and Manasseh, *
        stir up your strength and come to help us.
3   Restore us, O God of hosts; *
        show the light of your countenance, and we shall be saved.
4   O LORD God of hosts, *
        how long will you be angered
        despite the prayers of your people?
5   You have fed them with the bread of tears; *
        you have given them bowls of tears to drink.
6   You have made us the derision of our neighbors, *
        and our enemies laugh us to scorn.
7   Restore us, O God of hosts; *
        show the light of your countenance, and we shall be saved.

16 Let your hand be upon the man of your right hand, *
   the son of man you have made so strong for yourself.
17 And so will we never turn away from you; *
   give us life, that we may call upon your Name.
18 Restore us, O LORD God of hosts; *
   show the light of your countenance, and we shall be saved.

The Epistle   **1 Corinthians 1:3-9**

Grace to you and peace from God our Father and the Lord Jesus Christ. I give
thanks to my God always for you because of the grace of God that has been
given you in Christ Jesus, for in every way you have been enriched in him, in
speech and knowledge of every kind—just as the testimony of Christ has been
strengthened among you — so that you are not lacking in any spiritual gift as
you wait for the revealing of our Lord Jesus Christ. He will also strengthen
you to the end, so that you may be blameless on the day of our Lord Jesus
Christ. God is faithful; by him you were called into the fellowship of his Son,
Jesus Christ our Lord.

The Gospel   **Mark 13:24-37**

Jesus said, "But in those days, after that suffering, the sun will be darkened,
and the moon will not give its light, and the stars will be falling from heaven,
and the powers in the heavens will be shaken. Then they will see 'the Son of
Man coming in clouds' with great power and glory. Then he will send out the
angels, and gather his elect from the four winds, from the ends of the earth to
the ends of heaven. From the fig tree learn its lesson: as soon as its branch
becomes tender and puts forth its leaves, you know that summer is near. So
also, when you see these things taking place, you know that he is near, at the
very gates. Truly I tell you, this generation will not pass away until all these
things have taken place. Heaven and earth will pass away, but my words will
not pass away. But about that day or hour no one knows, neither the angels in
heaven, nor the Son, but only the Father. Beware, keep alert; for you do not
know when the time will come. It is like a man going on a journey, when he
leaves home and puts his slaves in charge, each with his work, and commands
the doorkeeper to be on the watch. Therefore, keep awake — for you do not
know when the master of the house will come, in the evening, or at midnight,
or at cockcrow, or at dawn, or else he may find you asleep when he comes
suddenly. And what I say to you I say to all: Keep awake."

Jeremiah 33:14-16
Psalm 25:1-9
1 Thessalonians 3:9-13
Luke 21:25-36

The Lesson   Jeremiah 33:14-16

The days are surely coming, says the LORD, when I will fulfill the promise I
made to the house of Israel and the house of Judah. In those days and at that
time I will cause a righteous Branch to spring up for David; and he shall
execute justice and righteousness in the land. In those days Judah will be
saved and Jerusalem will live in safety. And this is the name by which it will
be called: "The LORD is our righteousness."

The Response   Psalm 25:1-9

Psalm 25:1-9   *Ad te, Domine, levavi*
1   To you, O LORD, I lift up my soul;
      my God, I put my trust in you; *
         let me not be humiliated,
            nor let my enemies triumph over me.
2   Let none who look to you be put to shame; *
         let the treacherous be disappointed in their schemes.
3   Show me your ways, O LORD, *
         and teach me your paths.
4   Lead me in your truth and teach me, *
         for you are the God of my salvation;
         in you have I trusted all the day long.
5   Remember, O LORD, your compassion and love, *
         for they are from everlasting.
6   Remember not the sins of my youth and my transgressions; *
         remember me according to your love
         and for the sake of your goodness, O LORD.
7   Gracious and upright is the LORD; *
         therefore he teaches sinners in his way.
8   He guides the humble in doing right *
         and teaches his way to the lowly.
9   All the paths of the LORD are love and faithfulness *
         to those who keep his covenant and his testimonies.

The Epistle   **1 Thessalonians 3:9-13**

How can we thank God enough for you in return for all the joy that we feel before our God because of you? Night and day we pray most earnestly that we may see you face to face and restore whatever is lacking in your faith. Now may our God and Father himself and our Lord Jesus direct our way to you. And may the Lord make you increase and abound in love for one another and for all, just as we abound in love for you. And may he so strengthen your hearts in holiness that you may be blameless before our God and Father at the coming of our Lord Jesus with all his saints.

The Gospel   **Luke 21:25-36**

Jesus said, "There will be signs in the sun, the moon, and the stars, and on the earth distress among nations confused by the roaring of the sea and the waves. People will faint from fear and foreboding of what is coming upon the world, for the powers of the heavens will be shaken. Then they will see 'the Son of Man coming in a cloud' with power and great glory. Now when these things begin to take place, stand up and raise your heads, because your redemption is drawing near." Then he told them a parable: "Look at the fig tree and all the trees; as soon as they sprout leaves you can see for yourselves and know that summer is already near. So also, when you see these things taking place, you know that the kingdom of God is near. Truly I tell you, this generation will not pass away until all things have taken place. Heaven and earth will pass away, but my words will not pass away. Be on guard so that your hearts are not weighed down with dissipation and drunkenness and the worries of this life, and that day catch you unexpectedly, like a trap. For it will come upon all who live on the face of the whole earth. Be alert at all times, praying that you may have the strength to escape all these things that will take place, and to stand before the Son of Man."

SECOND SUNDAY OF ADVENT

The Collect

Merciful God, who sent your messengers the prophets to preach repentance and prepare the way for our salvation: Give us grace to heed their warnings and forsake our sins, that we may greet with joy the coming of Jesus Christ our Redeemer; who lives and reigns with you and the Holy Spirit, one God, now and for ever. *Amen.*

Year A
Isaiah 11:1-10
Psalm 72:1-7, 18-19
Romans 15:4-13
Matthew 3:1-12

The Lesson   Isaiah 11:1-10

A shoot shall come out from the stump of Jesse, and a branch shall grow out of his roots. The spirit of the Lord shall rest on him, the spirit of wisdom and understanding, the spirit of counsel and might, the spirit of knowledge and the fear of the LORD. His delight shall be in the fear of the LORD. He shall not judge by what his eyes see, or decide by what his ears hear; but with righteousness he shall judge the poor, and decide with equity for the meek of the earth; he shall strike the earth with the rod of his mouth, and with the breath of his lips he shall kill the wicked. Righteousness shall be the belt around his waist, and faithfulness the belt around his loins. The wolf shall live with the lamb, the leopard shall lie down with the kid, the calf and the lion and the fatling together, and a little child shall lead them. The cow and the bear shall graze, their young shall lie down together; and the lion shall eat straw like the ox. The nursing child shall play over the hole of the asp, and the weaned child shall put its hand on the adder's den. They will not hurt or destroy on all my holy mountain; for the earth will be full of the knowledge of the LORD as the waters cover the sea. On that day the root of Jesse shall stand as a signal to the peoples; the nations shall inquire of him, and his dwelling shall be glorious.

The Response   Psalm 72:1-7, 18-19

Psalm 72:1-7, 18-19   *Deus, judicium*

  1 Give the King your justice, O God, *
      and your righteousness to the King's Son;

  2 That he may rule your people righteously *
      and the poor with justice;

  3 That the mountains may bring prosperity to the people, *
      and the little hills bring righteousness.

  4 He shall defend the needy among the people; *
      he shall rescue the poor and crush the oppressor.

  5 He shall live as long as the sun and moon endure, *
      from one generation to another.

  6 He shall come down like rain upon the mown field, *
      like showers that water the earth.

7   In his time shall the righteous flourish; *
         there shall be abundance of peace till the moon shall
             be no more.
18   Blessed be the LORD God, the God of Israel, *
         who alone does wondrous deeds!
19   And blessed be his glorious Name for ever! *
         and may all the earth be filled with his glory.
         Amen. Amen.

The Epistle   Romans 15:4-13

Whatever was written in former days was written for our instruction, so that
by steadfastness and by the encouragement of the scriptures we might have
hope. May the God of steadfastness and encouragement grant you to live in
harmony with one another, in accordance with Christ Jesus, so that together
you may with one voice glorify the God and Father of our Lord Jesus Christ.
Welcome one another, therefore, just as Christ has welcomed you, for the
glory of God. For I tell you that Christ has become a servant of the circumcised on behalf of the truth of God in order that he might confirm the promises
given to the patriarchs, and in order that the Gentiles might glorify God for his
mercy. As it is written, "Therefore I will confess you among the Gentiles, and
sing praises to your name"; and again he says, "Rejoice, O Gentiles, with his
people"; and again, "Praise the Lord, all you Gentiles, and let all the peoples
praise him"; and again Isaiah says, "The root of Jesse shall come, the one who
rises to rule the Gentiles; in him the Gentiles shall hope." May the God of
hope fill you with all joy and peace in believing, so that you may abound in
hope by the power of the Holy Spirit.

The Gospel   Matthew 3:1-12

In those days John the Baptist appeared in the wilderness of Judea, proclaiming, "Repent, for the kingdom of heaven has come near." This is the one of
whom the prophet Isaiah spoke when he said, "The voice of one crying out in
the wilderness: 'Prepare the way of the Lord, make his paths straight.' " Now
John wore clothing of camel's hair with a leather belt around his waist, and
his food was locusts and wild honey. Then the people of Jerusalem and all
Judea were going out to him, and all the region along the Jordan, and they
were baptized by him in the river Jordan, confessing their sins. But when he
saw many Pharisees and Sadducees coming for baptism, he said to them,
"You brood of vipers! Who warned you to flee from the wrath to come? Bear
fruit worthy of repentance. Do not presume to say to yourselves, 'We have
Abraham as our ancestor'; for I tell you, God is able from these stones to
raise up children to Abraham. Even now the ax is lying at the root of the trees;
every tree therefore that does not bear good fruit is cut down and thrown into

the fire. I baptize you with water for repentance, but one who is more power-ful than I is coming after me; I am not worthy to carry his sandals. He will baptize you with the Holy Spirit and fire. His winnowing fork is in his hand, and he will clear his threshing floor and will gather his wheat into the granary; but the chaff he will burn with unquenchable fire."

Year B
Isaiah 40:1-11
Psalm 85:1-2, 8-13
2 Peter 3:8-15a
Mark 1:1-8

The Lesson   **Isaiah 40:1-11**

Comfort, O comfort my people, says your God. Speak tenderly to Jerusalem, and cry to her that she has served her term, that her penalty is paid, that she has received from the LORD's hand double for all her sins. A voice cries out: "In the wilderness prepare the way of the LORD, make straight in the desert a highway for our God. Every valley shall be lifted up, and every mountain and hill be made low; the uneven ground shall become level, and the rough places a plain. Then the glory of the LORD shall be revealed, and all people shall see it together, for the mouth of the LORD has spoken." A voice says, "Cry out!" And I said, "What shall I cry?" All people are grass, their constancy is like the flower of the field. The grass withers, the flower fades, when the breath of the LORD blows upon it; surely the people are grass. The grass withers, the flower fades; but the word of our God will stand forever. Get you up to a high mountain, O Zion, herald of good tidings; lift up your voice with strength, O Jerusalem, herald of good tidings, lift it up, do not fear; say to the cities of Judah, "Here is your God!" See, the Lord GOD comes with might, and his arm rules for him; his reward is with him, and his recompense before him. He will feed his flock like a shepherd; he will gather the lambs in his arms, and carry them in his bosom, and gently lead the mother sheep.

The Response   **Psalm 85:1-2, 8-13**

Psalm 85:1-2, 8-13   *Benedixisti, Domine*

1   You have been gracious to your land, O LORD, *
       you have restored the good fortune of Jacob.

2   You have forgiven the iniquity of your people *
       and blotted out all their sins.

8   I will listen to what the LORD God is saying, *
       for he is speaking peace to his faithful people
       and to those who turn their hearts to him.

9   Truly, his salvation is very near to those who fear him, *
        that his glory may dwell in our land.
10   Mercy and truth have met together; *
        righteousness and peace have kissed each other.
11   Truth shall spring up from the earth, *
        and righteousness shall look down from heaven.
12   The Lord will indeed grant prosperity, *
        and our land will yield its increase.
13   Righteousness shall go before him, *
        and peace shall be a pathway for his feet.

The Epistle   2 Peter 3:8-15*a*

Do not ignore this one fact, beloved, that with the Lord one day is like a
thousand years, and a thousand years are like one day. The Lord is not slow
about his promise, as some think of slowness, but is patient with you, not
wanting any to perish, but all to come to repentance. But the day of the Lord
will come like a thief, and then the heavens will pass away with a loud noise,
and the elements will be dissolved with fire, and the earth and everything that
is done on it will be disclosed. Since all these things are to be dissolved in this
way, what sort of persons ought you to be in leading lives of holiness and
godliness, waiting for and hastening the coming of the day of God, because of
which the heavens will be set ablaze and dissolved, and the elements will melt
with fire? But, in accordance with his promise, we wait for new heavens and a
new earth, where righteousness is at home. Therefore, beloved, while you are
waiting for these things, strive to be found by him at peace, without spot or
blemish; and regard the patience of our Lord as salvation.

The Gospel   Mark 1:1-8

The beginning of the good news of Jesus Christ, the Son of God. As it is
written in the prophet Isaiah, "See, I am sending my messenger ahead of you,
who will prepare your way; the voice of one crying out in the wilderness:
'Prepare the way of the Lord, make his paths straight,' " John the baptizer
appeared in the wilderness, proclaiming a baptism of repentance for the
forgiveness of sins. And people from the whole Judean countryside and all the
people of Jerusalem were going out to him, and were baptized by him in the
river Jordan, confessing their sins. Now John was clothed with camel's hair,
with a leather belt around his waist, and he ate locusts and wild honey. He
proclaimed, "The one who is more powerful than I is coming after me; I am
not worthy to stoop down and untie the thong of his sandals. I have baptized
you with water; but he will baptize you with the Holy Spirit."

Baruch 5:1-9 or *Malachi 3:1-4*
Canticle 4 or *16*
Philippians 1:3-11
Luke 3:1-6

The Lesson   Baruch 5:1-9 *or* Malachi 3:1-4
Baruch 5:1-9

Take off the garment of your sorrow and affliction, O Jerusalem, and put on forever the beauty of the glory from God. Put on the robe of the righteousness that comes from God; put on your head the diadem of the glory of the Everlasting; for God will show your splendor everywhere under heaven. For God will give you evermore the name, "Righteous Peace, Godly Glory." Arise, O Jerusalem, stand upon the height; look toward the east, and see your children gathered from west and east at the word of the Holy One, rejoicing that God has remembered them. For they went out from you on foot, led away by their enemies; but God will bring them back to you, carried in glory, as on a royal throne. For God has ordered that every high mountain and the everlasting hills be made low and the valleys filled up, to make level ground, so that Israel may walk safely in the glory of God. The woods and every fragrant tree have shaded Israel at God's command. For God will lead Israel with joy, in the light of his glory, with the mercy and righteousness that come from him.

or, Malachi 3:1-4

See, I am sending my messenger to prepare the way before me, and the Lord whom you seek will suddenly come to his temple. The messenger of the covenant in whom you delight — indeed, he is coming, says the LORD of hosts. But who can endure the day of his coming, and who can stand when he appears? For he is like a refiner's fire and like fullers' soap; he will sit as a refiner and purifier of silver, and he will purify the descendants of Levi and refine them like gold and silver, until they present offerings to the LORD in righteousness. Then the offering of Judah and Jerusalem will be pleasing to the LORD as in the days of old and as in former years.

The Response   **Canticle 4** *or* **16**
Canticle 4 *(Page 50 BCP)*

or, **Canticle 16**   **The Song of Zechariah** *Benedictus Dominus Deus*
Luke 1:68-79

Blessed be the Lord, the God of Israel; *
    he has come to his people and set them free.
He has raised up for us a mighty savior, *
    born of the house of his servant David.
Through his holy prophets he promised of old,
that he would save us from our enemies, *
    from the hands of all who hate us.
He promised to show mercy to our fathers *
    and to remember his holy covenant.
This was the oath he swore to our father Abraham, *
    to set us free from the hands of our enemies,
Free to worship him without fear, *
    holy and righteous in his sight
    all the days of our life.
You, my child, shall be called the prophet of the Most High, *
    for you will go before the Lord to prepare his way,
To give his people knowledge of salvation *
    by the forgiveness of their sins.
In the tender compassion of our God *
    the dawn from on high shall break upon us,
To shine on those who dwell in darkness and the
               shadow of death, *
    and to guide our feet into the way of peace.

The Epistle   **Philippians 1:3-11**

I thank my God every time I remember you, constantly praying with joy in every one of my prayers for all of you, because of your sharing in the gospel from the first day until now. I am confident of this, that the one who began a good work among you will bring it to completion by the day of Jesus Christ. It is right for me to think this way about all of you, because you hold me in your heart, for all of you share in God's grace with me, both in my imprisonment and in the defense and confirmation of the gospel. For God is my witness, how I long for all of you with the compassion of Christ Jesus. And this is my prayer, that your love may overflow more and more with knowledge and full insight to help you to determine what is best, so that in the day of Christ you may be pure and blameless, having produced the harvest of righteousness that comes through Jesus Christ for the glory and praise of God.

The Gospel   **Luke 3:1-6**

In the fifteenth year of the reign of Emperor Tiberius, when Pontius Pilate was
governor of Judea, and Herod was ruler of Galilee, and his brother Philip ruler
of the region of Ituraea and Trachonitis, and Lysanias ruler of Abilene, during
the high priesthood of Annas and Caiaphas, the word of God came to John son
of Zechariah in the wilderness. He went into all the region around the Jordan,
proclaiming a baptism of repentance for the forgiveness of sins, as it is written
in the book of the words of the prophet Isaiah, "The voice of one crying out in
the wilderness: 'Prepare the way of the Lord, make his paths straight. Every
valley shall be filled, and every mountain and hill shall be made low, and the
crooked shall be made straight, and the rough ways made smooth; and all
flesh shall see the salvation of God.' "

THIRD SUNDAY OF ADVENT

The Collect

Stir up your power, O Lord, and with great might come among us; and,
because we are sorely hindered by our sins, let your bountiful grace and mercy
speedily help and deliver us; through Jesus Christ our Lord, to whom, with
you and the Holy Spirit, be honor and glory, now and for ever. *Amen.*

Year A
Isaiah 35:1-10
Psalm 146:4-9 or *Canticle 3* or *15*
James 5:7-10
Matthew 11:2-11

The Lesson   **Isaiah 35:1-10**

The wilderness and the dry land shall be glad, the desert shall rejoice and
blossom; like the crocus it shall blossom abundantly, and rejoice with joy and
singing. The glory of Lebanon shall be given to it, the majesty of Carmel and
Sharon. They shall see the glory of the LORD, the majesty of our God.
Strengthen the weak hands, and make firm the feeble knees. Say to those who
are of a fearful heart, "Be strong, do not fear! Here is your God. He will come
with vengeance, with terrible recompense. He will come and save you." Then
the eyes of the blind shall be opened, and the ears of the deaf unstopped; then
the lame shall leap like a deer, and the tongue of the speechless sing for joy.
For waters shall break forth in the wilderness, and streams in the desert; the
burning sand shall become a pool, and the thirsty ground springs of water; the
haunt of jackals shall become a swamp, the grass shall become reeds and
rushes. A highway shall be there, and it shall be called the Holy Way; the
unclean shall not travel on it, but it shall be for God's people; no traveler, not
even fools, shall go astray. No lion shall be there, nor shall any ravenous beast

come up on it; they shall not be found there, but the redeemed shall walk there. And the ransomed of the LORD shall return, and come to Zion with singing; everlasting joy shall be upon their heads; they shall obtain joy and gladness, and sorrow and sighing shall flee away.

The Response Psalm 146:4-9 *or* **Canticle 3** *or* **15**

Psalm 146:4-9 *Lauda, anima mea*

4 Happy are they who have the God of Jacob for their help! *
    whose hope is in the LORD their God;
5 Who made heaven and earth, the seas, and all that is in them; *
    who keeps his promise for ever;
6 Who gives justice to those who are oppressed, *
    and food to those who hunger.
7 The LORD sets the prisoners free;
  the LORD opens the eyes of the blind; *
    the LORD lifts up those who are bowed down;
8 The LORD loves the righteous;
  the LORD cares for the stranger; *
    he sustains the orphan and widow,
    but frustrates the way of the wicked.
9 The LORD shall reign for ever, *
    your God, O Zion, throughout all generations.
    Hallelujah!

or, **Canticle 3** *(Page 50 BCP)*

or, **Canticle 15** **The Song of Mary** *Magnificat*
              Luke 1:46-55

My soul proclaims the greatness of the Lord,
my spirit rejoices in God my Savior; *
    for he has looked with favor on his lowly servant.
From this day all generations will call me blessed: *
    the Almighty has done great things for me,
    and holy is his Name.
He has mercy on those who fear him *
    in every generation.
He has shown the strength of his arm, *
    he has scattered the proud in their conceit.
He has cast down the mighty from their thrones, *
    and has lifted up the lowly.
He has filled the hungry with good things, *
    and the rich he has sent away empty.

He has come to the help of his servant Israel, *
    for he has remembered his promise of mercy,
The promise he made to our fathers, *
    to Abraham and his children for ever.

The Epistle   James 5:7-10

Be patient, therefore, beloved, until the coming of the Lord. The farmer waits
for the precious crop from the earth, being patient with it until it receives the
early and the late rains. You also must be patient. Strengthen your hearts, for
the coming of the Lord is near. Beloved, do not grumble against one another,
so that you may not be judged. See, the Judge is standing at the doors! As an
example of suffering and patience, beloved, take the prophets who spoke in the
name of the Lord.

The Gospel   Matthew 11:2-11

When John (the Baptist) heard in prison what the Messiah was doing, he sent
word by his disciples and said to him, "Are you the one who is to come, or are
we to wait for another?" Jesus answered them, "Go and tell John what you
hear and see: the blind receive their sight, the lame walk, the lepers are
cleansed, the deaf hear, the dead are raised, and the poor have good news
brought to them. And blessed is anyone who takes no offense at me." As they
went away, Jesus began to speak to the crowds about John: "What did you go
out into the wilderness to look at? A reed shaken by the wind? What then did
you go out to see? Someone dressed in soft robes? Look, those who wear soft
robes are in royal palaces. What then did you go out to see? A prophet? Yes, I
tell you, and more than a prophet. This is the one about whom it is written,
'See, I am sending my messenger ahead of you, who will prepare your way
before you.' Truly I tell you, among those born of women no one has arisen
greater than John the Baptist; yet the least in the kingdom of heaven is greater
than he."

Year B
Isaiah 61:1-4, 8-11
Psalm 126 or Canticle 3 or 15
1 Thessalonians 5:16-24
John 1:6-8, 19-28

The Lesson   Isaiah 61:1-4, 8-11

The spirit of the Lord GOD is upon me, because the LORD has anointed me; he
has sent me to bring good news to the oppressed, to bind up the brokenhearted, to proclaim liberty to the captives, and release to the prisoners; to
proclaim the year of the LORD's favor, and the day of vengeance of our God;

to comfort all who mourn; to provide for those who mourn in Zion — to give them a garland instead of ashes, the oil of gladness instead of mourning, the mantle of praise instead of a faint spirit. They will be called oaks of righteousness, the planting of the LORD, to display his glory. They shall build up the ancient ruins, they shall raise up the former devastations; they shall repair the ruined cities, the devastations of many generations. For I the LORD love justice, I hate robbery and wrongdoing; I will faithfully give them their recompense, and I will make an everlasting covenant with them. Their descendants shall be known among the nations, and their offspring among the peoples; all who see them shall acknowledge that they are a people whom the LORD has blessed. I will greatly rejoice in the LORD, my whole being shall exult in my God; for he has clothed me with the garments of salvation, he has covered me with the robe of righteousness, as a bridegroom decks himself with a garland, and as a bride adorns herself with her jewels. For as the earth brings forth its shoots, and as a garden causes what is sown in it to spring up, so the Lord GOD will cause righteousness and praise to spring up before all the nations.

The Response   **Psalm 126** *or* **Canticle 3** *or* **15**
Psalm 126   *In convertendo*

1   When the LORD restored the fortunes of Zion, *
        then were we like those who dream.
2   Then was our mouth filled with laughter, *
        and our tongue with shouts of joy.
3   Then they said among the nations, *
        "The LORD has done great things for them."
4   The LORD has done great things for us, *
        and we are glad indeed.
5   Restore our fortunes, O LORD, *
        like the watercourses of the Negev.
6   Those who sowed with tears *
        will reap with songs of joy.
7   Those who go out weeping, carrying the seed, *
        will come again with joy, shouldering their sheaves.

or, **Canticle 3**   *(Page 50 BCP)*

or, **Canticle 15**   **The Song of Mary**   *Magnificat*
                Luke 1:46-55
        My soul proclaims the greatness of the Lord,
        my spirit rejoices in God my Savior; *
            for he has looked with favor on his lowly servant.

From this day all generations will call me blessed: *
 the Almighty has done great things for me,
 and holy is his Name.
He has mercy on those who fear him *
 in every generation.
He has shown the strength of his arm, *
 he has scattered the proud in their conceit.
He has cast down the mighty from their thrones, *
 and has lifted up the lowly.
He has filled the hungry with good things, *
 and the rich he has sent away empty.
He has come to the help of his servant Israel, *
 for he has remembered his promise of mercy,
The promise he made to our fathers, *
 to Abraham and his children for ever.

The Epistle   1 Thessalonians 5:16-24

Rejoice always, pray without ceasing, give thanks in all circumstances; for
this is the will of God in Christ Jesus for you. Do not quench the Spirit. Do
not despise the words of prophets, but test everything; hold fast to what is
good; abstain from every form of evil. May the God of peace himself sanctify
you entirely; and may your spirit and soul and body be kept sound and
blameless at the coming of our Lord Jesus Christ. The one who calls you is
faithful, and he will do this.

The Gospel   John 1:6-8, 19-28

There was a man sent from God, whose name was John. He came as a witness
to testify to the light, so that all might believe through him. He himself was
not the light, but he came to testify to the light. This is the testimony given by
John when the Jews sent priests and Levites from Jerusalem to ask him, "Who
are you?" He confessed and did not deny it, but confessed, "I am not the
Messiah." And they asked him, "What then? Are you Elijah?" He said, "I am
not." "Are you the prophet?" He answered, "No." Then they said to him,
"Who are you? Let us have an answer for those who sent us. What do you say
about yourself?" He said, "I am the voice of one crying out in the wilderness,
'Make straight the way of the Lord,' " as the prophet Isaiah said. Now they
had been sent from the Pharisees. They asked him, "Why then are you baptizing if you are neither the Messiah, nor Elijah, nor the prophet?" John answered them, "I baptize with water. Among you stands one whom you do not
know, the one who is coming after me; I am not worthy to untie the thong of
his sandal." This took place in Bethany across the Jordan where John was
baptizing.

Year C

Zephaniah 3:14-20
Canticle 9
Philippians 4:4-7
Luke 3:7-18

The Lesson   **Zephaniah 3:14-20**

Sing aloud, O daughter Zion; shout, O Israel! Rejoice and exult with all your
heart, O daughter Jerusalem! The LORD has taken away the judgments against
you, he has turned away your enemies. The king of Israel, the LORD, is in your
midst; you shall fear disaster no more. On that day it shall be said to Jerusalem: Do not fear, O Zion; do not let your hands grow weak. The LORD, your
God, is in your midst, a warrior who gives victory; he will rejoice over you
with gladness, he will renew you in his love; he will exult over you with loud
singing as on a day of festival. I will remove disaster from you, so that you
will not bear reproach for it. I will deal with all your oppressors at that time.
And I will save the lame and gather the outcast, and I will change their shame
into praise and renown in all the earth. At that time I will bring you home, at
the time when I gather you; for I will make you renowned and praised among
all the peoples of the earth, when I restore your fortunes before your eyes, says
the LORD.

The Response   **Canticle 9**
Canticle 9   The First Song of Isaiah   *Ecce, Deus*
                         Isaiah 12:2-6
Surely, it is God who saves me; *
    I will trust in him and not be afraid.
For the Lord is my stronghold and my sure defense, *
    and he will be my Savior.
Therefore you shall draw water with rejoicing *
    from the springs of salvation.
And on that day you shall say, *
    Give thanks to the Lord and call upon his Name;
Make his deeds known among the peoples; *
    see that they remember that his Name is exalted.
Sing the praises of the Lord, for he has done great things, *
    and this is known in all the world.
Cry aloud, inhabitants of Zion, ring out your joy, *
    for the great one in the midst of you is the Holy One of Israel.

The Epistle   **Philippians 4:4-7**

Rejoice in the Lord always; again I will say, Rejoice. Let your gentleness be
known to everyone. The Lord is near. Do not worry about anything, but in
everything by prayer and supplication with thanksgiving let your requests be
made known to God. And the peace of God, which surpasses all understanding, will guard your hearts and your minds in Christ Jesus.

The Gospel   **Luke 3:7-18**

John said to the crowds that came out to be baptized by him, "You brood of
vipers! Who warned you to flee from the wrath to come? Bear fruits worthy of
repentance. Do not begin to say to yourselves, 'We have Abraham as our
ancestor'; for I tell you, God is able from these stones to raise up children to
Abraham. Even now the ax is lying at the root of the trees; every tree therefore
that does not bear good fruit is cut down and thrown into the fire." And the
crowds asked him, "What then should we do?" In reply he said to them,
"Whoever has two coats must share with anyone who has none; and whoever
has food must do likewise." Even tax collectors came to be baptized, and they
asked him, "Teacher, what should we do?" He said to them, "Collect no more
than the amount prescribed for you." Soldiers also asked him, "And we, what
should we do?" He said to them, "Do not extort money from anyone by threats
or false accusation, and be satisfied with your wages." As the people were
filled with expectation, and all were questioning in their hearts concerning
John, whether he might be the Messiah, John answered all of them by saying,
"I baptize you with water; but one who is more powerful than I is coming; I
am not worthy to untie the thong of his sandals. He will baptize you with the
Holy Spirit and fire. His winnowing fork is in his hand, to clear his threshing
floor and to gather the wheat into his granary; but the chaff he will burn with
unquenchable fire." So, with many other exhortations, he proclaimed the good
news to the people.

FOURTH SUNDAY OF ADVENT

The Collect

Purify our conscience, Almighty God, by your daily visitation, that your Son
Jesus Christ, at his coming, may find in us a mansion prepared for himself;
who lives and reigns with you, in the unity of the Holy Spirit, one God, now
and for ever. *Amen.*

Year A
Isaiah 7:10-16
Psalm 80:1-7, 16-18
Romans 1:1-7
Matthew 1:18-25

The Lesson   **Isaiah 7:10-16**

The LORD spoke to Ahaz, saying, Ask a sign of the LORD your God; let it be deep as Sheol or high as heaven. But Ahaz said, I will not ask, and I will not put the LORD to the test. Then Isaiah said: "Hear then, O house of David! Is it too little for you to weary mortals, that you weary my God also? Therefore the Lord himself will give you a sign. Look, the young woman is with child and shall bear a son, and shall name him Immanuel. He shall eat curds and honey by the time he knows how to refuse the evil and choose the good. For before the child knows how to refuse the evil and choose the good, the land before whose two kings you are in dread will be deserted."

The Response   **Psalm 80:1-7, 16-18**

Psalm 80:1-7, 16-18   *Qui regis Israel*

1   Hear, O Shepherd of Israel, leading Joseph like a flock; *
    shine forth, you that are enthroned upon the cherubim.
2   In the presence of Ephraim, Benjamin, and Manasseh, *
    stir up your strength and come to help us.
3   Restore us, O God of hosts; *
    show the light of your countenance, and we shall be saved.
4   O LORD God of hosts, *
    how long will you be angered
    despite the prayers of your people?
5   You have fed them with the bread of tears; *
    you have given them bowls of tears to drink.
6   You have made us the derision of our neighbors, *
    and our enemies laugh us to scorn.
7   Restore us, O God of hosts; *
    show the light of your countenance, and we shall be saved.
16   Let your hand be upon the man of your right hand, *
    the son of man you have made so strong for yourself.
17   And so will we never turn away from you; *
    give us life, that we may call upon your Name.
18   Restore us, O LORD God of hosts; *
    show the light of your countenance, and we shall be saved.

The Epistle   Romans 1:1-7

Paul, a servant of Jesus Christ, called to be an apostle, set apart for the gospel of God, which he promised beforehand through his prophets in the holy scriptures, the gospel concerning his Son, who was descended from David according to the flesh and was declared to be Son of God with power according to the spirit of holiness by resurrection from the dead, Jesus Christ our Lord, through whom we have received grace and apostleship to bring about the obedience of faith among all the Gentiles for the sake of his name, including yourselves who are called to belong to Jesus Christ, To all God's beloved in Rome, who are called to be saints: Grace to you and peace from God our Father and the Lord Jesus Christ.

The Gospel   Matthew 1:18-25

Now the birth of Jesus the Messiah took place in this way. When his mother Mary had been engaged to Joseph, but before they lived together, she was found to be with child from the Holy Spirit. Her husband Joseph, being a righteous man and unwilling to expose her to public disgrace, planned to dismiss her quietly. But just when he had resolved to do this, an angel of the Lord appeared to him in a dream and said, "Joseph, son of David, do not be afraid to take Mary as your wife, for the child conceived in her is from the Holy Spirit. She will bear a son, and you are to name him Jesus, for he will save his people from their sins." All this took place to fulfill what had been spoken by the Lord through the prophet: "Look, the virgin shall conceive and bear a son, and they shall name him Emmanuel," which means, "God is with us." When Joseph awoke from sleep, he did as the angel of the Lord commanded him; he took her as his wife, but had no marital relations with her until she had borne a son; and he named him Jesus.

Year B
2 Samuel 7:1-11, 16
Psalm 89:1-4, 19-26 or Canticle 3 or 15
Romans 16:25-27
Luke 1:26-38

The Lesson   2 Samuel 7:1-11, 16

Now when (David) the king was settled in his house, and the LORD had given him rest from all his enemies around him, the king said to the prophet Nathan, "See now, I am living in a house of cedar, but the ark of God stays in a tent." Nathan said to the king, "Go, do all that you have in mind; for the LORD is with you." But that same night the word of the LORD came to Nathan: Go and tell my servant David: Thus says the LORD: Are you the one to build me a house to live in? I have not lived in a house since the day I brought up the people of Israel from Egypt to this day, but I have been moving about in a tent and a tabernacle. Wherever I have moved about among all the people of Israel, did I ever speak a word with any of the tribal leaders of Israel, whom I commanded to shepherd my people Israel, saying, "Why have you not built me a house of cedar?" Now therefore thus you shall say to my servant David: Thus says the LORD of hosts: I took you from the pasture, from following the sheep to be prince over my people Israel; and I have been with you wherever you went, and have cut off all your enemies from before you; and I will make for you a great name, like the name of the great ones of the earth. And I will appoint a place for my people Israel and will plant them, so that they may live in their own place, and be disturbed no more; and evildoers shall afflict them no more, as formerly, from the time that I appointed judges over my people Israel; and I will give you rest from all your enemies. Moreover the LORD declares to you that the LORD will make you a house. Your house and your kingdom shall be made sure forever before me; your throne shall be established forever.

The Response   Psalm 89:1-4, 19-26
Psalm 89:1-4, 19-26   *Misericordias Domini*

1   Your love, O LORD, for ever will I sing; *
    from age to age my mouth will proclaim your faithfulness.
2   For I am persuaded that your love is established for ever; *
    you have set your faithfulness firmly in the heavens.
3   "I have made a covenant with my chosen one; *
    I have sworn an oath to David my servant:
4   'I will establish your line for ever, *
    and preserve your throne for all generations.'"
19 You spoke once in a vision and said to your faithful people: *
    "I have set the crown upon a warrior
    and have exalted one chosen out of the people.
20 I have found David my servant; *
    with my holy oil have I anointed him.
21 My hand will hold him fast *
    and my arm will make him strong.
22 No enemy shall deceive him, *
    nor any wicked man bring him down.
23 I will crush his foes before him *
    and strike down those who hate him.
24 My faithfulness and love shall be with him, *
    and he shall be victorious through my Name.

25 I shall make his dominion extend *
       from the Great Sea to the River.
26 He will say to me, 'You are my Father, *
       my God, and the rock of my salvation.'

or, **Canticle 3** *(Page 50 BCP)*

or, **Canticle 15 The Song of Mary** *Magnificat*
       Luke 1:46-55
       My soul proclaims the greatness of the Lord,
       my spirit rejoices in God my Savior; *
          for he has looked with favor on his lowly servant.
       From this day all generations will call me blessed: *
          the Almighty has done great things for me,
          and holy is his Name.
       He has mercy on those who fear him *
          in every generation.
       He has shown the strength of his arm, *
          he has scattered the proud in their conceit.
       He has cast down the mighty from their thrones, *
          and has lifted up the lowly.
       He has filled the hungry with good things, *
          and the rich he has sent away empty.
       He has come to the help of his servant Israel, *
          for he has remembered his promise of mercy,
       The promise he made to our fathers, *
          to Abraham and his children for ever.

The Epistle   Romans 16:25-27

Now to God who is able to strengthen you according to my gospel and the
proclamation of Jesus Christ, according to the revelation of the mystery that
was kept secret for long ages but is now disclosed, and through the prophetic
writings is made known to all the Gentiles, according to the command of the
eternal God, to bring about the obedience of faith — to the only wise God,
through Jesus Christ, to whom be the glory forever! Amen.

The Gospel   Luke 1:26-38

In the sixth month the angel Gabriel was sent by God to a town in Galilee
called Nazareth, to a virgin engaged to a man whose name was Joseph, of the
house of David. The virgin's name was Mary. And he came to her and said,
"Greetings, favored one! The Lord is with you." But she was much perplexed
by his words and pondered what sort of greeting this might be. The angel said

to her, "Do not be afraid, Mary, for you have found favor with God. And now, you will conceive in your womb and bear a son, and you will name him Jesus. He will be great, and will be called the Son of the Most High, and the Lord God will give to him the throne of his ancestor David. He will reign over the house of Jacob forever, and of his kingdom there will be no end." Mary said to the angel, "How can this be, since I am a virgin?" The angel said to her, "The Holy Spirit will come upon you, and the power of the Most High will over-shadow you; therefore the child to be born will be holy; he will be called Son of God. And now, your relative Elizabeth in her old age has also conceived a son; and this is the sixth month for her who was said to be barren. For nothing will be impossible with God." Then Mary said, "Here am I, the servant of the Lord; let it be with me according to your word." Then the angel departed from her.

Year C
*Micah 5:2-5*a
Canticle 3 or 15 or Psalm 80:1-7
Hebrews 10:5-10
Luke 1:39-45, (46-55)

The Lesson   **Micah 5:2-5***a*
But you, O Bethlehem of Ephrathah, who are one of the little clans of Judah, from you shall come forth for me one who is to rule in Israel, whose origin is from of old, from ancient days. Therefore he shall give them up until the time when she who is in labor has brought forth; then the rest of his kindred shall return to the people of Israel. And he shall stand and feed his flock in the strength of the LORD, in the majesty of the name of the LORD his God. And they shall live secure, for now he shall be great to the ends of the earth; and he shall be the one of peace.

The Response   **Canticle 3 or 15 or Psalm 80:1-7**
Canticle 3 *(Page 50 BCP)*

or, **Canticle 15   The Song of Mary**   *Magnificat*
                    Luke 1:46-55
My soul proclaims the greatness of the Lord,
my spirit rejoices in God my Savior; *
        for he has looked with favor on his lowly servant.
From this day all generations will call me blessed: *
        the Almighty has done great things for me,
        and holy is his Name.

He has mercy on those who fear him *
   in every generation.
He has shown the strength of his arm, *
   he has scattered the proud in their conceit.
He has cast down the mighty from their thrones, *
   and has lifted up the lowly.
He has filled the hungry with good things, *
   and the rich he has sent away empty.
He has come to the help of his servant Israel, *
   for he has remembered his promise of mercy,
The promise he made to our fathers, *
   to Abraham and his children for ever.

or, **Psalm 80:1-7**   *Qui regis Israel*

1   Hear, O Shepherd of Israel, leading Joseph like a flock; *
      shine forth, you that are enthroned upon the cherubim.
2   In the presence of Ephraim, Benjamin, and Manasseh, *
      stir up your strength and come to help us.
3   Restore us, O God of hosts; *
      show the light of your countenance, and we shall be saved.
4   O LORD God of hosts, *
      how long will you be angered
      despite the prayers of your people?
5   You have fed them with the bread of tears; *
      you have given them bowls of tears to drink.
6   You have made us the derision of our neighbors, *
      and our enemies laugh us to scorn.
7   Restore us, O God of hosts; *
      show the light of your countenance, and we shall be saved.

The Epistle   Hebrews 10:5-10

When Christ came into the world, he said, "Sacrifices and offerings you have
not desired, but a body you have prepared for me; in burnt offerings and sin
offerings you have taken no pleasure. Then I said, 'See, God, I have come to
do your will, O God' (in the scroll of the book it is written of me)." When he
said above, "You have neither desired nor taken pleasure in sacrifices and
offerings and burnt offerings and sin offerings" (these are offered according to
the law), then he added, "See, I have come to do your will." He abolishes the
first in order to establish the second. And it is by God's will that we have been
sanctified through the offering of the body of Jesus Christ once for all.

The Gospel   Luke 1:39-45 (46-55)
Luke 1:39-45

In those days Mary set out and went with haste to a Judean town in the hill country, where she entered the house of Zechariah and greeted Elizabeth. When Elizabeth heard Mary's greeting, the child leaped in her womb. And Elizabeth was filled with the Holy Spirit and exclaimed with a loud cry, "Blessed are you among women, and blessed is the fruit of your womb. And why has this happened to me, that the mother of my Lord comes to me? For as soon as I heard the sound of your greeting, the child in my womb leaped for joy. And blessed is she who believed that there would be a fulfillment of what was spoken to her by the Lord."

Luke 1:(46-55) [And Mary said, "My soul magnifies the Lord, and my spirit rejoices in God my Savior, for he has looked with favor on the lowliness of his servant. Surely, from now on all generations will call me blessed; for the Mighty One has done great things for me, and holy is his name. His mercy is for those who fear him from generation to generation. He has shown strength with his arm; he has scattered the proud in the thoughts of their hearts. He has brought down the powerful from their thrones, and lifted up the lowly; he has filled the hungry with good things, and sent the rich away empty. He has helped his servant Israel, in remembrance of his mercy, according to the promise he made to our ancestors, to Abraham and to his descendants forever."]

NATIVITY OF OUR LORD JESUS CHRIST (CHRISTMAS EVE & DAY)
DECEMBER 24 & 25

The Collect

O God, you make us glad by the yearly festival of the birth of your only Son Jesus Christ: Grant that we, who joyfully receive him as our Redeemer, may with sure confidence behold him when he comes to be our Judge; who lives and reigns with you and the Holy Spirit, one God, now and for ever. *Amen.*

or this

O God, you have caused this holy night to shine with the brightness of the true Light: Grant that we, who have known the mystery of that Light on earth, may also enjoy him perfectly in heaven; where with you and the Holy Spirit he lives and reigns, one God, in glory everlasting. *Amen.*

or this

Almighty God, you have given your only-begotten Son to take our nature upon him, and to be born [this day] of a pure virgin: Grant that we, who have been born again and made your children by adoption and grace, may daily be renewed by your Holy Spirit; through our Lord Jesus Christ, to whom with you and the same Spirit be honor and glory, now and for ever. *Amen.*

(Years A, B, and C — Propers I, II, and III)

Proper I - *Isaiah 9:2-7*
Psalm 96
Titus 2:11-14
Luke 2:1-14 (15-20)

The Lesson   **Isaiah 9:2-7**

The people who walked in darkness have seen a great light; those who lived in a land of deep darkness — on them light has shined. You have multiplied the nation, you have increased its joy; they rejoice before you as with joy at the harvest, as people exult when dividing plunder. For the yoke of their burden, and the bar across their shoulders, the rod of their oppressor, you have broken as on the day of Midian. For all the boots of the tramping warriors and all the garments rolled in blood shall be burned as fuel for the fire. For a child has been born for us, a son given to us; authority rests upon his shoulders; and he is named Wonderful Counselor, Mighty God, Everlasting Father, Prince of Peace. His authority shall grow continually, and there shall be endless peace for the throne of David and his kingdom. He will establish and uphold it with justice and with righteousness from this time onward and forevermore. The zeal of the LORD of hosts will do this.

The Response   **Psalm 96**

Psalm 96   *Cantate Domino*

1   Sing to the LORD a new song; *
    sing to the LORD, all the whole earth.
2   Sing to the LORD and bless his Name; *
    proclaim the good news of his salvation from day to day.
3   Declare his glory among the nations *
    and his wonders among all peoples.
4   For great is the LORD and greatly to be praised; *
    he is more to be feared than all gods.
5   As for all the gods of the nations, they are but idols; *
    but it is the LORD who made the heavens.

6 Oh, the majesty and magnificence of his presence! *
  Oh, the power and the splendor of his sanctuary!
7 Ascribe to the LORD, you families of the peoples; *
  ascribe to the LORD honor and power.
8 Ascribe to the LORD the honor due his Name; *
  bring offerings and come into his courts.
9 Worship the LORD in the beauty of holiness; *
  let the whole earth tremble before him.
10 Tell it out among the nations: "The LORD is King! *
  he has made the world so firm that it cannot be moved;
  he will judge the peoples with equity."
11 Let the heavens rejoice, and let the earth be glad;
  let the sea thunder and all that is in it; *
  let the field be joyful and all that is therein.
12 Then shall all the trees of the wood shout for joy
  before the LORD when he comes, *
  when he comes to judge the earth.
13 He will judge the world with righteousness *
  and the peoples with his truth.

The Epistle   Titus 2:11-14

The grace of God has appeared, bringing salvation to all, training us to
renounce impiety and worldly passions, and in the present age to live lives that
are self-controlled, upright, and godly, while we wait for the blessed hope and
the manifestation of the glory of our great God and Savior, Jesus Christ. He it
is who gave himself for us that he might redeem us from all iniquity and
purify for himself a people of his own who are zealous for good deeds.

The Gospel   Luke 2:1-14 (15-20)
Luke 2:1-14

In those days a decree went out from Emperor Augustus that all the world
should be registered. This was the first registration and was taken while
Quirinius was governor of Syria. All went to their own towns to be registered.
Joseph also went from the town of Nazareth in Galilee to Judea, to the city of
David called Bethlehem, because he was descended from the house and
family of David. He went to be registered with Mary, to whom he was engaged and who was expecting a child. While they were there, the time came
for her to deliver her child. And she gave birth to her firstborn son and
wrapped him in bands of cloth, and laid him in a manger, because there was
no place for them in the inn. In that region there were shepherds living in the
fields, keeping watch over their flock by night. Then an angel of the Lord
stood before them, and the glory of the Lord shone around them, and they

were terrified. But the angel said to them, "Do not be afraid; for see—I am bringing you good news of great joy for all the people: to you is born this day in the city of David a Savior, who is the Messiah, the Lord. This will be a sign for you: you will find a child wrapped in bands of cloth and lying in a manger." And suddenly there was with the angel a multitude of the heavenly host, praising God and saying, "Glory to God in the highest heaven, and on earth peace among those whom he favors!"

Luke 2:(15-20) [When the angels had left them and gone into heaven, the shepherds said to one another, "Let us go now to Bethlehem and see this thing that has taken place, which the Lord has made known to us." So they went with haste and found Mary and Joseph, and the child lying in the manger. When they saw this, they made known what had been told them about this child; and all who heard it were amazed at what the shepherds told them. But Mary treasured all these words and pondered them in her heart. The shepherds returned, glorifying and praising God for all they had heard and seen, as it had been told them.]

Proper II - *Isaiah 62:6-12*
Psalm 97
Titus 3:4-7
Luke 2:(1-7) 8-20

The Lesson   Isaiah 62:6-12

Upon your walls, O Jerusalem, I have posted sentinels; all day and all night they shall never be silent. You who remind the LORD, take no rest, and give him no rest until he establishes Jerusalem and makes it renowned throughout the earth. The LORD has sworn by his right hand and by his mighty arm: I will not again give your grain to be food for your enemies, and foreigners shall not drink the wine for which you have labored; but those who garner it shall eat it and praise the LORD, and those who gather it shall drink it in my holy courts. Go through, go through the gates, prepare the way for the people; build up, build up the highway, clear it of stones, lift up an ensign over the peoples. The LORD has proclaimed to the end of the earth: Say to daughter Zion, "See, your salvation comes; his reward is with him, and his recompense before him." They shall be called, "The Holy People, The Redeemed of the LORD"; and you shall be called, "Sought Out, A City Not Forsaken."

The Response

Psalm 97   *Dominus regnavit*

1   The LORD is King;
    let the earth rejoice; *
        let the multitude of the isles be glad.
2   Clouds and darkness are round about him, *
        righteousness and justice are the foundations of his throne.
3   A fire goes before him *
        and burns up his enemies on every side.
4   His lightnings light up the world; *
        the earth sees it and is afraid.
5   The mountains melt like wax at the presence of the LORD, *
        at the presence of the LORD of the whole earth.
6   The heavens declare his righteousness, *
        and all the peoples see his glory.
7   Confounded be all who worship carved images
    and delight in false gods! *
        Bow down before him, all you gods.
8   Zion hears and is glad, and the cities of Judah rejoice, *
        because of your judgments, O LORD.
9   For you are the LORD,
    most high over all the earth; *
        you are exalted far above all gods.
10 The LORD loves those who hate evil; *
        he preserves the lives of his saints
        and delivers them from the hand of the wicked.
11 Light has sprung up for the righteous, *
        and joyful gladness for those who are truehearted.
12 Rejoice in the LORD, you righteous, *
        and give thanks to his holy Name.

The Epistle   Titus 3:4-7

When the goodness and loving kindness of God our Savior appeared, he saved us, not because of any works of righteousness that we had done, but according to his mercy, through the water of rebirth and renewal by the Holy Spirit. This Spirit he poured out on us richly through Jesus Christ our Savior, so that, having been justified by his grace, we might become heirs according to the hope of eternal life.

The Gospel   Luke 2:(1-7) 8-20

Luke 2:(1-7) [In those days a decree went out from Emperor Augustus that all the world should be registered. This was the first registration and was taken while Quirinius was governor of Syria. All went to their own towns to be registered. Joseph also went from the town of Nazareth in Galilee to Judea, to the city of David called Bethlehem, because he was descended from the house and family of David. He went to be registered with Mary, to whom he was engaged and who was expecting a child. While they were there, the time came for her to deliver her child. And she gave birth to her firstborn son and wrapped him in bands of cloth, and laid him in a manger, because there was no place for them in the inn.]

Luke 2:8-20 In that region there were shepherds living in the fields, keeping watch over their flock by night. Then an angel of the Lord stood before them, and the glory of the Lord shone around them, and they were terrified. But the angel said to them, "Do not be afraid; for see — I am bringing you good news of great joy for all the people: to you is born this day in the city of David a Savior, who is the Messiah, the Lord. This will be a sign for you: you will find a child wrapped in bands of cloth and lying in a manger." And suddenly there was with the angel a multitude of the heavenly host, praising God and saying, "Glory to God in the highest heaven, and on earth peace among those whom he favors!" When the angels had left them and gone into heaven, the shepherds said to one another, "Let us go now to Bethlehem and see this thing that has taken place, which the Lord has made known to us." So they went with haste and found Mary and Joseph, and the child lying in the manger. When they saw this, they made known what had been told them about this child; and all who heard it were amazed at what the shepherds told them. But Mary treasured all these words and pondered them in her heart. The shepherds returned, glorifying and praising God for all they had heard and seen, as it had been told them.

Proper III - Isaiah 52:7-10
Psalm 98
Hebrews 1:1-4, (5-12)
John 1:1-14

The Lesson   **Isaiah 52:7-10**

How beautiful upon the mountains are the feet of the messenger who announces peace, who brings good news, who announces salvation, who says to Zion, "Your God reigns." Listen! Your sentinels lift up their voices, together they sing for joy; for in plain sight they see the return of the Lord to Zion. Break forth together into singing, you ruins of Jerusalem; for the Lord has comforted his people, he has redeemed Jerusalem. The Lord has bared his holy arm before the eyes of all the nations; and all the ends of the earth shall see the salvation of our God.

The Response   Psalm 98

Psalm 98   *Cantate Domino*

1   Sing to the LORD a new song, *
        for he has done marvelous things.
2   With his right hand and his holy arm *
        as he won for himself the victory.
3   The LORD has made known his victory; *
        his righteousness has he openly shown in
                the sight of the nations.
4   He remembers his mercy and faithfulness to
            the house of Israel, *
        and all the ends of the earth have seen the
            victory of our God.
5   Shout with joy to the LORD, all you lands; *
        lift up your voice, rejoice, and sing.
6   Sing to the LORD with the harp, *
        with the harp and the voice of song.
7   With trumpets and the sound of the horn *
        shout with joy before the King, the LORD.
8   Let the sea make a noise and all that is in it, *
        the lands and those who dwell therein.
9   Let the rivers clap their hands, *
        and let the hills ring out with joy before the LORD,
        when he comes to judge the earth.
10 In righteousness shall he judge the world *
        and the peoples with equity.

The Epistle   Hebrews 1:1-4, (5-12)

Long ago God spoke to our ancestors in many and various ways by the
prophets, but in these last days he has spoken to us by a Son, whom he
appointed heir of all things, through whom he also created the worlds. He is
the reflection of God's glory and the exact imprint of God's very being, and he
sustains all things by his powerful word. When he had made purification for
sins, he sat down at the right hand of the Majesty on high, having become as
much superior to angels as the name he has inherited is more excellent than
theirs.

Hebrews 1:(5-12) [For to which of the angels did God ever say, "You are my
Son; today I have begotten you"? Or again, "I will be his Father, and he will
be my Son"? And again, when he brings the firstborn into the world, he says,
"Let all God's angels worship him." Of the angels he says, "He makes his

angels winds, and his servants flames of fire." But of the Son he says, "Your throne, O God, is forever and ever, and the righteous scepter is the scepter of your kingdom. You have loved righteousness and hated wickedness; therefore God, your God, has anointed you with the oil of gladness beyond your companions." And, "In the beginning, Lord, you founded the earth, and the heavens are the work of your hands; they will perish, but you remain; they will all wear out like clothing; like a cloak you will roll them up, and like clothing they will be changed. But you are the same, and your years will never end."]

The Gospel   John 1:1-14

In the beginning was the Word, and the Word was with God, and the Word was God. He was in the beginning with God. All things came into being through him, and without him not one thing came into being. What has come into being in him was life, and the life was the light of all people. The light shines in the darkness, and the darkness did not overcome it. There was a man sent from God, whose name was John. He came as a witness to testify to the light, so that all might believe through him. He himself was not the light, but he came to testify to the light. The true light, which enlightens everyone, was coming into the world. He was in the world, and the world came into being through him; yet the world did not know him. He came to what was his own, and his own people did not accept him. But to all who received him, who believed in his name, he gave power to become children of God, who were born, not of blood or of the will of the flesh or of the will of man, but of God. And the Word became flesh and lived among us, and we have seen his glory, the glory as of a father's only son, full of grace and truth.

FIRST SUNDAY AFTER CHRISTMAS

The Collect

Almighty God, you have poured upon us the new light of your incarnate Word: Grant that this light, enkindled in our hearts, may shine forth in our lives; through Jesus Christ our Lord, who lives and reigns with you, in the unity of the Holy Spirit, one God, now and for ever. *Amen.*

Years A, B, and C
Isaiah 61:10—62:3
Psalm 147 or *147:13-21*
Galatians 3:23-25; 4:4-7
John 1:1-18

The Lesson   **Isaiah 61:10—62:3**

I will greatly rejoice in the LORD, my whole being shall exult in my God; for
he has clothed me with the garments of salvation, he has covered me with the
robe of righteousness, as a bridegroom decks himself with a garland, and as a
bride adorns herself with her jewels. For as the earth brings forth its shoots,
and as a garden causes what is sown in it to spring up, so the Lord GOD will
cause righteousness and praise to spring up before all the nations. For Zion's
sake I will not keep silent, and for Jerusalem's sake I will not rest, until her
vindication shines out like the dawn, and her salvation like a burning torch.
The nations shall see your vindication, and all the kings your glory; and you
shall be called by a new name that the mouth of the LORD will give. You shall
be a crown of beauty in the hand of the LORD, and a royal diadem in the hand
of your God.

The Response   **Psalm 147:(1-12) 13-21**

Psalm 147   *Laudate Dominum*

  [1   Hallelujah!
       How good it is to sing praises to our God! *
         how pleasant it is to honor him with praise!
  2   The LORD rebuilds Jerusalem; *
         he gathers the exiles of Israel.
  3   He heals the brokenhearted *
         and binds up their wounds.
  4   He counts the number of the stars *
         and calls them all by their names.
  5   Great is our LORD and mighty in power; *
         there is no limit to his wisdom.
  6   The LORD lifts up the lowly, *
         but casts the wicked to the ground.
  7   Sing to the LORD with thanksgiving; *
         make music to our God upon the harp.
  8   He covers the heavens with clouds *
         and prepares rain for the earth;
  9   He makes grass to grow upon the mountains *
         and green plants to serve mankind.
 10   He provides food for flocks and herds *
         and for the young ravens when they cry.
 11   He is not impressed by the might of a horse; *
         he has no pleasure in the strength of a man;
 12   But the LORD has pleasure in those who fear him, *
         in those who await his gracious favor.]

13 Worship the LORD, O Jerusalem; *
        praise your God, O Zion;

14 For he has strengthened the bars of your gates; *
        he has blessed your children within you.

15 He has established peace on your borders; *
        he satisfies you with the finest wheat.

16 He sends out his command to the earth, *
        and his word runs very swiftly.

17 He gives snow like wool; *
        he scatters hoarfrost like ashes.

18 He scatters his hail like bread crumbs; *
        who can stand against his cold?

19 He sends forth his word and melts them; *
        he blows with his wind, and the waters flow.

20 He declares his word to Jacob, *
        his statutes and his judgments to Israel.

21 He has not done so to any other nation; *
        to them he has not revealed his judgments.
        Hallelujah!

The Epistle   Galatians 3:23-25; 4:4-7

Now before faith came, we were imprisoned and guarded under the law until faith would be revealed. Therefore the law was our disciplinarian until Christ came, so that we might be justified by faith. But now that faith has come, we are no longer subject to a disciplinarian; but when the fullness of time had come, God sent his Son, born of a woman, born under the law, in order to redeem those who were under the law, so that we might receive adoption as children. And because you are children, God has sent the Spirit of his Son into our hearts, crying, "Abba! Father!" So you are no longer a slave but a child, and if a child then also an heir, through God.

The Gospel   John 1:1-18

In the beginning was the Word, and the Word was with God, and the Word was God. He was in the beginning with God. All things came into being through him, and without him not one thing came into being. What has come into being in him was life, and the life was the light of all people. The light shines in the darkness, and the darkness did not overcome it. There was a man sent from God, whose name was John. He came as a witness to testify to the light, so that all might believe through him. He himself was not the light, but he came to testify to the light. The true light, which enlightens everyone, was coming into the world. He was in the world, and the world came into being through him; yet the world did not know him. He came to what was his own, and his own people did not accept him. But to all who received him, who believed in his name, he gave power to become children of God, who were born, not of blood or of the will of the flesh or of the will of man, but of God. And the Word became flesh and lived among us, and we have seen his glory, the glory as of a father's only son, full of grace and truth. (John testified to him and cried out, "This was he of whom I said, 'He who comes after me ranks ahead of me because he was before me.' ") From his fullness we have all received, grace upon grace. The law indeed was given through Moses; grace and truth came through Jesus Christ. No one has ever seen God. It is God the only Son, who is close to the Father's heart, who has made him known.

HOLY NAME
(January 1)

The Collect
Eternal Father, you gave to your incarnate Son the holy name of Jesus to be the sign of our salvation: Plant in every heart, we pray, the love of him who is the Savior of the world, our Lord Jesus Christ; who lives and reigns with you and the Holy Spirit, one God, in glory everlasting. *Amen.*

Years A, B, and C
Numbers 6:22-27
Psalm 8
Galatians 4:4-7 or *Philippians 2:5-11*
Luke 2:15-21

The Lesson   Numbers 6:22-27
The LORD spoke to Moses, saying: Speak to Aaron and his sons, saying, Thus you shall bless the Israelites: You shall say to them, The LORD bless you and keep you; the LORD make his face to shine upon you, and be gracious to you; the LORD lift up his countenance upon you, and give you peace. So they shall put my name on the Israelites, and I will bless them.

The Response   Psalm 8
Psalm 8   *Domine, Dominus noster*
1   O LORD our Governor, *
       how exalted is your Name in all the world!
2   Out of the mouths of infants and children *
       your majesty is praised above the heavens.
3   You have set up a stronghold against your adversaries, *
       to quell the enemy and the avenger.
4   When I consider your heavens, the work of your fingers, *
       the moon and the stars you have set in their courses,

5   What is man that you should be mindful of him? *
        the son of man that you should seek him out?
6   You have made him but little lower than the angels; *
        you adorn him with glory and honor;
7   You give him mastery over the works of your hands; *
        you put all things under his feet:
8   All sheep and oxen, *
        even the wild beasts of the field,
9   The birds of the air, the fish of the sea, *
        and whatsoever walks in the paths of the sea.
10   O LORD our Governor, *
        how exalted is your Name in all the world!

The Epistle   Galatians 4:4-7 *or* Philippians 2:5-11
Galatians 4:4-7

When the fullness of time had come, God sent his Son, born of a woman, born under the law, in order to redeem those who were under the law, so that we might receive adoption as children. And because you are children, God has sent the Spirit of his Son into our hearts, crying, "Abba! Father!" So you are no longer a slave but a child, and if a child then also an heir, through God.

or, Philippians 2:5-11

Let the same mind be in you that was in Christ Jesus, who, though he was in the form of God, did not regard equality with God as something to be exploited, but emptied himself, taking the form of a slave, being born in human likeness. And being found in human form, he humbled himself and became obedient to the point of death — even death on a cross. Therefore God also highly exalted him and gave him the name that is above every name, so that at the name of Jesus every knee should bend, in heaven and on earth and under the earth, and every tongue should confess that Jesus Christ is Lord, to the glory of God the Father.

The Gospel   Luke 2:15-21

When the angels had left them and gone into heaven, the shepherds said to one another, "Let us go now to Bethlehem and see this thing that has taken place, which the Lord has made known to us." So they went with haste and found Mary and Joseph, and the child lying in the manger. When they saw this, they made known what had been told them about this child; and all who heard it were amazed at what the shepherds told them. But Mary treasured all these words and pondered them in her heart. The shepherds returned, glorifying and praising God for all they had heard and seen, as it had been told them. After eight days had passed, it was time to circumcise the child; and he was called Jesus, the name given by the angel before he was conceived in the womb.

SECOND SUNDAY AFTER CHRISTMAS

The Collect

O God, who wonderfully created, and yet more wonderfully restored, the dignity of human nature: Grant that we may share the divine life of him who humbled himself to share our humanity, your Son Jesus Christ; who lives and reigns with you, in the unity of the Holy Spirit, one God, for ever and ever. *Amen.*

Years A, B, and C
Jeremiah 31:7-14
Psalm 84 or 84:1-8
*Ephesians 1:3-6, 15-19*a
Matthew 2:13-15, 19-23 or *Luke 2:41-52* or *Matthew 2:1-12*

The Lesson   **Jeremiah 31:7-14**

Thus says the LORD: Sing aloud with gladness for Jacob, and raise shouts for the chief of the nations; proclaim, give praise, and say, "Save, O LORD, your people, the remnant of Israel." See, I am going to bring them from the land of the north, and gather them from the farthest parts of the earth, among them the blind and the lame, those with child and those in labor, together; a great company, they shall return here. With weeping they shall come, and with consolations I will lead them back, I will let them walk by brooks of water, in a straight path in which they shall not stumble; for I have become a father to Israel, and Ephraim is my firstborn. Hear the word of the LORD, O nations, and declare it in the coastlands far away; say, "He who scattered Israel will gather him, and will keep him as a shepherd a flock." For the LORD has ransomed Jacob, and has redeemed him from hands too strong for him. They shall come and sing aloud on the height of Zion, and they shall be radiant over the goodness of the LORD, over the grain, the wine, and the oil, and over the young of the flock and the herd; their life shall become like a watered garden, and they shall never languish again. Then shall the young women rejoice in the dance, and the young men and the old shall be merry. I will turn their mourning into joy, I will comfort them, and give them gladness for sorrow. I will give the priests their fill of fatness, and my people shall be satisfied with my bounty, says the LORD.

The Response   **Psalm 84:1-8 (9-12)**

Psalm 84   *Quam dilecta!*

    1   How dear to me is your dwelling, O LORD of hosts! *
            My soul has a desire and longing for the courts of
                the LORD;
            my heart and my flesh rejoice in the living God.

2   The sparrow has found her a house
    and the swallow a nest where she may lay her young; *
       by the side of your altars, O LORD of hosts,
       my King and my God.

3   Happy are they who dwell in your house! *
    they will always be praising you.

4   Happy are the people whose strength is in you! *
    whose hearts are set on the pilgrims' way.

5   Those who go through the desolate valley will find
       it a place of springs, *
    for the early rains have covered it with pools of water.

6   They will climb from height to height, *
    and the God of gods will reveal himself in Zion.

7   LORD God of hosts, hear my prayer; *
    hearken, O God of Jacob.

8   Behold our defender, O God; *
    and look upon the face of your Anointed.

[9   For one day in your courts is better than
       a thousand in my own room, *
    and to stand at the threshold of the house of my God
    than to dwell in the tents of the wicked.

10 For the LORD God is both sun and shield; *
    he will give grace and glory;

11 No good thing will the LORD withhold *
    from those who walk with integrity.

12 O LORD of hosts, *
    happy are they who put their trust in you!]

The Epistle   **Ephesians 1:3-6, 15-19***a*

Blessed be the God and Father of our Lord Jesus Christ, who has blessed us in Christ with every spiritual blessing in the heavenly places, just as he chose us in Christ before the foundation of the world to be holy and blameless before him in love. He destined us for adoption as his children through Jesus Christ, according to the good pleasure of his will, to the praise of his glorious grace that he freely bestowed on us in the Beloved. I have heard of your faith in the Lord Jesus and your love toward all the saints, and for this reason I do not cease to give thanks for you as I remember you in my prayers. I pray that the God of our Lord Jesus Christ, the Father of glory, may give you a spirit of wisdom and revelation as you come to know him, so that, with the eyes of your heart enlightened, you may know what is the hope to which he has called you, what are the riches of his glorious inheritance among the saints, and what is the immeasurable greatness of his power for us who believe.

The Gospel   Matthew 2:13-15, 19-23 *or* Luke 2:41-52
or Matthew 2:1-12

Matthew 2:13-15, 19-23

When the wise men who had come from the East had departed, an angel of the Lord appeared to Joseph in a dream and said, "Get up, take the child and his mother, and flee to Egypt, and remain there until I tell you; for Herod is about to search for the child, to destroy him." Then Joseph got up, took the child and his mother by night, and went to Egypt, and remained there until the death of Herod. This was to fulfill what had been spoken by the Lord through the prophet, "Out of Egypt I have called my son." When Herod died, an angel of the Lord suddenly appeared in a dream to Joseph in Egypt and said, "Get up, take the child and his mother, and go to the land of Israel, for those who were seeking the child's life are dead." Then Joseph got up, took the child and his mother, and went to the land of Israel. But when he heard that Archelaus was ruling over Judea in place of his father Herod, he was afraid to go there. And after being warned in a dream, he went away to the district of Galilee. There he made his home in a town called Nazareth, so that what had been spoken through the prophets might be fulfilled, "He will be called a Nazorean."

or

The Gospel   Luke 2:41-52

Now every year Jesus' parents went to Jerusalem for the festival of the Passover. And when he was twelve years old, they went up as usual for the festival. When the festival was ended and they started to return, the boy Jesus stayed behind in Jerusalem, but his parents did not know it. Assuming that he was in the group of travelers, they went a day's journey. Then they started to look for him among their relatives and friends. When they did not find him, they returned to Jerusalem to search for him. After three days they found him in the temple, sitting among the teachers, listening to them and asking them questions. And all who heard him were amazed at his understanding and his answers. When his parents saw him they were astonished; and his mother said to him, "Child, why have you treated us like this? Look, your father and I have been searching for you in great anxiety." He said to them, "Why were you searching for me? Did you not know that I must be in my Father's house?" But they did not understand what he said to them. Then he went down with them and came to Nazareth, and was obedient to them. His mother treasured all these things in her heart. And Jesus increased in wisdom and in years, and in divine and human favor.

or

The Gospel   Matthew 2:1-12

In the time of King Herod, after Jesus was born in Bethlehem of Judea, wise men from the East came to Jerusalem, asking, "Where is the child who has been born king of the Jews? For we observed his star at its rising, and have come to pay him homage." When King Herod heard this, he was frightened, and all Jerusalem with him; and calling together all the chief priests and scribes of the people, he inquired of them where the Messiah was to be born. They told him, "In Bethlehem of Judea; for so it has been written by the prophet: 'And you, Bethlehem, in the land of Judah, are by no means least among the rulers of Judah; for from you shall come a ruler who is to shepherd my people Israel.' " Then Herod secretly called for the wise men and learned from them the exact time when the star had appeared. Then he sent them to Bethlehem, saying, "Go and search diligently for the child; and when you have found him, bring me word so that I may also go and pay him homage." When they had heard the king, they set out; and there, ahead of them, went the star that they had seen at its rising, until it stopped over the place where the child was. When they saw that the star had stopped, they were overwhelmed with joy. On entering the house, they saw the child with Mary his mother; and they knelt down and paid him homage. Then, opening their treasure chests, they offered him gifts of gold, frankincense, and myrrh. And having been warned in a dream not to return to Herod, they left for their own country by another road.

THE EPIPHANY

The Collect

O God, by the leading of a star you manifested your only Son to the peoples of the earth: Lead us, who know you now by faith, to your presence, where we may see your glory face to face; through Jesus Christ our Lord, who lives and reigns with you and the Holy Spirit, one God, now and for ever. *Amen.*

Years A, B, and C
Isaiah 60:1-6
Psalm 72:1-7, 10-14
Ephesians 3:1-12
Matthew 2:1-12

The Lesson   Isaiah 60:1-6

Arise, shine; for your light has come, and the glory of the LORD has risen upon you. For darkness shall cover the earth, and thick darkness the peoples; but the LORD will arise upon you, and his glory will appear over you. Nations shall come to your light, and kings to the brightness of your dawn. Lift up your eyes and look around; they all gather together, they come to you; your sons shall come from far away, and your daughters shall be carried on their nurses' arms. Then you shall see and be radiant; your heart shall thrill and rejoice, because the abundance of the sea shall be brought to you, the wealth of the nations shall come to you. A multitude of camels shall cover you, the young camels of Midian and Ephah; all those from Sheba shall come. They shall bring gold and frankincense, and shall proclaim the praise of the LORD.

The Response   Psalm 72:1-7, 10-14

Psalm 72   *Deus, judicium*
1   Give the King your justice, O God, *
         and your righteousness to the King's Son;
2   That he may rule your people righteously *
         and the poor with justice;
3   That the mountains may bring prosperity to the people, *
         and the little hills bring righteousness.
4   He shall defend the needy among the people; *
         he shall rescue the poor and crush the oppressor.
5   He shall live as long as the sun and moon endure, *
         from one generation to another.
6   He shall come down like rain upon the mown field, *
         like showers that water the earth.
7   In his time shall the righteous flourish; *
         there shall be abundance of peace till the moon shall
                      be no more.
10   The kings of Tarshish and of the isles shall pay tribute, *
         and the kings of Arabia and Saba offer gifts.
11   All kings shall bow down before him, *
         and all the nations do him service.
12   For he shall deliver the poor who cries out in distress, *
         and the oppressed who has no helper.
13   He shall have pity on the lowly and poor; *
         he shall preserve the lives of the needy.
14   He shall redeem their lives from oppression and violence, *
         and dear shall their blood be in his sight.

The Epistle   Ephesians 3:1-12

This is the reason that I Paul am a prisoner for Christ Jesus for the sake of you Gentiles — for surely you have already heard of the commission of God's grace that was given me for you, and how the mystery was made known to me by revelation, as I wrote above in a few words, a reading of which will enable you to perceive my understanding of the mystery of Christ. In former generations this mystery was not made known to humankind, as it has now been revealed to his holy apostles and prophets by the Spirit: that is, the Gentiles have become fellow heirs, members of the same body, and sharers in the promise in Christ Jesus through the gospel. Of this gospel I have become a servant according to the gift of God's grace that was given me by the working of his power. Although I am the very least of all the saints, this grace was given to me to bring to the Gentiles the news of the boundless riches of Christ, and to make everyone see what is the plan of the mystery hidden for ages in God who created all things; so that through the church the wisdom of God in its rich variety might now be made known to the rulers and authorities in the heavenly places. This was in accordance with the eternal purpose that he has carried out in Christ Jesus our Lord, in whom we have access to God in boldness and confidence through faith in him.

The Gospel   Matthew 2:1-12

In the time of King Herod, after Jesus was born in Bethlehem of Judea, wise men from the East came to Jerusalem, asking, "Where is the child who has been born king of the Jews? For we observed his star at its rising, and have come to pay him homage." When King Herod heard this, he was frightened, and all Jerusalem with him; and calling together all the chief priests and scribes of the people, he inquired of them where the Messiah was to be born. They told him, "In Bethlehem of Judea; for so it has been written by the prophet: 'And you, Bethlehem, in the land of Judah, are by no means least among the rulers of Judah; for from you shall come a ruler who is to shepherd my people Israel.' " Then Herod secretly called for the wise men and learned from them the exact time when the star had appeared. Then he sent them to Bethlehem, saying, "Go and search diligently for the child; and when you have found him, bring me word so that I may also go and pay him homage." When they had heard the king, they set out; and there, ahead of them, went the star that they had seen at its rising, until it stopped over the place where the child was. When they saw that the star had stopped, they were overwhelmed with joy. On entering the house, they saw the child with Mary his mother; and they knelt down and paid him homage. Then, opening their treasure chests, they offered him gifts of gold, frankincense, and myrrh. And having been warned in a dream not to return to Herod, they left for their own country by another road.

FIRST SUNDAY AFTER THE EPIPHANY: THE BAPTISM OF OUR LORD

The Collect

Father in heaven, who at the baptism of Jesus in the River Jordan proclaimed him your beloved Son and anointed him with the Holy Spirit: Grant that all who are baptized into his Name may keep the covenant they have made, and boldly confess him as Lord and Savior; who with you and the Holy Spirit lives and reigns, one God, in glory everlasting. *Amen.*

Year A
Isaiah 42:1-9
Psalm 29
Acts 10:34-43
Matthew 3:13-17

The Lesson   Isaiah 42:1-9

Here is my servant, whom I uphold, my chosen, in whom my soul delights; I
have put my spirit upon him; he will bring forth justice to the nations. He will
not cry or lift up his voice, or make it heard in the street; a bruised reed he
will not break, and a dimly burning wick he will not quench; he will faithfully
bring forth justice. He will not grow faint or be crushed until he has established justice in the earth; and the coastlands wait for his teaching. Thus says
God, the LORD, who created the heavens and stretched them out, who spread
out the earth and what comes from it, who gives breath to the people upon it
and spirit to those who walk in it: I am the LORD, I have called you in righteousness, I have taken you by the hand and kept you; I have given you as a
covenant to the people, a light to the nations, to open the eyes that are blind, to
bring out the prisoners from the dungeon, from the prison those who sit in
darkness. I am the LORD, that is my name; my glory I give to no other, nor my
praise to idols. See, the former things have come to pass, and new things I
now declare; before they spring forth, I tell you of them.

The Response   Psalm 29

Psalm 29 *Afferte Domino*

1   Ascribe to the LORD, you gods, *
        ascribe to the LORD glory and strength.
2   Ascribe to the LORD the glory due his Name; *
        worship the LORD in the beauty of holiness.
3   The voice of the LORD is upon the waters;
    the God of glory thunders; *
        the LORD is upon the mighty waters.
4   The voice of the LORD is a powerful voice; *
        the voice of the LORD is a voice of splendor.
5   The voice of the LORD breaks the cedar trees; *
        the LORD breaks the cedars of Lebanon;
6   He makes Lebanon skip like a calf, *
        and Mount Hermon like a young wild ox.
7   The voice of the LORD splits the flames of fire;
    the voice of the LORD shakes the wilderness; *
        the LORD shakes the wilderness of Kadesh.

8   The voice of the Lord makes the oak trees writhe *
      and strips the forests bare.
9   And in the temple of the Lord *
      all are crying, "Glory!"
10 The Lord sits enthroned above the flood; *
      the Lord sits enthroned as King for evermore.
11 The Lord shall give strength to his people; *
      the Lord shall give his people the blessing of peace.

The Epistle   Acts 10:34-43

Peter began to speak to them: "I truly understand that God shows no partiality, but in every nation anyone who fears him and does what is right is acceptable to him. You know the message he sent to the people of Israel, preaching
peace by Jesus Christ — he is Lord of all. That message spread throughout
Judea, beginning in Galilee after the baptism that John announced: how God
anointed Jesus of Nazareth with the Holy Spirit and with power; how he went
about doing good and healing all who were oppressed by the devil, for God
was with him. We are witnesses to all that he did both in Judea and in Jerusalem. They put him to death by hanging him on a tree; but God raised him on
the third day and allowed him to appear, not to all the people but to us who
were chosen by God as witnesses, and who ate and drank with him after he
rose from the dead. He commanded us to preach to the people and to testify
that he is the one ordained by God as judge of the living and the dead. All the
prophets testify about him that everyone who believes in him receives forgiveness of sins through his name."

The Gospel   Matthew 3:13-17

Jesus came from Galilee to John at the Jordan, to be baptized by him. John
would have prevented him, saying, "I need to be baptized by you, and do you
come to me?" But Jesus answered him, "Let it be so now; for it is proper for
us in this way to fulfill all righteousness." Then he consented. And when Jesus
had been baptized, just as he came up from the water, suddenly the heavens
were opened to him and he saw the Spirit of God descending like a dove and
alighting on him. And a voice from heaven said, "This is my Son, the Beloved,
with whom I am well pleased."

Year B

Genesis 1:1-5
Psalm 29
Acts 19:1-7
Mark 1:4-11

The Lesson   Genesis 1:1-5

In the beginning when God created the heavens and the earth, the earth was a formless void and darkness covered the face of the deep, while a wind from God swept over the face of the waters. Then God said, "Let there be light"; and there was light. And God saw that the light was good; and God separated the light from the darkness. God called the light Day, and the darkness he called Night. And there was evening and there was morning, the first day.

The Response   Psalm 29

Psalm 29   *Afferte Domino*

1   Ascribe to the LORD, you gods, *
        ascribe to the LORD glory and strength.
2   Ascribe to the LORD the glory due his Name; *
        worship the LORD in the beauty of holiness.
3   The voice of the LORD is upon the waters;
    the God of glory thunders; *
        the LORD is upon the mighty waters.
4   The voice of the LORD is a powerful voice; *
        the voice of the LORD is a voice of splendor.
5   The voice of the LORD breaks the cedar trees; *
        the LORD breaks the cedars of Lebanon;
6   He makes Lebanon skip like a calf, *
        and Mount Hermon like a young wild ox.
7   The voice of the LORD splits the flames of fire;
    the voice of the LORD shakes the wilderness; *
        the LORD shakes the wilderness of Kadesh.
8   The voice of the LORD makes the oak trees writhe *
        and strips the forests bare.
9   And in the temple of the LORD *
        all are crying, "Glory!"
10   The LORD sits enthroned above the flood; *
        the LORD sits enthroned as King for evermore.
11   The LORD shall give strength to his people; *
        the LORD shall give his people the blessing of peace.

The Epistle   **Acts 19:1-7**

While Apollos was in Corinth, Paul passed through the interior regions and
came to Ephesus, where he found some disciples. He said to them, "Did you
receive the Holy Spirit when you became believers?" They replied, "No, we
have not even heard that there is a Holy Spirit." Then he said, "Into what then
were you baptized?" They answered, "Into John's baptism." Paul said, "John
baptized with the baptism of repentance, telling the people to believe in the
one who was to come after him, that is, in Jesus." On hearing this, they were
baptized in the name of the Lord Jesus. When Paul had laid his hands on
them, the Holy Spirit came upon them, and they spoke in tongues and prophesied — altogether there were about twelve of them.

The Gospel   **Mark 1:4-11**

John the baptizer appeared in the wilderness, proclaiming a baptism of
repentance for the forgiveness of sins. And people from the whole Judean
countryside and all the people of Jerusalem were going out to him, and were
baptized by him in the river Jordan, confessing their sins. Now John was
clothed with camel's hair, with a leather belt around his waist, and he ate
locusts and wild honey. He proclaimed, "The one who is more powerful than I
is coming after me; I am not worthy to stoop down and untie the thong of his
sandals. I have baptized you with water; but he will baptize you with the Holy
Spirit." In those days Jesus came from Nazareth of Galilee and was baptized
by John in the Jordan. And just as he was coming up out of the water, he saw
the heavens torn apart and the Spirit descending like dove on him. And a voice
came from heaven, "You are my Son, the Beloved; with you I am well
pleased."

Year C
Isaiah 43:1-7
Psalm 29
Acts 8:14-17
Luke 3:15-17, 21-22

The Lesson   **Isaiah 43:1-7**

Thus says the LORD, he who created you, O Jacob, he who formed you, O
Israel: Do not fear, for I have redeemed you; I have called you by name, you
are mine. When you pass through the waters, I will be with you; and through
the rivers, they shall not overwhelm you; when you walk through fire you
shall not be burned, and the flame shall not consume you. For I am the LORD
your God, the Holy One of Israel, your Savior. I give Egypt as your ransom,
Ethiopia and Seba in exchange for you. Because you are precious in my sight,

and honored, and I love you, I give people in return for you, nations in exchange for your life. Do not fear, for I am with you; I will bring your offspring from the east, and from the west I will gather you; I will say to the north, "Give them up," and to the south, "Do not withhold; bring my sons from far away and my daughters from the end of the earth—everyone who is called by my name, whom I created for my glory, whom I formed and made."

The Response   Psalm 29

Psalm 29   *Afferte Domino*

1   Ascribe to the LORD, you gods, *
        ascribe to the LORD glory and strength.
2   Ascribe to the LORD the glory due his Name; *
        worship the LORD in the beauty of holiness.
3   The voice of the LORD is upon the waters;
     the God of glory thunders; *
        the LORD is upon the mighty waters.
4   The voice of the LORD is a powerful voice; *
        the voice of the LORD is a voice of splendor.
5   The voice of the LORD breaks the cedar trees; *
        the LORD breaks the cedars of Lebanon;
6   He makes Lebanon skip like a calf, *
        and Mount Hermon like a young wild ox.
7   The voice of the LORD splits the flames of fire;
     the voice of the LORD shakes the wilderness; *
        the LORD shakes the wilderness of Kadesh.
8   The voice of the LORD makes the oak trees writhe *
        and strips the forests bare.
9   And in the temple of the LORD *
        all are crying, "Glory!"
10   The LORD sits enthroned above the flood; *
        the LORD sits enthroned as King for evermore.
11   The LORD shall give strength to his people; *
        the LORD shall give his people the blessing of peace.

The Epistle   Acts 8:14-17

Now when the apostles at Jerusalem heard that Samaria had accepted the word of God, they sent Peter and John to them. The two went down and prayed for them that they might receive the Holy Spirit (for as yet the Spirit had not come upon any of them; they had only been baptized in the name of the Lord Jesus). Then Peter and John laid their hands on them, and they received the Holy Spirit.

The Gospel   Luke 3:15-17, 21-22

As the people were filled with expectation, and all were questioning in their hearts concerning John, whether he might be the Messiah, John answered all of them by saying, "I baptize you with water; but one who is more powerful than I is coming; I am not worthy to untie the thong of his sandals. He will baptize you with the Holy Spirit and fire. His winnowing fork is in his hand, to clear his threshing floor and to gather the wheat into his granary; but the chaff he will burn with unquenchable fire." Now when all the people were baptized, and when Jesus also had been baptized and was praying, the heaven was opened, and the Holy Spirit descended upon him in bodily form like a dove. And a voice came from heaven, "You are my Son, the Beloved; with you I am well pleased."

SECOND SUNDAY AFTER THE EPIPHANY

The Collect

Almighty God, whose Son our Savior Jesus Christ is the light of the world: Grant that your people, illumined by your Word and Sacraments, may shine with the radiance of Christ's glory, that he may be known, worshiped, and obeyed to the ends of the earth; through Jesus Christ our Lord, who with you and the Holy Spirit lives and reigns, one God, now and for ever. *Amen.*

Year A
Isaiah 49:1-7
Psalm 40:1-12
1 Corinthians 1:1-9
John 1:29-42

The Lesson   Isaiah 49:1-7

Listen to me, O coastlands, pay attention, you peoples from far away! The LORD called me before I was born, while I was in my mother's womb he named me. He made my mouth like a sharp sword, in the shadow of his hand he hid me; he made me a polished arrow, in his quiver he hid me away. And he said to me, "You are my servant, Israel, in whom I will be glorified." But I said, "I have labored in vain, I have spent my strength for nothing and vanity; yet surely my cause is with the LORD, and my reward with my God." And now the LORD says, who formed me in the womb to be his servant, to bring Jacob back to him, and that Israel might be gathered to him, for I am honored in the sight of the LORD, and my God has become my strength — he says, "It is too light a thing that you should be my servant to raise up the tribes of Jacob and to restore the survivors of Israel; I will give you as a light to the nations, that my salvation may reach to the end of the earth." Thus says the LORD, the

Redeemer of Israel and his Holy One, to one deeply despised, abhorred by the nations, the slave of rulers, "Kings shall see and stand up, princes, and they shall prostrate themselves, because of the LORD, who is faithful, the Holy One of Israel, who has chosen you."

The Response   **Psalm 40:1-12**

Psalm 40:1-12   *Expectans, expectavi*

1   I waited patiently upon the LORD; *
        he stooped to me and heard my cry.

2   He lifted me out of the desolate pit, out of the mire and clay; *
        he set my feet upon a high cliff and made my footing sure.

3   He put a new song in my mouth,
    a song of praise to our God; *
            many shall see, and stand in awe,
            and put their trust in the LORD.

4   Happy are they who trust in the LORD! *
        they do not resort to evil spirits or turn to false gods.

5   Great things are they that you have done, O LORD my God!
    how great your wonders and your plans for us! *
        there is none who can be compared with you.

6   Oh, that I could make them known and tell them! *
        but they are more than I can count.

7   In sacrifice and offering you take no pleasure *
        (you have given me ears to hear you);

8   Burnt-offering and sin-offering you have not required, *
        and so I said, "Behold, I come.

9   In the roll of the book it is written concerning me: *
        'I love to do your will, O my God;
        your law is deep in my heart.'"

10 I proclaimed righteousness in the great congregation; *
        behold, I did not restrain my lips;
        and that, O LORD, you know.

11 Your righteousness have I not hidden in my heart;
    I have spoken of your faithfulness and your deliverance; *
            I have not concealed your love and faithfulness from the
                        great congregation.

12 You are the LORD;
    do not withhold your compassion from me; *
        let your love and your faithfulness keep me safe for ever.

The Epistle   **1 Corinthians 1:1-9**

Paul, called to be an apostle of Christ Jesus by the will of God, and our
brother Sosthenes, to the church of God that is in Corinth, to those who are
sanctified in Christ Jesus, called to be saints, together with all those who in
every place call on the name of our Lord Jesus Christ, both their Lord and
ours: Grace to you and peace from God our Father and the Lord Jesus Christ.
I give thanks to my God always for you because of the grace of God that has
been given you in Christ Jesus, for in every way you have been enriched in
him, in speech and knowledge of every kind — just as the testimony of Christ
has been strengthened among you — so that you are not lacking in any
spiritual gift as you wait for the revealing of our Lord Jesus Christ. He will
also strengthen you to the end, so that you may be blameless on the day of our
Lord Jesus Christ. God is faithful; by him you were called into the fellowship
of his Son, Jesus Christ our Lord.

The Gospel   **John 1:29-42**

The next day John saw Jesus coming toward him and declared, "Here is the
Lamb of God who takes away the sin of the world! This is he of whom I said,
'After me comes a man who ranks ahead of me because he was before me.' I
myself did not know him; but I came baptizing with water for this reason, that
he might be revealed to Israel." And John testified, "I saw the Spirit descending from heaven like a dove, and it remained on him. I myself did not know
him, but the one who sent me to baptize with water said to me, 'He on whom
you see the Spirit descend and remain is the one who baptizes with the Holy
Spirit.' And I myself have seen and have testified that this is the Son of God."
The next day John again was standing with two of his disciples, and as he
watched Jesus walk by, he exclaimed, "Look, here is the Lamb of God!" The
two disciples heard him say this, and they followed Jesus. When Jesus turned
and saw them following, he said to them, "What are you looking for?" They
said to him, "Rabbi" (which translated means Teacher), "where are you
staying?" He said to them, "Come and see." They came and saw where he was
staying, and they remained with him that day. It was about four o'clock in the
afternoon. One of the two who heard John speak and followed him was
Andrew, Simon Peter's brother. He first found his brother Simon and said to
him, "We have found the Messiah" (which is translated Anointed). He brought
Simon to Jesus, who looked at him and said, "You are Simon son of John. You
are to be called Cephas" (which is translated Peter).

Year B

1 Samuel 3:1-10 (11-20)
Psalm 139:1-5, 12-17
1 Corinthians 6:12-20
John 1:43-51

The Lesson   **1 Samuel 3:1-10 (11-20)**
1 Samuel 3:1-10

Now the boy Samuel was ministering to the LORD under Eli. The word of the LORD was rare in those days; visions were not widespread. At that time Eli, whose eyesight had begun to grow dim so that he could not see, was lying down in his room; the lamp of God had not yet gone out, and Samuel was lying down in the temple of the LORD, where the ark of God was. Then the LORD called, "Samuel! Samuel!" and he said, "Here I am!" and ran to Eli, and said, "Here I am, for you called me." But he said, "I did not call; lie down again." So he went and lay down. The LORD called again, "Samuel!" Samuel got up and went to Eli, and said, "Here I am, for you called me." But he said, "I did not call, my son; lie down again." Now Samuel did not yet know the LORD, and the word of the LORD had not yet been revealed to him. The LORD called Samuel again, a third time. And he got up and went to Eli, and said, "Here I am, for you called me." Then Eli perceived that the LORD was calling the boy. Therefore Eli said to Samuel, "Go, lie down; and if he calls you, you shall say, 'speak, LORD, for your servant is listening.'" So Samuel went and lay down in his place. Now the LORD came and stood there, calling as before, "Samuel! Samuel!" And Samuel said, "Speak, for your servant is listening."

1 Samuel 3:(11-20) [Then the LORD said to Samuel, "See, I am about to do something in Israel that will make both ears of anyone who hears of it tingle. On that day I will fulfill against Eli all that I have spoken concerning his house, from beginning to end. For I have told him that I am about to punish his house forever, for the iniquity that he knew, because his sons were blaspheming God, and he did not restrain them. Therefore I swear to the house of Eli that the iniquity of Eli's house shall not be expiated by sacrifice or offering forever." Samuel lay there until morning; then he opened the doors of the house of the LORD. Samuel was afraid to tell the vision to Eli. But Eli called Samuel and said, "Samuel, my son." He said, "Here I am." Eli said, "What was it that he told you? Do not hide it from me. May God do so to you and more also, if you hide anything from me of all that he told you." So Samuel told him everything and hid nothing from him. Then he said, "It is the LORD; let him do what seems good to him." As Samuel grew up, the LORD was with him and let none of his words fall to the ground. And all Israel from Dan to Beer-sheba knew that Samuel was a trustworthy prophet of the LORD.]

The Response   **Psalm 139:1-5, 12-17**

Psalm 139:1-5, 12-17   *Domine, probasti*

1   LORD, you have searched me out and known me; *
        you know my sitting down and my rising up;
        you discern my thoughts from afar.

2   You trace my journeys and my resting-places *
        and are acquainted with all my ways.

3   Indeed, there is not a word on my lips, *
        but you, O LORD, know it altogether.

4   You press upon me behind and before *
        and lay your hand upon me.

5   Such knowledge is too wonderful for me; *
        it is so high that I cannot attain to it.

12 For you yourself created my inmost parts;*
        you knit me together in my mother's womb.

13 I will thank you because I am marvelously made; *
        your works are wonderful, and I know it well.

14 My body was not hidden from you, *
        while I was being made in secret
        and woven in the depths of the earth.

15 Your eyes beheld my limbs, yet unfinished in the womb;
    all of them were written in your book; *
        they were fashioned day by day,
        when as yet there was none of them.

16 How deep I find your thoughts, O God! *
        how great is the sum of them!

17 If I were to count them, they would be more in number
                    than the sand; *
        to count them all, my life span would need to
                    be like yours.

The Epistle   **1 Corinthians 6:12-20**

"All things are lawful for me," but not all things are beneficial. "All things are
lawful for me," but I will not be dominated by anything. "Food is meant for
the stomach and the stomach for food," and God will destroy both one and the
other. The body is meant not for fornication but for the Lord, and the Lord for
the body. And God raised the Lord and will also raise us by his power. Do you
not know that your bodies are members of Christ? Should I therefore take the
members of Christ and make them members of a prostitute? Never! Do you
not know that whoever is united to a prostitute becomes one body with her?
For it is said, "The two shall be one flesh." But anyone united to the Lord

becomes one spirit with him. Shun fornication! Every sin that a person commits is outside the body; but the fornicator sins against the body itself. Or do you not know that your body is a temple of the Holy Spirit within you, which you have from God, and that you are not your own? For you were bought with a price; therefore glorify God in your body.

The Gospel   John 1:43-51
The next day Jesus decided to go to Galilee. He found Philip and said to him, "Follow me." Now Philip was from Bethsaida, the city of Andrew and Peter. Philip found Nathanael and said to him, "We have found him about whom Moses in the law and also the prophets wrote, Jesus son of Joseph from Nazareth." Nathanael said to him, "Can anything good come out of Nazareth?" Philip said to him, "Come and see." When Jesus saw Nathanael coming toward him, he said of him, "Here is truly an Israelite in whom there is no deceit!" Nathanael asked him, "Where did you get to know me?" Jesus answered, "I saw you under the fig tree before Philip called you." Nathanael replied, "Rabbi, you are the Son of God! You are the King of Israel!" Jesus answered, "Do you believe because I told you that I saw you under the fig tree? You will see greater things than these." And he said to him, "Very truly, I tell you, you will see heaven opened and the angels of God ascending and descending upon the Son of Man."

Year C
Isaiah 62:1-5
Psalm 36:5-10
1 Corinthians 12:1-11
John 2:1-11

The Lesson   Isaiah 62:1-5
For Zion's sake I will not keep silent, and for Jerusalem's sake I will not rest, until her vindication shines out like the dawn, and her salvation like a burning torch. The nations shall see your vindication, and all the kings your glory; and you shall be called by a new name that the mouth of the LORD will give. You shall be a crown of beauty in the hand of the LORD, and a royal diadem in the hand of your God. You shall no more be termed Forsaken, and your land shall no more be termed Desolate; but you shall be called My Delight Is in Her, and your land Married; for the LORD delights in you, and your land shall be married. For as a young man marries a young woman, so shall your builder marry you, and as the bridegroom rejoices over the bride, so shall your God rejoice over you.

The Response   Psalm 36:5-10

Psalm 36:5-10 *Dixit injustus*

5 Your love, O Lord, reaches to the heavens, *
    and your faithfulness to the clouds.
6 Your righteousness is like the strong mountains,
    your justice like the great deep; *
      you save both man and beast, O Lord.
7 How priceless is your love, O God! *
    your people take refuge under the
        shadow of your wings.
8 They feast upon the abundance of your house; *
    you give them drink from the river of your delights.
9 For with you is the well of life, *
    and in your light we see light.
10 Continue your loving-kindness to those who know you, *
    and your favor to those who are true of heart.

The Epistle   1 Corinthians 12:1-11

Now concerning spiritual gifts, brothers and sisters, I do not want you to be
uninformed. You know that when you were pagans, you were enticed and led
astray to idols that could not speak. Therefore I want you to understand that
no one speaking by the Spirit of God ever says "Let Jesus be cursed!" and no
one can say "Jesus is Lord" except by the Holy Spirit. Now there are varieties
of gifts, but the same Spirit; and there are varieties of services, but the same
Lord; and there are varieties of activities, but it is the same God who activates
all of them in everyone. To each is given the manifestation of the Spirit for the
common good. To one is given through the Spirit the utterance of wisdom, and
to another the utterance of knowledge according to the same Spirit, to another
faith by the same Spirit, to another gifts of healing by the one Spirit, to
another the working of miracles, to another prophecy, to another the discernment of spirits, to another various kinds of tongues, to another the interpretation of tongues. All these are activated by one and the same Spirit, who allots
to each one individually just as the Spirit chooses.

The Gospel   John 2:1-11

On the third day there was a wedding in Cana of Galilee, and the mother of
Jesus was there. Jesus and his disciples had also been invited to the wedding.
When the wine gave out, the mother of Jesus said to him, "They have no
wine." And Jesus said to her, "Woman, what concern is that to you and to me?
My hour has not yet come." His mother said to the servants, "Do whatever he
tells you." Now standing there were six stone water jars for the Jewish rites of
purification, each holding twenty or thirty gallons. Jesus said to them, "Fill the
jars with water." And they filled them up to the brim. He said to them, "Now

draw some out, and take it to the chief steward." So they took it. When the steward tasted the water that had become wine, and did not know where it came from (though the servants who had drawn the water knew), the steward called the bridegroom and said to him, "Everyone serves the good wine first, and then the inferior wine after the guests have become drunk. But you have kept the good wine until now." Jesus did this, the first of his signs, in Cana of Galilee, and revealed his glory; and his disciples believed in him.

THIRD SUNDAY AFTER THE EPIPHANY

The Collect

Give us grace, O Lord, to answer readily the call of our Savior Jesus Christ and proclaim to all people the Good News of his salvation, that we and the whole world may perceive the glory of his marvelous works; who lives and reigns with you and the Holy Spirit, one God, for ever and ever. *Amen.*

Year A
Isaiah 9:1-4
Psalm 27:1, 5-13
1 Corinthians 1:10-18
Matthew 4:12-23

The Lesson   **Isaiah 9:1-4**

There will be no gloom for those who were in anguish. In the former time he brought into contempt the land of Zebulun and the land of Naphtali, but in the latter time he will make glorious the way of the sea, the land beyond the Jordan, Galilee of the nations. The people who walked in darkness have seen a great light; those who lived in a land of deep darkness — on them light has shined. You have multiplied the nation, you have increased its joy; they rejoice before you as with joy at the harvest, as people exult when dividing plunder. For the yoke of their burden, and the bar across their shoulders, the rod of their oppressor, you have broken as on the day of Midian.

The Response   **Psalm 27:1, 5-13**

Psalm 27:1, 5-13   *Dominus illuminatio*

1   The Lord is my light and my salvation;
    whom then shall I fear? *
        the Lord is the strength of my life;
        of whom then shall I be afraid?

5   One thing have I asked of the Lord;
    one thing I seek; *
        that I may dwell in the house of the Lord all the days
            of my life;

6 To behold the fair beauty of the LORD *
   and to seek him in his temple.
7 For in the day of trouble he shall keep me safe
                    in his shelter; *
   he shall hide me in the secrecy of his dwelling
   and set me high upon a rock.
8 Even now he lifts up my head *
   above my enemies round about me.
9 Therefore I will offer in his dwelling an oblation
   with sounds of great gladness; *
   I will sing and make music to the LORD.
10 Hearken to my voice, O LORD, when I call; *
   have mercy on me and answer me.
11 You speak in my heart and say, "Seek my face." *
   Your face, LORD, will I seek.
12 Hide not your face from me, *
   nor turn away your servant in displeasure.
13 You have been my helper;
   cast me not away; *
   do not forsake me, O God of my salvation.

The Epistle   1 Corinthians 1:10-18

I appeal to you, brothers and sisters, by the name of our Lord Jesus Christ,
that all of you be in agreement and that there be no divisions among you, but
that you be united in the same mind and the same purpose. For it has been
reported to me by Chloe's people that there are quarrels among you, my
brothers and sisters. What I mean is that each of you says, "I belong to Paul,"
or "I belong to Apollos," or "I belong to Cephas," or "I belong to Christ." Has
Christ been divided? Was Paul crucified for you? Or were you baptized in the
name of Paul? I thank God that I baptized none of you except Crispus and
Gaius, so that no one can say that you were baptized in my name. (I did
baptize also the household of Stephanas; beyond that, I do not know whether I
baptized anyone else.) For Christ did not send me to baptize but to proclaim
the gospel, and not with eloquent wisdom, so that the cross of Christ might not
be emptied of its power. For the message about the cross is foolishness to
those who are perishing, but to us who are being saved it is the power of God.

The Gospel   Matthew 4:12-23

Now when Jesus heard that John had been arrested, he withdrew to Galilee.
He left Nazareth and made his home in Capernaum by the sea, in the territory
of Zebulun and Naphtali, so that what had been spoken through the prophet
Isaiah might be fulfilled: "Land of Zebulun, land of Naphtali, on the road by

the sea, across the Jordan, Galilee of the Gentiles — the people who sat in darkness have seen a great light, and for those who sat in the region and shadow of death light has dawned." From that time Jesus began to proclaim, "Repent, for the kingdom of heaven has come near." As he walked by the Sea of Galilee, he saw two brothers, Simon, who is called Peter, and Andrew his brother, casting a net into the sea — for they were fishermen. And he said to them, "Follow me, and I will make you fish for people." Immediately they left their nets and followed him. As he went from there, he saw two other brothers, James son of Zebedee and his brother John, in the boat with their father Zebedee, mending their nets, and he called them. Immediately they left the boat and their father, and followed him. Jesus went throughout Galilee, teaching in their synagogues and proclaiming the good news of the kingdom and curing every disease and every sickness among the people.

Year B
Jonah 3:1-5, 10
Psalm 62:6-14
1 Corinthians 7:29-31
Mark 1:14-20

The Lesson   **Jonah 3:1-5, 10**

The word of the LORD came to Jonah a second time, saying, "Get up, go to Nineveh, that great city, and proclaim to it the message that I tell you." So Jonah set out and went to Nineveh, according to the word of the LORD. Now Nineveh was an exceedingly large city, a three days' walk across. Jonah began to go into the city, going a day's walk. And he cried out, "Forty days more, and Nineveh shall be overthrown!" And the people of Nineveh believed God; they proclaimed a fast, and everyone, great and small, put on sackcloth. When God saw what they did, how they turned from their evil ways, God changed his mind about the calamity that he had said he would bring upon them; and he did not do it.

The Response   **Psalm 62:6-14**

Psalm 62:6-14 *Nonne Deo?*

6 For God alone my soul in silence waits; *
        truly, my hope is in him.

7 He alone is my rock and my salvation, *
        my stronghold, so that I shall not be shaken.

8 In God is my safety and my honor; *
        God is my strong rock and my refuge.

9 Put your trust in him always, O people, *
        pour out your hearts before him, for God is our refuge.

10 Those of high degree are but a fleeting breath, *
　　even those of low estate cannot be trusted.
11 On the scales they are lighter than a breath, *
　　all of them together.
12 Put no trust in extortion;
　in robbery take no empty pride; *
　　though wealth increase, set not your heart upon it.
13 God has spoken once, twice have I heard it, *
　　that power belongs to God.
14 Steadfast love is yours, O LORD, *
　　for you repay everyone according to his deeds.

The Epistle   1 Corinthians 7:29-31

I mean, brothers and sisters, the appointed time has grown short; from now
on, let even those who have wives be as though they had none, and those who
mourn as though they were not mourning, and those who rejoice as though
they were not rejoicing, and those who buy as though they had no possessions,
and those who deal with the world as though they had no dealings with it. For
the present form of this world is passing away.

The Gospel   Mark 1:14-20

Now after John (the Baptist) was arrested, Jesus came to Galilee, proclaiming
the good news of God, and saying, "The time is fulfilled, and the kingdom of
God has come near; repent, and believe in the good news." As Jesus passed
along by the Sea of Galilee, he saw Simon and his brother Andrew casting a
net into the sea—for they were fishermen. And Jesus said to them, "Follow me
and I will make you fish for people." And immediately they left their nets and
followed him. As he went a little farther, he saw James son of Zebedee and his
brother John, who were in their boat mending the nets. Immediately he called
them; and they left their father Zebedee in the boat with the hired men, and
followed him.

Year C
Nehemiah 8:1-3, 5-6, 8-10
Psalm 19
1 Corinthians 12:12-31a
Luke 4:14-21

The Lesson   Nehemiah 8:1-3, 5-6, 8-10

All the people (of Jerusalem) gathered together into the square before the
Water Gate. They told the scribe Ezra to bring the book of the law of Moses,

which the Lord had given to Israel. Accordingly, the priest Ezra brought the law before the assembly, both men and women and all who could hear with understanding. This was on the first day of the seventh month. He read from it facing the square before the Water Gate from early morning until midday, in the presence of the men and the women and those who could understand; and the ears of all the people were attentive to the book of the law. And Ezra opened the book in the sight of all the people, for he was standing above all the people; and when he opened it, all the people stood up. Then Ezra blessed the Lord, the great God, and all the people answered, "Amen, Amen," lifting up their hands. Then they bowed their heads and worshiped the Lord with their faces to the ground. So they read from the book, from the law of God, with interpretation. They gave the sense, so that the people understood the reading. And Nehemiah, who was the governor, and Ezra the priest and scribe, and the Levites who taught the people said to all the people, "This day is holy to the Lord your God; do not mourn or weep." For all the people wept when they heard the words of the law. Then he said to them, "Go your way, eat the fat and drink sweet wine and send portions of them to those for whom nothing is prepared, for this day is holy to our Lord; and do not be grieved, for the joy of the Lord is your strength."

The Response   Psalm 19

Psalm 19   *Caeli enarrant*

1   The heavens declare the glory of God, *
        and the firmament shows his handiwork.
2   One day tells its tale to another, *
        and one night imparts knowledge to another.
3   Although they have no words or language, *
        and their voices are not heard,
4   Their sound has gone out into all lands, *
        and their message to the ends of the world.
5   In the deep has he set a pavilion for the sun; *
        it comes forth like a bridegroom out of his chamber;
        it rejoices like a champion to run its course.
6   It goes forth from the uttermost edge of the heavens
    and runs about to the end of it again; *
        nothing is hidden from its burning heat.
7   The law of the Lord is perfect
                and revives the soul; *
        the testimony of the Lord is sure
                and gives wisdom to the innocent.
8   The statutes of the Lord are just
                and rejoice the heart; *

the commandment of the LORD is clear
and gives light to the eyes.
9　The fear of the LORD is clean
and endures for ever; *
the judgments of the LORD are true
and righteous altogether.
10　More to be desired are they than gold,
more than much fine gold, *
sweeter far than honey,
than honey in the comb.
11　By them also is your servant enlightened, *
and in keeping them there is great reward.
12　Who can tell how often he offends? *
cleanse me from my secret faults.
13　Above all, keep your servant from presumptuous sins;
let them not get dominion over me; *
then shall I be whole and sound,
and innocent of a great offense.
14　Let the words of my mouth and the meditation of my
heart be acceptable in your sight, *
O LORD, my strength and my redeemer.

The Epistle   1 Corinthians 12:12-31*a*

Just as the body is one and has many members, and all the members of the
body, though many, are one body, so it is with Christ. For in the one Spirit we
were all baptized into one body — Jews or Greeks, slaves or free — and we
were all made to drink of one Spirit. Indeed, the body does not consist of one
member but of many. If the foot would say, "Because I am not a hand, I do
not belong to the body," that would not make it any less a part of the body.
And if the ear would say, "Because I am not an eye, I do not belong to the
body," that would not make it any less a part of the body. If the whole body
were an eye, where would the hearing be? If the whole body were hearing,
where would the sense of smell be? But as it is, God arranged the members in
the body, each one of them, as he chose. If all were a single member, where
would the body be? As it is, there are many members, yet one body. The eye
cannot say to the hand, "I have no need of you," nor again the head to the feet,
"I have no need of you." On the contrary, the members of the body that seem
to be weaker are indispensable, and those members of the body that we think
less honorable we clothe with greater honor, and our less respectable members
are treated with greater respect; whereas our more respectable members do not
need this. But God has so arranged the body, giving the greater honor to the
inferior member, that there may be no dissension within the body, but the

members may have the same care for one another. If one member suffers, all suffer together with it; if one member is honored, all rejoice together with it. Now you are the body of Christ and individually members of it. And God has appointed in the church first apostles, second prophets, third teachers; then deeds of power, then gifts of healing, forms of assistance, forms of leadership, various kinds of tongues. Are all apostles? Are all prophets? Are all teachers? Do all work miracles? Do all possess gifts of healing? Do all speak in tongues? Do all interpret? But, strive for the greater gift.

The Gospel   **Luke 4:14-21**
Jesus, filled with the power of the Spirit, returned to Galilee, and a report about him spread through all the surrounding country. He began to teach in their synagogues and was praised by everyone. When he came to Nazareth, where he had been brought up, he went to the synagogue on the sabbath day, as was his custom. He stood up to read, and the scroll of the prophet Isaiah was given to him. He unrolled the scroll and found the place where it was written: "The Spirit of the Lord is upon me, because he has anointed me to bring good news to the poor. He has sent me to proclaim release to the captives and recovery of sight to the blind, to let the oppressed go free, to proclaim the year of the Lord's favor." And he rolled up the scroll, gave it back to the attendant, and sat down. The eyes of all in the synagogue were fixed on him. Then he began to say to them, "Today this scripture has been fulfilled in your hearing."

FOURTH SUNDAY AFTER THE EPIPHANY
The Collect
Almighty and everlasting God, you govern all things both in heaven and on earth: Mercifully hear the supplications of your people, and in our time grant us your peace; through Jesus Christ our Lord, who lives and reigns with you and the Holy Spirit, one God, for ever and ever. *Amen.*

Year A
Micah 6:1-8
Psalm 15
1 Corinthians 1:18-31
Matthew 5:1-12

The Lesson   **Micah 6:1-8**
Hear what the LORD says: Rise, plead your case before the mountains, and let the hills hear your voice. Hear, you mountains, the controversy of the LORD, and you enduring foundations of the earth; for the LORD has a controversy

with his people, and he will contend with Israel. "O my people, what have I done to you? In what have I wearied you? Answer me! For I brought you up from the land of Egypt, and redeemed you from the house of slavery; and I sent before you Moses, Aaron, and Miriam. O my people, remember now what King Balak of Moab devised, what Balaam son of Beor answered him, and what happened from Shittim to Gilgal, that you may know the saving acts of the LORD." With what shall I come before the LORD, and bow myself before God on high? Shall I come before him with burnt offerings, with calves a year old? Will the LORD be pleased with thousands of rams, with ten thousands of rivers of oil? Shall I give my firstborn for my transgression, the fruit of my body for the sin of my soul?" He has told you, O mortal, what is good; and what does the LORD require of you but to do justice, and to love kindness, and to walk humbly with your God?

The Response   **Psalm 15**

Psalm 15   *Domine, quis habitabit?*

1   LORD, who may dwell in your tabernacle? *
     who may abide upon your holy hill?
2   Whoever leads a blameless life and does what is right, *
     who speaks the truth from his heart.
3   There is no guile upon his tongue;
     he does no evil to his friend; *
     he does not heap contempt upon his neighbor.
4   In his sight the wicked is rejected, *
     but he honors those who fear the LORD.
5   He has sworn to do no wrong *
     and does not take back his word.
6   He does not give his money in hope of gain, *
     nor does he take a bribe against the innocent.
7   Whoever does these things *
     shall never be overthrown.

The Epistle   **1 Corinthians 1:18-31**

The message about the cross is foolishness to those who are perishing, but to us who are being saved it is the power of God. For it is written, "I will destroy the wisdom of the wise, and the discernment of the discerning I will thwart." Where is the one who is wise? Where is the scribe? Where is the debater of this age? Has not God made foolish the wisdom of the world? For since, in the wisdom of God, the world did not know God through wisdom, God decided, through the foolishness of our proclamation, to save those who believe. For Jews demand signs and Greeks desire wisdom, but we proclaim Christ cruci-fied, a stumbling block to Jews and foolishness to Gentiles, but to those who are the called, both Jews and Greeks, Christ the power of God and the wisdom of God. For God's foolishness is wiser than human wisdom, and God's weakness is stronger than human strength. Consider your own call, brothers and sisters: not many of you were wise by human standards, not many were powerful, not many were of noble birth. But God chose what is foolish in the world to shame the wise; God chose what is weak in the world to shame the strong; God chose what is low and despised in the world, things that are not, to reduce to nothing things that are, so that no one might boast in the presence of God. He is the source of your life in Christ Jesus, who became for us wisdom from God, and righteousness and sanctification and redemption, in order that, as it is written, "Let the one who boasts, boast in the Lord."

The Gospel   Matthew 5:1-12

When Jesus saw the crowds, he went up the mountain; and after he sat down, his disciples came to him. Then he began to speak, and taught them, saying: "Blessed are the poor in spirit, for theirs is the kingdom of heaven. Blessed are those who mourn, for they will be comforted. Blessed are the meek, for they will inherit the earth. Blessed are those who hunger and thirst for righteousness, for they will be filled. Blessed are the merciful, for they will receive mercy. Blessed are the pure in heart, for they will see God. Blessed are the peacemakers, for they will be called children of God. Blessed are those who are persecuted for righteousness' sake, for theirs is the kingdom of heaven. Blessed are you when people revile you and persecute you and utter all kinds of evil against you falsely on my account. Rejoice and be glad, for your reward is great in heaven, for in the same way they persecuted the prophets who were before you."

Year B
Deuteronomy 18:15-20
Psalm 111
1 Corinthians 8:1-13
Mark 1:21-28

The Lesson   Deuteronomy 18:15-20

The LORD your God will raise up for you a prophet like me from among your own people; you shall heed such a prophet. This is what you requested of the LORD your God at Horeb on the day of the assembly when you said: "If I hear the voice of the LORD my God any more, or ever again see this great fire, I will die." Then the LORD replied to me: "They are right in what they have said. I will raise up for them a prophet like you from among their own people; I will put my words in the mouth of the prophet, who shall speak to them everything that I command. Anyone who does not heed the words that the prophet shall speak in my name, I myself will hold accountable. But any prophet who speaks in the name of other gods, or who presumes to speak in my name a word that I have not commanded the prophet to speak—that prophet shall die."

The Response Psalm 111

Psalm 111 *Confitebor tibi*

1 Hallelujah!
   I will give thanks to the LORD with my whole heart, *
       in the assembly of the upright, in the congregation.
2 Great are the deeds of the LORD! *
       they are studied by all who delight in them.
3 His work is full of majesty and splendor, *
       and his righteousness endures for ever.
4 He makes his marvelous works to be remembered; *
       the LORD is gracious and full of compassion.
5 He gives food to those who fear him; *
       he is ever mindful of his covenant.
6 He has shown his people the power of his works *
       in giving them the lands of the nations.
7 The works of his hands are faithfulness and justice; *
       all his commandments are sure.
8 They stand fast for ever and ever, *
       because they are done in truth and equity.
9 He sent redemption to his people;
   he commanded his covenant for ever; *
       holy and awesome is his Name.
10 The fear of the LORD is the beginning of wisdom; *
       those who act accordingly have a good understanding;
       his praise endures for ever.

The Epistle 1 Corinthians 8:1-13

Now concerning food sacrificed to idols: we know that "all of us possess knowledge." Knowledge puffs up, but love builds up. Anyone who claims to know something does not yet have the necessary knowledge; but anyone who loves God is known by him. Hence, as to the eating of food offered to idols, we know that "no idol in the world really exists," and that "there is no God but one." Indeed, even though there may be so-called gods in heaven or on earth—as in fact there are many gods and many lords — yet for us there is one God, the Father, from whom are all things and for whom we exist, and one Lord, Jesus Christ, through whom are all things and through whom we exist. It is not everyone, however, who has this knowledge. Since some have become so accustomed to idols until now, they still think of the food they eat as food offered to an idol; and their conscience, being weak, is defiled. "Food will not bring us close to God." We are no worse off if we do not eat, and no better off if we do. But take care that this liberty of yours does not somehow become a stumbling block to the weak. For if others see you, who possess knowledge, eating in the temple of an idol, might they not, since their conscience is weak, be encouraged to the point of eating food sacrificed to idols? So by your knowledge those weak believers for whom Christ died are destroyed. But when you thus sin against members of your family, and wound their conscience when it is weak, you sin against Christ. Therefore, if food is a cause of their falling, I will never eat meat, so that I may not cause one of them to fall.

The Gospel   **Mark 1:21-28**
Jesus and his disciples went to Capernaum; and when the sabbath came, he entered the synagogue and taught. They were astounded at his teaching, for he taught them as one having authority, and not as the scribes. Just then there was in their synagogue a man with an unclean spirit, and he cried out, "What have you to do with us, Jesus of Nazareth? Have you come to destroy us? I know who you are, the Holy One of God." But Jesus rebuked him, saying, "Be silent, and come out of him!" And the unclean spirit, convulsing him and crying with a loud voice, came out of him. They were all amazed, and they kept on asking one another, "What is this? A new teaching — with authority! He commands even the unclean spirits, and they obey him." At once his fame began to spread throughout the surrounding region of Galilee.

Year C
Jeremiah 1:4-10
Psalm 71:1-6
1 Corinthians 13:1-13
Luke 4:21-30

The Lesson   **Jeremiah 1:4-10**
Now the word of the LORD came to me saying, "Before I formed you in the womb I knew you, and before you were born I consecrated you; I appointed you a prophet to the nations." Then I said, "Ah, Lord GOD! Truly I do not know how to speak, for I am only a boy." But the LORD said to me, "Do not say, 'I am only a boy'; for you shall go to all to whom I send you, and you shall speak whatever I command you. Do not be afraid of them, for I am with you to deliver you, says the LORD." Then the LORD put out his hand and

touched my mouth; and the LORD said to me, "Now I have put my words in your mouth. See, today I appoint you over nations and over kingdoms, to pluck up and to pull down, to destroy and to overthrow, to build and to plant."

The Response   Psalm 71:1-6

Psalm 71:1-6 *In te, Domine, speravi*

1   In you, O LORD, have I taken refuge; *
      let me never be ashamed.
2   In your righteousness, deliver me and set me free; *
      incline your ear to me and save me.
3   Be my strong rock, a castle to keep me safe; *
      you are my crag and my stronghold.
4   Deliver me, my God, from the hand of the wicked, *
      from the clutches of the evildoer and the oppressor.
5   For you are my hope, O LORD God, *
      my confidence since I was young.
6   I have been sustained by you ever since I was born;
      from my mother's womb you have been my strength; *
      my praise shall be always of you.

The Epistle   1 Corinthians 13:1-13

If I speak in the tongues of mortals and of angels, but do not have love, I am a noisy gong or a clanging cymbal. And if I have prophetic powers, and understand all mysteries and all knowledge, and if I have all faith, so as to remove mountains, but do not have love, I am nothing. If I give away all my possessions, and if I hand over my body so that I may boast, but do not have love, I gain nothing. Love is patient; love is kind; love is not envious or boastful or arrogant or rude. It does not insist on its own way; it is not irritable or resentful; it does not rejoice in wrongdoing, but rejoices in the truth. It bears all things, believes all things, hopes all things, endures all things. Love never ends. But as for prophecies, they will come to an end; as for tongues, they will cease; as for knowledge, it will come to an end. For we know only in part, and we prophesy only in part; but when the complete comes, the partial will come to an end. When I was a child, I spoke like a child, I thought like a child, I reasoned like a child; when I became an adult, I put an end to childish ways. For now we see in a mirror, dimly, but then we will see face to face. Now I know only in part; then I will know fully, even as I have been fully known. And now faith, hope, and love abide, these three; and the greatest of these is love.

The Gospel   Luke 4:21-30

Jesus began to say to them, "Today this scripture has been fulfilled in your hearing." All spoke well of him and were amazed at the gracious words that came from his mouth. They said, "Is not this Joseph's son?" He said to them, "Doubtless you will quote to me this proverb, 'Doctor, cure yourself!' And you will say, 'Do here also in your hometown the things that we have heard you did at Capernaum.' " And he said, "Truly I tell you, no prophet is accepted in the prophet's hometown. But the truth is, there were many widows in Israel in the time of Elijah, when the heaven was shut up three years and six months, and there was a severe famine over all the land; yet Elijah was sent to none of them except to a widow at Zarephath in Sidon. There were also many lepers in Israel in the time of the prophet Elisha, and none of them was cleansed except Naaman the Syrian." When they heard this, all in the synagogue were filled with rage. They got up, drove him out of the town, and led him to the brow of the hill on which their town was built, so that they might hurl him off the cliff. But he passed through the midst of them and went on his way.

FIFTH SUNDAY AFTER THE EPIPHANY
The Collect

Set us free, O God, from the bondage of our sins, and give us the liberty of that abundant life which you have made known to us in your Son our Savior Jesus Christ; who lives and reigns with you, in the unity of the Holy Spirit, one God, now and for ever. *Amen.*

Year A
Isaiah 58:1-9a, (9b-12)
Psalm 112:1-9 (10)
1 Corinthians 2:1-12, (13-16)
Matthew 5:13-20

The Lesson   Isaiah 58:1-9*a*, (9*b*-12)

Shout out, do not hold back! Lift up your voice like a trumpet! Announce to my people their rebellion, to the house of Jacob their sins. Yet day after day they seek me and delight to know my ways, as if they were a nation that practiced righteousness and did not forsake the ordinance of their God; they ask of me righteous judgments, they delight to draw near to God. "Why do we fast, but you do not see? Why humble ourselves, but you do not notice?" Look, you serve your own interest on your fast day, and oppress all your workers. Look, you fast only to quarrel and to fight and to strike with a wicked fist. Such fasting as you do today will not make your voice heard on high. Is such the fast that I choose, a day to humble oneself? Is it to bow down the head like a bulrush, and to lie in sackcloth and ashes? Will you call this a fast, a day acceptable to the LORD? Is not this the fast that I choose: to loose the bonds of injustice, to undo the thongs of the yoke, to let the oppressed go free, and to break every yoke? Is it not to share your bread with the hungry, and bring the homeless poor into your house; when you see the naked, to cover them, and not to hide yourself from your own kin? Then your light shall break forth like the dawn, and your healing shall spring up quickly; your vindicator shall go before you, the glory of the LORD shall be your rear guard. Then you shall call, and the LORD will answer; you shall cry for help, and he will say, Here I am.

Isaiah 58:(9b-12) [If you remove the yoke from among you, the pointing of the finger, the speaking of evil, if you offer your food to the hungry and satisfy the needs of the afflicted, then your light shall rise in the darkness and your gloom be like the noonday. The LORD will guide you continually, and satisfy your needs in parched places, and make your bones strong; and you shall be like a watered garden, like a spring of water, whose waters never fail. Your ancient ruins shall be rebuilt; you shall raise up the foundations of many generations; you shall be called the repairer of the breach, the restorer of streets to live in.]

The Response   Psalm 112:1-9, (10)

Psalm 112:1-9, (10)   *Beatus vir*

1   Hallelujah!
    Happy are they who fear the LORD *
        and have great delight in his commandments!
2   Their descendants will be mighty in the land; *
        the generation of the upright will be blessed.
3   Wealth and riches will be in their house, *
        and their righteousness will last for ever.
4   Light shines in the darkness for the upright; *
        the righteous are merciful and full of compassion.
5   It is good for them to be generous in lending *
        and to manage their affairs with justice.
6   For they will never be shaken; *
        the righteous will be kept in everlasting remembrance.
7   They will not be afraid of any evil rumors; *
        their heart is right;
        they put their trust in the LORD.
8   Their heart is established and will not shrink, *
        until they see their desire upon their enemies.

9   They have given freely to the poor, *
        and their righteousness stands fast for ever;
        they will hold up their head with honor.

[10   The wicked will see it and be angry;
        they will gnash their teeth and pine away; *
        the desires of the wicked will perish.]

The Epistle   1 Corinthians 2:1-12, (13-16)
1 Corinthians 2:1-12

When I came to you, brothers and sisters, I did not come proclaiming the
mystery of God to you in lofty words or wisdom. For I decided to know
nothing among you except Jesus Christ, and him crucified. And I came to you
in weakness and in fear and in much trembling. My speech and my proclamation were not with plausible words of wisdom, but with a demonstration of the
Spirit and of power, so that your faith might rest not on human wisdom but on
the power of God. Yet among the mature we do speak wisdom, though it is not
a wisdom of this age or of the rulers of this age, who are doomed to perish.
But we speak God's wisdom, secret and hidden, which God decreed before the
ages for our glory. None of the rulers of this age understood this; for if they
had, they would not have crucified the Lord of glory. But, as it is written,
"What no eye has seen, nor ear heard, nor the human heart conceived, what
God has prepared for those who love him"—these things God has revealed to
us through the Spirit; for the Spirit searches everything, even the depths of
God. For what human being knows what is truly human except the human
spirit that is within? So also no one comprehends what is truly God's except
the Spirit of God. Now we have received not the spirit of the world, but the
Spirit that is from God, so that we may understand the gifts bestowed on us
by God.

1 Corinthians 2:(13-16) [And we speak of these things in words not taught by
human wisdom but taught by the Spirit, interpreting spiritual things to those
who are spiritual. Those who are unspiritual do not receive the gifts of God's
Spirit, for they are foolishness to them, and they are unable to understand
them because they are spiritually discerned. Those who are spiritual discern
all things, and they are themselves subject to no one else's scrutiny. "For who
has known the mind of the Lord so as to instruct him?" But we have the mind
of Christ.]

The Gospel   Matthew 5:13-20

Jesus said, "You are the salt of the earth; but if salt has lost its taste, how can
its saltiness be restored? It is no longer good for anything, but is thrown out

and trampled under foot. You are the light of the world. A city built on a hill cannot be hid. No one after lighting a lamp puts it under the bushel basket, but on the lampstand, and it gives light to all in the house. In the same way, let your light shine before others, so that they may see your good works and give glory to your Father in heaven. Do not think that I have come to abolish the law or the prophets; I have come not to abolish but to fulfill. For truly I tell you, until heaven and earth pass away, not one letter, not one stroke of a letter, will pass from the law until all is accomplished. Therefore, whoever breaks one of the least of these commandments, and teaches others to do the same, will be called least in the kingdom of heaven; but whoever does them and teaches them will be called great in the kingdom of heaven. For I tell you, unless your righteousness exceeds that of the scribes and Pharisees, you will never enter the kingdom of heaven.

Year B
Isaiah 40:21-31
Psalm 147:1-12, 21c
1 Corinthians 9:16-23
Mark 1:29-39

The Lesson   **Isaiah 40:21-31**

Have you not known? Have you not heard? Has it not been told you from the beginning? Have you not understood from the foundations of the earth? It is he who sits above the circle of the earth, and its inhabitants are like grasshoppers; who stretches out the heavens like a curtain, and spreads them like a tent to live in; who brings princes to naught, and makes the rulers of the earth as nothing. Scarcely are they planted, scarcely sown, scarcely has their stem taken root in the earth, when he blows upon them, and they wither, and the tempest carries them off like stubble. To whom then will you compare me, or who is my equal? says the Holy One. Lift up your eyes on high and see: Who created these? He who brings out their host and numbers them, calling them all by name; because he is great in strength, mighty in power, not one is missing. Why do you say, O Jacob, and speak, O Israel, "My way is hidden from the LORD, and my right is disregarded by my God"? Have you not known? Have you not heard? The LORD is the everlasting God, the Creator of the ends of the earth. He does not faint or grow weary; his understanding is unsearchable. He gives power to the faint, and strengthens the powerless. Even youths will faint and be weary, and the young will fall exhausted; but those who wait for the LORD shall renew their strength, they shall mount up with wings like eagles, they shall run and not be weary, they shall walk and not faint.

The Response   Psalm 147:1-12, 21c

Psalm 147:1-12, 21c   *Laudate Dominum*

  1 Hallelujah!
     How good it is to sing praises to our God! *
       how pleasant it is to honor him with praise!

  2 The LORD rebuilds Jerusalem; *
     he gathers the exiles of Israel.

  3 He heals the brokenhearted *
     and binds up their wounds.

  4 He counts the number of the stars *
     and calls them all by their names.

  5 Great is our LORD and mighty in power; *
     there is no limit to his wisdom.

  6 The LORD lifts up the lowly, *
     but casts the wicked to the ground.

  7 Sing to the LORD with thanksgiving; *
     make music to our God upon the harp.

  8 He covers the heavens with clouds *
     and prepares rain for the earth;

  9 He makes grass to grow upon the mountains *
     and green plants to serve mankind.

10 He provides food for flocks and herds *
     and for the young ravens when they cry.

11 He is not impressed by the might of a horse; *
     he has no pleasure in the strength of a man;

12 But the LORD has pleasure in those who fear him, *
     in those who await his gracious favor. Hallelujah!

The Epistle   1 Corinthians 9:16-23

If I proclaim the gospel, this gives me no ground for boasting, for an obliga-
tion is laid on me, and woe to me if I do not proclaim the gospel! For if I do
this of my own will, I have a reward; but if not of my own will, I am entrusted with a commission. What then is my reward? Just this: that in my
proclamation I may make the gospel free of charge, so as not to make full use
of my rights in the gospel. For though I am free with respect to all, I have
made myself a slave to all, so that I might win more of them. To the Jews I
became as a Jew, in order to win Jews. To those under the law I became as
one under the law (though I myself am not under the law) so that I might win
those under the law. To those outside the law I became as one outside the law
(though I am not free from God's law but am under Christ's law) so that I
might win those outside the law. To the weak I became weak, so that I might

win the weak. I have become all things to all people, that I might by all means save some. I do it all for the sake of the gospel, so that I may share in its blessings.

The Gospel   Mark 1:29-39
Jesus left the synagogue, at Capernaum and entered the house of Simon and Andrew, with James and John. Now Simon's mother-in-law was in bed with a fever, and they told him about her at once. He came and took her by the hand and lifted her up. Then the fever left her, and she began to serve them. That evening, at sundown, they brought to him all who were sick or possessed with demons. And the whole city was gathered around the door. And he cured many who were sick with various diseases, and cast out many demons; and he would not permit the demons to speak, because they knew him. In the morning, while it was still very dark, he got up and went out to a deserted place, and there he prayed. And Simon and his companions hunted for him. When they found him, they said to him, "Everyone is searching for you." He answered, "Let us go on to the neighboring towns, so that I may proclaim the message there also; for that is what I came out to do." And he went throughout Galilee, proclaiming the message in their synagogues and casting out demons.

Year C
Isaiah 6:1-8, (9-13)
Psalm 138
1 Corinthians 15:1-11
Luke 5:1-11

The Lesson   Isaiah 6:1-8, (9-13)
Isaiah 6:1-8
In the year that King Uzziah died, I saw the Lord sitting on a throne, high and lofty; and the hem of his robe filled the temple. Seraphs were in attendance above him; each had six wings: with two they covered their faces, and with two they covered their feet, and with two they flew. And one called to another and said: "Holy, holy, holy is the LORD of hosts; the whole earth is full of his glory." The pivots on the thresholds shook at the voices of those who called, and the house filled with smoke. And I said: "Woe is me! I am lost, for I am a man of unclean lips, and I live among a people of unclean lips; yet my eyes have seen the King, the LORD of hosts!" Then one of the seraphs flew to me, holding a live coal that had been taken from the altar with a pair of tongs. The seraph touched my mouth with it and said: "Now that this has touched your

lips, your guilt has departed and your sin is blotted out." Then I heard the voice of the Lord saying, "Whom shall I send, and who will go for us?" And I said, "Here am I; send me!"

Isaiah 6:(9-13) [And he said, "Go and say to this people: 'Keep listening, but do not comprehend; keep looking, but do not understand.' Make the mind of this people dull, and stop their ears, and shut their eyes, so that they may not look with their eyes, and listen with their ears, and comprehend with their minds, and turn and be healed." Then I said, "How long, O Lord?" And he said: "Until cities lie waste without inhabitant, and houses without people, and the land is utterly desolate; until the LORD sends everyone far away, and vast is the emptiness in the midst of the land. Even if a tenth part remain in it, it will be burned again, like a terebinth or an oak whose stump remains standing when it is felled." The holy seed is its stump.]

The Response   Psalm 138

Psalm 138   *Confitebor tibi*

1   I will give thanks to you, O LORD, with my whole heart; *
    before the gods I will sing your praise.

2   I will bow down toward your holy temple
and praise your Name, *
    because of your love and faithfulness;

3   For you have glorified your Name *
    and your word above all things.

4   When I called, you answered me; *
    you increased my strength within me.

5   All the kings of the earth will praise you, O LORD, *
    when they have heard the words of your mouth.

6   They will sing of the ways of the LORD, *
    that great is the glory of the LORD.

7   Though the LORD be high, he cares for the lowly; *
    he perceives the haughty from afar.

8   Though I walk in the midst of trouble, you keep me safe; *
    you stretch forth your hand against the fury of my enemies;
    your right hand shall save me.

9   The LORD will make good his purpose for me; *
    O LORD, your love endures for ever;
    do not abandon the works of your hands.

The Epistle   **1 Corinthians 15:1-11**

Now I would remind you, brothers and sisters, of the good news that I proclaimed to you, which you in turn received, in which also you stand, through which also you are being saved, if you hold firmly to the message that I proclaimed to you — unless you have come to believe in vain. For I handed on to you as of first importance what I in turn had received: that Christ died for our sins in accordance with the scriptures, and that he was buried, and that he was raised on the third day in accordance with the scriptures, and that he appeared to Cephas, then to the twelve. Then he appeared to more than five hundred brothers and sisters at one time, most of whom are still alive, though some have died. Then he appeared to James, then to all the apostles. Last of all, as to one untimely born, he appeared also to me. For I am the least of the apostles, unfit to be called an apostle, because I persecuted the church of God. But by the grace of God I am what I am, and his grace toward me has not been in vain. On the contrary, I worked harder than any of them—though it was not I, but the grace of God that is with me. Whether then it was I or they, so we proclaim and so you have come to believe.

The Gospel   **Luke 5:1-11**

Once while Jesus was standing beside the lake of Gennesaret, and the crowd was pressing in on him to hear the word of God, he saw two boats there at the shore of the lake; the fishermen had gone out of them and were washing their nets. He got into one of the boats, the one belonging to Simon, and asked him to put out a little way from the shore. Then he sat down and taught the crowds from the boat. When he had finished speaking, he said to Simon, "Put out into the deep water and let down your nets for a catch." Simon answered, "Master, we have worked all night long but have caught nothing. Yet if you say so, I will let down the nets." When they had done this, they caught so many fish that their nets were beginning to break. So they signaled their partners in the other boat to come and help them. And they came and filled both boats, so that they began to sink. But when Simon Peter saw it, he fell down at Jesus' knees, saying, "Go away from me, Lord, for I am a sinful man!" For he and all who were with him were amazed at the catch of fish that they had taken; and so also were James and John, sons of Zebedee, who were partners with Simon. Then Jesus said to Simon, "Do not be afraid; from now on you will be catching people." When they had brought their boats to shore, they left everything and followed him.

SIXTH SUNDAY AFTER THE EPIPHANY

The Collect

O God, the strength of all who put their trust in you: Mercifully accept our prayers; and because in our weakness we can do nothing good without you, give us the help of your grace, that in keeping your commandments we may please you both in will and deed; through Jesus Christ our Lord, who lives and reigns with you and the Holy Spirit, one God, for ever and ever. *Amen.*

Year A
Deuteronomy 30:15-20 or Sirach 15:15-20
Psalm 119:1-8
1 Corinthians 3:1-9
Matthew 5:21-37

The Lesson   **Deuteronomy 30:15-20** *or* **Sirach 15:15-20**
Deuteronomy 30:15-20

Moses said: See, I have set before you today life and prosperity, death and adversity. If you obey the commandments of the LORD your God that I am commanding you today, by loving the LORD your God, walking in his ways, and observing his commandments, decrees, and ordinances, then you shall live and become numerous, and the LORD your God will bless you in the land that you are entering to possess. But if your heart turns away and you do not hear, but are led astray to bow down to other gods and serve them, I declare to you today that you shall perish; you shall not live long in the land that you are crossing the Jordan to enter and possess. I call heaven and earth to witness against you today that I have set before you life and death, blessings and curses. Choose life so that you and your descendants may live, loving the LORD your God, obeying him, and holding fast to him; for that means life to you and length of days, so that you may live in the land that the LORD swore to give to your ancestors, to Abraham, to Isaac, and to Jacob.

or, **Sirach 15:15-20**

If you choose, you can keep the commandments, and to act faithfully is a matter of your own choice. He has placed before you fire and water; stretch out your hand for whichever you choose. Before each person are life and death, and whichever one chooses will be given. For great is the wisdom of the Lord; he is mighty in power and sees everything; his eyes are on those who fear him, and he knows every human action. He has not commanded anyone to be wicked, and he has not given anyone permission to sin.

The Response   Psalm 119:1-8

Psalm 119:1-8   *Beati immaculati*

1   Happy are they whose way is blameless, *
      who walk in the law of the LORD!
2   Happy are they who observe his decrees *
      and seek him with all their hearts!
3   Who never do any wrong, *
      but always walk in his ways.
4   You laid down your commandments, *
      that we should fully keep them.
5   Oh, that my ways were made so direct *
      that I might keep your statutes!
6   Then I should not be put to shame, *
      when I regard all your commandments.
7   I will thank you with an unfeigned heart, *
      when I have learned your righteous judgments.
8   I will keep your statutes; *
      do not utterly forsake me.

The Epistle   1 Corinthians 3:1-9

Brothers and sisters, I could not speak to you as spiritual people, but rather as people of the flesh, as infants in Christ. I fed you with milk, not solid food, for you were not ready for solid food. Even now you are still not ready, for you are still of the flesh. For as long as there is jealousy and quarreling among you, are you not of the flesh, and behaving according to human inclinations? For when one says, "I belong to Paul," and another, "I belong to Apollos," are you not merely human? What then is Apollos? What is Paul? Servants through whom you came to believe, as the Lord assigned to each. I planted, Apollos watered, but God gave the growth. So neither the one who plants nor the one who waters is anything, but only God who gives the growth. The one who plants and the one who waters have a common purpose, and each will receive wages according to the labor of each. For we are God's servants, working together; you are God's field, God's building.

The Gospel   Matthew 5:21-37

Jesus said, "You have heard that it was said to those of ancient times, 'You shall not murder'; and 'whoever murders shall be liable to judgment.' But I say to you that if you are angry with a brother or sister, you will be liable to judgment; and if you insult a brother or sister, you will be liable to the council; and if you say, 'You fool,' you will be liable to the hell of fire. So when you are offering your gift at the altar, if you remember that your brother or sister has something against you, leave your gift there before the altar and go; first be reconciled to your brother or sister, and then come and offer your gift. Come to terms quickly with your accuser while you are on the way to court with him, or your accuser may hand you over to the judge, and the judge to the guard, and you will be thrown into prison. Truly I tell you, you will never get out until you have paid the last penny. "You have heard that it was said, 'You shall not commit adultery.' But I say to you that everyone who looks at a woman with lust has already committed adultery with her in his heart. If your right eye causes you to sin, tear it out and throw it away; it is better for you to lose one of your members than for your whole body to be thrown into hell. And if your right hand causes you to sin, cut it off and throw it away; it is better for you to lose one of your members than for your whole body to go into hell. "It was also said, 'Whoever divorces his wife, let him give her a certificate of divorce.' But I say to you that anyone who divorces his wife, except on the ground of unchastity, causes her to commit adultery; and whoever marries a divorced woman commits adultery. "Again, you have heard that it was said to those of ancient times, 'You shall not swear falsely, but carry out the vows you have made to the Lord.' But I say to you, Do not swear at all, either by heaven, for it is the throne of God, or by the earth, for it is his footstool, or by Jerusalem, for it is the city of the great King. And do not swear by your head, for you cannot make one hair white or black. Let your word be 'Yes, Yes' or 'No, No'; anything more than this comes from the evil one."

Year B
2 Kings 5:1-14
Psalm 30
1 Corinthians 9:24-27
Mark 1:40-45

The Lesson   **2 Kings 5:1-14**

Naaman, commander of the army of the king of Aram, was a great man and in high favor with his master, because by him the LORD had given victory to Aram. The man, though a mighty warrior, suffered from leprosy. Now the Arameans on one of their raids had taken a young girl captive from the land of Israel, and she served Naaman's wife. She said to her mistress, "If only my lord were with the prophet who is in Samaria! He would cure him of his leprosy." So Naaman went in and told his lord just what the girl from the land of Israel had said. And the king of Aram said, "Go then, and I will send along a letter to the king of Israel." He went, taking with him ten talents of silver, six thousand shekels of gold, and ten sets of garments. He brought the letter to the king of Israel, which read, "When this letter reaches you, know that I have sent to you my servant Naaman, that you may cure him of his leprosy." When the king of Israel read the letter, he tore his clothes and said, "Am I God, to give death or life, that this man sends word to me to cure a man of his leprosy? Just look and see how he is trying to pick a quarrel with me." But when Elisha the man of God heard that the king of Israel had torn his clothes, he sent a message to the king, "Why have you torn your clothes? Let him come to me, that he may learn that there is a prophet in Israel." So Naaman came with his horses and chariots, and halted at the entrance of Elisha's house. Elisha sent a messenger to him, saying, "Go, wash in the Jordan seven times, and your flesh shall be restored and you shall be clean." But Naaman became angry and went away, saying, "I thought that for me he would surely come out, and stand and call on the name of the LORD his God, and would wave his hand over the spot, and cure the leprosy! Are not Abana and Pharpar, the rivers of Damascus, better than all the waters of Israel? Could I not wash in them, and be clean?" He turned and went away in a rage. But his servants approached and said to him, "Father, if the prophet had commanded you to do something difficult, would you not have done it? How much more, when all he said to you was, 'Wash, and be clean'?" So he went down and immersed himself seven times in the Jordan, according to the word of the man of God; his flesh was restored like the flesh of a young boy, and he was clean.

The Response   Psalm 30

Psalm 30   *Exaltabo te, Domine*

1   I will exalt you, O LORD,
      because you have lifted me up *
          and have not let my enemies triumph over me.
2   O LORD my God, I cried out to you, *
          and you restored me to health.
3   You brought me up, O LORD, from the dead; *
          you restored my life as I was going down to the grave.
4   Sing to the LORD, you servants of his; *
          give thanks for the remembrance of his holiness.
5   For his wrath endures but the twinkling of an eye, *
          his favor for a lifetime.
6   Weeping may spend the night, *
          but joy comes in the morning.
7   While I felt secure, I said,
      "I shall never be disturbed. *
          You, LORD, with your favor, made me as strong as the mountains."
8   Then you hid your face, *
          and I was filled with fear.

9   I cried to you, O LORD; *
        I pleaded with the LORD, saying,
10   "What profit is there in my blood, if I go down to the Pit? *
        will the dust praise you or declare your faithfulness?
11   Hear, O LORD, and have mercy upon me; *
        O LORD, be my helper."
12   You have turned my wailing into dancing; *
        you have put off my sack-cloth and clothed me with joy.
13   Therefore my heart sings to you without ceasing; *
        O LORD my God, I will give you thanks for ever.

The Epistle   1 Corinthians 9:24-27

Do you not know that in a race the runners all compete, but only one receives the prize? Run in such a way that you may win it. Athletes exercise self-control in all things; they do it to receive a perishable wreath, but we an imperishable one. So I do not run aimlessly, nor do I box as though beating the air; but I punish my body and enslave it, so that after proclaiming to others I myself should not be disqualified.

The Gospel   Mark 1:40-45

A leper came to him begging Jesus, and kneeling he said to him, "If you choose, you can make me clean." Moved with pity, Jesus stretched out his hand and touched him, and said to him, "I do choose. Be made clean!" Immediately the leprosy left him, and he was made clean. After sternly warning him he sent him away at once, saying to him, "See that you say nothing to anyone; but go, show yourself to the priest, and offer for your cleansing what Moses commanded, as a testimony to them." But he went out and began to proclaim it freely, and to spread the word, so that Jesus could no longer go into a town openly, but stayed out in the country; and people came to him from every quarter.

Year C
Jeremiah 17:5-10
Psalm 1
1 Corinthians 15:12-20
Luke 6:17-26

The Lesson   Jeremiah 17:5-10

Thus says the LORD : Cursed are those who trust in mere mortals and make mere flesh their strength, whose hearts turn away from the LORD . They shall be like a shrub in the desert, and shall not see when relief comes. They shall live in the parched places of the wilderness, in an uninhabited salt land. Blessed are those who trust in the LORD, whose trust is the LORD. They shall be like a tree planted by water, sending out its roots by the stream. It shall not fear when heat comes, and its leaves shall stay green; in the year of drought it is not anxious, and it does not cease to bear fruit. The heart is devious above all else; it is perverse — who can understand it? I the LORD test the mind and search the heart, to give to all according to their ways, according to the fruit of their doings.

The Response   Psalm 1

Psalm 1   *Beatus vir qui non abiit*

1   Happy are they who have not walked in the counsel of
                                    the wicked, *
            nor lingered in the way of sinners,
            nor sat in the seats of the scornful!
2   Their delight is in the law of the LORD, *
            and they meditate on his law day and night.
3   They are like trees planted by streams of water,
            bearing fruit in due season, with leaves that do not wither; *
            everything they do shall prosper.
4   It is not so with the wicked; *
            they are like chaff which the wind blows away.
5   Therefore the wicked shall not stand upright when
                                    judgment comes, *
            nor the sinner in the council of the righteous.
6   For the LORD knows the way of the righteous, *
            but the way of the wicked is doomed.

The Epistle   1 Corinthians 15:12-20

Now if Christ is proclaimed as raised from the dead, how can some of you say there is no resurrection of the dead? If there is no resurrection of the dead, then Christ has not been raised; and if Christ has not been raised, then our proclamation has been in vain and your faith has been in vain. We are even found to be misrepresenting God, because we testified of God that he raised Christ — whom he did not raise if it is true that the dead are not raised. For if the dead are not raised, then Christ has not been raised. If Christ has not been raised, your faith is futile and you are still in your sins. Then those also who have died in Christ have perished. If for this life only we have hoped in Christ, we are of all people most to be pitied. But in fact Christ has been raised from the dead, the first fruits of those who have died.

The Gospel   **Luke 6:17-26**

Jesus came down with them and stood on a level place, with a great crowd of
his disciples and a great multitude of people from all Judea, Jerusalem, and
the coast of Tyre and Sidon. They had come to hear him and to be healed of
their diseases; and those who were troubled with unclean spirits were cured.
And all in the crowd were trying to touch him, for power came out from him
and healed all of them. Then he looked up at his disciples and said: "Blessed
are you who are poor, for yours is the kingdom of God. Blessed are you who
are hungry now, for you will be filled. Blessed are you who weep now, for you
will laugh. Blessed are you when people hate you, and when they exclude you,
revile you, and defame you on account of the Son of Man. Rejoice in that day
and leap for joy, for surely your reward is great in heaven; for that is what
their ancestors did to the prophets. But woe to you who are rich, for you have
received your consolation. Woe to you who are full now, for you will be
hungry. Woe to you who are laughing now, for you will mourn and weep. Woe
to you when all speak well of you, for that is what their ancestors did to the
false prophets."

SEVENTH SUNDAY AFTER THE EPIPHANY

The Collect

O Lord, you have taught us that without love whatever we do is worth nothing: Send your Holy Spirit and pour into our hearts your greatest gift, which
is love, the true bond of peace and of all virtue, without which whoever lives
is accounted dead before you. Grant this for the sake of your only Son Jesus
Christ, who lives and reigns with you and the Holy Spirit, one God, now and
for ever. *Amen.*

Year A
Leviticus 19:1-2, 9-18
Psalm 119:33-40
1 Corinthians 3:10-11, 16-23
Matthew 5:38-48

The Lesson   **Leviticus 19:1-2, 9-18**

The LORD spoke to Moses, saying: Speak to all the congregation of the people
of Israel and say to them: You shall be holy, for I the LORD your God am holy.
When you reap the harvest of your land, you shall not reap to the very edges
of your field, or gather the gleanings of your harvest. You shall not strip your
vineyard bare, or gather the fallen grapes of your vineyard; you shall leave
them for the poor and the alien: I am the LORD your God. You shall not steal;
you shall not deal falsely; and you shall not lie to one another. And you shall
not swear falsely by my name, profaning the name of your God; I am the

LORD. You shall not defraud your neighbor; you shall not steal; and you shall not keep for yourself the wages of a laborer until morning. You shall not revile the deaf or put a stumbling block before the blind; you shall fear your God: I am the LORD. You shall not render an unjust judgment; you shall not be partial to the poor or defer to the great: with justice you shall judge your neighbor. You shall not go around as a slanderer among your people, and you shall not profit by the blood of your neighbor: I am the LORD. You shall not hate in your heart anyone of your kin; you shall reprove your neighbor, or you will incur guilt yourself. You shall not take vengeance or bear a grudge against any of your people, but you shall love your neighbor as yourself: I am the LORD.

The Response   Psalm 119:33-40

Psalm 119:33-40   *Legem pone*

33   Teach me, O LORD, the way of your statutes, *
    and I shall keep it to the end.

34   Give me understanding, and I shall keep your law; *
    I shall keep it with all my heart.

35   Make me go in the path of your commandments, *
    for that is my desire.

36   Incline my heart to your decrees *
    and not to unjust gain.

37   Turn my eyes from watching what is worthless; *
    give me life in your ways.

38   Fulfill your promise to your servant, *
    which you make to those who fear you.

39   Turn away the reproach which I dread, *
    because your judgments are good.

40   Behold, I long for your commandments; *
    in your righteousness preserve my life.

The Epistle   1 Corinthians 3:10-11, 16-23

According to the grace of God given to me, like a skilled master builder I laid a foundation, and someone else is building on it. Each builder must choose with care how to build on it. For no one can lay any foundation other than the one that has been laid; that foundation is Jesus Christ. Do you not know that you are God's temple and that God's Spirit dwells in you? If anyone destroys God's temple, God will destroy that person. For God's temple is holy, and you are that temple. Do not deceive yourselves. If you think that you are wise in this age, you should become fools so that you may become wise. For the wisdom of this world is foolishness with God. For it is written, "He catches the wise in their craftiness," and again, "The Lord knows the thoughts of the wise, that they are futile." So let no one boast about human leaders. For all things are yours, whether Paul or Apollos or Cephas or the world or life or death or the present or the future — all belong to you, and you belong to Christ, and Christ belongs to God.

The Gospel   Matthew 5:38-48

Jesus said, "You have heard that it was said, 'An eye for an eye and a tooth for a tooth.' But I say to you, Do not resist an evildoer. But if anyone strikes you on the right cheek, turn the other also; and if anyone wants to sue you and take your coat, give your cloak as well; and if anyone forces you to go one mile, go also the second mile. Give to everyone who begs from you, and do not refuse anyone who wants to borrow from you. You have heard that it was said, 'You shall love your neighbor and hate your enemy.' But I say to you, Love your enemies and pray for those who persecute you, so that you may be children of your Father in heaven; for he makes his sun rise on the evil and on the good, and sends rain on the righteous and on the unrighteous. For if you love those who love you, what reward do you have? Do not even the tax collectors do the same? And if you greet only your brothers and sisters, what more are you doing than others? Do not even the Gentiles do the same? Be perfect, therefore, as your heavenly Father is perfect."

Year B
Isaiah 43:18-25
Psalm 41
2 Corinthians 1:18-22
Mark 2:1-12

The Lesson   Isaiah 43:18-25

Do not remember the former things, or consider the things of old. I am about to do a new thing; now it springs forth, do you not perceive it? I will make a way in the wilderness and rivers in the desert. The wild animals will honor me, the jackals and the ostriches; for I give water in the wilderness, rivers in the desert, to give drink to my chosen people, the people whom I formed for myself so that they might declare my praise. Yet you did not call upon me, O Jacob; but you have been weary of me, O Israel! You have not brought me your sheep for burnt offerings, or honored me with your sacrifices. I have not burdened you with offerings, or wearied you with frankincense. You have not bought me sweet cane with money, or satisfied me with the fat of your sacrifices. But you have burdened me with your sins; you have wearied me with your iniquities. I, I am He who blots out your transgressions for my own sake, and I will not remember your sins.

The Response

Psalm 41

Psalm 41   *Beatus qui intelligit*

1 Happy are they who consider the poor and needy! *
   the LORD will deliver them in the time of trouble.

2 The LORD preserves them and keeps them alive,
so that they may be happy in the land; *
   he does not hand them over to the will of their enemies.

3 The LORD sustains them on their sickbed *
   and ministers to them in their illness.

4 I said, "LORD, be merciful to me; *
   heal me, for I have sinned against you."

5 My enemies are saying wicked things about me: *
   "When will he die, and his name perish?"

6 Even if they come to see me, they speak empty words; *
their heart collects false rumors;
they go outside and spread them.

7 All my enemies whisper together about me *
   and devise evil against me.

8 "A deadly thing," they say, "has fastened on him; *
   he has taken to his bed and will never get up again."

9 Even my best friend, whom I trusted,
who broke bread with me, *
   has lifted up his heel and turned against me.

10 But you, O LORD, be merciful to me and raise me up, *
   and I shall repay them.

11 By this I know you are pleased with me, *
   that my enemy does not triumph over me.

12 In my integrity you hold me fast, *
   and shall set me before your face for ever.

13 Blessed be the LORD God of Israel, *
   from age to age. Amen. Amen.

The Epistle

2 Corinthians 1:18-22

As surely as God is faithful, our word to you has not been "Yes and No." For the Son of God, Jesus Christ, whom we proclaimed among you, Silvanus and Timothy and I, was not "Yes and No"; but in him it is always "Yes." For in him every one of God's promises is a "Yes." For this reason it is through him that we say the "Amen," to the glory of God. But it is God who establishes us with you in Christ and has anointed us, by putting his seal on us and giving us his Spirit in our hearts as a first installment.

The Gospel   **Mark 2:1-12**

When Jesus returned to Capernaum after some days, it was reported that he was at home. So many gathered around that there was no longer room for them, not even in front of the door; and he was speaking the word to them. Then some people came, bringing to him a paralyzed man, carried by four of them. And when they could not bring him to Jesus because of the crowd, they removed the roof above him; and after having dug through it, they let down the mat on which the paralytic lay. When Jesus saw their faith, he said to the paralytic, "Son, your sins are forgiven." Now some of the scribes were sitting there, questioning in their hearts, "Why does this fellow speak in this way? It is blasphemy! Who can forgive sins but God alone?" At once Jesus perceived in his spirit that they were discussing these questions among themselves; and he said to them, "Why do you raise such questions in your hearts? Which is easier, to say to the paralytic, 'Your sins are forgiven,' or to say, 'Stand up and take your mat and walk'? But so that you may know that the Son of Man has authority on earth to forgive sins" — he said to the paralytic — "I say to you, stand up, take your mat and go to your home." And he stood up, and immediately took the mat and went out before all of them; so that they were all amazed and glorified God, saying, "We have never seen anything like this!"

Year C
Genesis 45:3-11, 15
Psalm 37:1-12, 41-42
1 Corinthians 15:35-38, 42-50
Luke 6:27-38

The Lesson   **Genesis 45:3-11, 15**

Joseph said to his brothers, "I am Joseph. Is my father still alive?" But his brothers could not answer him, so dismayed were they at his presence. Then Joseph said to his brothers, "Come closer to me." And they came closer. He said, "I am your brother, Joseph, whom you sold into Egypt. And now do not be distressed, or angry with yourselves, because you sold me here; for God sent me before you to preserve life. For the famine has been in the land these two years; and there are five more years in which there will be neither plowing nor harvest. God sent me before you to preserve for you a remnant on earth, and to keep alive for you many survivors. So it was not you who sent me here, but God; he has made me a father to Pharaoh, and lord of all his house and ruler over all the land of Egypt. Hurry and go up to my father and say to him, 'Thus says your son Joseph, God has made me lord of all Egypt; come down to me, do not delay. You shall settle in the land of Goshen, and you shall be near me, you and your children and your children's children, as well as your flocks, your herds, and all that you have. I will provide for you there—since there are five more years of famine to come—so that you and your household, and all that you have, will not come to poverty.'" And he kissed all his brothers and wept upon them; and after that his brothers talked with him.

The Response   Psalm 37:1-12, 41-42

Psalm 37:1-12, 41-42   *Noli aemulari*

1   Do not fret yourself because of evildoers; *
        do not be jealous of those who do wrong.
2   For they shall soon wither like the grass, *
        and like the green grass fade away.
3   Put your trust in the LORD and do good; *
        dwell in the land and feed on its riches.
4   Take delight in the LORD, *
        and he shall give you your heart's desire.
5   Commit your way to the LORD and put your trust in him, *
        and he will bring it to pass.
6   He will make your righteousness as clear as the light *
        and your just dealing as the noonday.
7   Be still before the LORD *
        and wait patiently for him.
8   Do not fret yourself over the one who prospers, *
        the one who succeeds in evil schemes.
9   Refrain from anger, leave rage alone; *
        do not fret yourself; it leads only to evil.
10 For evildoers shall be cut off, *
        but those who wait upon the LORD shall possess the land.
11 In a little while the wicked shall be no more; *
        you shall search out their place, but they will not be there.
12 But the lowly shall possess the land; *
        they will delight in abundance of peace.
41 But the deliverance of the righteous comes from the LORD; *
        he is their stronghold in time of trouble.
42 The LORD will help them and rescue them; *
        he will rescue them from the wicked and deliver them,
        because they seek refuge in him.

The Epistle   1 Corinthians 15:35-38, 42-50

Someone will ask, "How are the dead raised? With what kind of body do they come?" Fool! What you sow does not come to life unless it dies. And as for what you sow, you do not sow the body that is to be, but a bare seed, perhaps of wheat or of some other grain. But God gives it a body as he has chosen, and to each kind of seed its own body. So it is with the resurrection of the

SEVENTH SUNDAY AFTER EPIPHANY — Year C   87

dead. What is sown is perishable, what is raised is imperishable. It is sown in dishonor, it is raised in glory. It is sown in weakness, it is raised in power. It is sown a physical body, it is raised a spiritual body. If there is a physical body, there is also a spiritual body. Thus it is written, "The first man, Adam, became a living being"; the last Adam became a life-giving spirit. But it is not the spiritual that is first, but the physical, and then the spiritual. The first man was from the earth, a man of dust; the second man is from heaven. As was the man of dust, so are those who are of the dust; and as is the man of heaven, so are those who are of heaven. Just as we have borne the image of the man of dust, we will also bear the image of the man of heaven. What I am saying, brothers and sisters, is this: flesh and blood cannot inherit the kingdom of God, nor does the perishable inherit the imperishable.

The Gospel   Luke 6:27-38

Jesus said, "I say to you that listen, Love your enemies, do good to those who hate you, bless those who curse you, pray for those who abuse you. If anyone strikes you on the cheek, offer the other also; and from anyone who takes away your coat do not withhold even your shirt. Give to everyone who begs from you; and if anyone takes away your goods, do not ask for them again. Do to others as you would have them do to you. If you love those who love you, what credit is that to you? For even sinners love those who love them. If you do good to those who do good to you, what credit is that to you? For even sinners do the same. If you lend to those from whom you hope to receive, what credit is that to you? Even sinners lend to sinners, to receive as much again. But love your enemies, do good, and lend, expecting nothing in return. Your reward will be great, and you will be children of the Most High; for he is kind to the ungrateful and the wicked. Be merciful, just as your Father is merciful. Do not judge, and you will not be judged; do not condemn, and you will not be condemned. Forgive, and you will be forgiven; give, and it will be given to you. A good measure, pressed down, shaken together, running over, will be put into your lap; for the measure you give will be the measure you get back."

EIGHTH SUNDAY AFTER THE EPIPHANY

The Collect

Most loving Father, whose will it is for us to give thanks for all things, to fear nothing but the loss of you, and to cast all our care on you who care for us: Preserve us from faithless fears and worldly anxieties, that no clouds of this mortal life may hide from us the light of that love which is immortal, and which you have manifested to us in your Son Jesus Christ our Lord; who lives and reigns with you, in the unity of the Holy Spirit, one God, now and for ever. *Amen.*

Year A
Isaiah 49:8-16a
Psalm 131
1 Corinthians 4:1-5
Matthew 6:24-34

The Lesson Isaiah 49:8-16*a*

Thus says the LORD: In a time of favor I have answered you, on a day of salvation I have helped you; I have kept you and given you as a covenant to the people, to establish the land, to apportion the desolate heritages; saying to the prisoners, "Come out," to those who are in darkness, "Show yourselves." They shall feed along the ways, on all the bare heights shall be their pasture; they shall not hunger or thirst, neither scorching wind nor sun shall strike them down, for he who has pity on them will lead them, and by springs of water will guide them. And I will turn all my mountains into a road, and my highways shall be raised up. Lo, these shall come from far away, and lo, these from the north and from the west, and these from the land of Syene. Sing for joy, O heavens, and exult, O earth; break forth, O mountains, into singing! For the LORD has comforted his people, and will have compassion on his suffering ones. But Zion said, "The LORD has forsaken me, my Lord has forgotten me." Can a woman forget her nursing child, or show no compassion for the child of her womb? Even these may forget, yet I will not forget you. See, I have inscribed you on the palms of my hands.

The Response Psalm 131

Psalm 131 *Domine, non est*

1 O LORD, I am not proud; *
   I have no haughty looks.
2 I do not occupy myself with great matters, *
   or with things that are too hard for me.
3 But I still my soul and make it quiet,
   like a child upon its mother's breast; *
   my soul is quieted within me.
4 O Israel, wait upon the LORD, *
   from this time forth for evermore.

The Epistle 1 Corinthians 4:1-5

Think of us in this way, as servants of Christ and stewards of God's mysteries. Moreover, it is required of stewards that they be found trustworthy. But with me it is a very small thing that I should be judged by you or by any human court. I do not even judge myself. I am not aware of anything against

EIGHTH SUNDAY AFTER EPIPHANY — Year A 89

myself, but I am not thereby acquitted. It is the Lord who judges me. Therefore do not pronounce judgment before the time, before the Lord comes, who will bring to light the things now hidden in darkness and will disclose the purposes of the heart. Then each one will receive commendation from God.

The Gospel   Matthew 6:24-34

Jesus said, "No one can serve two masters; for a slave will either hate the one and love the other, or be devoted to the one and despise the other. You cannot serve God and wealth. Therefore I tell you, do not worry about your life, what you will eat or what you will drink, or about your body, what you will wear. Is not life more than food, and the body more than clothing? Look at the birds of the air; they neither sow nor reap nor gather into barns, and yet your heavenly Father feeds them. Are you not of more value than they? And can any of you by worrying add a single hour to your span of life? And why do you worry about clothing? Consider the lilies of the field, how they grow; they neither toil nor spin, yet I tell you, even Solomon in all his glory was not clothed like one of these. But if God so clothes the grass of the field, which is alive today and tomorrow is thrown into the oven, will he not much more clothe you—you of little faith? Therefore do not worry, saying, 'What will we eat?' or 'What will we drink?' or 'What will we wear?' For it is the Gentiles who strive for all these things; and indeed your heavenly Father knows that you need all these things. But strive first for the kingdom of God and his righteousness, and all these things will be given to you as well. So do not worry about tomorrow, for tomorrow will bring worries of its own. Today's trouble is enough for today."

Year B
Hosea 2:14-20
Psalm 103:1-13, 22
2 Corinthians 3:1-6
Mark 2:13-22

The Lesson   Hosea 2:14-20

The LORD said to Hosea, "Therefore, I will now allure her, and bring her into the wilderness, and speak tenderly to her. From there I will give her her vineyards, and make the Valley of Achor a door of hope. There she shall respond as in the days of her youth, as at the time when she came out of the land of Egypt. On that day, says the LORD, you will call me, 'My husband,' and no longer will you call me, 'My Baal.' For I will remove the names of the Baals from her mouth, and they shall be mentioned by name no more. I will make for you a covenant on that day with the wild animals, the birds of the air, and the creeping things of the ground; and I will abolish the bow, the sword, and war from the land; and I will make you lie down in safety. And I will take you for my wife forever; I will take you for my wife in righteousness and in justice, in steadfast love, and in mercy. I will take you for my wife in faithfulness; and you shall know the LORD."

The Response   Psalm 103:1-13, 22

Psalm 103:1-13, 22   *Benedic, anima mea*

1   Bless the LORD, O my soul, *
  and all that is within me, bless his holy Name.
2   Bless the LORD, O my soul, *
  and forget not all his benefits.
3   He forgives all your sins *
  and heals all your infirmities;
4   He redeems your life from the grave *
  and crowns you with mercy and loving-kindness;
5   He satisfies you with good things, *
  and your youth is renewed like an eagle's.
6   The LORD executes righteousness *
  and judgment for all who are oppressed.
7   He made his ways known to Moses *
  and his works to the children of Israel.
8   The LORD is full of compassion and mercy, *
  slow to anger and of great kindness.
9   He will not always accuse us, *
  nor will he keep his anger for ever.
10   He has not dealt with us according to our sins, *
  nor rewarded us according to our wickedness.
11   For as the heavens are high above the earth, *
  so is his mercy great upon those who fear him.
12   As far as the east is from the west, *
  so far has he removed our sins from us.
13   As a father cares for his children, *
  so does the LORD care for those who fear him.
22   Bless the LORD, all you works of his,
 in all places of his dominion; *
  bless the LORD, O my soul.

The Epistle   2 Corinthians 3:1-6

Are we beginning to commend ourselves again? Surely we do not need, as some do, letters of recommendation to you or from you, do we? You your-selves are our letter, written on our hearts, to be known and read by all; and you show that you are a letter of Christ, prepared by us, written not with ink but with the Spirit of the living God, not on tablets of stone but on tablets of human hearts. Such is the confidence that we have through Christ toward God. Not that we are competent of ourselves to claim anything as coming from us; our competence is from God, who has made us competent to be ministers of a new covenant, not of letter but of spirit; for the letter kills, but the Spirit gives life.

The Gospel   Mark 2:13-22

Jesus went out again beside the sea; the whole crowd gathered around him, and he taught them. As he was walking along, he saw Levi son of Alphaeus sitting at the tax booth, and he said to him, "Follow me." And he got up and followed him. And as he sat at dinner in Levi's house, many tax collectors and sinners were also sitting with Jesus and his disciples — for there were many who followed him. When the scribes of the Pharisees saw that he was eating with sinners and tax collectors, they said to his disciples, "Why does he eat with tax collectors and sinners?" When Jesus heard this, he said to them, "Those who are well have no need of a physician, but those who are sick; I have come to call not the righteous but sinners." Now John's disciples and the Pharisees were fasting; and people came and said to him, "Why do John's disciples and the disciples of the Pharisees fast, but your disciples do not fast?" Jesus said to them, "The wedding guests cannot fast while the bridegroom is with them, can they? As long as they have the bridegroom with them, they cannot fast. The days will come when the bridegroom is taken away from them, and then they will fast on that day. No one sews a piece of unshrunk cloth on an old cloak; otherwise, the patch pulls away from it, the new from the old, and a worse tear is made. And no one puts new wine into old wineskins; otherwise, the wine will burst the skins, and the wine is lost, and so are the skins; but one puts new wine into fresh wineskins."

Year C
Sirach 27:4-7 or Isaiah 55:10-13
Psalm 92:1-4, 11-14
1 Corinthians 15:51-58
Luke 6:39-49

The Lesson   Sirach 27:4-7 *or* Isaiah 55:10-13
Sirach 27:4-7

When a sieve is shaken, the refuse appears; so do a person's faults when he speaks. The kiln tests the potter's vessels; so the test of a person is in his conversation. Its fruit discloses the cultivation of a tree; so a person's speech discloses the cultivation of his mind. Do not praise anyone before he speaks, for this is the way people are tested.

or, **Isaiah 55:10-13**

As the rain and the snow come down from heaven, and do not return there until they have watered the earth, making it bring forth and sprout, giving seed to the sower and bread to the eater, so shall my word be that goes out from my mouth; it shall not return to me empty, but it shall accomplish that which I purpose, and succeed in the thing for which I sent it. For you shall go out in joy, and be led back in peace; the mountains and the hills before you shall burst into song, and all the trees of the field shall clap their hands. Instead of the thorn shall come up the cypress; instead of the brier shall come up the myrtle; and it shall be to the LORD for a memorial, for an everlasting sign that shall not be cut off.

The Response   Psalm 92:1-4, 11-14

Psalm 92:1-4, 11-14   *Bonum est confiteri*

1   It is a good thing to give thanks to the LORD, *
          and to sing praises to your Name, O Most High;
2   To tell of your loving-kindness early in the morning *
          and of your faithfulness in the night season;
3   On the psaltery, and on the lyre, *
          and to the melody of the harp.
4   For you have made me glad by your acts, O LORD; *
          and I shout for joy because of the works of your hands.
11   The righteous shall flourish like a palm tree, *
          and shall spread abroad like a cedar of Lebanon.
12   Those who are planted in the house of the LORD *
          shall flourish in the courts of our God;
13   They shall still bear fruit in old age; *
          they shall be green and succulent;
14   That they may show how upright the LORD is, *
          my Rock, in whom there is no fault.

The Epistle   1 Corinthians 15:51-58

Listen, I will tell you a mystery! We will not all die, but we will all be changed, in a moment, in the twinkling of an eye, at the last trumpet. For the trumpet will sound, and the dead will be raised imperishable, and we will be changed. For this perishable body must put on imperishability, and this mortal body must put on immortality. When this perishable body puts on imperishability, and this mortal body puts on immortality, then the saying that is written will be fulfilled: "Death has been swallowed up in victory. Where, O death, is your victory? Where, O death, is your sting?" The sting of death is sin, and the power of sin is the law. But thanks be to God, who gives us the victory through our Lord Jesus Christ. Therefore, my beloved, be steadfast, immovable, always excelling in the work of the Lord, because you know that in the Lord your labor is not in vain.

The Gospel   Luke 6:39-49

Jesus told the people a parable: "Can a blind person guide a blind person? Will not both fall into a pit? A disciple is not above the teacher, but everyone who is fully qualified will be like the teacher. Why do you see the speck in your neighbor's eye, but do not notice the log in your own eye? Or how can you say to your neighbor, 'Friend, let me take out the speck in your eye,' when you yourself do not see the log in your own eye? You hypocrite, first take the log out of your own eye, and then you will see clearly to take the speck out of your neighbor's eye. No good tree bears bad fruit, nor again does a bad tree bear good fruit; for each tree is known by its own fruit. Figs are not gathered from thorns, nor are grapes picked from a bramble bush. The good person out of the good treasure of the heart produces good, and the evil person out of evil treasure produces evil; for it is out of the abundance of the heart that the mouth speaks. Why do you call me 'Lord, Lord,' and do not do what I tell you? I will show you what someone is like who comes to me, hears my words, and acts on them. That one is like a man building a house, who dug deeply and laid the foundation on rock; when a flood arose, the river burst against that house but could not shake it, because it had been well built. But the one who hears and does not act is like a man who built a house on the ground without a foundation. When the river burst against it, immediately it fell, and great was the ruin of that house."

LAST SUNDAY AFTER THE EPIPHANY

The Collect

O God, who before the passion of your only-begotten Son revealed his glory upon the holy mountain: Grant to us that we, beholding by faith the light of his countenance, may be strengthened to bear our cross, and be changed into his likeness from glory to glory; through Jesus Christ our Lord, who lives and reigns with you and the Holy Spirit, one God, for ever and ever. *Amen.*

Year A

Exodus 24:12-18
Psalm 2 or Psalm 99
2 Peter 1:16-21
Matthew 17:1-9

The Lesson　　　　　　　　　　　　　　　　**Exodus 24:12-18**

The LORD said to Moses, "Come up to me on the mountain, and wait there; and I will give you the tablets of stone, with the law and the commandment, which I have written for their instruction." So Moses set out with his assistant Joshua, and Moses went up into the mountain of God. To the elders he had said, "Wait here for us, until we come to you again; for Aaron and Hur are with you; whoever has a dispute may go to them." Then Moses went up on the mountain, and the cloud covered the mountain. The glory of the LORD settled on Mount Sinai, and the cloud covered it for six days; on the seventh day he called to Moses out of the cloud. Now the appearance of the glory of the LORD was like a devouring fire on the top of the mountain in the sight of the people of Israel. Moses entered the cloud, and went up on the mountain. Moses was on the mountain for forty days and forty nights.

The Response　　　　　　　　　　　　　　　　**Psalm 2 *or* 99**

Psalm 2　　*Quare fremuerunt gentes?*

1　Why are the nations in an uproar? *
　　　Why do the peoples mutter empty threats?
2　Why do the kings of the earth rise up in revolt,
　　and the princes plot together, *
　　　against the LORD and against his Anointed?
3　"Let us break their yoke," they say; *
　　　"let us cast off their bonds from us."
4　He whose throne is in heaven is laughing; *
　　　the LORD has them in derision.
5　Then he speaks to them in his wrath, *
　　　and his rage fills them with terror.
6　"I myself have set my king *
　　　upon my holy hill of Zion."
7　Let me announce the decree of the LORD: *
　　　he said to me, "You are my Son;
　　　this day have I begotten you.
8　Ask of me, and I will give you the nations for
　　　　　　　　　　your inheritance *
　　　and the ends of the earth for your possession.

9   You shall crush them with an iron rod *
     and shatter them like a piece of pottery."
10   And now, you kings, be wise; *
     be warned, you rulers of the earth.
11   Submit to the LORD with fear, *
     and with trembling bow before him;
12   Lest he be angry and you perish; *
     for his wrath is quickly kindled.
13   Happy are they all *
     who take refuge in him!

or, **Psalm 99**   *Dominus regnavit*

1   The LORD is King;
     let the people tremble; *
          he is enthroned upon the cherubim;
          let the earth shake.
2   The LORD is great in Zion; *
          he is high above all peoples.
3   Let them confess his Name, which is great and awesome; *
          he is the Holy One.
4   "O mighty King, lover of justice,
     you have established equity; *
          you have executed justice and righteousness in Jacob."
5   Proclaim the greatness of the LORD our God
     and fall down before his footstool; *
          he is the Holy One.
6   Moses and Aaron among his priests,
     and Samuel among those who call upon his Name, *
          they called upon the LORD, and he answered them.
7   He spoke to them out of the pillar of cloud; *
          they kept his testimonies and the decree that he gave them.
8   "O LORD our God, you answered them indeed; *
          you were a God who forgave them,
          yet punished them for their evil deeds."
9   Proclaim the greatness of the LORD our God
     and worship him upon his holy hill; *
          for the LORD our God is the Holy One.

The Epistle   **2 Peter 1:16-21**

We did not follow cleverly devised myths when we made known to you the
power and coming of our Lord Jesus Christ, but we had been eyewitnesses of
his majesty. For he received honor and glory from God the Father when that
voice was conveyed to him by the Majestic Glory, saying, "This is my Son,

my Beloved, with whom I am well pleased." We ourselves heard this voice come from heaven, while we were with him on the holy mountain. So we have the prophetic message more fully confirmed. You will do well to be attentive to this as to a lamp shining in a dark place, until the day dawns and the morning star rises in your hearts. First of all you must understand this, that no prophecy of scripture is a matter of one's own interpretation, because no prophecy ever came by human will, but men and women moved by the Holy Spirit spoke from God.

The Gospel   Matthew 17:1-9

Six days after Peter said that Jesus was the Christ, the Son of the living God, Jesus took with him Peter and James and his brother John and led them up a high mountain, by themselves. And he was transfigured before them, and his face shone like the sun, and his clothes became dazzling white. Suddenly there appeared to them Moses and Elijah, talking with him. Then Peter said to Jesus, "Lord, it is good for us to be here; if you wish, I will make three dwellings here, one for you, one for Moses, and one for Elijah." While he was still speaking, suddenly a bright cloud overshadowed them, and from the cloud a voice said, "This is my Son, the Beloved; with him I am well pleased; listen to him!" When the disciples heard this, they fell to the ground and were overcome by fear. But Jesus came and touched them, saying, "Get up and do not be afraid." And when they looked up, they saw no one except Jesus himself alone. As they were coming down the mountain, Jesus ordered them, "Tell no one about the vision until after the Son of Man has been raised from the dead."

Year B
2 Kings 2:1-12
Psalm 50:1-6
2 Corinthians 4:3-6
Mark 9:2-9

The Lesson   2 Kings 2:1-12

Now when the LORD was about to take Elijah up to heaven by a whirlwind, Elijah and Elisha were on their way from Gilgal. Elijah said to Elisha, "Stay here; for the LORD has sent me as far as Bethel." But Elisha said, "As the LORD lives, and as you yourself live, I will not leave you." So they went down to Bethel. The company of prophets who were in Bethel came out to Elisha, and said to him, "Do you know that today the LORD will take your master away from you?" And he said, "Yes, I know; keep silent." Elijah said to him, "Elisha, stay here; for the LORD has sent me to Jericho." But he said, "As the LORD lives, and as you yourself live, I will not leave you." So they came to

Jericho. The company of prophets who were at Jericho drew near to Elisha, and said to him, "Do you know that today the LORD will take your master away from you?" And he answered, "Yes, I know; be silent." Then Elijah said to him, "Stay here; for the LORD has sent me to the Jordan." But he said, "As the LORD lives, and as you yourself live, I will not leave you." So the two of them went on. Fifty men of the company of prophets also went, and stood at some distance from them, as they both were standing by the Jordan. Then Elijah took his mantle and rolled it up, and struck the water; the water was parted to the one side and to the other, until the two of them crossed on dry ground. When they had crossed, Elijah said to Elisha, "Tell me what I may do for you, before I am taken from you." Elisha said, "Please let me inherit a double share of your spirit." He responded, "You have asked a hard thing; yet, if you see me as I am being taken from you, it will be granted you; if not, it will not." As they continued walking and talking, a chariot of fire and horses of fire separated the two of them, and Elijah ascended in a whirlwind into heaven. Elisha kept watching and crying out, "Father, father! The chariots of Israel and its horsemen!" But when he could no longer see him, he grasped his own clothes and tore them in two pieces.

The Response   Psalm 50:1-6
Psalm 50:1-6 *Deus deorum*
1   The LORD, the God of gods, has spoken; *
        he has called the earth from the rising of the sun to
                                      its setting.
2   Out of Zion, perfect in its beauty, *
        God reveals himself in glory.
3   Our God will come and will not keep silence; *
        before him there is a consuming flame,
        and round about him a raging storm.
4   He calls the heavens and the earth from above *
        to witness the judgment of his people.
5   "Gather before me my loyal followers, *
        those who have made a covenant with me
        and sealed it with sacrifice."
6   Let the heavens declare the rightness of his cause; *
        for God himself is judge.

The Epistle   2 Corinthians 4:3-6
Even if our gospel is veiled, it is veiled to those who are perishing. In their case the god of this world has blinded the minds of the unbelievers, to keep them from seeing the light of the gospel of the glory of Christ, who is the image of God. For we do not proclaim ourselves; we proclaim Jesus Christ as

Lord and ourselves as your slaves for Jesus' sake. For it is the God who said, "Let light shine out of darkness," who has shone in our hearts to give the light of the knowledge of the glory of God in the face of Jesus Christ.

The Gospel   Mark 9:2-9

Six days later, Jesus took with him Peter and James and John, and led them up a high mountain apart, by themselves. And he was transfigured before them, and his clothes became dazzling white, such as no one on earth could bleach them. And there appeared to them Elijah with Moses, who were talking with Jesus. Then Peter said to Jesus, "Rabbi, it is good for us to be here; let us make three dwellings, one for you, one for Moses, and one for Elijah." He did not know what to say, for they were terrified. Then a cloud overshadowed them, and from the cloud there came a voice, "This is my Son, the Beloved; listen to him!" Suddenly when they looked around, they saw no one with them any more, but only Jesus. As they were coming down the mountain, he ordered them to tell no one about what they had seen, until after the Son of Man had risen from the dead.

Year C
Exodus 34:29-35
Psalm 99
2 Corinthians 3:12—4:2
Luke 9:28-36, (37-43)

The Lesson   Exodus 34:29-35

Moses came down from Mount Sinai. As he came down from the mountain with the two tablets of the covenant in his hand, Moses did not know that the skin of his face shone because he had been talking with God. When Aaron and all the Israelites saw Moses, the skin of his face was shining, and they were afraid to come near him. But Moses called to them; and Aaron and all the leaders of the congregation returned to him, and Moses spoke with them. Afterward all the Israelites came near, and he gave them in commandment all that the LORD had spoken with him on Mount Sinai. When Moses had finished speaking with them, he put a veil on his face; but whenever Moses went in before the LORD to speak with him, he would take the veil off, until he came out; and when he came out, and told the Israelites what he had been commanded, the Israelites would see the face of Moses, that the skin of his face was shining; and Moses would put the veil on his face again, until he went in to speak with him.

Psalm 99   *Dominus regnavit*

1   The LORD is King;
    let the people tremble; *
        he is enthroned upon the cherubim;
        let the earth shake.

2   The LORD is great in Zion; *
        he is high above all peoples.

3   Let them confess his Name, which is great and awesome; *
        he is the Holy One.

4   "O mighty King, lover of justice,
    you have established equity; *
        you have executed justice and righteousness in Jacob."

5   Proclaim the greatness of the LORD our God
    and fall down before his footstool; *
        he is the Holy One.

6   Moses and Aaron among his priests,
    and Samuel among those who call upon his Name, *
        they called upon the LORD, and he answered them.

7   He spoke to them out of the pillar of cloud; *
        they kept his testimonies and the decree that he gave them.

8   "O LORD our God, you answered them indeed; *
        you were a God who forgave them,
        yet punished them for their evil deeds."

9   Proclaim the greatness of the LORD our God
    and worship him upon his holy hill; *
        for the LORD our God is the Holy One.

The Epistle   **2 Corinthians 3:12—4:2**

Since, then, we have such a hope, we act with great boldness, not like Moses, who put a veil over his face to keep the people of Israel from gazing at the end of the glory that was being set aside. But their minds were hardened. Indeed, to this very day, when they hear the reading of the old covenant, that same veil is still there, since only in Christ is it set aside. Indeed, to this very day whenever Moses is read, a veil lies over their minds; but when one turns to the Lord, the veil is removed. Now the Lord is the Spirit, and where the Spirit of the Lord is, there is freedom. And all of us, with unveiled faces, seeing the glory of the Lord as though reflected in a mirror, are being transformed into the same image from one degree of glory to another; for this comes from the Lord, the Spirit. Therefore, since it is by God's mercy that we are engaged in this ministry, we do not lose heart. We have renounced the shameful things that one hides; we refuse to practice cunning or to falsify God's word; but by the open statement of the truth we commend ourselves to the conscience of everyone in the sight of God.

The Gospel   Luke 9:28-36, (37-43)
Luke 9:28-36

About eight days after these sayings Jesus took with him Peter and John and James, and went up on the mountain to pray. And while he was praying, the appearance of his face changed, and his clothes became dazzling white. Suddenly they saw two men, Moses and Elijah, talking to him. They appeared in glory and were speaking of his departure, which he was about to accomplish at Jerusalem. Now Peter and his companions were weighed down with sleep; but since they had stayed awake, they saw his glory and the two men who stood with him. Just as they were leaving him, Peter said to Jesus, "Master, it is good for us to be here; let us make three dwellings, one for you, one for Moses, and one for Elijah" — not knowing what he said. While he was saying this, a cloud came and overshadowed them; and they were terrified as they entered the cloud. Then from the cloud came a voice that said, "This is my Son, my Chosen; listen to him!" When the voice had spoken, Jesus was found alone. And they kept silent and in those days told no one any of the things they had seen.

Luke 9:(37-43) [On the next day, when they had come down from the mountain, a great crowd met him. Just then a man from the crowd shouted, "Teacher, I beg you to look at my son; he is my only child. Suddenly a spirit seizes him, and all at once he shrieks. It convulses him until he foams at the mouth; it mauls him and will scarcely leave him. I begged your disciples to cast it out, but they could not." Jesus answered, "You faithless and perverse generation, how much longer must I be with you and bear with you? Bring your son here." While he was coming, the demon dashed him to the ground in convulsions. But Jesus rebuked the unclean spirit, healed the boy, and gave him back to his father. And all were astounded at the greatness of God.]

THE FIRST DAY OF LENT,
or ASH WEDNESDAY

The Collect

Almighty and everlasting God, you hate nothing you have made and forgive the sins of all who are penitent: Create and make in us new and contrite hearts, that we, worthily lamenting our sins and acknowledging our wretchedness, may obtain of you, the God of all mercy, perfect remission and forgiveness; through Jesus Christ our Lord, who lives and reigns with you and the Holy Spirit, one God, for ever and ever. *Amen.*

Years A, B, C
Joel 2:1-2, 12-17 or *Isaiah 58:1-12*
Psalm 103 or *103:8-14*
2 Corinthians 5:20b—6:10
Matthew 6:1-6, 16-21

The Lesson   **Joel 2:1-2, 12-17** *or* **Isaiah 58:1-12**
Joel 2:1-2, 12-17

Blow the trumpet in Zion; sound the alarm on my holy mountain! Let all the inhabitants of the land tremble, for the day of the LORD is coming, it is near— a day of darkness and gloom, a day of clouds and thick darkness! Like blackness spread upon the mountains a great and powerful army comes; their like has never been from of old, nor will be again after them in ages to come. Yet even now, says the LORD, return to me with all your heart, with fasting, with weeping, and with mourning; rend your hearts and not your clothing. Return to the LORD, your God, for he is gracious and merciful, slow to anger, and abounding in steadfast love, and relents from punishing. Who knows whether he will not turn and relent, and leave a blessing behind him, a grain offering and a drink offering for the LORD, your God? Blow the trumpet in Zion; sanctify a fast; call a solemn assembly; gather the people. Sanctify the congregation; assemble the aged; gather the children, even infants at the breast. Let the bridegroom leave his room, and the bride her canopy. Between the vestibule and the altar let the priests, the ministers of the LORD, weep. Let them say, "Spare your people, O LORD, and do not make your heritage a mockery, a byword among the nations. Why should it be said among the peoples 'Where is their God?' "

or, **Isaiah 58:1-12**

Shout out, do not hold back! Lift up your voice like a trumpet! Announce to my people their rebellion, to the house of Jacob their sins. Yet day after day they seek me and delight to know my ways, as if they were a nation that practiced righteousness and did not forsake the ordinance of their God; they ask of me righteous judgments, they delight to draw near to God. "Why do we fast, but you do not see? Why humble ourselves, but you do not notice?" Look, you serve your own interest on your fast day, and oppress all your workers. Look, you fast only to quarrel and to fight and to strike with a wicked fist. Such fasting as you do today will not make your voice heard on high. Is such the fast that I choose, a day to humble oneself? Is it to bow down the head like a bulrush, and to lie in sackcloth and ashes? Will you call this a fast, a day acceptable to the LORD ? Is not this the fast that I choose: to loose the bonds of injustice, to undo the thongs of the yoke, to let the oppressed go free, and to break every yoke? Is it not to share your bread with the hungry, and bring the homeless poor into your house; when you see the naked, to cover them, and not to hide yourself from your own kin? Then your light shall break forth like the dawn, and your healing shall spring up quickly; your vindicator shall go before you, the glory of the LORD shall be your rear guard. Then you shall call, and the LORD will answer; you shall cry for help, and he will say, Here I am. If you remove the yoke from among you, the pointing of the finger, the speaking of evil, if you offer your food to the hungry and satisfy the needs of the afflicted, then your light shall rise in the darkness and your gloom be like the noonday. The LORD will guide you continually, and satisfy your needs in parched places, and make your bones strong; and you shall be like a watered garden, like a spring of water, whose waters never fail. Your ancient ruins shall be rebuilt; you shall raise up the foundations of many generations; you shall be called the repairer of the breach, the restorer of streets to live in.

The Response   **Psalm 103:(1-7), 8-14, (15-22)**

Psalm 103   *Benedic, anima mea*
[1   Bless the LORD, O my soul, *
        and all that is within me, bless his holy Name.
2   Bless the LORD, O my soul, *
        and forget not all his benefits.
3   He forgives all your sins *
        and heals all your infirmities;
4   He redeems your life from the grave *
        and crowns you with mercy and loving-kindness;
5   He satisfies you with good things, *
        and your youth is renewed like an eagle's.
6   The LORD executes righteousness *
        and judgment for all who are oppressed.
7   He made his ways known to Moses *
        and his works to the children of Israel.]

8   The LORD is full of compassion and mercy, *
        slow to anger and of great kindness.
9   He will not always accuse us, *
        nor will he keep his anger for ever.
10   He has not dealt with us according to our sins, *
        nor rewarded us according to our wickedness.
11   For as the heavens are high above the earth, *
        so is his mercy great upon those who fear him.
12   As far as the east is from the west, *
        so far has he removed our sins from us.

13 As a father cares for his children, *
        so does the Lord care for those who fear him.
14 For he himself knows whereof we are made; *
        he remembers that we are but dust.

[15 Our days are like the grass; *
        we flourish like a flower of the field;
16 When the wind goes over it, it is gone, *
        and its place shall know it no more.
17 But the merciful goodness of the Lord endures for ever
                            on those who fear him, *
        and his righteousness on children's children;
18 On those who keep his covenant *
        and remember his commandments and do them.
19 The Lord has set his throne in heaven, *
        and his kingship has dominion over all.
20 Bless the Lord, you angels of his,
    you mighty ones who do his bidding, *
        and hearken to the voice of his word.
21 Bless the Lord, all you his hosts, *
        you ministers of his who do his will.
22 Bless the Lord, all you works of his,
    in all places of his dominion; *
        bless the Lord, O my soul.]

The Epistle   2 Corinthians 5:20*b*—6:10

We entreat you on behalf of Christ, be reconciled to God. For our sake he
made him to be sin who knew no sin, so that in him we might become the
righteousness of God. As we work together with him, we urge you also not to
accept the grace of God in vain. For he says, "At an acceptable time I have
listened to you, and on a day of salvation I have helped you." See, now is the
acceptable time; see, now is the day of salvation! We are putting no obstacle
in anyone's way, so that no fault may be found with our ministry, but as
servants of God we have commended ourselves in every way: through great
endurance, in afflictions, hardships, calamities, beatings, imprisonments, riots,
labors, sleepless nights, hunger; by purity, knowledge, patience, kindness,
holiness of spirit, genuine love, truthful speech, and the power of God; with
the weapons of righteousness for the right hand and for the left; in honor and
dishonor, in ill repute and good repute. We are treated as impostors, and yet
are true; as unknown, and yet are well known; as dying, and see—we are
alive; as punished, and yet not killed; as sorrowful, yet always rejoicing; as
poor, yet making many rich; as having nothing, and yet possessing everything.

The Gospel **Matthew 6:1-6, 16-21**

Jesus said, "Beware of practicing your piety before others in order to be seen by them; for then you have no reward from your Father in heaven. So whenever you give alms, do not sound a trumpet before you, as the hypocrites do in the synagogues and in the streets, so that they may be praised by others. Truly I tell you, they have received their reward. But when you give alms, do not let your left hand know what your right hand is doing, so that your alms may be done in secret; and your Father who sees in secret will reward you. And whenever you pray, do not be like the hypocrites; for they love to stand and pray in the synagogues and at the street corners, so that they may be seen by others. Truly I tell you, they have received their reward. But whenever you pray, go into your room and shut the door and pray to your Father who is in secret; and your Father who sees in secret will reward you. And whenever you fast, do not look dismal, like the hypocrites, for they disfigure their faces so as to show others that they are fasting. Truly I tell you, they have received their reward. But when you fast, put oil on your head and wash your face, so that your fasting may be seen not by others but by your Father who is in secret; and your Father who sees in secret will reward you. Do not store up for yourselves treasures on earth, where moth and rust consume and where thieves break in and steal; but store up for yourselves treasures in heaven, where neither moth nor rust consumes and where thieves do not break in and steal. For where your treasure is, there your heart will be also."

FIRST SUNDAY IN LENT

The Collect

Almighty God, whose blessed Son was led by the Spirit to be tempted by Satan: Come quickly to help us who are assaulted by many temptations; and, as you know the weaknesses of each of us, let each one find you mighty to save; through Jesus Christ your Son our Lord, who lives and reigns with you and the Holy Spirit, one God, now and for ever. *Amen.*

Year A

Genesis 2:15-17; 3:1-7
Psalm 32
Romans 5:12-19
Matthew 4:1-11

The Lesson **Genesis 2:15-17; 3:1-7**

The LORD God took the man and put him in the garden of Eden to till it and keep it. And the LORD God commanded the man, "You may freely eat of every tree of the garden; but of the tree of the knowledge of good and evil you shall not eat, for in the day that you eat of it you shall die." Now the serpent was more crafty than any other wild animal that the LORD God had made. He said to the woman, "Did God say, 'You shall not eat from any tree in the garden'?" The woman said to the serpent, "We may eat of the fruit of the trees in the garden; but God said, 'You shall not eat of the fruit of the tree that is in the middle of the garden, nor shall you touch it, or you shall die.' " But the serpent said to the woman, "You will not die; for God knows that when you eat of it your eyes will be opened, and you will be like God, knowing good and evil." So when the woman saw that the tree was good for food, and that it was a delight to the eyes, and that the tree was to be desired to make one wise, she took of its fruit and ate; and she also gave some to her husband, who was with her, and he ate. Then the eyes of both were opened, and they knew that they were naked; and they sewed fig leaves together and made loincloths for themselves.

The Response   Psalm 32

Psalm 32   *Beati quorum*

1   Happy are they whose transgressions are forgiven, *
        and whose sin is put away!
2   Happy are they to whom the LORD imputes no guilt, *
        and in whose spirit there is no guile!
3   While I held my tongue, my bones withered away, *
        because of my groaning all day long.
4   For your hand was heavy upon me day and night; *
        my moisture was dried up as in the heat of summer.
5   Then I acknowledged my sin to you, *
        and did not conceal my guilt.
6   I said, "I will confess my transgressions to the LORD." *
        Then you forgave me the guilt of my sin.
7   Therefore all the faithful will make their prayers to you in
                        time of trouble; *
        when the great waters overflow, they shall not reach them.
8   You are my hiding-place;
    you preserve me from trouble; *
        you surround me with shouts of deliverance.
9   "I will instruct you and teach you in the way that you should go; *
        I will guide you with my eye.
10   Do not be like horse or mule, which have no understanding; *
        who must be fitted with bit and bridle,
        or else they will not stay near you."
11   Great are the tribulations of the wicked; *
        but mercy embraces those who trust in the LORD.

12   Be glad, you righteous, and rejoice in the LORD; *
      shout for joy, all who are true of heart.

The Epistle   Romans 5:12-19

Just as sin came into the world through one man, and death came through sin,
and so death spread to all because all have sinned - sin was indeed in the
world before the law, but sin is not reckoned when there is no law. Yet death
exercised dominion from Adam to Moses, even over those whose sins were not
like the transgression of Adam, who is a type of the one who was to come. But
the free gift is not like the trespass. For if the many died through the one
man's trespass, much more surely have the grace of God and the free gift in
the grace of the one man, Jesus Christ, abounded for the many. And the free
gift is not like the effect of the one man's sin. For the judgment following one
trespass brought condemnation, but the free gift following many trespasses
brings justification. If, because of the one man's trespass, death exercised
dominion through that one, much more surely will those who receive the
abundance of grace and the free gift of righteousness exercise dominion in life
through the one man, Jesus Christ. Therefore just as one man's trespass led to
condemnation for all, so one man's act of righteousness leads to justification
and life for all. For just as by the one man's disobedience the many were made
sinners, so by the one man's obedience the many will be made righteous.

The Gospel   Matthew 4:1-11

After he was baptized by John, Jesus was led up by the Spirit into the wilderness to be tempted by the devil. He fasted forty days and forty nights, and
afterwards he was famished. The tempter came and said to him, "If you are
the Son of God, command these stones to become loaves of bread." But he
answered, "It is written, 'One does not live by bread alone, but by every word
that comes from the mouth of God.' " Then the devil took him to the holy city
and placed him on the pinnacle of the temple, saying to him, "If you are the
Son of God, throw yourself down; for it is written, 'He will command his
angels concerning you,' and 'On their hands they will bear you up, so that you
will not dash your foot against a stone.' " Jesus said to him, "Again it is
written, 'Do not put the Lord your God to the test.' " Again, the devil took
him to a very high mountain and showed him all the kingdoms of the world
and their splendor; and he said to him, "All these I will give you, if you will
fall down and worship me." Jesus said to him, "Away with you Satan! for it is
written, 'Worship the Lord your God, and serve only him.' " Then the devil
left him, and suddenly angels came and waited on him.

Year B

Genesis 9:8-17
Psalm 25:1-9
1 Peter 3:18-22
Mark 1:9-15

The Lesson   Genesis 9:8-17

God said to Noah and to his sons with him, "As for me, I am establishing my covenant with you and your descendants after you, and with every living creature that is with you, the birds, the domestic animals, and every animal of the earth with you, as many as came out of the ark. I establish my covenant with you, that never again shall all flesh be cut off by the waters of a flood, and never again shall there be a flood to destroy the earth." God said, "This is the sign of the covenant that I make between me and you and every living creature that is with you, for all future generations: I have set my bow in the clouds, and it shall be a sign of the covenant between me and the earth. When I bring clouds over the earth and the bow is seen in the clouds, I will remember my covenant that is between me and you and every living creature of all flesh; and the waters shall never again become a flood to destroy all flesh. When the bow is in the clouds, I will see it and remember the everlasting covenant between God and every living creature of all flesh that is on the earth." God said to Noah, "This is the sign of the covenant that I have established between me and all flesh that is on the earth."

The Response   Psalm 25:1-9

Psalm 25:1-9   *Ad te, Domine, levavi*

1   To you, O LORD, I lift up my soul;
    my God, I put my trust in you; *
        let me not be humiliated,
        nor let my enemies triumph over me.

2   Let none who look to you be put to shame; *
        let the treacherous be disappointed in their schemes.

3   Show me your ways, O LORD, *
        and teach me your paths.

4   Lead me in your truth and teach me, *
        for you are the God of my salvation;
        in you have I trusted all the day long.

5   Remember, O LORD, your compassion and love, *
        for they are from everlasting.

6   Remember not the sins of my youth and my transgressions; *
        remember me according to your love
        and for the sake of your goodness, O LORD.

7   Gracious and upright is the LORD; *
       therefore he teaches sinners in his way.
8   He guides the humble in doing right *
       and teaches his way to the lowly.
9   All the paths of the LORD are love and faithfulness *
       to those who keep his covenant and his testimonies.

The Epistle   1 Peter 3:18-22

Christ also suffered for sins once for all, the righteous for the unrighteous, in order to bring you to God. He was put to death in the flesh, but made alive in the spirit, in which also he went and made a proclamation to the spirits in prison, who in former times did not obey, when God waited patiently in the days of Noah, during the building of the ark, in which a few, that is, eight persons, were saved through water. And baptism, which this prefigured, now saves you — not as a removal of dirt from the body, but as an appeal to God for a good conscience, through the resurrection of Jesus Christ, who has gone into heaven and is at the right hand of God, with angels, authorities, and powers made subject to him.

The Gospel   Mark 1:9-15

Jesus came from Nazareth of Galilee and was baptized by John in the Jordan. And just as he was coming up out of the water, he saw the heavens torn apart and the Spirit descending like a dove on him. And a voice came from heaven, "You are my Son, the Beloved; with you I am well pleased." And the Spirit immediately drove him out into the wilderness. He was in the wilderness forty days, tempted by Satan; and he was with the wild beasts; and the angels waited on him. Now after John was arrested, Jesus came to Galilee, proclaiming the good news of God, and saying, "The time is fulfilled, and the kingdom of God has come near; repent, and believe in the good news."

Year C

Deuteronomy 26:1-11
Psalm 91:1-2, 9-16
Romans 10:8b-13
Luke 4:1-13

The Lesson   Deuteronomy 26:1-11

Moses said, "When you have come into the land that the LORD your God is giving you as an inheritance to possess, and you possess it, and settle in it, you shall take some of the first of all the fruit of the ground, which you harvest from the land that the LORD your God is giving you, and you shall put it in a basket and go to the place that the LORD your God will choose as a dwelling for his name. You shall go to the priest who is in office at that time, and say to him, 'Today I declare to the LORD your God that I have come into the land that the LORD swore to our ancestors to give us.' When the priest takes the basket from your hand and sets it down before the altar of the LORD your God, you shall make this response before the LORD your God: 'A wandering Aramean was my ancestor; he went down into Egypt and lived there as an alien, few in number, and there he became a great nation, mighty and populous. When the Egyptians treated us harshly and afflicted us, by imposing hard labor on us, we cried to the LORD, the God of our ancestors; the LORD heard our voice and saw our affliction, our toil, and our oppression. The LORD brought us out of Egypt with a mighty hand and an outstretched arm, with a terrifying display of power, and with signs and wonders; and he brought us into this place and gave us this land, a land flowing with milk and honey. So now I bring the first of the fruit of the ground that you, O LORD, have given me.' You shall set it down before the LORD your God and bow down before the LORD your God. Then you, together with the Levites and the aliens who reside among you, shall celebrate with all the bounty that the LORD your God has given to you and to your house."

The Response   **Psalm 91:1-2, 9-16**

Psalm 91:1-2, 9-16   *Qui habitat*

1   He who dwells in the shelter of the Most High, *
         abides under the shadow of the Almighty.

2   He shall say to the LORD,
     "You are my refuge and my stronghold, *
         my God in whom I put my trust."

9   Because you have made the LORD your refuge, *
         and the Most High your habitation,

10   There shall no evil happen to you, *
         neither shall any plague come near your dwelling.

11   For he shall give his angels charge over you, *
         to keep you in all your ways.

12   They shall bear you in their hands, *
         lest you dash your foot against a stone.

13   You shall tread upon the lion and adder; *
         you shall trample the young lion and the serpent
                                        under your feet.

14   Because he is bound to me in love,
     therefore will I deliver him; *
         I will protect him, because he knows my Name.

15   He shall call upon me, and I will answer him; *
       I am with him in trouble;
       I will rescue him and bring him to honor.
16   With long life will I satisfy him, *
       and show him my salvation.

The Epistle   Romans 10:8*b*-13

"The word is near you, on your lips and in your heart" (that is, the word of
faith that we proclaim); because if you confess with your lips that Jesus is
Lord and believe in your heart that God raised him from the dead, you will be
saved. For one believes with the heart and so is justified, and one confesses
with the mouth and so is saved. The scripture says, "No one who believes in
him will be put to shame." For there is no distinction between Jew and Greek;
the same Lord is Lord of all and is generous to all who call on him. For,
"Everyone who calls on the name of the Lord shall be saved."

The Gospel   Luke 4:1-13

After his baptism, Jesus, full of the Holy Spirit, returned from the Jordan and
was led by the Spirit in the wilderness, where for forty days he was tempted
by the devil. He ate nothing at all during those days, and when they were over,
he was famished. The devil said to him, "If you are the Son of God, command
this stone to become a loaf of bread." Jesus answered him, "It is written, 'One
does not live by bread alone.' " Then the devil led him up and showed him in
an instant all the kingdoms of the world. And the devil said to him, "To you I
will give their glory and all this authority; for it has been given over to me,
and I give it to anyone I please. If you, then, will worship me, it will all be
yours." Jesus answered him, "It is written, 'Worship the Lord your God, and
serve only him.' " Then the devil took him to Jerusalem, and placed him on the
pinnacle of the temple, saying to him, "If you are the Son of God, throw
yourself down from here, for it is written, 'He will command his angels
concerning you, to protect you,' and 'On their hands they will bear you up, so
that you will not dash your foot against a stone.' " Jesus answered him, "It is
said, 'Do not put the Lord your God to the test.' " When the devil had finished
every test, he departed from him until an opportune time.

SECOND SUNDAY IN LENT

The Collect

O God, whose glory it is always to have mercy: Be gracious to all who have
gone astray from your ways, and bring them again with penitent hearts and
steadfast faith to embrace and hold fast the unchangeable truth of your Word,
Jesus Christ your Son; who with you and the Holy Spirit lives and reigns, one
God, for ever and ever. *Amen.*

Year A

*Genesis 12:1-4*a
Psalm 121
Romans 4:1-5, 13-17
John 3:1-17

The Lesson   **Genesis 12:1-4***a*

Now the LORD said to Abram, "Go from your country and your kindred and
your father's house to the land that I will show you. I will make of you a great
nation, and I will bless you, and make your name great, so that you will be a
blessing. I will bless those who bless you, and the one who curses you I will
curse; and in you all the families of the earth shall be blessed." So Abram
went, as the LORD had told him; and Lot went with him.

The Response   **Psalm 121**

Psalm 121   *Levavi oculos*

1   I lift up my eyes to the hills; *
        from where is my help to come?
2   My help comes from the LORD, *
        the maker of heaven and earth.
3   He will not let your foot be moved *
        and he who watches over you will not fall asleep.
4   Behold, he who keeps watch over Israel *
        shall neither slumber nor sleep;
5   The LORD himself watches over you; *
        the LORD is your shade at your right hand,
6   So that the sun shall not strike you by day, *
        nor the moon by night.
7   The LORD shall preserve you from all evil; *
        it is he who shall keep you safe.
8   The LORD shall watch over your going out and
                        your coming in, *
        from this time forth for evermore.

The Epistle   **Romans 4:1-5, 13-17**

What then are we to say was gained by Abraham, our ancestor according to
the flesh? For if Abraham was justified by works, he has something to boast
about, but not before God. For what does the scripture say? "Abraham
believed God, and it was reckoned to him as righteousness." Now to one who
works, wages are not reckoned as a gift but as something due. But to one who
without works trusts him who justifies the ungodly, such faith is reckoned as

righteousness. For the promise that he would inherit the world did not come to Abraham or to his descendants through the law but through the righteousness of faith. If it is the adherents of the law who are to be the heirs, faith is null and the promise is void. For the law brings wrath; but where there is no law, neither is there violation. For this reason it depends on faith, in order that the promise may rest on grace and be guaranteed to all his descendants, not only to the adherents of the law but also to those who share the faith of Abraham (for he is the father of all of us, as it is written, "I have made you the father of many nations") — in the presence of the God in whom he believed, who gives life to the dead and calls into existence the things that do not exist.

The Gospel   John 3:1-17

There was a Pharisee named Nicodemus, a leader of the Jews. He came to Jesus by night and said to him, "Rabbi, we know that you are a teacher who has come from God; for no one can do these signs that you do apart from the presence of God." Jesus answered him, "Very truly, I tell you, no one can see the kingdom of God without being born from above." Nicodemus said to him, "How can anyone be born after having grown old? Can one enter a second time into the mother's womb and be born?" Jesus answered, "Very truly, I tell you, no one can enter the kingdom of God without being born of water and Spirit. What is born of the flesh is flesh, and what is born of the Spirit is spirit. Do not be astonished that I said to you 'You must be born from above.' The wind blows where it chooses, and you hear the sound of it, but you do not know where it comes from or where it goes. So it is with everyone who is born of the Spirit." Nicodemus said to him, "How can these things be?" Jesus answered him, "Are you a teacher of Israel, and yet you do not understand these things? Very truly, I tell you, we speak of what we know and testify to what we have seen; yet you do not receive our testimony. If I have told you about earthly things and you do not believe, how can you believe if I tell you about heavenly things? No one has ascended into heaven except the one who descended from heaven, the Son of Man. And just as Moses lifted up the serpent in the wilderness, so must the Son of Man be lifted up, that whoever believes in him may have eternal life. For God so loved the world that he gave his only Son, so that everyone who believes in him may not perish but may have eternal life. Indeed, God did not send the Son into the world to condemn the world, but in order that the world might be saved through him."

Year B
Genesis 17:1-7, 15-16
Psalm 22:22-30
Romans 4:13-25
Mark 8:31-38

The Lesson   Genesis 17:1-7, 15-16

When Abram was ninety-nine years old, the LORD appeared to Abram, and said to him, "I am God Almighty; walk before me, and be blameless. And I will make my covenant between me and you, and will make you exceedingly numerous." Then Abram fell on his face; and God said to him, "As for me, this is my covenant with you: You shall be the ancestor of a multitude of nations. No longer shall your name be Abram, but your name shall be Abraham; for I have made you the ancestor of a multitude of nations. I will make you exceedingly fruitful; and I will make nations of you, and kings shall come from you. I will establish my covenant between me and you, and your offspring after you throughout their generations, for an everlasting covenant, to be God to you and to your offspring after you." God said to Abraham, "As for Sarai your wife, you shall not call her Sarai, but Sarah shall be her name. I will bless her, and moreover I will give you a son by her. I will bless her, and she shall give rise to nations; kings of peoples shall come from her."

The Response   Psalm 22:22-30

Psalm 22:22-30   *Deus, Deus meus*

22   Praise the LORD, you that fear him; *
           stand in awe of him, O offspring of Israel;
           all you of Jacob's line, give glory.
23   For he does not despise nor abhor the poor in their poverty;
           neither does he hide his face from them; *
           but when they cry to him he hears them.
24   My praise is of him in the great assembly; *
           I will perform my vows in the presence of those who
                          worship him.
25   The poor shall eat and be satisfied,
      and those who seek the LORD shall praise him: *
           "May your heart live for ever!"
26   All the ends of the earth shall remember and turn to
                          the LORD, *
           and all the families of the nations shall bow before him.
27   For kingship belongs to the LORD; *
           he rules over the nations.

28   To him alone all who sleep in the earth bow down
        in worship; *
      all who go down to the dust fall before him.
29   My soul shall live for him;
      my descendants shall serve him; *
      they shall be known as the LORD's for ever.
30   They shall come and make known to a people yet unborn *
      the saving deeds that he has done.

The Epistle   Romans 4:13-25

The promise that he would inherit the world did not come to Abraham or to his descendants through the law but through the righteousness of faith. If it is the adherents of the law who are to be the heirs, faith is null and the promise is void. For the law brings wrath; but where there is no law, neither is there violation. For this reason it depends on faith, in order that the promise may rest on grace and be guaranteed to all his descendants, not only to the adherents of the law but also to those who share the faith of Abraham (for he is the father of all of us, as it is written, "I have made you the father of many nations") — in the presence of the God in whom he believed, who gives life to the dead and calls into existence the things that do not exist. Hoping against hope, he believed that he would become "the father of many nations," according to what was said, "So numerous shall your descendants be." He did not weaken in faith when he considered his own body, which was already as good as dead (for he was about a hundred years old), or when he considered the barrenness of Sarah's womb. No distrust made him waver concerning the promise of God, but he grew strong in his faith as he gave glory to God, being fully convinced that God was able to do what he had promised. Therefore his faith "was reckoned to him as righteousness." Now the words, "it was reckoned to him," were written not for his sake alone, but for ours also. It will be reckoned to us who believe in him who raised Jesus our Lord from the dead, who was handed over to death for our trespasses and was raised for our justification.

The Gospel   Mark 8:31-38

Jesus began to teach them that the Son of Man must undergo great suffering, and be rejected by the elders, the chief priests, and the scribes, and be killed, and after three days rise again. He said all this quite openly. And Peter took him aside and began to rebuke him. But turning and looking at his disciples, he rebuked Peter and said, "Get behind me, Satan! For you are setting your mind not on divine things but on human things." He called the crowd with his disciples, and said to them, "If any want to become my followers, let them deny themselves and take up their cross and follow me. For those who want to save their life will lose it, and those who lose their life for my sake, and for the sake of the gospel, will save it. For what will it profit them to gain the whole world and forfeit their life? Indeed, what can they give in return for their life? Those who are ashamed of me and of my words in this adulterous and sinful generation, of them the Son of Man will also be ashamed when he comes in the glory of his Father with the holy angels."

Year C
Genesis 15:1-12, 17-18
Psalm 27
Philippians 3:17—4:1
Luke 13:31-35

The Lesson   **Genesis 15:1-12, 17-18**

The word of the LORD came to Abram in a vision, "Do not be afraid, Abram, I am your shield; your reward shall be very great." But Abram said, "O Lord GOD, what will you give me, for I continue childless, and the heir of my house is Eliezer of Damascus?" And Abram said, "You have given me no offspring, and so a slave born in my house is to be my heir." But the word of the LORD came to him, "This man shall not be your heir; no one but your very own issue shall be your heir." He brought him outside and said, "Look toward heaven and count the stars, if you are able to count them." Then he said to him, "So shall your descendants be." And he believed the LORD; and the LORD reckoned it to him as righteousness. Then he said to him, "I am the LORD who brought you from Ur of the Chaldeans, to give you this land to possess." But he said, "O Lord GOD, how am I to know that I shall possess it?" He said to him, "Bring me a heifer three years old, a female goat three years old, a ram three years old, a turtledove, and a young pigeon." He brought him all these and cut them in two, laying each half over against the other; but he did not cut the birds in two. And when birds of prey came down on the carcasses, Abram drove them away. As the sun was going down, a deep sleep fell upon Abram, and a deep and terrifying darkness descended upon him. When the sun had gone down and it was dark, a smoking fire pot and a flaming torch passed between these pieces. On that day the LORD made a covenant with Abram, saying, "To your descendants I give this land, from the river of Egypt to the great river, the river Euphrates."

The Response   **Psalm 27**

Psalm 27 *Dominus illuminatio*

1 The LORD is my light and my salvation;
   whom then shall I fear? *
        the LORD is the strength of my life;
        of whom then shall I be afraid?
2 When evildoers came upon me to eat up my flesh, *
        it was they, my foes and my adversaries, who
                            stumbled and fell.
3 Though an army should encamp against me, *
        yet my heart shall not be afraid;
4 And though war should rise up against me, *
        yet will I put my trust in him.
5 One thing have I asked of the LORD;
   one thing I seek; *
        that I may dwell in the house of the LORD all the days
                            of my life;
6 To behold the fair beauty of the LORD *
        and to seek him in his temple.
7 For in the day of trouble he shall keep me safe
                            in his shelter; *
        he shall hide me in the secrecy of his dwelling
        and set me high upon a rock.
8 Even now he lifts up my head *
        above my enemies round about me.
9 Therefore I will offer in his dwelling an oblation
   with sounds of great gladness; *
        I will sing and make music to the LORD.
10 Hearken to my voice, O LORD, when I call; *
        have mercy on me and answer me.
11 You speak in my heart and say, "Seek my face." *
        Your face, LORD, will I seek.
12 Hide not your face from me, *
        nor turn away your servant in displeasure.
13 You have been my helper;
    cast me not away; *
        do not forsake me, O God of my salvation.
14 Though my father and my mother forsake me, *
        the LORD will sustain me.
15 Show me your way, O LORD; *
        lead me on a level path, because of my enemies.

16 Deliver me not into the hand of my adversaries, *
       for false witnesses have risen up against me,
       and also those who speak malice.
17 What if I had not believed
       that I should see the goodness of the LORD *
       in the land of the living!
18 O tarry and await the LORD's pleasure;
       be strong, and he shall comfort your heart; *
       wait patiently for the LORD.

The Epistle   **Philippians 3:17—4:1**

Brothers and sisters, join in imitating me, and observe those who live according to the example you have in us. For many live as enemies of the cross of Christ; I have often told you of them, and now I tell you even with tears. Their end is destruction; their god is the belly; and their glory is in their shame; their minds are set on earthly things. But our citizenship is in heaven, and it is from there that we are expecting a Savior, the Lord Jesus Christ. He will transform the body of our humiliation that it may be conformed to the body of his glory, by the power that also enables him to make all things subject to himself. Therefore, my brothers and sisters, whom I love and long for, my joy and crown, stand firm in the Lord in this way, my beloved.

The Gospel   **Luke 13:31-35**

Some Pharisees came and said to him, "Get away from here, for Herod wants to kill you." He said to them, "Go and tell that fox for me, 'Listen, I am casting out demons and performing cures today and tomorrow, and on the third day I finish my work. Yet today, tomorrow, and the next day I must be on my way, because it is impossible for a prophet to be killed outside of Jerusalem.' Jerusalem, Jerusalem, the city that kills the prophets and stones those who are sent to it! How often have I desired to gather your children together as a hen gathers her brood under her wings, and you were not willing! See, your house is left to you. And I tell you, you will not see me until the time comes when you say, 'Blessed is the one who comes in the name of the Lord.' "

THIRD SUNDAY IN LENT

The Collect

Almighty God, you know that we have no power in ourselves to help ourselves: Keep us both outwardly in our bodies and inwardly in our souls, that we may be defended from all adversities which may happen to the body, and from all evil thoughts which may assault and hurt the soul; through Jesus Christ our Lord, who lives and reigns with you and the Holy Spirit, one God, for ever and ever. *Amen.*

Year A
Exodus 17:1-7
Psalm 95
Romans 5:1-11
John 4:5-42

The Lesson   Exodus 17:1-7

From the wilderness of Sin the whole congregation of the Israelites journeyed by stages, as the LORD commanded. They camped at Rephidim, but there was no water for the people to drink. The people quarreled with Moses, and said, "Give us water to drink." Moses said to them, "Why do your quarrel with me? Why do you test the LORD ?" But the people thirsted there for water; and the people complained against Moses and said, "Why did you bring us out of Egypt, to kill us and our children and livestock with thirst?" So Moses cried out to the LORD, "What shall I do with this people? They are almost ready to stone me." The LORD said to Moses, "Go on ahead of the people, and take some of the elders of Israel with you; take in your hand the staff with which you struck the Nile, and go. I will be standing there in front of you on the rock at Horeb. Strike the rock, and water will come out of it, so that the people may drink." Moses did so, in the sight of the elders of Israel. He called the place Massah and Meribah, because the Israelites quarreled and tested the LORD, saying, "Is the LORD among us or not?"

The Response   Psalm 95

Psalm 95   *Venite, exultemus*

1   Come, let us sing to the LORD; *
    let us shout for joy to the Rock of our salvation.
2   Let us come before his presence with thanksgiving *
    and raise a loud shout to him with psalms.
3   For the LORD is a great God, *
    and a great King above all gods.

4   In his hand are the caverns of the earth, *
       and the heights of the hills are his also.
5   The sea is his, for he made it, *
       and his hands have molded the dry land.
6   Come, let us bow down, and bend the knee, *
       and kneel before the LORD our Maker.
7   For he is our God,
     and we are the people of his pasture and the sheep of his hand. *
       Oh, that today you would hearken to his voice!
8   Harden not your hearts,
     as your forebears did in the wilderness, *
       at Meribah, and on that day at Massah,
       when they tempted me.
9   They put me to the test, *
       though they had seen my works.
10 Forty years long I detested that generation and said, *
       "This people are wayward in their hearts;
       they do not know my ways."
11 So I swore in my wrath, *
       "They shall not enter into my rest."

The Epistle   Romans 5:1-11

Since we are justified by faith, we have peace with God through our Lord
Jesus Christ, through whom we have obtained access to this grace in which we
stand; and we boast in our hope of sharing the glory of God. And not only
that, but we also boast in our sufferings, knowing that suffering produces
endurance, and endurance produces character, and character produces hope,
and hope does not disappoint us, because God's love has been poured into our
hearts through the Holy Spirit that has been given to us. For while we were
still weak, at the right time Christ died for the ungodly. Indeed, rarely will
anyone die for a righteous person — though perhaps for a good person
someone might actually dare to die. But God proves his love for us in that
while we still were sinners Christ died for us. Much more surely then, now
that we have been justified by his blood, will we be saved through him from
the wrath of God. For if while we were enemies, we were reconciled to God
through the death of his Son, much more surely, having been reconciled, will
we be saved by his life. But more than that, we even boast in God through our
Lord Jesus Christ, through whom we have now received reconciliation.

The Gospel   John 4:5-42

Jesus came to a Samaritan city called Sychar, near the plot of ground that
Jacob had given to his son Joseph. Jacob's well was there, and Jesus, tired out

by his journey, was sitting by the well. It was about noon. A Samaritan woman came to draw water, and Jesus said to her, "Give me a drink." (His disciples had gone to the city to buy food.) The Samaritan woman said to him, "How is it that you, a Jew, ask a drink of me, a woman of Samaria?" (Jews do not share things in common with Samaritans.) Jesus answered her, "If you knew the gift of God, and who it is that is saying to you, 'Give me a drink,' you would have asked him, and he would have given you living water." The woman said to him, "Sir, you have no bucket, and the well is deep. Where do you get that living water? Are you greater than our ancestor Jacob, who gave us the well, and with his sons and his flocks drank from it?" Jesus said to her, "Everyone who drinks of this water will be thirsty again, but those who drink of the water that I will give them will never be thirsty. The water that I will give will become in them a spring of water gushing up to eternal life." The woman said to him, "Sir, give me this water, so that I may never be thirsty or have to keep coming here to draw water." Jesus said to her, "Go, call your husband, and come back." The woman answered him, "I have no husband." Jesus said to her, "You are right in saying, 'I have no husband'; for you have had five husbands, and the one you have now is not your husband. What you have said is true!" The woman said to him, "Sir, I see that you are a prophet. Our ancestors worshiped on this mountain, but you say that the place where people must worship is in Jerusalem." Jesus said to her, "Woman, believe me, the hour is coming when you will worship the Father neither on this mountain nor in Jerusalem. You worship what you do not know; we worship what we know, for salvation is from the Jews. But the hour is coming, and is now here, when the true worshipers will worship the Father in spirit and truth, for the Father seeks such as these to worship him. God is spirit, and those who worship him must worship in spirit and truth." The woman said to him, "I know that Messiah is coming" (who is called Christ). "When he comes, he will proclaim all things to us." Jesus said to her, "I am he, the one who is speaking to you." Just then his disciples came. They were astonished that he was speaking with a woman, but no one said, "What do you want?" or, "Why are you speaking with her?" Then the woman left her water jar and went back to the city. She said to the people, "Come and see a man who told me every-thing I have ever done! He cannot be the Messiah, can he?" They left the city and were on their way to him. Meanwhile the disciples were urging him, "Rabbi, eat something." But he said to them, "I have food to eat that you do not know about." So the disciples said to one another, "Surely no one has brought him something to eat?" Jesus said to them, "My food is to do the will of him who sent me and to complete his work. Do you not say, 'Four months more, then comes the harvest'? But I tell you, look around you, and see how the fields are ripe for harvesting. The reaper is already receiving wages and is gathering fruit for eternal life, so that sower and reaper may rejoice together.

For here the saying holds true, 'One sows and another reaps.' I sent you to reap that for which you did not labor. Others have labored, and you have entered into their labor." Many Samaritans from that city believed in him because of the woman's testimony, "He told me everything I have ever done." So when the Samaritans came to him, they asked him to stay with them; and he stayed there two days. And many more believed because of his word. They said to the woman, "It is no longer because of what you said that we believe, for we have heard for ourselves, and we know that this is truly the Savior of the world."

Year B
Exodus 20:1-17
Psalm 19
1 Corinthians 1:18-25
John 2:13-22

The Lesson   Exodus 20:1-17

God spoke all these words: I am the LORD your God, who brought you out of the land of Egypt, out of the house of slavery; you shall have no other gods before me. You shall not make for yourself an idol, whether in the form of anything that is in heaven above, or that is on the earth beneath, or that is in the water under the earth. You shall not bow down to them or worship them; for I the LORD your God am a jealous God, punishing children for the iniquity of parents, to the third and the fourth generation of those who reject me, but showing steadfast love to the thousandth generation of those who love me and keep my commandments. You shall not make wrongful use of the name of the LORD your God, for the LORD will not acquit anyone who misuses his name. Remember the sabbath day, and keep it holy. Six days you shall labor and do all your work. But the seventh day is a sabbath to the LORD your God; you shall not do any work — you, your son or your daughter, your male or female slave, your livestock, or the alien resident in your towns. For in six days the LORD made heaven and earth, the sea, and all that is in them, but rested the seventh day; therefore the LORD blessed the sabbath day and consecrated it. Honor your father and your mother, so that your days may be long in the land that the LORD your God is giving you. You shall not murder. You shall not commit adultery. You shall not steal. You shall not bear false witness against your neighbor. You shall not covet your neighbor's house; you shall not covet your neighbor's wife, or male or female slave, or ox, or donkey, or anything that belongs to your neighbor.

Psalm 19   *Caeli enarrant*

1   The heavens declare the glory of God, *
      and the firmament shows his handiwork.
2   One day tells its tale to another, *
      and one night imparts knowledge to another.
3   Although they have no words or language, *
      and their voices are not heard,
4   Their sound has gone out into all lands, *
      and their message to the ends of the world.
5   In the deep has he set a pavilion for the sun; *
      it comes forth like a bridegroom out of his chamber;
      it rejoices like a champion to run its course.
6   It goes forth from the uttermost edge of the heavens
      and runs about to the end of it again; *
      nothing is hidden from its burning heat.
7   The law of the LORD is perfect
                  and revives the soul; *
      the testimony of the LORD is sure
                  and gives wisdom to the innocent.
8   The statutes of the LORD are just
                  and rejoice the heart; *
      the commandment of the LORD is clear
                  and gives light to the eyes.
9   The fear of the LORD is clean
                  and endures for ever; *
      the judgments of the LORD are true
                  and righteous altogether.
10 More to be desired are they than gold,
                  more than much fine gold, *
      sweeter far than honey,
                  than honey in the comb.
11 By them also is your servant enlightened, *
      and in keeping them there is great reward.
12 Who can tell how often he offends? *
      cleanse me from my secret faults.
13 Above all, keep your servant from presumptuous sins;
      let them not get dominion over me; *
      then shall I be whole and sound,
      and innocent of a great offense.
14 Let the words of my mouth and the meditation of my
                  heart be acceptable in your sight, *
      O LORD, my strength and my redeemer.

The Epistle   1 Corinthians 1:18-25

The message about the cross is foolishness to those who are perishing, but to
us who are being saved it is the power of God. For it is written, "I will destroy
the wisdom of the wise, and the discernment of the discerning I will thwart."
Where is the one who is wise? Where is the scribe? Where is the debater of
this age? Has not God made foolish the wisdom of the world? For since, in the
wisdom of God, the world did not know God through wisdom, God decided,
through the foolishness of our proclamation, to save those who believe. For
Jews demand signs and Greeks desire wisdom, but we proclaim Christ crucified, a stumbling block to Jews and foolishness to Gentiles, but to those who
are the called, both Jews and Greeks, Christ the power of God and the wisdom
of God. For God's foolishness is wiser than human wisdom, and God's
weakness is stronger than human strength.

The Gospel   John 2:13-22

The Passover of the Jews was near, and Jesus went up to Jerusalem. In the
temple he found people selling cattle, sheep, and doves, and the money changers seated at their tables. Making a whip of cords, he drove all of them out of
the temple, both the sheep and the cattle. He also poured out the coins of the
money changers and overturned their tables. He told those who were selling
the doves, "Take these things out of here! Stop making my Father's house a
marketplace!" His disciples remembered that it was written, "Zeal for your
house will consume me." The Jews then said to him, "What sign can you show
us for doing this?" Jesus answered them, "Destroy this temple, and in three
days I will raise it up." The Jews then said, "This temple has been under
construction for forty-six years, and will you raise it up in three days?" But he
was speaking of the temple of his body. After he was raised from the dead, his
disciples remembered that he had said this; and they believed the scripture and
the word that Jesus had spoken.

Year C
Exodus 3:1-15
Psalm 63:1-8
1 Corinthians 10:1-13
Luke 13:1-9

The Lesson   Exodus 3:1-15

Moses was keeping the flock of his father-in-law Jethro, the priest of Midian;
he led his flock beyond the wilderness, and came to Horeb, the mountain of
God. There the angel of the LORD appeared to him in a flame of fire out of a
bush; he looked, and the bush was blazing, yet it was not consumed. Then

Moses said, "I must turn aside and look at this great sight, and see why the bush is not burned up." When the Lord saw that he had turned aside to see, God called to him out of the bush, "Moses, Moses!" And he said, "Here I am." Then he said, "Come no closer! Remove the sandals from your feet, for the place on which you are standing is holy ground." He said further, "I am the God of your father, the God of Abraham, the God of Isaac, and the God of Jacob." And Moses hid his face, for he was afraid to look at God. Then the Lord said, "I have observed the misery of my people who are in Egypt; I have heard their cry on account of their taskmasters. Indeed, I know their sufferings, and I have come down to deliver them from the Egyptians, and to bring them up out of that land to a good and broad land, a land flowing with milk and honey, to the country of the Canaanites, the Hittites, the Amorites, the Perizzites, the Hivites, and the Jebusites. The cry of the Israelites has now come to me; I have also seen how the Egyptians oppress them. So come, I will send you to Pharaoh to bring my people, the Israelites, out of Egypt." But Moses said to God, "Who am I that I should go to Pharaoh, and bring the Israelites out of Egypt?" He said, "I will be with you; and this shall be the sign for you that it is I who sent you: when you have brought the people out of Egypt, you shall worship God on this mountain." But Moses said to God, "If I come to the Israelites and say to them, 'The God of your ancestors has sent me to you,' and they ask me, 'What is his name?' what shall I say to them?" God said to Moses, "I AM WHO I AM." He said further, "Thus you shall say to the Israelites, 'I AM has sent me to you.'" God also said to Moses, "Thus you shall say to the Israelites, 'The Lord, the God of your ancestors, the God of Abraham, the God of Isaac, and the God of Jacob, has sent me to you': This is my name forever, and this my title for all generations."

The Response   Psalm 63:1-8

Psalm 63   *Deus, Deus meus*

1   O God, you are my God; eagerly I seek you; *
        my soul thirsts for you, my flesh faints for you,
            as in a barren and dry land where there is no water.

2   Therefore I have gazed upon you in your holy place, *
        that I might behold your power and your glory.

3   For your loving-kindness is better than life itself; *
        my lips shall give you praise.

4   So will I bless you as long as I live *
        and lift up my hands in your Name.

5   My soul is content, as with marrow and fatness, *
        and my mouth praises you with joyful lips,

6   When I remember you upon my bed, *
        and meditate on you in the night watches.

7   For you have been my helper, *
        and under the shadow of your wings I will rejoice.
8   My soul clings to you; *
        your right hand holds me fast.

The Epistle   1 Corinthians 10:1-13

I do not want you to be unaware, brothers and sisters, that our ancestors were
all under the cloud, and all passed through the sea, and all were baptized into
Moses in the cloud and in the sea, and all ate the same spiritual food, and all
drank the same spiritual drink. For they drank from the spiritual rock that
followed them, and the rock was Christ. Nevertheless, God was not pleased
with most of them, and they were struck down in the wilderness. Now these
things occurred as examples for us, so that we might not desire evil as they
did. Do not become idolaters as some of them did; as it is written, "The people
sat down to eat and drink, and they rose up to play." We must not indulge in
sexual immorality as some of them did, and twenty-three thousand fell in a
single day. We must not put Christ to the test, as some of them did, and were
destroyed by serpents. And do not complain as some of them did, and were
destroyed by the destroyer. These things happened to them to serve as an
example, and they were written down to instruct us, on whom the ends of the
ages have come. So if you think you are standing, watch out that you do not
fall. No testing has overtaken you that is not common to everyone. God is
faithful, and he will not let you be tested beyond your strength, but with the
testing he will also provide the way out so that you may be able to endure it.

The Gospel   Luke 13:1-9

There were some present who told Jesus about the Galileans whose blood
Pilate had mingled with their sacrifices. He asked them, "Do you think that
because these Galileans suffered in this way they were worse sinners than all
other Galileans? No, I tell you; but unless you repent, you will all perish as
they did. Or those eighteen who were killed when the tower of Siloam fell on
them — do you think that they were worse offenders than all the others living
in Jerusalem? No, I tell you; but unless you repent, you will all perish just as
they did." Then he told this parable: "A man had a fig tree planted in his
vineyard; and he came looking for fruit on it and found none. So he said to the
gardener, 'See here! For three years I have come looking for fruit on this fig
tree, and still I find none. Cut it down! Why should it be wasting the soil?' He
replied, 'Sir, let it alone for one more year, until I dig around it and put
manure on it. If it bears fruit next year, well and good; but if not, you can cut
it down.' "

FOURTH SUNDAY IN LENT

The Collect

Gracious Father, whose blessed Son Jesus Christ came down from heaven to be the true bread which gives life to the world: Evermore give us this bread, that he may live in us, and we in him; who lives and reigns with you and the Holy Spirit, one God, now and for ever. *Amen.*

Year A
1 Samuel 16:1-13
Psalm 23
Ephesians 5:8-14
John 9:1-41

The Lesson   **1 Samuel 16:1-13**

The LORD said to Samuel, "How long will you grieve over Saul? I have rejected him from being king over Israel. Fill your horn with oil and set out; I will send you to Jesse the Bethlehemite, for I have provided for myself a king among his sons." Samuel said, "How can I go? If Saul hears of it, he will kill me." And the LORD said, "Take a heifer with you, and say, 'I have come to sacrifice to the LORD.' Invite Jesse to the sacrifice, and I will show you what you shall do; and you shall anoint for me the one whom I name to you." Samuel did what the LORD commanded, and came to Bethlehem. The elders of the city came to meet him trembling, and said, "Do you come peaceably?" He said, "Peaceably; I have come to sacrifice to the LORD; sanctify yourselves and come with me to the sacrifice." And he sanctified Jesse and his sons and invited them to the sacrifice. When they came, he looked on Eliab and thought, "Surely the LORD's anointed is now before the LORD." But the LORD said to Samuel, "Do not look on his appearance or on the height of his stature, because I have rejected him; for the LORD does not see as mortals see; they look on the outward appearance, but the LORD looks on the heart." Then Jesse called Abinadab, and made him pass before Samuel. He said, "Neither has the LORD chosen this one." Then Jesse made Shammah pass by. And he said, "Neither has the LORD chosen this one." Jesse made seven of his sons pass before Samuel, and Samuel said to Jesse, "The LORD has not chosen any of these." Samuel said to Jesse, "Are all your sons here?" And he said, "There remains yet the youngest, but he is keeping the sheep." And Samuel said to Jesse, "Send and bring him; for we will not sit down until he comes here." He sent and brought him in. Now he was ruddy, and had beautiful eyes, and was handsome. The LORD said, "Rise and anoint him; for this is the one." Then Samuel took the horn of oil, and anointed him in the presence of his brothers; and the spirit of the LORD came mightily upon David from that day forward. Samuel then set out and went to Ramah.

The Response   **Psalm 23**

Psalm 23   *Dominus regit me*

1   The LORD is my shepherd; *
        I shall not be in want.

2   He makes me lie down in green pastures *
        and leads me beside still waters.

3   He revives my soul *
        and guides me along right pathways for his Name's sake.

4   Though I walk through the valley of the shadow of death,
    I shall fear no evil; *
            for you are with me;
            your rod and your staff, they comfort me.

5   You spread a table before me in the presence of those
                    who trouble me; *
        you have anointed my head with oil,
        and my cup is running over.

6   Surely your goodness and mercy shall follow me all the days
                    of my life, *
        and I will dwell in the house of the LORD for ever.

The Epistle   **Ephesians 5:8-14**

Once you were darkness, but now in the Lord you are light. Live as children
of light—for the fruit of the light is found in all that is good and right and
true. Try to find out what is pleasing to the Lord. Take no part in the unfruit-
ful works of darkness, but instead expose them. For it is shameful even to
mention what such people do secretly; but everything exposed by the light
becomes visible, for everything that becomes visible is light. Therefore it says,
"Sleeper, awake! Rise from the dead, and Christ will shine on you."

The Gospel   **John 9:1-41**

As he walked along, Jesus saw a man blind from birth. His disciples asked
him, "Rabbi, who sinned, this man or his parents, that he was born blind?"
Jesus answered, "Neither this man nor his parents sinned; he was born blind
so that God's works might be revealed in him. We must work the works of him
who sent me while it is day; night is coming when no one can work. As long
as I am in the world, I am the light of the world." When he had said this, he
spat on the ground and made mud with the saliva and spread the mud on the
man's eyes, saying to him, "Go, wash in the pool of Siloam" (which means
Sent). Then he went and washed and came back able to see. The neighbors
and those who had seen him before as a beggar began to ask, "Is this not the
man who used to sit and beg?" Some were saying, "It is he." Others were
saying, "No, but it is someone like him." He kept saying, "I am the man." But

they kept asking him, "Then how were your eyes opened?" He answered, "The man called Jesus made mud, spread it on my eyes, and said to me, 'Go to Siloam and wash.' Then I went and washed and received my sight." They said to him, "Where is he?" He said, "I do not know." They brought to the Pharisees the man who had formerly been blind. Now it was a sabbath day when Jesus made the mud and opened his eyes. Then the Pharisees also began to ask him how he had received his sight. He said to them, "He put mud on my eyes. Then I washed, and now I see." Some of the Pharisees said, "This man is not from God, for he does not observe the sabbath." But others said, "How can a man who is a sinner perform such signs?" And they were divided. So they said again to the blind man, "What do you say about him? It was your eyes he opened." He said, "He is a prophet." The Jews did not believe that he had been blind and had received his sight until they called the parents of the man who had received his sight and asked them, "Is this your son, who you say was born blind? How then does he now see?" His parents answered, "We know that this is our son, and that he was born blind; but we do not know how it is that now he sees, nor do we know who opened his eyes. Ask him; he is of age. He will speak for himself." His parents said this because they were afraid of the Jews; for the Jews had already agreed that anyone who confessed Jesus to be the Messiah would be put out of the synagogue. Therefore his parents said, "He is of age; ask him." So for the second time they called the man who had been blind, and they said to him, "Give glory to God! We know that this man is a sinner." He answered, "I do not know whether he is a sinner. One thing I do know, that though I was blind, now I see." They said to him, "What did he do to you? How did he open your eyes?" He answered them, "I have told you already, and you would not listen. Why do you want to hear it again? Do you also want to become his disciples?" Then they reviled him, saying, "You are his disciple, but we are disciples of Moses. We know that God has spoken to Moses, but as for this man, we do not know where he comes from." The man answered, "Here is an astonishing thing! You do not know where he comes from, and yet he opened my eyes. We know that God does not listen to sinners, but he does listen to one who worships him and obeys his will. Never since the world began has it been heard that anyone opened the eyes of a person born blind. If this man were not from God, he could do nothing." They answered him, "You were born entirely in sins, and are you trying to teach us?" And they drove him out. Jesus heard that they had driven him out, and when he found him, he said, "Do you believe in the Son of Man?" He answered, "And who is he, sir? Tell me, so that I may believe in him." Jesus said to him, "You have seen him, and the one speaking with you is he." He said, "Lord, I believe." And he worshiped him. Jesus said, "I came into this world for judgment so that those who do not see may see, and those who do see may become blind." Some of the Pharisees near him heard this and said to him,

"Surely we are not blind, are we?" Jesus said to them, "If you were blind, you would not have sin. But now that you say, 'We see,' your sin remains."

Year B
Numbers 21:4-9
Psalm 107:1-3, 17-22
Ephesians 2:1-10
John 3:14-21

The Lesson   **Numbers 21:4-9**

From Mount Hor the Israelites set out by the way to the Red Sea, to go around the land of Edom; but the people became impatient on the way. The people spoke against God and against Moses, "Why have you brought us up out of Egypt to die in the wilderness? For there is no food and no water, and we detest this miserable food." Then the LORD sent poisonous serpents among the people, and they bit the people, so that many Israelites died. The people came to Moses and said, "We have sinned by speaking against the LORD and against you; pray to the LORD to take away the serpents from us." So Moses prayed for the people. And the LORD said to Moses, "Make a poisonous serpent, and set it on a pole; and everyone who is bitten shall look at it and live." So Moses made a serpent of bronze, and put it upon a pole; and whenever a serpent bit someone, that person would look at the serpent of bronze and live.

The Response   **Psalm 107:1-3, 17-22**

Psalm 107:1-3, 17-22   *Confitemini Domino*

1   Give thanks to the LORD, for he is good, *
        and his mercy endures for ever.
2   Let all those whom the LORD has redeemed proclaim *
        that he redeemed them from the hand of the foe.
3   He gathered them out of the lands; *
        from the east and from the west,
        from the north and from the south.
17   Some were fools and took to rebellious ways; *
        they were afflicted because of their sins.
18   They abhorred all manner of food *
        and drew near to death's door.
19   Then they cried to the LORD in their trouble, *
        and he delivered them from their distress.
20   He sent forth his word and healed them *
        and saved them from the grave.

21   Let them give thanks to the LORD for his mercy *
        and the wonders he does for his children.
22   Let them offer a sacrifice of thanksgiving *
        and tell of his acts with shouts of joy.

The Epistle   Ephesians 2:1-10

You were dead through the trespasses and sins in which you once lived,
following the course of this world, following the ruler of the power of the air,
the spirit that is now at work among those who are disobedient. All of us once
lived among them in the passions of our flesh, following the desires of flesh
and senses, and we were by nature children of wrath, like everyone else. But
God, who is rich in mercy, out of the great love with which he loved us even
when we were dead through our trespasses, made us alive together with Christ
— by grace you have been saved — and raised us up with him and seated us
with him in the heavenly places in Christ Jesus, so that in the ages to come he
might show the immeasurable riches of his grace in kindness toward us in
Christ Jesus. For by grace you have been saved through faith, and this is not
your own doing; it is the gift of God — not the result of works, so that no one
may boast. For we are what he has made us, created in Christ Jesus for good
works, which God prepared beforehand to be our way of life.

The Gospel   John 3:14-21

Jesus said, "Just as Moses lifted up the serpent in the wilderness, so must the
Son of Man be lifted up, that whoever believes in him may have eternal life.
For God so loved the world that he gave his only Son, so that everyone who
believes in him may not perish but may have eternal life. Indeed, God did not
send the Son into the world to condemn the world, but in order that the world
might be saved through him. Those who believe in him are not condemned;
but those who do not believe are condemned already, because they have not
believed in the name of the only Son of God. And this is the judgment, that the
light has come into the world, and people loved darkness rather than light
because their deeds were evil. For all who do evil hate the light and do not
come to the light, so that their deeds may not be exposed. But those who do
what is true come to the light, so that it may be clearly seen that their deeds
have been done in God."

Year C
Joshua 5:9-12
Psalm 32
2 Corinthians 5:16-21
Luke 15:1-3, 11b-32

The Lesson   Joshua 5:9-12

The LORD said to Joshua, "Today I have rolled away from you the disgrace of Egypt." And so that place is called Gilgal to this day. While the Israelites were camped in Gilgal they kept the passover in the evening on the fourteenth day of the month in the plains of Jericho. On the day after the passover, on that very day, they ate the produce of the land, unleavened cakes and parched grain. The manna ceased on the day they ate the produce of the land, and the Israelites no longer had manna; they ate the crops of the land of Canaan that year.

The Response   Psalm 32

Psalm 32 *Beati quorum*

1   Happy are they whose transgressions are forgiven, *
        and whose sin is put away!
2   Happy are they to whom the LORD imputes no guilt, *
        and in whose spirit there is no guile!
3   While I held my tongue, my bones withered away, *
        because of my groaning all day long.
4   For your hand was heavy upon me day and night; *
        my moisture was dried up as in the heat of summer.
5   Then I acknowledged my sin to you, *
        and did not conceal my guilt.
6   I said, "I will confess my transgressions to the LORD." *
        Then you forgave me the guilt of my sin.
7   Therefore all the faithful will make their prayers to you in
                            time of trouble; *
        when the great waters overflow, they shall not reach them.
8   You are my hiding-place;
    you preserve me from trouble; *
        you surround me with shouts of deliverance.
9   "I will instruct you and teach you in the way that you should go; *
        I will guide you with my eye.
10 Do not be like horse or mule, which have no understanding; *
        who must be fitted with bit and bridle,
        or else they will not stay near you."

11   Great are the tribulations of the wicked; *
        but mercy embraces those who trust in the LORD.
12   Be glad, you righteous, and rejoice in the LORD; *
        shout for joy, all who are true of heart.

The Epistle   2 Corinthians 5:16-21

We regard no one from a human point of view; even though we once knew
Christ from a human point of view, we know him no longer in that way. So if
anyone is in Christ, there is a new creation: everything old has passed away;
see, everything has become new! All this is from God, who reconciled us to
himself through Christ, and has given us the ministry of reconciliation; that is,
in Christ God was reconciling the world to himself, not counting their trespasses against them, and entrusting the message of reconciliation to us. So we
are ambassadors for Christ, since God is making his appeal through us; we
entreat you on behalf of Christ, be reconciled to God. For our sake he made
him to be sin who knew no sin, so that in him we might become the righteousness of God.

The Gospel   Luke 15:1-3, 11*b*-32

Now all the tax collectors and sinners were coming near to listen to Jesus.
And the Pharisees and the scribes were grumbling and saying, "This fellow
welcomes sinners and eats with them." So he told them this parable: Jesus
said, "There was a man who had two sons. The younger of them said to his
father, 'Father, give me the share of the property that will belong to me.' So he
divided his property between them. A few days later the younger son gathered
all he had and traveled to a distant country, and there he squandered his
property in dissolute living. When he had spent everything, a severe famine
took place throughout that country, and he began to be in need. So he went
and hired himself out to one of the citizens of that country, who sent him to his
fields to feed the pigs. He would gladly have filled himself with the pods that
the pigs were eating; and no one gave him anything. But when he came to
himself he said, 'How many of my father's hired hands have bread enough to
spare, but here I am dying of hunger! I will get up and go to my father, and I
will say to him, "Father, I have sinned against heaven and before you; I am no
longer worthy to be called your son; treat me like one of your hired hands." '
So he set off and went to his father. But while he was still far off, his father
saw him and was filled with compassion; he ran and put his arms around him
and kissed him. Then the son said to him, 'Father, I have sinned against
heaven and before you; I am no longer worthy to be called your son.' But the
father said to his slaves, 'Quickly, bring out a robe — the best one — and put
it on him; put a ring on his finger and sandals on his feet. And get the fatted
calf and kill it, and let us eat and celebrate; for this son of mine was dead and

is alive again; he was lost and is found!' And they began to celebrate. Now his elder son was in the field; and when he came and approached the house, he heard music and dancing. He called one of the slaves and asked what was going on. He replied, 'Your brother has come, and your father has killed the fatted calf, because he has got him back safe and sound.' Then he became angry and refused to go in. His father came out and began to plead with him. But he answered his father, 'Listen! For all these years I have been working like a slave for you, and I have never disobeyed your command; yet you have never given me even a young goat so that I might celebrate with my friends. But when this son of yours came back, who has devoured your property with prostitutes, you killed the fatted calf for him!' Then the father said to him, 'Son, you are always with me, and all that is mine is yours. But we had to celebrate and rejoice, because this brother of yours was dead and has come to life; he was lost and has been found.' "

FIFTH SUNDAY IN LENT

The Collect
Almighty God, you alone can bring into order the unruly wills and affections of sinners: Grant your people grace to love what you command and desire what you promise; that, among the swift and varied changes of the world, our hearts may surely there be fixed where true joys are to be found; through Jesus Christ our Lord, who lives and reigns with you and the Holy Spirit, one God, now and for ever. *Amen.*

Year A
Ezekiel 37:1-14
Psalm 130
Romans 8:6-11
John 11:1-45

The Lesson   **Ezekiel 37:1-14**
The hand of the LORD came upon me, and he brought me out by the spirit of the LORD and set me down in the middle of a valley; it was full of bones. He led me all around them; there were very many lying in the valley, and they were very dry. He said to me, "Mortal, can these bones live?" I answered, "O Lord GOD, you know." Then he said to me, "Prophesy to these bones, and say to them: O dry bones, hear the word of the LORD. Thus says the Lord GOD to these bones: I will cause breath to enter you, and you shall live. I will lay sinews on you, and will cause flesh to come upon you, and cover you with skin, and put breath in you, and you shall live; and you shall know that I am the LORD." So I prophesied as I had been commanded; and as I prophesied, suddenly there was a noise, a rattling, and the bones came together, bone to its

bone. I looked, and there were sinews on them, and flesh had come upon them, and skin had covered them; but there was no breath in them. Then he said to me, "Prophesy to the breath, prophesy, mortal, and say to the breath: Thus says the Lord GOD: Come from the four winds, O breath, and breathe upon these slain, that they may live." I prophesied as he commanded me, and the breath came into them, and they lived, and stood on their feet, a vast multitude. Then he said to me, "Mortal, these bones are the whole house of Israel. They say, 'Our bones are dried up, and our hope is lost; we are cut off completely.' Therefore prophesy, and say to them, Thus says the Lord GOD: I am going to open your graves, and bring you up from your graves, O my people; and I will bring you back to the land of Israel. And you shall know that I am the LORD, when I open your graves, and bring you up from your graves, O my people. I will put my spirit within you, and you shall live, and I will place you on your own soil; then you shall know that I, the LORD, have spoken and will act," says the LORD.

The Response   Psalm 130

Psalm 130   *De profundis*

1   Out of the depths have I called to you, O LORD;
    LORD, hear my voice; *
        let your ears consider well the voice of my supplication.
2   If you, LORD, were to note what is done amiss, *
        O LORD, who could stand?
3   For there is forgiveness with you; *
        therefore you shall be feared.
4   I wait for the LORD; my soul waits for him; *
        in his word is my hope.
5   My soul waits for the LORD,
    more than watchmen for the morning, *
        more than watchmen for the morning.
6   O Israel, wait for the LORD, *
        for with the LORD there is mercy;
7   With him there is plenteous redemption, *
        and he shall redeem Israel from all their sins.

The Epistle   Romans 8:6-11

To set the mind on the flesh is death, but to set the mind on the Spirit is life and peace. For this reason the mind that is set on the flesh is hostile to God; it does not submit to God's law — indeed it cannot, and those who are in the flesh cannot please God. But you are not in the flesh; you are in the Spirit, since the Spirit of God dwells in you. Anyone who does not have the Spirit of Christ does not belong to him. But if Christ is in you, though the body is dead because of sin, the Spirit is life because of righteousness. If the Spirit of him who raised Jesus from the dead dwells in you, he who raised Christ from the dead will give life to your mortal bodies also through his Spirit that dwells in you.

The Gospel   John 11:1-45

Now a certain man was ill, Lazarus of Bethany, the village of Mary and her sister Martha. Mary was the one who anointed the Lord with perfume and wiped his feet with her hair; her brother Lazarus was ill. So the sisters sent a message to Jesus, "Lord, he whom you love is ill." But when Jesus heard it, he said, "This illness does not lead to death; rather it is for God's glory, so that the Son of God may be glorified through it." Accordingly, though Jesus loved Martha and her sister and Lazarus, after having heard that Lazarus was ill, he stayed two days longer in the place where he was. Then after this he said to the disciples, "Let us go to Judea again." The disciples said to him, "Rabbi, the Jews were just now trying to stone you, and are you going there again?" Jesus answered, "Are there not twelve hours of daylight? Those who walk during the day do not stumble, because they see the light of this world. But those who walk at night stumble, because the light is not in them." After saying this, he told them, "Our friend Lazarus has fallen asleep, but I am going there to awaken him." The disciples said to him, "Lord, if he has fallen asleep, he will be all right." Jesus, however, had been speaking about his death, but they thought that he was referring merely to sleep. Then Jesus told them plainly, "Lazarus is dead. For your sake I am glad I was not there, so that you may believe. But let us go to him." Thomas, who was called the Twin, said to his fellow disciples, "Let us also go, that we may die with him." When Jesus arrived, he found that Lazarus had already been in the tomb four days. Now Bethany was near Jerusalem, some two miles away, and many of the Jews had come to Martha and Mary to console them about their brother. When Martha heard that Jesus was coming, she went and met him, while Mary stayed at home. Martha said to Jesus, "Lord, if you had been here, my brother would not have died. But even now I know that God will give you whatever you ask of him." Jesus said to her, "Your brother will rise again." Martha said to him, "I know that he will rise again in the resurrection on the last day." Jesus said to her, "I am the resurrection and the life. Those who believe in me, even though they die, will live, and everyone who lives and believes in me will never die. Do you believe this?" She said to him, "Yes, Lord, I believe that you are the Messiah, the Son of God, the one coming into the world." When she had said this, she went back and called her sister Mary, and told her privately, "The Teacher is here and is calling for you." And when she heard it, she got up quickly and went to him. Now Jesus had not yet come to the village, but was still at the place where Martha had met him. The Jews who were with her in the house, consoling her, saw Mary get up quickly and go out. They followed her, because they thought that she was going to the tomb to weep there. When Mary came where Jesus was and saw him, she knelt at his feet and said to him, "Lord, if you had been here, my brother would not have died." When Jesus saw her weeping, and the Jews who came with her also weeping, he was greatly disturbed in spirit and deeply moved. He said, "Where have you laid him?" They said to him, "Lord, come and see." Jesus began to weep. So the Jews said, "See how he loved him!" But some of them said, "Could not he who opened the eyes of the blind man have kept this man from dying?" Then Jesus, again greatly disturbed, came to the tomb. It was a cave, and a stone was lying against it. Jesus said, "Take away the stone." Martha, the sister of the dead man, said to him, "Lord, already there is a stench because he has been dead four days." Jesus said to her, "Did I not tell you that if you believed, you would see the glory of God?" So they took away the stone. And Jesus looked upward and said, "Father, I thank you for having heard me. I knew that you always hear me, but I have said this for the sake of the crowd standing here, so that they may believe that you sent me." When he had said this, he cried with a loud voice, "Lazarus, come out!" The dead man came out, his hands and feet bound with strips of cloth, and his face wrapped in a cloth. Jesus said to them, "Unbind him, and let him go." Many of the Jews therefore, who had come with Mary and had seen what Jesus did, believed in him.

Year B
Jeremiah 31:31-34
Psalm 51:1-13 or Psalm 119:9-16
Hebrews 5:5-10
John 12:20-33

The Lesson   **Jeremiah 31:31-34**

The days are surely coming, says the LORD, when I will make a new covenant with the house of Israel and the house of Judah. It will not be like the covenant that I made with their ancestors when I took them by the hand to bring them out of the land of Egypt — a covenant that they broke, though I was their husband, says the LORD. But this is the covenant that I will make with the house of Israel after those days, says the LORD: I will put my law within them, and I will write it on their hearts; and I will be their God, and they shall be my people. No longer shall they teach one another, or say to each other, "Know the LORD," for they shall all know me, from the least of them to the greatest, says the LORD; for I will forgive their iniquity, and remember their sin no more.

The Response   **Psalm 51:1-13** *or* **Psalm 119:9-16**

Psalm 51:1-13   *Miserere mei, Deus*

1   Have mercy on me, O God, according to your
            loving-kindness; *
        in your great compassion blot out my offenses.

2   Wash me through and through from my wickedness *
        and cleanse me from my sin.

3   For I know my transgressions, *
        and my sin is ever before me.

4   Against you only have I sinned *
        and done what is evil in your sight.

5   And so you are justified when you speak *
        and upright in your judgment.

6   Indeed, I have been wicked from my birth, *
        a sinner from my mother's womb.

7   For behold, you look for truth deep within me, *
        and will make me understand wisdom secretly.

8   Purge me from my sin, and I shall be pure; *
        wash me, and I shall be clean indeed.

9   Make me hear of joy and gladness, *
        that the body you have broken may rejoice.

10   Hide your face from my sins *
        and blot out all my iniquities.

11   Create in me a clean heart, O God, *
        and renew a right spirit within me.

12   Cast me not away from your presence *
        and take not your holy Spirit from me.

13   Give me the joy of your saving help again*
        and sustain me with your bountiful Spirit.

or, **Psalm 119:9-16**   *In quo corrigit?*

9   How shall a young man cleanse his way? *
        By keeping to your words.

10   With my whole heart I seek you; *
        let me not stray from your commandments.

11   I treasure your promise in my heart, *
        that I may not sin against you.

12   Blessed are you, O Lord; *
        instruct me in your statutes.

13   With my lips will I recite *
        all the judgments of your mouth.

14 I have taken greater delight in the way of your decrees *
     than in all manner of riches.
15 I will meditate on your commandments *
     and give attention to your ways.
16 My delight is in your statutes; *
     I will not forget your word.

The Epistle   Hebrews 5:5-10

Christ did not glorify himself in becoming a high priest, but was appointed by
the one who said to him, "You are my Son, today I have begotten you"; as he
says also in another place, "You are a priest forever, according to the order of
Melchizedek." In the days of his flesh, Jesus offered up prayers and supplications, with loud cries and tears, to the one who was able to save him from
death, and he was heard because of his reverent submission. Although he was
a Son, he learned obedience through what he suffered; and having been made
perfect, he became the source of eternal salvation for all who obey him,
having been designated by God a high priest according to the order of
Melchizedek.

The Gospel   John 12:20-33

Now among those who went up to worship at the festival were some Greeks.
They came to Philip, who was from Bethsaida in Galilee, and said to him,
"Sir, we wish to see Jesus." Philip went and told Andrew; then Andrew and
Philip went and told Jesus. Jesus answered them, "The hour has come for the
Son of Man to be glorified. Very truly, I tell you, unless a grain of wheat falls
into the earth and dies, it remains just a single grain; but if it dies, it bears
much fruit. Those who love their life lose it, and those who hate their life in
this world will keep it for eternal life. Whoever serves me must follow me, and
where I am, there will my servant be also. Whoever serves me, the Father will
honor. Now my soul is troubled. And what should I say — 'Father, save me
from this hour'? No, it is for this reason that I have come to this hour. Father,
glorify your name." Then a voice came from heaven, "I have glorified it, and I
will glorify it again." The crowd standing there heard it and said that it was
thunder. Others said, "An angel has spoken to him." Jesus answered, "This
voice has come for your sake, not for mine. Now is the judgment of this
world; now the ruler of this world will be driven out. And I, when I am lifted
up from the earth, will draw all people to myself." He said this to indicate the
kind of death he was to die.

Isaiah 43:16-21
Psalm 126
Philippians 3:4b-14
John 12:1-8

The Lesson   Isaiah 43:16-21

Thus says the LORD, who makes a way in the sea, a path in the mighty waters,
who brings out chariot and horse, army and warrior; they lie down, they
cannot rise, they are extinguished, quenched like a wick: Do not remember the
former things, or consider the things of old. I am about to do a new thing; now
it springs forth, do you not perceive it? I will make a way in the wilderness
and rivers in the desert. The wild animals will honor me, the jackals and the
ostriches; for I give water in the wilderness, rivers in the desert, to give drink
to my chosen people, the people whom I formed for myself so that they might
declare my praise.

The Response   Psalm 126

Psalm 126   *In convertendo*

   1   When the LORD restored the fortunes of Zion, *
        then were we like those who dream.
   2   Then was our mouth filled with laughter, *
        and our tongue with shouts of joy.
   3   Then they said among the nations, *
        "The LORD has done great things for them."
   4   The LORD has done great things for us, *
        and we are glad indeed.
   5   Restore our fortunes, O LORD, *
        like the watercourses of the Negev.
   6   Those who sowed with tears *
        will reap with songs of joy.
   7   Those who go out weeping, carrying the seed, *
        will come again with joy, shouldering their sheaves.

The Epistle   Philippians 3:4b-14

If anyone else has reason to be confident in the flesh, I have more: circumcised
on the eighth day, a member of the people of Israel, of the tribe of Benjamin, a
Hebrew born of Hebrews; as to the law, a Pharisee; as to zeal, a persecutor of
the church; as to righteousness under the law, blameless. Yet whatever gains I
had, these I have come to regard as loss because of Christ. More than that, I
regard everything as loss because of the surpassing value of knowing Christ

Jesus my Lord. For his sake I have suffered the loss of all things, and I regard them as rubbish, in order that I may gain Christ and be found in him, not having a righteousness of my own that comes from the law, but one that comes through faith in Christ, the righteousness from God based on faith. I want to know Christ and the power of his resurrection and the sharing of his sufferings by becoming like him in his death, if somehow I may attain the resurrection from the dead. Not that I have already obtained this or have already reached the goal; but I press on to make it my own, because Christ Jesus has made me his own. Beloved, I do not consider that I have made it my own; but this one thing I do: forgetting what lies behind and straining forward to what lies ahead, I press on toward the goal for the prize of the heavenly call of God in Christ Jesus.

The Gospel   John 12:1-8

Six days before the Passover Jesus came to Bethany, the home of Lazarus, whom he had raised from the dead. There they gave a dinner for him. Martha served, and Lazarus was one of those at the table with him. Mary took a pound of costly perfume made of pure nard, anointed Jesus' feet, and wiped them with her hair. The house was filled with the fragrance of the perfume. But Judas Iscariot, one of his disciples (the one who was about to betray him), said, "Why was this perfume not sold for three hundred denarii and the money given to the poor?" (He said this not because he cared about the poor, but because he was a thief; he kept the common purse and used to steal what was put into it.) Jesus said, "Leave her alone. She bought it so that she might keep it for the day of my burial. You always have the poor with you, but you do not always have me."

THE SUNDAY OF THE PASSION: PALM SUNDAY

The Collect

Almighty and everliving God, in your tender love for the human race you sent your Son our Savior Jesus Christ to take upon him our nature, and to suffer death upon the cross, giving us the example of his great humility: Mercifully grant that we may walk in the way of his suffering, and also share in his resurrection; through Jesus Christ our Lord, who lives and reigns with you and the Holy Spirit, one God, for ever and ever. *Amen.*

Year A
Liturgy of the Palms
Matthew 21:1-11
Psalm 118:1-2, 19-29
Liturgy of the Word
Isaiah 50:4-9a
Psalm 31:9-16
Philippians 2:5-11
Matthew 26:14—27:66 or *Matthew 27:11-54*

The Liturgy of the Palms

The Lesson   **Matthew 21:1-11**

When they had come near Jerusalem and had reached Bethphage, at the Mount of Olives, Jesus sent two disciples, saying to them, "Go into the village ahead of you, and immediately you will find a donkey tied, and a colt with her; untie them and bring them to me. If anyone says anything to you, just say this, 'The Lord needs them.' And he will send them immediately." This took place to fulfill what had been spoken through the prophet, saying, "Tell the daughter of Zion, Look, your king is coming to you, humble, and mounted on a donkey, and on a colt, the foal of a donkey." The disciples went and did as Jesus had directed them; they brought the donkey and the colt, and put their cloaks on them, and he sat on them. A very large crowd spread their cloaks on the road, and others cut branches from the trees and spread them on the road. The crowds that went ahead of him and that followed were shouting, "Hosanna to the Son of David! Blessed is the one who comes in the name of the Lord! Hosanna in the highest heaven!" When he entered Jerusalem, the whole city was in turmoil, asking, "Who is this?" The crowds were saying, "This is the prophet Jesus from Nazareth in Galilee."

At the Procession   **Psalm 118:1-2, 19-29**

Psalm 118:1-2, 19-29   *Confitemini Domino*

1   Give thanks to the LORD, for he is good; *
         his mercy endures for ever.
2   Let Israel now proclaim, *
         "His mercy endures for ever."
19   Open for me the gates of righteousness; *
         I will enter them;
         I will offer thanks to the LORD.
20   "This is the gate of the LORD; *
         he who is righteous may enter."

21 I will give thanks to you, for you answered me *
    and have become my salvation.
22 The same stone which the builders rejected *
    has become the chief cornerstone.
23 This is the LORD's doing, *
    and it is marvelous in our eyes.
24 On this day the LORD has acted; *
    we will rejoice and be glad in it.
25 Hosanna, LORD, hosanna! *
    LORD, send us now success.
26 Blessed is he who comes in the name of the LORD; *
    we bless you from the house of the LORD.
27 God is the LORD; he has shined upon us; *
    form a procession with branches up to the horns of the altar.
28 "You are my God, and I will thank you; *
    you are my God, and I will exalt you."
29 Give thanks to the LORD, for he is good; *
    his mercy endures for ever.

The Liturgy of the Word

The Lesson   **Isaiah 50:4-9a**

The Lord GOD has given me the tongue of a teacher, that I may know how to sustain the weary with a word. Morning by morning he wakens — wakens my ear to listen as those who are taught. The Lord GOD has opened my ear, and I was not rebellious, I did not turn backward. I gave my back to those who struck me, and my cheeks to those who pulled out the beard; I did not hide my face from insult and spitting. The Lord GOD helps me; therefore I have not been disgraced; therefore I have set my face like flint, and I know that I shall not be put to shame; he who vindicates me is near. Who will contend with me? Let us stand up together. Who are my adversaries? Let them confront me. It is the Lord GOD who helps me; who will declare me guilty?

The Response   **Psalm 31:9-16**

Psalm 31 *In te, Domine, speravi*

9 Have mercy on me, O LORD, for I am in trouble; *
    my eye is consumed with sorrow,
    and also my throat and my belly.
10 For my life is wasted with grief,
    and my years with sighing; *
    my strength fails me because of affliction,
    and my bones are consumed.

11 I have become a reproach to all my enemies and
                                  even to my neighbors,
    a dismay to those of my acquaintance; *
      when they see me in the street they avoid me.
12 I am forgotten like a dead man, out of mind; *
      I am as useless as a broken pot.
13 For I have heard the whispering of the crowd;
fear is all around; *
      they put their heads together against me;
      they plot to take my life.
14 But as for me, I have trusted in you, O LORD. *
      I have said, "You are my God.
15 My times are in your hand; *
      rescue me from the hand of my enemies,
      and from those who persecute me.
16 Make your face to shine upon your servant, *
      and in your loving-kindness save me."

The Epistle   Philippians 2:5-11

Let the same mind be in you that was in Christ Jesus, who, though he was in the form of God, did not regard equality with God as something to be exploited, but emptied himself, taking the form of a slave, being born in human likeness. And being found in human form, he humbled himself and became obedient to the point of death — even death on a cross. Therefore God also highly exalted him and gave him the name that is above every name, so that at the name of Jesus every knee should bend, in heaven and on earth and under the earth, and every tongue should confess that Jesus Christ is Lord, to the glory of God the Father.

The Gospel   Matthew 26:14—27:66 *or* Matthew 27:11-54
Matthew 26:14—27:66

One of the twelve, who was called Judas Iscariot, went to the chief priests and said, "What will you give me if I betray him to you?" They paid him thirty pieces of silver. And from that moment he began to look for an opportunity to betray him. On the first day of Unleavened Bread the disciples came to Jesus, saying, "Where do you want us to make the preparations for you to eat the Passover?" He said, "Go into the city to a certain man, and say to him, 'The Teacher says, My time is near; I will keep the Passover at your house with my disciples.' " So the disciples did as Jesus had directed them, and they prepared the Passover meal. When it was evening, he took his place with the twelve; and while they were eating, he said, "Truly I tell you, one of you will betray me." And they became greatly distressed and began to say to him one after another, "Surely not I, Lord?" He answered, "The one who has dipped his hand into the bowl with me will betray me. The Son of Man goes as it is written of him, but woe to that one by whom the Son of Man is betrayed! It would have been better for that one not to have been born." Judas, who betrayed him, said, "Surely not I, Rabbi?" He replied, "You have said so." While they were eating, Jesus took a loaf of bread, and after blessing it he broke it, gave it to the disciples, and said, "Take, eat; this is my body." Then he took a cup, and after giving thanks he gave it to them, saying, "Drink from it, all of you; for this is my blood of the covenant, which is poured out for many for the forgiveness of sins. I tell you, I will never again drink of this fruit of the vine until that day when I drink it new with you in my Father's kingdom." When they had sung the hymn, they went out to the Mount of Olives. Then Jesus said to them, "You will all become deserters because of me this night; for it is written, 'I will strike the shepherd, and the sheep of the flock will be scattered.' But after I am raised up, I will go ahead of you to Galilee." Peter said to him, "Though all become deserters because of you, I will never desert you." Jesus said to him, "Truly I tell you, this very night, before the cock crows, you will deny me three times." Peter said to him, "Even though I must die with you, I will not deny you." And so said all the disciples. Then Jesus went with them to a place called Gethsemane; and he said to his disciples, "Sit here while I go over there and pray." He took with him Peter and the two sons of Zebedee, and began to be grieved and agitated. Then he said to them, "I am deeply grieved, even to death; remain here, and stay awake with me." And going a little farther, he threw himself on the ground and prayed, "My Father, if it is possible, let this cup pass from me; yet not what I want but what you want." Then he came to the disciples and found them sleeping; and he said to Peter, "So, could you not stay awake with me one hour? Stay awake and pray that you may not come into the time of trial; the spirit indeed is willing, but the flesh is weak." Again he went away for the second time and prayed, "My Father, if this cannot pass unless I drink it, your will be done." Again he came and found them sleeping, for their eyes were heavy. So leaving them again, he went away and prayed for the third time, saying the same words. Then he came to the disciples and said to them, "Are you still sleeping and taking your rest? See, the hour is at hand, and the Son of Man is betrayed into the hands of sinners. Get up, let us be going. See, my betrayer is at hand." While he was still speaking, Judas, one of the twelve, arrived; with him was a large crowd with swords and clubs, from the chief priests and the elders of the people. Now the betrayer had given them a sign, saying, "The one I will kiss is the man; arrest him." At once he came up to Jesus and said, "Greetings, Rabbi!" and kissed him. Jesus said to him, "Friend, do what you are here to do." Then they came and laid hands on Jesus and arrested him. Suddenly, one of those with Jesus put his hand on his sword, drew it, and struck the slave of the high priest, cutting off his ear. Then Jesus said to him, "Put your sword back into its place; for all who take the sword will perish by the sword. Do you think that I cannot appeal to my Father, and he will at once send me more than twelve legions of angels? But how then would the scriptures be fulfilled, which say it must happen in this way?" At that hour Jesus said to the crowds, "Have you come out with swords and clubs to arrest me as though I were a bandit? Day after day I sat in the temple teaching, and you did not arrest me. But all this has taken place, so that the scriptures of the prophets may be fulfilled." Then all the disciples deserted him and fled. Those who had arrested Jesus took him to Caiaphas the high priest, in whose house the scribes and the elders had gathered. But Peter was following him at a distance, as far as the courtyard of the high priest; and going inside, he sat with the guards in order to see how this would end. Now the chief priests and the whole council were looking for false testimony against Jesus so that they might put him to death, but they found none, though many false witnesses came forward. At last two came forward and said, "This fellow said, 'I am able to destroy the temple of God and to build it in three days.' " The high priest stood up and said, "Have you no answer? What is it that they testify against you?" But Jesus was silent. Then the high priest said to him, "I put you under oath before the living God, tell us if you are the Messiah, the Son of God." Jesus said to him, "You have said so. But I tell you, From now on you will see the Son of Man seated at the right hand of Power and coming on the clouds of heaven." Then the high priest tore his clothes and said, "He has blasphemed! Why do we still need witnesses? You have now heard his blasphemy. What is your verdict?" They answered, "He deserves death." Then they spat in his face and struck him; and some slapped him, saying, "Prophesy to us, you Messiah! Who is it that struck you?" Now Peter was sitting outside in the courtyard. A servant-girl came to him and said, "You also were with Jesus the Galilean." But he denied it before all of them, saying, "I do not know what you are talking about." When he went out to the porch, another servant-girl saw him, and she said to the bystanders, "This man was with Jesus of Nazareth." Again he denied it with an oath, "I do not know the man." After a little while the bystanders came up and said to Peter, "Certainly you are also one of them, for your accent betrays you." Then he began to curse, and he swore an oath, "I do not know the man!" At that moment the cock crowed. Then Peter remembered what Jesus had said: "Before the cock crows, you will deny me three times." And he went out and wept bitterly. When morning came, all the chief priests and the elders of the people conferred together against Jesus in order to bring about his death. They bound him, led him away, and handed him over to Pilate the governor. When Judas, his betrayer, saw that Jesus was condemned, he repented and brought back the thirty pieces of silver to the chief priests and the elders. He said, "I have sinned by betraying innocent blood." But they said, "What is that to us? See to it yourself." Throwing down the pieces of silver in the temple, he departed; and he went and hanged himself. But the chief priests, taking the pieces of silver, said, "It is not lawful to put them into the treasury, since they are blood money." After conferring together, they used them to buy the potter's field as a place to bury foreigners. For this reason that field has been called the Field of Blood to this day. Then was fulfilled what had been spoken through the prophet Jeremiah, "And they took the thirty pieces of silver, the price of the one on whom a price had been set, on whom some of the people of Israel had set a price, and they gave them for the potter's field, as the Lord commanded me." Now Jesus stood before the governor; and the governor asked him, "Are you the King of the Jews?" Jesus said, "You say so." But when he was accused by the chief priests and elders, he did not answer. Then Pilate said to him, "Do you not hear how many accusations they make against you?" But he gave him no answer, not even to a single charge, so that the governor was greatly amazed. Now at the festival the governor was accustomed to release a prisoner for the crowd, anyone whom they wanted. At that time they had a notorious prisoner, called Jesus Barabbas. So after they had gathered, Pilate said to them, "Whom do you want me to release for you, Jesus Barabbas or Jesus who is called the Messiah?" For he realized that it was out of jealousy that they had handed him over. While he was sitting on the judgment seat, his wife sent word to him, "Have nothing to do with that innocent man, for today I have suffered a great deal because of a dream about him." Now the chief priests and the elders persuaded the crowds to ask for Barabbas and to have Jesus killed. The governor again said to them, "Which of the two do you want me to release for you?" And they said, "Barabbas." Pilate said to them, "Then what should I do with Jesus who is called the Messiah?" All of them said, "Let him be crucified!" Then he asked, "Why, what evil has he done?" But they shouted all the more, "Let him be crucified!" So when Pilate saw that he could do nothing, but rather that a riot was beginning, he took some water and washed his hands before the crowd, saying, "I am innocent of this man's blood; see to it yourselves." Then the people as a whole answered, "His blood be on us and on our children!" So he released Barabbas for them; and after flogging Jesus, he handed him over to be crucified. Then the soldiers of the governor took Jesus into the governor's headquarters, and they gathered the whole cohort around him. They stripped him and put a scarlet robe on him, and after twisting some thorns into a crown, they put it on his head. They put a reed in his right hand and knelt before him and mocked him, saying, "Hail, King of the Jews!" They spat on him, and took the reed and struck him on the head. After mocking him, they stripped him of the robe and put his own clothes on him. Then they led him away to crucify him. As they went out, they came upon a man from Cyrene named Simon; they compelled this man to carry his cross. And when they came to a place called Golgotha (which means Place of a Skull), they offered him wine to drink, mixed with gall; but when he tasted it, he would not drink it. And when they had crucified him, they divided his clothes among themselves by casting lots; then they sat down there and kept watch over him. Over his head they put the charge against him, which read, "This is Jesus, the King of the Jews." Then two bandits were crucified with him, one on his right and one on his left. Those who passed by derided him, shaking their heads and saying, "You who would destroy the temple and build it in three days, save yourself! If you are the Son of God, come down from the cross." In the same way the chief priests also, along with the scribes and elders, were mocking him, saying, "He saved others; he cannot save himself. He is the King of Israel; let him come down from the cross now, and we will believe in him. He trusts in God; let God deliver him now, if he wants to; for he said, 'I am God's Son.' " The bandits who were crucified with him also taunted him in the same way. From noon on, darkness came over the whole land until three in the afternoon. And about three o'clock Jesus cried with a loud voice, "Eli, Eli, lema sabachthani?" that is, "My God, my God, why have you forsaken me?" When some of the bystanders heard it, they said, "This man is calling for Elijah." At once one of them ran and got a sponge, filled it with sour wine, put it on a stick, and gave it to him to drink. But the others said, "Wait, let us see whether Elijah will come to save him." Then Jesus cried again with a loud voice and breathed his last. At that moment the curtain of the temple was torn in two, from top to bottom. The earth shook, and the rocks were split. The tombs also were opened, and many bodies of the saints who had fallen asleep were raised. After his resurrection they came out of the tombs and entered the holy city and appeared to many. Now when the centurion and those with him, who were keeping watch over Jesus, saw the earthquake and what took place, they were terrified and said, "Truly this man was God's Son!" Many women were also there, looking on from a distance; they had followed Jesus from Galilee and had provided for him. Among them were Mary Magdalene, and Mary the mother of James and Joseph, and the mother of the sons of Zebedee. When it was evening, there came a rich man from Arimathea, named Joseph, who was also a disciple of Jesus. He went to Pilate and asked for the body Jesus; then Pilate ordered it to be given to him. So Joseph took the body and wrapped it in a clean linen cloth and laid it in his own new tomb, which he had hewn in the rock. He then rolled a great stone to the door of the tomb and went away. Mary Magdalene and the other Mary were there, sitting opposite the tomb. The next day, that is, after the day of Preparation, the chief priests and the Pharisees gathered before Pilate and said, "Sir, we remember what that impostor said while he was still alive, 'After three days I will rise again.' Therefore command the tomb to be made secure until the third day; otherwise his disciples may go and steal him away, and tell the people, 'He has been raised from the dead,' and the last deception would be worse than the first." Pilate said to them, "You have a guard of soldiers; go, make it as secure as you can." So they went with the guard and made the tomb secure by sealing the stone.

or, **Matthew 27:11-54**

Now Jesus stood before the governor; and the governor asked him, "Are you the King of the Jews?" Jesus said, "You say so." But when he was accused by the chief priests and elders, he did not answer. Then Pilate said to him, "Do you not hear how many accusations they make against you?" But he gave him no answer, not even to a single charge, so that the governor was greatly amazed. Now at the festival the governor was accustomed to release a prisoner for the crowd, anyone whom they wanted. At that time they had a notorious prisoner, called Jesus Barabbas. So after they had gathered, Pilate said to them, "Whom do you want me to release for you, Jesus Barabbas or Jesus who is called the Messiah?" For he realized that it was out of jealousy that they had handed him over. While he was sitting on the judgment seat, his wife sent word to him, "Have nothing to do with that innocent man, for today I have suffered a great deal because of a dream about him." Now the chief priests and the elders persuaded the crowds to ask for Barabbas and to have Jesus killed. The governor again said to them, "Which of the two do you want me to release for you?" And they said, "Barabbas." Pilate said to them, "Then what should I do with Jesus who is called the Messiah?" All of them said, "Let him be crucified!" Then he asked, "Why, what evil has he done?" But they shouted all the more, "Let him be crucified!" So when Pilate saw that he could do nothing, but rather that a riot was beginning, he took some water and washed his hands before the crowd, saying, "I am innocent of this man's blood; see to it yourselves." Then the people as a whole answered, "His blood be on us and on our children!" So he released Barabbas for them; and after flogging Jesus, he handed him over to be crucified. Then the soldiers of the governor took Jesus into the governor's headquarters, and they gathered the whole cohort around him. They stripped him and put a scarlet robe on him, and after twisting some thorns into a crown, they put it on his head. They put a reed in his right hand and knelt before him and mocked him, saying, "Hail, King of the Jews!" They spat on him, and took the reed and struck him on the head. After mocking him, they stripped him of the robe and put his own clothes on him. Then they led him away to crucify him. As they went out, they came upon a man from Cyrene named Simon; they compelled this man to carry his cross. And when they came to a place called Golgotha (which means Place of a Skull), they offered him wine to drink, mixed with gall; but when he tasted it, he would not drink it. And when they had crucified him, they divided his clothes among themselves by casting lots; then they sat down there and kept watch over him. Over his head they put the charge against him, which read, "This is Jesus, the King of the Jews." Then two bandits were crucified with him, one on his right and one on his left. Those who passed by derided him, shaking their heads and saying, "You who would destroy the temple and build it in three days, save yourself! If you are the Son of God, come down from the cross." In the same way the chief priests also, along with the scribes and elders, were mocking him, saying, "He saved others; he cannot save himself. He is the King of Israel; let him come down from the cross now, and we will believe in him. He trusts in God; let God deliver him now, if he wants to; for he said, 'I am God's Son.' " The bandits who were crucified with him also taunted him in the same way. From noon on, darkness came over the whole land until three in the afternoon. And about three o'clock Jesus cried with a loud voice, "Eli, Eli, lema sabachthani?" that is, "My God, my God, why have you forsaken me?" When some of the bystanders heard it, they said, "This man is calling for Elijah." At once one of them ran and got a sponge, filled it with sour wine, put it on a stick, and gave it to him to drink. But the others said, "Wait, let us see whether Elijah will come to save him." Then Jesus cried again with a loud voice and breathed his last. At that moment the curtain of the temple was torn in two, from top to bottom. The earth shook, and the rocks were split. The tombs also were opened, and many bodies of the saints who had fallen asleep were raised. After his resurrection they came out of the tombs and entered the holy city and appeared to many. Now when the centurion and those with him, who were keeping watch over Jesus, saw the earthquake and what took place, they were terrified and said, "Truly this man was God's Son!"

Year B
Liturgy of the Palms
Mark 11:1-11 or *John 12:12-16*
Psalm 118:1-2, 19-29
Liturgy of the Word
Isaiah 50:4-9a
Psalm 31:9-16
Philippians 2:5-11
Mark 14:1—15:47 or *Mark 15:1-39, (40-47)*

Liturgy of the Palms

The Lessons   **Mark 11:1-11** *or* **John 12:12-16**
Mark 11:1-11

When Jesus and his disciples were approaching Jerusalem, at Bethphage and Bethany, near the Mount of Olives, he sent two of his disciples and said to them, "Go into the village ahead of you, and immediately as you enter it, you will find tied there a colt that has never been ridden; untie it and bring it. If anyone says to you, 'Why are you doing this?' just say this, 'The Lord needs it and will send it back here immediately.' " They went away and found a colt tied near a door, outside in the street. As they were untying it, some of the bystanders said to them, "What are you doing, untying the colt?" They told them what Jesus had said; and they allowed them to take it. Then they brought the colt to Jesus and threw their cloaks on it; and he sat on it. Many people spread their cloaks on the road, and others spread leafy branches that they had cut in the fields. Then those who went ahead and those who followed were shouting, "Hosanna! Blessed is the one who comes in the name of the Lord! Blessed is the coming kingdom of our ancestor David! Hosanna in the highest heaven!" Then he entered Jerusalem and went into the temple; and when he had looked around at everything, as it was already late, he went out to Bethany with the twelve.

or, **John 12:12-16**

The next day the great crowd that had come to the festival heard that Jesus was coming to Jerusalem. So they took branches of palm trees and went out to meet him, shouting, "Hosanna! Blessed is the one who comes in the name of the Lord—the King of Israel!" Jesus found a young donkey and sat on it; as it is written: "Do not be afraid, daughter of Zion. Look, your king is coming, sitting on a donkey's colt!" His disciples did not understand these things at first; but when Jesus was glorified, then they remembered that these things had been written of him and had been done to him.

The Response   **Psalm 118:1-2, 19-29**

Psalm 118:1-2, 19-29   *Confitemini Domino*

  1   Give thanks to the LORD, for he is good; *
       his mercy endures for ever.

  2   Let Israel now proclaim, *
       "His mercy endures for ever."

 19   Open for me the gates of righteousness; *
       I will enter them;
       I will offer thanks to the LORD.

 20   "This is the gate of the LORD; *
       he who is righteous may enter."

 21   I will give thanks to you, for you answered me *
       and have become my salvation.

 22   The same stone which the builders rejected *
       has become the chief cornerstone.

 23   This is the LORD's doing, *
       and it is marvelous in our eyes.

 24   On this day the LORD has acted; *
       we will rejoice and be glad in it.

 25   Hosanna, LORD, hosanna! *
       LORD, send us now success.

 26   Blessed is he who comes in the name of the LORD; *
       we bless you from the house of the LORD.

27　God is the Lord; he has shined upon us; *
　　　form a procession with branches up to the horns of the altar.

28　"You are my God, and I will thank you; *
　　　you are my God, and I will exalt you."

29　Give thanks to the Lord, for he is good; *
　　　his mercy endures for ever.

Liturgy of the Word

The Lesson   **Isaiah 50:4-9***a*

The Lord God has given me the tongue of a teacher, that I may know how to
sustain the weary with a word. Morning by morning he wakens—wakens my
ear to listen as those who are taught. The Lord God has opened my ear, and I
was not rebellious, I did not turn backward. I gave my back to those who
struck me, and my cheeks to those who pulled out the beard; I did not hide my
face from insult and spitting. The Lord God helps me; therefore I have not
been disgraced; therefore I have set my face like flint, and I know that I shall
not be put to shame; he who vindicates me is near. Who will contend with me?
Let us stand up together. Who are my adversaries? Let them confront me. It
is the Lord God who helps me; who will declare me guilty?

The Response   **Psalm 31:9-16**

Psalm 31:9-16　*In te, Domine, speravi*

9　Have mercy on me, O Lord, for I am in trouble; *
　　　my eye is consumed with sorrow,
　　　and also my throat and my belly.

10　For my life is wasted with grief,
　　and my years with sighing; *
　　　my strength fails me because of affliction,
　　　and my bones are consumed.

11　I have become a reproach to all my enemies and
　　　　　　　　even to my neighbors,
　　a dismay to those of my acquaintance; *
　　　when they see me in the street they avoid me.

12　I am forgotten like a dead man, out of mind; *
　　　I am as useless as a broken pot.

13　For I have heard the whispering of the crowd;
　　fear is all around; *
　　　they put their heads together against me;
　　　they plot to take my life.

14　But as for me, I have trusted in you, O Lord. *
　　　I have said, "You are my God.

15 My times are in your hand; *

    rescue me from the hand of my enemies,

    and from those who persecute me.

16 Make your face to shine upon your servant, *

    and in your loving-kindness save me."

The Epistle   Philippians 2:5-11

Let the same mind be in you that was in Christ Jesus, who, though he was in the form of God, did not regard equality with God as something to be exploited, but emptied himself, taking the form of a slave, being born in human likeness. And being found in human form, he humbled himself and became obedient to the point of death — even death on a cross. Therefore God also highly exalted him and gave him the name that is above every name, so that at the name of Jesus every knee should bend, in heaven and on earth and under the earth, and every tongue should confess that Jesus Christ is Lord, to the glory of God the Father.

The Gospel   Mark 14:1—15:47 *or* Mark 15:1-39, (40-47)
Mark 14:1—15:47

It was two days before the Passover and the festival of Unleavened Bread. The chief priests and the scribes were looking for a way to arrest Jesus by stealth and kill him; for they said, "Not during the festival, or there may be a riot among the people." While he was at Bethany in the house of Simon the leper, as he sat at the table, a woman came with an alabaster jar of very costly ointment of nard, and she broke open the jar and poured the ointment on his head. But some were there who said to one another in anger, "Why was the ointment wasted in this way? For this ointment could have been sold for more than three hundred denarii, and the money given to the poor." And they scolded her. But Jesus said, "Let her alone; why do you trouble her? She has performed a good service for me. For you always have the poor with you, and you can show kindness to them whenever you wish; but you will not always have me. She has done what she could; she has anointed my body beforehand for its burial. Truly I tell you, wherever the good news is proclaimed in the whole world, what she has done will be told in remembrance of her." Then Judas Iscariot, who was one of the twelve, went to the chief priests in order to betray him to them. When they heard it, they were greatly pleased, and promised to give him money. So he began to look for an opportunity to betray him. On the first day of Unleavened Bread, when the Passover lamb is sacrificed, his disciples said to him, "Where do you want us to go and make the preparations for you to eat the Passover?" So he sent two of his disciples, saying to them, "Go into the city, and a man carrying a jar of water will meet you; follow him, and wherever he enters, say to the owner of the house, 'The Teacher asks, Where is my guest room where I may eat the Passover with my disciples?' He will show you a large room upstairs, furnished and ready. Make preparations for us there." So the disciples set out and went to the city, and found everything as he had told them; and they prepared the Passover meal. When it was evening, he came with the twelve. And when they had taken their places and were eating, Jesus said, "Truly I tell you, one of you will betray me, one who is eating with me." They began to be distressed and to say to him one after another, "Surely, not I?" He said to them, "It is one of the twelve, one who is dipping bread into the bowl with me. For the Son of Man goes as it is written of him, but woe to that one by whom the Son of Man is betrayed! It would have been better for that one not to have been born." While they were eating, he took a loaf of bread, and after blessing it he broke it, gave it to them, and said, "Take; this is my body." Then he took a cup, and after giving thanks he gave it to them, and all of them drank from it. He said to them, "This is my blood of the covenant, which is poured out for many. Truly I tell you, I will never again drink of the fruit of the vine until that day when I drink it new in the kingdom of God." When they had sung the hymn, they went out to the Mount of Olives. And Jesus said to them, "You will all become deserters; for it is written, 'I will strike the shepherd, and the sheep will be scattered.' But after I am raised up, I will go before you to Galilee." Peter said to him, "Even though all become deserters, I will not." Jesus said to him, "Truly I tell you, this day, this very night, before the cock crows twice, you will deny me three times." But he said vehemently, "Even though I must die with you, I will not deny you." And all of them said the same. They went to a place called Gethsemane; and he said to his disciples, "Sit here while I pray." He took with him Peter and James and John, and began to be distressed and agitated. And said to them, "I am deeply grieved, even to death; remain here, and keep awake." And going a little farther, he threw himself on the ground and prayed that, if it were possible, the hour might pass from him. He said, "Abba, Father, for you all things are possible; remove this cup from me; yet, not what I want, but what you want." He came and found them sleeping; and he said to Peter, "Simon, are you asleep? Could you not keep awake one hour? Keep awake and pray that you may not come into the time of trial; the spirit indeed is willing, but the flesh is weak." And again he went away and prayed, saying the same words. And once more he came and found them sleeping, for their eyes were very heavy; and they did not know what to say to him. He came a third time and said to them, "Are you still sleeping and taking your rest? Enough! The hour has come; the Son of Man is betrayed into the hands of sinners. Get up, let us be going. See, my betrayer is at hand." Immediately, while he was still speaking, Judas, one of the twelve, arrived; and with him there was a crowd with swords and clubs, from the chief priests, the scribes, and the elders. Now the betrayer had given them a sign, saying, "The one I will kiss is the man; arrest him and lead him away under guard." So when he came, he went up to him at once and said, "Rabbi!" and kissed him. Then they laid hands on him and arrested him. But one of those who stood near drew his sword and struck the slave of the high priest, cutting off his ear. Then Jesus said to them, "Have you come out with swords and clubs to arrest me as though I were a bandit? Day after day I was with you in the temple teaching, and you did not arrest me. But let the scriptures be fulfilled." All of them deserted him and fled. A certain young man was following him, wearing nothing but a linen cloth. They caught hold of him, but he left the linen cloth and ran off naked. They took Jesus to the high priest; and all the chief priests, the elders, and the scribes were assembled. Peter had followed him at a distance, right into the courtyard of the high priest; and he was sitting with the guards, warming himself at the fire. Now the chief priests and the whole council were looking for testimony against Jesus to put him to death; but they found none. For many gave false testimony against him, and their testimony did not agree. Some stood up and gave false testimony against him, saying, "We heard him say, 'I will destroy this temple that is made with hands, and in three days I will build another, not made with hands.' " But even on this point their testimony did not agree. Then the high priest stood up before them and asked Jesus, "Have you no answer? What is it that they testify against you?" But he was silent and did not answer. Again the high priest asked him, "Are you the Messiah, the Son of the Blessed One?" Jesus said, "I am; and 'you will see the Son of Man seated at the right hand of the Power,' and 'coming with the clouds of heaven.' " Then the high priest tore his clothes and said, "Why do we still need witnesses? You have heard his blasphemy! What is your decision?" All of them condemned him as deserving death. Some began to spit on him, to blindfold him, and to strike him, saying to him, "Prophesy!" The guards also took him over and beat him. While Peter was below in the courtyard, one of the servant-girls of the high priest came by. When she saw Peter warming himself, she stared at him and said, "You also were with Jesus, the man from Nazareth." But he denied it, saying, "I do not know or understand what you are talking about." And he went out into the forecourt. Then the cock crowed. And the servant-girl, on seeing him, began again to say to the bystanders, "This man is one of them." But again he denied it. Then after a little while the bystanders again said to Peter, "Certainly you are one of them; for you are a Galilean." But he began to curse, and he swore an oath, "I do not know this man you are talking about." At that moment the cock crowed for the second time. Then Peter remembered that Jesus had said to him, "Before the cock crows twice, you will deny me three times." And he broke down and wept. As soon as it was morning, the chief priests held a consultation with the elders and scribes and the whole council. They bound Jesus, led him away, and handed him over to Pilate. Pilate asked him, "Are you the King of the Jews?" He answered him, "You say so." Then the chief priests accused him of many things. Pilate asked him again, "Have you no answer? See how many charges they bring against you." But Jesus made no further reply, so that Pilate was amazed. Now at the festival he used to release a prisoner for them, anyone for whom they asked. Now a man called Barabbas was in prison with the rebels who had committed murder during the insurrection. So the crowd came and began to ask Pilate to do for them according to his custom. Then he answered them, "Do you want me to release for you the King of the Jews?" For he realized that it was out of jealousy that the chief priests had handed him over. But the chief priests stirred up the crowd to have him release Barabbas for them instead. Pilate spoke to them again, "Then what do you wish me to do with the man you call the King of the Jews?" They shouted back, "Crucify him!" Pilate asked them, "Why, what evil has he done?" But they shouted all the more, "Crucify him!" So Pilate, wishing to satisfy the crowd, released Barabbas for them; and after flogging Jesus, he handed him over to be crucified. Then the soldiers led him into the courtyard of the palace (that is, the governor's headquarters); and they called together the whole cohort. And they clothed him in a purple cloak; and after twisting some thorns into a crown, they put it on him. And they began saluting him, "Hail, King of the Jews!" They struck his head with a reed, spat upon him, and knelt down in homage to him. After mocking him, they stripped him of the purple cloak and put his own clothes on him. Then they led him out to crucify him. They compelled a passer-by, who was coming in from the country, to carry his cross; it was Simon of Cyrene, the father of Alexander and Rufus. Then they brought Jesus to the place called Golgotha (which means the place of a skull). And they offered him wine mixed with myrrh; but he did not take it. And they crucified him, and divided his clothes among them, casting lots to decide what each should take. It was nine o'clock in the morning when they crucified him. The inscription of the charge against him read, "The King of the Jews." And with him they crucified two bandits, one on his right and one on his left. Those who passed by derided him, shaking their heads and saying, "Aha! You who would destroy the temple and build it in three days, save yourself, and come down from the cross!" In the same way the chief priests, along with the scribes, were also mocking him among themselves and saying, "He saved others; he cannot save himself. Let the Messiah, the King of Israel, come down from the cross now, so that we may see and believe." Those who were crucified with him also taunted him. When it was noon, darkness came over the whole land until three in the afternoon. At three o'clock Jesus cried out with a loud voice, "Eloi, Eloi, lema sabachthani?" which means, "My God, my God, why have you forsaken me?" When some of the bystanders heard it, they said, "Listen, he is calling for Elijah." And someone ran, filled a sponge with sour wine, put it on a stick, and gave it to him to drink, saying, "Wait, let us see whether Elijah will come to take him down." Then Jesus gave a loud cry and breathed his last. And the curtain of the temple was torn in two, from top to bottom. Now when the centurion, who stood facing him, saw that in this way he breathed his last, he said, "Truly this man was God's Son!" There were also women looking on from a distance; among them were Mary Magdalene, and Mary the mother of James the younger and of Joses, and Salome. These used to follow him and provided for him when he was in

Galilee; and there were many other women who had come up with him to Jerusalem. When evening had come, and since it was the day of Preparation, that is, the day before the sabbath, Joseph of Arimathea, a respected member of the council, who was also himself waiting expectantly for the kingdom of God, went boldly to Pilate and asked for the body of Jesus. Then Pilate wondered if he were already dead; and summoning the centurion, he asked him whether he had been dead for some time. When he learned from the centurion that he was dead, he granted the body to Joseph. Then Joseph bought a linen cloth, and taking down the body, wrapped it in the linen cloth, and laid it in a tomb that had been hewn out of the rock. He then rolled a stone against the door of the tomb. Mary Magdalene and Mary the mother of Joses saw where the body was laid.

or, **Mark 15:1-39, (40-47)**
Mark 15:1-39

As soon as it was morning, the chief priests held a consultation with the elders and scribes and the whole council. They bound Jesus, led him away, and handed him over to Pilate. Pilate asked him, "Are you the King of the Jews?" He answered him, "You say so." Then the chief priests accused him of many things. Pilate asked him again, "Have you no answer? See how many charges they bring against you." But Jesus made no further reply, so that Pilate was amazed. Now at the festival he used to release a prisoner for them, anyone for whom they asked. Now a man called Barabbas was in prison with the rebels who had committed murder during the insurrection. So the crowd came and began to ask Pilate to do for them according to his custom. Then he answered them, "Do you want me to release for you the King of the Jews?" For he realized that it was out of jealousy that the chief priests had handed him over. But the chief priests stirred up the crowd to have him release Barabbas for them instead. Pilate spoke to them again, "Then what do you wish me to do with the man you call the King of the Jews?" They shouted back, "Crucify him!" Pilate asked them, "Why, what evil has he done?" But they shouted all the more, "Crucify him!" So Pilate, wishing to satisfy the crowd, released Barabbas for them; and after flogging Jesus, he handed him over to be crucified. Then the soldiers led him into the courtyard of the palace (that is, the governor's headquarters); and they called together the whole cohort. And they clothed him in a purple cloak; and after twisting some thorns into a crown, they put it on him. And they began saluting him, "Hail, King of the Jews!" They struck his head with a reed, spat upon him, and knelt down in homage to him. After mocking him, they stripped him of the purple cloak and put his own clothes on him. Then they led him out to crucify him. They compelled a passer-by, who was coming in from the country, to carry his cross; it was Simon of Cyrene, the father of Alexander and Rufus. Then they brought Jesus to the place called Golgotha (which means the place of a skull). And they offered him wine mixed with myrrh; but he did not take it. And they crucified him, and divided his clothes among them, casting lots to decide what each should take. It was nine o'clock in the morning when they crucified him. The inscription of the charge against him read, "The King of the Jews." And with him they crucified two bandits, one on his right and one on his left. Those who passed by derided him, shaking their heads and saying, "Aha! You who would destroy the temple and build it in three days, save yourself, and come down from the cross!" In the same way the chief priests, along with the scribes, were also mocking him among themselves and saying, "He saved others; he cannot save himself. Let the Messiah, the King of Israel, come down from the cross now, so that we may see and believe." Those who were crucified with him also taunted him. When it was noon, darkness came over the whole land until three in the afternoon. At three o'clock Jesus cried out with a loud voice, "Eloi, Eloi, lema sabachthani?" which means, "My God, my God, why have you forsaken me?" When some of the bystanders heard it, they said, "Listen, he is calling for Elijah." And someone ran, filled a sponge with sour wine, put it on a stick, and gave it to him to drink, saying, "Wait, let us see whether Elijah will come to take him down." Then Jesus gave a loud cry and breathed his last. And the curtain of the temple was torn in two, from top to bottom. Now when the centurion, who stood facing him, saw that in this way he breathed his last, he said, "Truly this man was God's Son!"

Mark 15:(40-47) [There were also women looking on from a distance; among them were Mary Magdalene, and Mary the mother of James the younger and of Joses, and Salome. These used to follow him and provided for him when he was in Galilee; and there were many other women who had come up with him to Jerusalem. When evening had come, and since it was the day of Preparation, that is, the day before the sabbath, Joseph of Arimathea, a respected member of the council, who was also himself waiting expectantly for the kingdom of God, went boldly to Pilate and asked for the body of Jesus. Then Pilate wondered if he were already dead; and summoning the centurion, he asked him whether he had been dead for some time. When he learned from the centurion that he was dead, he granted the body to Joseph. Then Joseph bought a linen cloth, and taking down the body, wrapped it in the linen cloth, and laid it in a tomb that had been hewn out of the rock. He then rolled a stone against the door of the tomb. Mary Magdalene and Mary the mother of Joses saw where the body was laid.]

Year C

Liturgy of the Palms

Luke 19:28-40
Psalm 118:1-2, 19-29

Liturgy of the Word

Isaiah 50:4-9a
Psalm 31:9-16
Philippians 2:5-11
Luke 22:14—23:56 or *Luke 23:1-49*

Liturgy of the Palms

The Lesson   **Luke 19:28-40**

After Jesus had said this, Jesus went on ahead, going up to Jerusalem. When he had come near Bethphage and Bethany, at the place called the Mount of Olives, he sent two of the disciples, saying, "Go into the village ahead of you, and as you enter it you will find tied there a colt that has never been ridden. Untie it and bring it here. If anyone asks you, 'Why are you untying it?' just say this, 'The Lord needs it.' " So those who were sent departed and found it as he had told them. As they were untying the colt, its owners asked them, "Why are you untying the colt?" They said, "The Lord needs it." Then they brought it to Jesus; and after throwing their cloaks on the colt, they set Jesus on it. As he rode along, people kept spreading their cloaks on the road. As he was now approaching the path down from the Mount of Olives, the whole multitude of the disciples began to praise God joyfully with a loud voice for all the deeds of power that they had seen, saying, "Blessed is the king who comes in the name of the Lord! Peace in heaven, and glory in the highest heaven!" Some of the Pharisees in the crowd said to him, "Teacher, order your disciples to stop." He answered, "I tell you, if these were silent, the stones would shout out."

The Response   **Psalm 118:1-2, 19-29**

Psalm 118:1-2, 19-29   *Confitemini Domino*

1   Give thanks to the Lord, for he is good; *
        his mercy endures for ever.
2   Let Israel now proclaim, *
        "His mercy endures for ever."
19   Open for me the gates of righteousness; *
        I will enter them;
        I will offer thanks to the Lord.
20   "This is the gate of the Lord; *
        he who is righteous may enter."

21   I will give thanks to you, for you answered me *
        and have become my salvation.

22   The same stone which the builders rejected *
        has become the chief cornerstone.

23   This is the LORD's doing, *
        and it is marvelous in our eyes.

24   On this day the LORD has acted; *
        we will rejoice and be glad in it.

25   Hosanna, LORD, hosanna! *
        LORD, send us now success.

26   Blessed is he who comes in the name of the LORD; *
        we bless you from the house of the LORD.

27   God is the LORD; he has shined upon us; *
        form a procession with branches up to the horns of the altar.

28   "You are my God, and I will thank you; *
        you are my God, and I will exalt you."

29   Give thanks to the LORD, for he is good; *
        his mercy endures for ever.

Liturgy of the Word

The Lesson   **Isaiah 50:4-9*a***

The Lord GOD has given me the tongue of a teacher, that I may know how to sustain the weary with a word. Morning by morning he wakens — wakens my ear to listen as those who are taught. The Lord GOD has opened my ear, and I was not rebellious, I did not turn backward. I gave my back to those who struck me, and my cheeks to those who pulled out the beard; I did not hide my face from insult and spitting. The Lord GOD helps me; therefore I have not been disgraced; therefore I have set my face like flint, and I know that I shall not be put to shame; he who vindicates me is near. Who will contend with me? Let us stand up together. Who are my adversaries? Let them confront me. It is the Lord GOD who helps me; who will declare me guilty?

The Response   **Psalm 31:9-16**

Psalm 31:9-16   *In te, Domine, speravi*

  9   Have mercy on me, O LORD, for I am in trouble; *
        my eye is consumed with sorrow,
        and also my throat and my belly.

10   For my life is wasted with grief,
      and my years with sighing; *
        my strength fails me because of affliction,
        and my bones are consumed.

11 I have become a reproach to all my enemies and
          even to my neighbors,
  a dismay to those of my acquaintance; *
     when they see me in the street they avoid me.

12 I am forgotten like a dead man, out of mind; *
     I am as useless as a broken pot.

13 For I have heard the whispering of the crowd;
  fear is all around; *
       they put their heads together against me;
       they plot to take my life.

14 But as for me, I have trusted in you, O LORD. *
     I have said, "You are my God.

15 My times are in your hand; *
     rescue me from the hand of my enemies,
     and from those who persecute me.

16 Make your face to shine upon your servant, *
     and in your loving-kindness save me."

The Epistle   Philippians 2:5-11

Let the same mind be in you that was in Christ Jesus, who, though he was in the form of God, did not regard equality with God as something to be exploited, but emptied himself, taking the form of a slave, being born in human likeness. And being found in human form, he humbled himself and became obedient to the point of death — even death on a cross. Therefore God also highly exalted him and gave him the name that is above every name, so that at the name of Jesus every knee should bend, in heaven and on earth and under the earth, and every tongue should confess that Jesus Christ is Lord, to the glory of God the Father.

The Gospel   Luke 22:14—23:56 *or* Luke 23:1-49
Luke 22:14—23:56

When the hour (for the Passover meal) came, Jesus took his place at the table, and the apostles with him. He said to them, "I have eagerly desired to eat this Passover with you before I suffer; for I tell you, I will not eat it until it is fulfilled in the kingdom of God." Then he took a cup, and after giving thanks he said, "Take this and divide it among yourselves; for I tell you that from now on I will not drink of the fruit of the vine until the kingdom of God comes." Then he took a loaf of bread, and when he had given thanks, he broke it and gave it to them, saying, "This is my body, which is given for you. Do this in remembrance of me." And he did the same with the cup after supper, saying, "This cup that is poured out for you is the new covenant in my blood. But see, the one who betrays me is with me, and his hand is on the table. For the Son of Man is going as it has been determined, but woe to that one by whom he is betrayed!" Then they began to ask one another, which one of them it could be who would do this. A dispute also arose among them as to which one of them was to be regarded as the greatest. But he said to them, "The kings of the Gentiles lord it over them; and those in authority over them are called benefactors. But not so with you; rather the greatest among you must become like the youngest, and the leader like one who serves. For who is greater, the one who is at the table or the one who serves? Is it not the one at the table? But I am among you as one who serves. You are those who have stood by me in my trials; and I confer on you, just as my Father has conferred on me, a kingdom, so that you may eat and drink at my table in my kingdom, and you will sit on thrones judging the twelve tribes of Israel. Simon, Simon, listen! Satan has demanded to sift all of you like wheat, but I have prayed for you that your own faith may not fail; and you, when once you have turned back, strengthen your brothers." And he said to him, "Lord, I am ready to go with you to prison and to death!" Jesus said, "I tell you, Peter, the cock will not crow this day, until you have denied three times that you know me." He said to them, "When I sent you out without a purse, bag, or sandals, did you lack anything?" They said, "No, not a thing." He said to them, "But now, the one who has a purse must take it, and likewise a bag. And the one who has no sword must sell his cloak and buy one. For I tell you, this scripture must be fulfilled in me, 'And he was counted among the lawless'; and indeed what is written about me is being fulfilled." They said, "Lord, look, here are two swords." He replied, "It is enough." He came out and went, as was his custom, to the Mount of Olives; and the disciples followed him. When he reached the place, he said to them, "Pray that you may not come into the time of trial." Then he withdrew from them about a stone's throw, knelt down, and prayed, "Father, if you are willing, remove this cup from me; yet, not my will but yours be done." Then an angel from heaven appeared to him and gave him strength. In his anguish he prayed more earnestly, and his sweat became like great drops of blood falling down on the ground. When he got up from prayer, he came to the disciples and found them sleeping because of grief, and he said to them, "Why are you sleeping? Get up and pray that you may not come into the time of trial." While he was still speaking, suddenly a crowd came, and the one called Judas, one of the twelve, was leading them. He approached Jesus to kiss him; but Jesus said to him, "Judas, is it with a kiss that you are betraying the Son of Man?" When those who were around him saw what was coming, they asked, "Lord, should we strike with the sword?" Then one of them struck the slave of the high priest and cut off his right ear. But Jesus said, "No more of this!" And he touched his ear and healed him. Then Jesus said to the chief priests, the officers of the temple police, and the elders who had come for him, "Have you come out with swords and clubs as if I were a bandit? When I was with you day after day in the temple, you did not lay hands on me. But this is your hour, and the power of darkness!" Then they seized him and led him away, bringing him into the high priest's house. But Peter was following at a distance. When they had kindled a fire in the middle of the courtyard and sat down together, Peter sat among them. Then a servant-girl, seeing him in the firelight, stared at him and said, "This man also was with him." But he denied it, saying, "Woman, I do not know him." A little later someone else, on seeing him, said, "You also are one of them." But Peter said, "Man, I am not!" Then about an hour later still another kept insisting, "Surely this man also was with him; for he is a Galilean." But Peter said, "Man, I do not know what you are talking about!" At that moment, while he was still speaking, the cock crowed. The Lord turned and looked at Peter. Then Peter remembered the word of the Lord, how he had said to him, "Before the cock crows today, you will deny me three times." And he went out and wept bitterly. Now the men who were holding Jesus began to mock him and beat him; they also blindfolded him and kept asking him, "Prophesy! Who is it that struck you?" They kept heaping many other insults on him. When day came, the assembly of the elders of the people, both chief priests and scribes, gathered together, and they brought him to their council. They said, "If you are the Messiah, tell us." He replied, "If I tell you, you will not believe; and if I question you, you will not answer. But from now on the Son of Man will be seated at the right hand of the power of God." All of them asked, "Are you, then, the Son of God?" He said to them, "You say that I am." Then they said, "What further testimony do we need? We have heard it ourselves from his own lips!" Then the assembly rose as a body and brought Jesus before Pilate. They began to accuse him, saying, "We found this man perverting our nation, forbidding us to pay taxes to the emperor, and saying that he himself is the Messiah, a king." Then Pilate asked him, "Are you the king of the Jews?" He answered, "You say so." Then Pilate said to the chief priests and the crowds, "I find no basis for an accusation against this man." But they were insistent and said, "He stirs up the people by teaching throughout all Judea, from Galilee where he began even to this place." When Pilate heard this, he asked whether the man was a Galilean. And when he learned that he was under Herod's jurisdiction, he sent him off to Herod, who was himself in Jerusalem at that time. When Herod saw Jesus, he was very glad, for he had been wanting to see him for a long time, because he had heard about him and was hoping to see him perform some sign. He questioned him at some length, but Jesus gave him no answer. The chief priests and the scribes stood by, vehemently accusing him. Even Herod with his soldiers treated him with contempt and mocked him; then he put an elegant robe on him, and sent him back to Pilate. That same day Herod and Pilate became friends with each other; before this they had been enemies. Pilate then called together the chief priests, the leaders, and the people, and said to them, "You brought me this man as one who was perverting the people; and here I have examined him in your presence and have not found this man guilty of any of your charges against him. Neither has Herod, for he sent him back to us. Indeed, he has done nothing to deserve death. I will therefore have him flogged and release him." Then they all shouted out together, "Away with this fellow! Release Barabbas for us!" (This was a man who had been put in prison for an insurrection that had taken place in the city, and for murder.) Pilate, wanting to release Jesus, addressed them again; but they kept shouting, "Crucify, crucify him!" A third time he said to them, "Why, what evil has he done? I have found in him no ground for the sentence of death; I will therefore have him flogged and then release him." But they kept urgently demanding with loud shouts that he should be crucified; and their voices prevailed. So Pilate gave his verdict that their demand should be granted. He released the man they asked for, the one who had been put in prison for insurrection and murder, and he handed Jesus over as they wished. As they led him away, they seized a man, Simon of Cyrene, who was coming from the country, and they laid the cross on him, and made him carry it behind Jesus. A great number of the people followed him, and among them were women who were beating their breasts and wailing for him. But Jesus turned to them and said, "Daughters of Jerusalem, do not weep for me, but weep for yourselves and for your children. For the days are surely coming when they will say, 'Blessed are the barren, and the wombs that never bore, and the breasts that never nursed.' Then they will begin to say to the mountains, 'Fall on us'; and to the hills, 'Cover us.' For if they do this when the wood is green, what will happen when it is dry?" Two others also, who were criminals, were led away to be put to death with him. When they came to the place that is called The Skull, they crucified Jesus there with the criminals, one on his right and one on his left. Then Jesus said, "Father, forgive them; for they do not know what they are doing." And they cast lots to divide his clothing. And the people stood by, watching; but the leaders scoffed at him, saying, "He saved others; let him save himself if he is the Messiah of God, his chosen one!" The soldiers also mocked him, coming up and offering him sour wine, and saying, "If you are the King of the Jews, save yourself!" There was also an inscription over him, "This is the King of the Jews." One of the criminals who were hanged there kept deriding him and saying, "Are you not the Messiah? Save yourself and us!" But the other rebuked him, saying, "Do you not fear God, since you are under the same sentence of condemnation? And we indeed have been condemned justly, for we are getting what we deserve for our deeds, but this man has done nothing wrong." Then he said, "Jesus, remember me when you come into your kingdom." He replied, "Truly I tell you, today you will be with me in Paradise." It was now about noon, and darkness came over the whole land until three in the afternoon, while the sun's light failed; and the curtain of the temple was torn in two. Then Jesus, crying with a loud voice, said, "Father, into your hands I commend my spirit." Having said this, he breathed his last. When the centurion saw what had taken place, he praised God and said,

"Certainly this man was innocent." And when all the crowds who had gathered there for this spectacle saw what had taken place, they returned home, beating their breasts. But all his acquaintances, including the women who had followed him from Galilee, stood at a distance, watching these things. Now there was a good and righteous man named Joseph, who, though a member of the council, had not agreed to their plan and action. He came from the Jewish town of Arimathea, and he was waiting expectantly for the kingdom of God. This man went to Pilate and asked for the body of Jesus. Then he took it down, wrapped it in a linen cloth, and laid it in a rock-hewn tomb where no one had ever been laid. It was the day of Preparation, and the sabbath was beginning. The women who had come with him from Galilee followed, and they saw the tomb and how his body was laid. Then they returned, and prepared spices and ointments. On the sabbath they rested according to the commandment.

or, Luke 23:1-49

The assembly of elders rose as a body and brought Jesus before Pilate. They began to accuse him, saying, "We found this man perverting our nation, forbidding us to pay taxes to the emperor, and saying that he himself is the Messiah, a king." Then Pilate asked him, "Are you the king of the Jews?" He answered, "You say so." Then Pilate said to the chief priests and the crowds, "I find no basis for an accusation against this man." But they were insistent and said, "He stirs up the people by teaching throughout all Judea, from Galilee where he began even to this place." When Pilate heard this, he asked whether the man was a Galilean. And when he learned that he was under Herod's jurisdiction, he sent him off to Herod, who was himself in Jerusalem at that time. When Herod saw Jesus, he was very glad, for he had been wanting to see him for a long time, because he had heard about him and was hoping to see him perform some sign. He questioned him at some length, but Jesus gave him no answer. The chief priests and the scribes stood by, vehemently accusing him. Even Herod with his soldiers treated him with contempt and mocked him; then he put an elegant robe on him, and sent him back to Pilate. That same day Herod and Pilate became friends with each other; before this they had been enemies. Pilate then called together the chief priests, the leaders, and the people, and said to them, "You brought me this man as one who was perverting the people; and here I have examined him in your presence and have not found this man guilty of any of your charges against him. Neither has Herod, for he sent him back to us. Indeed, he has done nothing to deserve death. I will therefore have him flogged and release him." Then they all shouted out together, "Away with this fellow! Release Barabbas for us!" (This was a man who had been put in prison for an insurrection that had taken place in the city, and for murder.) Pilate, wanting to release Jesus, addressed them again; but they kept shouting, "Crucify, crucify him!" A third time he said to them, "Why, what evil has he done? I have found in him no ground for the sentence of death; I will therefore have him flogged and then release him." But they kept urgently demanding with loud shouts that he should be crucified; and their voices prevailed. So Pilate gave his verdict that their demand should be granted. He released the man they asked for, the one who had been put in prison for insurrection and murder, and he handed Jesus over as they wished. As they led him away, they seized a man, Simon of Cyrene, who was coming from the country, and they laid the cross on him, and made him carry it behind Jesus. A great number of the people followed him, and among them were women who were beating their breasts and wailing for him. But Jesus turned to them and said, "Daughters of Jerusalem, do not weep for me, but weep for yourselves and for your children. For the days are surely coming when they will say, 'Blessed are the barren, and the wombs that never bore, and the breasts that never nursed.' Then they will begin to say to the mountains, 'Fall on us'; and to the hills, 'Cover us.' For if they do this when the wood is green, what will happen when it is dry?" Two others also, who were criminals, were led away to be put to death with him. When they came to the place that is called The Skull, they crucified Jesus there with the criminals, one on his right and one on his left. Then Jesus said, "Father, forgive them; for they do not know what they are doing." And they cast lots to divide his clothing. And the people stood by, watching; but the leaders scoffed at him, saying, "He saved others; let him save himself if he is the Messiah of God, his chosen one!" The soldiers also mocked him, coming up and offering him sour wine, and saying, "If you are the King of the Jews, save yourself!" There was also an inscription over him, "This is the King of the Jews." One of the criminals who were hanged there kept deriding him and saying, "Are you not the Messiah? Save yourself and us!" But the other rebuked him, saying, "Do you not fear God, since you are under the same sentence of condemnation? And we indeed have been condemned justly, for we are getting what we deserve for our deeds, but this man has done nothing wrong." Then he said, "Jesus, remember me when you come into your kingdom." He replied, "Truly I tell you, today you will be with me in Paradise." It was now about noon, and darkness came over the whole land until three in the afternoon, while the sun's light failed; and the curtain of the temple was torn in two. Then Jesus, crying with a loud voice, said, "Father, into your hands I commend my spirit." Having said this, he breathed his last. When the centurion saw what had taken place, he praised God and said, "Certainly this man was innocent." And when all the crowds who had gathered there for this spectacle saw what had taken place, they returned home, beating their breasts. But all his acquaintances, including the women who had followed him from Galilee, stood at a distance, watching these things.

MONDAY IN HOLY WEEK

The Collect

Almighty God, whose most dear Son went not up to joy but first he suffered pain, and entered not into glory before he was crucified: Mercifully grant that we, walking in the way of the cross, may find it none other than the way of life and peace; through Jesus Christ your Son our Lord, who lives and reigns with you and the Holy Spirit, one God, for ever and ever. *Amen.*

Years A, B, and C
Isaiah 42:1-9
Psalm 36:5-11
Hebrews 9:11-15
John 12:1-11

The Lesson   **Isaiah 42:1-9**

Here is my servant, whom I uphold, my chosen, in whom my soul delights; I have put my spirit upon him; he will bring forth justice to the nations. He will not cry or lift up his voice, or make it heard in the street; a bruised reed he will not break, and a dimly burning wick he will not quench; he will faithfully bring forth justice. He will not grow faint or be crushed until he has established justice in the earth; and the coastlands wait for his teaching. Thus says God, the LORD, who created the heavens and stretched them out, who spread out the earth and what comes from it, who gives breath to the people upon it and spirit to those who walk in it: I am the LORD, I have called you in righteousness, I have taken you by the hand and kept you; I have given you as a covenant to the people, a light to the nations, to open the eyes that are blind, to bring out the prisoners from the dungeon, from the prison those who sit in darkness. I am the LORD, that is my name; my glory I give to no other, nor my praise to idols. See, the former things have come to pass, and new things I now declare; before they spring forth, I tell you of them.

The Response   **Psalm 36:5-11**

Psalm 36:5-11   *Dixit injustus*

5   Your love, O LORD, reaches to the heavens, *
    and your faithfulness to the clouds.

6   Your righteousness is like the strong mountains,
    your justice like the great deep; *
      you save both man and beast, O LORD.

7   How priceless is your love, O God! *
    your people take refuge under the
        shadow of your wings.

8   They feast upon the abundance of your house; *
        you give them drink from the river of your delights.
9   For with you is the well of life, *
        and in your light we see light.
10 Continue your loving-kindness to those who know you, *
        and your favor to those who are true of heart.
11 Let not the foot of the proud come near me, *
        nor the hand of the wicked push me aside.

The Epistle   Hebrews 9:11-15

When Christ came as a high priest of the good things that have come, then
through the greater and perfect tent (not made with hands, that is, not of this
creation), he entered once for all into the Holy Place, not with the blood of
goats and calves, but with his own blood, thus obtaining eternal redemption.
For if the blood of goats and bulls, with the sprinkling of the ashes of a heifer,
sanctifies those who have been defiled so that their flesh is purified, how much
more will the blood of Christ, who through the eternal Spirit offered himself
without blemish to God, purify our conscience from dead works to worship
the living God! For this reason he is the mediator of a new covenant, so that
those who are called may receive the promised eternal inheritance, because a
death has occurred that redeems them from the transgressions under the first
covenant.

The Gospel   John 12:1-11

Six days before the Passover Jesus came to Bethany, the home of Lazarus,
whom he had raised from the dead. There they gave a dinner for him. Martha
served, and Lazarus was one of those at the table with him. Mary took a
pound of costly perfume made of pure nard, anointed Jesus' feet, and wiped
them with her hair. The house was filled with the fragrance of the perfume.
But Judas Iscariot, one of his disciples (the one who was about to betray him),
said, "Why was this perfume not sold for three hundred denarii and the money
given to the poor?" (He said this not because he cared about the poor, but
because he was a thief; he kept the common purse and used to steal what was
put into it.) Jesus said, "Leave her alone. She bought it so that she might keep
it for the day of my burial. You always have the poor with you, but you do not
always have me." When the great crowd of the Jews learned that he was there,
they came not only because of Jesus but also to see Lazarus, whom he had
raised from the dead. So the chief priests planned to put Lazarus to death as
well, since it was on account of him that many of the Jews were deserting and
were believing in Jesus.

TUESDAY IN HOLY WEEK

The Collect

O God, by the passion of your blessed Son you made an instrument of shameful death to be for us the means of life: Grant us so to glory in the cross of Christ, that we may gladly suffer shame and loss for the sake of your Son our Savior Jesus Christ; who lives and reigns with you and the Holy Spirit, one God, for ever and ever. *Amen.*

Years A, B, and C
Isaiah 49:1-7
Psalm 71:1-14
1 Corinthians 1:18-31
John 12:20-36

The Lesson   Isaiah 49:1-7

Listen to me, O coastlands, pay attention, you peoples from far away! The LORD called me before I was born, while I was in my mother's womb he named me. He made my mouth like a sharp sword, in the shadow of his hand he hid me; he made me a polished arrow, in his quiver he hid me away. And he said to me, "You are my servant, Israel, in whom I will be glorified." But I said, "I have labored in vain, I have spent my strength for nothing and vanity; yet surely my cause is with the LORD, and my reward with my God." And now the LORD says, who formed me in the womb to be his servant, to bring Jacob back to him, and that Israel might be gathered to him, for I am honored in the sight of the LORD, and my God has become my strength—he says, "It is too light a thing that you should be my servant to raise up the tribes of Jacob and to restore the survivors of Israel; I will give you as a light to the nations, that my salvation may reach to the end of the earth." Thus says the LORD, the Redeemer of Israel and his Holy One, to one deeply despised, abhorred by the nations, the slave of rulers, "Kings shall see and stand up, princes, and they shall prostrate themselves, because of the LORD, who is faithful, the Holy One of Israel, who has chosen you."

The Response   Psalm 71:1-14

Psalm 71:1-14   *In te, Domine, speravi*

   1   In you, O LORD, have I taken refuge; *
         let me never be ashamed.
   2   In your righteousness, deliver me and set me free; *
         incline your ear to me and save me.
   3   Be my strong rock, a castle to keep me safe; *
         you are my crag and my stronghold.

4 Deliver me, my God, from the hand of the wicked, *
   from the clutches of the evildoer and the oppressor.

5 For you are my hope, O Lord God, *
   my confidence since I was young.

6 I have been sustained by you ever since I was born;
   from my mother's womb you have been my strength; *
   my praise shall be always of you.

7 I have become a portent to many; *
   but you are my refuge and my strength.

8 Let my mouth be full of your praise *
   and your glory all the day long.

9 Do not cast me off in my old age; *
   forsake me not when my strength fails.

10 For my enemies are talking against me, *
   and those who lie in wait for my life take counsel together.

11 They say, "God has forsaken him;
   go after him and seize him; *
   because there is none who will save."

12 O God, be not far from me; *
   come quickly to help me, O my God.

13 Let those who set themselves against me be put to shame and
                be disgraced; *
   let those who seek to do me evil be covered with scorn
                and reproach.

14 But I shall always wait in patience, *
   and shall praise you more and more.

The Epistle   1 Corinthians 1:18-31

The message about the cross is foolishness to those who are perishing, but to
us who are being saved it is the power of God. For it is written, "I will destroy
the wisdom of the wise, and the discernment of the discerning I will thwart."
Where is the one who is wise? Where is the scribe? Where is the debater of
this age? Has not God made foolish the wisdom of the world? For since, in the
wisdom of God, the world did not know God through wisdom, God decided,
through the foolishness of our proclamation, to save those who believe. For
Jews demand signs and Greeks desire wisdom, but we proclaim Christ crucified, a stumbling block to Jews and foolishness to Gentiles, but to those who
are the called, both Jews and Greeks, Christ the power of God and the wisdom
of God. For God's foolishness is wiser than human wisdom, and God's
weakness is stronger than human strength. Consider your own call, brothers
and sisters: not many of you were wise by human standards, not many were
powerful, not many were of noble birth. But God chose what is foolish in the

world to shame the wise; God chose what is weak in the world to shame the strong; God chose what is low and despised in the world, things that are not, to reduce to nothing things that are, so that no one might boast in the presence of God. He is the source of your life in Christ Jesus, who became for us wisdom from God, and righteousness and sanctification and redemption, in order that, as it is written, "Let the one who boasts, boast in the Lord."

The Gospel   John 12:20-36

Among those who went up to worship at the festival were some Greeks. They came to Philip, who was from Bethsaida in Galilee, and said to him, "Sir, we wish to see Jesus." Philip went and told Andrew; then Andrew and Philip went and told Jesus. Jesus answered them, "The hour has come for the Son of Man to be glorified. Very truly, I tell you, unless a grain of wheat falls into the earth and dies, it remains just a single grain; but if it dies, it bears much fruit. Those who love their life lose it, and those who hate their life in this world will keep it for eternal life. Whoever serves me must follow me, and where I am, there will my servant be also. Whoever serves me, the Father will honor. Now my soul is troubled. And what should I say—'Father, save me from this hour'? No, it is for this reason that I have come to this hour. Father, glorify your name." Then a voice came from heaven, "I have glorified it, and I will glorify it again." The crowd standing there heard it and said that it was thunder. Others said, "An angel has spoken to him." Jesus answered, "This voice has come for your sake, not for mine. Now is the judgment of this world; now the ruler of this world will be driven out. And I, when I am lifted up from the earth, will draw all people to myself." He said this to indicate the kind of death he was to die. The crowd answered him, "We have heard from the law that the Messiah remains forever. How can you say that the Son of Man must be lifted up? Who is this Son of Man?" Jesus said to them, "The light is with you for a little longer. Walk while you have the light, so that the darkness may not overtake you. If you walk in the darkness, you do not know where you are going. While you have the light, believe in the light, so that you may become children of light." After Jesus had said this, he departed and hid from them.

WEDNESDAY IN HOLY WEEK

The Collect

Lord God, whose blessed Son our Savior gave his body to be whipped and his face to be spit upon: Give us grace to accept joyfully the sufferings of the present time, confident of the glory that shall be revealed; through Jesus Christ your Son our Lord, who lives and reigns with you and the Holy Spirit, one God, for ever and ever. *Amen.*

Years A, B, and C
*Isaiah 50:4-9*a
Psalm 70
Hebrews 12:1-3
John 13:21-32

The Lesson   Isaiah 50:4-9*a*

The Lord GOD has given me the tongue of a teacher, that I may know how to
sustain the weary with a word. Morning by morning he wakens — wakens my
ear to listen as those who are taught. The Lord GOD has opened my ear, and I
was not rebellious, I did not turn backward. I gave my back to those who
struck me, and my cheeks to those who pulled out the beard; I did not hide my
face from insult and spitting. The Lord GOD helps me; therefore I have not
been disgraced; therefore I have set my face like flint, and I know that I shall
not be put to shame; he who vindicates me is near. Who will contend with me?
Let us stand up together. Who are my adversaries? Let them confront me. It is
the Lord GOD who helps me; who will declare me guilty?

The Response   Psalm 70

Psalm 70   *Deus, in adjutorium*

1   Be pleased, O God, to deliver me; *
    O LORD, make haste to help me.
2   Let those who seek my life be ashamed
    and altogether dismayed; *
        let those who take pleasure in my misfortune
        draw back and be disgraced.
3   Let those who say to me "Aha!" and gloat over me turn back, *
        because they are ashamed.
4   Let all who seek you rejoice and be glad in you; *
        let those who love your salvation say for ever,
        "Great is the LORD!"
5   But as for me, I am poor and needy; *
        come to me speedily, O God.
6   You are my helper and my deliverer; *
        O LORD, do not tarry.

The Epistle   Hebrews 12:1-3

Since we are surrounded by so great a cloud of witnesses, let us also lay aside
every weight and the sin that clings so closely, and let us run with perseverance the race that is set before us, looking to Jesus the pioneer and perfecter of
our faith, who for the sake of the joy that was set before him endured the
cross, disregarding its shame, and has taken his seat at the right hand of the

throne of God. Consider him who endured such hostility against himself from sinners, so that you may not grow weary or lose heart.

The Gospel   John 13:21-32

Jesus was troubled in spirit, and declared, "Very truly, I tell you, one of you will betray me." The disciples looked at one another, uncertain of whom he was speaking. One of his disciples — the one whom Jesus loved — was reclining next to him; Simon Peter therefore motioned to him to ask Jesus of whom he was speaking. So while reclining next to Jesus, he asked him, "Lord, who is it?" Jesus answered, "It is the one to whom I give this piece of bread when I have dipped it in the dish." So when he had dipped the piece of bread, he gave it to Judas son of Simon Iscariot. After he received the piece of bread, Satan entered into him. Jesus said to him, "Do quickly what you are going to do." Now no one at the table knew why he said this to him. Some thought that, because Judas had the common purse, Jesus was telling him, "Buy what we need for the festival"; or, that he should give something to the poor. So, after receiving the piece of bread, he immediately went out. And it was night. When he had gone out, Jesus said, "Now the Son of Man has been glorified, and God has been glorified in him. If God has been glorified in him, God will also glorify him in himself and will glorify him at once."

MAUNDY THURSDAY

The Collect

Almighty Father, whose dear Son, on the night before he suffered, instituted the Sacrament of his Body and Blood: Mercifully grant that we may receive it thankfully in remembrance of Jesus Christ our Lord, who in these holy mysteries gives us a pledge of eternal life; and who now lives and reigns with you and the Holy Spirit, one God, for ever and ever. *Amen.*

Years A, B, and C
Exodus 12:1-4, (5-10), 11-14
Psalm 116:1, 10-17
1 Corinthians 11:23-26
John 13:1-17, 31b-35

The Lesson   Exodus 12:1-4, (5-10), 11-14
Exodus 12:1-4

The LORD said to Moses and Aaron in the land of Egypt: This month shall mark for you the beginning of months; it shall be the first month of the year for you. Tell the whole congregation of Israel that on the tenth of this month they are to take a lamb for each family, a lamb for each household. If a household is too small for a whole lamb, it shall join its closest neighbor in obtaining one; the lamb shall be divided in proportion to the number of people who eat of it.

Exodus 12:(5-10)

[Your lamb shall be without blemish, a year-old male; you may take it from the sheep or from the goats. You shall keep it until the fourteenth day of this month; then the whole assembled congregation of Israel shall slaughter it at twilight. They shall take some of the blood and put it on the two doorposts and the lintel of the houses in which they eat it. They shall eat the lamb that same night; they shall eat it roasted over the fire with unleavened bread and bitter herbs. Do not eat any of it raw or boiled in water, but roasted over the fire, with its head, legs, and inner organs. You shall let none of it remain until the morning; anything that remains until the morning you shall burn.]

Exodus 12:11-14

This is how you shall eat it: your loins girded, your sandals on your feet, and your staff in your hand; and you shall eat it hurriedly. It is the passover of the LORD. For I will pass through the land of Egypt that night, and I will strike down every firstborn in the land of Egypt, both human beings and animals; on all the gods of Egypt I will execute judgments: I am the LORD. The blood shall be a sign for you on the houses where you live: when I see the blood, I will pass over you, and no plague shall destroy you when I strike the land of Egypt. This day shall be a day of remembrance for you. You shall celebrate it as a festival to the LORD; throughout your generations you shall observe it as a perpetual ordinance.

The Response   Psalm 116:1, 10-17

Psalm 116:1, 10-17   *Dilexi, quoniam*

  1   I love the LORD, because he has heard the voice of
           my supplication, *
       because he has inclined his ear to me whenever
           I called upon him.

10   How shall I repay the LORD *
       for all the good things he has done for me?

11   I will lift up the cup of salvation *
       and call upon the Name of the LORD.

12   I will fulfill my vows to the LORD *
       in the presence of all his people.

13   Precious in the sight of the LORD *
       is the death of his servants.

14 O Lord, I am your servant; *
        I am your servant and the child of your handmaid;
        you have freed me from my bonds.
15 I will offer you the sacrifice of thanksgiving *
        and call upon the Name of the Lord.
16 I will fulfill my vows to the Lord *
        in the presence of all his people,
17 In the courts of the Lord's house, *
        in the midst of you, O Jerusalem.

The Epistle   1 Corinthians 11:23-26

I received from the Lord what I also handed on to you, that the Lord Jesus on the night when he was betrayed took a loaf of bread, and when he had given thanks, he broke it and said, "This is my body that is for you. Do this in remembrance of me." In the same way he took the cup also, after supper, saying, "This cup is the new covenant in my blood. Do this, as often as you drink it, in remembrance of me." For as often as you eat this bread and drink the cup, you proclaim the Lord's death until he comes.

The Gospel   John 13:1-17, 31b-35

Before the festival of the Passover, Jesus knew that his hour had come to depart from this world and go to the Father. Having loved his own who were in the world, he loved them to the end. The devil had already put it into the heart of Judas son of Simon Iscariot to betray him. And during supper Jesus, knowing that the Father had given all things into his hands, and that he had come from God and was going to God, got up from the table, took off his outer robe, and tied a towel around himself. Then he poured water into a basin and began to wash the disciples' feet and to wipe them with the towel that was tied around him. He came to Simon Peter, who said to him, "Lord, are you going to wash my feet?" Jesus answered, "You do not know now what I am doing, but later you will understand." Peter said to him, "You will never wash my feet." Jesus answered, "Unless I wash you, you have no share with me." Simon Peter said to him, "Lord, not my feet only but also my hands and my head!" Jesus said to him, "One who has bathed does not need to wash, except for the feet, but is entirely clean. And you are clean, though not all of you." For he knew who was to betray him; for this reason he said, "Not all of you are clean." After he had washed their feet, had put on his robe, and had returned to the table, he said to them, "Do you know what I have done to you? You call me Teacher and Lord—and you are right, for that is what I am. So if I, your Lord and Teacher, have washed your feet, you also ought to wash one another's feet. For I have set you an example, that you also should do as I have done to you. Very truly, I tell you, servants are not greater than their master, nor are messengers greater than the one who sent them. If you know these things, you are blessed if you do them. Now the Son of Man has been glorified, and God has been glorified in him. If God has been glorified in him, God will also glorify him in himself and will glorify him at once. Little children, I am with you only a little longer. You will look for me; and as I said to the Jews so now I say to you, 'Where I am going, you cannot come.' I give you a new commandment, that you love one another. Just as I have loved you, you also should love one another. By this everyone will know that you are my disciples, if you have love for one another."

GOOD FRIDAY

The Collect

Almighty God, we pray you graciously to behold this your family, for whom our Lord Jesus Christ was willing to be betrayed, and given into the hands of sinners, and to suffer death upon the cross; who now lives and reigns with you and the Holy Spirit, one God, for ever and ever. *Amen.*

Years A, B, and C
Isaiah 52:13—53:12
Psalm 22
Hebrews 10:16-25 or *Hebrews 4:14-16; 5:7-9*
John 18:1—19:42

The Lesson   **Isaiah 52:13—53:12**

See, my servant shall prosper; he shall be exalted and lifted up, and shall be very high. Just as there were many who were astonished at him — so marred was his appearance, beyond human semblance, and his form beyond that of mortals—so he shall startle many nations; kings shall shut their mouths because of him; for that which had not been told them they shall see, and that which they had not heard they shall contemplate. Who has believed what we have heard? And to whom has the arm of the LORD been revealed? For he grew up before him like a young plant, and like a root out of dry ground; he had no form or majesty that we should look at him, nothing in his appearance that we should desire him. He was despised and rejected by others; a man of suffering and acquainted with infirmity; and as one from whom others hide their faces he was despised, and we held him of no account. Surely he has borne our infirmities and carried our diseases; yet we accounted him stricken, struck down by God, and afflicted. But he was wounded for our transgressions, crushed for our iniquities; upon him was the punishment that made us whole, and by his bruises we are healed. All we like sheep have gone astray; we have all turned to our own way, and the LORD has laid on him the iniquity of us all. He was oppressed, and he was afflicted, yet he did not open his mouth; like a lamb that is led to the slaughter, and like a sheep that before its shearers is silent, so he did not open his mouth. By a perversion of justice he was taken away. Who could have imagined his future? For he was cut off from the land of the living, stricken for the transgression of my people. They made his grave with the wicked and his tomb with the rich, although he had done no violence, and there was no deceit in his mouth. Yet it was the will of the Lord to crush him with pain. When you make his life an offering for sin, he shall see his offspring, and shall prolong his days; through him the will of the Lord shall prosper. Out of his anguish he shall see light; he shall find satisfaction through his knowledge. The righteous one, my servant, shall make many righteous, and he shall bear their iniquities. Therefore I will allot him a portion with the great, and he shall divide the spoil with the strong; because he poured out himself to death, and was numbered with the transgressors; yet he bore the sin of many, and made intercession for the transgressors.

The Response   Psalm 22

Psalm 22   *Deus, Deus meus*

1   My God, my God, why have you forsaken me? *
        and are so far from my cry
        and from the words of my distress?

2   O my God, I cry in the daytime, but you do not answer; *
        by night as well, but I find no rest.

3   Yet you are the Holy One, *
        enthroned upon the praises of Israel.

4   Our forefathers put their trust in you; *
        they trusted, and you delivered them.

5   They cried out to you and were delivered; *
        they trusted in you and were not put to shame.

6   But as for me, I am a worm and no man, *
        scorned by all and despised by the people.

7   All who see me laugh me to scorn; *
        they curl their lips and wag their heads, saying,

8   "He trusted in the Lord; let him deliver him; *
        let him rescue him, if he delights in him."

9   Yet you are he who took me out of the womb, *
        and kept me safe upon my mother's breast.

10   I have been entrusted to you ever since I was born; *
        you were my God when I was still in my mother's womb.

11   Be not far from me, for trouble is near, *
        and there is none to help.

12 Many young bulls encircle me; *
      strong bulls of Bashan surround me.
13 They open wide their jaws at me, *
      like a ravening and a roaring lion.
14 I am poured out like water;
    all my bones are out of joint; *
      my heart within my breast is melting wax.
15 My mouth is dried out like a pot-sherd;
    my tongue sticks to the roof of my mouth; *
      and you have laid me in the dust of the grave.
16 Packs of dogs close me in,
    and gangs of evildoers circle around me; *
      they pierce my hands and my feet;
      I can count all my bones.
17 They stare and gloat over me; *
      they divide my garments among them;
      they cast lots for my clothing.
18 Be not far away, O LORD; *
      you are my strength; hasten to help me.
19 Save me from the sword, *
      my life from the power of the dog.
20 Save me from the lion's mouth, *
      my wretched body from the horns of wild bulls.
21 I will declare your Name to my brethren; *
      in the midst of the congregation I will praise you.
22 Praise the LORD, you that fear him; *
      stand in awe of him, O offspring of Israel;
      all you of Jacob's line, give glory.
23 For he does not despise nor abhor the poor in their poverty;
    neither does he hide his face from them; *
      but when they cry to him he hears them.
24 My praise is of him in the great assembly; *
      I will perform my vows in the presence of those who
        worship him.
25 The poor shall eat and be satisfied,
    and those who seek the LORD shall praise him: *
      "May your heart live for ever!"
26 All the ends of the earth shall remember and turn to the LORD, *
      and all the families of the nations shall bow before him.
27 For kingship belongs to the LORD; *
      he rules over the nations.
28 To him alone all who sleep in the earth bow down
        in worship; *

all who go down to the dust fall before him.

29 My soul shall live for him;
      my descendants shall serve him; *
         they shall be known as the LORD's for ever.

30 They shall come and make known to a people yet unborn *
         the saving deeds that he has done.

The Epistle   Hebrews 10:16-25 *or* Hebrews 4:14-16, 5:7-9
Hebrews 10:16-25

The Holy Spirit testifies saying: "This is the covenant that I will make with
them after those days, says the Lord: I will put my laws in their hearts, and I
will write them on their minds," he also adds, "I will remember their sins and
their lawless deeds no more." Where there is forgiveness of these, there is no
longer any offering for sin. Therefore, my friends, since we have confidence to
enter the sanctuary by the blood of Jesus, by the new and living way that he
opened for us through the curtain (that is, through his flesh), and since we
have a great priest over the house of God, let us approach with a true heart in
full assurance of faith, with our hearts sprinkled clean from an evil conscience
and our bodies washed with pure water. Let us hold fast to the confession of
our hope without wavering, for he who has promised is faithful. And let us
consider how to provoke one another to love and good deeds, not neglecting to
meet together, as is the habit of some, but encouraging one another, and all the
more as you see the Day approaching.

or, Hebrews 4:14-16, 5:7-9

Since we have a great high priest who has passed through the heavens, Jesus,
the Son of God, let us hold fast to our confession. For we do not have a high
priest who is unable to sympathize with our weaknesses, but we have one who
in every respect has been tested as we are, yet without sin. Let us therefore
approach the throne of grace with boldness, so that we may receive mercy and
find grace to help in time of need. In the days of his flesh, Jesus offered up
prayers and supplications, with loud cries and tears, to the one who was able
to save him from death, and he was heard because of his reverent submission.
Although he was a Son, he learned obedience through what he suffered; and
having been made perfect, he became the source of eternal salvation for all
who obey him.

The Gospel   John 18:1—19:42

Jesus went out with his disciples across the Kidron valley to a place where
there was a garden, which he and his disciples entered. Now Judas, who
betrayed him, also knew the place, because Jesus often met there with his
disciples. So Judas brought a detachment of soldiers together with police from

the chief priests and the Pharisees, and they came there with lanterns and torches and weapons. Then Jesus, knowing all that was to happen to him, came forward and asked them, "Whom are you looking for?" They answered, "Jesus of Nazareth." Jesus replied, "I am he." Judas, who betrayed him, was standing with them. When Jesus said to them, "I am he," they stepped back and fell to the ground. Again he asked them, "Whom are you looking for?" And they said, "Jesus of Nazareth." Jesus answered, "I told you that I am he. So if you are looking for me, let these men go." This was to fulfill the word that he had spoken, "I did not lose a single one of those whom you gave me." Then Simon Peter, who had a sword, drew it, struck the high priest's slave, and cut off his right ear. The slave's name was Malchus. Jesus said to Peter, "Put your sword back into its sheath. Am I not to drink the cup that the Father has given me?" So the soldiers, their officer, and the Jewish police arrested Jesus and bound him. First they took him to Annas, who was the father-in-law of Caiaphas, the high priest that year. Caiaphas was the one who had advised the Jews that it was better to have one person die for the people. Simon Peter and another disciple followed Jesus. Since that disciple was known to the high priest, he went with Jesus into the courtyard of the high priest, but Peter was standing outside at the gate. So the other disciple, who was known to the high priest, went out, spoke to the woman who guarded the gate, and brought Peter in. The woman said to Peter, "You are not also one of this man's disciples, are you?" He said, "I am not." Now the slaves and the police had made a charcoal fire because it was cold, and they were standing around it and warming themselves. Peter also was standing with them and warming himself. Then the high priest questioned Jesus about his disciples and about his teaching. Jesus answered, "I have spoken openly to the world; I have always taught in synagogues and in the temple, where all the Jews come together. I have said nothing in secret. Why do you ask me? Ask those who heard what I said to them; they know what I said." When he had said this, one of the police standing nearby struck Jesus on the face, saying, "Is that how you answer the high priest?" Jesus answered, "If I have spoken wrongly, testify to the wrong. But if I have spoken rightly, why do you strike me?" Then Annas sent him bound to Caiaphas the high priest. Now Simon Peter was standing and warming himself. They asked him, "You are not also one of his disciples, are you?" He denied it and said, "I am not." One of the slaves of the high priest, a relative of the man whose ear Peter had cut off, asked, "Did I not see you in the garden with him?" Again Peter denied it, and at that moment the cock crowed. Then they took Jesus from Caiaphas to Pilate's headquarters. It was early in the morning. They themselves did not enter the headquarters, so as to avoid ritual defilement and to be able to eat the Passover. So Pilate went out to them and said, "What accusation do you bring against this man?" They answered, "If this man were not a criminal, we would not have handed him over to you." Pilate said to them, "Take him yourselves and judge him according to your law." The Jews replied, "We are not permitted to put anyone to death." (This was to fulfill what Jesus had said when he indicated the kind of death he was to die.) Then Pilate entered the headquarters again, summoned Jesus, and asked him, "Are you the King of the Jews?" Jesus answered, "Do you ask this on your own, or did others tell you about me?" Pilate replied, "I am not a Jew, am I? Your own nation and the chief priests have handed you over to me. What have you done?" Jesus answered, "My kingdom is not from this world. If my kingdom were from this world, my followers would be fighting to keep me from being handed over to the Jews. But as it is, my kingdom is not from here." Pilate asked him, "So you are a king?" Jesus answered, "You say that I am a king. For this I was born, and for this I came into the world, to testify to the truth. Everyone who belongs to the truth listens to my voice." Pilate asked him, "What is truth?" After he had said this, he went out to the Jews again and told them, "I find no case against him. But you have a custom that I release someone for you at the Passover. Do you want me to release for you the King of the Jews?" They shouted in reply, "Not this man, but Barabbas!" Now Barabbas was a bandit. Then Pilate took Jesus and had him flogged. And the soldiers wove a crown of thorns and put it on his head, and they dressed him in a purple robe. They kept coming up to him, saying, "Hail, King of the Jews!" and striking him on the face. Pilate went out again and said to them, "Look, I am bringing him out to you to let you know that I find no case against him." So Jesus came out, wearing the crown of thorns and the purple robe. Pilate said to them, "Here is the man!" When the chief priests and the police saw him, they shouted, "Crucify him! Crucify him!" Pilate said to them, "Take him yourselves and crucify him; I find no case against him." The Jews answered him, "We have a law, and according to that law he ought to die because he has claimed to be the Son of God." Now when Pilate heard this, he was more afraid than ever. He entered his headquarters again and asked Jesus, "Where are you from?" But Jesus gave him no answer. Pilate therefore said to him, "Do you refuse to speak to me? Do you not know that I have power to release you, and power to crucify you?" Jesus answered him, "You would have no power over me unless it had been given you from above; therefore the one who handed me over to you is guilty of a greater sin." From then on Pilate tried to release him, but the Jews cried out, "If you release this man, you are no friend of the emperor. Everyone who claims to be a king sets himself against the emperor." When Pilate heard these words, he brought Jesus outside and sat on the judge's bench at a place called The Stone Pavement, or in Hebrew Gabbatha. Now it was the day of Preparation for the Passover; and it was about noon. He said to the Jews, "Here is your King!" They cried out, "Away with him! Away with him! Crucify him!" Pilate asked them, "Shall I crucify your King?" The chief priests answered,

"We have no king but the emperor." Then he handed him over to them to be crucified. So they took Jesus; and carrying the cross by himself, he went out to what is called The Place of the Skull, which in Hebrew is called Golgotha. There they crucified him, and with him two others, one on either side, with Jesus between them. Pilate also had an inscription written and put on the cross. It read, "Jesus of Nazareth, the King of the Jews." Many of the Jews read this inscription, because the place where Jesus was crucified was near the city; and it was written in Hebrew, in Latin, and in Greek. Then the chief priests of the Jews said to Pilate, "Do not write, 'The King of the Jews,' but 'This man said, 'I am the King of the Jews.' '" Pilate answered, "What I have written I have written." When the soldiers had crucified Jesus, they took his clothes and divided them into four parts, one for each soldier. They also took his tunic; now the tunic was seamless, woven in one piece from the top. So they said to one another, "Let us not tear it, but cast lots for it to see who will get it." This was to fulfill what the scripture says, "They divided my clothes among themselves, and for my clothing they cast lots." And that is what the soldiers did. Meanwhile, standing near the cross of Jesus were his mother, and his mother's sister, Mary the wife of Clopas, and Mary Magdalene. When Jesus saw his mother and the disciple whom he loved standing beside her, he said to his mother, "Woman, here is your son." Then he said to the disciple, "Here is your mother." And from that hour the disciple took her into his own home. After this, when Jesus knew that all was now finished, he said (in order to fulfill the scripture), "I am thirsty." A jar full of sour wine was standing there. So they put a sponge full of the wine on a branch of hyssop and held it to his mouth. When Jesus had received the wine, he said, "It is finished." Then he bowed his head and gave up his spirit. Since it was the day of Preparation, the Jews did not want the bodies left on the cross during the sabbath, especially because that sabbath was a day of great solemnity. So they asked Pilate to have the legs of the crucified men broken and the bodies removed. Then the soldiers came and broke the legs of the first and of the other who had been crucified with him. But when they came to Jesus and saw that he was already dead, they did not break his legs. Instead, one of the soldiers pierced his side with a spear, and at once blood and water came out. (He who saw this has testified so that you also may believe. His testimony is true, and he knows that he tells the truth.) These things occurred so that the scripture might be fulfilled, "None of his bones shall be broken." And again another passage of scripture says, "They will look on the one whom they have pierced." After these things, Joseph of Arimathea, who was a disciple of Jesus, though a secret one because of his fear of the Jews, asked Pilate to let him take away the body of Jesus. Pilate gave him permission; so he came and removed his body. Nicodemus, who had at first come to Jesus by night, also came, bringing a mixture of myrrh and aloes, weighing about a hundred pounds. They took the body of Jesus and wrapped it with the spices in linen cloths, according to the burial custom of the Jews. Now there was a garden in the place where he was crucified, and in the garden there was a new tomb in which no one had ever been laid. And so, because it was the Jewish day of Preparation, and the tomb was nearby, they laid Jesus there.

HOLY SATURDAY

The Collect

O God, Creator of heaven and earth: Grant that, as the crucified body of your dear Son was laid in the tomb and rested on this holy Sabbath, so we may await with him the coming of the third day, and rise with him to newness of life; who now lives and reigns with you and the Holy Spirit, one God, for ever and ever. *Amen.*

Years A, B, and C
Job 14:1-14 or *Lamentations 3:1-9, 19-24*
Psalm 31:1-4, 15-16
1 Peter 4:1-8
Matthew 27:57-66 or *John 19:38-42*

The Lesson   **Job 14:1-14** *or* **Lamentations 3:1-9, 19-24**
Job 14:1-14

Job said: "A mortal, born of woman, few of days and full of trouble, comes up like a flower and withers, flees like a shadow and does not last. Do you fix your eyes on such a one? Do you bring me into judgment with you? Who can bring a clean thing out of an unclean? No one can. Since their days are determined, and the number of their months is known to you, and you have appointed the bounds that they cannot pass, look away from them, and desist, that they may enjoy, like laborers, their days. For there is hope for a tree, if it is cut down, that it will sprout again, and that its shoots will not cease. Though its root grows old in the earth, and its stump dies in the ground, yet at the scent of water it will bud and put forth branches like a young plant. But mortals die, and are laid low; humans expire, and where are they? As waters fail from a lake, and a river wastes away and dries up, so mortals lie down and do not rise again; until the heavens are no more, they will not awake or be roused out of their sleep. Oh that you would hide me in Sheol, that you would conceal me until your wrath is past, that you would appoint me a set time, and remember me! If mortals die, will they live again? All the days of my service I would wait until my release should come."

or, **Lamentations 3:1-9, 19-24**

I am one who has seen affliction under the rod of God's wrath; he has driven and brought me into darkness without any light; against me alone he turns his hand, again and again, all day long. He has made my flesh and my skin waste away, and broken my bones; he has besieged and enveloped me with bitterness and tribulation; he has made me sit in darkness like the dead of long ago. He has walled me about so that I cannot escape; he has put heavy chains on me; though I call and cry for help, he shuts out my prayer; he has blocked my ways with hewn stones, he has made my paths crooked. The thought of my affliction and my homelessness is wormwood and gall! My soul continually thinks of it and is bowed down within me. But this I call to mind, and therefore I have hope: The steadfast love of the LORD never ceases, his mercies never come to an end; they are new every morning; great is your faithfulness. "The LORD is my portion," says my soul, "therefore I will hope in him."

The Response   **Psalm 31:1-4, 15-16**

Psalm 31:1-4, 15-16   *In te, Domine, speravi*

1   In you, O LORD, have I taken refuge;
      let me never be put to shame; *
            deliver me in your righteousness.

2   Incline your ear to me; *
            make haste to deliver me.

3   Be my strong rock, a castle to keep me safe,
      for you are my crag and my stronghold; *
            for the sake of your Name, lead me and guide me.

4   Take me out of the net that they have secretly set for me, *
            for you are my tower of strength.

15   My times are in your hand; *
            rescue me from the hand of my enemies,
            and from those who persecute me.

16   Make your face to shine upon your servant, *
            and in your loving-kindness save me."

The Epistle   **1 Peter 4:1-8**

Since Christ suffered in the flesh, arm yourselves also with the same intention (for whoever has suffered in the flesh has finished with sin), so as to live for the rest of your earthly life no longer by human desires but by the will of God. You have already spent enough time in doing what the Gentiles like to do, living in licentiousness, passions, drunkenness, revels, carousing, and lawless idolatry. They are surprised that you no longer join them in the same excesses of dissipation, and so they blaspheme. But they will have to give an accounting to him who stands ready to judge the living and the dead. For this is the reason the gospel was proclaimed even to the dead, so that, though they had been judged in the flesh as everyone is judged, they might live in the spirit as God does. The end of all things is near; therefore be serious and discipline yourselves for the sake of your prayers. Above all, maintain constant love for one another, for love covers a multitude of sins.

The Gospel   Matthew 27:57-66 *or* John 19:38-42
Matthew 27:57-66

When it was evening, there came a rich man from Arimathea, named Joseph, who was also a disciple of Jesus. He went to Pilate and asked for the body of Jesus; then Pilate ordered it to be given to him. So Joseph took the body and wrapped it in a clean linen cloth and laid it in his own new tomb, which he had hewn in the rock. He then rolled a great stone to the door of the tomb and went away. Mary Magdalene and the other Mary were there, sitting opposite the tomb. The next day, that is, after the day of Preparation, the chief priests and the Pharisees gathered before Pilate and said, "Sir, we remember what that impostor said while he was still alive, 'After three days I will rise again.' Therefore command the tomb to be made secure until the third day; otherwise his disciples may go and steal him away, and tell the people, 'He has been raised from the dead,' and the last deception would be worse than the first." Pilate said to them, "You have a guard of soldiers; go, make it as secure as you can." So they went with the guard and made the tomb secure by sealing the stone.

or, John 19:38-42

Joseph of Arimathea, who was a disciple of Jesus, though a secret one because of his fear of the Jews, asked Pilate to let him take away the body of Jesus. Pilate gave him permission; so he came and removed his body. Nicodemus, who had at first come to Jesus by night, also came, bringing a mixture of myrrh and aloes, weighing about a hundred pounds. They took the body of Jesus and wrapped it with the spices in linen cloths, according to the burial custom of the Jews. Now there was a garden in the place where he was crucified, and in the garden there was a new tomb in which no one had ever been laid. And so, because it was the Jewish day of Preparation, and the tomb was nearby, they laid Jesus there.

THE GREAT VIGIL OF EASTER
EASTER VIGIL

The Collect

Almighty God, who for our redemption gave your only-begotten Son to the death of the cross, and by his glorious resurrection delivered us from the power of our enemy; Grant us so to die daily to sin, that we may evermore live with him in the joy of his resurrection; through Jesus Christ your Son our Lord, who lives and reigns with you and the Holy Spirit, one God, now and for ever. *Amen.*

or this

O God, who made this most holy night to shine with the glory of the Lord's resurrection: Stir up in your Church that Spirit of adoption which is given to us in Baptism, that we, being renewed both in body and mind, may worship you in sincerity and truth; through Jesus Christ our Lord, who lives and reigns with you, in the unity of the Holy Spirit, one God, now and for ever. *Amen.*

Years A, B, and C

(At least two of the following Lessons are read, of which one is always the Lesson from Exodus. After each Lesson, the Psalm or Canticle listed, or some other suitable psalm, canticle, or hymn may be sung.)

Old Testament Readings and Responses

Genesis 1:1—2:4a and Psalm 136:1-9, 23-26
Genesis 7:1-5, 11-18; 8:6-18; 9:8-13 and Psalm 46
Genesis 22:1-18 and Psalm 16
Exodus 14:10-31; 15:20-21 and Canticle 8
Isaiah 55:1-11 and Canticle 9
Baruch 3:9-15, 32—4:4 or Proverbs 8:1-8, 19-21; 9:4b-6
and Psalm 19
Ezekiel 36:24-28 and Psalm 42 and 43
Ezekiel 37:1-14 and Psalm 143
Zephaniah 3:14-20 and Psalm 98

At the Eucharist
Romans 6:3-11
Psalm 114

Gospel - Year A	Gospel - Year B	Gospel - Year C
Matthew 28:1-10	*Mark 16:1-8*	*Luke 24:1-12*

The Lesson   **Genesis 1:1—2:4a**

In the beginning when God created the heavens and the earth, the earth was a
formless void and darkness covered the face of the deep, while a wind from
God swept over the face of the waters. Then God said, "Let there be light";
and there was light. And God saw that the light was good; and God separated
the light from the darkness. God called the light Day, and the darkness he
called Night. And there was evening and there was morning, the first day. And
God said, "Let there be a dome in the midst of the waters, and let it separate
the waters from the waters." So God made the dome and separated the waters
that were under the dome from the waters that were above the dome. And it
was so. God called the dome Sky. And there was evening and there was
morning, the second day. And God said, "Let the waters under the sky be
gathered together into one place, and let the dry land appear." And it was so.
God called the dry land Earth, and the waters that were gathered together he
called Seas. And God saw that it was good. Then God said, "Let the earth put
forth vegetation: plants yielding seed, and fruit trees of every kind on earth
that bear fruit with the seed in it." And it was so. The earth brought forth
vegetation: plants yielding seed of every kind, and trees of every kind bearing
fruit with the seed in it. And God saw that it was good. And there was evening
and there was morning, the third day. And God said, "Let there be lights in the
dome of the sky to separate the day from the night; and let them be for signs
and for seasons and for days and years, and let them be lights in the dome of
the sky to give light upon the earth." And it was so. God made the two great
lights—the greater light to rule the day and the lesser light to rule the night—
and the stars. God set them in the dome of the sky to give light upon the earth,
to rule over the day and over the night, and to separate the light from the
darkness. And God saw that it was good. And there was evening and there
was morning, the fourth day. And God said, "Let the waters bring forth
swarms of living creatures, and let birds fly above the earth across the dome
of the sky." So God created the great sea monsters and every living creature
that moves, of every kind, with which the waters swarm, and every winged
bird of every kind. And God saw that it was good. God blessed them, saying,
"Be fruitful and multiply and fill the waters in the seas, and let birds multiply
on the earth." And there was evening and there was morning, the fifth day.
And God said, "Let the earth bring forth living creatures of every kind: cattle
and creeping things and wild animals of the earth of every kind." And it was
so. God made the wild animals of the earth of every kind, and the cattle of
every kind, and everything that creeps upon the ground of every kind. And
God saw that it was good. Then God said, "Let us make humankind in our
image, according to our likeness; and let them have dominion over the fish of
the sea, and over the birds of the air, and over the cattle, and over all the wild
animals of the earth, and over every creeping thing that creeps upon the

earth." So God created humankind in his image, in the image of God he created them; male and female he created them. God blessed them, and God said to them, "Be fruitful and multiply, and fill the earth and subdue it; and have dominion over the fish of the sea and over the birds of the air and over every living thing that moves upon the earth." God said, "See, I have given you every plant yielding seed that is upon the face of all the earth, and every tree with seed in its fruit; you shall have them for food. And to every beast of the earth, and to every bird of the air, and to everything that creeps on the earth, everything that has the breath of life, I have given every green plant for food." And it was so. God saw everything that he had made, and indeed, it was very good. And there was evening and there was morning, the sixth day. Thus the heavens and the earth were finished, and all their multitude. And on the seventh day God finished the work that he had done, and he rested on the seventh day from all the work that he had done. So God blessed the seventh day and hallowed it, because on it God rested from all the work that he had done in creation. These are the generations of the heavens and the earth when they were created.

The Response   **Psalm 136:1-9, 23-26**

Psalm 136:1-9, 23-26   *Confitemini*

1   Give thanks to the LORD, for he is good, *
        for his mercy endures for ever.
2   Give thanks to the God of gods, *
        for his mercy endures for ever.
3   Give thanks to the LORD of LORDS, *
        for his mercy endures for ever.
4   Who only does great wonders, *
        for his mercy endures for ever;
5   Who by wisdom made the heavens, *
        for his mercy endures for ever;
6   Who spread out the earth upon the waters, *
        for his mercy endures for ever;
7   Who created great lights, *
        for his mercy endures for ever;
8   The sun to rule the day, *
        for his mercy endures for ever;
9   The moon and the stars to govern the night, *
        for his mercy endures for ever.
23 Who remembered us in our low estate, *
        for his mercy endures for ever;
24 And delivered us from our enemies, *
        for his mercy endures for ever;

25 Who gives food to all creatures, *
   for his mercy endures for ever.
26 Give thanks to the God of heaven, *
   for his mercy endures for ever.

The Lesson   **Genesis 7:1-5, 11-18; 8:6-18; 9:8-13**

The LORD said to Noah, "Go into the ark, you and all your household, for I have seen that you alone are righteous before me in this generation. Take with you seven pairs of all clean animals, the male and its mate; and a pair of the animals that are not clean, the male and its mate; and seven pairs of the birds of the air also, male and female, to keep their kind alive on the face of all the earth. For in seven days I will send rain on the earth for forty days and forty nights; and every living thing that I have made I will blot out from the face of the ground." And Noah did all that the LORD had commanded him. In the six hundredth year of Noah's life, in the second month, on the seventeenth day of the month, on that day all the fountains of the great deep burst forth, and the windows of the heavens were opened. The rain fell on the earth forty days and forty nights. On the very same day Noah with his sons, Shem and Ham and Japheth, and Noah's wife and the three wives of his sons entered the ark, they and every wild animal of every kind, and all domestic animals of every kind, and every creeping thing that creeps on the earth, and every bird of every kind — every bird, every winged creature. They went into the ark with Noah, two and two of all flesh in which there was the breath of life. And those that entered, male and female of all flesh, went in as God had commanded him; and the LORD shut him in. The flood continued forty days on the earth; and the waters increased, and bore up the ark, and it rose high above the earth. The waters swelled and increased greatly on the earth; and the ark floated on the face of the waters. At the end of forty days Noah opened the window of the ark that he had made and sent out the raven; and it went to and fro until the waters were dried up from the earth. Then he sent out the dove from him, to see if the waters had subsided from the face of the ground; but the dove found no place to set its foot, and it returned to him to the ark, for the waters were still on the face of the whole earth. So he put out his hand and took it and brought it into the ark with him. He waited another seven days, and again he sent out the dove from the ark; and the dove came back to him in the evening, and there in its beak was a freshly plucked olive leaf; so Noah knew that the waters had subsided from the earth. Then he waited another seven days, and sent out the dove; and it did not return to him anymore. In the six hundred first year, in the first month, the first day of the month, the waters were dried up from the earth; and Noah removed the covering of the ark, and looked, and saw that the face of the ground was drying. In the second month, on the twenty-seventh day of the month, the earth was dry. Then God said to Noah,

"Go out of the ark, you and your wife, and your sons and your sons' wives with you. Bring out with you every living thing that is with you of all flesh—birds and animals and every creeping thing that creeps on the earth—so that they may abound on the earth, and be fruitful and multiply on the earth." So Noah went out with his sons and his wife and his sons' wives. Then God said to Noah and to his sons with him, "As for me, I am establishing my covenant with you and your descendants after you, and with every living creature that is with you, the birds, the domestic animals, and every animal of the earth with you, as many as came out of the ark. I establish my covenant with you, that never again shall all flesh be cut off by the waters of a flood, and never again shall there be a flood to destroy the earth." God said, "This is the sign of the covenant that I make between me and you and every living creature that is with you, for all future generations: I have set my bow in the clouds, and it shall be a sign of the covenant between me and the earth."

The Response   Psalm 46

Psalm 46   *Deus noster refugium*

1   God is our refuge and strength, *
        a very present help in trouble.
2   Therefore we will not fear, though the earth be moved, *
        and though the mountains be toppled into the
                depths of the sea;
3   Though its waters rage and foam, *
        and though the mountains tremble at its tumult.
4   The LORD of hosts is with us; *
        the God of Jacob is our stronghold.
5   There is a river whose streams make glad the city of God, *
        the holy habitation of the Most High.
6   God is in the midst of her;
    she shall not be overthrown; *
        God shall help her at the break of day.
7   The nations make much ado, and the kingdoms are shaken; *
        God has spoken, and the earth shall melt away.
8   The LORD of hosts is with us; *
        the God of Jacob is our stronghold.
9   Come now and look upon the works of the LORD, *
        what awesome things he has done on earth.
10 It is he who makes war to cease in all the world; *
        he breaks the bow, and shatters the spear,
        and burns the shields with fire.

11   "Be still, then, and know that I am God; *
        I will be exalted among the nations;
        I will be exalted in the earth."
12   The LORD of hosts is with us; *
        the God of Jacob is our stronghold.

The Lesson   Genesis 22:1-18

God tested Abraham. He said to him, "Abraham!" And he said, "Here I am."
He said, "Take your son, your only son Isaac, whom you love, and go to the
land of Moriah, and offer him there as a burnt offering on one of the mountains that I shall show you." So Abraham rose early in the morning, saddled
his donkey, and took two of his young men with him, and his son Isaac; he cut
the wood for the burnt offering, and set out and went to the place in the
distance that God had shown him. On the third day Abraham looked up and
saw the place far away. Then Abraham said to his young men, "Stay here with
the donkey; the boy and I will go over there; we will worship, and then we will
come back to you." Abraham took the wood of the burnt offering and laid it
on his son Isaac, and he himself carried the fire and the knife. So the two of
them walked on together. Isaac said to his father Abraham, "Father!" And he
said, "Here I am, my son." He said, "The fire and the wood are here, but
where is the lamb for a burnt offering?" Abraham said, "God himself will
provide the lamb for a burnt offering, my son." So the two of them walked on
together. When they came to the place that God had shown him, Abraham
built an altar there and laid the wood in order. He bound his son Isaac, and
laid him on the altar, on top of the wood. Then Abraham reached out his hand
and took the knife to kill his son. But the angel of the LORD called to him from
heaven, and said, "Abraham, Abraham!" And he said, "Here I am." He said,
"Do not lay your hand on the boy or do anything to him; for now I know that
you fear God, since you have not withheld your son, your only son, from me."
And Abraham looked up and saw a ram, caught in a thicket by its horns.
Abraham went and took the ram and offered it up as a burnt offering instead
of his son. So Abraham called that place "The LORD will provide"; as it is said
to this day, "On the mount of the LORD it shall be provided." The angel of the
LORD called to Abraham a second time from heaven, and said, "By myself I
have sworn, says the LORD: Because you have done this, and have not withheld your son, your only son, I will indeed bless you, and I will make your
offspring as numerous as the stars of heaven and as the sand that is on the
seashore. And your offspring shall possess the gate of their enemies, and by
your offspring shall all the nations of the earth gain blessing for themselves,
because you have obeyed my voice."

The Response   **Psalm 16**

Psalm 16   *Conserva me, Domine*

1   Protect me, O God, for I take refuge in you; *
      I have said to the LORD, "You are my LORD,
      my good above all other."
2   All my delight is upon the godly that are in the land, *
      upon those who are noble among the people.
3   But those who run after other gods *
      shall have their troubles multiplied.
4   Their libations of blood I will not offer, *
      nor take the names of their gods upon my lips.
5   O LORD, you are my portion and my cup; *
      it is you who uphold my lot.
6   My boundaries enclose a pleasant land; *
      indeed, I have a goodly heritage.
7   I will bless the LORD who gives me counsel; *
      my heart teaches me, night after night.
8   I have set the LORD always before me; *
      because he is at my right hand I shall not fall.
9   My heart, therefore, is glad, and my spirit rejoices; *
      my body also shall rest in hope.
10 For you will not abandon me to the grave, *
      nor let your holy one see the Pit.
11 You will show me the path of life; *
      in your presence there is fullness of joy,
      and in your right hand are pleasures for evermore.

The Lesson   **Exodus 14:10-31; 15:20-21**

As Pharaoh drew near, the Israelites looked back, and there were the Egyptians advancing on them. In great fear the Israelites cried out to the Lord. They said to Moses, "Was it because there were no graves in Egypt that you have taken us away to die in the wilderness? What have you done to us, bringing us out of Egypt? Is this not the very thing we told you in Egypt, 'Let us alone and let us serve the Egyptians'? For it would have been better for us to serve the Egyptians than to die in the wilderness." But Moses said to the people, "Do not be afraid, stand firm, and see the deliverance that the LORD will accomplish for you today; for the Egyptians whom you see today you shall never see again. The LORD will fight for you, and you have only to keep still." Then the LORD said to Moses, "Why do you cry out to me? Tell the Israelites to go forward. But you lift up your staff, and stretch out your hand over the sea and divide it, that the Israelites may go into the sea on dry ground. Then I will harden the hearts of the Egyptians so that they will go in after them; and so I will gain glory for myself over Pharaoh and all his army, his chariots, and his chariot drivers. And the Egyptians shall know that I am the Lord, when I have gained glory for myself over Pharaoh, his chariots, and his chariot drivers." The angel of God who was going before the Israelite army moved and went behind them; and the pillar of cloud moved from in front of them and took its place behind them. It came between the army of Egypt and the army of Israel. And so the cloud was there with the darkness, and it lit up the night; one did not come near the other all night. Then Moses stretched out his hand over the sea. The LORD drove the sea back by a strong east wind all night, and turned the sea into dry land; and the waters were divided. The Israelites went into the sea on dry ground, the waters forming a wall for them on their right and on their left. The Egyptians pursued, and went into the sea after them, all of Pharaoh's horses, chariots, and chariot drivers. At the morning watch the LORD in the pillar of fire and cloud looked down upon the Egyptian army, and threw the Egyptian army into panic. He clogged their chariot wheels so that they turned with difficulty. The Egyptians said, "Let us flee from the Israelites, for the LORD is fighting for them against Egypt." Then the LORD said to Moses, "Stretch out your hand over the sea, so that the water may come back upon the Egyptians, upon their chariots and chariot drivers." So Moses stretched out his hand over the sea, and at dawn the sea returned to its normal depth. As the Egyptians fled before it, the LORD tossed the Egyptians into the sea. The waters returned and covered the chariots and the chariot drivers, the entire army of Pharaoh that had followed them into the sea; not one of them remained. But the Israelites walked on dry ground through the sea, the waters forming a wall for them on their right and on their left. Thus the LORD saved Israel that day from the Egyptians; and Israel saw the Egyptians dead on the seashore. Israel saw the great work that the LORD did against the Egyptians. So the people feared the LORD and believed in the LORD and in his servant Moses. Then the prophet Miriam, Aaron's sister, took a tambourine in her hand; and all the women went out after her with tambourines and with dancing. And Miriam sang to them: "Sing to the LORD, for he has triumphed gloriously; horse and rider he has thrown into the sea."

The Response   **Canticle 8**
Canticle 8   The Song of Moses   *Cantemus Domino*
Exodus 15:1-6, 11-13, 17-18

I will sing to the Lord, for he is lofty and uplifted; *
    the horse and its rider has he hurled into the sea.
The Lord is my strength and my refuge; *
    the Lord has become my Savior.

This is my God and I will praise him, *
   the God of my people and I will exalt him.
The Lord is a mighty warrior; *
   Yahweh is his Name.
The chariots of Pharaoh and his army has he hurled into the sea; *
   the finest of those who bear armor have been
      drowned in the Red Sea.
The fathomless deep has overwhelmed them; *
   they sank into the depths like a stone.
Your right hand, O Lord, is glorious in might; *
   your right hand, O Lord, has overthrown the enemy.
Who can be compared with you, O Lord, among the gods? *
   who is like you, glorious in holiness,
      awesome in renown, and worker of wonders?
You stretched forth your right hand; *
   the earth swallowed them up.
With your constant love you led the people you redeemed; *
   with your might you brought them in safety to
      your holy dwelling.
You will bring them in and plant them *
   on the mount of your possession,
The resting-place you have made for yourself, O Lord, *
   the sanctuary, O Lord, that your hand has established.
The Lord shall reign *
   for ever and for ever.

The Lesson   Isaiah 55:1-11

Ho, everyone who thirsts, come to the waters; and you that have no money,
come, buy and eat! Come, buy wine and milk without money and without
price. Why do you spend your money for that which is not bread, and your
labor for that which does not satisfy? Listen carefully to me, and eat what is
good, and delight yourselves in rich food. Incline your ear, and come to me;
listen, so that you may live. I will make with you an everlasting covenant, my
steadfast, sure love for David. See, I made him a witness to the peoples, a
leader and commander for the peoples. See, you shall call nations that you do
not know, and nations that do not know you shall run to you, because of the
LORD your God, the Holy One of Israel, for he has glorified you. Seek the
LORD while he may be found, call upon him while he is near; let the wicked
forsake their way, and the unrighteous their thoughts; let them return to the
LORD, that he may have mercy on them, and to our God, for he will abundantly pardon. For my thoughts are not your thoughts, nor are your ways my
ways, says the LORD. For as the heavens are higher than the earth, so are my
ways higher than your ways and my thoughts than your thoughts. For as the

rain and the snow come down from heaven, and do not return there until they have watered the earth, making it bring forth and sprout, giving seed to the sower and bread to the eater, so shall my word be that goes out from my mouth; it shall not return to me empty, but it shall accomplish that which I purpose, and succeed in the thing for which I sent it.

The Response   Canticle 9
Canticle 9   The First Song of Isaiah   *Ecce, Deus*
                 Isaiah 12:2-6

Surely, it is God who saves me; *
    I will trust in him and not be afraid.
For the Lord is my stronghold and my sure defense, *
    and he will be my Savior.
Therefore you shall draw water with rejoicing *
    from the springs of salvation.
And on that day you shall say, *
    Give thanks to the Lord and call upon his Name;
Make his deeds known among the peoples; *
    see that they remember that his Name is exalted.
Sing the praises of the Lord, for he has done great things, *
    and this is known in all the world.
Cry aloud, inhabitants of Zion, ring out your joy, *
    for the great one in the midst of you is the Holy One of Israel.

The Lesson   Baruch 3:9-15, 32—4:4
                                     or Proverbs 8:1-8, 19-21; 9:4*b*-6
Baruch 3:9-15, 32—4:4
Hear the commandments of life, O Israel; give ear, and learn wisdom! Why is it, O Israel, why is it that you are in the land of your enemies, that you are growing old in a foreign country, that you are defiled with the dead, that you are counted among those in Hades? You have forsaken the fountain of wisdom. If you had walked in the way of God, you would be living in peace forever. Learn where there is wisdom, where there is strength, where there is understanding, so that you may at the same time discern where there is length of days, and life, where there is light for the eyes, and peace. Who has found her place? And who has entered her storehouses? But the one who knows all things knows her, he found her by his understanding. The one who prepared the earth for all time filled it with four-footed creatures; the one who sends forth the light, and it goes; he called it, and it obeyed him, trembling; the stars shone in their watches, and were glad; he called them, and they said, "Here we are!" They shone with gladness for him who made them. This is our God; no other can be compared to him. He found the whole way to knowledge, and

gave her to his servant Jacob and to Israel, whom he loved. Afterwards she appeared on earth and lived with humankind. She is the book of the commandments of God, the law that endures forever. All who hold her fast will live, and those who forsake her will die. Turn, O Jacob, and take her; walk toward the shining of her light. Do not give your glory to another, or your advantages to an alien people. Happy are we, O Israel, for we know what is pleasing to God.

or, Proverbs 8:1-8, 19-21; 9:4b-6

Does not wisdom call, and does not understanding raise her voice? On the heights, beside the way, at the crossroads she takes her stand; beside the gates in front of the town, at the entrance of the portals she cries out: "To you, O people, I call, and my cry is to all that live. O simple ones, learn prudence; acquire intelligence, you who lack it. Hear, for I will speak noble things, and from my lips will come what is right; for my mouth will utter truth; wickedness is an abomination to my lips. All the words of my mouth are righteous; there is nothing twisted or crooked in them. My fruit is better than gold, even fine gold, and my yield than choice silver. I walk in the way of righteousness, along the paths of justice, endowing with wealth those who love me, and filling their treasuries." To those without sense she says, "Come, eat of my bread and drink of the wine I have mixed. Lay aside immaturity, and live, and walk in the way of insight."

The Response   Psalm 19
Psalm 19   *Caeli enarrant*

1   The heavens declare the glory of God, *
        and the firmament shows his handiwork.
2   One day tells its tale to another, *
        and one night imparts knowledge to another.
3   Although they have no words or language, *
        and their voices are not heard,
4   Their sound has gone out into all lands, *
        and their message to the ends of the world.
5   In the deep has he set a pavilion for the sun; *
        it comes forth like a bridegroom out of his chamber;
        it rejoices like a champion to run its course.
6   It goes forth from the uttermost edge of the heavens
    and runs about to the end of it again; *
        nothing is hidden from its burning heat.
7   The law of the LORD is perfect
    and revives the soul; *
        the testimony of the LORD is sure
        and gives wisdom to the innocent.

8   The statutes of the LORD are just
     and rejoice the heart; *
          the commandment of the LORD is clear
          and gives light to the eyes.
9   The fear of the LORD is clean
     and endures for ever; *
          the judgments of the LORD are true
          and righteous altogether.
10   More to be desired are they than gold,
     more than much fine gold, *
          sweeter far than honey,
          than honey in the comb.
11   By them also is your servant enlightened, *
          and in keeping them there is great reward.
12   Who can tell how often he offends? *
          cleanse me from my secret faults.
13   Above all, keep your servant from presumptuous sins;
     let them not get dominion over me; *
          then shall I be whole and sound,
          and innocent of a great offense.
14   Let the words of my mouth and the meditation of my
     heart be acceptable in your sight, *
          O LORD, my strength and my redeemer.

The Lesson   Ezekiel 36:24-28

Thus says the Lord GOD: I will take you from the nations, and gather you
from all the countries, and bring you into your own land. I will sprinkle clean
water upon you, and you shall be clean from all your uncleannesses, and from
all your idols I will cleanse you. A new heart I will give you, and a new spirit
I will put within you; and I will remove from your body the heart of stone and
give you a heart of flesh. I will put my spirit within you, and make you follow
my statutes and be careful to observe my ordinances. Then you shall live in
the land that I gave to your ancestors; and you shall be my people, and I will
be your God.

The Response   Psalm 42 and 43
Psalm 42   *Quemadmodum*
     1   As the deer longs for the water-brooks, *
               so longs my soul for you, O God.
     2   My soul is athirst for God, athirst for the living God; *
               when shall I come to appear before the presence of God?

3   My tears have been my food day and night, *
      while all day long they say to me,
      "Where now is your God?"

4   I pour out my soul when I think on these things: *
      how I went with the multitude and led them into the house of God,

5   With the voice of praise and thanksgiving, *
      among those who keep holy-day.

6   Why are you so full of heaviness, O my soul? *
      and why are you so disquieted within me?

7   Put your trust in God; *
      for I will yet give thanks to him,
      who is the help of my countenance, and my God.

8   My soul is heavy within me; *
      therefore I will remember you from the land of Jordan,
      and from the peak of Mizar among the heights of Hermon.

9   One deep calls to another in the noise of your cataracts; *
      all your rapids and floods have gone over me.

10   The LORD grants his loving-kindness in the daytime; *
      in the night season his song is with me,
      a prayer to the God of my life.

11   I will say to the God of my strength,
      "Why have you forgotten me? *
      and why do I go so heavily while the enemy oppresses me?"

12   While my bones are being broken, *
      my enemies mock me to my face;

13   All day long they mock me *
      and say to me, "Where now is your God?"

14   Why are you so full of heaviness, O my soul? *
      and why are you so disquieted within me?

15   Put your trust in God; *
      for I will yet give thanks to him,
      who is the help of my countenance, and my God.

Psalm 43   *Judica me, Deus*

1   Give judgment for me, O God,
      and defend my cause against an ungodly people; *
      deliver me from the deceitful and the wicked.

2   For you are the God of my strength;
      why have you put me from you? *
      and why do I go so heavily while the enemy oppresses me?

3   Send out your light and your truth, that they may lead me, *
      and bring me to your holy hill
      and to your dwelling;

4   That I may go to the altar of God,
     to the God of my joy and gladness; *
       and on the harp I will give thanks to you, O God my God.
5   Why are you so full of heaviness, O my soul? *
       and why are you so disquieted within me?
6   Put your trust in God; *
       for I will yet give thanks to him,
       who is the help of my countenance, and my God.

The Lesson   Ezekiel 37:1-14

The hand of the LORD came upon me, and he brought me out by the spirit of
the LORD and set me down in the middle of a valley; it was full of bones. He
led me all around them; there were very many lying in the valley, and they
were very dry. He said to me, "Mortal, can these bones live?" I answered, "O
Lord GOD, you know." Then he said to me, "Prophesy to these bones, and say
to them: O dry bones, hear the word of the LORD. Thus says the Lord GOD to
these bones: I will cause breath to enter you, and you shall live. I will lay
sinews on you, and will cause flesh to come upon you, and cover you with
skin, and put breath in you, and you shall live; and you shall know that I am
the LORD." So I prophesied as I had been commanded; and as I prophesied,
suddenly there was a noise, a rattling, and the bones came together, bone to its
bone. I looked, and there were sinews on them, and flesh had come upon them,
and skin had covered them; but there was no breath in them. Then he said to
me, "Prophesy to the breath, prophesy, mortal, and say to the breath: Thus
says the Lord GOD: Come from the four winds, O breath, and breathe upon
these slain, that they may live." I prophesied as he commanded me, and the
breath came into them, and they lived, and stood on their feet, a vast multitude. Then he said to me, "Mortal, these bones are the whole house of Israel.
They say, 'Our bones are dried up, and our hope is lost; we are cut off completely.' Therefore prophesy, and say to them, Thus says the Lord GOD: I am
going to open your graves, and bring you up from your graves, O my people;
and I will bring you back to the land of Israel. And you shall know that I am
the LORD, when I open your graves, and bring you up from your graves, O my
people. I will put my spirit within you, and you shall live, and I will place you
on your own soil; then you shall know that I, the LORD, have spoken and will
act," says the LORD.

The Response   Psalm 143

Psalm 143   *Domine, exaudi*
1   LORD, hear my prayer,
     and in your faithfulness heed my supplications; *
       answer me in your righteousness.
2   Enter not into judgment with your servant, *
       for in your sight shall no one living be justified.

3   For my enemy has sought my life;
    he has crushed me to the ground; *
        he has made me live in dark places like those who are long dead.
4   My spirit faints within me; *
        my heart within me is desolate.
5   I remember the time past;
    I muse upon all your deeds; *
        I consider the works of your hands.
6   I spread out my hands to you; *
        my soul gasps to you like a thirsty land.
7   O Lord, make haste to answer me; my spirit fails me; *
        do not hide your face from me
        or I shall be like those who go down to the Pit.
8   Let me hear of your loving-kindness in the morning,
    for I put my trust in you; *
        show me the road that I must walk,
        for I lift up my soul to you.
9   Deliver me from my enemies, O Lord, *
        for I flee to you for refuge.
10   Teach me to do what pleases you, for you are my God; *
        let your good Spirit lead me on level ground.
11   Revive me, O Lord, for your Name's sake; *
        for your righteousness' sake, bring me out of trouble.
12   Of your goodness, destroy my enemies
    and bring all my foes to naught, *
        for truly I am your servant.

The Lesson   Zephaniah 3:14-20

Sing aloud, O daughter Zion; shout, O Israel! Rejoice and exult with all your
heart, O daughter Jerusalem! The Lord has taken away the judgments against
you, he has turned away your enemies. The king of Israel, the Lord, is in your
midst; you shall fear disaster no more. On that day it shall be said to Jerusalem: Do not fear, O Zion; do not let your hands grow weak. The Lord, your
God, is in your midst, a warrior who gives victory; he will rejoice over you
with gladness, he will renew you in his love; he will exult over you with loud
singing as on a day of festival. I will remove disaster from you, so that you
will not bear reproach for it. I will deal with all your oppressors at that time.
And I will save the lame and gather the outcast, and I will change their shame
into praise and renown in all the earth. At that time I will bring you home, at
the time when I gather you; for I will make you renowned and praised among
all the peoples of the earth, when I restore your fortunes before your eyes,
says the Lord.

The Response

Psalm 98   *Cantate Domino*

1   Sing to the LORD a new song, *
        for he has done marvelous things.
2   With his right hand and his holy arm *
        has he won for himself the victory.
3   The LORD has made known his victory; *
        his righteousness has he openly shown in
            the sight of the nations.
4   He remembers his mercy and faithfulness to
            the house of Israel, *
    and all the ends of the earth have seen the
            victory of our God.
5   Shout with joy to the LORD, all you lands; *
        lift up your voice, rejoice, and sing.
6   Sing to the LORD with the harp, *
        with the harp and the voice of song.
7   With trumpets and the sound of the horn *
        shout with joy before the King, the LORD.
8   Let the sea make a noise and all that is in it, *
        the lands and those who dwell therein.
9   Let the rivers clap their hands, *
        and let the hills ring out with joy before the LORD,
        when he comes to judge the earth.
10 In righteousness shall he judge the world *
        and the peoples with equity.

The Epistle   **Romans 6:3-11**

Do you not know that all of us who have been baptized into Christ Jesus were
baptized into his death? Therefore we have been buried with him by baptism
into death, so that, just as Christ was raised from the dead by the glory of the
Father, so we too might walk in newness of life. For if we have been united
with him in a death like his, we will certainly be united with him in a resurrection like his. We know that our old self was crucified with him so that the
body of sin might be destroyed, and we might no longer be enslaved to sin.
For whoever has died is freed from sin. But if we have died with Christ, we
believe that we will also live with him. We know that Christ, being raised from
the dead, will never die again; death no longer has dominion over him. The
death he died, he died to sin, once for all; but the life he lives, he lives to God.
So you also must consider yourselves dead to sin and alive to God in Christ
Jesus.

EASTER VIGIL — Years A, B, and C   **201**

The Response   **Psalm 114**

Psalm 114   *In exitu Israel*

1   Hallelujah!
    When Israel came out of Egypt, *
        the house of Jacob from a people of strange speech,
2   Judah became God's sanctuary *
        and Israel his dominion.
3   The sea beheld it and fled; *
        Jordan turned and went back.
4   The mountains skipped like rams, *
        and the little hills like young sheep.
5   What ailed you, O sea, that you fled? *
        O Jordan, that you turned back?
6   You mountains, that you skipped like rams? *
        you little hills like young sheep?
7   Tremble, O earth, at the presence of the LORD, *
        at the presence of the God of Jacob,
8   Who turned the hard rock into a pool of water *
        and flint-stone into a flowing spring.

Year A

The Gospel   **Matthew 28:1-10**

After the sabbath, as the first day of the week was dawning, Mary Magdalene
and the other Mary went to see the tomb. And suddenly there was a great
earthquake; for an angel of the Lord, descending from heaven, came and rolled
back the stone and sat on it. His appearance was like lightning, and his
clothing white as snow. For fear of him the guards shook and became like
dead men. But the angel said to the women, "Do not be afraid; I know that
you are looking for Jesus who was crucified. He is not here; for he has been
raised, as he said. Come, see the place where he lay. Then go quickly and tell
his disciples, 'He has been raised from the dead, and indeed he is going ahead
of you to Galilee; there you will see him.' This is my message for you." So
they left the tomb quickly with fear and great joy, and ran to tell his disciples.
Suddenly Jesus met them and said, "Greetings!" And they came to him, took
hold of his feet, and worshiped him. Then Jesus said to them, "Do not be
afraid; go and tell my brothers to go to Galilee; there they will see me."

Year B

The Gospel   **Mark 16:1-8**

When the sabbath was over, Mary Magdalene, and Mary the mother of James, and Salome bought spices, so that they might go and anoint him. And very early on the first day of the week, when the sun had risen, they went to the tomb. They had been saying to one another, "Who will roll away the stone for us from the entrance to the tomb?" When they looked up, they saw that the stone, which was very large, had already been rolled back. As they entered the tomb, they saw a young man, dressed in a white robe, sitting on the right side; and they were alarmed. But he said to them, "Do not be alarmed; you are looking for Jesus of Nazareth, who was crucified. He has been raised; he is not here. Look, there is the place they laid him. But go, tell his disciples and Peter that he is going ahead of you to Galilee; there you will see him, just as he told you." So they went out and fled from the tomb, for terror and amazement had seized them; and they said nothing to anyone, for they were afraid.

Year C

The Gospel   **Luke 24:1-12**

On the first day of the week, at early dawn, the women came to the tomb, taking the spices that they had prepared. They found the stone rolled away from the tomb, but when they went in, they did not find the body. While they were perplexed about this, suddenly two men in dazzling clothes stood beside them. The women were terrified and bowed their faces to the ground, but the men said to them, "Why do you look for the living among the dead? He is not here, but has risen. Remember how he told you, while he was still in Galilee, that the Son of Man must be handed over to sinners, and be crucified, and on the third day rise again." Then they remembered his words, and returning from the tomb, they told all this to the eleven and to all the rest. Now it was Mary Magdalene, Joanna, Mary the mother of James, and the other women with them who told this to the apostles. But these words seemed to them an idle tale, and they did not believe them. But Peter got up and ran to the tomb; stooping and looking in, he saw the linen cloths by themselves; then he went home, amazed at what had happened.

EASTER DAY

The Collect

O God, who for our redemption gave your only-begotten Son to the death of the cross, and by his glorious resurrection delivered us from the power of our enemy: Grant us so to die daily to sin, that we may evermore live with him in the joy of his resurrection; through Jesus Christ your Son our Lord, who lives and reigns with you and the Holy Spirit, one God, now and for ever. *Amen.*

or this

O God, who made this most holy night to shine with the glory of the Lord's resurrection: Stir up in your Church that Spirit of adoption which is given to us in Baptism, that we, being renewed both in body and mind, may worship you in sincerity and truth; through Jesus Christ our Lord, who lives and reigns with you, in the unity of the Holy Spirit, one God, now and for ever. *Amen.*

or this

Almighty God, who through your only-begotten Son Jesus Christ overcame death and opened to us the gate of everlasting life: Grant that we, who celebrate with joy the day of the Lord's resurrection, may be raised from the death of sin by your life-giving Spirit; through Jesus Christ our Lord, who lives and reigns with you and the Holy Spirit, one God, now and for ever. *Amen.*

Year A
Acts 10:34-43 or *Jeremiah 31:1-6*
Psalm 118:1-2, 14-24
Colossians 3:1-4 or *Acts 10:34-43*
John 20:1-18 or *Matthew 28:1-10*

The Lesson　　　　　　　　　　**Acts 10:34-43** *or* **Jeremiah 31:1-6**
Acts 10:34-43

Peter began to speak to them: "I truly understand that God shows no partiality, but in every nation anyone who fears him and does what is right is acceptable to him. You know the message he sent to the people of Israel, preaching peace by Jesus Christ — he is Lord of all. That message spread throughout Judea, beginning in Galilee after the baptism that John announced: how God anointed Jesus of Nazareth with the Holy Spirit and with power; how he went about doing good and healing all who were oppressed by the devil, for God was with him. We are witnesses to all that he did both in Judea and in Jerusalem. They put him to death by hanging him on a tree; but God raised him on the third day and allowed him to appear, not to all the people but to us who were chosen by God as witnesses, and who ate and drank with him after he rose from the dead. He commanded us to preach to the people and to testify that he is the one ordained by God as judge of the living and the dead. All the prophets testify about him that everyone who believes in him receives forgiveness of sins through his name."

or, **Jeremiah 31:1-6**

At that time, says the Lord, I will be the God of all the families of Israel, and they shall be my people. Thus says the Lord: The people who survived the sword found grace in the wilderness; when Israel sought for rest, the Lord appeared to him from far away. I have loved you with an everlasting love; therefore I have continued my faithfulness to you. Again I will build you, and you shall be built, O virgin Israel! Again you shall take your tambourines, and go forth in the dance of the merrymakers. Again you shall plant vineyards on the mountains of Samaria; the planters shall plant, and shall enjoy the fruit. For there shall be a day when sentinels will call in the hill country of Ephraim: "Come, let us go up to Zion, to the Lord our God."

The Response   **Psalm 118:1-2, 14-24**

Psalm 118:1-2, 14-24   *Confitemini Domino*

1   Give thanks to the Lord, for he is good; *
       his mercy endures for ever.

2   Let Israel now proclaim, *
       "His mercy endures for ever."

14   The Lord is my strength and my song, *
       and he has become my salvation.

15   There is a sound of exultation and victory *
       in the tents of the righteous:

16   "The right hand of the Lord has triumphed! *
       the right hand of the Lord is exalted!
       the right hand of the Lord has triumphed!"

17   I shall not die, but live, *
       and declare the works of the Lord.

18   The Lord has punished me sorely, *
       but he did not hand me over to death.

19   Open for me the gates of righteousness; *
       I will enter them;
       I will offer thanks to the Lord.

20   "This is the gate of the Lord; *
       he who is righteous may enter."

21   I will give thanks to you, for you answered me *
       and have become my salvation.

22   The same stone which the builders rejected *
       has become the chief cornerstone.

23   This is the Lord's doing, *
       and it is marvelous in our eyes.

24   On this day the Lord has acted; *
       we will rejoice and be glad in it.

The Epistle   **Colossians 3:1-4** *or* **Acts 10:34-43**
Colossians 3:1-4

If you have been raised with Christ, seek the things that are above, where
Christ is, seated at the right hand of God. Set your minds on things that are
above, not on things that are on earth, for you have died, and your life is
hidden with Christ in God. When Christ who is your life is revealed, then you
also will be revealed with him in glory.

or, **Acts 10:34-43**

Peter began to speak to them: "I truly understand that God shows no partiality, but in every nation anyone who fears him and does what is right is acceptable to him. You know the message he sent to the people of Israel, preaching
peace by Jesus Christ — he is Lord of all. That message spread throughout
Judea, beginning in Galilee after the baptism that John announced: how God
anointed Jesus of Nazareth with the Holy Spirit and with power; how he went
about doing good and healing all who were oppressed by the devil, for God
was with him. We are witnesses to all that he did both in Judea and in Jerusalem. They put him to death by hanging him on a tree; but God raised him on
the third day and allowed him to appear, not to all the people but to us who
were chosen by God as witnesses, and who ate and drank with him after he
rose from the dead. He commanded us to preach to the people and to testify
that he is the one ordained by God as judge of the living and the dead. All the
prophets testify about him that everyone who believes in him receives forgiveness of sins through his name."

The Gospel   **John 20:1-18** *or* **Matthew 28:1-10**
John 20:1-18

Early on the first day of the week, while it was still dark, Mary Magdalene
came to the tomb and saw that the stone had been removed from the tomb. So
she ran and went to Simon Peter and the other disciple, the one whom Jesus
loved, and said to them, "They have taken the Lord out of the tomb, and we
do not know where they have laid him." Then Peter and the other disciple set
out and went toward the tomb. The two were running together, but the other
disciple outran Peter and reached the tomb first. He bent down to look in and
saw the linen wrappings lying there, but he did not go in. Then Simon Peter
came, following him, and went into the tomb. He saw the linen wrappings
lying there, and the cloth that had been on Jesus' head, not lying with the linen
wrappings but rolled up in a place by itself. Then the other disciple, who
reached the tomb first, also went in, and he saw and believed; for as yet they
did not understand the scripture, that he must rise from the dead. Then the
disciples returned to their homes. But Mary stood weeping outside the tomb.

As she wept, she bent over to look into the tomb; and she saw two angels in white, sitting where the body of Jesus had been lying, one at the head and the other at the feet. They said to her, "Woman, why are you weeping?" She said to them, "They have taken away my Lord, and I do not know where they have laid him." When she had said this, she turned around and saw Jesus standing there, but she did not know that it was Jesus. Jesus said to her, "Woman, why are you weeping? Whom are you looking for?" Supposing him to be the gardener, she said to him, "Sir, if you have carried him away, tell me where you have laid him, and I will take him away." Jesus said to her, "Mary!" She turned and said to him in Hebrew, "Rabbouni!" (which means Teacher). Jesus said to her, "Do not hold on to me, because I have not yet ascended to the Father. But go to my brothers and say to them, 'I am ascending to my Father and your Father, to my God and your God.' " Mary Magdalene went and announced to the disciples, "I have seen the Lord"; and she told them that he had said these things to her.

or, Matthew 28:1-10

After the sabbath, as the first day of the week was dawning, Mary Magdalene and the other Mary went to see the tomb. And suddenly there was a great earthquake; for an angel of the Lord, descending from heaven, came and rolled back the stone and sat on it. His appearance was like lightning, and his clothing white as snow. For fear of him the guards shook and became like dead men. But the angel said to the women, "Do not be afraid; I know that you are looking for Jesus who was crucified. He is not here; for he has been raised, as he said. Come, see the place where he lay. Then go quickly and tell his disciples, 'He has been raised from the dead, and indeed he is going ahead of you to Galilee; there you will see him.' This is my message for you." So they left the tomb quickly with fear and great joy, and ran to tell his disciples. Suddenly Jesus met them and said, "Greetings!" And they came to him, took hold of his feet, and worshiped him. Then Jesus said to them, "Do not be afraid; go and tell my brothers to go to Galilee; there they will see me."

Year B

Acts 10:34-43 or Isaiah 25:6-9
Psalm 118:1-2, 14-24
1 Corinthians 15:1-11 or Acts 10:34-43
John 20:1-18 or Mark 16:1-8

The Lesson   **Acts 10:34-43** *or* **Isaiah 25:6-9**
Acts 10:34-43

Then Peter began to speak to them: "I truly understand that God shows no partiality, but in every nation anyone who fears him and does what is right is acceptable to him. You know the message he sent to the people of Israel, preaching peace by Jesus Christ — he is Lord of all. That message spread throughout Judea, beginning in Galilee after the baptism that John announced: how God anointed Jesus of Nazareth with the Holy Spirit and with power; how he went about doing good and healing all who were oppressed by the devil, for God was with him. We are witnesses to all that he did both in Judea and in Jerusalem. They put him to death by hanging him on a tree; but God raised him on the third day and allowed him to appear, not to all the people but to us who were chosen by God as witnesses, and who ate and drank with him after he rose from the dead. He commanded us to preach to the people and to testify that he is the one ordained by God as judge of the living and the dead. All the prophets testify about him that everyone who believes in him receives forgiveness of sins through his name."

or, **Isaiah 25:6-9**

On this mountain the LORD of hosts will make for all peoples a feast of rich food, a feast of well-aged wines, of rich food filled with marrow, of well-aged wines strained clear. And he will destroy on this mountain the shroud that is cast over all peoples, the sheet that is spread over all nations; he will swallow up death forever. Then the Lord GOD will wipe away the tears from all faces, and the disgrace of his people he will take away from all the earth, for the LORD has spoken. It will be said on that day, Lo, this is our God; we have waited for him, so that he might save us. This is the LORD for whom we have waited; let us be glad and rejoice in his salvation.

The Response   **Psalm 118:1-2, 14-24**
Psalm 118:1-2, 14-24   *Confitemini Domino*

   1   Give thanks to the LORD, for he is good; *
           his mercy endures for ever.
   2   Let Israel now proclaim, *
           "His mercy endures for ever."

14 The LORD is my strength and my song, *
    and he has become my salvation.

15 There is a sound of exultation and victory *
    in the tents of the righteous:

16 "The right hand of the LORD has triumphed! *
    the right hand of the LORD is exalted!
    the right hand of the LORD has triumphed!"

17 I shall not die, but live, *
    and declare the works of the LORD.

18 The LORD has punished me sorely, *
    but he did not hand me over to death.

19 Open for me the gates of righteousness; *
    I will enter them;
    I will offer thanks to the LORD.

20 "This is the gate of the LORD; *
    he who is righteous may enter."

21 I will give thanks to you, for you answered me *
    and have become my salvation.

22 The same stone which the builders rejected *
    has become the chief cornerstone.

23 This is the LORD's doing, *
    and it is marvelous in our eyes.

24 On this day the LORD has acted; *
    we will rejoice and be glad in it.

The Epistle   **1 Corinthians 15:1-11** *or* **Acts 10:34-43**

1 Corinthians 15:1-11

Now I would remind you, brothers and sisters, of the good news that I proclaimed to you, which you in turn received, in which also you stand, through which also you are being saved, if you hold firmly to the message that I proclaimed to you—unless you have come to believe in vain. For I handed on to you as of first importance what I in turn had received: that Christ died for our sins in accordance with the scriptures, and that he was buried, and that he was raised on the third day in accordance with the scriptures, and that he appeared to Cephas, then to the twelve. Then he appeared to more than five hundred brothers and sisters at one time, most of whom are still alive, though some have died. Then he appeared to James, then to all the apostles. Last of all, as to one untimely born, he appeared also to me. For I am the least of the apostles, unfit to be called an apostle, because I persecuted the church of God. But by the grace of God I am what I am, and his grace toward me has not been in vain. On the contrary, I worked harder than any of them — though it was not I, but the grace of God that is with me. Whether then it was I or they, so we proclaim and so you have come to believe.

or, **Acts 10:34-43**

Peter began to speak to them: "I truly understand that God shows no partiality, but in every nation anyone who fears him and does what is right is acceptable to him. You know the message he sent to the people of Israel, preaching peace by Jesus Christ — he is Lord of all. That message spread throughout Judea, beginning in Galilee after the baptism that John announced: how God anointed Jesus of Nazareth with the Holy Spirit and with power; how he went about doing good and healing all who were oppressed by the devil, for God was with him. We are witnesses to all that he did both in Judea and in Jerusalem. They put him to death by hanging him on a tree; but God raised him on the third day and allowed him to appear, not to all the people but to us who were chosen by God as witnesses, and who ate and drank with him after he rose from the dead. He commanded us to preach to the people and to testify that he is the one ordained by God as judge of the living and the dead. All the prophets testify about him that everyone who believes in him receives forgiveness of sins through his name."

The Gospel   **John 20:1-18** *or* **Mark 16:1-8**
John 20:1-18

Early on the first day of the week, while it was still dark, Mary Magdalene came to the tomb and saw that the stone had been removed from the tomb. So she ran and went to Simon Peter and the other disciple, the one whom Jesus loved, and said to them, "They have taken the Lord out of the tomb, and we do not know where they have laid him." Then Peter and the other disciple set out and went toward the tomb. The two were running together, but the other disciple outran Peter and reached the tomb first. He bent down to look in and saw the linen wrappings lying there, but he did not go in. Then Simon Peter came, following him, and went into the tomb. He saw the linen wrappings lying there, and the cloth that had been on Jesus' head, not lying with the linen wrappings but rolled up in a place by itself. Then the other disciple, who reached the tomb first, also went in, and he saw and believed; for as yet they did not understand the scripture, that he must rise from the dead. Then the disciples returned to their homes. But Mary stood weeping outside the tomb. As she wept, she bent over to look into the tomb; and she saw two angels in white, sitting where the body of Jesus had been lying, one at the head and the other at the feet. They said to her, "Woman, why are you weeping?" She said to them, "They have taken away my Lord, and I do not know where they have laid him." When she had said this, she turned around and saw Jesus standing there, but she did not know that it was Jesus. Jesus said to her, "Woman, why are you weeping? Whom are you looking for?" Supposing him to be the gardener, she said to him, "Sir, if you have carried him away, tell me where you have laid him, and I will take him away." Jesus said to her, "Mary!" She turned and said to him in Hebrew, "Rabbouni!" (which means Teacher). Jesus said to her, "Do not hold on to me, because I have not yet ascended to the Father. But go to my brothers and say to them, 'I am ascending to my Father and your Father, to my God and your God.' " Mary Magdalene went and announced to the disciples, "I have seen the Lord"; and she told them that he had said these things to her.

or, Mark 16:1-8

When the sabbath was over, Mary Magdalene, and Mary the mother of James, and Salome bought spices, so that they might go and anoint him. And very early on the first day of the week, when the sun had risen, they went to the tomb. They had been saying to one another, "Who will roll away the stone for us from the entrance to the tomb?" When they looked up, they saw that the stone, which was very large, had already been rolled back. As they entered the tomb, they saw a young man, dressed in a white robe, sitting on the right side; and they were alarmed. But he said to them, "Do not be alarmed; you are looking for Jesus of Nazareth, who was crucified. He has been raised; he is not here. Look, there is the place they laid him. But go, tell his disciples and Peter that he is going ahead of you to Galilee; there you will see him, just as he told you." So they went out and fled from the tomb, for terror and amazement had seized them; and they said nothing to anyone, for they were afraid.

Year C
Acts 10:34-43 or Isaiah 65:17-25
Psalm 118:1-2, 14-24
1 Corinthians 15:19-26 or Acts 10:34-43
John 20:1-18 or Luke 24:1-12

The Lesson   **Acts 10:34-43 *or* Isaiah 65:17-25**
Acts 10:34-43

Peter began to speak to them: "I truly understand that God shows no partiality, but in every nation anyone who fears him and does what is right is acceptable to him. You know the message he sent to the people of Israel, preaching peace by Jesus Christ — he is Lord of all. That message spread throughout Judea, beginning in Galilee after the baptism that John announced: how God anointed Jesus of Nazareth with the Holy Spirit and with power; how he went about doing good and healing all who were oppressed by the devil, for God was with him. We are witnesses to all that he did both in Judea and in Jerusalem. They put him to death by hanging him on a tree; but God raised him on the third day and allowed him to appear, not to all the people but to us who were chosen by God as witnesses, and who ate and drank with him after he rose from the dead. He commanded us to preach to the people and to testify that he is the one ordained by God as judge of the living and the dead. All the prophets testify about him that everyone who believes in him receives forgiveness of sins through his name."

or, **Isaiah 65:17-25**

Thus says the Lord GOD: I am about to create new heavens and a new earth; the former things shall not be remembered or come to mind. But be glad and rejoice forever in what I am creating; for I am about to create Jerusalem as a joy, and its people as a delight. I will rejoice in Jerusalem, and delight in my people; no more shall the sound of weeping be heard in it, or the cry of distress. No more shall there be in it an infant that lives but a few days, or an old person who does not live out a lifetime; for one who dies at a hundred years will be considered a youth, and one who falls short of a hundred will be considered accursed. They shall build houses and inhabit them; they shall plant vineyards and eat their fruit. They shall not build and another inhabit; they shall not plant and another eat; for like the days of a tree shall the days of my people be, and my chosen shall long enjoy the work of their hands. They shall not labor in vain, or bear children for calamity; for they shall be off-spring blessed by the LORD — and their descendants as well. Before they call I will answer, while they are yet speaking I will hear. The wolf and the lamb shall feed together, the lion shall eat straw like the ox; but the serpent—its food shall be dust! They shall not hurt or destroy on all my holy mountain, says the LORD.

The Response   **Psalm 118:1-2, 14-24**

Psalm 118: 1-2, 14-24   *Confitemini Domino*

  1   Give thanks to the LORD, for he is good; *
        his mercy endures for ever.

  2   Let Israel now proclaim, *
        "His mercy endures for ever."

 14   The LORD is my strength and my song, *
        and he has become my salvation.

 15   There is a sound of exultation and victory *
        in the tents of the righteous:

 16   "The right hand of the LORD has triumphed! *
        the right hand of the LORD is exalted!
        the right hand of the LORD has triumphed!"

 17   I shall not die, but live, *
        and declare the works of the LORD.

 18   The LORD has punished me sorely, *
        but he did not hand me over to death.

19   Open for me the gates of righteousness; *
       I will enter them;
       I will offer thanks to the LORD.
20   "This is the gate of the LORD; *
       he who is righteous may enter."
21   I will give thanks to you, for you answered me *
       and have become my salvation.
22   The same stone which the builders rejected *
       has become the chief cornerstone.
23   This is the LORD's doing, *
       and it is marvelous in our eyes.
24   On this day the LORD has acted; *
       we will rejoice and be glad in it.

The Epistle   1 Corinthians 15:19-26 *or* Acts 10:34-43
1 Corinthians 15:19-26

If for this life only we have hoped in Christ, we are of all people most to be pitied. But in fact Christ has been raised from the dead, the first fruits of those who have died. For since death came through a human being, the resurrection of the dead has also come through a human being; for as all die in Adam, so all will be made alive in Christ. But each in his own order: Christ the first fruits, then at his coming those who belong to Christ. Then comes the end, when he hands over the kingdom to God the Father, after he has destroyed every ruler and every authority and power. For he must reign until he has put all his enemies under his feet. The last enemy to be destroyed is death.

or, Acts 10:34-43

Peter began to speak to them: "I truly understand that God shows no partiality, but in every nation anyone who fears him and does what is right is acceptable to him. You know the message he sent to the people of Israel, preaching peace by Jesus Christ — he is Lord of all. That message spread throughout Judea, beginning in Galilee after the baptism that John announced: how God anointed Jesus of Nazareth with the Holy Spirit and with power; how he went about doing good and healing all who were oppressed by the devil, for God was with him. We are witnesses to all that he did both in Judea and in Jerusalem. They put him to death by hanging him on a tree; but God raised him on the third day and allowed him to appear, not to all the people but to us who were chosen by God as witnesses, and who ate and drank with him after he rose from the dead. He commanded us to preach to the people and to testify that he is the one ordained by God as judge of the living and the dead. All the prophets testify about him that everyone who believes in him receives forgiveness of sins through his name."

The Gospel
John 20:1-18

John 20:1-18 *or* Luke 24:1-12

Early on the first day of the week, while it was still dark, Mary Magdalene came to the tomb and saw that the stone had been removed from the tomb. So she ran and went to Simon Peter and the other disciple, the one whom Jesus loved, and said to them, "They have taken the Lord out of the tomb, and we do not know where they have laid him." Then Peter and the other disciple set out and went toward the tomb. The two were running together, but the other disciple outran Peter and reached the tomb first. He bent down to look in and saw the linen wrappings lying there, but he did not go in. Then Simon Peter came, following him, and went into the tomb. He saw the linen wrappings lying there, and the cloth that had been on Jesus' head, not lying with the linen wrappings but rolled up in a place by itself. Then the other disciple, who reached the tomb first, also went in, and he saw and believed; for as yet they did not understand the scripture, that he must rise from the dead. Then the disciples returned to their homes. But Mary stood weeping outside the tomb. As she wept, she bent over to look into the tomb; and she saw two angels in white, sitting where the body of Jesus had been lying, one at the head and the other at the feet. They said to her, "Woman, why are you weeping?" She said to them, "They have taken away my Lord, and I do not know where they have laid him." When she had said this, she turned around and saw Jesus standing there, but she did not know that it was Jesus. Jesus said to her, "Woman, why are you weeping? Whom are you looking for?" Supposing him to be the gardener, she said to him, "Sir, if you have carried him away, tell me where you have laid him, and I will take him away." Jesus said to her, "Mary!" She turned and said to him in Hebrew, "Rabbouni!" (which means Teacher). Jesus said to her, "Do not hold on to me, because I have not yet ascended to the Father. But go to my brothers and say to them, 'I am ascending to my Father and your Father, to my God and your God.' " Mary Magdalene went and announced to the disciples, "I have seen the Lord"; and she told them that he had said these things to her.

or, Luke 24:1-12

On the first day of the week, at early dawn, the women came to the tomb, taking the spices that they had prepared. They found the stone rolled away from the tomb, but when they went in, they did not find the body. While they were perplexed about this, suddenly two men in dazzling clothes stood beside them. The women were terrified and bowed their faces to the ground, but the men said to them, "Why do you look for the living among the dead? He is not here, but has risen. Remember how he told you, while he was still in Galilee, that the Son of Man must be handed over to sinners, and be crucified, and on the third day rise again." Then they remembered his words, and returning from the tomb, they told all this to the eleven and to all the rest. Now it was Mary Magdalene, Joanna, Mary the mother of James, and the other women with them who told this to the apostles. But these words seemed to them an idle tale, and they did not believe them. But Peter got up and ran to the tomb; stooping and looking in, he saw the linen cloths by themselves; then he went home, amazed at what had happened.

EASTER EVENING SERVICE

Years A, B, and C
Isaiah 25:6-9
Psalm 114
1 Corinthians 5:6b-8
Luke 24:13-49

The Lesson   **Isaiah 25:6-9**

On this mountain the LORD of hosts will make for all peoples a feast of rich food, a feast of well-aged wines, of rich food filled with marrow, of well-aged wines strained clear. And he will destroy on this mountain the shroud that is cast over all peoples, the sheet that is spread over all nations; he will swallow up death forever. Then the Lord GOD will wipe away the tears from all faces, and the disgrace of his people he will take away from all the earth, for the LORD has spoken. It will be said on that day, Lo, this is our God; we have waited for him, so that he might save us. This is the LORD for whom we have waited; let us be glad and rejoice in his salvation.

The Response   **Psalm 114**

Psalm 114   *In exitu Israel*

1   Hallelujah!
    When Israel came out of Egypt, *
        the house of Jacob from a people of strange speech,
2   Judah became God's sanctuary *
        and Israel his dominion.
3   The sea beheld it and fled; *
        Jordan turned and went back.
4   The mountains skipped like rams, *
        and the little hills like young sheep.
5   What ailed you, O sea, that you fled? *
        O Jordan, that you turned back?
6   You mountains, that you skipped like rams? *
        you little hills like young sheep?

7 Tremble, O earth, at the presence of the LORD, *
    at the presence of the God of Jacob,

8 Who turned the hard rock into a pool of water *
    and flint-stone into a flowing spring.

The Epistle   1 Corinthians 5:6b-8

Do you not know that a little yeast leavens the whole batch of dough? Clean out the old yeast so that you may be a new batch, as you really are unleavened. For our paschal lamb, Christ, has been sacrificed. Therefore, let us celebrate the festival, not with the old yeast, the yeast of malice and evil, but with the unleavened bread of sincerity and truth.

The Gospel   Luke 24:13-49

On the first day of the week, two of Jesus' followers were going to a village called Emmaus, about seven miles from Jerusalem, and talking with each other about all these things that had happened. While they were talking and discussing, Jesus himself came near and went with them, but their eyes were kept from recognizing him. And he said to them, "What are you discussing with each other while you walk along?" They stood still, looking sad. Then one of them, whose name was Cleopas, answered him, "Are you the only stranger in Jerusalem who does not know the things that have taken place there in these days?" He asked them, "What things?" They replied, "The things about Jesus of Nazareth, who was a prophet mighty in deed and word before God and all the people, and how our chief priests and leaders handed him over to be condemned to death and crucified him. But we had hoped that he was the one to redeem Israel. Yes, and besides all this, it is now the third day since these things took place. Moreover, some women of our group astounded us. They were at the tomb early this morning, and when they did not find his body there, they came back and told us that they had indeed seen a vision of angels who said that he was alive. Some of those who were with us went to the tomb and found it just as the women had said; but they did not see him." Then he said to them, "Oh, how foolish you are, and how slow of heart to believe all that the prophets have declared! Was it not necessary that the Messiah should suffer these things and then enter into his glory?" Then beginning with Moses and all the prophets, he interpreted to them the things about himself in all the scriptures. As they came near the village to which they were going, he walked ahead as if he were going on. But they urged him strongly, saying, "Stay with us, because it is almost evening and the day is now nearly over." So he went in to stay with them. When he was at the table with them, he took bread, blessed and broke it, and gave it to them. Then their eyes were opened, and they recognized him; and he vanished from their sight. They said to each other, "Were not our hearts burning within us while he was talking to us on the road, while he was opening the scriptures to us?" That same hour they got up and returned to Jerusalem; and they found the eleven and their companions gathered together. They were saying, "The Lord has risen indeed, and he has appeared to Simon!" Then they told what had happened on the road, and how he had been made known to them in the breaking of the bread. While they were talking about this, Jesus himself stood among them and said to them, "Peace be with you." They were startled and terrified, and thought that they were seeing a ghost. He said to them, "Why are you frightened, and why do doubts arise in your hearts? Look at my hands and my feet; see that it is I myself. Touch me and see; for a ghost does not have flesh and bones as you see that I have." And when he had said this, he showed them his hands and his feet. While in their joy they were disbelieving and still wondering, he said to them, "Have you anything here to eat?" They gave him a piece of broiled fish, and he took it and ate in their presence. Then he said to them, "These are my words that I spoke to you while I was still with you—that everything written about me in the law of Moses, the prophets, and the psalms must be fulfilled." Then he opened their minds to understand the scriptures, and he said to them, "Thus it is written, that the Messiah is to suffer and to rise from the dead on the third day, and that repentance and forgiveness of sins is to be proclaimed in his name to all nations, beginning from Jerusalem. You are witnesses of these things. And see, I am sending upon you what my Father promised; so stay here in the city until you have been clothed with power from on high."

MONDAY IN EASTER WEEK

The Collect

Grant, we pray, Almighty God, that we who celebrate with awe the Paschal feast may be found worthy to attain to everlasting joys; through Jesus Christ our Lord, who lives and reigns with you and the Holy Spirit, one God, now and for ever. *Amen.*

Years A, B, and C
Acts 2:14, 22b-32
Psalm 16:8-11 or 118:19-24
Matthew 28:9-15

The Lesson   **Acts 2:14, 22b-32**

Peter, standing with the eleven, raised his voice and addressed them, "Men of Judea and all who live in Jerusalem, let this be known to you, and listen to what I say. Jesus of Nazareth, a man attested to you by God with deeds of power, wonders, and signs that God did through him among you, as you yourselves know — this man, handed over to you according to the definite plan and foreknowledge of God, you crucified and killed by the hands of those outside the law. But God raised him up, having freed him from death, because it was impossible for him to be held in its power. For David says concerning him, 'I saw the Lord always before me, for he is at my right hand so that I will not be shaken; therefore my heart was glad, and my tongue rejoiced; moreover my flesh will live in hope. For you will not abandon my soul to Hades, or let your Holy One experience corruption. You have made known to me the ways of life; you will make me full of gladness with your presence.' Fellow Israelites, I may say to you confidently of our ancestor David that he both died and was buried, and his tomb is with us to this day. Since he was a prophet, he knew that God had sworn with an oath to him that he would put one of his descendants on his throne. Foreseeing this, David spoke of the resurrection of the Messiah, saying, 'He was not abandoned to Hades, nor did his flesh experience corruption.' This Jesus God raised up, and of that all of us are witnesses."

The Response   **Psalm 16:8-11** *or* **Psalm 118:19-24**
Psalm 16:8-11   *Conserva me, Domine*

8   I have set the LORD always before me; *
        because he is at my right hand I shall not fall.
9   My heart, therefore, is glad, and my spirit rejoices; *
        my body also shall rest in hope.
10   For you will not abandon me to the grave, *
        nor let your holy one see the Pit.
11   You will show me the path of life; *
        in your presence there is fullness of joy,
        and in your right hand are pleasures for evermore.

or, **Psalm 118:19-24**   *Confitemini Domino*

19   Open for me the gates of righteousness; *
        I will enter them;
        I will offer thanks to the LORD.
20   "This is the gate of the LORD; *
        he who is righteous may enter."
21   I will give thanks to you, for you answered me *
        and have become my salvation.
22   The same stone which the builders rejected *
        has become the chief cornerstone.
23   This is the LORD's doing, *
        and it is marvelous in our eyes.

24   On this day the LORD has acted; *
      we will rejoice and be glad in it.

The Gospel   Matthew 28:9-15

Jesus met Mary Magdalene and the other Mary and said, "Greetings!" And they came to him, took hold of his feet, and worshiped him. Then Jesus said to them, "Do not be afraid; go and tell my brothers to go to Galilee; there they will see me." While they were going, some of the guard went into the city and told the chief priests everything that had happened. After the priests had assembled with the elders, they devised a plan to give a large sum of money to the soldiers, telling them, "You must say, 'His disciples came by night and stole him away while we were asleep.' If this comes to the governor's ears, we will satisfy him and keep you out of trouble." So they took the money and did as they were directed. And this story is still told among the Jews to this day.

TUESDAY IN EASTER WEEK

The Collect

O God, who by the glorious resurrection of your Son Jesus Christ destroyed death and brought life and immortality to light: Grant that we, who have been raised with him, may abide in his presence and rejoice in the hope of eternal glory; through Jesus Christ our Lord, to whom, with you and the Holy Spirit, be dominion and praise for ever and ever. *Amen.*

Years A, B, and C
Acts 2:36-41
Psalm 33:18-22 or *Psalm 118:19-24*
John 20:11-18

The Lesson   Acts 2:36-41

Peter said, "Therefore let the entire house of Israel know with certainty that God has made him both Lord and Messiah, this Jesus whom you crucified." Now when they heard this, they were cut to the heart and said to Peter and to the other apostles, "Brothers, what should we do?" Peter said to them, "Repent, and be baptized every one of you in the name of Jesus Christ so that your sins may be forgiven; and you will receive the gift of the Holy Spirit. For the promise is for you, for your children, and for all who are far away, everyone whom the Lord our God calls to him." And he testified with many other arguments and exhorted them, saying, "Save yourselves from this corrupt generation." So those who welcomed his message were baptized, and that day about three thousand persons were added.

The Response   Psalm 33:18-22 *or* Psalm 118:19-24

Psalm 33:18-22   *Exultate, justi*

18   Behold, the eye of the Lord is upon those who fear him, *
        on those who wait upon his love,
19   To pluck their lives from death, *
        and to feed them in time of famine.
20   Our soul waits for the Lord; *
        he is our help and our shield.
21   Indeed, our heart rejoices in him, *
        for in his holy Name we put our trust.
22   Let your loving-kindness, O Lord, be upon us, *
        as we have put our trust in you.

or, **Psalm 118:19-24**   *Confitemini Domino*

19   Open for me the gates of righteousness; *
        I will enter them;
        I will offer thanks to the Lord.
20   "This is the gate of the Lord; *
        he who is righteous may enter."
21   I will give thanks to you, for you answered me *
        and have become my salvation.
22   The same stone which the builders rejected *
        has become the chief cornerstone.
23   This is the Lord's doing, *
        and it is marvelous in our eyes.
24   On this day the Lord has acted; *
        we will rejoice and be glad in it.

The Gospel   John 20:11-18

Mary Magdalene stood weeping outside the tomb. As she wept, she bent over
to look into the tomb; and she saw two angels in white, sitting where the body
of Jesus had been lying, one at the head and the other at the feet. They said to
her, "Woman, why are you weeping?" She said to them, "They have taken
away my Lord, and I do not know where they have laid him." When she had
said this, she turned around and saw Jesus standing there, but she did not
know that it was Jesus. Jesus said to her, "Woman, why are you weeping?
Whom are you looking for?" Supposing him to be the gardener, she said to
him, "Sir, if you have carried him away, tell me where you have laid him, and
I will take him away." Jesus said to her, "Mary!" She turned and said to him
in Hebrew, "Rabbouni!" (which means Teacher). Jesus said to her, "Do not
hold on to me, because I have not yet ascended to the Father. But go to my
brothers and say to them, 'I am ascending to my Father and your Father, to

my God and your God.'" Mary Magdalene went and announced to the disciples, "I have seen the Lord"; and she told them that he had said these things to her.

WEDNESDAY IN EASTER WEEK

The Collect

O God, whose blessed Son made himself known to his disciples in the breaking of bread: Open the eyes of our faith, that we may behold him in all his redeeming work; who lives and reigns with you, in the unity of the Holy Spirit, one God, now and for ever. *Amen.*

Years A, B, and C
Acts 3:1-10
Psalm 105:1-8 or 118:19-24
Luke 24:13-35

The Lesson   **Acts 3:1-10**

One day Peter and John were going up to the temple at the hour of prayer, at three o'clock in the afternoon. And a man lame from birth was being carried in. People would lay him daily at the gate of the temple called the Beautiful Gate so that he could ask for alms from those entering the temple. When he saw Peter and John about to go into the temple, he asked them for alms. Peter looked intently at him, as did John, and said, "Look at us." And he fixed his attention on them, expecting to receive something from them. But Peter said, "I have no silver or gold, but what I have I give you; in the name of Jesus Christ of Nazareth, stand up and walk." And he took him by the right hand and raised him up; and immediately his feet and ankles were made strong. Jumping up, he stood and began to walk, and he entered the temple with them, walking and leaping and praising God. All the people saw him walking and praising God, and they recognized him as the one who used to sit and ask for alms at the Beautiful Gate of the temple; and they were filled with wonder and amazement at what had happened to him.

The Response   **Psalm 105:1-8**

Psalm 105:1-8   *Confitemini Domino*
1   Give thanks to the LORD and call upon his Name; *
        make known his deeds among the peoples.
2   Sing to him, sing praises to him, *
        and speak of all his marvelous works.
3   Glory in his holy Name; *
        let the hearts of those who seek the LORD rejoice.

4   Search for the LORD and his strength; *
        continually seek his face.
5   Remember the marvels he has done, *
        his wonders and the judgments of his mouth,
6   O offspring of Abraham his servant, *
        O children of Jacob his chosen.
7   He is the LORD our God; *
        his judgments prevail in all the world.
8   He has always been mindful of his covenant, *
        the promise he made for a thousand generations:

or, **Psalm 118:19-24**   *Confitemini Domino*

19   Open for me the gates of righteousness; *
        I will enter them;
        I will offer thanks to the LORD.
20   "This is the gate of the LORD; *
        he who is righteous may enter."
21   I will give thanks to you, for you answered me *
        and have become my salvation.
22   The same stone which the builders rejected *
        has become the chief cornerstone.
23   This is the LORD's doing, *
        and it is marvelous in our eyes.
24   On this day the LORD has acted; *
        we will rejoice and be glad in it.

The Gospel   Luke 24:13-35

On the first day of the week, two of Jesus' followers were going to a village called Emmaus, about seven miles from Jerusalem, and talking with each other about all these things that had happened. While they were talking and discussing, Jesus himself came near and went with them, but their eyes were kept from recognizing him. And he said to them, "What are you discussing with each other while you walk along?" They stood still, looking sad. Then one of them, whose name was Cleopas, answered him, "Are you the only stranger in Jerusalem who does not know the things that have taken place there in these days?" He asked them, "What things?" They replied, "The things about Jesus of Nazareth, who was a prophet mighty in deed and word before God and all the people, and how our chief priests and leaders handed him over to be condemned to death and crucified him. But we had hoped that he was the one to redeem Israel. Yes, and besides all this, it is now the third day since these things took place. Moreover, some women of our group astounded us. They were at the tomb early this morning, and when they did not find his body there, they came back and told us that they had indeed seen a vision of angels who said that he was alive. Some of those who were with us went to the tomb and found it just as the women had said; but they did not see him." Then he said to them, "Oh, how foolish you are, and how slow of heart to believe all that the prophets have declared! Was it not necessary that the Messiah should suffer these things and then enter into his glory?" Then beginning with Moses and all the prophets, he interpreted to them the things about himself in all the scriptures. As they came near the village to which they were going, he walked ahead as if he were going on. But they urged him strongly, saying, "Stay with us, because it is almost evening and the day is now nearly over." So he went in to stay with them. When he was at the table with them, he took bread, blessed and broke it, and gave it to them. Then their eyes were opened, and they recognized him; and he vanished from their sight. They said to each other, "Were not our hearts burning within us while he was talking to us on the road, while he was opening the scriptures to us?" That same hour they got up and returned to Jerusalem; and they found the eleven and their companions gathered together. They were saying, "The Lord has risen indeed, and he has appeared to Simon!" Then they told what had happened on the road, and how he had been made known to them in the breaking of the bread.

THURSDAY IN EASTER WEEK

The Collect
Almighty and everlasting God, who in the Paschal mystery established the new covenant of reconciliation: Grant that all who have been reborn into the fellowship of Christ's Body may show forth in their lives what they profess by their faith; through Jesus Christ our Lord, who lives and reigns with you and the Holy Spirit, one God, for ever and ever. *Amen.*

Years A, B, and C
Acts 3:11-26
Psalm 8 or Psalm 114 or Psalm 118:19-24
Luke 24:36b-48

The Lesson   Acts 3:11-26
While the lame man (who had been healed) clung to Peter and John, all the people ran together to them in the portico called Solomon's Portico, utterly astonished. When Peter saw it, he addressed the people, "You Israelites, why do you wonder at this, or why do you stare at us, as though by our own power or piety we had made him walk? The God of Abraham, the God of Isaac, and the God of Jacob, the God of our ancestors has glorified his servant Jesus, whom you handed over and rejected in the presence of Pilate, though he had

decided to release him. But you rejected the Holy and Righteous One and asked to have a murderer given to you, and you killed the Author of life, whom God raised from the dead. To this we are witnesses. And by faith in his name, his name itself has made this man strong, whom you see and know; and the faith that is through Jesus has given him this perfect health in the presence of all of you. And now, friends, I know that you acted in ignorance, as did also your rulers. In this way God fulfilled what he had foretold through all the prophets, that his Messiah would suffer. Repent therefore, and turn to God so that your sins may be wiped out, so that times of refreshing may come from the presence of the Lord, and that he may send the Messiah appointed for you, that is, Jesus, who must remain in heaven until the time of universal restoration that God announced long ago through his holy prophets. Moses said, 'The Lord your God will raise up for you from your own people a prophet like me. You must listen to whatever he tells you. And it will be that everyone who does not listen to that prophet will be utterly rooted out of the people.' And all the prophets, as many as have spoken, from Samuel and those after him, also predicted these days. You are the descendants of the prophets and of the covenant that God gave to your ancestors, saying to Abraham, 'And in your descendants all the families of the earth shall be blessed.' When God raised up his servant, he sent him first to you, to bless you by turning each of you from your wicked ways."

The Response   **Psalm 8** *or* **Psalm 114** *or* **Psalm 118:19-24**
Psalm 8   *Domine, Dominus noster*

1   O LORD our Governor, *
        how exalted is your Name in all the world!
2   Out of the mouths of infants and children *
        your majesty is praised above the heavens.
3   You have set up a stronghold against your adversaries, *
        to quell the enemy and the avenger.
4   When I consider your heavens, the work of your fingers, *
        the moon and the stars you have set in their courses,
5   What is man that you should be mindful of him? *
        the son of man that you should seek him out?
6   You have made him but little lower than the angels; *
        you adorn him with glory and honor;
7   You give him mastery over the works of your hands; *
        you put all things under his feet:
8   All sheep and oxen, *
        even the wild beasts of the field,
9   The birds of the air, the fish of the sea, *
        and whatsoever walks in the paths of the sea.

10   O Lord our Governor, *
         how exalted is your Name in all the world!

or, **Psalm 114**   *In exitu Israel*

1   Hallelujah!
         When Israel came out of Egypt, *
             the house of Jacob from a people of strange speech,
2   Judah became God's sanctuary *
         and Israel his dominion.
3   The sea beheld it and fled; *
         Jordan turned and went back.
4   The mountains skipped like rams, *
         and the little hills like young sheep.
5   What ailed you, O sea, that you fled? *
         O Jordan, that you turned back?
6   You mountains, that you skipped like rams? *
         you little hills like young sheep?
7   Tremble, O earth, at the presence of the Lord, *
         at the presence of the God of Jacob,
8   Who turned the hard rock into a pool of water *
         and flint-stone into a flowing spring.

or, **Psalm 118:19-24**   *Confitemini Domino*

19   Open for me the gates of righteousness; *
         I will enter them;
         I will offer thanks to the Lord.
20   "This is the gate of the Lord; *
         he who is righteous may enter."
21   I will give thanks to you, for you answered me *
         and have become my salvation.
22   The same stone which the builders rejected *
         has become the chief cornerstone.
23   This is the Lord's doing, *
         and it is marvelous in our eyes.
24   On this day the Lord has acted; *
         we will rejoice and be glad in it.

The Gospel   Luke 24:36*b*-48

Jesus himself appeared and stood among the eleven and said to them, "Peace
be with you." They were startled and terrified, and thought that they were
seeing a ghost. He said to them, "Why are you frightened, and why do doubts
arise in your hearts? Look at my hands and my feet; see that it is I myself.

Touch me and see; for a ghost does not have flesh and bones as you see that I have." And when he had said this, he showed them his hands and his feet. While in their joy they were disbelieving and still wondering, he said to them, "Have you anything here to eat?" They gave him a piece of broiled fish, and he took it and ate in their presence. Then he said to them, "These are my words that I spoke to you while I was still with you — that everything written about me in the law of Moses, the prophets, and the psalms must be fulfilled." Then he opened their minds to understand the scriptures, and he said to them, "Thus it is written, that the Messiah is to suffer and to rise from the dead on the third day, and that repentance and forgiveness of sins is to be proclaimed in his name to all nations, beginning from Jerusalem. You are witnesses of these things."

FRIDAY IN EASTER WEEK

The Collect
Almighty Father, who gave your only Son to die for our sins and to rise for our justification: Give us grace so to put away the leaven of malice and wickedness, that we may always serve you in pureness of living and truth; through Jesus Christ your Son our Lord, who lives and reigns with you and the Holy Spirit, one God, now and for ever. *Amen.*

Years A, B, and C
Acts 4:1-12
Psalm 116:1-8 or *Psalm 118:19-24*
John 21:1-14

The Lesson   Acts 4:1-12
While Peter and John were speaking to the people, the priests, the captain of the temple, and the Sadducees came to them, much annoyed because they were teaching the people and proclaiming that in Jesus there is the resurrection of the dead. So they arrested them and put them in custody until the next day, for it was already evening. But many of those who heard the word believed; and they numbered about five thousand. The next day their rulers, elders, and scribes assembled in Jerusalem, with Annas the high priest, Caiaphas, John, and Alexander, and all who were of the high-priestly family. When they had made the prisoners stand in their midst, they inquired, "By what power or by what name did you do this?" Then Peter, filled with the Holy Spirit, said to them, "Rulers of the people and elders, if we are questioned today because of a good deed done to someone who was sick and are asked how this man has been healed, let it be known to all of you, and to all the people of Israel, that this man is standing before you in good health by the name of Jesus Christ of Nazareth, whom you crucified, whom God raised from the dead. This Jesus is

'the stone that was rejected by you, the builders; it has become the corner-stone.' There is salvation in no one else, for there is no other name under heaven given among mortals by which we must be saved."

The Response   **Psalm 116:1-8** *or* **Psalm 118:19-24**
Psalm 116:1-8 *Dilexi, quoniam*

1   I love the LORD, because he has heard the voice of
                  my supplication, *
            because he has inclined his ear to me whenever
            I called upon him.
2   The cords of death entangled me;
      the grip of the grave took hold of me; *
            I came to grief and sorrow.
3   Then I called upon the Name of the LORD: *
            "O LORD, I pray you, save my life."
4   Gracious is the LORD and righteous; *
            our God is full of compassion.
5   The LORD watches over the innocent; *
            I was brought very low, and he helped me.
6   Turn again to your rest, O my soul, *
            for the LORD has treated you well.
7   For you have rescued my life from death, *
            my eyes from tears, and my feet from stumbling.
8   I will walk in the presence of the LORD *
            in the land of the living.

or, **Psalm 118:19-24** *Confitemini Domino*

19   Open for me the gates of righteousness; *
            I will enter them;
            I will offer thanks to the LORD.
20   "This is the gate of the LORD; *
            he who is righteous may enter."
21   I will give thanks to you, for you answered me *
            and have become my salvation.
22   The same stone which the builders rejected *
            has become the chief cornerstone.
23   This is the LORD's doing, *
            and it is marvelous in our eyes.
24   On this day the LORD has acted; *
            we will rejoice and be glad in it.

The Gospel   **John 21:1-14**

Jesus showed himself again to the disciples by the Sea of Tiberias; and he
showed himself in this way. Gathered there together were Simon Peter,
Thomas called the Twin, Nathanael of Cana in Galilee, the sons of Zebedee,
and two others of his disciples. Simon Peter said to them, "I am going fishing." They said to him, "We will go with you." They went out and got into the
boat, but that night they caught nothing. Just after daybreak, Jesus stood on
the beach; but the disciples did not know that it was Jesus. Jesus said to them,
"Children, you have no fish, have you?" They answered him, "No." He said to
them, "Cast the net to the right side of the boat, and you will find some." So
they cast it, and now they were not able to haul it in because there were so
many fish. That disciple whom Jesus loved said to Peter, "It is the Lord!"
When Simon Peter heard that it was the Lord, he put on some clothes, for he
was naked, and jumped into the sea. But the other disciples came in the boat,
dragging the net full of fish, for they were not far from the land, only about a
hundred yards off. When they had gone ashore, they saw a charcoal fire there,
with fish on it, and bread. Jesus said to them, "Bring some of the fish that you
have just caught." So Simon Peter went aboard and hauled the net ashore, full
of large fish, a hundred fifty-three of them; and though there were so many,
the net was not torn. Jesus said to them, "Come and have breakfast." Now
none of the disciples dared to ask him, "Who are you?" because they knew it
was the Lord. Jesus came and took the bread and gave it to them, and did the
same with the fish. This was now the third time that Jesus appeared to the
disciples after he as raised from the dead.

SATURDAY IN EASTER WEEK

The Collect

We thank you, heavenly Father, that you have delivered us from the dominion
of sin and death and brought us into the kingdom of your Son; and we pray
that, as by his death he has recalled us to life, so by his love he may raise us
to eternal joys; who lives and reigns with you, in the unity of the Holy Spirit,
one God, now and for ever. *Amen.*

Years A, B, and C
Acts 4:13-21
Psalm 118:14-18 or *Psalm 118:19-24*
Mark 16:9-15, 20

The Lesson   **Acts 4:13-21**

When the rulers and elders saw the boldness of Peter and John and realized
that they were uneducated and ordinary men, they were amazed and recognized them as companions of Jesus. When they saw the man who had been

cured standing beside them, they had nothing to say in opposition. So they ordered them to leave the council while they discussed the matter with one another. They said, "What will we do with them? For it is obvious to all who live in Jerusalem that a notable sign has been done through them; we cannot deny it. But to keep it from spreading further among the people, let us warn them to speak no more to anyone in this name." So they called them and ordered them not to speak or teach at all in the name of Jesus. But Peter and John answered them, "Whether it is right in God's sight to listen to you rather than to God, you must judge; for we cannot keep from speaking about what we have seen and heard." After threatening them again, they let them go, finding no way to punish them because of the people, for all of them praised God for what had happened.

The Response **Psalm 118:14-18** *or* **Psalm 118:19-24**

Psalm 118:14-18 *Confitemini Domino*

14 The LORD is my strength and my song, *
     and he has become my salvation.
15 There is a sound of exultation and victory *
     in the tents of the righteous:
16 "The right hand of the LORD has triumphed! *
     the right hand of the LORD is exalted!
     the right hand of the LORD has triumphed!"
17 I shall not die, but live, *
     and declare the works of the LORD.
18 The LORD has punished me sorely, *
     but he did not hand me over to death.

Psalm 118:19-24 *Confitemini Domino*

19 Open for me the gates of righteousness; *
     I will enter them;
     I will offer thanks to the LORD.
20 "This is the gate of the LORD; *
     he who is righteous may enter."
21 I will give thanks to you, for you answered me *
     and have become my salvation.
22 The same stone which the builders rejected *
     has become the chief cornerstone.
23 This is the LORD's doing, *
     and it is marvelous in our eyes.
24 On this day the LORD has acted; *
     we will rejoice and be glad in it.

The Gospel   **Mark 16:9-15, 20**

After Jesus rose early on the first day of the week, he appeared first to Mary
Magdalene, from whom he had cast out seven demons. She went out and told
those who had been with him, while they were mourning and weeping. But
when they heard that he was alive and had been seen by her, they would not
believe it. After this he appeared in another form to two of them, as they were
walking into the country. And they went back an told the rest, but they did not
believe them. Later he appeared to the eleven themselves as they were sitting
at the table; and he upbraided them for their lack of faith and stubbornness,
because they had not believed those who saw him after he had risen. And he
said to them, "Go into all the world and proclaim the good news to the whole
creation." And they went out and proclaimed the good news everywhere, while
the Lord worked with them and confirmed the message by the signs that
accompanied it.

SECOND SUNDAY OF EASTER

The Collect

Almighty and everlasting God, who in the Paschal mystery established the
new covenant of reconciliation: Grant that all who have been reborn into the
fellowship of Christ's Body may show forth in their lives what they profess by
their faith; through Jesus Christ our Lord, who lives and reigns with you and
the Holy Spirit, one God, for ever and ever. *Amen.*

Year A
Acts 2:14a, 22-32
Psalm 16
1 Peter 1:3-9
John 20:19-31

The Lesson   **Acts 2:14a, 22-32**

Peter, standing with the eleven, raised his voice and addressed them, "You that
are Israelites, listen to what I have to say: Jesus of Nazareth, a man attested to
you by God with deeds of power, wonders, and signs that God did through
him among you, as you yourselves know — this man, handed over to you
according to the definite plan and foreknowledge of God, you crucified and
killed by the hands of those outside the law. But God raised him up, having
freed him from death, because it was impossible for him to be held in its
power. For David says concerning him, 'I saw the Lord always before me, for
he is at my right hand so that I will not be shaken; therefore my heart was
glad, and my tongue rejoiced; moreover my flesh will live in hope. For you
will not abandon my soul to Hades, or let your Holy One experience corrup-

tion. You have made known to me the ways of life; you will make me full of gladness with your presence.' Fellow Israelites, I may say to you confidently of our ancestor David that he both died and was buried, and his tomb is with us to this day. Since he was a prophet, he knew that God had sworn with an oath to him that he would put one of his descendants on his throne. Foreseeing this, David spoke of the resurrection of the Messiah, saying, 'He was not abandoned to Hades, nor did his flesh experience corruption.' This Jesus God raised up, and of that all of us are witnesses."

The Response   Psalm 16

Psalm 16   *Conserva me, Domine*

1   Protect me, O God, for I take refuge in you; *
         I have said to the LORD, "You are my LORD,
         my good above all other."
2   All my delight is upon the godly that are in the land, *
         upon those who are noble among the people.
3   But those who run after other gods *
         shall have their troubles multiplied.
4   Their libations of blood I will not offer, *
         nor take the names of their gods upon my lips.
5   O LORD, you are my portion and my cup; *
         it is you who uphold my lot.
6   My boundaries enclose a pleasant land; *
         indeed, I have a goodly heritage.
7   I will bless the LORD who gives me counsel; *
         my heart teaches me, night after night.
8   I have set the LORD always before me; *
         because he is at my right hand I shall not fall.
9   My heart, therefore, is glad, and my spirit rejoices; *
         my body also shall rest in hope.
10 For you will not abandon me to the grave, *
         nor let your holy one see the Pit.
11 You will show me the path of life; *
         in your presence there is fullness of joy,
         and in your right hand are pleasures for evermore.

The Epistle   1 Peter 1:3-9

Blessed be the God and Father of our Lord Jesus Christ! By his great mercy he has given us a new birth into a living hope through the resurrection of Jesus Christ from the dead, and into an inheritance that is imperishable, undefiled, and unfading, kept in heaven for you, who are being protected by the power of God through faith for a salvation ready to be revealed in the last time. In this you rejoice, even if now for a little while you have had to suffer various trials, so that the genuineness of your faith — being more precious than gold that, though perishable, is tested by fire — may be found to result in praise and glory and honor when Jesus Christ is revealed. Although you have not seen him, you love him; and even though you do not see him now, you believe in him and rejoice with an indescribable and glorious joy, for you are receiving the outcome of your faith, the salvation of your souls.

The Gospel   John 20:19-31

When it was evening of the day of Resurrection, the first day of the week, and the doors of the house where the disciples had met were locked for fear of the Jews, Jesus came and stood among them and said, "Peace be with you." After he said this, he showed them his hands and his side. Then the disciples re-joiced when they saw the Lord. Jesus said to them again, "Peace be with you. As the Father has sent me, so I send you." When he had said this, he breathed on them and said to them, "Receive the Holy Spirit. If you forgive the sins of any, they are forgiven them; if you retain the sins of any, they are retained." But Thomas (who was called the Twin), one of the twelve, was not with them when Jesus came. So the other disciples told him, "We have seen the Lord." But he said to them, "Unless I see the mark of the nails in his hands, and put my finger in the mark of the nails and my hand in his side, I will not believe." A week later his disciples were again in the house, and Thomas was with them. Although the doors were shut, Jesus came and stood among them and said, "Peace be with you." Then he said to Thomas, "Put your finger here and see my hands. Reach out your hand and put it in my side. Do not doubt but believe." Thomas answered him, "My Lord and my God!" Jesus said to him, "Have you believed because you have seen me? Blessed are those who have not seen and yet have come to believe." Now Jesus did many other signs in the presence of his disciples, which are not written in this book. But these are written so that you may come to believe that Jesus is the Messiah, the Son of God, and that through believing you may have life in his name.

Year B
Acts 4:32-35
Psalm 133
1 John 1:1—2:2
John 20:19-31

The Lesson   Acts 4:32-35

Now the whole group of those who believed were of one heart and soul, and no one claimed private ownership of any possessions, but everything they owned was held in common. With great power the apostles gave their testimony to the resurrection of the Lord Jesus, and great grace was upon them all. There was not a needy person among them, for as many as owned lands or houses sold them and brought the proceeds of what was sold. They laid it at the apostles' feet, and it was distributed to each as any had need.

The Response   Psalm 133

Psalm 133   *Ecce, quam bonum!*

1   Oh, how good and pleasant it is, *
    when brethren live together in unity!

2   It is like fine oil upon the head *
    that runs down upon the beard,

3   Upon the beard of Aaron, *
    and runs down upon the collar of his robe.

4   It is like the dew of Hermon *
    that falls upon the hills of Zion.

5   For there the LORD has ordained the blessing: *
    life for evermore.

The Epistle   1 John 1:1—2:2

We declare to you what was from the beginning, what we have heard, what we have seen with our eyes, what we have looked at and touched with our hands, concerning the word of life — this life was revealed, and we have seen it and testify to it, and declare to you the eternal life that was with the Father and was revealed to us — we declare to you what we have seen and heard so that you also may have fellowship with us; and truly our fellowship is with the Father and with his Son Jesus Christ. We are writing these things so that our joy may be complete. This is the message we have heard from him and proclaim to you, that God is light and in him there is no darkness at all. If we say that we have fellowship with him while we are walking in darkness, we lie and do not do what is true; but if we walk in the light as he himself is in the light, we have fellowship with one another, and the blood of Jesus his Son cleanses us from all sin. If we say that we have no sin, we deceive ourselves, and the truth is not in us. If we confess our sins, he who is faithful and just will forgive us our sins and cleanse us from all unrighteousness. If we say that we have not sinned, we make him a liar, and his word is not in us. My little children, I am writing these things to you so that you may not sin. But if anyone does sin, we have an advocate with the Father, Jesus Christ the righteous; and he is the atoning sacrifice for our sins, and not for ours only but also for the sins of the whole world.

The Gospel   **John 20:19-31**

When it was evening of the day of Resurrection, the first day of the week, and the doors of the house where the disciples had met were locked for fear of the Jews, Jesus came and stood among them and said, "Peace be with you." After he said this, he showed them his hands and his side. Then the disciples rejoiced when they saw the Lord. Jesus said to them again, "Peace be with you. As the Father has sent me, so I send you." When he had said this, he breathed on them and said to them, "Receive the Holy Spirit. If you forgive the sins of any, they are forgiven them; if you retain the sins of any, they are retained." But Thomas (who was called the Twin), one of the twelve, was not with them when Jesus came. So the other disciples told him, "We have seen the Lord." But he said to them, "Unless I see the mark of the nails in his hands, and put my finger in the mark of the nails and my hand in his side, I will not believe." A week later his disciples were again in the house, and Thomas was with them. Although the doors were shut, Jesus came and stood among them and said, "Peace be with you." Then he said to Thomas, "Put your finger here and see my hands. Reach out your hand and put it in my side. Do not doubt but believe." Thomas answered him, "My Lord and my God!" Jesus said to him, "Have you believed because you have seen me? Blessed are those who have not seen and yet have come to believe." Now Jesus did many other signs in the presence of his disciples, which are not written in this book. But these are written so that you may come to believe that Jesus is the Messiah, the Son of God, and that through believing you may have life in his name.

Year C

Acts 5:27-32
Psalm 118:14-29 or *Psalm 150*
Revelation 1:4-8
John 20:19-31

The Lesson   **Acts 5:27-32**

When the temple police had brought the apostles, they had them stand before the council. The high priest questioned them, saying, "We gave you strict orders not to teach in this name, yet here you have filled Jerusalem with your teaching and you are determined to bring this man's blood on us." But Peter and the apostles answered, "We must obey God rather than any human authority. The God of our ancestors raised up Jesus, whom you had killed by hanging him on a tree. God exalted him at his right hand as Leader and Savior that he might give repentance to Israel and forgiveness of sins. And we are witnesses to these things, and so is the Holy Spirit whom God has given to those who obey him."

The Response   **Psalm 118:14-29** *or* **Psalm 150**

Psalm 118:14-29   *Confitemini Domino*

14   The LORD is my strength and my song, *
       and he has become my salvation.

15   There is a sound of exultation and victory *
       in the tents of the righteous:

16   "The right hand of the LORD has triumphed! *
       the right hand of the LORD is exalted!
       the right hand of the LORD has triumphed!"

17   I shall not die, but live, *
       and declare the works of the LORD.

18   The LORD has punished me sorely, *
       but he did not hand me over to death.

19   Open for me the gates of righteousness; *
       I will enter them;
       I will offer thanks to the LORD.

20   "This is the gate of the LORD; *
       he who is righteous may enter."

21   I will give thanks to you, for you answered me *
       and have become my salvation.

22   The same stone which the builders rejected *
       has become the chief cornerstone.

23   This is the LORD's doing, *
       and it is marvelous in our eyes.

24   On this day the LORD has acted; *
       we will rejoice and be glad in it.

25   Hosanna, LORD, hosanna! *
       LORD, send us now success.

26   Blessed is he who comes in the name of the LORD; *
       we bless you from the house of the LORD.

27   God is the LORD; he has shined upon us; *
       form a procession with branches up to the horns of the altar.

28   "You are my God, and I will thank you; *
       you are my God, and I will exalt you."

29   Give thanks to the LORD, for he is good; *
       his mercy endures for ever.

or, **Psalm 150**   *Laudate Dominum*

1   Hallelujah!
    Praise God in his holy temple; *
       praise him in the firmament of his power.

2   Praise him for his mighty acts; *
     praise him for his excellent greatness.
3   Praise him with the blast of the ram's-horn; *
     praise him with lyre and harp.
4   Praise him with timbrel and dance; *
     praise him with strings and pipe.
5   Praise him with resounding cymbals; *
     praise him with loud-clanging cymbals.
6   Let everything that has breath *
     praise the LORD.
     Hallelujah!

The Epistle   Revelation 1:4-8

John to the seven churches that are in Asia: Grace to you and peace from him
who is and who was and who is to come, and from the seven spirits who are
before his throne, and from Jesus Christ, the faithful witness, the firstborn of
the dead, and the ruler of the kings of the earth. To him who loves us and freed
us from our sins by his blood, and made us to be a kingdom, priests serving
his God and Father, to him be glory and dominion forever and ever. Amen.
Look! He is coming with the clouds; every eye will see him, even those who
pierced him; and on his account all the tribes of the earth will wail. So it is to
be. Amen. "I am the Alpha and the Omega," says the Lord God, who is and
who was and who is to come, the Almighty.

The Gospel   John 20:19-31

When it was evening of the day of Resurrection, the first day of the week, and
the doors of the house where the disciples had met were locked for fear of the
Jews, Jesus came and stood among them and said, "Peace be with you." After
he said this, he showed them his hands and his side. Then the disciples rejoiced when they saw the Lord. Jesus said to them again, "Peace be with you.
As the Father has sent me, so I send you." When he had said this, he breathed
on them and said to them, "Receive the Holy Spirit. If you forgive the sins of
any, they are forgiven them; if you retain the sins of any, they are retained."
But Thomas (who was called the Twin), one of the twelve, was not with them
when Jesus came. So the other disciples told him, "We have seen the Lord."
But he said to them, "Unless I see the mark of the nails in his hands, and put
my finger in the mark of the nails and my hand in his side, I will not believe."
A week later his disciples were again in the house, and Thomas was with
them. Although the doors were shut, Jesus came and stood among them and
said, "Peace be with you." Then he said to Thomas, "Put your finger here and
see my hands. Reach out your hand and put it in my side. Do not doubt but

believe." Thomas answered him, "My Lord and my God!" Jesus said to him, "Have you believed because you have seen me? Blessed are those who have not seen and yet have come to believe." Now Jesus did many other signs in the presence of his disciples, which are not written in this book. But these are written so that you may come to believe that Jesus is the Messiah, the Son of God, and that through believing you may have life in his name.

THIRD SUNDAY OF EASTER

The Collect

O God, whose blessed Son made himself known to his disciples in the breaking of bread: Open the eyes of our faith, that we may behold him in all his redeeming work; who lives and reigns with you, in the unity of the Holy Spirit, one God, now and for ever. *Amen.*

Year A
Acts 2:14a, 36-41
Psalm 116:1-3, 10-17
1 Peter 1:17-23
Luke 24:13-35

The Lesson   **Acts 2:14*a*, 36-41**

Peter, standing with the eleven, raised his voice and addressed them, "Therefore let the entire house of Israel know with certainty that God has made him both Lord and Messiah, this Jesus whom you crucified." Now when they heard this, they were cut to the heart and said to Peter and to the other apostles, "Brothers, what should we do?" Peter said to them, "Repent, and be baptized every one of you in the name of Jesus Christ so that your sins may be forgiven; and you will receive the gift of the Holy Spirit. For the promise is for you, for your children, and for all who are far away, everyone whom the Lord our God calls to him." And he testified with many other arguments and exhorted them, saying, "Save yourselves from this corrupt generation." So those who welcomed his message were baptized, and that day about three thousand persons were added.

The Response   **Psalm 116:1-3, 10-17**

Psalm 116:1-3, 10-17   *Dilexi, quoniam*

1   I love the LORD, because he has heard the voice of
                my supplication, *
      because he has inclined his ear to me whenever
                I called upon him.

2   The cords of death entangled me;
        the grip of the grave took hold of me; *
            I came to grief and sorrow.
3   Then I called upon the Name of the LORD: *
            "O LORD, I pray you, save my life."
10 How shall I repay the LORD *
            for all the good things he has done for me?
11 I will lift up the cup of salvation *
            and call upon the Name of the LORD.
12 I will fulfill my vows to the LORD *
            in the presence of all his people.
13 Precious in the sight of the LORD *
            is the death of his servants.
14 O LORD, I am your servant; *
            I am your servant and the child of your handmaid;
            you have freed me from my bonds.
15 I will offer you the sacrifice of thanksgiving *
            and call upon the Name of the LORD.
16 I will fulfill my vows to the LORD *
            in the presence of all his people,
17 In the courts of the LORD's house, *
            in the midst of you, O Jerusalem.
            Hallelujah!

The Epistle   1 Peter 1:17-23

If you invoke as Father the one who judges all people impartially according to
their deeds, live in reverent fear during the time of your exile. You know that
you were ransomed from the futile ways inherited from your ancestors, not
with perishable things like silver or gold, but with the precious blood of
Christ, like that of a lamb without defect or blemish. He was destined before
the foundation of the world, but was revealed at the end of the ages for your
sake. Through him you have come to trust in God, who raised him from the
dead and gave him glory, so that your faith and hope are set on God. Now that
you have purified your souls by your obedience to the truth so that you have
genuine mutual love, love one another deeply from the heart. You have been
born anew, not of perishable but of imperishable seed, through the living and
enduring word of God.

The Gospel   Luke 24:13-35

On the first day of the week, two of Jesus' followers were going to a village
called Emmaus, about seven miles from Jerusalem, and talking with each
other about all these things that had happened. While they were talking and

discussing, Jesus himself came near and went with them, but their eyes were kept from recognizing him. And he said to them, "What are you discussing with each other while you walk along?" They stood still, looking sad. Then one of them, whose name was Cleopas, answered him, "Are you the only stranger in Jerusalem who does not know the things that have taken place there in these days?" He asked them, "What things?" They replied, "The things about Jesus of Nazareth, who was a prophet mighty in deed and word before God and all the people, and how our chief priests and leaders handed him over to be condemned to death and crucified him. But we had hoped that he was the one to redeem Israel. Yes, and besides all this, it is now the third day since these things took place. Moreover, some women of our group astounded us. They were at the tomb early this morning, and when they did not find his body there, they came back and told us that they had indeed seen a vision of angels who said that he was alive. Some of those who were with us went to the tomb and found it just as the women had said; but they did not see him." Then he said to them, "Oh, how foolish you are, and how slow of heart to believe all that the prophets have declared! Was it not necessary that the Messiah should suffer these things and then enter into his glory?" Then beginning with Moses and all the prophets, he interpreted to them the things about himself in all the scriptures. As they came near the village to which they were going, he walked ahead as if he were going on. But they urged him strongly, saying, "Stay with us, because it is almost evening and the day is now nearly over." So he went in to stay with them. When he was at the table with them, he took bread, blessed and broke it, and gave it to them. Then their eyes were opened, and they recognized him; and he vanished from their sight. They said to each other, "Were not our hearts burning within us while he was talking to us on the road, while he was opening the scriptures to us?" That same hour they got up and returned to Jerusalem; and they found the eleven and their companions gathered together. They were saying, "The Lord has risen indeed, and he has appeared to Simon!" Then they told what had happened on the road, and how he had been made known to them in the breaking of the bread.

Year B
Acts 3:12-19
Psalm 4
1 John 3:1-7
Luke 24:36b-48

The Lesson   **Acts 3:12-19**

When Peter saw the wonder and amazement caused by his healing of the lame man, he addressed the people, "You Israelites, why do you wonder at this, or why do you stare at us, as though by our own power or piety we had made him walk? The God of Abraham, the God of Isaac, and the God of Jacob, the God of our ancestors has glorified his servant Jesus, whom you handed over and rejected in the presence of Pilate, though he had decided to release him. But you rejected the Holy and Righteous One and asked to have a murderer given to you, and you killed the Author of life, whom God raised from the dead. To this we are witnesses. And by faith in his name, his name itself has made this man strong, whom you see and know; and the faith that is through Jesus has given him this perfect health in the presence of all of you. And now, friends, I know that you acted in ignorance, as did also your rulers. In this way God fulfilled what he had foretold through all the prophets, that his Messiah would suffer. Repent therefore, and turn to God so that your sins may be wiped out."

The Response   Psalm 4

Psalm 4   *Cum invocarem*

1   Answer me when I call, O God, defender of my cause; *
        you set me free when I am hard-pressed;
        have mercy on me and hear my prayer.

2   "You mortals, how long will you dishonor my glory; *
        how long will you worship dumb idols
        and run after false gods?"

3   Know that the LORD does wonders for the faithful; *
        when I call upon the LORD, he will hear me.

4   Tremble, then, and do not sin; *
        speak to your heart in silence upon your bed.

5   Offer the appointed sacrifices *
        and put your trust in the LORD.

6   Many are saying,
        "Oh, that we might see better times!" *
        Lift up the light of your countenance upon us, O LORD.

7   You have put gladness in my heart, *
        more than when grain and wine and oil increase.

8   I lie down in peace; at once I fall asleep; *
        for only you, LORD, make me dwell in safety.

The Epistle   1 John 3:1-7

See what love the Father has given us, that we should be called children of God; and that is what we are. The reason the world does not know us is that it did not know him. Beloved, we are God's children now; what we will be has not yet been revealed. What we do know is this: when he is revealed, we will be like him, for we will see him as he is. And all who have this hope in him purify themselves, just as he is pure. Everyone who commits sin is guilty of lawlessness; sin is lawlessness. You know that he was revealed to take away sins, and in him there is no sin. No one who abides in him sins; no one who sins has either seen him or known him. Little children, let no one deceive you. Everyone who does what is right is righteous, just as he is righteous.

The Gospel   Luke 24:36*b*-48

While the disciples were telling how they had seen Jesus risen from the dead, Jesus himself stood among them and said to them, "Peace be with you." They were startled and terrified, and thought that they were seeing a ghost. He said to them, "Why are you frightened, and why do doubts arise in your hearts? Look at my hands and my feet; see that it is I myself. Touch me and see; for a ghost does not have flesh and bones as you see that I have." And when he had said this, he showed them his hands and his feet. While in their joy they were disbelieving and still wondering, he said to them, "Have you anything here to eat?" They gave him a piece of broiled fish, and he took it and ate in their presence. Then he said to them, "These are my words that I spoke to you while I was still with you—that everything written about me in the law of Moses, the prophets, and the psalms must be fulfilled." Then he opened their minds to understand the scriptures, and he said to them, "Thus it is written, that the Messiah is to suffer and to rise from the dead on the third day, and that repentance and forgiveness of sins is to be proclaimed in his name to all nations, beginning from Jerusalem. You are witnesses of these things."

Year C
Acts 9:1-6, (7-20)
Psalm 30
Revelation 5:11-14
John 21:1-19

The Lesson   Acts 9:1-6, (7-20)
Acts 9:1-6

Saul, still breathing threats and murder against the disciples of the Lord, went to the high priest and asked him for letters to the synagogues at Damascus, so that if he found any who belonged to the Way, men or women, he might bring them bound to Jerusalem. Now as he was going along and approaching Damascus, suddenly a light from heaven flashed around him. He fell to the ground and heard a voice saying to him, "Saul, Saul, why do you persecute me?" He asked, "Who are you, Lord?" The reply came, "I am Jesus, whom you are persecuting. But get up and enter the city, and you will be told what you are to do."

Acts 9:(7-20) [The men who were traveling with him stood speechless because they heard the voice but saw no one. Saul got up from the ground, and though his eyes were open, he could see nothing; so they led him by the hand and brought him into Damascus. For three days he was without sight, and neither ate nor drank. Now there was a disciple in Damascus named Ananias. The Lord said to him in a vision, "Ananias." He answered, "Here I am, Lord." The Lord said to him, "Get up and go to the street called Straight, and at the house of Judas look for a man of Tarsus named Saul. At this moment he is praying, and he has seen in a vision a man named Ananias come in and lay his hands on him so that he might regain his sight." But Ananias answered, "Lord, I have heard from many about this man, how much evil he has done to your saints in Jerusalem; and here he has authority from the chief priests to bind all who invoke your name." But the Lord said to him, "Go, for he is an instrument whom I have chosen to bring my name before Gentiles and kings and before the people of Israel; I myself will show him how much he must suffer for the sake of my name." So Ananias went and entered the house. He laid his hands on Saul and said, "Brother Saul, the Lord Jesus, who appeared to you on your way here, has sent me so that you may regain your sight and be filled with the Holy Spirit." And immediately something like scales fell from his eyes, and his sight was restored. Then he got up and was baptized, and after taking some food, he regained his strength. For several days he was with the disciples in Damascus, and immediately he began to proclaim Jesus in the synagogues, saying, "He is the Son of God."]

The Response   Psalm 30

Psalm 30   *Exaltabo te, Domine*

1   I will exalt you, O LORD,
      because you have lifted me up *
          and have not let my enemies triumph over me.

2   O LORD my God, I cried out to you, *
          and you restored me to health.

3   You brought me up, O LORD, from the dead; *
          you restored my life as I was going down to the grave.

4   Sing to the LORD, you servants of his; *
          give thanks for the remembrance of his holiness.

5   For his wrath endures but the twinkling of an eye, *
          his favor for a lifetime.

6   Weeping may spend the night, *
          but joy comes in the morning.

7   While I felt secure, I said,
      "I shall never be disturbed. *
          You, LORD, with your favor, made me as strong as
              the mountains."

8   Then you hid your face, *
       and I was filled with fear.

9   I cried to you, O LORD; *
       I pleaded with the LORD, saying,

10   "What profit is there in my blood, if I go down to the Pit? *
       will the dust praise you or declare your faithfulness?

11   Hear, O LORD, and have mercy upon me; *
       O LORD, be my helper."

12   You have turned my wailing into dancing; *
       you have put off my sack-cloth and clothed me with joy.

13   Therefore my heart sings to you without ceasing; *
       O LORD my God, I will give you thanks for ever.

The Epistle   Revelation 5:11-14

I, John, looked, and I heard the voice of many angels surrounding the throne and the living creatures and the elders; they numbered myriads of myriads and thousands of thousands, singing with full voice, "Worthy is the Lamb that was slaughtered to receive power and wealth and wisdom and might and honor and glory and blessing!" Then I heard every creature in heaven and on earth and under the earth and in the sea, and all that is in them, singing, "To the one seated on the throne and to the Lamb be blessing and honor and glory and might forever and ever!" And the four living creatures said, "Amen!" And the elders fell down and worshiped.

The Gospel   John 21:1-19

Jesus showed himself again to the disciples by the Sea of Tiberias; and he showed himself in this way. Gathered there together were Simon Peter, Thomas called the Twin, Nathanael of Cana in Galilee, the sons of Zebedee, and two others of his disciples. Simon Peter said to them, "I am going fishing." They said to him, "We will go with you." They went out and got into the boat, but that night they caught nothing. Just after daybreak, Jesus stood on the beach; but the disciples did not know that it was Jesus. Jesus said to them, "Children, you have no fish, have you?" They answered him, "No." He said to them, "Cast the net to the right side of the boat, and you will find some." So they cast it, and now they were not able to haul it in because there were so many fish. That disciple whom Jesus loved said to Peter, "It is the Lord!" When Simon Peter heard that it was the Lord, he put on some clothes, for he was naked, and jumped into the sea. But the other disciples came in the boat, dragging the net full of fish, for they were not far from the land, only about a hundred yards off. When they had gone ashore, they saw a charcoal fire there, with fish on it, and bread. Jesus said to them, "Bring some of the fish that you have just caught." So Simon Peter went aboard and hauled the net ashore, full of large fish, a hundred fifty-three of them; and though there were so many, the net was not torn. Jesus said to them, "Come and have breakfast." Now none of the disciples dared to ask him, "Who are you?" because they knew it was the Lord. Jesus came and took the bread and gave it to them, and did the same with the fish. This was now the third time that Jesus appeared to the disciples after he was raised from the dead. When they had finished breakfast, Jesus said to Simon Peter, "Simon son of John, do you love me more than these?" He said to him, "Yes, Lord; you know that I love you." Jesus said to him, "Feed my lambs." A second time he said to him, "Simon son of John, do you love me?" He said to him, "Yes, Lord; you know that I love you." Jesus said to him, "Tend my sheep." He said to him the third time, "Simon son of John, do you love me?" Peter felt hurt because he said to him the third time, "Do you love me?" And he said to him, "Lord, you know everything; you know that I love you." Jesus said to him, "Feed my sheep. Very truly, I tell you, when you were younger, you used to fasten your own belt and to go wherever you wished. But when you grow old, you will stretch out your hands, and someone else will fasten a belt around you and take you where you do not wish to go." (He said this to indicate the kind of death by which he would glorify God.) After this he said to him, "Follow me."

FOURTH SUNDAY OF EASTER

The Collect
O God, whose Son Jesus is the good shepherd of your people: Grant that when we hear his voice we may know him who calls us each by name, and follow where he leads; who, with you and the Holy Spirit, lives and reigns, one God, for ever and ever. *Amen.*

Year A
Acts 2:42-47
Psalm 23
1 Peter 2:19-25
John 10:1-10

The Lesson   **Acts 2:42-47**
The believers devoted themselves to the apostles' teaching and fellowship, to the breaking of bread and the prayers. Awe came upon everyone, because many wonders and signs were being done by the apostles. All who believed were together and had all things in common; they would sell their possessions and goods and distribute the proceeds to all, as any had need. Day by day, as they spent much time together in the temple, they broke bread at home and ate their food with glad and generous hearts, praising God and having the good-will of all the people. And day by day the Lord added to their number those who were being saved.

The Response   **Psalm 23**

Psalm 23 *Dominus regit me*

1   The LORD is my shepherd; *
      I shall not be in want.
2   He makes me lie down in green pastures *
      and leads me beside still waters.
3   He revives my soul *
      and guides me along right pathways for his Name's sake.
4   Though I walk through the valley of the shadow of death,
    I shall fear no evil; *
        for you are with me;
        your rod and your staff, they comfort me.
5   You spread a table before me in the presence of those
                    who trouble me; *
      you have anointed my head with oil,
      and my cup is running over.
6   Surely your goodness and mercy shall follow me all the days
                    of my life, *
      and I will dwell in the house of the LORD for ever.

The Epistle   **1 Peter 2:19-25**

It is a credit to you if, being aware of God, you endure pain while suffering unjustly. If you endure when you are beaten for doing wrong, what credit is that? But if you endure when you do right and suffer for it, you have God's approval. For to this you have been called, because Christ also suffered for you, leaving you an example, so that you should follow in his steps. "He committed no sin, and no deceit was found in his mouth." When he was abused, he did not return abuse; when he suffered, he did not threaten; but he entrusted himself to the one who judges justly. He himself bore our sins in his body on the cross, so that, free from sins, we might live for righteousness; by his wounds you have been healed. For you were going astray like sheep, but now you have returned to the shepherd and guardian of your souls.

The Gospel   **John 10:1-10**

Jesus said, "Very truly, I tell you, anyone who does not enter the sheepfold by the gate but climbs in by another way is a thief and a bandit. The one who enters by the gate is the shepherd of the sheep. The gatekeeper opens the gate for him, and the sheep hear his voice. He calls his own sheep by name and leads them out. When he has brought out all his own, he goes ahead of them, and the sheep follow him because they know his voice. They will not follow a stranger, but they will run from him because they do not know the voice of strangers." Jesus used this figure of speech with them, but they did not understand what he was saying to them. So again Jesus said to them, "Very truly, I tell you, I am the gate for the sheep. All who came before me are thieves and bandits; but the sheep did not listen to them. I am the gate. Whoever enters by me will be saved, and will come in and go out and find pasture. The thief comes only to steal and kill and destroy. I came that they may have life, and have it abundantly."

Year B
Acts 4:5-12
Psalm 23
1 John 3:16-24
John 10:11-18

The Lesson   Acts 4:5-12

The next day their rulers, elders, and scribes assembled in Jerusalem, with Annas the high priest, Caiaphas, John, and Alexander, and all who were of the high-priestly family. When they had made the prisoners stand in their midst, they inquired, "By what power or by what name did you do this?" Then Peter, filled with the Holy Spirit, said to them, "Rulers of the people and elders, if we are questioned today because of a good deed done to someone who was sick and are asked how this man has been healed, let it be known to all of you, and to all the people of Israel, that this man is standing before you in good health by the name of Jesus Christ of Nazareth, whom you crucified, whom God raised from the dead. This Jesus is 'the stone that was rejected by you, the builders; it has become the cornerstone.' There is salvation in no one else, for there is no other name under heaven given among mortals by which we must be saved."

The Response   Psalm 23

Psalm 23   *Dominus regit me*

1   The LORD is my shepherd; *
        I shall not be in want.
2   He makes me lie down in green pastures *
        and leads me beside still waters.
3   He revives my soul *
        and guides me along right pathways for his Name's sake.
4   Though I walk through the valley of the shadow of death,
     I shall fear no evil; *
            for you are with me;
            your rod and your staff, they comfort me.

5   You spread a table before me in the presence of those
who trouble me; *
you have anointed my head with oil,
and my cup is running over.
6   Surely your goodness and mercy shall follow me all the days
of my life, *
and I will dwell in the house of the LORD for ever.

The Epistle   1 John 3:16-24

We know love by this, that he laid down his life for us—and we ought to lay
down our lives for one another. How does God's love abide in anyone who has
the world's goods and sees a brother or sister in need and yet refuses help?
Little children, let us love, not in word or speech, but in truth and action. And
by this we will know that we are from the truth and will reassure our hearts
before him whenever our hearts condemn us; for God is greater than our
hearts, and he knows everything. Beloved, if our hearts do not condemn us, we
have boldness before God; and we receive from him whatever we ask, because
we obey his commandments and do what pleases him. And this is his commandment, that we should believe in the name of his Son Jesus Christ and
love one another, just as he has commanded us. All who obey his commandments abide in him, and he abides in them. And by this we know that he
abides in us, by the Spirit that he has given us.

The Gospel   John 10:11-18

Jesus said, "I am the good shepherd. The good shepherd lays down his life for
the sheep. The hired hand, who is not the shepherd and does not own the
sheep, sees the wolf coming and leaves the sheep and runs away—and the
wolf snatches them and scatters them. The hired hand runs away because a
hired hand does not care for the sheep. I am the good shepherd. I know my
own and my own know me, just as the Father knows me and I know the
Father. And I lay down my life for the sheep. I have other sheep that do not
belong to this fold. I must bring them also, and they will listen to my voice. So
there will be one flock, one shepherd. For this reason the Father loves me,
because I lay down my life in order to take it up again. No one takes it from
me, but I lay it down of my own accord. I have power to lay it down, and I
have power to take it up again. I have received this command from my
Father."

Year C

Acts 9:36-43
Psalm 23
Revelation 7:9-17
John 10:22-30

The Lesson   **Acts 9:36-43**

Now in Joppa there was a disciple whose name was Tabitha, which in Greek is Dorcas. She was devoted to good works and acts of charity. At that time she became ill and died. When they had washed her, they laid her in a room upstairs. Since Lydda was near Joppa, the disciples, who heard that Peter was there, sent two men to him with the request, "Please come to us without delay." So Peter got up and went with them; and when he arrived, they took him to the room upstairs. All the widows stood beside him, weeping and showing tunics and other clothing that Dorcas had made while she was with them. Peter put all of them outside, and then he knelt down and prayed. He turned to the body and said, "Tabitha, get up." Then she opened her eyes, and seeing Peter, she sat up. He gave her his hand and helped her up. Then calling the saints and widows, he showed her to be alive. This became known throughout Joppa, and many believed in the Lord. Meanwhile he stayed in Joppa for some time with a certain Simon, a tanner.

The Response   **Psalm 23**

Psalm 23   *Dominus regit me*

1   The LORD is my shepherd; *
        I shall not be in want.
2   He makes me lie down in green pastures *
        and leads me beside still waters.
3   He revives my soul *
        and guides me along right pathways for his Name's sake.
4   Though I walk through the valley of the shadow of death,
    I shall fear no evil; *
        for you are with me;
        your rod and your staff, they comfort me.
5   You spread a table before me in the presence of those
                    who trouble me; *
        you have anointed my head with oil,
        and my cup is running over.
6   Surely your goodness and mercy shall follow me all the days
                    of my life, *
        and I will dwell in the house of the LORD for ever.

The Epistle **Revelation 7:9-17**

I looked, and there was a great multitude that no one could count, from every nation, from all tribes and peoples and languages, standing before the throne and before the Lamb, robed in white, with palm branches in their hands. They cried out in a loud voice, saying, "Salvation belongs to our God who is seated on the throne, and to the Lamb!" And all the angels stood around the throne and around the elders and the four living creatures, and they fell on their faces before the throne and worshiped God, singing, "Amen! Blessing and glory and wisdom and thanksgiving and honor and power and might be to our God forever and ever! Amen." Then one of the elders addressed me, saying, "Who are these, robed in white, and where have they come from?" I said to him, "Sir, you are the one that knows." Then he said to me, "These are they who have come out of the great ordeal; they have washed their robes and made them white in the blood of the Lamb. For this reason they are before the throne of God, and worship him day and night within his temple, and the one who is seated on the throne will shelter them. They will hunger no more, and thirst no more; the sun will not strike them, nor any scorching heat; for the Lamb at the center of the throne will be their shepherd, and he will guide them to springs of the water of life, and God will wipe away every tear from their eyes."

The Gospel **John 10:22-30**

It was the festival of the Dedication at Jerusalem. It was winter, and Jesus was walking in the temple, in the portico of Solomon. So the Jews gathered around him and said to him, "How long will you keep us in suspense? If you are the Messiah, tell us plainly." Jesus answered, "I have told you, and you do not believe. The works that I do in my Father's name testify to me; but you do not believe, because you do not belong to my sheep. My sheep hear my voice. I know them, and they follow me. I give them eternal life, and they will never perish. No one will snatch them out of my hand. What my Father has given me is greater than all else, and no one can snatch it out of the Father's hand. The Father and I are one."

FIFTH SUNDAY OF EASTER

The Collect

Almighty God, whom truly to know is everlasting life: Grant us so perfectly to know your Son Jesus Christ to be the way, the truth, and the life, that we may steadfastly follow his steps in the way that leads to eternal life; through Jesus Christ your Son our Lord, who lives and reigns with you, in the unity of the Holy Spirit, one God, for ever and ever. *Amen.*

Year A

Acts 7:55-60
Psalm 31:1-5, 15-16
1 Peter 2:2-10
John 14:1-14

The Lesson
Acts 7:55-60

Filled with the Holy Spirit, Stephen gazed into heaven and saw the glory of God and Jesus standing at the right hand of God. "Look," he said, "I see the heavens opened and the Son of Man standing at the right hand of God!" But they covered their ears, and with a loud shout all rushed together against him. Then they dragged him out of the city and began to stone him; and the witnesses laid their coats at the feet of a young man named Saul. While they were stoning Stephen, he prayed, "Lord Jesus, receive my spirit." Then he knelt down and cried out in a loud voice, "Lord, do not hold this sin against them." When he had said this, he died.

The Response
Psalm 31:1-5, 15-16

Psalm 31:1-5, 15-16   *In te, Domine, speravi*

1   In you, O LORD, have I taken refuge;
        let me never be put to shame; *
            deliver me in your righteousness.
2   Incline your ear to me; *
        make haste to deliver me.
3   Be my strong rock, a castle to keep me safe,
        for you are my crag and my stronghold; *
            for the sake of your Name, lead me and guide me.
4   Take me out of the net that they have secretly set for me, *
        for you are my tower of strength.
5   Into your hands I commend my spirit, *
        for you have redeemed me,
        O LORD, O God of truth.
15   My times are in your hand; *
        rescue me from the hand of my enemies,
        and from those who persecute me.
16   Make your face to shine upon your servant, *
        and in your loving-kindness save me."

The Epistle
1 Peter 2:2-10

Like newborn infants, long for the pure, spiritual milk, so that by it you may grow into salvation — if indeed you have tasted that the Lord is good. Come to him, a living stone, though rejected by mortals yet chosen and precious in God's sight, and like living stones, let yourselves be built into a spiritual house, to be a holy priesthood, to offer spiritual sacrifices acceptable to God through Jesus Christ. For it stands in scripture: "See, I am laying in Zion a stone, a cornerstone chosen and precious; and whoever believes in him will not be put to shame." To you then who believe, he is precious; but for those who do not believe, "The stone that the builders rejected has become the very head of the corner," and "A stone that makes them stumble, and a rock that makes them fall." They stumble because they disobey the word, as they were destined to do. But you are a chosen race, a royal priesthood, a holy nation, God's own people, in order that you may proclaim the mighty acts of him who called you out of darkness into his marvelous light. Once you were not a people, but now you are God's people; once you had not received mercy, but now you have received mercy.

The Gospel John 14:1-14

Jesus said, "Do not let your hearts be troubled. Believe in God, believe also in me. In my Father's house there are many dwelling places. If it were not so, would I have told you that I go to prepare a place for you? And if I go and prepare a place for you, I will come again and will take you to myself, so that where I am, there you may be also. And you know the way to the place where I am going." Thomas said to him, "Lord, we do not know where you are going. How can we know the way?" Jesus said to him, "I am the way, and the truth, and the life. No one comes to the Father except through me. If you know me, you will know my Father also. From now on you do know him and have seen him." Philip said to him, "Lord, show us the Father, and we will be satisfied." Jesus said to him, "Have I been with you all this time, Philip, and you still do not know me? Whoever has seen me has seen the Father. How can you say, 'Show us the Father'? Do you not believe that I am in the Father and the Father is in me? The words that I say to you I do not speak on my own; but the Father who dwells in me does his works. Believe me that I am in the Father and the Father is in me; but if you do not, then believe me because of the works themselves. Very truly, I tell you, the one who believes in me will also do the works that I do and, in fact, will do greater works than these because I am going to the Father. I will do whatever you ask in my name, so that the Father may be glorified in the Son. If in my name you ask me for anything, I will do it."

Year B

Acts 8:26-40
Psalm 22:24-30
1 John 4:7-21
John 15:1-8

The Lesson   **Acts 8:26-40**

An angel of the Lord said to Philip, "Get up and go toward the south to the road that goes down from Jerusalem to Gaza." (This is a wilderness road.) So he got up and went. Now there was an Ethiopian eunuch, a court official of the Candace, queen of the Ethiopians, in charge of her entire treasury. He had come to Jerusalem to worship and was returning home; seated in his chariot, he was reading the prophet Isaiah. Then the Spirit said to Philip, "Go over to this chariot and join it." So Philip ran up to it and heard him reading the prophet Isaiah. He asked, "Do you understand what you are reading?" He replied, "How can I, unless someone guides me?" And he invited Philip to get in and sit beside him. Now the passage of the scripture that he was reading was this: "Like a sheep he was led to the slaughter, and like a lamb silent before its shearer, so he does not open his mouth. In his humiliation justice was denied him. Who can describe his generation? For his life is taken away from the earth." The eunuch asked Philip, "About whom, may I ask you, does the prophet say this, about himself or about someone else?" Then Philip began to speak, and starting with this scripture, he proclaimed to him the good news about Jesus. As they were going along the road, they came to some water; and the eunuch said, "Look, here is water! What is to prevent me from being baptized?" He commanded the chariot to stop, and both of them, Philip and the eunuch, went down into the water, and Philip baptized him. When they came up out of the water, the Spirit of the Lord snatched Philip away; the eunuch saw him no more, and went on his way rejoicing. But Philip found himself at Azotus, and as he was passing through the region, he proclaimed the good news to all the towns until he came to Caesarea.

The Response   **Psalm 22:24-30**

Psalm 22:24-30   *Deus, Deus meus*

24   My praise is of him in the great assembly; *
         I will perform my vows in the presence of those who
                  worship him.
25   The poor shall eat and be satisfied,
         and those who seek the LORD shall praise him: *
              "May your heart live for ever!"
26   All the ends of the earth shall remember and turn to
                  the LORD, *
         and all the families of the nations shall bow before him.

27   For kingship belongs to the Lord; *
        he rules over the nations.
28   To him alone all who sleep in the earth bow down
                    in worship; *
        all who go down to the dust fall before him.
29   My soul shall live for him;
        my descendants shall serve him; *
        they shall be known as the Lord's for ever.
30   They shall come and make known to a people yet unborn *
        the saving deeds that he has done.

The Epistle   1 John 4:7-21

Beloved, let us love one another, because love is from God; everyone who
loves is born of God and knows God. Whoever does not love does not know
God, for God is love. God's love was revealed among us in this way: God sent
his only Son into the world so that we might live through him. In this is love,
not that we loved God but that he loved us and sent his Son to be the atoning
sacrifice for our sins. Beloved, since God loved us so much, we also ought to
love one another. No one has ever seen God; if we love one another, God lives
in us, and his love is perfected in us. By this we know that we abide in him
and he in us, because he has given us of his Spirit. And we have seen and do
testify that the Father has sent his Son as the Savior of the world. God abides
in those who confess that Jesus is the Son of God, and they abide in God. So
we have known and believe the love that God has for us. God is love, and
those who abide in love abide in God, and God abides in them. Love has been
perfected among us in this: that we may have boldness on the day of judgment, because as he is, so are we in this world. There is no fear in love, but
perfect love casts out fear; for fear has to do with punishment, and whoever
fears has not reached perfection in love. We love because he first loved us.
Those who say, "I love God," and hate their brothers or sisters, are liars; for
those who do not love a brother or sister whom they have seen, cannot love
God whom they have not seen. The commandment we have from him is this:
those who love God must love their brothers and sisters also.

The Gospel   John 15:1-8

Jesus said, "I am the true vine, and my Father is the vinegrower. He removes
every branch in me that bears no fruit. Every branch that bears fruit he prunes
to make it bear more fruit. You have already been cleansed by the word that I
have spoken to you. Abide in me as I abide in you. Just as the branch cannot
bear fruit by itself unless it abides in the vine, neither can you unless you
abide in me. I am the vine, you are the branches. Those who abide in me and I
in them bear much fruit, because apart from me you can do nothing. Whoever

does not abide in me is thrown away like a branch and withers; such branches are gathered, thrown into the fire, and burned. If you abide in me, and my words abide in you, ask for whatever you wish, and it will be done for you. My Father is glorified by this, that you bear much fruit and become my disciples.

Year C
Acts 11:1-18
Psalm 148
Revelation 21:1-6
John 13:31-35

The Lesson   Acts 11:1-18

Now the apostles and the believers who were in Judea heard that the Gentiles had also accepted the word of God. So when Peter went up to Jerusalem, the circumcised believers criticized him, saying, "Why did you go to uncircumcised men and eat with them?" Then Peter began to explain it to them, step by step, saying, "I was in the city of Joppa praying, and in a trance I saw a vision. There was something like a large sheet coming down from heaven, being lowered by its four corners; and it came close to me. As I looked at it closely I saw four-footed animals, beasts of prey, reptiles, and birds of the air. I also heard a voice saying to me, 'Get up, Peter; kill and eat.' But I replied, 'By no means, Lord; for nothing profane or unclean has ever entered my mouth.' But a second time the voice answered from heaven, 'What God has made clean, you must not call profane.' This happened three times; then everything was pulled up again to heaven. At that very moment three men, sent to me from Caesarea, arrived at the house where we were. The Spirit told me to go with them and not to make a distinction between them and us. These six brothers also accompanied me, and we entered the man's house. He told us how he had seen the angel standing in his house and saying, 'Send to Joppa and bring Simon, who is called Peter; he will give you a message by which you and your entire household will be saved.' And as I began to speak, the Holy Spirit fell upon them just as it had upon us at the beginning. And I remembered the word of the Lord, how he had said, 'John baptized with water, but you will be baptized with the Holy Spirit.' If then God gave them the same gift that he gave us when we believed in the Lord Jesus Christ, who was I that I could hinder God?" When they heard this, they were silenced. And they praised God, saying, "Then God has given even to the Gentiles the repentance that leads to life."

Psalm 148   *Laudate Dominum*

1   Hallelujah!
      Praise the LORD from the heavens; *
         praise him in the heights.

2   Praise him, all you angels of his; *
         praise him, all his host.

3   Praise him, sun and moon; *
         praise him, all you shining stars.

4   Praise him, heaven of heavens, *
         and you waters above the heavens.

5   Let them praise the Name of the LORD; *
         for he commanded, and they were created.

6   He made them stand fast for ever and ever; *
         he gave them a law which shall not pass away.

7   Praise the LORD from the earth, *
         you sea-monsters and all deeps;

8   Fire and hail, snow and fog, *
         tempestuous wind, doing his will;

9   Mountains and all hills, *
         fruit trees and all cedars;

10   Wild beasts and all cattle, *
         creeping things and winged birds;

11   Kings of the earth and all peoples, *
         princes and all rulers of the world;

12   Young men and maidens, *
         old and young together.

13   Let them praise the Name of the LORD, *
         for his Name only is exalted,
         his splendor is over earth and heaven.

14   He has raised up strength for his people
      and praise for all his loyal servants, *
         the children of Israel, a people who are near him.
         Hallelujah!

The Epistle   **Revelation 21:1-6**

I, John, saw a new heaven and a new earth; for the first heaven and the first
earth had passed away, and the sea was no more. And I saw the holy city, the
new Jerusalem, coming down out of heaven from God, prepared as a bride
adorned for her husband. And I heard a loud voice from the throne saying,
"See, the home of God is among mortals. He will dwell with them as their
God; they will be his peoples, and God himself will be with them; he will wipe

every tear from their eyes. Death will be no more; mourning and crying and pain will be no more, for the first things have passed away." And the one who was seated on the throne said, "See, I am making all things new." Also he said, "Write this, for these words are trustworthy and true." Then he said to me, "It is done! I am the Alpha and the Omega, the beginning and the end. To the thirsty I will give water as a gift from the spring of the water of life."

The Gospel   John 13:31-35

At the last supper, when Judas had gone out, Jesus said, "Now the Son of Man has been glorified, and God has been glorified in him. If God has been glorified in him, God will also glorify him in himself and will glorify him at once. Little children, I am with you only a little longer. You will look for me; and as I said to the Jews so now I say to you, 'Where I am going, you cannot come.' I give you a new commandment, that you love one another. Just as I have loved you, you also should love one another. By this everyone will know that you are my disciples, if you have love for one another."

SIXTH SUNDAY OF EASTER

The Collect

O God, you have prepared for those who love you such good things as surpass our understanding: Pour into our hearts such love towards you, that we, loving you in all things and above all things, may obtain your promises, which exceed all that we can desire; through Jesus Christ our Lord, who lives and reigns with you and the Holy Spirit, one God, for ever and ever. *Amen.*

Year A
Acts 17:22-31
Psalm 66:7-18
1 Peter 3:13-22
John 14:15-21

The Lesson   Acts 17:22-31

Paul stood in front of the Areopagus and said, "Athenians, I see how extremely religious you are in every way. For as I went through the city and looked carefully at the objects of your worship, I found among them an altar with the inscription, 'To an unknown god.' What therefore you worship as unknown, this I proclaim to you. The God who made the world and everything in it, he who is Lord of heaven and earth, does not live in shrines made by human hands, nor is he served by human hands, as though he needed anything, since he himself gives to all mortals life and breath and all things. From one ancestor he made all nations to inhabit the whole earth, and he allotted the times of their existence and the boundaries of the places where they would live, so that they would search for God and perhaps grope for him and find him—though indeed he is not far from each one of us. For 'In him we live and move and have our being'; as even some of your own poets have said, 'For we too are his offspring.' Since we are God's offspring, we ought not to think that the deity is like gold, or silver, or stone, an image formed by the art and imagination of mortals. While God has overlooked the times of human ignorance, now he commands all people everywhere to repent, because he has fixed a day on which he will have the world judged in righteousness by a man whom he has appointed, and of this he has given assurance to all by raising him from the dead."

The Response   Psalm 66:7-18

Psalm 66:7-18   *Jubilate Deo*

 7 Bless our God, you peoples; *
   make the voice of his praise to be heard;
 8 Who holds our souls in life, *
   and will not allow our feet to slip.
 9 For you, O God, have proved us; *
   you have tried us just as silver is tried.
 10 You brought us into the snare; *
   you laid heavy burdens upon our backs.
 11 You let enemies ride over our heads;
  we went through fire and water; *
   but you brought us out into a place of refreshment.
 12 I will enter your house with burnt-offerings
  and will pay you my vows, *
   which I promised with my lips
   and spoke with my mouth when I was in trouble.
 13 I will offer you sacrifices of fat beasts
  with the smoke of rams; *
   I will give you oxen and goats.
 14 Come and listen, all you who fear God, *
   and I will tell you what he has done for me.
 15 I called out to him with my mouth, *
   and his praise was on my tongue.
 16 If I had found evil in my heart, *
   the LORD would not have heard me;
 17 But in truth God has heard me; *
   he has attended to the voice of my prayer.
 18 Blessed be God, who has not rejected my prayer, *
   nor withheld his love from me.

The Epistle   1 Peter 3:13-22

Now who will harm you if you are eager to do what is good? But even if you
do suffer for doing what is right, you are blessed. Do not fear what they fear,
and do not be intimidated, but in your hearts sanctify Christ as Lord. Always
be ready to make your defense to anyone who demands from you an accounting for the hope that is in you; yet do it with gentleness and reverence. Keep
your conscience clear, so that, when you are maligned, those who abuse you
for your good conduct in Christ may be put to shame. For it is better to suffer
for doing good, if suffering should be God's will, than to suffer for doing evil.
For Christ also suffered for sins once for all, the righteous for the unrighteous,
in order to bring you to God. He was put to death in the flesh, but made alive
in the spirit, in which also he went and made a proclamation to the spirits in
prison, who in former times did not obey, when God waited patiently in the
days of Noah, during the building of the ark, in which a few, that is, eight
persons, were saved through water. And baptism, which this prefigured, now
saves you—not as a removal of dirt from the body, but as an appeal to God
for a good conscience, through the resurrection of Jesus Christ, who has gone
into heaven and is at the right hand of God, with angels, authorities, and
powers made subject to him.

The Gospel   John 14:15-21

Jesus said to his disciples, "If you love me, you will keep my commandments.
And I will ask the Father, and he will give you another Advocate, to be with
you forever. This is the Spirit of truth, whom the world cannot receive,
because it neither sees him nor knows him. You know him, because he abides
with you, and he will be in you. I will not leave you orphaned; I am coming to
you. In a little while the world will no longer see me, but you will see me;
because I live, you also will live. On that day you will know that I am in my
Father, and you in me, and I in you. They who have my commandments and
keep them are those who love me; and those who love me will be loved by my
Father, and I will love them and reveal myself to them."

Year B

Acts 10:44-48
Psalm 98
1 John 5:1-6
John 15:9-17

The Lesson   Acts 10:44-48

While Peter was still speaking, the Holy Spirit fell upon all who heard the
word. The circumcised believers who had come with Peter were astounded
that the gift of the Holy Spirit had been poured out even on the Gentiles, for
they heard them speaking in tongues and extolling God. Then Peter said, "Can

anyone withhold the water for baptizing these people who have received the Holy Spirit just as we have?" So he ordered them to be baptized in the name of Jesus Christ. Then they invited him to stay for several days.

The Response   Psalm 98

Psalm 98   *Cantate Domino*

1   Sing to the LORD a new song, *
    for he has done marvelous things.
2   With his right hand and his holy arm *
    has he won for himself the victory.
3   The LORD has made known his victory; *
    his righteousness has he openly shown in
        the sight of the nations.
4   He remembers his mercy and faithfulness to
        the house of Israel, *
    and all the ends of the earth have seen the
        victory of our God.
5   Shout with joy to the LORD, all you lands; *
    lift up your voice, rejoice, and sing.
6   Sing to the LORD with the harp, *
    with the harp and the voice of song.
7   With trumpets and the sound of the horn *
    shout with joy before the King, the LORD.
8   Let the sea make a noise and all that is in it, *
    the lands and those who dwell therein.
9   Let the rivers clap their hands, *
    and let the hills ring out with joy before the LORD,
    when he comes to judge the earth.
10   In righteousness shall he judge the world *
    and the peoples with equity.

The Epistle   1 John 5:1-6

Everyone who believes that Jesus is the Christ has been born of God, and everyone who loves the parent loves the child. By this we know that we love the children of God, when we love God and obey his commandments. For the love of God is this, that we obey his commandments. And his commandments are not burdensome, for whatever is born of God conquers the world. And this is the victory that conquers the world, our faith. Who is it that conquers the world but the one who believes that Jesus is the Son of God? This is the one who came by water and blood, Jesus Christ, not with the water only but with the water and the blood. And the Spirit is the one that testifies, for the Spirit is the truth.

The Gospel   **John 15:9-17**

Jesus said to his disciples, "As the Father has loved me, so I have loved you; abide in my love. If you keep my commandments, you will abide in my love, just as I have kept my Father's commandments and abide in his love. I have said these things to you so that my joy may be in you, and that your joy may be complete. This is my commandment, that you love one another as I have loved you. No one has greater love than this, to lay down one's life for one's friends. You are my friends if you do what I command you. I do not call you servants any longer, because the servant does not know what the master is doing; but I have called you friends, because I have made known to you everything that I have heard from my Father. You did not choose me but I chose you. And I appointed you to go and bear fruit, fruit that will last, so that the Father will give you whatever you ask him in my name. I am giving you these commands so that you may love one another."

Year C
Acts 16:9-15
Psalm 67
Revelation 21:10, 22—22:5
John 14:23-29 or *John 5:1-9*

The Lesson   **Acts 16:9-15**

During the night Paul had a vision: there stood a man of Macedonia pleading with him and saying, "Come over to Macedonia and help us." When he had seen the vision, we immediately tried to cross over to Macedonia, being convinced that God had called us to proclaim the good news to them. We set sail from Troas and took a straight course to Samothrace, the following day to Neapolis, and from there to Philippi, which is a leading city of the district of Macedonia and a Roman colony. We remained in this city for some days. On the sabbath day we went outside the gate by the river, where we supposed there was a place of prayer; and we sat down and spoke to the women who had gathered there. A certain woman named Lydia, a worshiper of God, was listening to us; she was from the city of Thyatira and a dealer in purple cloth. The Lord opened her heart to listen eagerly to what was said by Paul. When she and her household were baptized, she urged us, saying, "If you have judged me to be faithful to the Lord, come and stay at my home." And she prevailed upon us.

The Response   **Psalm 67**

Psalm 67   *Deus misereatur*

1   May God be merciful to us and bless us, *
      show us the light of his countenance and come to us.

2 Let your ways be known upon earth, *
    your saving health among all nations.
3 Let the peoples praise you, O God; *
    let all the peoples praise you.
4 Let the nations be glad and sing for joy, *
    for you judge the peoples with equity
    and guide all the nations upon earth.
5 Let the peoples praise you, O God; *
    let all the peoples praise you.
6 The earth has brought forth her increase; *
    may God, our own God, give us his blessing.
7 May God give us his blessing, *
    and may all the ends of the earth stand in awe of him.

The Epistle   **Revelation 21:10, 22—22:5**

In the spirit the angel carried me away to a great, high mountain and showed me the holy city Jerusalem coming down out of heaven from God. I saw no temple in the city, for its temple is the Lord God the Almighty and the Lamb. And the city has no need of sun or moon to shine on it, for the glory of God is its light, and its lamp is the Lamb. The nations will walk by its light, and the kings of the earth will bring their glory into it. Its gates will never be shut by day—and there will be no night there. People will bring into it the glory and the honor of the nations. But nothing unclean will enter it, nor anyone who practices abomination or falsehood, but only those who are written in the Lamb's book of life. Then the angel showed me the river of the water of life, bright as crystal, flowing from the throne of God and of the Lamb through the middle of the street of the city. On either side of the river, is the tree of life with its twelve kinds of fruit, producing its fruit each month; and the leaves of the tree are for the healing of the nations. Nothing accursed will be found there any more. But the throne of God and of the Lamb will be in it, and his servants will worship him; they will see his face, and his name will be on their foreheads. And there will be no more night; they need no light of lamp or sun, for the Lord God will be their light, and they will reign forever and ever.

The Gospel   **John 14:23-29** *or* **John 5:1-9**
John 14:23-29

Jesus said to Judas (not Iscariot), "Those who love me will keep my word, and my Father will love them, and we will come to them and make our home with them. Whoever does not love me does not keep my words; and the word that you hear is not mine, but is from the Father who sent me. I have said these things to you while I am still with you. But the Advocate, the Holy Spirit, whom the Father will send in my name, will teach you everything, and remind you of all that I have said to you. Peace I leave with you; my peace I give to you. I do not give to you as the world gives. Do not let your hearts be troubled, and do not let them be afraid. You heard me say to you, 'I am going away, and I am coming to you.' If you loved me, you would rejoice that I am going to the Father, because the Father is greater than I. And now I have told you this before it occurs, so that when it does occur, you may believe."

or, **John 5:1-9**

After Jesus healed the son of the royal official, there was a festival of the Jews, and Jesus went up to Jerusalem. Now in Jerusalem by the Sheep Gate there is a pool, called in Hebrew Beth-zatha, which has five porticoes. In these lay many invalids—blind, lame, and paralyzed. One man was there who had been ill for thirty-eight years. When Jesus saw him lying there and knew that he had been there a long time, he said to him, "Do you want to be made well?" The sick man answered him, "Sir, I have no one to put me into the pool when the water is stirred up; and while I am making my way, someone else steps down ahead of me." Jesus said to him, "Stand up, take your mat and walk." At once the man was made well, and he took up his mat and began to walk. Now that day was a sabbath.

ASCENSION DAY

The Collect

Almighty God, whose blessed Son our Savior Jesus Christ ascended far above all heavens that he might fill all things: Mercifully give us faith to perceive that, according to his promise, he abides with his Church on earth, even to the end of the ages; through Jesus Christ our Lord, who lives and reigns with you and the Holy Spirit, one God, in glory everlasting. *Amen.*

or this

Grant, we pray, Almighty God, that as we believe your only-begotten Son our Lord Jesus Christ to have ascended into heaven, so we may also in heart and mind there ascend, and with him continually dwell; who lives and reigns with you and the Holy Spirit, one God, for ever and ever. *Amen.*

Years A, B, and C
Acts 1:1-11
Psalm 47 or *Psalm 93*
Ephesians 1:15-23
Luke 24:44-53

The Lesson   **Acts 1:1-11**

In the first book, Theophilus, I wrote about all that Jesus did and taught from
the beginning until the day when he was taken up to heaven, after giving
instructions through the Holy Spirit to the apostles whom he had chosen. After
his suffering he presented himself alive to them by many convincing proofs,
appearing to them during forty days and speaking about the kingdom of God.
While staying with them, he ordered them not to leave Jerusalem, but to wait
there for the promise of the Father. "This," he said, "is what you have heard
from me; for John baptized with water, but you will be baptized with the Holy
Spirit not many days from now." So when they had come together, they asked
him, "Lord, is this the time when you will restore the kingdom to Israel?" He
replied, "It is not for you to know the times or periods that the Father has set
by his own authority. But you will receive power when the Holy Spirit has
come upon you; and you will be my witnesses in Jerusalem, in all Judea and
Samaria, and to the end of the earth." When he had said this, as they were
watching, he was lifted up, and a cloud took him out of their sight. While he
was going and they were gazing up toward heaven, suddenly two men in white
robes stood by them. They said, "Men of Galilee, why do you stand looking
up toward heaven? This Jesus, who has been taken up from you into heaven,
will come in the same way as you saw him go into heaven."

The Response   **Psalm 47** *or* **Psalm 93**

Psalm 47   *Omnes gentes, plaudite*

1   Clap your hands, all you peoples; *
        shout to God with a cry of joy.
2   For the LORD Most High is to be feared; *
        he is the great King over all the earth.
3   He subdues the peoples under us, *
        and the nations under our feet.
4   He chooses our inheritance for us, *
        the pride of Jacob whom he loves.
5   God has gone up with a shout, *
        the LORD with the sound of the ram's-horn.
6   Sing praises to God, sing praises; *
        sing praises to our King, sing praises.
7   For God is King of all the earth; *
        sing praises with all your skill.
8   God reigns over the nations; *
        God sits upon his holy throne.
9   The nobles of the peoples have gathered together *
        with the people of the God of Abraham.
10 The rulers of the earth belong to God, *
        and he is highly exalted.

or, **Psalm 93** *Dominus regnavit*

1 The LORD is King;
   he has put on splendid apparel; *
      the LORD has put on his apparel
      and girded himself with strength.

2 He has made the whole world so sure *
      that it cannot be moved;

3 Ever since the world began, your throne has been established; *
      you are from everlasting.

4 The waters have lifted up, O LORD,
   the waters have lifted up their voice; *
      the waters have lifted up their pounding waves.

5 Mightier than the sound of many waters,
   mightier than the breakers of the sea, *
      mightier is the LORD who dwells on high.

6 Your testimonies are very sure, *
      and holiness adorns your house, O LORD,
      for ever and for evermore.

The Epistle   **Ephesians 1:15-23**

I have heard of your faith in the Lord Jesus and your love toward all the
saints, and for this reason I do not cease to give thanks for you as I remember
you in my prayers. I pray that the God of our Lord Jesus Christ, the Father of
glory, may give you a spirit of wisdom and revelation as you come to know
him, so that, with the eyes of your heart enlightened, you may know what is
the hope to which he has called you, what are the riches of his glorious
inheritance among the saints, and what is the immeasurable greatness of his
power for us who believe, according to the working of his great power. God
put this power to work in Christ when he raised him from the dead and seated
him at his right hand in the heavenly places, far above all rule and authority
and power and dominion, and above every name that is named, not only in this
age but also in the age to come. And he has put all things under his feet and
has made him the head over all things for the church, which is his body, the
fullness of him who fills all in all.

The Gospel   **Luke 24:44-53**

Jesus said to his disciples, "These are my words that I spoke to you while I
was still with you—that everything written about me in the law of Moses, the
prophets, and the psalms must be fulfilled." Then he opened their minds to
understand the scriptures, and he said to them, "Thus it is written, that the
Messiah is to suffer and to rise from the dead on the third day, and that
repentance and forgiveness of sins is to be proclaimed in his name to all

nations, beginning from Jerusalem. You are witnesses of these things. I am sending upon you what my Father promised; so stay here in the city until you have been clothed with power from on high." Then he led them out as far as Bethany, and, lifting up his hands, he blessed them. While he was blessing them, he withdrew from them and was carried up into heaven. And they worshiped him, and returned to Jerusalem with great joy; and they were continually in the temple blessing God.

SEVENTH SUNDAY OF EASTER

The Collect

O God, the King of glory, you have exalted your only Son Jesus Christ with great triumph to your kingdom in heaven: Do not leave us comfortless, but send us your Holy Spirit to strengthen us, and exalt us to that place where our Savior Christ has gone before; who lives and reigns with you and the Holy Spirit, one God, in glory everlasting. *Amen.*

Year A

Acts 1:6-14
Psalm 68:1-10, 33-36
1 Peter 4:12-14; 5:6-11
John 17:1-11

The Lesson   Acts 1:6-14

When the apostles had come together, they asked Jesus, "Lord, is this the time when you will restore the kingdom to Israel?" He replied, "It is not for you to know the times or periods that the Father has set by his own authority. But you will receive power when the Holy Spirit has come upon you; and you will be my witnesses in Jerusalem, in all Judea and Samaria, and to the ends of the earth." When he had said this, as they were watching, he was lifted up, and a cloud took him out of their sight. While he was going and they were gazing up toward heaven, suddenly two men in white robes stood by them. They said, "Men of Galilee, why do you stand looking up toward heaven? This Jesus, who has been taken up from you into heaven, will come in the same way as you saw him go into heaven." Then they returned to Jerusalem from the mount called Olivet, which is near Jerusalem, a sabbath day's journey away. When they had entered the city, they went to the room upstairs where they were staying, Peter, and John, and James, and Andrew, Philip and Thomas, Bartholomew and Matthew, James son of Alphaeus, and Simon the Zealot, and Judas son of James. All these were constantly devoting themselves to prayer, together with certain women, including Mary the mother of Jesus, as well as his brothers.

The Response   **Psalm 68:1-10, 33-36**

Psalm 68:1-10, 33-36   *Exsurgat Deus*

1   Let God arise, and let his enemies be scattered; *
    let those who hate him flee before him.

2   Let them vanish like smoke when the wind drives it away; *
    as the wax melts at the fire, so let the wicked perish at
                          the presence of God.

3   But let the righteous be glad and rejoice before God; *
    let them also be merry and joyful.

4   Sing to God, sing praises to his Name;
    exalt him who rides upon the heavens; *
    Yahweh is his Name, rejoice before him!

5   Father of orphans, defender of widows, *
    God in his holy habitation!

6   God gives the solitary a home and brings forth prisoners
                          into freedom; *
    but the rebels shall live in dry places.

7   O God, when you went forth before your people, *
    when you marched through the wilderness,

8   The earth shook, and the skies poured down rain,
    at the presence of God, the God of Sinai, *
    at the presence of God, the God of Israel.

9   You sent a gracious rain, O God, upon your inheritance; *
    you refreshed the land when it was weary.

10 Your people found their home in it; *
    in your goodness, O God, you have made provision
                          for the poor.

33 Sing to God, O kingdoms of the earth; *
    sing praises to the LORD.

34 He rides in the heavens, the ancient heavens; *
    he sends forth his voice, his mighty voice.

35 Ascribe power to God; *
    his majesty is over Israel;
    his strength is in the skies.

36 How wonderful is God in his holy places! *
    the God of Israel giving strength and power to his people!
    Blessed be God!

The Epistle   **1 Peter 4:12-14; 5:6-11**

Beloved, do not be surprised at the fiery ordeal that is taking place among you
to test you, as though something strange were happening to you. But rejoice
insofar as you are sharing Christ's sufferings, so that you may also be glad

and shout for joy when his glory is revealed. If you are reviled for the name of Christ, you are blessed, because the spirit of glory, which is the Spirit of God, is resting on you. Humble yourselves therefore under the mighty hand of God, so that he may exalt you in due time. Cast all your anxiety on him, because he cares for you. Discipline yourselves, keep alert. Like a roaring lion your adversary the devil prowls around, looking for someone to devour. Resist him, steadfast in your faith, for you know that your brothers and sisters in all the world are undergoing the same kinds of suffering. And after you have suffered for a little while, the God of all grace, who has called you to his eternal glory in Christ, will himself restore, support, strengthen, and establish you. To him be the power forever and ever. Amen.

The Gospel   John 17:1-11

Jesus looked up to heaven and said, "Father, the hour has come; glorify your Son so that the Son may glorify you, since you have given him authority over all people, to give eternal life to all whom you have given him. And this is eternal life, that they may know you, the only true God, and Jesus Christ whom you have sent. I glorified you on earth by finishing the work that you gave me to do. So now, Father, glorify me in your own presence with the glory that I had in your presence before the world existed. I have made your name known to those whom you gave me from the world. They were yours, and you gave them to me, and they have kept your word. Now they know that every-thing you have given me is from you; for the words that you gave to me I have given to them, and they have received them and know in truth that I came from you; and they have believed that you sent me. I am asking on their behalf; I am not asking on behalf of the world, but on behalf of those whom you gave me, because they are yours. All mine are yours, and yours are mine; and I have been glorified in them. And now I am no longer in the world, but they are in the world, and I am coming to you. Holy Father, protect them in your name that you have given me, so that they may be one, as we are one."

Year B
Acts 1:15-17, 21-26
Psalm 1
1 John 5:9-13
John 17:6-19

The Lesson   Acts 1:15-17, 21-26

In the days following the Ascension, Peter stood up among the believers (together the crowd numbered about one hundred twenty persons) and said, "Friends, the scripture had to be fulfilled, which the Holy Spirit through

David foretold concerning Judas, who became a guide for those who arrested Jesus—for he was numbered among us and was allotted his share in this ministry. So one of the men who have accompanied us during all the time that the Lord Jesus went in and out among us, beginning from the baptism of John until the day when he was taken up from us—one of these must become a witness with us to his resurrection." So they proposed two, Joseph called Barsabbas, who was also known as Justus, and Matthias. Then they prayed and said, "Lord, you know everyone's heart. Show us which one of these two you have chosen to take the place in this ministry and apostleship from which Judas turned aside to go to his own place." And they cast lots for them, and the lot fell on Matthias; and he was added to the eleven apostles.

The Response   Psalm 1

Psalm 1   *Beatus vir qui non abiit*

1   Happy are they who have not walked in the counsel of
             the wicked, *
          nor lingered in the way of sinners,
          nor sat in the seats of the scornful!
2   Their delight is in the law of the LORD, *
          and they meditate on his law day and night.
3   They are like trees planted by streams of water,
          bearing fruit in due season, with leaves that do not wither; *
          everything they do shall prosper.
4   It is not so with the wicked; *
          they are like chaff which the wind blows away.
5   Therefore the wicked shall not stand upright when
             judgment comes, *
          nor the sinner in the council of the righteous.
6   For the LORD knows the way of the righteous, *
          but the way of the wicked is doomed.

The Epistle   1 John 5:9-13

If we receive human testimony, the testimony of God is greater; for this is the testimony of God that he has testified to his Son. Those who believe in the Son of God have the testimony in their hearts. Those who do not believe in God have made him a liar by not believing in the testimony that God has given concerning his Son. And this is the testimony: God gave us eternal life, and this life is in his Son. Whoever has the Son has life; whoever does not have the Son of God does not have life. I write these things to you who believe in the name of the Son of God, so that you may know that you have eternal life.

The Gospel   John 17:6-19

Jesus prayed, "I have made your name known to those whom you gave me from the world. They were yours, and you gave them to me, and they have kept your word. Now they know that everything you have given me is from you; for the words that you gave to me I have given to them, and they have received them and know in truth that I came from you; and they have believed that you sent me. I am asking on their behalf; I am not asking on behalf of the world, but on behalf of those whom you gave me, because they are yours. All mine are yours, and yours are mine; and I have been glorified in them. And now I am no longer in the world, but they are in the world, and I am coming to you. Holy Father, protect them in your name that you have given me, so that they may be one, as we are one. While I was with them, I protected them in your name that you have given me. I guarded them, and not one of them was lost except the one destined to be lost, so that the scripture might be fulfilled. But now I am coming to you, and I speak these things in the world so that they may have my joy made complete in themselves. I have given them your word, and the world has hated them because they do not belong to the world, just as I do not belong to the world. I am not asking you to take them out of the world, but I ask you to protect them from the evil one. They do not belong to the world, just as I do not belong to the world. Sanctify them in the truth; your word is truth. As you have sent me into the world, so I have sent them into the world. And for their sakes I sanctify myself, so that they also may be sanctified in truth."

Year C
Acts 16:16-34
Psalm 97
Revelation 22:12-14, 16-17, 20-21
John 17:20-26

The Lesson   Acts 16:16-34

One day, as we (Paul and his traveling companions) were going to the place of prayer, we met a slave girl who had a spirit of divination and brought her owners a great deal of money by fortune-telling. While she followed Paul and us, she would cry out, "These men are slaves of the Most High God, who proclaim to you a way of salvation." She kept doing this for many days. But Paul, very much annoyed, turned and said to the spirit, "I order you in the name of Jesus Christ to come out of her." And it came out that very hour. But when her owners saw that their hope of making money was gone, they seized Paul and Silas and dragged them into the marketplace before the authorities. When they had brought them before the magistrates, they said, "These men are disturbing our city; they are Jews and are advocating customs that are not lawful for us as Romans to adopt or observe." The crowd joined in attacking them, and the magistrates had them stripped of their clothing and ordered them to be beaten with rods. After they had given them a severe flogging, they threw them into prison and ordered the jailer to keep them securely. Following these instructions, he put them in the innermost cell and fastened their feet in the stocks. About midnight Paul and Silas were praying and singing hymns to God, and the prisoners were listening to them. Suddenly there was an earthquake, so violent that the foundations of the prison were shaken; and immediately all the doors were opened and everyone's chains were unfastened. When the jailer woke up and saw the prison doors wide open, he drew his sword and was about to kill himself, since he supposed that the prisoners had escaped. But Paul shouted in a loud voice, "Do not harm yourself, for we are all here." The jailer called for lights, and rushing in, he fell down trembling before Paul and Silas. Then he brought them outside and said, "Sirs, what must I do to be saved?" They answered, "Believe on the Lord Jesus, and you will be saved, you and your household." They spoke the word of the Lord to him and to all who were in his house. At the same hour of the night he took them and washed their wounds; then he and his entire family were baptized without delay. He brought them up into the house and set food before them; and he and his entire household rejoiced that he had become a believer in God.

The Response   Psalm 97

Psalm 97   *Dominus regnavit*

 1   The LORD is King;
      let the earth rejoice; *
          let the multitude of the isles be glad.
 2   Clouds and darkness are round about him, *
          righteousness and justice are the foundations of his throne.
 3   A fire goes before him *
          and burns up his enemies on every side.
 4   His lightnings light up the world; *
          the earth sees it and is afraid.
 5   The mountains melt like wax at the presence of the LORD, *
          at the presence of the LORD of the whole earth.
 6   The heavens declare his righteousness, *
          and all the peoples see his glory.
 7   Confounded be all who worship carved images
      and delight in false gods! *
          Bow down before him, all you gods.
 8   Zion hears and is glad, and the cities of Judah rejoice, *
          because of your judgments, O LORD.

9   For you are the LORD,
        most high over all the earth; *
            you are exalted far above all gods.

10 The LORD loves those who hate evil; *
        he preserves the lives of his saints
        and delivers them from the hand of the wicked.

11 Light has sprung up for the righteous, *
        and joyful gladness for those who are truehearted.

12 Rejoice in the LORD, you righteous, *
        and give thanks to his holy Name.

The Epistle   Revelation 22:12-14, 16-17, 20-21

Jesus said, "See, I am coming soon; my reward is with me, to repay according
to everyone's work. I am the Alpha and the Omega, the first and the last, the
beginning and the end." Blessed are those who wash their robes, so that they
will have the right to the tree of life and may enter the city by the gates. "It is
I, Jesus, who sent my angel to you with this testimony for the churches. I am
the root and the descendant of David, the bright morning star." The Spirit and
the bride say, "Come." And let everyone who hears say, "Come." And let
everyone who is thirsty come. Let anyone who wishes take the water of life as
a gift. The one who testifies to these things says, "Surely I am coming soon."
Amen. Come, Lord Jesus! The grace of the Lord Jesus be with all the saints.
Amen.

The Gospel   John 17:20-26

Jesus prayed for his disciples and then he said, "I ask not only on behalf of
these, but also on behalf of those who will believe in me through their word,
that they may all be one. As you, Father, are in me and I am in you, may they
also be in us, so that the world may believe that you have sent me. The glory
that you have given me I have given them, so that they may be one, as we are
one, I in them and you in me, that they may become completely one, so that
the world may know that you have sent me and have loved them even as you
have loved me. Father, I desire that those also, whom you have given me, may
be with me where I am, to see my glory, which you have given me because
you loved me before the foundation of the world. "Righteous Father, the world
does not know you, but I know you; and these know that you have sent me. I
made your name known to them, and I will make it known, so that the love
with which you have loved me may be in them, and I in them."

VIGIL OF PENTECOST

The Collect

Almighty God, on this day you opened the way of eternal life to every race
and nation by the promised gift of your Holy Spirit: Shed abroad this gift
throughout the world by the preaching of the Gospel, that it may reach to the
ends of the earth; through Jesus Christ our Lord, who lives and reigns with
you, in the unity of the Holy Spirit, one God, for ever and ever. *Amen.*

or this

O God, who on this day taught the hearts of your faithful people by sending to
them the light of your Holy Spirit: Grant us by the same Spirit to have a right
judgment in all things, and evermore to rejoice in his holy comfort; through
Jesus Christ your Son our Lord, who lives and reigns with you, in the unity of
the Holy Spirit, one God, for ever and ever. *Amen.*

Early or Vigil Service
Years A, B, and C
Genesis 11:1-9 and Psalm 33:12-22
or *Exodus 19:1-9a, 16-20a; 20:18-20 and Canticle 2 or 13*
or *Ezekiel 37:1-14 and Psalm 130*
or *Joel 2:28-32 and Canticle 9*
Acts 2:1-11 or Romans 8:14-17, 22-27 and Psalm 104:25-32
John 7:37-39a

The Lesson   **Genesis 11:1-9**

Now the whole earth had one language and the same words. And as they
migrated from the east, they came upon a plain in the land of Shinar and
settled there. And they said to one another, "Come, let us make bricks, and
burn them thoroughly." And they had brick for stone, and bitumen for mortar.
Then they said, "Come, let us build ourselves a city, and a tower with its top
in the heavens, and let us make a name for ourselves; otherwise we shall be
scattered abroad upon the face of the whole earth." The LORD came down to
see the city and the tower, which mortals had built. And the LORD said, "Look,
they are one people, and they have all one language; and this is only the
beginning of what they will do; nothing that they propose to do will now be
impossible for them. Come, let us go down, and confuse their language there,
so that they will not understand one another's speech." So the LORD scattered
them abroad from there over the face of all the earth, and they left off building
the city. Therefore it was called Babel, because there the LORD confused the

language of all the earth; and from there the LORD scattered them abroad over the face of all the earth.

The Response   Psalm 33:12-22

Psalm 33:12-22   *Exultate, justi*

12   Happy is the nation whose God is the LORD! *
          happy the people he has chosen to be his own!
13   The LORD looks down from heaven, *
          and beholds all the people in the world.
14   From where he sits enthroned he turns his gaze *
          on all who dwell on the earth.
15   He fashions all the hearts of them *
          and understands all their works.
16   There is no king that can be saved by a mighty army;
          a strong man is not delivered by his great strength.
17   The horse is a vain hope for deliverance; *
          for all its strength it cannot save.
18   Behold, the eye of the LORD is upon those who fear him, *
          on those who wait upon his love,
19   To pluck their lives from death, *
          and to feed them in time of famine.
20   Our soul waits for the LORD; *
          he is our help and our shield.
21   Indeed, our heart rejoices in him, *
          for in his holy Name we put our trust.
22   Let your loving-kindness, O LORD, be upon us, *
          as we have put our trust in you.

or, **Exodus 19:1-9a, 16-20a; 20:18-20**

On the third new moon after the Israelites had gone out of the land of Egypt, on that very day, they came into the wilderness of Sinai. They had journeyed from Rephidim, entered the wilderness of Sinai, and camped in the wilderness; Israel camped there in front of the mountain. Then Moses went up to God; the LORD called to him from the mountain, saying, "Thus you shall say to the house of Jacob, and tell the Israelites: You have seen what I did to the Egyptians, and how I bore you on eagles' wings and brought you to myself. Now therefore, if you obey my voice and keep my covenant, you shall be my treasured possession out of all the peoples. Indeed, the whole earth is mine, but you shall be for me a priestly kingdom and a holy nation. These are the words that you shall speak to the Israelites." So Moses came, summoned the elders of the people, and set before them all these words that the Lord had commanded him. The people all answered as one: "Everything that the LORD has spoken we will do." Moses reported the words of the people to the LORD. Then the LORD said to Moses, "I am going to come to you in a dense cloud, in order that the people may hear when I speak with you and so trust you ever after." On the morning of the third day there was thunder and lightning, as well as a thick cloud on the mountain, and a blast of a trumpet so loud that all the people who were in the camp trembled. Moses brought the people out of the camp to meet God. They took their stand at the foot of the mountain. Now Mount Sinai was wrapped in smoke, because the LORD had descended upon it in fire; the smoke went up like the smoke of a kiln, while the whole mountain shook violently. As the blast of the trumpet grew louder and louder, Moses would speak and God would answer him in thunder. When the LORD descended upon Mount Sinai, all the people witnessed the thunder and lightning, the sound of the trumpet, and the mountain smoking, they were afraid and trembled and stood at a distance, and said to Moses, "You speak to us, and we will listen; but do not let God speak to us, or we will die." Moses said to the people, "Do not be afraid; for God has come only to test you and to put the fear of him upon you so that you do not sin."

The Response   **Canticle 2** or **13**
Canticle 2   *(Page 49 BCP)*

Canticle 13   A Song of Praise   *Benedictus es, Domine*
Song of the Three Young Men, 29-34

Glory to you, Lord God of our fathers; *
    you are worthy of praise; glory to you.
Glory to you for the radiance of your holy Name; *
    we will praise you and highly exalt you for ever.
Glory to you in the splendor of your temple; *
    on the throne of your majesty, glory to you.
Glory to you, seated between the Cherubim; *
    we will praise you and highly exalt you for ever.
Glory to you, beholding the depths; *
    in the high vault of heaven, glory to you.
Glory to you, Father, Son, and Holy Spirit; *
    we will praise you and highly exalt you for ever.

or, Ezekiel 37:1-14

The hand of the LORD came upon me, and he brought me out by the spirit of the LORD and set me down in the middle of a valley; it was full of bones. He led me all around them; there were very many lying in the valley, and they were very dry. He said to me, "Mortal, can these bones live?" I answered, "O Lord GOD, you know." Then he said to me, "Prophesy to these bones, and say to them: O dry bones, hear the word of the LORD. Thus says the Lord GOD to these bones: I will cause breath to enter you, and you shall live. I will lay sinews on you, and will cause flesh to come upon you, and cover you with skin, and put breath in you, and you shall live; and you shall know that I am the LORD." So I prophesied as I had been commanded; and as I prophesied, suddenly there was a noise, a rattling, and the bones came together, bone to its bone. I looked, and there were sinews on them, and flesh had come upon them, and skin had covered them; but there was no breath in them. Then he said to me, "Prophesy to the breath, prophesy, mortal, and say to the breath: Thus says the Lord GOD: Come from the four winds, O breath, and breathe upon these slain, that they may live." I prophesied as he commanded me, and the breath came into them, and they lived, and stood on their feet, a vast multitude. Then he said to me, "Mortal, these bones are the whole house of Israel. They say, 'Our bones are dried up, and our hope is lost; we are cut off completely.' Therefore prophesy, and say to them, Thus says the Lord GOD: I am going to open your graves, and bring you up from your graves, O my people; and I will bring you back to the land of Israel. And you shall know that I am the LORD, when I open your graves, and bring you up from your graves, O my people. I will put my spirit within you, and you shall live, and I will place you on your own soil; then you shall know that I, the LORD, have spoken and will act," says the LORD.

The Response   Psalm 130
Psalm 130   *De profundis*

1   Out of the depths have I called to you, O LORD;
    LORD, hear my voice; *
        let your ears consider well the voice of my supplication.
2   If you, LORD, were to note what is done amiss, *
        O LORD, who could stand?
3   For there is forgiveness with you; *
        therefore you shall be feared.
4   I wait for the LORD; my soul waits for him; *
        in his word is my hope.
5   My soul waits for the LORD,
    more than watchmen for the morning, *
        more than watchmen for the morning.
6   O Israel, wait for the LORD, *
        for with the LORD there is mercy;
7   With him there is plenteous redemption, *
        and he shall redeem Israel from all their sins.

or, **Joel 2:28-32**

The Lᴏʀᴅ said: I will pour out my spirit on all flesh; your sons and your daughters shall prophesy, your old men shall dream dreams, and your young men shall see visions. Even on the male and female slaves, in those days, I will pour out my spirit. I will show portents in the heavens and on the earth, blood and fire and columns of smoke. The sun shall be turned to darkness, and the moon to blood, before the great and terrible day of the Lᴏʀᴅ comes. Then everyone who calls on the name of the Lord shall be saved; for in Mount Zion and in Jerusalem there shall be those who escape, as the Lord has said, and among the survivors shall be those whom the Lord calls.

The Response   **Canticle 9**

Canticle 9   The First Song of Isaiah   *Ecce, Deus*
                    Isaiah 12:2-6

Surely, it is God who saves me; *
    I will trust in him and not be afraid.
For the Lord is my stronghold and my sure defense, *
    and he will be my Savior.
Therefore you shall draw water with rejoicing *
    from the springs of salvation.
And on that day you shall say, *
    Give thanks to the Lord and call upon his Name;
Make his deeds known among the peoples; *
    see that they remember that his Name is exalted.
Sing the praises of the Lord, for he has done great things, *
    and this is known in all the world.
Cry aloud, inhabitants of Zion, ring out your joy, *
    for the great one in the midst of you is the Holy One of Israel.

or, **Acts 2-1-11**

When the day of Pentecost had come, they were all together in one place. And suddenly from heaven there came a sound like the rush of a violent wind, and it filled the entire house where they were sitting. Divided tongues, as of fire, appeared among them, and a tongue rested on each of them. All of them were filled with the Holy Spirit and began to speak in other languages, as the Spirit gave them ability. Now there were devout Jews from every nation under heaven living in Jerusalem. And at this sound the crowd gathered and was bewildered, because each one heard them speaking in the native language of each. Amazed and astonished, they asked, "Are not all these who are speaking Galileans? And how is it that we hear, each of us, in our own native language? Parthians, Medes, Elamites, and residents of Mesopotamia, Judea and Cappadocia, Pontus and Asia, Phrygia and Pamphylia, Egypt and the parts of

Libya belonging to Cyrene, and visitors from Rome, both Jews and proselytes, Cretans and Arabs—in our own languages we hear them speaking about God's deeds of power."

or, **Romans 8:14-17, 22-27**

All who are led by the Spirit of God are children of God. For you did not receive a spirit of slavery to fall back into fear, but you have received a spirit of adoption. When we cry, "Abba! Father!" it is that very Spirit bearing witness with our spirit that we are children of God, and if children, then heirs, heirs of God and joint heirs with Christ — if, in fact, we suffer with him so that we may also be glorified with him. We know that the whole creation has been groaning in labor pains until now; and not only the creation, but we ourselves, who have the first fruits of the Spirit, groan inwardly while we wait for adoption, the redemption of our bodies. For in hope we were saved. Now hope that is seen is not hope. For who hopes for what is seen? But if we hope for what we do not see, we wait for it with patience. Likewise the Spirit helps us in our weakness; for we do not know how to pray as we ought, but that very Spirit intercedes with sighs too deep for words. And God, who searches the heart, knows what is the mind of the Spirit, because the Spirit intercedes for the saints according to the will of God.

The Response   Psalm 104:25-32

Psalm 104:25-32 *Benedic, anima mea*

25   O LORD, how manifold are your works! *
             in wisdom you have made them all;
             the earth is full of your creatures.
26   Yonder is the great and wide sea
         with its living things too many to number, *
             creatures both small and great.
27   There move the ships,
         and there is that Leviathan, *
             which you have made for the sport of it.
28   All of them look to you *
             to give them their food in due season.
29   You give it to them; they gather it; *
             you open your hand, and they are filled with good things.
30   You hide your face, and they are terrified; *
             you take away their breath,
             and they die and return to their dust.
31   You send forth your Spirit, and they are created; *
             and so you renew the face of the earth.

32   May the glory of the LORD endure for ever; *
     may the LORD rejoice in all his works.

The Gospel   John 7:37-39*a*

On the last day of the festival, the great day, while Jesus was standing there,
he cried out, "Let anyone who is thirsty come to me, and let the one who
believes in me drink. As the scripture has said, 'Out of the believer's heart
shall flow rivers of living water.' " Now he said this about the Spirit, which
believers in him were to receive.

· DAY OF PENTECOST

The Collect

Almighty God, on this day you opened the way of eternal life to every race
and nation by the promised gift of your Holy Spirit: Shed abroad this gift
throughout the world by the preaching of the Gospel, that it may reach to the
ends of the earth; through Jesus Christ our Lord, who lives and reigns with
you, in the unity of the Holy Spirit, one God, for ever and ever. *Amen.*

or this

O God, who on this day taught the hearts of your faithful people by sending to
them the light of your Holy Spirit: Grant us by the same Spirit to have a right
judgment in all things, and evermore to rejoice in his holy comfort; through
Jesus Christ your Son our Lord, who lives and reigns with you, in the unity of
the Holy Spirit, one God, for ever and ever. *Amen.*

Year A

*(If the passage from Numbers is chosen for the First Reading, the passage from
Acts is used as the Second Reading.)*

Acts 2:1-21 or *Numbers 11:24-30*
*Psalm 104:25-35, 37*b
1 *Corinthians 12:3*b-13 or *Acts 2:1-21*
John 20:19-23 or *John 7:37-39*

The Lesson   Acts 2:1-21 or Numbers 11:24-30
Acts 2:1-21

When the day of Pentecost had come, they were all together in one place. And
suddenly from heaven there came a sound like the rush of a violent wind, and
it filled the entire house where they were sitting. Divided tongues, as of fire,
appeared among them, and a tongue rested on each of them. All of them were
filled with the Holy Spirit and began to speak in other languages, as the Spirit

gave them ability. Now there were devout Jews from every nation under heaven living in Jerusalem. And at this sound the crowd gathered and was bewildered, because each one heard them speaking in the native language of each. Amazed and astonished, they asked, "Are not all these who are speaking Galileans? And how is it that we hear, each of us, in our own native language? Parthians, Medes, Elamites, and residents of Mesopotamia, Judea and Cappadocia, Pontus and Asia, Phrygia and Pamphylia, Egypt and the parts of Libya belonging to Cyrene, and visitors from Rome, both Jews and proselytes, Cretans and Arabs—in our own languages we hear them speaking about God's deeds of power." All were amazed and perplexed, saying to one another, "What does this mean?" But others sneered and said, "They are filled with new wine." But Peter, standing with the eleven, raised his voice and addressed them, "Men of Judea and all who live in Jerusalem, let this be known to you, and listen to what I say. Indeed, these are not drunk, as you suppose, for it is only nine o'clock in the morning. No, this is what was spoken through the prophet Joel: 'In the last days it will be, God declares, that I will pour out my Spirit upon all flesh, and your sons and your daughters shall prophesy, and your young men shall see visions, and your old men shall dream dreams. Even upon my slaves, both men and women, in those days I will pour out my Spirit; and they shall prophesy. And I will show portents in the heaven above and signs on the earth below, blood, and fire, and smoky mist. The sun shall be turned to darkness and the moon to blood, before the coming of the Lord's great and glorious day. Then everyone who calls on the name of the Lord shall be saved.' "

or, **Numbers 11:24-30**

Moses went out and told the people the words of the LORD; and he gathered seventy elders of the people, and placed them all around the tent. Then the LORD came down in the cloud and spoke to him, and took some of the spirit that was on him and put it on the seventy elders; and when the spirit rested upon them, they prophesied. But they did not do so again. Two men remained in the camp, one named Eldad, and the other named Medad, and the spirit rested on them; they were among those registered, but they had not gone out to the tent, and so they prophesied in the camp. And a young man ran and told Moses, "Eldad and Medad are prophesying in the camp." And Joshua son of Nun, the assistant of Moses, one of his chosen men, said, "My lord Moses, stop them!" But Moses said to him, "Are you jealous for my sake? Would that all the Lord's people were prophets, and that the LORD would put his spirit on them!" And Moses and the elders of Israel returned to the camp.

The Response — Psalm 104:25-35, 37b

Psalm 104:25-35, 37b   *Benedic, anima mea*

25   O Lord, how manifold are your works! *
      in wisdom you have made them all;
      the earth is full of your creatures.

26   Yonder is the great and wide sea
      with its living things too many to number, *
      creatures both small and great.

27   There move the ships,
      and there is that Leviathan, *
      which you have made for the sport of it.

28   All of them look to you *
      to give them their food in due season.

29   You give it to them; they gather it; *
      you open your hand, and they are filled with good things.

30   You hide your face, and they are terrified; *
      you take away their breath,
      and they die and return to their dust.

31   You send forth your Spirit, and they are created; *
      and so you renew the face of the earth.

32   May the glory of the Lord endure for ever; *
      may the Lord rejoice in all his works.

33   He looks at the earth and it trembles; *
      he touches the mountains and they smoke.

34   I will sing to the Lord as long as I live; *
      I will praise my God while I have my being.

35   May these words of mine please him; *
      I will rejoice in the Lord. Hallelujah!

The Epistle — 1 Corinthians 12:3b-13 *or* Acts 2:1-21

1 Corinthians 12:3b-13

No one can say "Jesus is Lord" except by the Holy Spirit. Now there are varieties of gifts, but the same Spirit; and there are varieties of services, but the same Lord; and there are varieties of activities, but it is the same God who activates all of them in everyone. To each is given the manifestation of the Spirit for the common good. To one is given through the Spirit the utterance of wisdom, and to another the utterance of knowledge according to the same Spirit, to another faith by the same Spirit, to another gifts of healing by the one Spirit, to another the working of miracles, to another prophecy, to another the discernment of spirits, to another various kinds of tongues, to another the interpretation of tongues. All these are activated by one and the same Spirit, who allots to each one individually just as the Spirit chooses. For just as the body is one and has many members, and all the members of the body, though many, are one body, so it is with Christ. For in the one Spirit we were all baptized into one body — Jews or Greeks, slaves or free — and we were all made to drink of one Spirit.

or, Acts 2:1-21

When the day of Pentecost had come, the apostles were all together in one place. And suddenly from heaven there came a sound like the rush of a violent wind, and it filled the entire house where they were sitting. Divided tongues, as of fire, appeared among them, and a tongue rested on each of them. All of them were filled with the Holy Spirit and began to speak in other languages, as the Spirit gave them ability. Now there were devout Jews from every nation under heaven living in Jerusalem. And at this sound the crowd gathered and was bewildered, because each one heard them speaking in the native language of each. Amazed and astonished, they asked, "Are not all these who are speaking Galileans? And how is it that we hear, each of us, in our own native language? Parthians, Medes, Elamites, and residents of Mesopotamia, Judea and Cappadocia, Pontus and Asia, Phrygia and Pamphylia, Egypt and the parts of Libya belonging to Cyrene, and visitors from Rome, both Jews and proselytes, Cretans and Arabs—in our own languages we hear them speaking about God's deeds of power." All were amazed and perplexed, saying to one another, "What does this mean?" But others sneered and said, "They are filled with new wine." But Peter, standing with the eleven, raised his voice and addressed them, "Men of Judea and all who live in Jerusalem, let this be known to you, and listen to what I say. Indeed, these are not drunk, as you suppose, for it is only nine o'clock in the morning. No, this is what was spoken through the prophet Joel: 'In the last days it will be, God declares, that I will pour out my Spirit upon all flesh, and your sons and your daughters shall prophesy, and your young men shall see visions, and your old men shall dream dreams. Even upon my slaves, both men and women, in those days I will pour out my Spirit; and they shall prophesy. And I will show portents in the heaven above and signs on the earth below, blood, and fire, and smoky mist. The sun shall be turned to darkness and the moon to blood, before the coming of the Lord's great and glorious day. Then everyone who calls on the name of the Lord shall be saved.' "

The Gospel   John 20:19-23 *or* John 7:37-39
John 20:19-23

When it was evening of the day of Resurrection, the first day of the week, and the doors of the house where the disciples had met were locked for fear of the Jews, Jesus came and stood among them and said, "Peace be with you." After he said this, he showed them his hands and his side. Then the disciples rejoiced when they saw the Lord. Jesus said to them again, "Peace be with you. As the Father has sent me, so I send you." When he had said this, he breathed on them and said to them, "Receive the Holy Spirit. If you forgive the sins of any, they are forgiven them; if you retain the sins of any, they are retained."

or, John 7:37-39

On the last day of the festival, the great day, while Jesus was standing there, he cried out, "Let anyone who is thirsty come to me, and let the one who believes in me drink. As the scripture has said, 'Out of the believer's heart shall flow rivers of living water.' " Now he said this about the Spirit, which believers in him were to receive; for as yet there was no Spirit, because Jesus was not yet glorified.

Year B

(If the passage from Ezekiel is chosen for the First Reading, the passage from Acts is used as the Second Reading)

Acts 2:1-21 or Ezekiel 37:1-14
Psalm 104:25-35, 37b
Romans 8:22-27 or Acts 2:1-21
John 15:26-27; 16:4b-15

The Lesson   **Acts 2:1-21 *or* Ezekiel 37:1-14**
Acts 2:1-21

When the day of Pentecost had come, they were all together in one place. And suddenly from heaven there came a sound like the rush of a violent wind, and it filled the entire house where they were sitting. Divided tongues, as of fire, appeared among them, and a tongue rested on each of them. All of them were filled with the Holy Spirit and began to speak in other languages, as the Spirit gave them ability. Now there were devout Jews from every nation under heaven living in Jerusalem. And at this sound the crowd gathered and was bewildered, because each one heard them speaking in the native language of each. Amazed and astonished, they asked, "Are not all these who are speaking Galileans? And how is it that we hear, each of us, in our own native language? Parthians, Medes, Elamites, and residents of Mesopotamia, Judea and Cappadocia, Pontus and Asia, Phrygia and Pamphylia, Egypt and the parts of Libya belonging to Cyrene, and visitors from Rome, both Jews and proselytes, Cretans and Arabs — in our own languages we hear them speaking about God's deeds of power." All were amazed and perplexed, saying to one another, "What does this mean?" But others sneered and said, "They are filled with new wine." But Peter, standing with the eleven, raised his voice and addressed them, "Men of Judea and all who live in Jerusalem, let this be known to you, and listen to what I say. Indeed, these are not drunk, as you suppose, for it is only nine o'clock in the morning. No, this is what was spoken through the prophet Joel: 'In the last days it will be, God declares, that I will pour out my Spirit upon all flesh, and your sons and your daughters shall prophesy, and your young men shall see visions, and your old men shall dream dreams. Even upon my slaves, both men and women, in those days I will pour out my Spirit; and they shall prophesy. And I will show portents in the heaven above and signs on the earth below, blood, and fire, and smoky mist. The sun shall be turned to darkness and the moon to blood, before the coming of the Lord's great and glorious day. Then everyone who calls on the name of the Lord shall be saved.' "

or, Ezekiel 37:1-14

The hand of the LORD came upon me, and he brought me out by the spirit of the LORD and set me down in the middle of a valley; it was full of bones. He led me all around them; there were very many lying in the valley, and they were very dry. He said to me, "Mortal, can these bones live?" I answered, "O Lord GOD, you know." Then he said to me, "Prophesy to these bones, and say to them: O dry bones, hear the word of the LORD. Thus says the Lord GOD to these bones: I will cause breath to enter you, and you shall live. I will lay sinews on you, and will cause flesh to come upon you, and cover you with skin, and put breath in you, and you shall live; and you shall know that I am the LORD." So I prophesied as I had been commanded; and as I prophesied, suddenly there was a noise, a rattling, and the bones came together, bone to its bone. I looked, and there were sinews on them, and flesh had come upon them, and skin had covered them; but there was no breath in them. Then he said to me, "Prophesy to the breath, prophesy, mortal, and say to the breath: Thus says the Lord GOD: Come from the four winds, O breath, and breathe upon these slain, that they may live." I prophesied as he commanded me, and the breath came into them, and they lived, and stood on their feet, a vast multitude. Then he said to me, "Mortal, these bones are the whole house of Israel. They say, 'Our bones are dried up, and our hope is lost; we are cut off completely.' Therefore prophesy, and say to them, Thus says the Lord GOD: I am going to open your graves, and bring you up from your graves, O my people; and I will bring you back to the land of Israel. And you shall know that I am the LORD, when I open your graves, and bring you up from your graves, O my people. I will put my spirit within you, and you shall live, and I will place you on your own soil; then you shall know that I, the LORD, have spoken and will act," says the LORD.

The Response　　　　　　　　　　　**Psalm 104:25-35, 37*b***

Psalm 104:25-35, 37*b*　　*Benedic, anima mea*

25　O LORD, how manifold are your works! *
　　　　in wisdom you have made them all;
　　　　the earth is full of your creatures.
26　Yonder is the great and wide sea
　　　with its living things too many to number, *
　　　　creatures both small and great.
27　There move the ships,
　　　and there is that Leviathan, *
　　　　which you have made for the sport of it.
28　All of them look to you *
　　　　to give them their food in due season.
29　You give it to them; they gather it; *
　　　　you open your hand, and they are filled with good things.
30　You hide your face, and they are terrified; *
　　　　you take away their breath,
　　　　and they die and return to their dust.
31　You send forth your Spirit, and they are created; *
　　　　and so you renew the face of the earth.
32　May the glory of the LORD endure for ever; *
　　　　may the LORD rejoice in all his works.
33　He looks at the earth and it trembles; *
　　　　he touches the mountains and they smoke.
34　I will sing to the LORD as long as I live; *
　　　　I will praise my God while I have my being.
35　May these words of mine please him; *
　　　　I will rejoice in the LORD. Hallelujah!

The Epistle　　　　　　　**Romans 8:22-27** *or* **Acts 2:1-21**
Romans 8:22-27

We know that the whole creation has been groaning in labor pains until now;
and not only the creation, but we ourselves, who have the first fruits of the
Spirit, groan inwardly while we wait for adoption, the redemption of our
bodies. For in hope we were saved. Now hope that is seen is not hope. For
who hopes for what is seen? But if we hope for what we do not see, we wait
for it with patience. Likewise the Spirit helps us in our weakness; for we do
not know how to pray as we ought, but that very Spirit intercedes with sighs
too deep for words. And God, who searches the heart, knows what is the mind
of the Spirit, because the Spirit intercedes for the saints according to the will
of God.

or, **Acts 2:1-21**

When the day of Pentecost had come, they were all together in one place. And suddenly from heaven there came a sound like the rush of a violent wind, and it filled the entire house where they were sitting. Divided tongues, as of fire, appeared among them, and a tongue rested on each of them. All of them were filled with the Holy Spirit and began to speak in other languages, as the Spirit gave them ability. Now there were devout Jews from every nation under heaven living in Jerusalem. And at this sound the crowd gathered and was bewildered, because each one heard them speaking in the native language of each. Amazed and astonished, they asked, "Are not all these who are speaking Galileans? And how is it that we hear, each of us, in our own native language? Parthians, Medes, Elamites, and residents of Mesopotamia, Judea and Cappadocia, Pontus and Asia, Phrygia and Pamphylia, Egypt and the parts of Libya belonging to Cyrene, and visitors from Rome, both Jews and proselytes, Cretans and Arabs—in our own languages we hear them speaking about God's deeds of power." All were amazed and perplexed, saying to one another, "What does this mean?" But others sneered and said, "They are filled with new wine." But Peter, standing with the eleven, raised his voice and addressed them, "Men of Judea and all who live in Jerusalem, let this be known to you, and listen to what I say. Indeed, these are not drunk, as you suppose, for it is only nine o'clock in the morning. No, this is what was spoken through the prophet Joel: 'In the last days it will be, God declares, that I will pour out my Spirit upon all flesh, and your sons and your daughters shall prophesy, and your young men shall see visions, and your old men shall dream dreams. Even upon my slaves, both men and women, in those days I will pour out my Spirit; and they shall prophesy. And I will show portents in the heaven above and signs on the earth below, blood, and fire, and smoky mist. The sun shall be turned to darkness and the moon to blood, before the coming of the Lord's great and glorious day. Then everyone who calls on the name of the Lord shall be saved.' "

The Gospel   **John 15:26-27, 16:4***b***-15**

Jesus said, "When the Advocate comes, whom I will send to you from the Father, the Spirit of truth who comes from the Father, he will testify on my behalf. You also are to testify because you have been with me from the beginning. I did not say these things to you from the beginning, because I was with you. But now I am going to him who sent me; yet none of you asks me, 'Where are you going?' But because I have said these things to you, sorrow has filled your hearts. Nevertheless I tell you the truth: it is to your advantage that I go away, for if I do not go away, the Advocate will not come to you; but if I go, I will send him to you. And when he comes, he will prove the world wrong about sin and righteousness and judgment: about sin, because they do not believe in me; about righteousness, because I am going to the Father and you will see me no longer; about judgment, because the ruler of this world has been condemned. I still have many things to say to you, but you cannot bear them now. When the Spirit of truth comes, he will guide you into all the truth; for he will not speak on his own, but will speak whatever he hears, and he will declare to you the things that are to come. He will glorify me, because he will take what is mine and declare it to you. All that the Father has is mine. For this reason I said that he will take what is mine and declare it to you."

Year C

(If the passage from Genesis is chosen for the First Reading, the passage from Acts is used as the Second Reading)

Acts 2:1-21 or *Genesis 11:1-9*
*Psalm 104:25-35, 37*b
Romans 8:14-17 or *Acts 2:1-21*
John 14:8-17, (25-27)

The Lesson   **Acts 2:1-21** *or* **Genesis 11:1-9**
Acts 2:1-21

When the day of Pentecost had come, they were all together in one place. And suddenly from heaven there came a sound like the rush of a violent wind, and it filled the entire house where they were sitting. Divided tongues, as of fire, appeared among them, and a tongue rested on each of them. All of them were filled with the Holy Spirit and began to speak in other languages, as the Spirit gave them ability. Now there were devout Jews from every nation under heaven living in Jerusalem. And at this sound the crowd gathered and was bewildered, because each one heard them speaking in the native language of each. Amazed and astonished, they asked, "Are not all these who are speaking Galileans? And how is it that we hear, each of us, in our own native language? Parthians, Medes, Elamites, and residents of Mesopotamia, Judea and Cappadocia, Pontus and Asia, Phrygia and Pamphylia, Egypt and the parts of Libya belonging to Cyrene, and visitors from Rome, both Jews and proselytes, Cretans and Arabs—in our own languages we hear them speaking about God's deeds of power." All were amazed and perplexed, saying to one another, "What does this mean?" But others sneered and said, "They are filled with new wine." But Peter, standing with the eleven, raised his voice and addressed them, "Men of Judea and all who live in Jerusalem, let this be known to you, and listen to what I say. Indeed, these are not drunk, as you suppose, for it is only nine o'clock in the morning. No, this is what was spoken through the prophet Joel: 'In the last days it will be, God declares, that I will pour out my Spirit upon all flesh, and your sons and your daughters shall prophesy, and your young men shall see visions, and your old men shall dream dreams. Even upon my slaves, both men and women, in those days I will pour out my Spirit;

and they shall prophesy. And I will show portents in the heaven above and signs on the earth below, blood, and fire, and smoky mist. The sun shall be turned to darkness and the moon to blood, before the coming of the Lord's great and glorious day. Then everyone who calls on the name of the Lord shall be saved.' "

or, **Genesis 11:1-9**

Now the whole earth had one language and the same words. And as they migrated from the east, they came upon a plain in the land of Shinar and settled there. And they said to one another, "Come, let us make bricks, and burn them thoroughly." And they had brick for stone, and bitumen for mortar. Then they said, "Come, let us build ourselves a city, and a tower with its top in the heavens, and let us make a name for ourselves; otherwise we shall be scattered abroad upon the face of the whole earth." The LORD came down to see the city and the tower, which mortals had built. And the LORD said, "Look, they are one people, and they have all one language; and this is only the beginning of what they will do; nothing that they propose to do will now be impossible for them. Come, let us go down, and confuse their language there, so that they will not understand one another's speech." So the LORD scattered them abroad from there over the face of all the earth, and they left off building the city. Therefore it was called Babel, because there the LORD confused the language of all the earth; and from there the LORD scattered them abroad over the face of all the earth.

The Response   **Psalm 104:25-35, 37*b***

Psalm 104:25-35, 37*b*   *Benedic, anima mea*

25   O LORD, how manifold are your works! *
      in wisdom you have made them all;
      the earth is full of your creatures.

26   Yonder is the great and wide sea
    with its living things too many to number, *
      creatures both small and great.

27   There move the ships,
    and there is that Leviathan, *
      which you have made for the sport of it.

28   All of them look to you *
      to give them their food in due season.

29   You give it to them; they gather it; *
      you open your hand, and they are filled with good things.

30   You hide your face, and they are terrified; *
      you take away their breath,
      and they die and return to their dust.

31 You send forth your Spirit, and they are created; *
        and so you renew the face of the earth.
32 May the glory of the LORD endure for ever; *
        may the LORD rejoice in all his works.
33 He looks at the earth and it trembles; *
        he touches the mountains and they smoke.
34 I will sing to the LORD as long as I live; *
        I will praise my God while I have my being.
35 May these words of mine please him; *
        I will rejoice in the LORD. Hallelujah!

The Epistle   Romans 8:14-17 *or* Acts 2:1-21
Romans 8:14-17

All who are led by the Spirit of God are children of God. For you did not
receive a spirit of slavery to fall back into fear, but you have received a spirit
of adoption. When we cry, "Abba! Father!" it is that very Spirit bearing
witness with our spirit that we are children of God, and if children, then heirs,
heirs of God and joint heirs with Christ — if, in fact, we suffer with him so
that we may also be glorified with him.

or, Acts 2:1-21

When the day of Pentecost had come, they were all together in one place. And
suddenly from heaven there came a sound like the rush of a violent wind, and
it filled the entire house where they were sitting. Divided tongues, as of fire,
appeared among them, and a tongue rested on each of them. All of them were
filled with the Holy Spirit and began to speak in other languages, as the Spirit
gave them ability. Now there were devout Jews from every nation under
heaven living in Jerusalem. And at this sound the crowd gathered and was
bewildered, because each one heard them speaking in the native language of
each. Amazed and astonished, they asked, "Are not all these who are speaking
Galileans? And how is it that we hear, each of us, in our own native language?
Parthians, Medes, Elamites, and residents of Mesopotamia, Judea and
Cappadocia, Pontus and Asia, Phrygia and Pamphylia, Egypt and the parts of
Libya belonging to Cyrene, and visitors from Rome, both Jews and proselytes,
Cretans and Arabs—in our own languages we hear them speaking about
God's deeds of power." All were amazed and perplexed, saying to one another,
"What does this mean?" But others sneered and said, "They are filled with
new wine." But Peter, standing with the eleven, raised his voice and addressed
them, "Men of Judea and all who live in Jerusalem, let this be known to you,
and listen to what I say. Indeed, these are not drunk, as you suppose, for it is
only nine o'clock in the morning. No, this is what was spoken through the
prophet Joel: 'In the last days it will be, God declares, that I will pour out my

Spirit upon all flesh, and your sons and your daughters shall prophesy, and your young men shall see visions, and your old men shall dream dreams. Even upon my slaves, both men and women, in those days I will pour out my Spirit; and they shall prophesy. And I will show portents in the heaven above and signs on the earth below, blood, and fire, and smoky mist. The sun shall be turned to darkness and the moon to blood, before the coming of the Lord's great and glorious day. Then everyone who calls on the name of the Lord shall be saved.' "

The Gospel   John 14:8-17, (25-27)
John 14:8-17

Jesus said, "If you know me, you will know my Father also. From now on you do know him and have seen him." Philip said to him, "Lord, show us the Father, and we will be satisfied." Jesus said to him, "Have I been with you all this time, Philip, and you still do not know me? Whoever has seen me has seen the Father. How can you say, 'Show us the Father'? Do you not believe that I am in the Father and the Father is in me? The words that I say to you I do not speak on my own; but the Father who dwells in me does his works. Believe me that I am in the Father and the Father is in me; but if you do not, then believe me because of the works themselves. Very truly, I tell you, the one who believes in me will also do the works that I do and, in fact, will do greater works than these, because I am going to the Father. I will do whatever you ask in my name, so that the Father may be glorified in the Son. If in my name you ask me for anything, I will do it. If you love me, you will keep my commandments. And I will ask the Father, and he will give you another Advocate, to be with you forever. This is the Spirit of truth, whom the world cannot receive, because it neither sees him nor knows him. You know him, because he abides with you, and he will be in you."

John 14:(25-27) "[I have said these things to you while I am still with you. But the Advocate, the Holy Spirit, whom the Father will send in my name, will teach you everything, and remind you of all that I have said to you. Peace I leave with you; my peace I give to you. I do not give to you as the world gives. Do not let your hearts be troubled, and do not let them be afraid.]"

SEASON AFTER PENTECOST *(Ordinary Time)*

TRINITY SUNDAY
(THE FIRST SUNDAY AFTER PENTECOST)

The Collect

Almighty and everlasting God, you have given to us your servants grace, by the confession of a true faith, to acknowledge the glory of the eternal Trinity, and in the power of your divine Majesty to worship the Unity: Keep us steadfast in this faith and worship, and bring us at last to see you in your one and eternal glory, O Father; who with the Son and the Holy Spirit live and reign, one God, for ever and ever. *Amen.*

Year A
*Genesis 1:1—2:4*a
Psalm 8 or *Canticle 2* or *13*
2 Corinthians 13:11-13
Matthew 28:16-20

The Lesson   **Genesis 1:1—2:4***a*

In the beginning when God created the heavens and the earth, the earth was a formless void and darkness covered the face of the deep, while a wind from God swept over the face of the waters. Then God said, "Let there be light"; and there was light. And God saw that the light was good; and God separated the light from the darkness. God called the light Day, and the darkness he called Night. And there was evening and there was morning, the first day. And God said, "Let there be a dome in the midst of the waters, and let it separate the waters from the waters." So God made the dome and separated the waters that were under the dome from the waters that were above the dome. And it was so. God called the dome Sky. And there was evening and there was morning, the second day. And God said, "Let the waters under the sky be gathered together into one place, and let the dry land appear." And it was so. God called the dry land Earth, and the waters that were gathered together he called Seas. And God saw that it was good. Then God said, "Let the earth put forth vegetation: plants yielding seed, and fruit trees of every kind on earth that bear fruit with the seed in it." And it was so. The earth brought forth vegetation: plants yielding seed of every kind, and trees of every kind bearing fruit with the seed in it. And God saw that it was good. And there was evening and there was morning, the third day. And God said, "Let there be lights in the dome of the sky to separate the day from the night; and let them be for signs and for seasons and for days and years, and let them be lights in the dome of the sky to give light upon the earth." And it was so. God made the two great lights—the greater light to rule the day and the lesser light to rule the night—

and the stars. God set them in the dome of the sky to give light upon the earth, to rule over the day and over the night, and to separate the light from the darkness. And God saw that it was good. And there was evening and there was morning, the fourth day. And God said, "Let the waters bring forth swarms of living creatures, and let birds fly above the earth across the dome of the sky." So God created the great sea monsters and every living creature that moves, of every kind, with which the waters swarm, and every winged bird of every kind. And God saw that it was good. God blessed them, saying, "Be fruitful and multiply and fill the waters in the seas, and let birds multiply on the earth." And there was evening and there was morning, the fifth day. And God said, "Let the earth bring forth living creatures of every kind: cattle and creeping things and wild animals of the earth of every kind." And it was so. God made the wild animals of the earth of every kind, and the cattle of every kind, and everything that creeps upon the ground of every kind. And God saw that it was good. Then God said, "Let us make humankind in our image, according to our likeness; and let them have dominion over the fish of the sea, and over the birds of the air, and over the cattle, and over all the wild animals of the earth, and over every creeping thing that creeps upon the earth." So God created humankind in his image, in the image of God he created them; male and female he created them. God blessed them, and God said to them, "Be fruitful and multiply, and fill the earth and subdue it; and have dominion over the fish of the sea and over the birds of the air and over every living thing that moves upon the earth." God said, "See, I have given you every plant yielding seed that is upon the face of all the earth, and every tree with seed in its fruit; you shall have them for food. And to every beast of the earth, and to every bird of the air, and to everything that creeps on the earth, everything that has the breath of life, I have given every green plant for food." And it was so. God saw everything that he had made, and indeed, it was very good. And there was evening and there was morning, the sixth day. Thus the heavens and the earth were finished, and all their multitude. And on the seventh day God finished the work that he had done, and he rested on the seventh day from all the work that he had done. So God blessed the seventh day and hallowed it, because on it God rested from all the work that he had done in creation. These are the generations of the heavens and the earth when they were created.

The Response   **Psalm 8** or **Canticle 2** or **13**

Psalm 8 *Domine, Dominus noster*

1   O LORD our Governor, *
          how exalted is your Name in all the world!

2   Out of the mouths of infants and children *
          your majesty is praised above the heavens.

3   You have set up a stronghold against your adversaries, *
          to quell the enemy and the avenger.

4   When I consider your heavens, the work of your fingers, *
        the moon and the stars you have set in their courses,

5   What is man that you should be mindful of him? *
        the son of man that you should seek him out?

6   You have made him but little lower than the angels; *
        you adorn him with glory and honor;

7   You give him mastery over the works of your hands; *
        you put all things under his feet:

8   All sheep and oxen, *
        even the wild beasts of the field,

9   The birds of the air, the fish of the sea, *
        and whatsoever walks in the paths of the sea.

10   O Lord our Governor, *
        how exalted is your Name in all the world!

or, **Canticle 2**   *(Page 49 BCP)*

or, **Canticle 13   A Song of Praise**   *Benedictus es, Domine*
                                    Song of the Three Young Men, 29-34

Glory to you, Lord God of our fathers; *
    you are worthy of praise; glory to you.
Glory to you for the radiance of your holy Name; *
    we will praise you and highly exalt you for ever.
Glory to you in the splendor of your temple; *
    on the throne of your majesty, glory to you.
Glory to you, seated between the Cherubim; *
    we will praise you and highly exalt you for ever.
Glory to you, beholding the depths; *
    in the high vault of heaven, glory to you.
Glory to you, Father, Son, and Holy Spirit; *
    we will praise you and highly exalt you for ever.

The Epistle   2 Corinthians 13:11-13

Finally, brothers and sisters, farewell. Put things in order, listen to my appeal,
agree with one another, live in peace; and the God of love and peace will be
with you. Greet one another with a holy kiss. All the saints greet you. The
grace of the Lord Jesus Christ, the love of God, and the communion of the
Holy Spirit be with all of you.

The Gospel   Matthew 28:16-20

The eleven disciples went to Galilee, to the mountain to which Jesus had
directed them. When they saw him, they worshiped him; but some doubted.
And Jesus came and said to them, "All authority in heaven and on earth has

been given to me. Go therefore and make disciples of all nations, baptizing them in the name of the Father and of the Son and of the Holy Spirit, and teaching them to obey everything that I have commanded you. And remember, I am with you always, to the end of the age."

Year B
Isaiah 6:1-8
Psalm 29 or *Canticle 2* or *13*
Romans 8:12-17
John 3:1-17

The Lesson   **Isaiah 6:1-8**

In the year that King Uzziah died, I saw the Lord sitting on a throne, high and lofty; and the hem of his robe filled the temple. Seraphs were in attendance above him; each had six wings: with two they covered their faces, and with two they covered their feet, and with two they flew. And one called to another and said: "Holy, holy, holy is the LORD of hosts; the whole earth is full of his glory." The pivots on the thresholds shook at the voices of those who called, and the house filled with smoke. And I said: "Woe is me! I am lost, for I am a man of unclean lips, and I live among a people of unclean lips; yet my eyes have seen the King, the LORD of hosts!" Then one of the seraphs flew to me, holding a live coal that had been taken from the altar with a pair of tongs. The seraph touched my mouth with it and said: "Now that this has touched your lips, your guilt has departed and your sin is blotted out." Then I heard the voice of the Lord saying, "Whom shall I send, and who will go for us?" And I said, "Here am I; send me!"

The Response   **Psalm 29** *or* **Canticle 2** *or* **13**

Psalm 29   *Afferte Domino*

1   Ascribe to the LORD, you gods, *
        ascribe to the LORD glory and strength.
2   Ascribe to the LORD the glory due his Name; *
        worship the LORD in the beauty of holiness.
3   The voice of the LORD is upon the waters;
    the God of glory thunders; *
        the LORD is upon the mighty waters.
4   The voice of the LORD is a powerful voice; *
        the voice of the LORD is a voice of splendor.
5   The voice of the LORD breaks the cedar trees; *
        the LORD breaks the cedars of Lebanon;
6   He makes Lebanon skip like a calf, *
        and Mount Hermon like a young wild ox.

7   The voice of the LORD splits the flames of fire;
      the voice of the LORD shakes the wilderness; *
         the LORD shakes the wilderness of Kadesh.

8   The voice of the LORD makes the oak trees writhe *
      and strips the forests bare.

9   And in the temple of the LORD *
      all are crying, "Glory!"

10   The LORD sits enthroned above the flood; *
      the LORD sits enthroned as King for evermore.

11   The LORD shall give strength to his people; *
      the LORD shall give his people the blessing of peace.

or, **Canticle 2**   *(Page 49 BCP)*

or, **Canticle 13   A Song of Praise**   *Benedictus es, Domine*
                                Song of the Three Young Men, 29-34

    Glory to you, Lord God of our fathers; *
      you are worthy of praise; glory to you.
    Glory to you for the radiance of your holy Name; *
      we will praise you and highly exalt you for ever.
    Glory to you in the splendor of your temple; *
      on the throne of your majesty, glory to you.
    Glory to you, seated between the Cherubim; *
      we will praise you and highly exalt you for ever.
    Glory to you, beholding the depths; *
      in the high vault of heaven, glory to you.
    Glory to you, Father, Son, and Holy Spirit; *
      we will praise you and highly exalt you for ever.

The Epistle   Romans 8:12-17

Brothers and sisters, we are debtors, not to the flesh, to live according to the flesh — for if you live according to the flesh, you will die; but if by the Spirit you put to death the deeds of the body, you will live. For all who are led by the Spirit of God are children of God. For you did not receive a spirit of slavery to fall back into fear, but you have received a spirit of adoption. When we cry, "Abba! Father!" it is that very Spirit bearing witness with our spirit that we are children of God, and if children, then heirs, heirs of God and joint heirs with Christ — if, in fact, we suffer with him so that we may also be glorified with him.

The Gospel   John 3:1-17

Now there was a Pharisee named Nicodemus, a leader of the Jews. He came to Jesus by night and said to him, "Rabbi, we know that you are a teacher who

294   TRINITY SUNDAY — Year B

has come from God; for no one can do these signs that you do apart from the presence of God." Jesus answered him, "Very truly, I tell you, no one can see the kingdom of God without being born from above." Nicodemus said to him, "How can anyone be born after having grown old? Can one enter a second time into the mother's womb and be born?" Jesus answered, "Very truly, I tell you, no one can enter the kingdom of God without being born of water and Spirit. What is born of the flesh is flesh, and what is born of the Spirit is spirit. Do not be astonished that I said to you, 'You must be born from above.' The wind blows where it chooses, and you hear the sound of it, but you do not know where it comes from or where it goes. So it is with everyone who is born of the Spirit." Nicodemus said to him, "How can these things be?" Jesus answered him, "Are you a teacher of Israel, and yet you do not understand these things? Very truly, I tell you, we speak of what we know and testify to what we have seen; yet you do not receive our testimony. If I have told you about earthly things and you do not believe, how can you believe if I tell you about heavenly things? No one has ascended into heaven except the one who descended from heaven, the Son of Man. And just as Moses lifted up the serpent in the wilderness, so must the Son of Man be lifted up, that whoever believes in him may have eternal life. For God so loved the world that he gave his only Son, so that everyone who believes in him may not perish but may have eternal life. Indeed, God did not send the Son into the world to condemn the world, but in order that the world might be saved through him."

Year C
Proverbs 8:1-4, 22-31
Psalm 8 or *Canticle 2* or *13*
Romans 5:1-5
John 16:12-15

The Lesson   **Proverbs 8:1-4, 22-31**

Does not wisdom call, and does not understanding raise her voice? On the heights, beside the way, at the crossroads she takes her stand; beside the gates in front of the town, at the entrance of the portals she cries out: "To you, O people, I call, and my cry is to all that live. The LORD created me at the beginning of his work, the first of his acts of long ago. Ages ago I was set up, at the first, before the beginning of the earth. When there were no depths I was brought forth, when there were no springs abounding with water. Before the mountains had been shaped, before the hills, I was brought forth — when he had not yet made earth and fields, or the world's first bits of soil. When he established the heavens, I was there, when he drew a circle on the face of the deep, when he made firm the skies above, when he established the fountains of the deep, when he assigned to the sea its limit, so that the waters might not transgress his command, when he marked out the foundations of the earth, then I was beside him, like a master worker; and I was daily his delight, rejoicing before him always, rejoicing in his inhabited world and delighting in the human race."

The Response   Psalm 8 *or* Canticle 2 *or* 13
Psalm 8   *Domine, Dominus noster*
  1   O LORD our Governor, *
        how exalted is your Name in all the world!
  2   Out of the mouths of infants and children *
        your majesty is praised above the heavens.
  3   You have set up a stronghold against your adversaries, *
        to quell the enemy and the avenger.
  4   When I consider your heavens, the work of your fingers, *
        the moon and the stars you have set in their courses,
  5   What is man that you should be mindful of him? *
        the son of man that you should seek him out?
  6   You have made him but little lower than the angels; *
        you adorn him with glory and honor;
  7   You give him mastery over the works of your hands; *
        you put all things under his feet:
  8   All sheep and oxen, *
        even the wild beasts of the field,
  9   The birds of the air, the fish of the sea, *
        and whatsoever walks in the paths of the sea.
  10 O LORD our Governor, *
        how exalted is your Name in all the world!

or, **Canticle 2**   *(Page 49 BCP)*

or, **Canticle 13   A Song of Praise**   *Benedictus es, Domine*
                              Song of the Three Young Men, 29-34
        Glory to you, Lord God of our fathers; *
          you are worthy of praise; glory to you.
        Glory to you for the radiance of your holy Name; *
          we will praise you and highly exalt you for ever.
        Glory to you in the splendor of your temple; *
          on the throne of your majesty, glory to you.
        Glory to you, seated between the Cherubim; *
          we will praise you and highly exalt you for ever.
        Glory to you, beholding the depths; *
          in the high vault of heaven, glory to you.

Glory to you, Father, Son, and Holy Spirit; *
we will praise you and highly exalt you for ever.

The Epistle   Romans 5:1-5

Since we are justified by faith, we have peace with God through our Lord
Jesus Christ, through whom we have obtained access to this grace in which we
stand; and we boast in our hope of sharing the glory of God. And not only
that, but we also boast in our sufferings, knowing that suffering produces
endurance, and endurance produces character, and character produces hope,
and hope does not disappoint us, because God's love has been poured into our
hearts through the Holy Spirit that has been given to us.

The Gospel   John 16:12-15

Jesus said to his disciples, "I still have many things to say to you, but you
cannot bear them now. When the Spirit of truth comes, he will guide you into
all the truth; for he will not speak on his own, but will speak whatever he
hears, and he will declare to you the things that are to come. He will glorify
me, because he will take what is mine and declare it to you. All that the Father
has is mine. For this reason I said that he will take what is mine and declare it
to you."

*(If the Sunday between May 24 and 28 inclusive follows Trinity Sunday, the Proper
for the Eighth Sunday after the Epiphany is used).*

PROPER 4

Sunday between May 29 and June 4 inclusive (if after Trinity Sunday)
The Collect

O God, your never-failing providence sets in order all things both in heaven
and earth: Put away from us, we entreat you, all hurtful things, and give us
those things which are profitable for us; through Jesus Christ our Lord, who
lives and reigns with you and the Holy Spirit, one God, for ever and ever.
Amen.

Year A

Genesis 6:9-22; 7:24; 8:14-19 **or**   ✛ *Deuteronomy 11:18-21,*
Psalm 46   *26-28*
                                              ✛ *Psalm 31:1-5, 19-24*
Romans 1:16-17; 3:22b-28, (29-31)
Matthew 7:21-29

The Lesson   **Genesis 6:9-22, 7:24; 8:14-19**

These are the descendants of Noah. Noah was a righteous man, blameless in
his generation; Noah walked with God. And Noah had three sons, Shem,
Ham, and Japheth. Now the earth was corrupt in God's sight, and the earth
was filled with violence. And God saw that the earth was corrupt; for all flesh
had corrupted its ways upon the earth. And God said to Noah, "I have determined to make an end of all flesh, for the earth is filled with violence because
of them; now I am going to destroy them along with the earth. Make yourself
an ark of cypress wood; make rooms in the ark, and cover it inside and out
with pitch. This is how you are to make it: the length of the ark three hundred
cubits, its width fifty cubits, and its height thirty cubits. Make a roof for the
ark, and finish it to a cubit above; and put the door of the ark in its side; make
it with lower, second, and third decks. For my part, I am going to bring a
flood of waters on the earth, to destroy from under heaven all flesh in which is
the breath of life; everything that is on the earth shall die. But I will establish
my covenant with you; and you shall come into the ark, you, your sons, your
wife, and your sons' wives with you. And of every living thing, of all flesh,
you shall bring two of every kind into the ark, to keep them alive with you;
they shall be male and female. Of the birds according to their kinds, and of the
animals according to their kinds, of every creeping thing of the ground according to its kind, two of every kind shall come in to you, to keep them alive.
Also take with you every kind of food that is eaten, and store it up; and it shall
serve as food for you and for them." Noah did this; he did all that God commanded him. And the waters swelled on the earth for one hundred fifty days.
In the second month, on the twenty-seventh day of the month, the earth was
dry. Then God said to Noah, "Go out of the ark, you and your wife, and your
sons and your sons' wives with you. Bring out with you every living thing that
is with you of all flesh — birds and animals and every creeping thing that
creeps on the earth — so that they may abound on the earth, and be fruitful
and multiply on the earth." So Noah went out with his sons and his wife and
his sons' wives. And every animal, every creeping thing, and every bird,
everything that moves on the earth, went out of the ark by families.

The Response   **Psalm 46**

Psalm 46   *Deus noster refugium*

   1   God is our refuge and strength, *
           a very present help in trouble.
   2   Therefore we will not fear, though the earth be moved, *
           and though the mountains be toppled into the
                     depths of the sea;
   3   Though its waters rage and foam, *
           and though the mountains tremble at its tumult.

4   The Lord of hosts is with us; *
     the God of Jacob is our stronghold.

5   There is a river whose streams make glad the city of God, *
     the holy habitation of the Most High.

6   God is in the midst of her;
   she shall not be overthrown; *
     God shall help her at the break of day.

7   The nations make much ado, and the kingdoms are shaken; *
     God has spoken, and the earth shall melt away.

8   The Lord of hosts is with us; *
     the God of Jacob is our stronghold.

9   Come now and look upon the works of the Lord, *
     what awesome things he has done on earth.

10 It is he who makes war to cease in all the world; *
     he breaks the bow, and shatters the spear,
     and burns the shields with fire.

11 "Be still, then, and know that I am God; *
     I will be exalted among the nations;
     I will be exalted in the earth."

12 The Lord of hosts is with us; *
     the God of Jacob is our stronghold.

or, ☩ **The Lesson**   **Deuteronomy 11:18-21, 26-28**

Moses said: You shall put these words of mine in your heart and soul, and you shall bind them as a sign on your hand, and fix them as an emblem on your forehead. Teach them to your children, talking about them when you are at home and when you are away, when you lie down and when you rise. Write them on the doorposts of your house and on your gates, so that your days and the days of your children may be multiplied in the land that the Lord swore to your ancestors to give them, as long as the heavens are above the earth. See, I am setting before you today a blessing and a curse: the blessing, if you obey the commandments of the Lord your God that I am commanding you today; and the curse, if you do not obey the commandments of the Lord your God, but turn from the way that I am commanding you today, to follow other gods that you have not known.

☩ **The Response**   **Psalm 31:1-5, 19-24**

Psalm 31:1-5, 19-24   *In te, Domine, speravi*

1   In you, O Lord, have I taken refuge;
   let me never be put to shame; *
     deliver me in your righteousness.

2　Incline your ear to me; *
　　make haste to deliver me.
3　Be my strong rock, a castle to keep me safe,
　　for you are my crag and my stronghold; *
　　　for the sake of your Name, lead me and guide me.
4　Take me out of the net that they have secretly set for me, *
　　for you are my tower of strength.
5　Into your hands I commend my spirit, *
　　for you have redeemed me,
　　O Lord, O God of truth.
19　How great is your goodness, O Lord!
　　which you have laid up for those who fear you; *
　　　which you have done in the sight of all
　　　for those who put their trust in you.
20　You hide them in the covert of your presence from those
　　　　　who slander them; *
　　　you keep them in your shelter from the strife of tongues.
21　Blessed be the Lord! *
　　for he has shown me the wonders of his love in a
　　　　　besieged city.
22　Yet I said in my alarm,
　　"I have been cut off from the sight of your eyes." *
　　　Nevertheless, you heard the sound of my entreaty
　　　when I cried out to you.
23　Love the Lord, all you who worship him; *
　　the Lord protects the faithful,
　　　but repays to the full those who act haughtily.
24　Be strong and let your heart take courage, *
　　all you who wait for the Lord.

The Epistle　　　　　　　　**Romans 1:16-17; 3:22b-28, (29-31)**

I am not ashamed of the gospel; it is the power of God for salvation to everyone who has faith, to the Jew first and also to the Greek. For in it the righteousness of God is revealed through faith for faith; as it is written, "The one
who is righteous will live by faith." For there is no distinction, since all have
sinned and fall short of the glory of God; they are now justified by his grace
as a gift, through the redemption that is in Christ Jesus, whom God put
forward as a sacrifice of atonement by his blood, effective through faith. He
did this to show his righteousness, because in his divine forbearance he had
passed over the sins previously committed; it was to prove at the present time
that he himself is righteous and that he justifies the one who has faith in Jesus.
Then what becomes of boasting? It is excluded. By what law? By that of

works? No, but by the law of faith. For we hold that a person is justified by faith apart from works prescribed by the law.

Romans 1:(29-31) [Or is God the God of Jews only? Is he not the God of Gentiles also? Yes, of Gentiles also, since God is one; and he will justify the circumcised on the ground of faith and the uncircumcised through that same faith. Do we then overthrow the law by this faith? By no means! On the contrary, we uphold the law.]

The Gospel   Matthew 7:21-29

Jesus said, "Not everyone who says to me, 'Lord, Lord,' will enter the kingdom of heaven, but only the one who does the will of my Father in heaven. On that day many will say to me, 'Lord, Lord, did we not prophesy in your name, and cast out demons in your name, and do many deeds of power in your name?' Then I will declare to them, 'I never knew you; go away from me, you evildoers.' Everyone then who hears these words of mine and acts on them will be like a wise man who built his house on rock. The rain fell, the floods came, and the winds blew and beat on that house, but it did not fall, because it had been founded on rock. And everyone who hears these words of mine and does not act on them will be like a foolish man who built his house on sand. The rain fell, and the floods came, and the winds blew and beat against that house, and it fell — and great was its fall!" Now when Jesus had finished saying these things, the crowds were astounded at his teaching, for he taught them as one having authority, and not as their scribes.

Year B

1 Samuel 3:1-10, (11-20)   **or**   ✝ *Deuteronomy 5:12-15*
Psalm 139:1-5, 12-17   ✝ *Psalm 81:1-10*
                      2 Corinthians 4:5-12
                      Mark 2:23—3:6

The Lesson   1 Samuel 3:1-10, (11-20)

Now the boy Samuel was ministering to the LORD under Eli. The word of the LORD was rare in those days; visions were not widespread. At that time Eli, whose eyesight had begun to grow dim so that he could not see, was lying down in his room; the lamp of God had not yet gone out, and Samuel was lying down in the temple of the LORD, where the ark of God was. Then the LORD called, "Samuel! Samuel!" and he said, "Here I am!" and ran to Eli, and said, "Here I am, for you called me." But he said, "I did not call; lie down again." So he went and lay down. The LORD called again, "Samuel!" Samuel got up and went to Eli, and said, "Here I am, for you called me." But he said, "I did not call, my son; lie down again." Now Samuel did not yet know the

LORD, and the word of the LORD had not yet been revealed to him. The LORD called Samuel again, a third time. And he got up and went to Eli, and said, "Here I am, for you called me." Then Eli perceived that the LORD was calling the boy. Therefore Eli said to Samuel, "Go, lie down; and if he calls you, you shall say, 'Speak, LORD, for your servant is listening.' " So Samuel went and lay down in his place. Now the LORD came and stood there, calling as before, "Samuel! Samuel!" And Samuel said, "Speak, for your servant is listening."

1 Samuel 3:(11-20) [Then the LORD said to Samuel, "See, I am about to do something in Israel that will make both ears of anyone who hears of it tingle. On that day I will fulfill against Eli all that I have spoken concerning his house, from beginning to end. For I have told him that I am about to punish his house forever, for the iniquity that he knew, because his sons were blaspheming God, and he did not restrain them. Therefore I swear to the house of Eli that the iniquity of Eli's house shall not be expiated by sacrifice or offering forever." Samuel lay there until morning; then he opened the doors of the house of the LORD. Samuel was afraid to tell the vision to Eli. But Eli called Samuel and said, "Samuel, my son." He said, "Here I am." Eli said, "What was it that he told you? Do not hide it from me. May God do so to you and more also, if you hide anything from me of all that he told you." So Samuel told him everything and hid nothing from him. Then he said, "It is the LORD; let him do what seems good to him." As Samuel grew up, the LORD was with him and let none of his words fall to the ground. And all Israel from Dan to Beer-sheba knew that Samuel was a trustworthy prophet of the LORD.]

The Response   **Psalm 139:1-5, 12-17**

Psalm 139:1-5, 12-17   *Domine, probasti*

1   LORD, you have searched me out and known me; *
        you know my sitting down and my rising up;
        you discern my thoughts from afar.

2   You trace my journeys and my resting-places *
        and are acquainted with all my ways.

3   Indeed, there is not a word on my lips, *
        but you, O LORD, know it altogether.

4   You press upon me behind and before *
        and lay your hand upon me.

5   Such knowledge is too wonderful for me; *
        it is so high that I cannot attain to it.

12   For you yourself created my inmost parts; *
        you knit me together in my mother's womb.

13   I will thank you because I am marvelously made; *
        your works are wonderful, and I know it well.

14 My body was not hidden from you, *
    while I was being made in secret
    and woven in the depths of the earth.
15 Your eyes beheld my limbs, yet unfinished in the womb;
    all of them were written in your book; *
    they were fashioned day by day,
    when as yet there was none of them.
16 How deep I find your thoughts, O God! *
    how great is the sum of them!
17 If I were to count them, they would be more in number
    than the sand; *
    to count them all, my life span would need to
    be like yours.

or, ✠ The Lesson   Deuteronomy 5:12-15

Moses said: Observe the sabbath day and keep it holy, as the LORD your God commanded you. Six days you shall labor and do all your work. But the seventh day is a sabbath to the LORD your God; you shall not do any work — you, or your son or your daughter, or your male or female slave, or your ox or your donkey, or any of your livestock, or the resident alien in your towns, so that your male and female slave may rest as well as you. Remember that you were a slave in the land of Egypt, and the LORD your God brought you out from there with a mighty hand and an outstretched arm; therefore the LORD your God commanded you to keep the sabbath day.

✠ The Response   Psalm 81:1-10

Psalm 81:1-10   *Exultate Deo*
1 Sing with joy to God our strength *
    and raise a loud shout to the God of Jacob.
2 Raise a song and sound the timbrel, *
    the merry harp, and the lyre.
3 Blow the ram's-horn at the new moon, *
    and at the full moon, the day of our feast.
4 For this is a statute for Israel, *
    a law of the God of Jacob.
5 He laid it as a solemn charge upon Joseph, *
    when he came out of the land of Egypt.
6 I heard an unfamiliar voice saying *
    "I eased his shoulder from the burden;
    his hands were set free from bearing the load."
7 You called on me in trouble, and I saved you; *
    I answered you from the secret place of thunder
    and tested you at the waters of Meribah.

8 Hear, O my people, and I will admonish you: *
 O Israel, if you would but listen to me!
9 There shall be no strange god among you; *
 you shall not worship a foreign god.
10 I am the LORD your God,
 who brought you out of the land of Egypt and said, *
 "Open your mouth wide, and I will fill it."

The Epistle   2 Corinthians 4:5-12

We do not proclaim ourselves; we proclaim Jesus Christ as Lord and ourselves as your slaves for Jesus' sake. For it is the God who said, "Let light
shine out of darkness," who has shone in our hearts to give the light of the
knowledge of the glory of God in the face of Jesus Christ. But we have this
treasure in clay jars, so that it may be made clear that this extraordinary
power belongs to God and does not come from us. We are afflicted in every
way, but not crushed; perplexed, but not driven to despair; persecuted, but not
forsaken; struck down, but not destroyed; always carrying in the body the
death of Jesus, so that the life of Jesus may also be made visible in our bodies.
For while we live, we are always being given up to death for Jesus' sake, so
that the life of Jesus may be made visible in our mortal flesh. So death is at
work in us, but life in you.

The Gospel   Mark 2:23—3:6

One sabbath Jesus was going through the grainfields; and as they made their
way his disciples began to pluck heads of grain. The Pharisees said to him,
"Look, why are they doing what is not lawful on the sabbath?" And he said to
them, "Have you never read what David did when he and his companions
were hungry and in need of food? He entered the house of God, when Abiathar
was high priest, and ate the bread of the Presence, which it is not lawful for
any but the priests to eat, and he gave some to his companions." Then he said
to them, "The sabbath was made for humankind, and not humankind for the
sabbath; so the Son of Man is lord even of the sabbath." Again he entered the
synagogue, and a man was there who had a withered hand. They watched him
to see whether he would cure him on the sabbath, so that they might accuse
him. And he said to the man who had the withered hand, "Come forward."
Then he said to them, "Is it lawful to do good or to do harm on the sabbath, to
save life or to kill?" But they were silent. He looked around at them with
anger; he was grieved at their hardness of heart and said to the man, "Stretch
out your hand." He stretched it out, and his hand was restored. The Pharisees
went out and immediately conspired with the Herodians against him, how to
destroy him.

Year C

1 Kings 18:20-21, (22-29), 30-39	**or**	✝ 1 Kings 8:22-23, 41-43
		✝ Psalm 96:1-9

Psalm 96

Galatians 1:1-12
Luke 7:1-10

The Lesson   1 Kings 18:20-21, (22-29), 30-39
1 Kings 18:20-21

Ahab sent to all the Israelites, and assembled the prophets at Mount Carmel. Elijah then came near to all the people, and said, "How long will you go limping with two different opinions? If the LORD is God, follow him; but if Baal, then follow him." The people did not answer him a word.

1 Kings 18:(22-29) [Then Elijah said to the people, "I, even I only, am left a prophet of the LORD; but Baal's prophets number four hundred fifty. Let two bulls be given to us; let them choose one bull for themselves, cut it in pieces, and lay it on the wood, but put no fire to it; I will prepare the other bull and lay it on the wood, but put no fire to it. Then you call on the name of your god and I will call on the name of the LORD; the god who answers by fire is indeed God." All the people answered, "Well spoken!" Then Elijah said to the prophets of Baal, "Choose for yourselves one bull and prepare it first, for you are many; then call on the name of your god, but put no fire to it." So they took the bull that was given them, prepared it, and called on the name of Baal from morning until noon, crying, "O Baal, answer us!" But there was no voice, and no answer. They limped about the altar that they had made. At noon Elijah mocked them, saying, "Cry aloud! Surely he is a god; either he is meditating, or he has wandered away, or he is on a journey, or perhaps he is asleep and must be awakened." Then they cried aloud and, as was their custom, they cut themselves with swords and lances until the blood gushed out over them. As midday passed, they raved on until the time of the offering of the oblation, but there was no voice, no answer, and no response.]

1 Kings 18:30-39 Then Elijah said to all the people, "Come closer to me"; and all the people came closer to him. First he repaired the altar of the LORD that had been thrown down; Elijah took twelve stones, according to the number of the tribes of the sons of Jacob, to whom the word of the LORD came, saying, "Israel shall be your name"; with the stones he built an altar in the name of the LORD. Then he made a trench around the altar, large enough to contain two measures of seed. Next he put the wood in order, cut the bull in pieces, and laid it on the wood. He said, "Fill four jars with water and pour it on the burnt offering and on the wood." Then he said, "Do it a second time"; and they did it a second time. Again he said, "Do it a third time"; and they did it a third time, so that the water ran all around the altar, and filled the trench also with water. At the time of the offering of the oblation, the prophet Elijah came near and said, "O LORD, God of Abraham, Isaac, and Israel, let it be known this day that you are God in Israel, that I am your servant, and that I have done all these things at your bidding. Answer me, O LORD, answer me, so that this people may know that you, O LORD, are God, and that you have turned their hearts back." Then the fire of the LORD fell and consumed the burnt offering, the wood, the stones, and the dust, and even licked up the water that was in the trench. When all the people saw it, they fell on their faces and said, "The LORD indeed is God; the LORD indeed is God."

The Response   Psalm 96

Psalm 96   *Cantate Domino*

  1   Sing to the LORD a new song; *
       sing to the LORD, all the whole earth.

  2   Sing to the LORD and bless his Name; *
       proclaim the good news of his salvation from day to day.

  3   Declare his glory among the nations *
       and his wonders among all peoples.

  4   For great is the LORD and greatly to be praised; *
       he is more to be feared than all gods.

  5   As for all the gods of the nations, they are but idols; *
       but it is the LORD who made the heavens.

  6   Oh, the majesty and magnificence of his presence! *
       Oh, the power and the splendor of his sanctuary!

  7   Ascribe to the LORD, you families of the peoples; *
       ascribe to the LORD honor and power.

  8   Ascribe to the LORD the honor due his Name; *
       bring offerings and come into his courts.

  9   Worship the LORD in the beauty of holiness; *
       let the whole earth tremble before him.

10   Tell it out among the nations: "The LORD is King! *
       he has made the world so firm that it cannot be moved;
       he will judge the peoples with equity."

11   Let the heavens rejoice, and let the earth be glad;
       let the sea thunder and all that is in it; *
       let the field be joyful and all that is therein.

12   Then shall all the trees of the wood shout for joy
       before the LORD when he comes, *
       when he comes to judge the earth.

13   He will judge the world with righteousness *
        and the peoples with his truth.

or, ✛ **The Lesson**   **1 Kings 8:22-23, 41-43**

Solomon stood before the altar of the Lord in the presence of all the assembly of Israel, and spread out his hands to heaven. He said, "O Lord, God of Israel, there is no God like you in heaven above or on earth beneath, keeping covenant and steadfast love for your servants who walk before you with all their heart. Likewise when a foreigner, who is not of your people Israel, comes from a distant land because of your name — for they shall hear of your great name, your mighty hand, and your outstretched arm — when a foreigner comes and prays toward this house, then hear in heaven your dwelling place, and do according to all that the foreigner calls to you, so that all the peoples of the earth may know your name and fear you, as do your people Israel, and so that they may know that your name has been invoked on this house that I have built."

✛ **The Response**   **Psalm 96:1-9**

Psalm 96:1-9   *Cantate Domino*

1   Sing to the LORD a new song; *
        sing to the LORD, all the whole earth.
2   Sing to the LORD and bless his Name; *
        proclaim the good news of his salvation from day to day.
3   Declare his glory among the nations *
        and his wonders among all peoples.
4   For great is the LORD and greatly to be praised; *
        he is more to be feared than all gods.
5   As for all the gods of the nations, they are but idols; *
        but it is the LORD who made the heavens.
6   Oh, the majesty and magnificence of his presence! *
        Oh, the power and the splendor of his sanctuary!
7   Ascribe to the LORD, you families of the peoples; *
        ascribe to the LORD honor and power.
8   Ascribe to the LORD the honor due his Name; *
        bring offerings and come into his courts.
9   Worship the LORD in the beauty of holiness; *
        let the whole earth tremble before him.

The Epistle   **Galatians 1:1-12**

Paul an apostle — sent neither by human commission nor from human authorities, but through Jesus Christ and God the Father, who raised him from the dead—and all the members of God's family who are with me, To the churches of Galatia: Grace to you and peace from God our Father and the Lord Jesus Christ, who gave himself for our sins to set us free from the present evil age, according to the will of our God and Father, to whom be the glory forever and ever. Amen. I am astonished that you are so quickly deserting the one who called you in the grace of Christ and are turning to a different gospel — not that there is another gospel, but there are some who are confusing you and want to pervert the gospel of Christ. But even if we or an angel from heaven should proclaim to you a gospel contrary to what we proclaimed to you, let that one be accursed! As we have said before, so now I repeat, if anyone proclaims to you a gospel contrary to what you received, let that one be accursed! Am I now seeking human approval, or God's approval? Or am I trying to please people? If I were still pleasing people, I would not be a servant of Christ. For I want you to know, brothers and sisters, that the gospel that was proclaimed by me is not of human origin; for I did not receive it from a human source, nor was I taught it, but I received it through a revelation of Jesus Christ.

The Gospel   Luke 7:1-10

After Jesus had finished all his sayings in the hearing of the people, he entered Capernaum. A centurion there had a slave whom he valued highly, and who was ill and close to death. When he heard about Jesus, he sent some Jewish elders to him, asking him to come and heal his slave. When they came to Jesus, they appealed to him earnestly, saying, "He is worthy of having you do this for him, for he loves our people, and it is he who built our synagogue for us." And Jesus went with them, but when he was not far from the house, the centurion sent friends to say to him, "Lord, do not trouble yourself, for I am not worthy to have you come under my roof; therefore I did not presume to come to you. But only speak the word, and let my servant be healed. For I also am a man set under authority, with soldiers under me; and I say to one, 'Go,' and he goes, and to another, 'Come,' and he comes, and to my slave, 'Do this,' and the slave does it." When Jesus heard this he was amazed at him, and turning to the crowd that followed him, he said, "I tell you, not even in Israel have I found such faith." When those who had been sent returned to the house, they found the slave in good health.

PROPER 5

Sunday between June 5 and June 11 inclusive (if after Trinity Sunday)
The Collect
O God, from whom all good proceeds: Grant that by your inspiration we may think those things that are right, and by your merciful guiding may do them; through Jesus Christ our Lord, who lives and reigns with you and the Holy Spirit, one God, for ever and ever. *Amen.*

Genesis 12:1-9 **or** ✣ *Hosea 5:15—6:6*
Psalm 33:1-12   ✣ *Psalm 50:7-15*

Romans 4:13-25
Matthew 9:9-13, 18-26

The Lesson   Genesis 12:1-9

The LORD said to Abram, "Go from your country and your kindred and your father's house to the land that I will show you. I will make of you a great nation, and I will bless you, and make your name great, so that you will be a blessing. I will bless those who bless you, and the one who curses you I will curse; and in you all the families of the earth shall be blessed." So Abram went, as the LORD had told him; and Lot went with him. Abram was seventy-five years old when he departed from Haran. Abram took his wife Sarai and his brother's son Lot, and all the possessions that they had gathered, and the persons whom they had acquired in Haran; and they set forth to go to the land of Canaan. When they had come to the land of Canaan, Abram passed through the land to the place at Shechem, to the oak of Moreh. At that time the Canaanites were in the land. Then the LORD appeared to Abram, and said, "To your offspring I will give this land." So he built there an altar to the LORD, who had appeared to him. From there he moved on to the hill country on the east of Bethel, and pitched his tent, with Bethel on the west and Ai on the east; and there he built an altar to the LORD and invoked the name of the LORD. And Abram journeyed on by stages toward the Negeb.

The Response   Psalm 33:1-12

Psalm 33:1-12 *Exultate, justi*

1 Rejoice in the LORD, you righteous; *
   it is good for the just to sing praises.
2 Praise the LORD with the harp; *
   play to him upon the psaltery and lyre.
3 Sing for him a new song; *
   sound a fanfare with all your skill upon the trumpet.
4 For the word of the LORD is right, *
   and all his works are sure.
5 He loves righteousness and justice; *
   the loving-kindness of the LORD fills the whole earth.
6 By the word of the LORD were the heavens made, *
   by the breath of his mouth all the heavenly hosts.
7 He gathers up the waters of the ocean as in a water-skin *
   and stores up the depths of the sea.
8 Let all the earth fear the LORD; *
   let all who dwell in the world stand in awe of him.

9   For he spoke, and it came to pass; *
       he commanded, and it stood fast.
10   The LORD brings the will of the nations to naught; *
       he thwarts the designs of the peoples.
11   But the LORD's will stands fast for ever, *
       and the designs of his heart from age to age.
12   Happy is the nation whose God is the LORD! *
       happy the people he has chosen to be his own!

or, ✠ **The Lesson**   **Hosea 5:15—6:6**

The LORD said: I will return again to my place until they acknowledge their guilt and seek my face. In their distress they will beg my favor: "Come, let us return to the LORD; for it is he who has torn, and he will heal us; he has struck down, and he will bind us up. After two days he will revive us; on the third day he will raise us up, that we may live before him. Let us know, let us press on to know the LORD; his appearing is as sure as the dawn; he will come to us like the showers, like the spring rains that water the earth." What shall I do with you, O Ephraim? What shall I do with you, O Judah? Your love is like a morning cloud, like the dew that goes away early. Therefore I have hewn them by the prophets, I have killed them by the words of my mouth, and my judgment goes forth as the light. For I desire steadfast love and not sacrifice, the knowledge of God rather than burnt offerings.

✠ **The Response**   **Psalm 50:7-15**

Psalm 50:7-15   *Deus deorum*
7   Hear, O my people, and I will speak:
     "O Israel, I will bear witness against you; *
       for I am God, your God.
8   I do not accuse you because of your sacrifices; *
       your offerings are always before me.
9   I will take no bull-calf from your stalls, *
       nor he-goats out of your pens;
10   For all the beasts of the forest are mine, *
       the herds in their thousands upon the hills.
11   I know every bird in the sky, *
       and the creatures of the fields are in my sight.
12   If I were hungry, I would not tell you, *
       for the whole world is mine and all that is in it.
13   Do you think I eat the flesh of bulls, *
       or drink the blood of goats?
14   Offer to God a sacrifice of thanksgiving *
       and make good your vows to the Most High.

15   Call upon me in the day of trouble; *
    I will deliver you, and you shall honor me."

The Epistle   Romans 4:13-25

The promise that he would inherit the world did not come to Abraham or to his descendants through the law but through the righteousness of faith. If it is the adherents of the law who are to be the heirs, faith is null and the promise is void. For the law brings wrath; but where there is no law, neither is there violation. For this reason it depends on faith, in order that the promise may rest on grace and be guaranteed to all his descendants, not only to the adherents of the law but also to those who share the faith of Abraham (for he is the father of all of us, as it is written, "I have made you the father of many nations") — in the presence of the God in whom he believed, who gives life to the dead and calls into existence the things that do not exist. Hoping against hope, he believed that he would become "the father of many nations," according to what was said, "So numerous shall your descendants be." He did not weaken in faith when he considered his own body, which was already as good as dead (for he was about a hundred years old), or when he considered the barrenness of Sarah's womb. No distrust made him waver concerning the promise of God, but he grew strong in his faith as he gave glory to God, being fully convinced that God was able to do what he had promised. Therefore his faith "was reckoned to him as righteousness." Now the words, "it was reckoned to him," were written not for his sake alone, but for ours also. It will be reckoned to us who believe in him who raised Jesus our Lord from the dead, who was handed over to death for our trespasses and was raised for our justification.

The Gospel   Matthew 9:9-13, 18-26

Jesus saw a man called Matthew sitting at the tax booth; and he said to him, "Follow me." And he got up and followed him. And as he sat at dinner in the house, many tax collectors and sinners came and were sitting with him and his disciples. When the Pharisees saw this, they said to his disciples, "Why does your teacher eat with tax collectors and sinners?" But when he heard this, he said, "Those who are well have no need of a physician, but those who are sick. Go and learn what this means, 'I desire mercy, not sacrifice.' For I have come to call not the righteous but sinners." While he was saying these things to them, suddenly a leader of the synagogue came in and knelt before him, saying, "My daughter has just died; but come and lay your hand on her, and she will live." And Jesus got up and followed him, with his disciples. Then suddenly a woman who had been suffering from hemorrhages for twelve years came up behind him and touched the fringe of his cloak, for she said to herself, "If I only touch his cloak, I will be made well." Jesus turned, and seeing her he said, "Take heart, daughter; your faith has made you well." And instantly the woman was made well. When Jesus came to the leader's house and saw the flute players and the crowd making a commotion, he said, "Go away; for the girl is not dead but sleeping." And they laughed at him. But when the crowd had been put outside, he went in and took her by the hand, and the girl got up. And the report of this spread throughout that district.

Year B

1 Samuel 8:4-11, (12-15),	**or**	✠ *Genesis 3:8-15*
16-20, (11:14-15)		✠ *Psalm 130*
Psalm 138		

2 Corinthians 4:13—5:1
Mark 3:20-35

The Lesson   1 Samuel 8:4-11, (12-15), 16-20, (11:14-15)
1 Samuel 8:4-11

All the elders of Israel gathered together and came to Samuel at Ramah, and said to him, "You are old and your sons do not follow in your ways; appoint for us, then, a king to govern us, like other nations." But the thing displeased Samuel when they said, "Give us a king to govern us." Samuel prayed to the LORD, and the LORD said to Samuel, "Listen to the voice of the people in all that they say to you; for they have not rejected you, but they have rejected me from being king over them. Just as they have done to me, from the day I brought them up out of Egypt to this day, forsaking me and serving other gods, so also they are doing to you. Now then, listen to their voice; only—you shall solemnly warn them, and show them the ways of the king who shall reign over them." So Samuel reported all the words of the LORD to the people who were asking him for a king. He said, "These will be the ways of the king who will reign over you: he will take your sons and appoint them to his chariots and to be his horsemen, and to run before his chariots;

1 Samuel 8:(12-15) [and he will appoint for himself commanders of thousands and commanders of fifties, and some to plow his ground and to reap his harvest, and to make his implements of war and the equipment of his chariots. He will take your daughters to be perfumers and cooks and bakers. He will take the best of your fields and vineyards and olive orchards and give them to his courtiers. He will take one-tenth of your grain and of your vineyards and give it to his officers and his courtiers.]

1 Samuel 8:16-20 He will take your male and female slaves, and the best of your cattle and donkeys, and put them to his work. He will take one-tenth of your flocks, and you shall be his slaves. And in that day you will cry out because of your king, whom you have chosen for yourselves; but the LORD will not answer you in that day." But the people refused to listen to the voice of Samuel; they said, "No! but we are determined to have a king over us, so that we also may be like other nations, and that our king may govern us and go out before us and fight our battles."

1 Samuel (11:14-15) [Samuel said to the people, "Come, let us go to Gilgal and there renew the kingship." So all the people went to Gilgal, and there they made Saul king before the LORD in Gilgal. There they sacrificed offerings of well-being before the LORD, and there Saul and all the Israelites rejoiced greatly.]

The Response   Psalm 138

Psalm 138   *Confitebor tibi*

1   I will give thanks to you, O LORD, with my whole heart; *
        before the gods I will sing your praise.
2   I will bow down toward your holy temple
    and praise your Name, *
        because of your love and faithfulness;
3   For you have glorified your Name *
        and your word above all things.
4   When I called, you answered me; *
        you increased my strength within me.
5   All the kings of the earth will praise you, O LORD, *
        when they have heard the words of your mouth.
6   They will sing of the ways of the LORD, *
        that great is the glory of the LORD.
7   Though the LORD be high, he cares for the lowly; *
        he perceives the haughty from afar.
8   Though I walk in the midst of trouble, you keep me safe; *
        you stretch forth your hand against the fury of my enemies;
        your right hand shall save me.
9   The LORD will make good his purpose for me; *
        O LORD, your love endures for ever;
        do not abandon the works of your hands

or, ✚ **The Lesson**   **Genesis 3:8-15**

They heard the sound of the LORD God walking in the garden at the time of the evening breeze, and the man and his wife hid themselves from the presence of the LORD God among the trees of the garden. But the LORD God called to the man, and said to him, "Where are you?" He said, "I heard the sound of you in the garden, and I was afraid, because I was naked; and I hid myself." He said,

"Who told you that you were naked? Have you eaten from the tree of which I commanded you not to eat?" The man said, "The woman whom you gave to be with me, she gave me fruit from the tree, and I ate." Then the LORD God said to the woman, "What is this that you have done?" The woman said, "The serpent tricked me, and I ate." The LORD God said to the serpent, "Because you have done this, cursed are you among all animals and among all wild creatures; upon your belly you shall go, and dust you shall eat all the days of your life. I will put enmity between you and the woman, and between your offspring and hers; he will strike your head, and you will strike his heel."

✝ The Response   Psalm 130

Psalm 130   *De profundis*

1   Out of the depths have I called to you, O LORD;
      LORD, hear my voice; *
          let your ears consider well the voice of my supplication.
2   If you, LORD, were to note what is done amiss, *
          O LORD, who could stand?
3   For there is forgiveness with you; *
          therefore you shall be feared.
4   I wait for the LORD; my soul waits for him; *
          in his word is my hope.
5   My soul waits for the LORD,
      more than watchmen for the morning, *
          more than watchmen for the morning.
6   O Israel, wait for the LORD, *
          for with the LORD there is mercy;
7   With him there is plenteous redemption, *
          and he shall redeem Israel from all their sins.

The Epistle   2 Corinthians 4:13—5:1

Just as we have the same spirit of faith that is in accordance with scripture — "I believed, and so I spoke" — we also believe, and so we speak, because we know that the one who raised the Lord Jesus will raise us also with Jesus, and will bring us with you into his presence. Yes, everything is for your sake, so that grace, as it extends to more and more people, may increase thanksgiving, to the glory of God. So we do not lose heart. Even though our outer nature is wasting away, our inner nature is being renewed day by day. For this slight momentary affliction is preparing us for an eternal weight of glory beyond all measure, because we look not at what can be seen but at what cannot be seen; for what can be seen is temporary, but what cannot be seen is eternal. For we know that if the earthly tent we live in is destroyed, we have a building from God, a house not made with hands, eternal in the heavens.

The Gospel   Mark 3:20-35

The crowd came together again, so that Jesus and his disciples could not even
eat. When his family heard it, they went out to restrain him, for people were
saying, "He has gone out of his mind." And the scribes who came down from
Jerusalem said, "He has Beelzebul, and by the ruler of the demons he casts out
demons." And he called them to him, and spoke to them in parables, "How
can Satan cast out Satan? If a kingdom is divided against itself, that kingdom
cannot stand. And if a house is divided against itself, that house will not be
able to stand. And if Satan has risen up against himself and is divided, he
cannot stand, but his end has come. But no one can enter a strong man's house
and plunder his property without first tying up the strong man; then indeed the
house can be plundered. Truly I tell you, people will be forgiven for their sins
and whatever blasphemies they utter; but whoever blasphemes against the
Holy Spirit can never have forgiveness, but is guilty of an eternal sin"— for
they had said, "He has an unclean spirit." Then his mother and his brothers
came; and standing outside, they sent to him and called him. A crowd was
sitting around him; and they said to him, "Your mother and your brothers and
sisters are outside, asking for you." And he replied, "Who are my mother and
my brothers?" And looking at those who sat around him, he said, "Here are
my mother and my brothers! Whoever does the will of God is my brother and
sister and mother."

Year C

1 Kings 17:8-16, (17-24)   **or**   ✝ *1 Kings 17:17-24*
Psalm 146   ✝ *Psalm 30*
Galatians 1:11-24
Luke 7:11-17

The Lesson   1 Kings 17:8-16, (17-24)
1 Kings 17:8-16

Then the word of the LORD came to Elijah, saying, "Go now to Zarephath,
which belongs to Sidon, and live there; for I have commanded a widow there
to feed you." So he set out and went to Zarephath. When he came to the gate
of the town, a widow was there gathering sticks; he called to her and said,
"Bring me a little water in a vessel, so that I may drink." As she was going to
bring it, he called to her and said, "Bring me a morsel of bread in your hand."
but she said, "As the LORD your God lives, I have nothing baked, only a
handful of meal in a jar, and a little oil in a jug; I am now gathering a couple
of sticks, so that I may go home and prepare it for myself and my son, that we
may eat it, and die." Elijah said to her, "Do not be afraid; go and do as you
have said; but first make me a little cake of it and bring it to me, and afterwards make something for yourself and your son. For thus says the LORD the

God of Israel: The jar of meal will not be emptied and the jug of oil will not fail until the day that the LORD sends rain on the earth." She went and did as Elijah said, so that she as well as he and her household ate for many days. The jarof meal was not emptied, nether did the jug of oil fail, according to the word of the LORD that he spoke by Elijah.

1 Kings 17:(17-24) [The son of the woman, the mistress of the house, became ill; his illness was so severe that there was no breath left in him. She then said to Elijah, "What have you against me, O man of God? You have come to me to bring my sin to remembrance, and to cause the death of my son!" But he said to her, "Give me your son." He took him from her bosom, carried him up into the upper chamber where he was lodging, and laid him on his own bed. He cried out to the Lord, "O Lord my God, have you brought calamity even upon the widow with whom I am staying, by killing her son?" Then he stretched himself upon the child three times, and cried out to the Lord, "O Lord my God, let this child's life come into him again." The Lord listened to the voice of Elijah; the life of the child came into him again, and he revived. Elijah took the child, brought him down from the upper chamber into the house, and gave him to his mother; then Elijah said, "See, your son is alive." So the woman said to Elijah, "Now I know that you are a man of God, and that the word of the Lord in your mouth is truth."]

The Response   Psalm 146

Psalm 146   *Lauda, anima mea*
1   Hallelujah!
    Praise the LORD, O my soul! *
    I will praise the LORD as long as I live;
        I will sing praises to my God while I have my being.
2   Put not your trust in rulers, nor in any child of earth, *
        for there is no help in them.
3   When they breathe their last, they return to earth, *
        and in that day their thoughts perish.
4   Happy are they who have the God of Jacob for their help! *
        whose hope is in the LORD their God;
5   Who made heaven and earth, the seas, and all that is in them; *
        who keeps his promise for ever;
6   Who gives justice to those who are oppressed, *
        and food to those who hunger.
7   The LORD sets the prisoners free;
    the LORD opens the eyes of the blind; *
        the LORD lifts up those who are bowed down;

8   The LORD loves the righteous;
      the LORD cares for the stranger; *
          he sustains the orphan and widow,
          but frustrates the way of the wicked.
9   The LORD shall reign for ever, *
      your God, O Zion, throughout all generations.
      Hallelujah!

or, ✝ The Lesson   1 Kings 17:17-24

The son of the woman, the mistress of the house, became ill; his illness was so
severe that there was no breath left in him. She then said to Elijah, "What
have you against me, O man of God? You have come to me to bring my sin to
remembrance, and to cause the death of my son!" But he said to her, "Give me
your son." He took him from her bosom, carried him up into the upper
chamber where he was lodging, and laid him on his own bed. He cried out to
the Lord, "O Lord my God, have you brought calamity even upon the widow
with whom I am staying, by killing her son?" Then he stretched himself upon
the child three times, and cried out to the Lord, "O Lord my God, let this
child's life come into him again." The Lord listened to the voice of Elijah; the
life of the child came into him again, and he revived. Elijah took the child,
brought him down from the upper chamber into the house, and gave him to his
mother; then Elijah said, "See, your son is alive." So the woman said to
Elijah, "Now I know that you are a man of God, and that the word of the Lord
in your mouth is truth."

✝ The Response   Psalm 30

Psalm 30   *Exaltabo te, Domine*
   1   I will exalt you, O LORD,
          because you have lifted me up *
             and have not let my enemies triumph over me.
   2   O LORD my God, I cried out to you, *
             and you restored me to health.
   3   You brought me up, O LORD, from the dead; *
             you restored my life as I was going down to the grave.
   4   Sing to the LORD, you servants of his; *
             give thanks for the remembrance of his holiness.
   5   For his wrath endures but the twinkling of an eye, *
             his favor for a lifetime.
   6   Weeping may spend the night, *
             but joy comes in the morning.

7   While I felt secure, I said,
    "I shall never be disturbed. *
        You, LORD, with your favor, made me as strong as
            the mountains."
8   Then you hid your face, *
    and I was filled with fear.
9   I cried to you, O LORD; *
    I pleaded with the LORD, saying,
10 "What profit is there in my blood, if I go down to the Pit? *
    will the dust praise you or declare your faithfulness?
11 Hear, O LORD, and have mercy upon me; *
    O LORD, be my helper."
12 You have turned my wailing into dancing; *
    you have put off my sack-cloth and clothed me with joy.
13 Therefore my heart sings to you without ceasing; *
    O LORD my God, I will give you thanks for ever.

The Epistle   Galatians 1:11-24

I want you to know, brothers and sisters, that the gospel that was proclaimed
by me is not of human origin; for I did not receive it from a human source, nor
was I taught it, but I received it through a revelation of Jesus Christ. You have
heard, no doubt, of my earlier life in Judaism. I was violently persecuting the
church of God and was trying to destroy it. I advanced in Judaism beyond
many among my people of the same age, for I was far more zealous for the
traditions of my ancestors. But when God, who had set me apart before I was
born and called me through his grace, was pleased to reveal his Son to me, so
that I might proclaim him among the Gentiles, I did not confer with any
human being, nor did I go up to Jerusalem to those who were already apostles
before me, but I went away at once into Arabia, and afterwards I returned to
Damascus. Then after three years I did go up to Jerusalem to visit Cephas and
stayed with him fifteen days; but I did not see any other apostle except James
the Lord's brother. In what I am writing to you, before God, I do not lie! Then
I went into the regions of Syria and Cilicia, and I was still unknown by sight
to the churches of Judea that are in Christ; they only heard it said, "The one
who formerly was persecuting us is now proclaiming the faith he once tried to
destroy." And they glorified God because of me.

The Gospel   Luke 7:11-17

Soon after healing the centurion's slave, Jesus went to a town called Nain, and
his disciples and a large crowd went with him. As he approached the gate of
the town, a man who had died was being carried out. He was his mother's
only son, and she was a widow; and with her was a large crowd from the

town. When the Lord saw her, he had compassion for her and said to her, "Do not weep." Then he came forward and touched the bier, and the bearers stood still. And he said, "Young man, I say to you, rise!" The dead man sat up and began to speak, and Jesus gave him to his mother. Fear seized all of them; and they glorified God, saying, "A great prophet has risen among us!" and "God has looked favorably on his people!" This word about him spread throughout Judea and all the surrounding country.

PROPER 6

Sunday between June 12 and June 18 inclusive (if after Trinity Sunday)

The Collect

Keep, O Lord, your household the Church in your steadfast faith and love, that through your grace we may proclaim your truth with boldness, and minister your justice with compassion; for the sake of our Savior Jesus Christ, who lives and reigns with you and the Holy Spirit, one God, now and for ever. *Amen.*

Year A

Genesis 18:1-15, (21:1-7)	**or**	✢ *Exodus 19:2-8a*
Psalm 116:1, 10-17		✢ *Psalm 100*
	Romans 5:1-8	
	Matthew 9:35—10:8, (9-23)	

The Lesson   **Genesis 18:1-15, (21:1-7)**
Genesis 18:1-15

The LORD appeared to Abraham by the oaks of Mamre, as he sat at the entrance of his tent in the heat of the day. He looked up and saw three men standing near him. When he saw them, he ran from the tent entrance to meet them, and bowed down to the ground. He said, "My lord, if I find favor with you, do not pass by your servant. Let a little water be brought, and wash your feet, and rest yourselves under the tree. Let me bring a little bread, that you may refresh yourselves, and after that you may pass on—since you have come to your servant." So they said, "Do as you have said." And Abraham hastened into the tent to Sarah, and said, "Make ready quickly three measures of choice flour, knead it, and make cakes." Abraham ran to the herd, and took a calf, tender and good, and gave it to the servant, who hastened to prepare it. Then he took curds and milk and the calf that he had prepared, and set it before them; and he stood by them under the tree while they ate. They said to him, "Where is your wife Sarah?" And he said, "There, in the tent." Then one said, "I will surely return to you in due season, and your wife Sarah shall have a son." And Sarah was listening at the tent entrance behind him. Now Abraham and Sarah were old, advanced in age; it had ceased to be with Sarah after the manner of women. So Sarah laughed to herself, saying, "After I have grown old, and my husband is old, shall I have pleasure?" The LORD said to Abraham, "Why did Sarah laugh, and say, 'Shall I indeed bear a child, now that I am old?' Is anything too wonderful for the LORD? At the set time I will return to you, in due season, and Sarah shall have a son." But Sarah denied, saying, "I did not laugh"; for she was afraid. He said, "Oh yes, you did laugh."

Genesis (21:1-7) [The LORD dealt with Sarah as he had said, and the LORD did for Sarah as he had promised. Sarah conceived and bore Abraham a son in his old age, at the time of which God had spoken to him. Abraham gave the name Isaac to his son whom Sarah bore him. And Abraham circumcised his son Isaac when he was eight days old, as God had commanded him. Abraham was a hundred years old when his son Isaac was born to him. Now Sarah said, "God has brought laughter for me; everyone who hears will laugh with me." And she said, "Who would ever have said to Abraham that Sarah would nurse children? Yet I have borne him a son in his old age."]

The Response   **Psalm 116:1, 10-17**
Psalm 116:1-2, 10-17   *Dilexi, quoniam*
1   I love the LORD, because he has heard the voice of
                    my supplication, *
            because he has inclined his ear to me whenever
                    I called upon him.
10   How shall I repay the LORD *
            for all the good things he has done for me?
11   I will lift up the cup of salvation *
            and call upon the Name of the LORD.
12   I will fulfill my vows to the LORD *
            in the presence of all his people.
13   Precious in the sight of the LORD *
            is the death of his servants.
14   O LORD, I am your servant; *
            I am your servant and the child of your handmaid;
            you have freed me from my bonds.
15   I will offer you the sacrifice of thanksgiving *
            and call upon the Name of the LORD.
16   I will fulfill my vows to the LORD *
            in the presence of all his people,
17   In the courts of the LORD's house, *
            in the midst of you, O Jerusalem.
            Hallelujah!

or, ✠ **The Lesson** Exodus 19:2-8*a*

The people of Israel had journeyed from Rephidim, entered the wilderness of Sinai, and camped in the wilderness; Israel camped there in front of the mountain. Then Moses went up to God; the Lord called to him from the mountain, saying, "Thus you shall say to the house of Jacob, and tell the Israelites: You have seen what I did to the Egyptians, and how I bore you on eagles' wings and brought you to myself. Now therefore, if you obey my voice and keep my covenant, you shall be my treasured possession out of all the peoples. Indeed, the whole earth is mine, but you shall be for me a priestly kingdom and a holy nation. These are the words that you shall speak to the Israelites." So Moses came, summoned the elders of the people, and set before them all these words that the Lord had commanded him. The people all answered as one: "Everything that the Lord has spoken we will do."

✠ **The Response** **Psalm 100**

Psalm 100 *Jubilate Deo*

1 Be joyful in the LORD, all you lands; *
  serve the LORD with gladness
  and come before his presence with a song.

2 Know this: The LORD himself is God; *
  he himself has made us, and we are his;
  we are his people and the sheep of his pasture.

3 Enter his gates with thanksgiving;
  go into his courts with praise; *
  give thanks to him and call upon his Name.

4 For the LORD is good;
  his mercy is everlasting; *
  and his faithfulness endures from age to age.

The Epistle **Romans 5:1-8**

Since we are justified by faith, we have peace with God through our Lord Jesus Christ, through whom we have obtained access to this grace in which we stand; and we boast in our hope of sharing the glory of God. And not only that, but we also boast in our sufferings, knowing that suffering produces endurance, and endurance produces character, and character produces hope, and hope does not disappoint us, because God's love has been poured into our hearts through the Holy Spirit that has been given to us. For while we were still weak, at the right time Christ died for the ungodly. Indeed, rarely will anyone die for a righteous person — though perhaps for a good person someone might actually dare to die. But God proves his love for us in that while we still were sinners Christ died for us.

The Gospel Matthew 9:35—10:8 (9-23)
Matthew 9:35—10:8

Jesus went about all the cities and villages, teaching in their synagogues, and proclaiming the good news of the kingdom, and curing every disease and every sickness. When he saw the crowds, he had compassion for them, because they were harassed and helpless, like sheep without a shepherd. Then he said to his disciples, "The harvest is plentiful, but the laborers are few; therefore ask the Lord of the harvest to send out laborers into his harvest." Then Jesus summoned his twelve disciples and gave them authority over unclean spirits, to cast them out, and to cure every disease and every sickness. These are the names of the twelve apostles: first, Simon, also known as Peter, and his brother Andrew; James son of Zebedee, and his brother John; Philip and Bartholomew; Thomas and Matthew the tax collector; James son of Alphaeus, and Thaddaeus; Simon the Cananaean, and Judas Iscariot, the one who betrayed him. These twelve Jesus sent out with the following instructions: "Go nowhere among the Gentiles, and enter no town of the Samaritans, but go rather to the lost sheep of the house of Israel. As you go, proclaim the good news, 'The kingdom of heaven has come near.' Cure the sick, raise the dead, cleanse the lepers, cast out demons. You received without payment; give without payment."

Matthew 10:(9-23) ["Take no gold, or silver, or copper in your belts, no bag for your journey, or two tunics, or sandals, or a staff; for laborers deserve their food. Whatever town or village you enter, find out who in it is worthy, and stay there until you leave. As you enter the house, greet it. If the house is worthy, let your peace come upon it; but if it is not worthy, let your peace return to you. If anyone will not welcome you or listen to your words, shake off the dust from your feet as you leave that house or town. Truly I tell you, it will be more tolerable for the land of Sodom and Gomorrah on the day of judgment than for that town. See, I am sending you out like sheep into the midst of wolves; so be wise as serpents and innocent as doves. Beware of them, for they will hand you over to councils and flog you in their synagogues; and you will be dragged before governors and kings because of me, as a testimony to them and the Gentiles. When they hand you over, do not worry about how you are to speak or what you are to say; for what you are to say will be given to you at that time; for it is not you who speak, but the Spirit of your Father speaking through you. Brother will betray brother to death, and a father his child, and children will rise against parents and have them put to death; and you will be hated by all because of my name. But the one who endures to the end will be saved. When they persecute you in one town, flee to the next; for truly I tell you, you will not have gone through all the towns of Israel before the Son of Man comes."]

Year B

1 Samuel 15:34—16:13   **or**   ✝ *Ezekiel 17:22-24*

Psalm 20   ✝ *Psalm 92:1-4, 11-14*

2 Corinthians 5:6-10, (11-13), 14-17

Mark 4:26-34

The Lesson   **1 Samuel 15:34—16:13**

Samuel went to Ramah; and Saul went up to his house in Gibeah of Saul. Samuel did not see Saul again until the day of his death, but Samuel grieved over Saul. And the LORD was sorry that he had made Saul king over Israel. The LORD said to Samuel, "How long will you grieve over Saul? I have rejected him from being king over Israel. Fill your horn with oil and set out; I will send you to Jesse the Bethlehemite, for I have provided for myself a king among his sons." Samuel said, "How can I go? If Saul hears of it, he will kill me." And the LORD said, "Take a heifer with you, and say, 'I have come to sacrifice to the LORD.' Invite Jesse to the sacrifice, and I will show you what you shall do; and you shall anoint for me the one whom I name to you." Samuel did what the LORD commanded, and came to Bethlehem. The elders of the city came to meet him trembling, and said, "Do you come peaceably?" He said, "Peaceably; I have come to sacrifice to the LORD; sanctify yourselves and come with me to the sacrifice." And he sanctified Jesse and his sons and invited them to the sacrifice. When they came, he looked on Eliab and thought, "Surely the LORD's anointed is now before the LORD." But the LORD said to Samuel, "Do not look on his appearance or on the height of his stature, because I have rejected him; for the LORD does not see as mortals see; they look on the outward appearance, but the LORD looks on the heart." Then Jesse called Abinadab, and made him pass before Samuel. He said, "Neither has the LORD chosen this one." Then Jesse made Shammah pass by. And he said, "Neither has the LORD chosen this one." Jesse made seven of his sons pass before Samuel, and Samuel said to Jesse, "The LORD has not chosen any of these." Samuel said to Jesse, "Are all your sons here?" And he said, "There remains yet the youngest, but he is keeping the sheep." And Samuel said to Jesse, "Send and bring him; for we will not sit down until he comes here." He sent and brought him in. Now he was ruddy, and had beautiful eyes, and was handsome. The LORD said, "Rise and anoint him; for this is the one." Then Samuel took the horn of oil, and anointed him in the presence of his brothers; and the spirit of the LORD came mightily upon David from that day forward. Samuel then set out and went to Ramah.

The Response   **Psalm 20**

Psalm 20   *Exaudiat te Dominus*

1   May the LORD answer you in the day of trouble, *
        the Name of the God of Jacob defend you;
2   Send you help from his holy place *
        and strengthen you out of Zion;
3   Remember all your offerings *
        and accept your burnt sacrifice;
4   Grant you your heart's desire *
        and prosper all your plans.
5   We will shout for joy at your victory
    and triumph in the Name of our God; *
        may the LORD grant all your requests.
6   Now I know that the LORD gives victory to his anointed; *
        he will answer him out of his holy heaven,
        with the victorious strength of his right hand.
7   Some put their trust in chariots and some in horses, *
        but we will call upon the Name of the LORD our God.
8   They collapse and fall down, *
        but we will arise and stand upright.
9   O LORD, give victory to the king *
        and answer us when we call.

or, ☩ **The Lesson**   **Ezekiel 17:22-24**

Thus says the Lord GOD: I myself will take a sprig from the lofty top of a
cedar; I will set it out. I will break off a tender one from the topmost of its
young twigs; I myself will plant it on a high and lofty mountain. On the
mountain height of Israel I will plant it, in order that it may produce boughs
and bear fruit, and become a noble cedar. Under it every kind of bird will live;
in the shade of its branches will nest winged creatures of every kind. All the
trees of the field shall know that I am the LORD. I bring low the high tree, I
make high the low tree; I dry up the green tree and make the dry tree flourish.
I the LORD have spoken; I will accomplish it.

☩ **The Response**   **Psalm 92:1-4, 11-14**

Psalm 92:1-4, 11-14   *Bonum est confiteri*

1   It is a good thing to give thanks to the LORD, *
        and to sing praises to your Name, O Most High;
2   To tell of your loving-kindness early in the morning *
        and of your faithfulness in the night season;

3   On the psaltery, and on the lyre, *
    and to the melody of the harp.
4   For you have made me glad by your acts, O LORD; *
    and I shout for joy because of the works of your hands
11 The righteous shall flourish like a palm tree, *
    and shall spread abroad like a cedar of Lebanon.
12 Those who are planted in the house of the LORD *
    shall flourish in the courts of our God;
13 They shall still bear fruit in old age; *
    they shall be green and succulent;
14 That they may show how upright the LORD is, *
    my Rock, in whom there is no fault.

The Epistle   2 Corinthians 5:6-10, (11-13), 14-17
2 Corinthians 5:6-10

We are always confident; even though we know that while we are at home in
the body we are away from the Lord — for we walk by faith, not by sight.
Yes, we do have confidence, and we would rather be away from the body and
at home with the Lord. So whether we are at home or away, we make it our
aim to please him. For all of us must appear before the judgment seat of
Christ, so that each may receive recompense for what has been done in the
body, whether good or evil.

2 Corinthians 5:(11-13) [Therefore, knowing the fear of the Lord, we try
to persuade others; but we ourselves are well known to God, and I hope that
we are also well known to your consciences. We are not commending ourselves to you again, but giving you an opportunity to boast about us, so that
you may be able to answer those who boast in outward appearance and not in
the heart. For if we are beside ourselves, it is for God; if we are in our right
mind, it is for you.]

2 Corinthians 5:14-17 For the love of Christ urges us on, because we are
convinced that one has died for all; therefore all have died. And he died for all,
so that those who live might live no longer for themselves, but for him who
died and was raised for them. From now on, therefore, we regard no one from
a human point of view; even though we once knew Christ from a human point
of view, we know him no longer in that way. So if anyone is in Christ, there is
a new creation: everything old has passed away; see, everything has become
new!

The Gospel   Mark 4:26-34

Jesus said, "The kingdom of God is as if someone would scatter seed on the ground, and would sleep and rise night and day, and the seed would sprout and grow, he does not know how. The earth produces of itself, first the stalk, then the head, then the full grain in the head. But when the grain is ripe, at once he goes in with his sickle, because the harvest has come." He also said, "With what can we compare the kingdom of God, or what parable will we use for it? It is like a mustard seed, which, when sown upon the ground, is the smallest of all the seeds on earth; yet when it is sown it grows up and becomes the greatest of all shrubs, and puts forth large branches, so that the birds of the air can make nests in its shade." With many such parables he spoke the word to them, as they were able to hear it; he did not speak to them except in parables, but he explained everything in private to his disciples.

Year C

1 Kings 21:1-10, (11-14),   **or**   ✝ *2 Samuel 11:26—12:10,*
15-21a   *13-15*
Psalm 5:1-8   ✝ *Psalm 32*

Galatians 2:15-21
Luke 7:36—8:3

The Lesson   1 Kings 21:1-10, (11-14), 15-21a
1 Kings 21:1-10

The following events took place: Naboth the Jezreelite had a vineyard in Jezreel, beside the palace of King Ahab of Samaria. And Ahab said to Naboth, "Give me your vineyard, so that I may have it for a vegetable garden, because it is near my house; I will give you a better vineyard for it; or, if it seems good to you, I will give you its value in money." But Naboth said to Ahab, "The LORD forbid that I should give you my ancestral inheritance." Ahab went home resentful and sullen because of what Naboth the Jezreelite had said to him; for he had said, "I will not give you my ancestral inheritance." He lay down on his bed, turned away his face, and would not eat. His wife Jezebel came to him and said, "Why are you so depressed that you will not eat?" He said to her, "Because I spoke to Naboth the Jezreelite and said to him, 'Give me your vineyard for money; or else, if you prefer, I will give you another vineyard for it'; but he answered, 'I will not give you my vineyard.'" His wife Jezebel said to him, "Do you now govern Israel? Get up, eat some food, and be cheerful; I will give you the vineyard of Naboth the Jezreelite." So she wrote letters in Ahab's name and sealed them with his seal; she sent the letters to the elders and the nobles who lived with Naboth in his city. She wrote in the letters, "Proclaim a fast, and seat Naboth at the head of the assembly; seat two scoundrels opposite him, and have them bring a charge against him, saying, 'You have cursed God and the king.' Then take him out, and stone him to death."

1 Kings 21:(11-14) [The men of his city, the elders and the nobles who lived in his city, did as Jezebel had sent word to them. Just as it was written in the letters that she had sent to them, they proclaimed a fast and seated Naboth at the head of the assembly. The two scoundrels came in and sat opposite him; and the scoundrels brought a charge against Naboth, in the presence of the people, saying, "Naboth cursed God and the king." So they took him outside the city, and stoned him to death. Then they sent to Jezebel, saying, "Naboth has been stoned; he is dead."]

1 Kings 21:15-21a As soon as Jezebel heard that Naboth had been stoned and was dead, Jezebel said to Ahab, "Go, take possession of the vineyard of Naboth the Jezreelite, which he refused to give you for money; for Naboth is not alive, but dead." As soon as Ahab heard that Naboth was dead, Ahab set out to go down to the vineyard of Naboth the Jezreelite, to take possession of it. Then the word of the LORD came to Elijah the Tishbite, saying: Go down to meet King Ahab of Israel, who rules in Samaria; he is now in the vineyard of Naboth, where he has gone to take possession. You shall say to him, "Thus says the LORD: Have you killed, and also taken possession?" You shall say to him, "Thus says the LORD: In the place where dogs licked up the blood of Naboth, dogs will also lick up your blood." Ahab said to Elijah, "Have you found me, O my enemy?" He answered, "I have found you. Because you have sold yourself to do what is evil in the sight of the LORD, I will bring disaster on you."

The Response   Psalm 5:1-8

Psalm 5:1-8   *Verba mea auribus*

1   Give ear to my words, O LORD; *
        consider my meditation.
2   Hearken to my cry for help, my King and my God, *
        for I make my prayer to you.
3   In the morning, LORD, you hear my voice; *
        early in the morning I make my appeal and watch for you.
4   For you are not a God who takes pleasure in wickedness, *
        and evil cannot dwell with you.
5   Braggarts cannot stand in your sight; *
        you hate all those who work wickedness.
6   You destroy those who speak lies; *
        the bloodthirsty and deceitful, O LORD, you abhor.

7   But as for me, through the greatness of your mercy I will
                go into your house; *
         I will bow down toward your holy temple in awe of you.
8   Lead me, O LORD, in your righteousness,
         because of those who lie in wait for me; *
                make your way straight before me.

or, ☩ **The Lesson**   **2 Samuel 11:26—12:10, 13-15**

When the wife of Uriah heard that her husband was dead, she made lamentation for him. When the mourning was over, David sent and brought her to his
house, and she became his wife, and bore him a son. But the thing that David
had done displeased the LORD, and the LORD sent Nathan to David. He came to
him, and said to him, "There were two men in a certain city, the one rich and
the other poor. The rich man had very many flocks and herds; but the poor
man had nothing but one little ewe lamb, which he had bought. He brought it
up, and it grew up with him and with his children; it used to eat of his meager
fare, and drink from his cup, and lie in his bosom, and it was like a daughter
to him. Now there came a traveler to the rich man, and he was loath to take
one of his own flock or herd to prepare for the wayfarer who had come to him,
but he took the poor man's lamb, and prepared that for the guest who had
come to him." Then David's anger was greatly kindled against the man. He
said to Nathan, "As the LORD lives, the man who has done this deserves to die;
he shall restore the lamb fourfold, because he did this thing, and because he
had no pity." Nathan said to David, "You are the man! Thus says the LORD,
the God of Israel: I anointed you king over Israel, and I rescued you from the
hand of Saul; I gave you your master's house, and your master's wives into
your bosom, and gave you the house of Israel and of Judah; and if that had
been too little, I would have added as much more. Why have you despised the
word of the LORD, to do what is evil in his sight? You have struck down Uriah
the Hittite with the sword, and have taken his wife to be your wife, and have
killed him with the sword of the Ammonites. Now therefore the sword shall
never depart from your house, for you have despised me, and have taken the
wife of Uriah the Hittite to be your wife." David said to Nathan, "I have
sinned against the LORD." Nathan said to David, "Now the LORD has put away
your sin; you shall not die. Nevertheless, because by this deed you have
utterly scorned the LORD, the child that is born to you shall die." Then Nathan
went to his house. The LORD struck the child that Uriah's wife bore to David
and it became very ill.

Psalm 32   *Beati quorum*

1   Happy are they whose transgressions are forgiven, *
        and whose sin is put away!
2   Happy are they to whom the LORD imputes no guilt, *
        and in whose spirit there is no guile!
3   While I held my tongue, my bones withered away, *
        because of my groaning all day long.
4   For your hand was heavy upon me day and night; *
        my moisture was dried up as in the heat of summer.
5   Then I acknowledged my sin to you, *
        and did not conceal my guilt.
6   I said, "I will confess my transgressions to the LORD." *
        Then you forgave me the guilt of my sin.
7   Therefore all the faithful will make their prayers to you in
                        time of trouble; *
        when the great waters overflow, they shall not reach them.
8   You are my hiding-place;
    you preserve me from trouble; *
        you surround me with shouts of deliverance.
9   "I will instruct you and teach you in the way that you should go; *
        I will guide you with my eye.
10 Do not be like horse or mule, which have no understanding; *
        who must be fitted with bit and bridle,
        or else they will not stay near you."
11 Great are the tribulations of the wicked; *
        but mercy embraces those who trust in the LORD.
12 Be glad, you righteous, and rejoice in the LORD; *
        shout for joy, all who are true of heart.

The Epistle   Galatians 2:15-21

We ourselves are Jews by birth and not Gentile sinners; yet we know that a
person is justified not by the works of the law but through faith in Jesus
Christ. And we have come to believe in Christ Jesus, so that we might be
justified by faith in Christ, and not by doing the works of the law, because no
one will be justified by the works of the law. But if, in our effort to be justified
in Christ, we ourselves have been found to be sinners, is Christ then a servant
of sin? Certainly not! But if I build up again the very things that I once tore
down, then I demonstrate that I am a transgressor. For through the law I died
to the law, so that I might live to God. I have been crucified with Christ; and it
is no longer I who live, but it is Christ who lives in me. And the life I now live
in the flesh I live by faith in the Son of God, who loved me and gave himself

for me. I do not nullify the grace of God; for if justification comes through the law, then Christ died for nothing.

The Gospel   Luke 7:36—8:3

One of the Pharisees asked Jesus to eat with him, and he went into the Pharisee's house and took his place at the table. And a woman in the city, who was a sinner, having learned that he was eating in the Pharisee's house, brought an alabaster jar of ointment. She stood behind him at his feet, weeping, and began to bathe his feet with her tears and to dry them with her hair. Then she continued kissing his feet and anointing them with the ointment. Now when the Pharisee who had invited him saw it, he said to himself, "If this man were a prophet, he would have known who and what kind of woman this is who is touching him — that she is a sinner." Jesus spoke up and said to him, "Simon, I have something to say to you." "Teacher," he replied, "Speak." "A certain creditor had two debtors; one owed five hundred denarii, and the other fifty. When they could not pay, he canceled the debts for both of them. Now which of them will love him more?" Simon answered, "I suppose the one for whom he canceled the greater debt." And Jesus said to him, "You have judged rightly." Then turning toward the woman, he said to Simon, "Do you see this woman? I entered your house; you gave me no water for my feet, but she has bathed my feet with her tears and dried them with her hair. You gave me no kiss, but from the time I came in she has not stopped kissing my feet. You did not anoint my head with oil, but she has anointed my feet with ointment. Therefore, I tell you, her sins, which were many, have been forgiven; hence she has shown great love. But the one to whom little is forgiven, loves little." Then he said to her, "Your sins are forgiven." But those who were at the table with him began to say among themselves, "Who is this who even forgives sins?" And he said to the woman, "Your faith has saved you; go in peace." Soon afterwards he went on through cities and villages, proclaiming and bringing the good news of the kingdom of God. The twelve were with him, as well as some women who had been cured of evil spirits and infirmities: Mary, called Magdalene, from whom seven demons had gone out, and Joanna, the wife of Herod's steward Chuza, and Susanna, and many others, who provided for them out of their resources.

PROPER 7

Sunday between June 19 and June 25 inclusive (if after Trinity Sunday)

The Collect

O Lord, make us have perpetual love and reverence for your holy Name, for you never fail to help and govern those whom you have set upon the sure foundation of your loving-kindness; through Jesus Christ our Lord, who lives and reigns with you and the Holy Spirit, one God, for ever and ever. *Amen.*

Year A

Genesis 21:8-21	**or**	✝ *Jeremiah 20:7-13*
Psalm 86:1-10, 16-17		✝ *Psalm 69:8-11, (12-17), 18-20*

Romans 6:1b-11

Matthew 10:24-39

The Lesson   Genesis 21:8-21

The child grew, and was weaned; and Abraham made a great feast on the day that Isaac was weaned. But Sarah saw the son of Hagar the Egyptian, whom she had borne to Abraham, playing with her son Isaac. So she said to Abraham, "Cast out this slave woman with her son; for the son of this slave woman shall not inherit along with my son Isaac." The matter was very distressing to Abraham on account of his son. But God said to Abraham, "Do not be distressed because of the boy and because of your slave woman; whatever Sarah says to you, do as she tells you, for it is through Isaac that offspring shall be named for you. As for the son of the slave woman, I will make a nation of him also, because he is your offspring." So Abraham rose early in the morning, and took bread and a skin of water, and gave it to Hagar, putting it on her shoulder, along with the child, and sent her away. And she departed, and wandered about in the wilderness of Beer-sheba. When the water in the skin was gone, she cast the child under one of the bushes. Then she went and sat down opposite him a good way off, about the distance of a bowshot; for she said, "Do not let me look on the death of the child." And as she sat opposite him, she lifted up her voice and wept. And God heard the voice of the boy; and the angel of God called to Hagar from heaven, and said to her, "What troubles you, Hagar? Do not be afraid; for God has heard the voice of the boy where he is. Come, lift up the boy and hold him fast with your hand, for I will make a great nation of him." Then God opened her eyes and she saw a well of water. She went, and filled the skin with water, and gave the boy a drink. God was with the boy, and he grew up; he lived in the wilderness, and became an expert with the bow. He lived in the wilderness of Paran; and his mother got a wife for him from the land of Egypt.

The Response   Psalm 86:1-10, 16-17

Psalm 86:1-10, 16-17   *Inclina, Domine*

1   Bow down your ear, O Lord, and answer me, *
        for I am poor and in misery.

2   Keep watch over my life, for I am faithful; *
        save your servant who puts his trust in you.

3   Be merciful to me, O Lord, for you are my God; *
        I call upon you all the day long.

PROPER 7 - *June 19 - June 25* — **Year A**   **331**

4   Gladden the soul of your servant, *
      for to you, O LORD, I lift up my soul.

5   For you, O LORD, are good and forgiving, *
      and great is your love toward all who call upon you.

6   Give ear, O LORD, to my prayer, *
      and attend to the voice of my supplications.

7   In the time of my trouble I will call upon you, *
      for you will answer me.

8   Among the gods there is none like you, O LORD, *
      nor anything like your works.

9   All nations you have made will come and
                     worship you, O LORD, *
      and glorify your Name.

10 For you are great;
   you do wondrous things; *
      and you alone are God.

16 Turn to me and have mercy upon me; *
      give your strength to your servant;
      and save the child of your handmaid.

17 Show me a sign of your favor,
   so that those who hate me may see it and be ashamed; *
      because you, O LORD, have helped me and comforted me.

or, ✛ **The Lesson**   **Jeremiah 20:7-13**

O LORD, you have enticed me, and I was enticed; you have overpowered me, and you have prevailed. I have become a laughingstock all day long; everyone mocks me. For whenever I speak, I must cry out, I must shout, "Violence and destruction!" For the word of the LORD has become for me a reproach and derision all day long. If I say, "I will not mention him, or speak any more in his name," then within me there is something like a burning fire shut up in my bones; I am weary with holding it in, and I cannot. For I hear many whispering: "Terror is all around! Denounce him! Let us denounce him!" All my close friends are watching for me to stumble. "Perhaps he can be enticed, and we can prevail against him, and take our revenge on him." But the LORD is with me like a dread warrior; therefore my persecutors will stumble, and they will not prevail. They will be greatly shamed, for they will not succeed. Their eternal dishonor will never be forgotten. O LORD of hosts, you test the righteous, you see the heart and the mind; let me see your retribution upon them, for to you I have committed my cause. Sing to the LORD; praise the LORD! For he has delivered the life of the needy from the hands of evildoers.

✠ **The Response**   **Psalm 69:8-11, (12-17), 18-20**

Psalm 69:8-11, (12-17), 18-20   *Salvum me fac*

8   Surely, for your sake have I suffered reproach, *
        and shame has covered my face.
9   I have become a stranger to my own kindred, *
        an alien to my mother's children.
10   Zeal for your house has eaten me up; *
        the scorn of those who scorn you has fallen upon me.
11   I humbled myself with fasting, *
        but that was turned to my reproach.

[12   I put on sack-cloth also, *
        and became a byword among them.
13   Those who sit at the gate murmur against me, *
        and the drunkards make songs about me.
14   But as for me, this is my prayer to you, *
        at the time you have set, O LORD:
15   "In your great mercy, O God, *
        answer me with your unfailing help.
16   Save me from the mire; do not let me sink; *
        let me be rescued from those who hate me
        and out of the deep waters.
17   Let not the torrent of waters wash over me,
        neither let the deep swallow me up; *
        do not let the Pit shut its mouth upon me.]

18   Answer me, O LORD, for your love is kind; *
        in your great compassion, turn to me."
19   "Hide not your face from your servant; *
        be swift and answer me, for I am in distress.
20   Draw near to me and redeem me; *
        because of my enemies deliver me."

The Epistle   **Romans 6:1b-11**

Should we continue in sin in order that grace may abound? By no means! How
can we who died to sin go on living in it? Do you not know that all of us who
have been baptized into Christ Jesus were baptized into his death? Therefore
we have been buried with him by baptism into death, so that, just as Christ
was raised from the dead by the glory of the Father, so we too might walk in
newness of life. For if we have been united with him in a death like his, we
will certainly be united with him in a resurrection like his. We know that our
old self was crucified with him so that the body of sin might be destroyed, and

we might no longer be enslaved to sin. For whoever has died is freed from sin. But if we have died with Christ, we believe that we will also live with him. We know that Christ, being raised from the dead, will never die again; death no longer has dominion over him. The death he died, he died to sin, once for all; but the life he lives, he lives to God. So you also must consider yourselves dead to sin and alive to God in Christ Jesus.

The Gospel   Matthew 10:24-39

Jesus said to his disciples, "A disciple is not above the teacher, nor a slave above the master; it is enough for the disciple to be like the teacher, and the slave like the master. If they have called the master of the house Beelzebul, how much more will they malign those of his household! So have no fear of them; for nothing is covered up that will not be uncovered, and nothing secret that will not become known. What I say to you in the dark, tell in the light; and what you hear whispered, proclaim from the housetops. Do not fear those who kill the body but cannot kill the soul; rather fear him who can destroy both soul and body in hell. Are not two sparrows sold for a penny? Yet not one of them will fall to the ground apart from your Father. And even the hairs of your head are all counted. So do not be afraid; you are of more value than many sparrows. Everyone therefore who acknowledges me before others, I also will acknowledge before my Father in heaven; but whoever denies me before others, I also will deny before my Father in heaven. Do not think that I have come to bring peace to the earth; I have not come to bring peace, but a sword. For I have come to set a man against his father, and a daughter against her mother, and a daughter-in-law against her mother-in-law; and one's foes will be members of one's own household. Whoever loves father or mother more than me is not worthy of me; and whoever loves son or daughter more than me is not worthy of me; and whoever does not take up the cross and follow me is not worthy of me. Those who find their life will lose it, and those who lose their life for my sake will find it."

Year B

1 Samuel 17:(1a, 4-11, 19-23),   **or**   ✠ *Job 38:1-11*
              32-49   ✠ *Psalm 107:1-3, 23-32*
Psalm 9:9-20
or
1 Samuel 17:57—18:5, 10-16
Psalm 133

                    2 Corinthians 6:1-13
                    Mark 4:35-41

The Lesson   **1 Samuel 17:(1a, 4-11, 19-23), 32-49**

1 Samuel 17:(1a, 4-11, 19-23) [Now the Philistines gathered their armies for battle. And there came out from the camp of the Philistines a champion named Goliath, of Gath, whose height was six cubits and a span. He had a helmet of bronze on his head, and he was armed with a coat of mail; the weight of the coat was five thousand shekels of bronze. He had greaves of bronze on his legs and a javelin of bronze slung between his shoulders. The shaft of his spear was like a weaver's beam, and his spear's head weighed six hundred shekels of iron; and his shield-bearer went before him. He stood and shouted to the ranks of Israel, "Why have you come out to draw up for battle? Am I not a Philistine, and are you not servants of Saul? Choose a man for yourselves, and let him come down to me. If he is able to fight with me and kill me, then we will be your servants; but if I prevail against him and kill him, then you shall be our servants and serve us." And the Philistine said, "Today I defy the ranks of Israel! Give me a man, that we may fight together." When Saul and all Israel heard these words of the Philistine, they were dismayed and greatly afraid. Now Saul, and they, and all the men of Israel, were in the valley of Elah, fighting with the Philistines. David rose early in the morning, left the sheep with a keeper, took the provisions, and went as Jesse had commanded him. He came to the encampment as the army was going forth to the battle line, shouting the war cry. Israel and the Philistines drew up for battle, army against army. David left the things in charge of the keeper of the baggage, ran to the ranks, and went and greeted his brothers. As he talked with them, the champion, the Philistine of Gath, Goliath by name, came up out of the ranks of the Philistines, and spoke the same words as before. And David heard him.]

1 Samuel 17:32-49 David said to Saul, "Let no one's heart fail because of him; your servant will go and fight with this Philistine." Saul said to David, "You are not able to go against this Philistine to fight with him; for you are just a boy, and he has been a warrior from his youth." But David said to Saul, "Your servant used to keep sheep for his father; and whenever a lion or a bear came, and took a lamb from the flock, I went after it and struck it down, rescuing the lamb from its mouth; and if it turned against me, I would catch it by the jaw, strike it down, and kill it. Your servant has killed both lions and bears; and this uncircumcised Philistine shall be like one of them, since he has defied the armies of the living God." David said, "The LORD, who saved me from the paw of the lion and from the paw of the bear, will save me from the hand of this Philistine." So Saul said to David, "Go, and may the LORD be with you!" Saul clothed David with his armor; he put a bronze helmet on his head and clothed him with a coat of mail. David strapped Saul's sword over the armor, and he tried in vain to walk, for he was not used to them. Then David said to Saul, "I cannot walk with these; for I am not used to them." So David removed them. Then he took his staff in his hand, and chose five smooth stones from the wadi, and put them in his shepherd's bag, in the pouch; his sling was in his hand, and he drew near to the Philistine. The Philistine came on and drew near to David, with his shield-bearer in front of him. When the Philistine looked and saw David, he disdained him, for he was only a youth, ruddy and handsome in appearance. The Philistine said to David, "Am I a dog, that you come to me with sticks?" And the Philistine cursed David by his gods. The Philistine said to David, "Come to me, and I will give your flesh to the birds of the air and to the wild animals of the field." But David said to the Philistine, "You come to me with sword and spear and javelin; but I come to you in the name of the LORD of hosts, the God of the armies of Israel, whom you have defied. This very day the LORD will deliver you into my hand, and I will strike you down and cut off your head; and I will give the dead bodies of the Philistine army this very day to the birds of the air and to the wild animals of the earth, so that all the earth may know that there is a God in Israel, and that all this assembly may know that the LORD does not save by sword and spear; for the battle is the LORD's and he will give you into our hand." When the Philistine drew nearer to meet David, David ran quickly toward the battle line to meet the Philistine. David put his hand in his bag, took out a stone, slung it, and struck the Philistine on his forehead; the stone sank into his forehead, and he fell face down on the ground.

The Response   Psalm 9:9-20

Psalm 9:9-20 *Confitebor tibi*

9   The LORD will be a refuge for the oppressed, *
        a refuge in time of trouble.
10   Those who know your Name will put their trust in you, *
        for you never forsake those who seek you, O LORD.
11   Sing praise to the LORD who dwells in Zion; *
        proclaim to the peoples the things he has done.
12   The Avenger of blood will remember them; *
        he will not forget the cry of the afflicted.
13   Have pity on me, O LORD; *
        see the misery I suffer from those who hate me,
        O you who lift me up from the gate of death;
14   So that I may tell of all your praises
     and rejoice in your salvation *
        in the gates of the city of Zion.
15   The ungodly have fallen into the pit they dug, *
        and in the snare they set is their own foot caught.

16 The LORD is known by his acts of justice; *
       the wicked are trapped in the works of their own hands.
17 The wicked shall be given over to the grave, *
       and also all the peoples that forget God.
18 For the needy shall not always be forgotten, *
       and the hope of the poor shall not perish for ever.
19 Rise up, O LORD, let not the ungodly have the upper hand; *
       let them be judged before you.
20 Put fear upon them, O LORD; *
       let the ungodly know they are but mortal.

or, **The Lesson**   **1 Samuel 17:57—18:5, 10-16**

On David's return from killing the Philistine, Abner took him and brought him
before Saul, with the head of the Philistine in his hand. Saul said to him,
"Whose son are you, young man?" And David answered, "I am the son of
your servant Jesse the Bethlehemite." When David had finished speaking to
Saul, the soul of Jonathan was bound to the soul of David, and Jonathan loved
him as his own soul. Saul took him that day and would not let him return to
his father's house. Then Jonathan made a covenant with David, because he
loved him as his own soul. Jonathan stripped himself of the robe that he was
wearing, and gave it to David, and his armor, and even his sword and his bow
and his belt. David went out and was successful wherever Saul sent him; as a
result, Saul set him over the army. And all the people, even the servants of
Saul, approved. The next day an evil spirit from God rushed upon Saul, and
he raved within his house, while David was playing the lyre, as he did day by
day. Saul had his spear in his hand; and Saul threw the spear, for he thought,
"I will pin David to the wall." But David eluded him twice. Saul was afraid of
David, because the LORD was with him but had departed from Saul. So Saul
removed him from his presence, and made him a commander of a thousand;
and David marched out and came in, leading the army. David had success in
all his undertakings; for the LORD was with him. When Saul saw that he had
great success, he stood in awe of him. But all Israel and Judah loved David;
for it was he who marched out and came in leading them.

The Response   **Psalm 133**

Psalm 133 *Ecce, quam bonum!*
   1 Oh, how good and pleasant it is, *
          when brethren live together in unity!
   2 It is like fine oil upon the head *
          that runs down upon the beard,
   3 Upon the beard of Aaron, *
          and runs down upon the collar of his robe.

4   It is like the dew of Hermon *
         that falls upon the hills of Zion.
5   For there the LORD has ordained the blessing: *
         life for evermore.

or, ✠ The Lesson   Job 38:1-11

The LORD answered Job out of the whirlwind: "Who is this that darkens counsel by words without knowledge? Gird up your loins like a man, I will question you, and you shall declare to me. Where were you when I laid the foundation of the earth? Tell me, if you have understanding. Who determined its measurements — surely you know! Or who stretched the line upon it? On what were its bases sunk, or who laid its cornerstone when the morning stars sang together and all the heavenly beings shouted for joy? Or who shut in the sea with doors when it burst out from the womb? — when I made the clouds its garment, and thick darkness its swaddling band, and prescribed bounds for it, and set bars and doors, and said, 'Thus far shall you come, and no farther, and here shall your proud waves be stopped'?"

✠ The Response   Psalm 107:1-3, 23-32

Psalm 107:1-3, 23-32   *Confitemini Domino*
    1   Give thanks to the LORD, for he is good, *
             and his mercy endures for ever.
    2   Let all those whom the LORD has redeemed proclaim *
             that he redeemed them from the hand of the foe.
    3   He gathered them out of the lands; *
             from the east and from the west,
             from the north and from the south.
   23   Some went down to the sea in ships *
             and plied their trade in deep waters;
   24   They beheld the works of the LORD *
             and his wonders in the deep.
   25   Then he spoke, and a stormy wind arose, *
             which tossed high the waves of the sea.
   26   They mounted up to the heavens and fell back to the depths; *
             their hearts melted because of their peril.
   27   They reeled and staggered like drunkards *
             and were at their wits' end.
   28   Then they cried to the LORD in their trouble, *
             and he delivered them from their distress.
   29   He stilled the storm to a whisper *
             and quieted the waves of the sea.

30   Then were they glad because of the calm, *
       and he brought them to the harbor they were bound for.
31   Let them give thanks to the LORD for his mercy *
       and the wonders he does for his children.
32   Let them exalt him in the congregation of the people *
       and praise him in the council of the elders.

The Epistle   2 Corinthians 6:1-13

As we work together with him, we urge you also not to accept the grace of God in vain. For he says, "At an acceptable time I have listened to you, and on a day of salvation I have helped you." See, now is the acceptable time; see, now is the day of salvation! We are putting no obstacle in anyone's way, so that no fault may be found with our ministry, but as servants of God we have commended ourselves in every way: through great endurance, in afflictions, hardships, calamities, beatings, imprisonments, riots, labors, sleepless nights, hunger; by purity, knowledge, patience, kindness, holiness of spirit, genuine love, truthful speech, and the power of God; with the weapons of righteousness for the right hand and for the left; in honor and dishonor, in ill repute and good repute. We are treated as impostors, and yet are true; as unknown, and yet are well known; as dying, and see — we are alive; as punished, and yet not killed; as sorrowful, yet always rejoicing; as poor, yet making many rich; as having nothing, and yet possessing everything. We have spoken frankly to you Corinthians; our heart is wide open to you. There is no restriction in our affections, but only in yours. In return — I speak as to children — open wide your hearts also.

The Gospel   Mark 4:35-41

On that day, when evening had come, Jesus said to his disciples, "Let us go across to the other side." And leaving the crowd behind, they took him with them in the boat, just as he was. Other boats were with him. A great windstorm arose, and the waves beat into the boat, so that the boat was already being swamped. But he was in the stern, asleep on the cushion; and they woke him up and said to him, "Teacher, do you not care that we are perishing?" He woke up and rebuked the wind, and said to the sea, "Peace! Be still!" Then the wind ceased, and there was a dead calm. He said to them, "Why are you afraid? Have you still no faith?" And they were filled with great awe and said to one another, "Who then is this, that even the wind and the sea obey him?"

Year C

1 Kings 19:1-4, (5-7), 8-15a	**or**	✝ *Isaiah 65:1-9*
Psalm 42 and *43*		✝ *Psalm 22:18-27*

Galatians 3:23-29
Luke 8:26-39

The Lesson   1 Kings 19:1-4, (5-7), 8-15*a*
1 Kings 19:1-4

Ahab told Jezebel all that Elijah had done, and how he had killed all the prophets with the sword. Then Jezebel sent a messenger to Elijah, saying, "So may the gods do to me, and more also, if I do not make your life like the life of one of them by this time tomorrow." Then he was afraid; he got up and fled for his life, and came to Beer-sheba, which belongs to Judah; he left his servant there. But he himself went a day's journey into the wilderness, and came and sat down under a solitary broom tree. He asked that he might die: "It is enough; now, O LORD, take away my life, for I am no better than my ancestors."

1 Kings 19:(5-7) [Then he lay down under the broom tree and fell asleep. Suddenly an angel touched him and said to him, "Get up and eat." He looked, and there at his head was a cake baked on hot stones, and a jar of water. He ate and drank, and lay down again. The angel of the LORD came a second time, touched him, and said, "Get up and eat, otherwise the journey will be too much for you."]

1 Kings 19:8-15*a* He got up, and ate and drank; then he went in the strength of that food forty days and forty nights to Horeb the mount of God. At that place he came to a cave, and spent the night there. Then the word of the LORD came to him, saying, "What are you doing here, Elijah?" He answered, "I have been very zealous for the LORD, the God of hosts; for the Israelites have forsaken your covenant, thrown down your altars, and killed your prophets with the sword. I alone am left, and they are seeking my life, to take it away." He said, "Go out and stand on the mountain before the LORD, for the LORD is about to pass by." Now there was a great wind, so strong that it was splitting mountains and breaking rocks in pieces before the LORD, but the LORD was not in the wind; and after the wind an earthquake, but the LORD was not in the earthquake; and after the earthquake a fire, but the LORD was not in the fire; and after the fire a sound of sheer silence. When Elijah heard it, he wrapped his face in his mantle and went out and stood at the entrance of the cave. Then there came a voice to him that said, "What are you doing here, Elijah?" He answered, "I have been very zealous for the LORD, the God of hosts; for the

Israelites have forsaken your covenant, thrown down your altars, and killed your prophets with the sword. I alone am left, and they are seeking my life, to take it away." Then the LORD said to him, "Go, return on your way to the wilderness of Damascus."

The Response   Psalm 42 and 43
Psalm 42 *Quemadmodum*

1 As the deer longs for the water-brooks, *
      so longs my soul for you, O God.
2 My soul is athirst for God, athirst for the living God; *
      when shall I come to appear before the presence of God?
3 My tears have been my food day and night, *
      while all day long they say to me,
      "Where now is your God?"
4 I pour out my soul when I think on these things: *
      how I went with the multitude and led them into the
            house of God,
5 With the voice of praise and thanksgiving, *
      among those who keep holy-day.
6 Why are you so full of heaviness, O my soul? *
      and why are you so disquieted within me?
7 Put your trust in God; *
      for I will yet give thanks to him,
      who is the help of my countenance, and my God.
8 My soul is heavy within me; *
      therefore I will remember you from the land of Jordan,
      and from the peak of Mizar among the heights of Hermon.
9 One deep calls to another in the noise of your cataracts; *
      all your rapids and floods have gone over me.
10 The LORD grants his loving-kindness in the daytime; *
      in the night season his song is with me,
      a prayer to the God of my life.
11 I will say to the God of my strength,
      "Why have you forgotten me? *
      and why do I go so heavily while the enemy
            oppresses me?"
12 While my bones are being broken, *
      my enemies mock me to my face;
13 All day long they mock me *
      and say to me, "Where now is your God?"
14 Why are you so full of heaviness, O my soul? *
      and why are you so disquieted within me?

15   Put your trust in God; *
            for I will yet give thanks to him,
            who is the help of my countenance, and my God.

Psalm 43   *Judica me, Deus*

1   Give judgment for me, O God,
            and defend my cause against an ungodly people; *
            deliver me from the deceitful and the wicked.

2   For you are the God of my strength;
            why have you put me from you? *
            and why do I go so heavily while the enemy oppresses me?

3   Send out your light and your truth, that they may lead me, *
            and bring me to your holy hill
            and to your dwelling;

4   That I may go to the altar of God,
            to the God of my joy and gladness; *
            and on the harp I will give thanks to you, O God my God.

5   Why are you so full of heaviness, O my soul? *
            and why are you so disquieted within me?

6   Put your trust in God; *
            for I will yet give thanks to him,
            who is the help of my countenance, and my God.

or, ✟ **The Lesson**   **Isaiah 65:1-9**

The Lord spoke: I was ready to be sought out by those who did not ask, to be
found by those who did not seek me. I said, "Here I am, here I am," to a
nation that did not call on my name. I held out my hands all day long to a
rebellious people, who walk in a way that is not good, following their own
devices; a people who provoke me to my face continually, sacrificing in
gardens and offering incense on bricks; who sit inside tombs, and spend the
night in secret places; who eat swine's flesh, with broth of abominable things
in their vessels; who say, "Keep to yourself, do not come near me, for I am too
holy for you." These are a smoke in my nostrils, a fire that burns all day long.
See, it is written before me: I will not keep silent, but I will repay; I will
indeed repay into their laps their iniquities and their ancestors' iniquities
together, says the LORD; because they offered incense on the mountains and
reviled me on the hills, I will measure into their laps full payment for their
actions. Thus says the LORD: As the wine is found in the cluster, and they say,
"Do not destroy it, for there is a blessing in it," so I will do for my servants'
sake, and not destroy them all. I will bring forth descendants from Jacob, and
from Judah inheritors of my mountains; my chosen shall inherit it, and my
servants shall settle there.

✠ **The Response**   **Psalm 22:18-27**

Psalm 22:18-27   *Deus, Deus meus*

18   Be not far away, O LORD; *
　　　you are my strength; hasten to help me.
19   Save me from the sword, *
　　　my life from the power of the dog.
20   Save me from the lion's mouth, *
　　　my wretched body from the horns of wild bulls.
21   I will declare your Name to my brethren; *
　　　in the midst of the congregation I will praise you.
22   Praise the LORD, you that fear him; *
　　　stand in awe of him, O offspring of Israel;
　　　all you of Jacob's line, give glory.
23   For he does not despise nor abhor the poor in their poverty;
　　　neither does he hide his face from them; *
　　　but when they cry to him he hears them.
24   My praise is of him in the great assembly; *
　　　I will perform my vows in the presence of those who
　　　　　　worship him.
25   The poor shall eat and be satisfied,
　　　and those who seek the LORD shall praise him: *
　　　"May your heart live for ever!"
26   All the ends of the earth shall remember and turn to the LORD, *
　　　and all the families of the nations shall bow before him.
27   For kingship belongs to the LORD; *
　　　he rules over the nations.

The Epistle   **Galatians 3:23-29**

Now before faith came, we were imprisoned and guarded under the law until faith would be revealed. Therefore the law was our disciplinarian until Christ came, so that we might be justified by faith. But now that faith has come, we are no longer subject to a disciplinarian, for in Christ Jesus you are all children of God through faith. As many of you as were baptized into Christ have clothed yourselves with Christ. There is no longer Jew or Greek, there is no longer slave or free, there is no longer male and female; for all of you are one in Christ Jesus. And if you belong to Christ, then you are Abraham's offspring, heirs according to the promise.

The Gospel   **Luke 8:26-39**

Jesus and his disciples arrived at the country of the Gerasenes, which is opposite Galilee. As he stepped out on land, a man of the city who had demons met him. For a long time he had worn no clothes, and he did not live in a house but in the tombs. When he saw Jesus, he fell down before him and shouted at the top of his voice, "What have you to do with me, Jesus, Son of the Most High God? I beg you, do not torment me" — for Jesus had commanded the unclean spirit to come out of the man. (For many times it had seized him; he was kept under guard and bound with chains and shackles, but he would break the bonds and be driven by the demon into the wilds.) Jesus then asked him, "What is your name?" He said, "Legion"; for many demons had entered him. They begged him not to order them to go back into the abyss. Now there on the hillside a large herd of swine was feeding; and the demons begged Jesus to let them enter these. So he gave them permission. Then the demons came out of the man and entered the swine, and the herd rushed down the steep bank into the lake and was drowned. When the swineherds saw what had happened, they ran off and told it in the city and in the country. Then people came out to see what had happened, and when they came to Jesus, they found the man from whom the demons had gone sitting at the feet of Jesus, clothed and in his right mind. And they were afraid. Those who had seen it told them how the one who had been possessed by demons had been healed. Then all the people of the surrounding country of the Gerasenes asked Jesus to leave them; for they were seized with great fear. So he got into the boat and returned. The man from whom the demons had gone begged that he might be with him; but Jesus sent him away, saying, "Return to your home, and declare how much God has done for you." So he went away, proclaiming throughout the city how much Jesus had done for him.

PROPER 8

Sunday between June 26 and July 2 inclusive

The Collect

Almighty God, you have built your Church upon the foundation of the apostles and prophets, Jesus Christ himself being the chief cornerstone: Grant us so to be joined together in unity of spirit by their teaching, that we may be made a holy temple acceptable to you; through Jesus Christ our Lord, who lives and reigns with you and the Holy Spirit, one God, for ever and ever. *Amen.*

Year A

Genesis 22:1-14	**or**	✠ *Jeremiah 28:5-9*
Psalm 13		✠ *Psalm 89:1-4, 15-18*
	Romans 6:12-23	
	Matthew 10:40-42	

The Lesson   Genesis 22:1-14

God tested Abraham. He said to him, "Abraham!" And he said, "Here I am." He said, "Take your son, your only son Isaac, whom you love, and go to the land of Moriah, and offer him there as a burnt offering on one of the mountains that I shall show you." So Abraham rose early in the morning, saddled his donkey, and took two of his young men with him, and his son Isaac; he cut the wood for the burnt offering, and set out and went to the place in the distance that God had shown him. On the third day Abraham looked up and saw the place far away. Then Abraham said to his young men, "Stay here with the donkey; the boy and I will go over there; we will worship, and then we will come back to you." Abraham took the wood of the burnt offering and laid it on his son Isaac, and he himself carried the fire and the knife. So the two of them walked on together. Isaac said to his father Abraham, "Father!" And he said, "Here I am, my son." He said, "The fire and the wood are here, but where is the lamb for a burnt offering?" Abraham said, "God himself will provide the lamb for a burnt offering, my son." So the two of them walked on together. When they came to the place that God had shown him, Abraham built an altar there and laid the wood in order. He bound his son Isaac, and laid him on the altar, on top of the wood. Then Abraham reached out his hand and took the knife to kill his son. But the angel of the LORD called to him from heaven, and said, "Abraham, Abraham!" And he said, "Here I am." He said, "Do not lay your hand on the boy or do anything to him; for now I know that you fear God, since you have not withheld your son, your only son, from me." And Abraham looked up and saw a ram, caught in a thicket by its horns. Abraham went and took the ram and offered it up as a burnt offering instead of his son. So Abraham called that place "The LORD will provide"; as it is said to this day, "On the mount of the LORD it shall be provided."

The Response   Psalm 13

Psalm 13   *Usquequo, Domine?*

1   How long, O LORD?
      will you forget me for ever? *
         how long will you hide your face from me?
2   How long shall I have perplexity in my mind,
      and grief in my heart, day after day? *
         how long shall my enemy triumph over me?
3   Look upon me and answer me, O LORD my God; *
         give light to my eyes, lest I sleep in death;
4   Lest my enemy say, "I have prevailed over him," *
         and my foes rejoice that I have fallen.
5   But I put my trust in your mercy; *
         my heart is joyful because of your saving help.
6   I will sing to the LORD, for he has dealt with me richly; *
         I will praise the Name of the LORD Most High.

or, ✠ **The Lesson**   **Jeremiah 28:5-9**

The prophet Jeremiah spoke to the prophet Hananiah in the presence of the priests and all the people who were standing in the house of the LORD; and the prophet Jeremiah said, "Amen! May the LORD do so; may the LORD fulfill the words that you have prophesied, and bring back to this place from Babylon the vessels of the house of the LORD, and all the exiles. But listen now to this word that I speak in your hearing and in the hearing of all the people. The prophets who preceded you and me from ancient times prophesied war, famine, and pestilence against many countries and great kingdoms. As for the prophet who prophesies peace, when the word of that prophet comes true, then it will be known that the LORD has truly sent the prophet."

✠ **The Response**   **Psalm 89:1-4, 15-18**

Psalm 89:1-4, 15-18   *Misericordias Domini*

1   Your love, O LORD, for ever will I sing; *
        from age to age my mouth will proclaim your faithfulness.
2   For I am persuaded that your love is established for ever; *
        you have set your faithfulness firmly in the heavens.
3   "I have made a covenant with my chosen one; *
        I have sworn an oath to David my servant:
4   'I will establish your line for ever, *
        and preserve your throne for all generations.'"
15 Happy are the people who know the festal shout! *
        they walk, O LORD, in the light of your presence.
16 They rejoice daily in your Name; *
        they are jubilant in your righteousness.
17 For you are the glory of their strength, *
        and by your favor our might is exalted.
18 Truly, the LORD is our ruler; *
        the Holy One of Israel is our King.

The Epistle   **Romans 6:12-23**

Do not let sin exercise dominion in your mortal bodies, to make you obey their passions. No longer present your members to sin as instruments of wickedness, but present yourselves to God as those who have been brought from death to life, and present your members to God as instruments of righteousness. For sin will have no dominion over you, since you are not under law but under grace. What then? Should we sin because we are not under law but under grace? By no means! Do you not know that if you present yourselves to anyone as obedient slaves, you are slaves of the one whom you obey, either of sin, which leads to death, or of obedience, which leads to righteousness? But thanks be to God that you, having once been slaves of sin, have become obedient from the heart to the form of teaching to which you were entrusted, and that you, having been set free from sin, have become slaves of righteousness. I am speaking in human terms because of your natural limitations. For just as you once presented your members as slaves to impurity and to greater and greater iniquity, so now present your members as slaves to righteousness for sanctification. When you were slaves of sin, you were free in regard to righteousness. So what advantage did you then get from the things of which you now are ashamed? The end of those things is death. But now that you have been freed from sin and enslaved to God, the advantage you get is sanctification. The end is eternal life. For the wages of sin is death, but the free gift of God is eternal life in Christ Jesus our Lord.

The Gospel   Matthew 10:40-42

Jesus said, "Whoever welcomes you welcomes me, and whoever welcomes me welcomes the one who sent me. Whoever welcomes a prophet in the name of a prophet will receive a prophet's reward; and whoever welcomes a righteous person in the name of a righteous person will receive the reward of the righteous; and whoever gives even a cup of cold water to one of these little ones in the name of a disciple — truly I tell you, none of these will lose their reward."

Year B

2 Samuel 1:1, 17-27	**or**	✛ *Wisdom of Solomon 1:13-15;*
Psalm 130		*2:23-24*
		✛ *Lamentations 3:21-33*
		or *Psalm 30*

2 Corinthians 8:7-15
Mark 5:21-43

The Lesson   2 Samuel 1:1, 17-27

After the death of Saul, when David had returned from defeating the Amalekites, David remained two days in Ziklag. David intoned this lamentation over Saul and his son Jonathan. (He ordered that The Song of the Bow be taught to the people of Judah; it is written in the Book of Jashar.) He said: Your glory, O Israel, lies slain upon your high places! How the mighty have fallen! Tell it not in Gath, proclaim it not in the streets of Ashkelon; or the daughters of the Philistines will rejoice, the daughters of the uncircumcised will exult. You mountains of Gilboa, let there be no dew or rain upon you, nor bounteous fields! For there the shield of the mighty was defiled, the shield of Saul, anointed with oil no more. From the blood of the slain, from the fat of the mighty, the bow of Jonathan did not turn back, nor the sword of Saul return empty. Saul and Jonathan, beloved and lovely! In life and in death they were not divided; they were swifter than eagles, they were stronger than lions.

O daughters of Israel, weep over Saul, who clothed you with crimson, in luxury, who put ornaments of gold on your apparel. How the mighty have fallen in the midst of the battle! Jonathan lies slain upon your high places. I am distressed for you, my brother Jonathan; greatly beloved were you to me; your love to me was wonderful, passing the love of women. How the mighty have fallen, and the weapons of war perished!

The Response   Psalm 130

Psalm 130   *De profundis*

1   Out of the depths have I called to you, O LORD;
    LORD, hear my voice; *
        let your ears consider well the voice of my supplication.
2   If you, LORD, were to note what is done amiss, *
        O LORD, who could stand?
3   For there is forgiveness with you; *
        therefore you shall be feared.
4   I wait for the LORD; my soul waits for him; *
        in his word is my hope.
5   My soul waits for the LORD,
    more than watchmen for the morning, *
        more than watchmen for the morning.
6   O Israel, wait for the LORD, *
        for with the LORD there is mercy;
7   With him there is plenteous redemption, *
        and he shall redeem Israel from all their sins.

or, ✛ The Lesson   Wisdom of Solomon 1:13-15; 2:23-24
✛ Wisdom of Solomon 1:13-15; 2:23-24

God did not make death, and he does not delight in the death of the living. For he created all things so that they might exist; the generative forces of the world are wholesome, and there is no destructive poison in them, and the dominion of Hades is not on earth. For righteousness is immortal. God created us for incorruption, and made us in the image of his own eternity, but through the devil's envy death entered the world, and those who belong to his company experience it.

✛ The Response   Lamentations 3:21-33

This I call to mind, and therefore I have hope: The steadfast love of the LORD never ceases, His mercies never come to an end; they are new every morning; great is your faithfulness. "The LORD is my portion," says my soul, "therefore I will hope in him." The LORD is good to those who wait for him, to the soul that seeks him. It is good that one should wait quietly for the salvation of the

LORD. It is good for one to bear the yoke in youth, to sit alone in silence when the Lord has imposed it, to put one's mouth to the dust (there may yet be hope), to give one's cheek to the smiter, and be filled with insults. For the Lord will not reject forever. Although he causes grief, he will have compassion according to the abundance of his steadfast love; for he does not willingly afflict or grieve anyone.

or, **Psalm 30**

Psalm 30   *Exaltabo te, Domine*

1   I will exalt you, O LORD,
      because you have lifted me up *
         and have not let my enemies triumph over me.
2   O LORD my God, I cried out to you, *
         and you restored me to health.
3   You brought me up, O LORD, from the dead; *
         you restored my life as I was going down to the grave.
4   Sing to the LORD, you servants of his; *
         give thanks for the remembrance of his holiness.
5   For his wrath endures but the twinkling of an eye, *
         his favor for a lifetime.
6   Weeping may spend the night, *
         but joy comes in the morning.
7   While I felt secure, I said,
      "I shall never be disturbed. *
         You, LORD, with your favor, made me as strong as
               the mountains."
8   Then you hid your face, *
         and I was filled with fear.
9   I cried to you, O LORD; *
         I pleaded with the LORD, saying,
10   "What profit is there in my blood, if I go down to the Pit? *
         will the dust praise you or declare your faithfulness?
11   Hear, O LORD, and have mercy upon me; *
         O LORD, be my helper."
12   You have turned my wailing into dancing; *
         you have put off my sack-cloth and clothed me with joy.
13   Therefore my heart sings to you without ceasing; *
         O LORD my God, I will give you thanks for ever.

The Epistle   2 Corinthians 8:7-15

As you excel in everything — in faith, in speech, in knowledge, in utmost eagerness, and in our love for you — so we want you to excel also in this generous undertaking. I do not say this as a command, but I am testing the genuineness of your love against the earnestness of others. For you know the generous act of our Lord Jesus Christ, that though he was rich, yet for your sakes he became poor, so that by his poverty you might become rich. And in this matter I am giving my advice: it is appropriate for you who began last year not only to do something but even to desire to do something — now finish doing it, so that your eagerness may be matched by completing it according to your means. For if the eagerness is there, the gift is acceptable according to what one has — not according to what one does not have. I do not mean that there should be relief for others and pressure on you, but it is a question of a fair balance between your present abundance and their need, so that their abundance may be for your need, in order that there may be a fair balance. As it is written, "The one who had much did not have too much, and the one who had little did not have too little."

The Gospel   Mark 5:21-43

When Jesus had crossed again in the boat to the other side, a great crowd gathered around him; and he was by the sea. Then one of the leaders of the synagogue named Jairus came and, when he saw him, fell at his feet and begged him repeatedly, "My little daughter is at the point of death. Come and lay your hands on her, so that she may be made well, and live." So he went with him. And a large crowd followed him and pressed in on him. Now there was a woman who had been suffering from hemorrhages for twelve years. She had endured much under many physicians, and had spent all that she had; and she was no better, but rather grew worse. She had heard about Jesus, and came up behind him in the crowd and touched his cloak, for she said, "If I but touch his clothes, I will be made well." Immediately her hemorrhage stopped; and she felt in her body that she was healed of her disease. Immediately aware that power had gone forth from him, Jesus turned about in the crowd and said, "Who touched my clothes?" And his disciples said to him, "You see the crowd pressing in on you; how can you say, 'Who touched me?' " He looked all around to see who had done it. But the woman, knowing what had happened to her, came in fear and trembling, fell down before him, and told him the whole truth. He said to her, "Daughter, your faith has made you well; go in peace, and be healed of your disease." While he was still speaking, some people came from the leader's house to say, "Your daughter is dead. Why trouble the teacher any further?" But overhearing what they said, Jesus said to the leader of the synagogue, "Do not fear, only believe." He allowed no one to follow him except Peter, James, and John, the brother of James. When they came to the house of the leader of the synagogue, he saw a commotion, people weeping and wailing loudly. When he had entered, he said to them, "Why do you make a commotion and weep? The child is not dead but sleeping." And they laughed at him. Then he put them all outside, and took the child's father and mother and those who were with him, and went in where the child was. He took her by the hand and said to her, "Talitha cum," which means, "Little girl, get up!" And immediately the girl got up and began to walk about (she was twelve years of age). At this they were overcome with amazement. He strictly ordered them that no one should know this, and told them to give her something to eat.

Year C

2 Kings 2:1-2, 6-14 **or** ✟ *1 Kings 19:15-16, 19-21*
Psalm 77:1-2, 11-20 ✟ *Psalm 16*

Galatians 5:1, 13-25
Luke 9:51-62

The Lesson   **2 Kings 2:1-2, 6-14**

Now when the LORD was about to take Elijah up to heaven by a whirlwind, Elijah and Elisha were on their way from Gilgal. Elijah said to Elisha, "Stay here; for the LORD has sent me as far as Bethel." But Elisha said, "As the LORD lives, and as you yourself live, I will not leave you." So they went down to Bethel. Then Elijah said to him, "Stay here; for the LORD has sent me to the Jordan." But he said, "As the LORD lives, and as you yourself live, I will not leave you." So the two of them went on. Fifty men of the company of prophets also went, and stood at some distance from them, as they both were standing by the Jordan. Then Elijah took his mantle and rolled it up, and struck the water; the water was parted to the one side and to the other, until the two of them crossed on dry ground. When they had crossed, Elijah said to Elisha, "Tell me what I may do for you, before I am taken from you." Elisha said, "Please let me inherit a double share of your spirit." He responded, "You have asked a hard thing; yet, if you see me as I am being taken from you, it will be granted you; if not, it will not." As they continued walking and talking, a chariot of fire and horses of fire separated the two of them, and Elijah ascended in a whirlwind into heaven. Elisha kept watching and crying out, "Father, father! The chariots of Israel and its horsemen!" But when he could no longer see him, he grasped his own clothes and tore them in two pieces. He picked up the mantle of Elijah that had fallen from him, and went back and stood on the bank of the Jordan. He took the mantle of Elijah that had fallen from him, and struck the water, saying, "Where is the LORD, the God of Elijah?" When he had struck the water, the water was parted to the one side and to the other, and Elisha went over.

The Response   **Psalm 77:1-2, 11-20**

Psalm 77:1-2, 11-20   *Voce mea ad Dominum*

 1 I will cry aloud to God; *
        I will cry aloud, and he will hear me.
 2 In the day of my trouble I sought the LORD; *
        my hands were stretched out by night and did not tire;
        I refused to be comforted.
11 I will remember the works of the LORD, *
        and call to mind your wonders of old time.
12 I will meditate on all your acts *
        and ponder your mighty deeds.
13 Your way, O God, is holy; *
        who is so great a god as our God?
14 You are the God who works wonders *
        and have declared your power among the peoples.
15 By your strength you have redeemed your people, *
        the children of Jacob and Joseph.
16 The waters saw you, O God;
    the waters saw you and trembled; *
        the very depths were shaken.
17 The clouds poured out water;
    the skies thundered; *
        your arrows flashed to and fro;
18 The sound of your thunder was in the whirlwind;
    your lightnings lit up the world; *
        the earth trembled and shook.
19 Your way was in the sea,
    and your paths in the great waters, *
        yet your footsteps were not seen.
20 You led your people like a flock *
        by the hand of Moses and Aaron.

or, ✟ **The Lesson**   **1 Kings 19:15-16, 19-21**

The LORD said to Elijah, "Go, return on your way to the wilderness of Damascus; when you arrive, you shall anoint Hazael as king over Aram. Also you shall anoint Jehuson of Nimshi as king over Israel; and you shall anoint Elisha son of Shaphat of Abel-meholah as prophet in your place." So he set out from there, and found Elisha son of Shaphat, who was plowing. There were twelve yoke of oxen ahead of him, and he was with the twelfth. Elijah passed by him and threw his mantle over him. He left the oxen, ran after Elijah, and said, "Let me kiss my father and my mother, and then I will follow you." Then Elijah said to him, "Go back again; for what have I done to you?" He returned from following him, took the yoke of oxen, and slaughtered them; using the equipment from the oxen, he boiled their flesh, and gave it to the people, and they ate. Then he set out and followed Elijah, and became his servant.

✚ The Response   Psalm 16

Psalm 16 *Conserva me, Domine*

1 Protect me, O God, for I take refuge in you; *
      I have said to the LORD, "You are my LORD,
         my good above all other."
2 All my delight is upon the godly that are in the land, *
      upon those who are noble among the people.
3 But those who run after other gods *
      shall have their troubles multiplied.
4 Their libations of blood I will not offer, *
      nor take the names of their gods upon my lips.
5 O LORD, you are my portion and my cup; *
      it is you who uphold my lot.
6 My boundaries enclose a pleasant land; *
      indeed, I have a goodly heritage.
7 I will bless the LORD who gives me counsel; *
      my heart teaches me, night after night.
8 I have set the LORD always before me; *
      because he is at my right hand I shall not fall.
9 My heart, therefore, is glad, and my spirit rejoices; *
      my body also shall rest in hope.
10 For you will not abandon me to the grave, *
      nor let your holy one see the Pit.
11 You will show me the path of life; *
      in your presence there is fullness of joy,
      and in your right hand are pleasures for evermore.

The Epistle   Galatians 5:1, 13-25

For freedom Christ has set us free. Stand firm, therefore, and do not submit again to a yoke of slavery. For you were called to freedom, brothers and sisters; only do not use your freedom as an opportunity for self-indulgence, but through love become slaves to one another. For the whole law is summed up in a single commandment, "You shall love your neighbor as yourself." If, however, you bite and devour one another, take care that you are not consumed by one another. Live by the Spirit, I say, and do not gratify the desires of the flesh. For what the flesh desires is opposed to the Spirit, and what the Spirit desires is opposed to the flesh; for these are opposed to each other, to prevent you from doing what you want. But if you are led by the Spirit, you are not subject to the law. Now the works of the flesh are obvious: fornication, impurity, licentiousness, idolatry, sorcery, enmities, strife, jealousy, anger, quarrels, dissensions, factions, envy, drunkenness, carousing, and things like these. I am warning you, as I warned you before: those who do such things will not inherit the kingdom of God. By contrast, the fruit of the Spirit is love, joy, peace, patience, kindness, generosity, faithfulness, gentleness, and self-control. There is no law against such things. And those who belong to Christ Jesus have crucified the flesh with its passions and desires. If we live by the Spirit, let us also be guided by the Spirit.

The Gospel   Luke 9:51-62

When the days drew near for Jesus to be taken up, he set his face to go to Jerusalem. And he sent messengers ahead of him. On their way they entered a village of the Samaritans to make ready for him; but they did not receive him, because his face was set toward Jerusalem. When his disciples James and John saw it, they said, "Lord, do you want us to command fire to come down from heaven and consume them?" But he turned and rebuked them. Then they went on to another village. As they were going along the road, someone said to him, "I will follow you wherever you go." And Jesus said to him, "Foxes have holes, and birds of the air have nests; but the Son of Man has nowhere to lay his head." To another he said, "Follow me." But he said, "Lord, first let me go and bury my father." But Jesus said to him, "Let the dead bury their own dead; but as for you, go and proclaim the kingdom of God." Another said, "I will follow you, Lord; but let me first say farewell to those at my home." Jesus said to him, "No one who puts a hand to the plow and looks back is fit for the kingdom of God."

PROPER 9

Sunday between July 3 and July 9 inclusive

The Collect

O God, you have taught us to keep all your commandments by loving you and our neighbor: Grant us the grace of your Holy Spirit, that we may be devoted to you with our whole heart, and united to one another with pure affection; through Jesus Christ our Lord, who lives and reigns with you and the Holy Spirit, one God, for ever and ever. *Amen.*

Year A

Genesis 24:34-38, 42-49, 58-67	**or**	✝ *Zechariah 9:9-12*
Psalm 45:11-18		✝ *Psalm 145:8-15*
or *Song of Solomon 2:8-13*		

Romans 7:15-25a
Matthew 11:16-19, 25-30

The Lesson   Genesis 24:34-38, 42-49, 58-67

The servant said, "I am Abraham's servant. The LORD has greatly blessed my master, and he has become wealthy; he has given him flocks and herds, silver and gold, male and female slaves, camels and donkeys. And Sarah my master's wife bore a son to my master when she was old; and he has given him all that he has. My master made me swear, saying, 'You shall not take a wife for my son from the daughters of the Canaanites, in whose land I live; but you shall go to my father's house, to my kindred, and get a wife for my son.' I came today to the spring, and said, 'O LORD, the God of my master Abraham, if now you will only make successful the way I am going! I am standing here by the spring of water; let the young woman who comes out to draw, to whom I shall say, "Please give me a little water from your jar to drink," and who will say to me, "Drink, and I will draw for your camels also" — let her be the woman whom the LORD has appointed for my master's son. Before I had finished speaking in my heart, there was Rebekah coming out with her water jar on her shoulder; and she went down to the spring, and drew. I said to her, 'Please let me drink.' She quickly let down her jar from her shoulder, and said, 'Drink, and I will also water your camels.' So I drank, and she also watered the camels. Then I asked her, 'Whose daughter are you?' She said, 'The daughter of Bethuel, Nahor's son, whom Milcah bore to him.' So I put the ring on her nose, and the bracelets on her arms. Then I bowed my head and worshiped the LORD, and blessed the LORD, the God of my master Abraham, who had led me by the right way to obtain the daughter of my master's kinsman for his son. Now then, if you will deal loyally and truly with my master, tell me; and if not, tell me, so that I may turn either to the right hand or to the left." And they called Rebekah, and said to her, "Will you go with this man?" She said, "I will." So they sent away their sister Rebekah and her nurse along with Abraham's servant and his men. And they blessed Rebekah and said to her, "May you, our sister, become thousands of myriads; may your offspring gain possession of the gates of their foes." Then Rebekah and her maids rose up, mounted the camels, and followed the man; thus the servant took Rebekah, and went his way. Now Isaac had come from Beer-lahai-roi, and was settled in the Negeb. Isaac went out in the evening to walk in the field; and looking up, he saw camels coming. And Rebekah looked up, and when she saw Isaac, she slipped quickly from the camel, and said to the servant, "Who is the man over there, walking in the field to meet us?" The servant said, "It is my master." So she took her veil and covered herself. And the servant told Isaac all the things that he had done. Then Isaac brought her into his mother Sarah's tent. He took Rebekah, and she became his wife; and he loved her. So Isaac was comforted after his mother's death.

The Response   **Psalm 45:11-18**

Psalm 45:11-18   *Eructavit cor meum*

11 "Hear, O daughter; consider and listen closely; *
        forget your people and your father's house.

12 The king will have pleasure in your beauty; *
        he is your master; therefore do him honor.

13 The people of Tyre are here with a gift; *
        the rich among the people seek your favor."

14 All glorious is the princess as she enters; *
        her gown is cloth-of-gold.

15 In embroidered apparel she is brought to the king; *
        after her the bridesmaids follow in procession.

16 With joy and gladness they are brought, *
        and enter into the palace of the king.

17 "In place of fathers, O king, you shall have sons; *
        you shall make them princes over all the earth.

18 I will make your name to be remembered
    from one generation to another; *
        therefore nations will praise you for ever and ever."

or, **Song of Solomon 2:8-13**

8   The voice of my beloved! Look, he comes,
        leaping upon the mountains, bounding over the hills.

9   My beloved is like a gazelle or a young stag.
        Look, there he stands behind our wall, gazing in at the windows,
        looking through the lattice.

10 My beloved speaks and says to me:
        "Arise, my love, my fair one, and come away;

11 for now the winter is past, the rain is over and gone.

12 The flowers appear on the earth; the time of singing has come,
        and the voice of the turtledove is heard in our land.

13 The fig tree puts forth its figs, and the vines are in blossom;
        they give forth fragrance.
        Arise, my love, my fair one, and come away."

or, ✠ **The Lesson**   **Zechariah 9:9-12**

Rejoice greatly, O daughter Zion! Shout aloud, O daughter Jerusalem! Lo,
your king comes to you; triumphant and victorious is he, humble and riding on
a donkey, on a colt, the foal of a donkey. He will cut off the chariot from
Ephraim and the war horse from Jerusalem; and the battle bow shall be cut
off, and he shall command peace to the nations; his dominion shall be from
sea to sea, and from the River to the ends of the earth. As for you also,

because of the blood of my covenant with you, I will set your prisoners free from the waterless pit. Return to your stronghold, O prisoners of hope; today I declare that I will restore to you double.

✟ The Response   Psalm 145:8-15

Psalm 145:8-15   *Exaltabo te, Deus*

8   The LORD is gracious and full of compassion, *
      slow to anger and of great kindness.
9   The LORD is loving to everyone *
      and his compassion is over all his works.
10   All your works praise you, O LORD, *
      and your faithful servants bless you.
11   They make known the glory of your kingdom *
      and speak of your power;
12   That the peoples may know of your power *
      and the glorious splendor of your kingdom.
13   Your kingdom is an everlasting kingdom; *
      your dominion endures throughout all ages.
14   The LORD is faithful in all his words *
      and merciful in all his deeds.
15   The LORD upholds all those who fall; *
      he lifts up those who are bowed down.

The Epistle   Romans 7:15-25*a*

I do not understand my own actions. For I do not do what I want, but I do the very thing I hate. Now if I do what I do not want, I agree that the law is good. But in fact it is no longer I that do it, but sin that dwells within me. For I know that nothing good dwells within me, that is, in my flesh. I can will what is right, but I cannot do it. For I do not do the good I want, but the evil I do not want is what I do. Now if I do what I do not want, it is no longer I that do it, but sin that dwells within me. So I find it to be a law that when I want to do what is good, evil lies close at hand. For I delight in the law of God in my inmost self, but I see in my members another law at war with the law of my mind, making me captive to the law of sin that dwells in my members. Wretched man that I am! Who will rescue me from this body of death? Thanks be to God through Jesus Christ our Lord!

The Gospel   Matthew 11:16-19, 25-30

Jesus said to the crowd, "But to what will I compare this generation? It is like children sitting in the marketplaces and calling to one another, 'We played the flute for you, and you did not dance; we wailed, and you did not mourn.' For

John came neither eating nor drinking, and they say, 'He has a demon'; the Son of Man came eating and drinking, and they say, 'Look, a glutton and a drunkard, a friend of tax collectors and sinners!' Yet wisdom is vindicated by her deeds." At that time Jesus said, "I thank you, Father, Lord of heaven and earth, because you have hidden these things from the wise and the intelligent and have revealed them to infants; yes, Father, for such was your gracious will. All things have been handed over to me by my Father; and no one knows the Son except the Father, and no one knows the Father except the Son and anyone to whom the Son chooses to reveal him. Come to me, all you that are weary and are carrying heavy burdens, and I will give you rest. Take my yoke upon you, and learn from me; for I am gentle and humble in heart, and you will find rest for your souls. For my yoke is easy, and my burden is light."

Year B

2 Samuel 5:1-5, 9-10	**or**	☩ Ezekiel 2:1-5
Psalm 48		☩ Psalm 123

2 Corinthians 12:2-10
Mark 6:1-13

The Lesson   **2 Samuel 5:1-5, 9-10**

All the tribes of Israel came to David at Hebron, and said, "Look, we are your bone and flesh. For some time, while Saul was king over us, it was you who led out Israel and brought it in. The LORD said to you: It is you who shall be shepherd of my people Israel, you who shall be ruler over Israel." So all the elders of Israel came to the king at Hebron; and King David made a covenant with them at Hebron before the LORD, and they anointed David king over Israel. David was thirty years old when he began to reign, and he reigned forty years. At Hebron he reigned over Judah seven years and six months; and at Jerusalem he reigned over all Israel and Judah thirty-three years. David occupied the stronghold, and named it the city of David. David built the city all around from the Millo inward. And David became greater and greater, for the LORD, the God of hosts, was with him.

The Response   **Psalm 48**

Psalm 48   *Magnus Dominus*

1   Great is the LORD, and highly to be praised; *
        in the city of our God is his holy hill.
2   Beautiful and lofty, the joy of all the earth, is the
                hill of Zion, *
        the very center of the world and the city of the great King.
3   God is in her citadels; *
        he is known to be her sure refuge.

4   Behold, the kings of the earth assembled *
      and marched forward together.
5   They looked and were astounded; *
      they retreated and fled in terror.
6   Trembling seized them there; *
      they writhed like a woman in childbirth,
      like ships of the sea when the east wind shatters them.
7   As we have heard, so have we seen,
      in the city of the LORD of hosts, in the city of our God; *
      God has established her for ever.
8   We have waited in silence on your loving-kindness, O God, *
      in the midst of your temple.
9   Your praise, like your Name, O God, reaches to
                              the world's end; *
      your right hand is full of justice.
10   Let Mount Zion be glad
      and the cities of Judah rejoice, *
      because of your judgments.
11   Make the circuit of Zion;
      walk round about her; *
      count the number of her towers.
12   Consider well her bulwarks;
      examine her strongholds; *
      that you may tell those who come after.
13   This God is our God for ever and ever; *
      he shall be our guide for evermore.

or, ✛ The Lesson   Ezekiel 2:1-5

The LORD said to me: O mortal, stand up on your feet, and I will speak with
you. And when he spoke to me, a spirit entered into me and set me on my feet;
and I heard him speaking to me. He said to me, Mortal, I am sending you to
the people of Israel, to a nation of rebels who have rebelled against me; they
and their ancestors have transgressed against me to this very day. The descendants are impudent and stubborn. I am sending you to them, and you shall say
to them, "Thus says the Lord GOD." Whether they hear or refuse to hear (for
they are a rebellious house), they shall know that there has been a prophet
among them.

✛ The Response   Psalm 123

Psalm 123   *Ad te levavi oculos meos*
1   To you I lift up my eyes, *
      to you enthroned in the heavens.

2　As the eyes of servants look to the hand of their masters, *
　　　and the eyes of a maid to the hand of her mistress,
3　So our eyes look to the LORD our God, *
　　　until he show us his mercy.
4　Have mercy upon us, O LORD, have mercy, *
　　　for we have had more than enough of contempt,
5　Too much of the scorn of the indolent rich, *
　　　and of the derision of the proud.

The Epistle　　　　　　　　　　　　　2 Corinthians 12:2-10

I know a person in Christ who fourteen years ago was caught up to the third
heaven — whether in the body or out of the body I do not know; God knows.
And I know that such a person — whether in the body or out of the body I do
not know; God knows — was caught up into Paradise and heard things that
are not to be told, that no mortal is permitted to repeat. On behalf of such a
one I will boast, but on my own behalf I will not boast, except of my weaknesses. But if I wish to boast, I will not be a fool, for I will be speaking the
truth. But I refrain from it, so that no one may think better of me than what is
seen in me or heard from me, even considering the exceptional character of the
revelations. Therefore, to keep me from being too elated, a thorn was given me
in the flesh, a messenger of Satan to torment me, to keep me from being too
elated. Three times I appealed to the Lord about this, that it would leave me,
but he said to me, "My grace is sufficient for you, for power is made perfect
in weakness." So, I will boast all the more gladly of my weaknesses, so that
the power of Christ may dwell in me. Therefore I am content with weaknesses,
insults, hardships, persecutions, and calamities for the sake of Christ; for
whenever I am weak, then I am strong.

The Gospel　　　　　　　　　　　　　　　　Mark 6:1-13

Jesus came to his hometown, and his disciples followed him. On the sabbath
he began to teach in the synagogue, and many who heard him were astounded.
They said, "Where did this man get all this? What is this wisdom that has
been given to him? What deeds of power are being done by his hands! Is not
this the carpenter, the son of Mary and brother of James and Joses and Judas
and Simon, and are not his sisters here with us?" And they took offense at
him. Then Jesus said to them, "Prophets are not without honor, except in their
hometown, and among their own kin, and in their own house." And he could
do no deed of power there, except that he laid his hands on a few sick people
and cured them. And he was amazed at their unbelief. Then he went about
among the villages teaching. He called the twelve and began to send them out
two by two, and gave them authority over the unclean spirits. He ordered them
to take nothing for their journey except a staff; no bread, no bag, no money in

their belts; but to wear sandals and not to put on two tunics. He said to them, "Wherever you enter a house, stay there until you leave the place. If any place will not welcome you and they refuse to hear you, as you leave, shake off the dust that is on your feet as a testimony against them." So they went out and proclaimed that all should repent. They cast out many demons, and anointed with oil many who were sick and cured them.

Year C

2 Kings 5:1-14	**or**	✝ *Isaiah 66:10-14*
Psalm 30		✝ *Psalm 66:1-8*

Galatians 6:(1-6), 7-16
Luke 10:1-11, 16-20

The Lesson   **2 Kings 5:1-14**

Naaman, commander of the army of the king of Aram, was a great man and in high favor with his master, because by him the LORD had given victory to Aram. The man, though a mighty warrior, suffered from leprosy. Now the Arameans on one of their raids had taken a young girl captive from the land of Israel, and she served Naaman's wife. She said to her mistress, "If only my lord were with the prophet who is in Samaria! He would cure him of his leprosy." So Naaman went in and told his lord just what the girl from the land of Israel had said. And the king of Aram said, "Go then, and I will send along a letter to the king of Israel." He went, taking with him ten talents of silver, six thousand shekels of gold, and ten sets of garments. He brought the letter to the king of Israel, which read, "When this letter reaches you, know that I have sent to you my servant Naaman, that you may cure him of his leprosy." When the king of Israel read the letter, he tore his clothes and said, "Am I God, to give death or life, that this man sends word to me to cure a man of his leprosy? Just look and see how he is trying to pick a quarrel with me." But when Elisha the man of God heard that the king of Israel had torn his clothes, he sent a message to the king, "Why have you torn your clothes? Let him come to me, that he may learn that there is a prophet in Israel." So Naaman came with his horses and chariots, and halted at the entrance of Elisha's house. Elisha sent a messenger to him, saying, "Go, wash in the Jordan seven times, and your flesh shall be restored and you shall be clean." But Naaman became angry and went away, saying, "I thought that for me he would surely come out, and stand and call on the name of the LORD his God, and would wave his hand over the spot, and cure the leprosy! Are not Abana and Pharpar, the rivers of Damascus, better than all the waters of Israel? Could I not wash in them, and be clean?" He turned and went away in a rage. But his servants approached and said to him, "Father, if the prophet had commanded you to do something difficult, would you not have done it? How much more, when all he said to you was, 'Wash, and be clean'?" So he went down and immersed himself seven times in the Jordan, according to the word of the man of God; his flesh was restored like the flesh of a young boy, and he was clean.

The Response   Psalm 30

Psalm 30   *Exaltabo te, Domine*

1   I will exalt you, O LORD,
        because you have lifted me up *
            and have not let my enemies triumph over me.

2   O LORD my God, I cried out to you, *
        and you restored me to health.

3   You brought me up, O LORD, from the dead; *
        you restored my life as I was going down to the grave.

4   Sing to the LORD, you servants of his; *
        give thanks for the remembrance of his holiness.

5   For his wrath endures but the twinkling of an eye, *
        his favor for a lifetime.

6   Weeping may spend the night, *
        but joy comes in the morning.

7   While I felt secure, I said,
    "I shall never be disturbed. *
        You, LORD, with your favor, made me as strong as the mountains."

8   Then you hid your face, *
        and I was filled with fear.

9   I cried to you, O LORD; *
        I pleaded with the LORD, saying,

10 "What profit is there in my blood, if I go down to the Pit? *
        will the dust praise you or declare your faithfulness?

11 Hear, O LORD, and have mercy upon me; *
        O LORD, be my helper."

12 You have turned my wailing into dancing; *
        you have put off my sack-cloth and clothed me with joy.

13 Therefore my heart sings to you without ceasing; *
        O LORD my God, I will give you thanks for ever.

or, ☩ The Lesson   Isaiah 66:10-14

Thus says the LORD: Rejoice with Jerusalem, and be glad for her, all you who love her; rejoice with her in joy, all you who mourn over her — that you may nurse and be satisfied from her consoling breast; that you may drink deeply with delight from her glorious bosom. For thus says the LORD: I will extend prosperity to her like a river, and the wealth of the nations like an overflowing stream; and you shall nurse and be carried on her arm, and dandled on her knees. As a mother comforts her child, so I will comfort you; you shall be comforted in Jerusalem. You shall see, and your heart shall rejoice; your bodies shall flourish like the grass; and it shall be known that the hand of the LORD is with his servants, and his indignation is against his enemies.

✠ The Response   Psalm 66:1-8

Psalm 66:1-8   *Jubilate Deo*

1   Be joyful in God, all you lands; *
        sing the glory of his Name;
        sing the glory of his praise.

2   Say to God, "How awesome are your deeds! *
        because of your great strength your enemies
                cringe before you.

3   All the earth bows down before you, *
        sings to you, sings out your Name."

4   Come now and see the works of God, *
        how wonderful he is in his doing toward all people.

5   He turned the sea into dry land,
        so that they went through the water on foot, *
        and there we rejoiced in him.

6   In his might he rules for ever;
        his eyes keep watch over the nations; *
        let no rebel rise up against him.

7   Bless our God, you peoples; *
        make the voice of his praise to be heard;

8   Who holds our souls in life, *
        and will not allow our feet to slip.

The Epistle   Galatians 6:(1-6), 7-16

Galatians 6:(1-6)

[My friends, if anyone is detected in a transgression, you who have received the Spirit should restore such a one in a spirit of gentleness. Take care that you yourselves are not tempted. Bear one another's burdens, and in this way you will fulfill the law of Christ. For if those who are nothing think they are something, they deceive themselves. All must test their own work; then that work, rather than their neighbor's work, will become a cause for pride. For all must carry their own loads. Those who are taught the word must share in all good things with their teacher.]

Galatians 6:7-16 Do not be deceived; God is not mocked, for you reap whatever you sow. If you sow to your own flesh, you will reap corruption from the flesh; but if you sow to the Spirit, you will reap eternal life from the Spirit. So let us not grow weary in doing what is right, for we will reap at harvest time, if we do not give up. So then, whenever we have an opportunity, let us work for the good of all, and especially for those of the family of faith. See what large letters I make when I am writing in my own hand! It is those who want to make a good showing in the flesh that try to compel you to be circumcised — only that they may not be persecuted for the cross of Christ. Even the circumcised do not themselves obey the law, but they want you to be circumcised so that they may boast about your flesh. May I never boast of anything except the cross of our Lord Jesus Christ, by which the world has been crucified to me, and I to the world. For neither circumcision nor uncircumcision is anything; but a new creation is everything! As for those who will follow this rule — peace be upon them, and mercy, and upon the Israel of God.

The Gospel   **Luke 10:1-11, 16-20**

The Lord appointed seventy others and sent them on ahead of him in pairs to every town and place where he himself intended to go. He said to them, "The harvest is plentiful, but the laborers are few; therefore ask the Lord of the harvest to send out laborers into his harvest. Go on your way. See, I am sending you out like lambs into the midst of wolves. Carry no purse, no bag, no sandals; and greet no one on the road. Whatever house you enter, first say, 'Peace to this house!' And if anyone is there who shares in peace, your peace will rest on that person; but if not, it will return to you. Remain in the same house, eating and drinking whatever they provide, for the laborer deserves to be paid. Do not move about from house to house. Whenever you enter a town and its people welcome you, eat what is set before you; cure the sick who are there, and say to them, 'The kingdom of God has come near to you.' But whenever you enter a town and they do not welcome you, go out into its streets and say, 'Even the dust of your town that clings to our feet, we wipe off in protest against you. Yet know this: the kingdom of God has come near.' Whoever listens to you listens to me, and whoever rejects you rejects me, and whoever rejects me rejects the one who sent me." The seventy returned with joy, saying, "Lord, in your name even the demons submit to us!" He said to them, "I watched Satan fall from heaven like a flash of lightning. See, I have given you authority to tread on snakes and scorpions, and over all the power of the enemy; and nothing will hurt you. Nevertheless, do not rejoice at this, that the spirits submit to you, but rejoice that your names are written in heaven."

PROPER 10

Sunday between July 10 and July 16 inclusive

The Collect

O Lord, mercifully receive the prayers of your people who call upon you, and grant that they may know and understand what things they ought to do, and also may have grace and power faithfully to accomplish them; through Jesus Christ our Lord, who lives and reigns with you and the Holy Spirit, one God, now and for ever. *Amen.*

Year A

Genesis 25:19-34	**or**	✠ *Isaiah 55:10-13*
Psalm 119:105-112		✠ *Psalm 65:(1-8), 9-14*

Romans 8:1-11
Matthew 13:1-9, 18-23

The Lesson   Genesis 25:19-34

These are the descendants of Isaac, Abraham's son: Abraham was the father of Isaac, and Isaac was forty years old when he married Rebekah, daughter of Bethuel the Aramean of Paddan-aram, sister of Laban the Aramean. Isaac prayed to the LORD for his wife, because she was barren; and the LORD granted his prayer, and his wife Rebekah conceived. The children struggled together within her; and she said, "If it is to be this way, why do I live?" So she went to inquire of the LORD. And the LORD said to her, "Two nations are in your womb, and two peoples born of you shall be divided; the one shall be stronger than the other, the elder shall serve the younger." When her time to give birth was at hand, there were twins in her womb. The first came out red, all his body like a hairy mantle; so they named him Esau. Afterward his brother came out, with his hand gripping Esau's heel; so he was named Jacob. Isaac was sixty years old when she bore them. When the boys grew up, Esau was a skillful hunter, a man of the field, while Jacob was a quiet man, living in tents. Isaac loved Esau, because he was fond of game; but Rebekah loved Jacob. Once when Jacob was cooking a stew, Esau came in from the field, and he was famished. Esau said to Jacob, "Let me eat some of that red stuff, for I am famished!" (Therefore he was called Edom.) Jacob said, "First sell me your birthright." Esau said, "I am about to die; of what use is a birthright to me?" Jacob said, "Swear to me first." So he swore to him, and sold his birthright to Jacob. Then Jacob gave Esau bread and lentil stew, and he ate and drank, and rose and went his way. Thus Esau despised his birthright.

The Response   **Psalm 119:105-112**

Psalm 119:105-112   *Lucerna pedibus meis*

105   Your word is a lantern to my feet *
         and a light upon my path.

106   I have sworn and am determined *
         to keep your righteous judgments.

107   I am deeply troubled; *
         preserve my life, O LORD, according to your word.

108   Accept, O LORD, the willing tribute of my lips, *
         and teach me your judgments.

109   My life is always in my hand, *
         yet I do not forget your law.

110   The wicked have set a trap for me, *
         but I have not strayed from your commandments.

111   Your decrees are my inheritance for ever; *
         truly, they are the joy of my heart.

112   I have applied my heart to fulfill your statutes *
         for ever and to the end.

or, ✟ **The Lesson**   **Isaiah 55:10-13**

As the rain and the snow come down from heaven, and do not return there until they have watered the earth, making it bring forth and sprout, giving seed to the sower and bread to the eater, so shall my word be that goes out from my mouth; it shall not return to me empty, but it shall accomplish that which I purpose, and succeed in the thing for which I sent it. For you shall go out in joy, and be led back in peace; the mountains and the hills before you shall burst into song, and all the trees of the field shall clap their hands. Instead of the thorn shall come up the cypress; instead of the brier shall come up the myrtle; and it shall be to the LORD for a memorial, for an everlasting sign that shall not be cut off.

✟ **The Response**   **Psalm 65:(1-8) 9-14**

Psalm 65:(1-8) 9-14   *Te decet hymnus*

[1   You are to be praised, O God, in Zion; *
         to you shall vows be performed in Jerusalem.

2   To you that hear prayer shall all flesh come, *
         because of their transgressions.

3   Our sins are stronger than we are, *
         but you will blot them out.

4   Happy are they whom you choose
         and draw to your courts to dwell there! *

they will be satisfied by the beauty of your house,
by the holiness of your temple.
5   Awesome things will you show us in your righteousness,
O God of our salvation, *
O Hope of all the ends of the earth
and of the seas that are far away.
6   You make fast the mountains by your power; *
they are girded about with might.
7   You still the roaring of the seas, *
the roaring of their waves,
and the clamor of the peoples.
8   Those who dwell at the ends of the earth will tremble at your
marvelous signs; *
you make the dawn and the dusk to sing for joy.]

9   You visit the earth and water it abundantly;
you make it very plenteous; *
the river of God is full of water.
10 You prepare the grain, *
for so you provide for the earth.
11 You drench the furrows and smooth out the ridges; *
with heavy rain you soften the ground and bless its increase.
12 You crown the year with your goodness, *
and your paths overflow with plenty.
13 May the fields of the wilderness be rich for grazing, *
and the hills be clothed with joy.
14 May the meadows cover themselves with flocks,
and the valleys cloak themselves with grain; *
let them shout for joy and sing.

The Epistle   Romans 8:1-11

There is no condemnation for those who are in Christ Jesus. For the law of the
Spirit of life in Christ Jesus has set you free from the law of sin and of death.
For God has done what the law, weakened by the flesh, could not do: by
sending his own Son in the likeness of sinful flesh, and to deal with sin, he
condemned sin in the flesh, so that the just requirement of the law might be
fulfilled in us, who walk not according to the flesh but according to the Spirit.
For those who live according to the flesh set their minds on the things of the
flesh, but those who live according to the Spirit set their minds on the things
of the Spirit. To set the mind on the flesh is death, but to set the mind on the
Spirit is life and peace. For this reason the mind that is set on the flesh is
hostile to God; it does not submit to God's law — indeed it cannot, and those

who are in the flesh cannot please God. But you are not in the flesh; you are in the Spirit, since the Spirit of God dwells in you. Anyone who does not have the Spirit of Christ does not belong to him. But if Christ is in you, though the body is dead because of sin, the Spirit is life because of righteousness. If the Spirit of him who raised Jesus from the dead dwells in you, he who raised Christ from the dead will give life to your mortal bodies also through his Spirit that dwells in you.

The Gospel   Matthew 13:1-9, 18-23

Jesus went out of the house and sat beside the sea. Such great crowds gathered around him that he got into a boat and sat there, while the whole crowd stood on the beach. And he told them many things in parables, saying: "Listen! A sower went out to sow. And as he sowed, some seeds fell on the path, and the birds came and ate them up. Other seeds fell on rocky ground, where they did not have much soil, and they sprang up quickly, since they had no depth of soil. But when the sun rose, they were scorched; and since they had no root, they withered away. Other seeds fell among thorns, and the thorns grew up and choked them. Other seeds fell on good soil and brought forth grain, some a hundredfold, some sixty, some thirty. Let anyone with ears listen! Hear then the parable of the sower. When anyone hears the word of the kingdom and does not understand it, the evil one comes and snatches away what is sown in the heart; this is what was sown on the path. As for what was sown on rocky ground, this is the one who hears the word and immediately receives it with joy; yet such a person has no root, but endures only for a while, and when trouble or persecution arises on account of the word, that person immediately falls away. As for what was sown among thorns, this is the one who hears the word, but the cares of the world and the lure of wealth choke the word, and it yields nothing. But as for what was sown on good soil, this is the one who hears the word and understands it, who indeed bears fruit and yields, in one case a hundredfold, in another sixty, and in another thirty."

Year B

2 Samuel 6:1-5, 12b-19   **or**   ✝ *Amos 7:7-15*
Psalm 24   ✝ *Psalm 85:8-13*

Ephesians 1:3-14
Mark 6:14-29

The Lesson   2 Samuel 6:1-5, 12b-19

David again gathered all the chosen men of Israel, thirty thousand. David and all the people with him set out and went from Baale-judah, to bring up from there the ark of God, which is called by the name of the LORD of hosts who is enthroned on the cherubim. They carried the ark of God on a new cart, and brought it out of the house of Abinadab, which was on the hill. Uzzah and

Ahio, the sons of Abinadab, were driving the new cart with the ark of God; and Ahio went in front of the ark. David and all the house of Israel were dancing before the Lord with all their might, with song and lyres and harps and tambourines and castanets and cymbals. "The Lord has blessed the household of Obed-edom and all that belongs to him, because of the ark of God." So David went and brought up the ark of God from the house of Obed-edom to the city of David with rejoicing; and when those who bore the ark of the Lord had gone six paces, he sacrificed an ox and a fatling. David danced before the Lord with all his might; David was girded with a linen ephod. So David and all the house of Israel brought up the ark of the Lord with shouting, and with the sound of the trumpet. As the ark of the Lord came into the city of David, Michal daughter of Saul looked out of the window, and saw King David leaping and dancing before the Lord; and she despised him in her heart. They brought in the ark of the Lord, and set it in its place, inside the tent that David had pitched for it; and David offered burnt offerings and offerings of well-being before the Lord. When David had finished offering the burnt offerings and the offerings of well-being, he blessed the people in the name of the Lord of hosts, and distributed food among all the people, the whole multitude of Israel, both men and women, to each a cake of bread, a portion of meat, and a cake of raisins. Then all the people went back to their homes.

The Response   Psalm 24
Psalm 24   *Domini est terra*

1   The earth is the Lord's and all that is in it, *
       the world and all who dwell therein.
2   For it is he who founded it upon the seas *
       and made it firm upon the rivers of the deep.
3   "Who can ascend the hill of the Lord? *
       and who can stand in his holy place?"
4   "Those who have clean hands and a pure heart, *
       who have not pledged themselves to falsehood,
       nor sworn by what is a fraud.
5   They shall receive a blessing from the Lord *
       and a just reward from the God of their salvation."
6   Such is the generation of those who seek him, *
       of those who seek your face, O God of Jacob.
7   Lift up your heads, O gates;
   lift them high, O everlasting doors; *
       and the King of glory shall come in.
8   "Who is this King of glory?" *
       "The Lord, strong and mighty,
       the Lord, mighty in battle."

9   Lift up your heads, O gates;
       lift them high, O everlasting doors; *
          and the King of glory shall come in.
10   "Who is he, this King of glory?"
       "The LORD of hosts,
          he is the King of glory."

or, ☩ **The Lesson**   Amos 7:7-15

This is what the Lord GOD showed me: the Lord was standing beside a wall
built with a plumb line, with a plumb line in his hand. And the LORD said to
me, "Amos, what do you see?" And I said, "A plumb line." Then the Lord
said, "See, I am setting a plumb line in the midst of my people Israel; I will
never again pass them by; the high places of Isaac shall be made desolate, and
the sanctuaries of Israel shall be laid waste, and I will rise against the house of
Jeroboam with the sword." Then Amaziah, the priest of Bethel, sent to King
Jeroboam of Israel, saying, "Amos has conspired against you in the very
center of the house of Israel; the land is not able to bear all his words. For
thus Amos has said, 'Jeroboam shall die by the sword, and Israel must go into
exile away from his land.' " And Amaziah said to Amos, "O seer, go, flee
away to the land of Judah, earn your bread there, and prophesy there; but
never again prophesy at Bethel, for it is the king's sanctuary, and it is a temple
of the kingdom." Then Amos answered Amaziah, "I am no prophet, nor a
prophet's son; but I am a herdsman, and a dresser of sycamore trees, and the
LORD took me from following the flock, and the LORD said to me, 'Go, prophesy to my people Israel.' "

☩ **The Response**   Psalm 85:8-13

Psalm 85:8-13   *Benedixisti, Domine*
   8   I will listen to what the LORD God is saying, *
          for he is speaking peace to his faithful people
          and to those who turn their hearts to him.
   9   Truly, his salvation is very near to those who fear him, *
          that his glory may dwell in our land.
  10   Mercy and truth have met together; *
          righteousness and peace have kissed each other.
  11   Truth shall spring up from the earth, *
          and righteousness shall look down from heaven.
  12   The LORD will indeed grant prosperity, *
          and our land will yield its increase.
  13   Righteousness shall go before him, *
          and peace shall be a pathway for his feet.

The Epistle   **Ephesians 1:3-14**

Blessed be the God and Father of our Lord Jesus Christ, who has blessed us in Christ with every spiritual blessing in the heavenly places, just as he chose us in Christ before the foundation of the world to be holy and blameless before him in love. He destined us for adoption as his children through Jesus Christ, according to the good pleasure of his will, to the praise of his glorious grace that he freely bestowed on us in the Beloved. In him we have redemption through his blood, the forgiveness of our trespasses, according to the riches of his grace that he lavished on us. With all wisdom and insight he has made known to us the mystery of his will, according to his good pleasure that he set forth in Christ, as a plan for the fullness of time, to gather up all things in him, things in heaven and things on earth. In Christ we have also obtained an inheritance, having been destined according to the purpose of him who accomplishes all things according to his counsel and will, so that we, who were the first to set our hope on Christ, might live for the praise of his glory. In him you also, when you had heard the word of truth, the gospel of your salvation, and had believed in him, were marked with the seal of the promised Holy Spirit; this is the pledge of our inheritance toward redemption as God's own people, to the praise of his glory.

The Gospel   **Mark 6:14-29**

King Herod heard of the deeds of power, for Jesus' name had become known. Some were saying, "John the baptizer has been raised from the dead; and for this reason these powers are at work in him." But others said, "It is Elijah." And others said, "It is a prophet, like one of the prophets of old." But when Herod heard of it, he said, "John, whom I beheaded, has been raised." For Herod himself had sent men who arrested John, bound him, and put him in prison on account of Herodias, his brother Philip's wife, because Herod had married her. For John had been telling Herod, "It is not lawful for you to have your brother's wife." And Herodias had a grudge against him, and wanted to kill him. But she could not, for Herod feared John, knowing that he was a righteous and holy man, and he protected him. When he heard him, he was greatly perplexed; and yet he liked to listen to him. But an opportunity came when Herod on his birthday gave a banquet for his courtiers and officers and for the leaders of Galilee. When his daughter Herodias came in and danced, she pleased Herod and his guests; and the king said to the girl, "Ask me for whatever you wish, and I will give it." And he solemnly swore to her, "Whatever you ask me, I will give you, even half of my kingdom." She went out and said to her mother, "What should I ask for?" She replied, "The head of John the baptizer." Immediately she rushed back to the king and requested, "I want you to give me at once the head of John the Baptist on a platter." The king was deeply grieved; yet out of regard for his oaths and for the guests, he did not want to refuse her. Immediately the king sent a soldier of the guard with orders to bring John's head. He went and beheaded him in the prison, brought his head on a platter, and gave it to the girl. Then the girl gave it to her mother. When his disciples heard about it, they came and took his body, and laid it in a tomb.

Year C

Amos 7:7-17	**or**	✝ *Deuteronomy 30:9-14*
Psalm 82		✝ *Psalm 25:1-9*

Colossians 1:1-14
Luke 10:25-37

The Lesson   Amos 7:7-17

This is what the Lord GOD showed me: the Lord was standing beside a wall built with a plumb line, with a plumb line in his hand. And the LORD said to me, "Amos, what do you see?" And I said, "A plumb line." Then the Lord said, "See, I am setting a plumb line in the midst of my people Israel; I will never again pass them by; the high places of Isaac shall be made desolate, and the sanctuaries of Israel shall be laid waste, and I will rise against the house of Jeroboam with the sword." Then Amaziah, the priest of Bethel, sent to King Jeroboam of Israel, saying, "Amos has conspired against you in the very center of the house of Israel; the land is not able to bear all his words. For thus Amos has said, 'Jeroboam shall die by the sword, and Israel must go into exile away from his land.'" And Amaziah said to Amos, "O seer, go, flee away to the land of Judah, earn your bread there, and prophesy there; but never again prophesy at Bethel, for it is the king's sanctuary, and it is a temple of the kingdom." Then Amos answered Amaziah, "I am no prophet, nor a prophet's son; but I am a herdsman, and a dresser of sycamore trees, and the LORD took me from following the flock, and the LORD said to me, 'Go, prophesy to my people Israel.' Now therefore hear the word of the LORD. You say, 'Do not prophesy against Israel, and do not preach against the house of Isaac.' Therefore thus says the LORD: 'Your wife shall become a prostitute in the city, and your sons and your daughters shall fall by the sword, and your land shall be parceled out by line; you yourself shall die in an unclean land, and Israel shall surely go into exile away from its land.'"

The Response   Psalm 82

Psalm 82   *Deus stetit*

1   God takes his stand in the council of heaven; *
         he gives judgment in the midst of the gods:

2　"How long will you judge unjustly, *
　　and show favor to the wicked?

3　Save the weak and the orphan; *
　　defend the humble and needy;

4　Rescue the weak and the poor; *
　　deliver them from the power of the wicked.

5　They do not know, neither do they understand;
　　they go about in darkness; *
　　　all the foundations of the earth are shaken.

6　Now I say to you, 'You are gods, *
　　and all of you children of the Most High;

7　Nevertheless, you shall die like mortals, *
　　and fall like any prince.'"

8　Arise, O God, and rule the earth, *
　　for you shall take all nations for your own.

or, ✠ **The Lesson**　　　　　　　　　**Deuteronomy 30:9-14**

Moses said: The Lord your God will make you abundantly prosperous in all your undertakings, in the fruit of your body, in the fruit of your livestock, and in the fruit of your soil. For the Lord will again take delight in prospering you, just as he delighted in prospering your ancestors, when you obey the Lord your God by observing his commandments and decrees that are written in this book of the law, because you turn to the Lord your God with all your heart and with all your soul. Surely, this commandment that I am commanding you today is not too hard for you, nor is it too far away. It is not in heaven, that you should say, "Who will go up to heaven for us, and get it for us so that we may hear it and observe it?" Neither is it beyond the sea, that you should say, "Who will cross to the other side of the sea for us, and get it for us so that we may hear it and observe it?" No, the word is very near to you; it is in your mouth and in your heart for you to observe.

✠ **The Response**　　　　　　　　　　　**Psalm 25:1-9**

Psalm 25:1-9　*Ad te, Domine, levavi*

1　To you, O Lord, I lift up my soul;
　　my God, I put my trust in you; *
　　　let me not be humiliated,
　　　nor let my enemies triumph over me.

2　Let none who look to you be put to shame; *
　　let the treacherous be disappointed in their schemes.

3　Show me your ways, O Lord, *
　　and teach me your paths.

4   Lead me in your truth and teach me, *
     for you are the God of my salvation;
     in you have I trusted all the day long.

5   Remember, O LORD, your compassion and love, *
     for they are from everlasting.

6   Remember not the sins of my youth and my transgressions; *
     remember me according to your love
     and for the sake of your goodness, O LORD.

7   Gracious and upright is the LORD; *
     therefore he teaches sinners in his way.

8   He guides the humble in doing right *
     and teaches his way to the lowly.

9   All the paths of the LORD are love and faithfulness *
     to those who keep his covenant and his testimonies.

The Epistle   Colossians 1:1-14

Paul, an apostle of Christ Jesus by the will of God, and Timothy our brother, to the saints and faithful brothers and sisters in Christ in Colossae: Grace to you and peace from God our Father. In our prayers for you we always thank God, the Father of our Lord Jesus Christ, for we have heard of your faith in Christ Jesus and of the love that you have for all the saints, because of the hope laid up for you in heaven. You have heard of this hope before in the word of the truth, the gospel that has come to you. Just as it is bearing fruit and growing in the whole world, so it has been bearing fruit among yourselves from the day you heard it and truly comprehended the grace of God. This you learned from Epaphras, our beloved fellow servant. He is a faithful minister of Christ on your behalf, and he has made known to us your love in the Spirit. For this reason, since the day we heard it, we have not ceased praying for you and asking that you may be filled with the knowledge of God's will in all spiritual wisdom and understanding, so that you may lead lives worthy of the Lord, fully pleasing to him, as you bear fruit in every good work and as you grow in the knowledge of God. May you be made strong with all the strength that comes from his glorious power, and may you be prepared to endure everything with patience, while joyfully giving thanks to the Father, who has enabled you to share in the inheritance of the saints in the light. He has rescued us from the power of darkness and transferred us into the kingdom of his beloved Son, in whom we have redemption, the forgiveness of sins.

The Gospel   Luke 10:25-37

A lawyer stood up to test Jesus. "Teacher," he said, "what must I do to inherit eternal life?" Jesus said to him, "What is written in the law? What do you read there?" He answered, "You shall love the Lord your God with all your heart, and with all your soul, and with all your strength, and with all your mind; and your neighbor as yourself." And Jesus said to him, "You have given the right answer; do this, and you will live." But wanting to justify himself, he asked Jesus, "And who is my neighbor?" Jesus replied, "A man was going down from Jerusalem to Jericho, and fell into the hands of robbers, who stripped him, beat him, and went away, leaving him half dead. Now by chance a priest was going down that road; and when he saw him, he passed by on the other side. So likewise a Levite, when he came to the place and saw him, passed by on the other side. But a Samaritan while traveling came near him; and when he saw him, he was moved with pity. He went to him and bandaged his wounds, having poured oil and wine on them. Then he put him on his own animal, brought him to an inn, and took care of him. The next day he took out two denarii, gave them to the innkeeper, and said, 'Take care of him; and when I come back, I will repay you whatever more you spend.' Which of these three, do you think, was a neighbor to the man who fell into the hands of the robbers?" He said, "The one who showed him mercy." Jesus said to him, "Go and do likewise."

PROPER 11

Sunday between July 17 and July 23 inclusive

The Collect

Almighty God, the fountain of all wisdom, you know our necessities before we ask and our ignorance in asking: Have compassion on our weakness, and mercifully give us those things which for our unworthiness we dare not, and for our blindness we cannot ask; through the worthiness of your Son Jesus Christ our Lord, who lives and reigns with you and the Holy Spirit, one God, now and for ever. *Amen.*

Year A

*Genesis 28:10-19*a   **or**   ✠ *Wisdom of Solomon 12:13,*
Psalm 139:1-11, 22-23   *16-19*
                                                          or ✠ *Isaiah 44:6-8*
                                                          ✠ *Psalm 86:11-17*
Romans 8:12-25
Matthew 13:24-30, 36-43

The Lesson   Genesis 28:10-19*a*

Jacob left Beer-sheba and went toward Haran. He came to a certain place and stayed there for the night, because the sun had set. Taking one of the stones of the place, he put it under his head and lay down in that place. And he dreamed that there was a ladder set up on the earth, the top of it reaching to heaven; and the angels of God were ascending and descending on it. And the LORD stood beside him and said, "I am the LORD, the God of Abraham your father and the God of Isaac; the land on which you lie I will give to you and to your offspring; and your offspring shall be like the dust of the earth, and you shall spread abroad to the west and to the east and to the north and to the south; and all the families of the earth shall be blessed in you and in your offspring. Know that I am with you and will keep you wherever you go, and will bring you back to this land; for I will not leave you until I have done what I have promised you." Then Jacob woke from his sleep and said, "Surely the LORD is in this place — and I did not know it!" And he was afraid, and said, "How awesome is this place! This is none other than the house of God, and this is the gate of heaven." So Jacob rose early in the morning, and he took the stone that he had put under his head and set it up for a pillar and poured oil on the top of it. He called that place Bethel.

The Response   Psalm 139:1-11, 22-23

Psalm 139:1-11, 22-23 *Domine, probasti*

1 LORD, you have searched me out and known me; *
        you know my sitting down and my rising up;
        you discern my thoughts from afar.

2 You trace my journeys and my resting-places *
        and are acquainted with all my ways.

3 Indeed, there is not a word on my lips, *
        but you, O LORD, know it altogether.

4 You press upon me behind and before *
        and lay your hand upon me.

5 Such knowledge is too wonderful for me; *
        it is so high that I cannot attain to it.

6 Where can I go then from your Spirit? *
        where can I flee from your presence?

7 If I climb up to heaven, you are there; *
        if I make the grave my bed, you are there also.

8 If I take the wings of the morning *
        and dwell in the uttermost parts of the sea,

9 Even there your hand will lead me *
        and your right hand hold me fast.

10 If I say, "Surely the darkness will cover me, *
        and the light around me turn to night,"

11 Darkness is not dark to you;
        the night is as bright as the day; *
        darkness and light to you are both alike.

22   Search me out, O God, and know my heart; *
          try me and know my restless thoughts.
23   Look well whether there be any wickedness in me *
          and lead me in the way that is everlasting.

or, ✛ **The Lesson**   **Wisdom of Solomon 12:13, 16-19**
                                              or **Isaiah 44:6-8**
Wisdom of Solomon 12:13, 16-19

There is no god besides you, whose care is for all people, to whom you should
prove that you have not judged unjustly; For your strength is the source of
righteousness, and your sovereignty over all causes you to spare all. For you
show your strength when people doubt the completeness of your power, and
you rebuke any insolence among those who know it. Although you are sovereign in strength, you judge with mildness, and with great forbearance you
govern us; for you have power to act whenever you choose. Through such
works you have taught your people that the righteous must be kind, and you
have filled your children with good hope, because you give repentance for
sins.

or, ✛ **Isaiah 44:6-8**

Thus says the Lord, the King of Israel, and his Redeemer, the Lord of hosts: I
am the first and I am the last; besides me there is no god. Who is like me? Let
them proclaim it, let them declare and set it forth before me. Who has announced from of old the things to come? Let them tell us what is yet to be. Do
not fear, or be afraid; have I not told you from of old and declared it? You are
my witnesses! Is there any god besides me? There is no other rock; I know not
one.

✛ **The Response**   **Psalm 86:11-17**

Psalm 86:11-17 *Inclina, Domine*
    11   Teach me your way, O Lord,
              and I will walk in your truth; *
                  knit my heart to you that I may fear your Name.
    12   I will thank you, O Lord my God, with all my heart, *
                  and glorify your Name for evermore.
    13   For great is your love toward me; *
                  you have delivered me from the nethermost Pit.
    14   The arrogant rise up against me, O God,
              and a band of violent men seeks my life; *
                  they have not set you before their eyes.

15 But you, O LORD, are gracious and full of compassion, *
       slow to anger, and full of kindness and truth.
16 Turn to me and have mercy upon me; *
       give your strength to your servant;
       and save the child of your handmaid.
17 Show me a sign of your favor,
       so that those who hate me may see it and be ashamed; *
       because you, O LORD, have helped me and comforted me.

The Epistle   Romans 8:12-25

Brothers and sisters, we are debtors, not to the flesh, to live according to the flesh — for if you live according to the flesh, you will die; but if by the Spirit you put to death the deeds of the body, you will live. For all who are led by the Spirit of God are children of God. For you did not receive a spirit of slavery to fall back into fear, but you have received a spirit of adoption. When we cry, "Abba! Father!" it is that very Spirit bearing witness with our spirit that we are children of God, and if children, then heirs, heirs of God and joint heirs with Christ — if, in fact, we suffer with him so that we may also be glorified with him. I consider that the sufferings of this present time are not worth comparing with the glory about to be revealed to us. For the creation waits with eager longing for the revealing of the children of God; for the creation was subjected to futility, not of its own will but by the will of the one who subjected it, in hope that the creation itself will be set free from its bondage to decay and will obtain the freedom of the glory of the children of God. We know that the whole creation has been groaning in labor pains until now; and not only the creation, but we ourselves, who have the first fruits of the Spirit, groan inwardly while we wait for adoption, the redemption of our bodies. For in hope we were saved. Now hope that is seen is not hope. For who hopes for what is seen? But if we hope for what we do not see, we wait for it with patience.

The Gospel   Matthew 13:24-30, 36-43

Jesus put before them another parable: "The kingdom of heaven may be compared to someone who sowed good seed in his field; but while everybody was asleep, an enemy came and sowed weeds among the wheat, and then went away. So when the plants came up and bore grain, then the weeds appeared as well. And the slaves of the householder came and said to him, 'Master, did you not sow good seed in your field? Where, then, did these weeds come from?' He answered, 'An enemy has done this.' The slaves said to him, 'Then do you want us to go and gather them?' But he replied, 'No; for in gathering the weeds you would uproot the wheat along with them. Let both of them grow together until the harvest; and at harvest time I will tell the reapers,

Collect the weeds first and bind them in bundles to be burned, but gather the wheat into my barn.' " Then he left the crowds and went into the house. And his disciples approached him, saying, "Explain to us the parable of the weeds of the field." He answered, "The one who sows the good seed is the Son of Man; the field is the world, and the good seed are the children of the kingdom; the weeds are the children of the evil one, and the enemy who sowed them is the devil; the harvest is the end of the age, and the reapers are angels. Just as the weeds are collected and burned up with fire, so will it be at the end of the age. The Son of Man will send his angels, and they will collect out of his kingdom all causes of sin and all evildoers, and they will throw them into the furnace of fire, where there will be weeping and gnashing of teeth. Then the righteous will shine like the sun in the kingdom of their Father. Let anyone with ears listen!'"

Year B

| 2 Samuel 7:1-14a | **or** | ✝ Jeremiah 23:1-6 |
| Psalm 89:20-37 | | ✝ Psalm 23 |

Ephesians 2:11-22
Mark 6:30-34, 53-56

The Lesson   2 Samuel 7:1-14*a*

When (David) the king was settled in his house, and the LORD had given him rest from all his enemies around him, the king said to the prophet Nathan, "See now, I am living in a house of cedar, but the ark of God stays in a tent." Nathan said to the king, "Go, do all that you have in mind; for the LORD is with you." But that same night the word of the LORD came to Nathan: Go and tell my servant David: Thus says the LORD: Are you the one to build me a house to live in? I have not lived in a house since the day I brought up the people of Israel from Egypt to this day, but I have been moving about in a tent and a tabernacle. Wherever I have moved about among all the people of Israel, did I ever speak a word with any of the tribal leaders of Israel, whom I commanded to shepherd my people Israel, saying, "Why have you not built me a house of cedar?" Now therefore thus you shall say to my servant David: Thus says the LORD of hosts: I took you from the pasture, from following the sheep to be prince over my people Israel; and I have been with you wherever you went, and have cut off all your enemies from before you; and I will make for you a great name, like the name of the great ones of the earth. And I will appoint a place for my people Israel and will plant them, so that they may live in their own place, and be disturbed no more; and evildoers shall afflict them no more, as formerly, from the time that I appointed judges over my people Israel; and I will give you rest from all your enemies. Moreover the LORD declares to you that the LORD will make you a house. When your days are fulfilled and you lie down with your ancestors, I will raise up your offspring after you, who shall come forth from your body, and I will establish his kingdom. He shall build a house for my name, and I will establish the throne of his kingdom forever. I will be a father to him, and he shall be a son to me.

The Response   Psalm 89:20-37

Psalm 89:20-37   *Tunc locutus es*

20   "I have found David my servant; *
         with my holy oil have I anointed him.
21   My hand will hold him fast *
         and my arm will make him strong.
22   No enemy shall deceive him, *
         nor any wicked man bring him down.
23   I will crush his foes before him *
         and strike down those who hate him.
24   My faithfulness and love shall be with him, *
         and he shall be victorious through my Name.
25   I shall make his dominion extend *
         from the Great Sea to the River.
26   He will say to me, 'You are my Father, *
         my God, and the rock of my salvation.'
27   I will make him my firstborn *
         and higher than the kings of the earth.
28   I will keep my love for him for ever, *
         and my covenant will stand firm for him.
29   I will establish his line for ever *
         and his throne as the days of heaven."
30   "If his children forsake my law *
         and do not walk according to my judgments;
31   If they break my statutes *
         and do not keep my commandments;
32   I will punish their transgressions with a rod *
         and their iniquities with the lash;
33   But I will not take my love from him, *
         nor let my faithfulness prove false.
34   I will not break my covenant, *
         nor change what has gone out of my lips.
35   Once for all I have sworn by my holiness: *
         'I will not lie to David.
36   His line shall endure for ever *
         and his throne as the sun before me;

37   It shall stand fast for evermore like the moon, *
     the abiding witness in the sky.'"

or, ✙ **The Lesson**   **Jeremiah 23:1-6**

Woe to the shepherds who destroy and scatter the sheep of my pasture! says
the LORD. Therefore thus says the LORD, the God of Israel, concerning the
shepherds who shepherd my people: It is you who have scattered my flock,
and have driven them away, and you have not attended to them. So I will
attend to you for your evil doings, says the LORD. Then I myself will gather
the remnant of my flock out of all the lands where I have driven them, and I
will bring them back to their fold, and they shall be fruitful and multiply. I
will raise up shepherds over them who will shepherd them, and they shall not
fear any longer, or be dismayed, nor shall any be missing, says the LORD. The
days are surely coming, says the LORD, when I will raise up for David a
righteous Branch, and he shall reign as king and deal wisely, and shall execute
justice and righteousness in the land. In his days Judah will be saved and
Israel will live in safety. And this is the name by which he will be called: "The
LORD is our righteousness."

✙ **The Response**   **Psalm 23**

Psalm 23   *Dominus regit me*

1   The LORD is my shepherd; *
      I shall not be in want.
2   He makes me lie down in green pastures *
      and leads me beside still waters.
3   He revives my soul *
      and guides me along right pathways for his Name's sake.
4   Though I walk through the valley of the shadow of death,
    I shall fear no evil; *
        for you are with me;
        your rod and your staff, they comfort me.
5   You spread a table before me in the presence of those
                        who trouble me; *
        you have anointed my head with oil,
        and my cup is running over.
6   Surely your goodness and mercy shall follow me all the days
                        of my life, *
        and I will dwell in the house of the LORD for ever.

The Epistle   **Ephesians 2:11-22**

Remember that at one time you Gentiles by birth, called "the uncircumcision"
by those who are called "the circumcision" — a physical circumcision made

in the flesh by human hands — remember that you were at that time without Christ, being aliens from the commonwealth of Israel, and strangers to the covenants of promise, having no hope and without God in the world. But now in Christ Jesus you who once were far off have been brought near by the blood of Christ. For he is our peace; in his flesh he has made both groups into one and has broken down the dividing wall, that is, the hostility between us. He has abolished the law with its commandments and ordinances, that he might create in himself one new humanity in place of the two, thus making peace, and might reconcile both groups to God in one body through the cross, thus putting to death that hostility through it. So he came and proclaimed peace to you who were far off and peace to those who were near; for through him both of us have access in one Spirit to the Father. So then you are no longer strangers and aliens, but you are citizens with the saints and also members of the household of God, built upon the foundation of the apostles and prophets, with Christ Jesus himself as the cornerstone. In him the whole structure is joined together and grows into a holy temple in the Lord; in whom you also are built together spiritually into a dwelling place for God.

The Gospel   Mark 6:30-34, 53-56

The apostles gathered around Jesus, and told him all that they had done and taught. He said to them, "Come away to a deserted place all by yourselves and rest a while." For many were coming and going, and they had no leisure even to eat. And they went away in the boat to a deserted place by themselves. Now many saw them going and recognized them, and they hurried there on foot from all the towns and arrived ahead of them. As he went ashore, he saw a great crowd; and he had compassion for them, because they were like sheep without a shepherd; and he began to teach them many things. When they had crossed over, they came to land at Gennesaret and moored the boat. When they got out of the boat, people at once recognized him, and rushed about that whole region and began to bring the sick on mats to wherever they heard he was. And wherever he went, into villages or cities or farms, they laid the sick in the marketplaces, and begged him that they might touch even the fringe of his cloak; and all who touched it were healed.

Year C

Amos 8:1-12	**or**	✝ *Genesis 18:1-10a*
Psalm 52		✝ *Psalm 15*

Colossians 1:15-28
Luke 10:38-42

The Lesson   Amos 8:1-12

This is what the Lord GOD showed me—a basket of summer fruit. He said, "Amos, what do you see?" And I said, "A basket of summer fruit." Then the

LORD said to me, "The end has come upon my people Israel; I will never again pass them by. The songs of the temple shall become wailings in that day," says the Lord GOD; "the dead bodies shall be many, cast out in every place. Be silent!" Hear this, you that trample on the needy, and bring to ruin the poor of the land, saying, "When will the new moon be over so that we may sell grain; and the sabbath, so that we may offer wheat for sale? We will make the ephah small and the shekel great, and practice deceit with false balances, buying the poor for silver and the needy for a pair of sandals, and selling the sweepings of the wheat." The LORD has sworn by the pride of Jacob: Surely I will never forget any of their deeds. Shall not the land tremble on this account, and everyone mourn who lives in it, and all of it rise like the Nile, and be tossed about and sink again, like the Nile of Egypt? On that day, says the Lord GOD, I will make the sun go down at noon, and darken the earth in broad daylight. I will turn your feasts into mourning, and all your songs into lamentation; I will bring sackcloth on all loins, and baldness on every head; I will make it like the mourning for an only son, and the end of it like a bitter day. The time is surely coming, says the Lord GOD, when I will send a famine on the land; not a famine of bread, or a thirst for water, but of hearing the words of the LORD. They shall wander from sea to sea, and from north to east; they shall run to and fro, seeking the word of the LORD, but they shall not find it.

The Response   Psalm 52

Psalm 52   *Quid gloriaris?*

1   You tyrant, why do you boast of wickedness *
        against the godly all day long?
2   You plot ruin;
    your tongue is like a sharpened razor, *
        O worker of deception.
3   You love evil more than good *
        and lying more than speaking the truth.
4   You love all words that hurt, *
        O you deceitful tongue.
5   Oh, that God would demolish you utterly, *
        topple you, and snatch you from your dwelling,
        and root you out of the land of the living!
6   The righteous shall see and tremble, *
        and they shall laugh at him, saying,
7   "This is the one who did not take God for a refuge, *
        but trusted in great wealth
        and relied upon wickedness."
8   But I am like a green olive tree in the house of God; *
        I trust in the mercy of God for ever and ever.

9   I will give you thanks for what you have done *
        and declare the goodness of your Name in the presence
            of the godly.

or, ✠ **The Lesson**   **Genesis 18:1-10***a*

The LORD appeared to Abraham by the oaks of Mamre, as he sat at the
entrance of his tent in the heat of the day. He looked up and saw three men
standing near him. When he saw them, he ran from the tent entrance to meet
them, and bowed down to the ground. He said, "My lord, if I find favor with
you, do not pass by your servant. Let a little water be brought, and wash your
feet, and rest yourselves under the tree. Let me bring a little bread, that you
may refresh yourselves, and after that you may pass on — since you have
come to your servant." So they said, "Do as you have said." And Abraham
hastened into the tent to Sarah, and said, "Make ready quickly three measures
of choice flour, knead it, and make cakes." Abraham ran to the herd, and took
a calf, tender and good, and gave it to the servant, who hastened to prepare it.
Then he took curds and milk and the calf that he had prepared, and set it
before them; and he stood by them under the tree while they ate. They said to
him, "Where is your wife Sarah?" And he said, "There, in the tent." Then one
said, "I will surely return to you in due season, and your wife Sarah shall have
a son."

✠ **The Response**   **Psalm 15**

Psalm 15   *Domine, quis habitabit?*

1   LORD, who may dwell in your tabernacle? *
        who may abide upon your holy hill?
2   Whoever leads a blameless life and does what is right, *
        who speaks the truth from his heart.
3   There is no guile upon his tongue;
    he does no evil to his friend; *
        he does not heap contempt upon his neighbor.
4   In his sight the wicked is rejected, *
        but he honors those who fear the LORD.
5   He has sworn to do no wrong *
        and does not take back his word.
6   He does not give his money in hope of gain, *
        nor does he take a bribe against the innocent.
7   Whoever does these things *
        shall never be overthrown.

The Epistle   **Colossians 1:15-28**

Jesus is the image of the invisible God, the firstborn of all creation; for in him
all things in heaven and on earth were created, things visible and invisible,

whether thrones or dominions or rulers or powers — all things have been created through him and for him. He himself is before all things, and in him all things hold together. He is the head of the body, the church; he is the beginning, the firstborn from the dead, so that he might come to have first place in everything. For in him all the fullness of God was pleased to dwell, and through him God was pleased to reconcile to himself all things, whether on earth or in heaven, by making peace through the blood of his cross. And you who were once estranged and hostile in mind, doing evil deeds, he has now reconciled in his fleshly body through death, so as to present you holy and blameless and irreproachable before him — provided that you continue securely established and steadfast in the faith, without shifting from the hope promised by the gospel that you heard, which has been proclaimed to every creature under heaven. I, Paul, became a servant of this gospel. I am now rejoicing in my sufferings for your sake, and in my flesh I am completing what is lacking in Christ's afflictions for the sake of his body, that is, the church. I became its servant according to God's commission that was given to me for you, to make the word of God fully known, the mystery that has been hidden throughout the ages and generations but has now been revealed to his saints. To them God chose to make known how great among the Gentiles are the riches of the glory of this mystery, which is Christ in you, the hope of glory. It is he whom we proclaim, warning everyone and teaching everyone in all wisdom, so that we may present everyone mature in Christ.

The Gospel   Luke 10:38-42

As Jesus and his disciples went on their way, Jesus entered a certain village, where a woman named Martha welcomed him into her home. She had a sister named Mary, who sat at the Lord's feet and listened to what he was saying. But Martha was distracted by her many tasks; so she came to him and asked, "Lord, do you not care that my sister has left me to do all the work by myself? Tell her then to help me." But the Lord answered her, "Martha, Martha, you are worried and distracted by many things; there is need of only one thing. Mary has chosen the better part, which will not be taken away from her."

PROPER 12

Sunday between July 24 and July 30 inclusive

The Collect

O God, the protector of all who trust in you, without whom nothing is strong, nothing is holy: Increase and multiply upon us your mercy; that, with you as our ruler and guide, we may so pass through things temporal, that we lose not the things eternal; through Jesus Christ our Lord, who lives and reigns with you and the Holy Spirit, one God, for ever and ever. *Amen.*

Year A

Genesis 29:15-28
Psalm 105:1-11, 45b
or Psalm 128

or

✝ 1 Kings 3:5-12
✝ Psalm 119:129-136

Romans 8:26-39
Matthew 13:31-33, 44-52

The Lesson   Genesis 29:15-28

Laban said to Jacob, "Because you are my kinsman, should you therefore
serve me for nothing? Tell me, what shall your wages be?" Now Laban had
two daughters; the name of the elder was Leah, and the name of the younger
was Rachel. Leah's eyes were lovely, and Rachel was graceful and beautiful.
Jacob loved Rachel; so he said, "I will serve you seven years for your younger
daughter Rachel." Laban said, "It is better that I give her to you than that I
should give her to any other man; stay with me." So Jacob served seven years
for Rachel, and they seemed to him but a few days because of the love he had
for her. Then Jacob said to Laban, "Give me my wife that I may go in to her,
for my time is completed." So Laban gathered together all the people of the
place, and made a feast. But in the evening he took his daughter Leah and
brought her to Jacob; and he went in to her. (Laban gave his maid Zilpah to
his daughter Leah to be her maid.) When morning came, it was Leah! And
Jacob said to Laban, "What is this you have done to me? Did I not serve with
you for Rachel? Why then have you deceived me?" Laban said, "This is not
done in our country — giving the younger before the firstborn. Complete the
week of this one, and we will give you the other also in return for serving me
another seven years." Jacob did so, and completed her week; then Laban gave
him his daughter Rachel as a wife.

The Response   Psalm 105:1-11, 45b *or* Psalm 128
Psalm 105:1-11, 45b   *Confitemini Domino*

1   Give thanks to the LORD and call upon his Name; *
        make known his deeds among the peoples.
2   Sing to him, sing praises to him, *
        and speak of all his marvelous works.
3   Glory in his holy Name; *
        let the hearts of those who seek the LORD rejoice.
4   Search for the LORD and his strength; *
        continually seek his face.
5   Remember the marvels he has done, *
        his wonders and the judgments of his mouth,

6   O offspring of Abraham his servant, *
     O children of Jacob his chosen.

7   He is the Lord our God; *
     his judgments prevail in all the world.

8   He has always been mindful of his covenant, *
     the promise he made for a thousand generations:

9   The covenant he made with Abraham, *
     the oath that he swore to Isaac,

10   Which he established as a statute for Jacob, *
     an everlasting covenant for Israel,

11   Saying, "To you will I give the land of Canaan *
     to be your allotted inheritance." Hallelujah!

or, Psalm 128   *Beati omnes*

1   Happy are they all who fear the Lord, *
     and who follow in his ways!

2   You shall eat the fruit of your labor; *
     happiness and prosperity shall be yours.

3   Your wife shall be like a fruitful vine within your house, *
     your children like olive shoots round about your table.

4   The man who fears the Lord *
     shall thus indeed be blessed.

5   The Lord bless you from Zion, *
     and may you see the prosperity of Jerusalem all the days
        of your life.

6   May you live to see your children's children; *
     may peace be upon Israel.

or, ☩ The Lesson   1 Kings 3:5-12

At Gibeon the Lord appeared to Solomon in a dream by night; and God said,
"Ask what I should give you." And Solomon said, "You have shown great and
steadfast love to your servant my father David, because he walked before you
in faithfulness, in righteousness, and in uprightness of heart toward you; and
you have kept for him this great and steadfast love, and have given him a son
to sit on his throne today. And now, O Lord my God, you have made your
servant king in place of my father David, although I am only a little child; I do
not know how to go out or come in. And your servant is in the midst of the
people whom you have chosen, a great people, so numerous they cannot be
numbered or counted. Give your servant therefore an understanding mind to
govern your people, able to discern between good and evil; for who can
govern this your great people?" It pleased the Lord that Solomon had asked
this. God said to him, "Because you have asked this, and have not asked for

yourself long life or riches, or for the life of your enemies, but have asked for yourself understanding to discern what is right, I now do according to your word. Indeed I give you a wise and discerning mind; no one like you has been before you and no one like you shall arise after you."

✙ The Response   Psalm 119:129-136

Psalm 119:129-136 *Mirabilia*

129   Your decrees are wonderful; *
            therefore I obey them with all my heart.
130   When your word goes forth it gives light; *
            it gives understanding to the simple.
131   I open my mouth and pant; *
            I long for your commandments.
132   Turn to me in mercy, *
            as you always do to those who love your Name.
133   Steady my footsteps in your word; *
            let no iniquity have dominion over me.
134   Rescue me from those who oppress me, *
            and I will keep your commandments.
135   Let your countenance shine upon your servant *
            and teach me your statutes.
136   My eyes shed streams of tears, *
            because people do not keep your law.

The Epistle   Romans 8:26-39

The Spirit helps us in our weakness; for we do not know how to pray as we ought, but that very Spirit intercedes with sighs too deep for words. And God, who searches the heart, knows what is the mind of the Spirit, because the Spirit intercedes for the saints according to the will of God. We know that all things work together for good for those who love God, who are called according to his purpose. For those whom he foreknew he also predestined to be conformed to the image of his Son, in order that he might be the firstborn within a large family. And those whom he predestined he also called; and those whom he called he also justified; and those whom he justified he also glorified. What then are we to say about these things? If God is for us, who is against us? He who did not withhold his own Son, but gave him up for all of us, will he not with him also give us everything else? Who will bring any charge against God's elect? It is God who justifies. Who is to condemn? It is Christ Jesus, who died, yes, who was raised, who is at the right hand of God, who indeed intercedes for us. Who will separate us from the love of Christ? Will hardship, or distress, or persecution, or famine, or nakedness, or peril, or sword? As it is written, "For your sake we are being killed all day long; we are accounted as sheep to be slaughtered." No, in all these things we are more than conquerors through him who loved us. For I am convinced that neither death, nor life, nor angels, nor rulers, nor things present, nor things to come, nor powers, nor height, nor depth, nor anything else in all creation, will be able to separate us from the love of God in Christ Jesus our Lord.

The Gospel   Matthew 13:31-33, 44-52

Jesus put before them another parable: "The kingdom of heaven is like a mustard seed that someone took and sowed in his field; it is the smallest of all the seeds, but when it has grown it is the greatest of shrubs and becomes a tree, so that the birds of the air come and make nests in its branches." He told them another parable: "The kingdom of heaven is like yeast that a woman took and mixed in with three measures of flour until all of it was leavened. The kingdom of heaven is like treasure hidden in a field, which someone found and hid; then in his joy he goes and sells all that he has and buys that field. Again, the kingdom of heaven is like a merchant in search of fine pearls; on finding one pearl of great value, he went and sold all that he had and bought it. Again, the kingdom of heaven is like a net that was thrown into the sea and caught fish of every kind; when it was full, they drew it ashore, sat down, and put the good into baskets but threw out the bad. So it will be at the end of the age. The angels will come out and separate the evil from the righteous and throw them into the furnace of fire, where there will be weeping and gnashing of teeth. Have you understood all this?" They answered, "Yes." And he said to them, "Therefore every scribe who has been trained for the kingdom of heaven is like the master of a household who brings out of his treasure what is new and what is old."

Year B

2 Samuel 11:1-15   **or**   ✛ *2 Kings 4:42-44*
Psalm 14   ✛ *Psalm 145:10-19*
Ephesians 3:14-21
John 6:1-21

The Lesson   2 Samuel 11:1-15

In the spring of the year, the time when kings go out to battle, David sent Joab with his officers and all Israel with him; they ravaged the Ammonites, and besieged Rabbah. But David remained at Jerusalem. It happened, late one afternoon, when David rose from his couch and was walking about on the roof of the king's house, that he saw from the roof a woman bathing; the woman was very beautiful. David sent someone to inquire about the woman. It was reported, "This is Bathsheba daughter of Eliam, the wife of Uriah the Hittite."

So David sent messengers to get her, and she came to him, and he lay with her. (Now she was purifying herself after her period.) Then she returned to her house. The woman conceived; and she sent and told David, "I am pregnant." So David sent word to Joab, "Send me Uriah the Hittite." And Joab sent Uriah to David. When Uriah came to him, David asked how Joab and the people fared, and how the war was going. Then David said to Uriah, "Go down to your house, and wash your feet." Uriah went out of the king's house, and there followed him a present from the king. But Uriah slept at the entrance of the king's house with all the servants of his lord, and did not go down to his house. When they told David, "Uriah did not go down to his house," David said to Uriah, "You have just come from a journey. Why did you not go down to your house?" Uriah said to David, "The ark and Israel and Judah remain in booths; and my lord Joab and the servants of my lord are camping in the open field; shall I then go to my house, to eat and to drink, and to lie with my wife? As you live, and as your soul lives, I will not do such a thing." Then David said to Uriah, "Remain here today also, and tomorrow I will send you back." So Uriah remained in Jerusalem that day. On the next day, David invited him to eat and drink in his presence and made him drunk; and in the evening he went out to lie on his couch with the servants of his lord, but he did not go down to his house. In the morning David wrote a letter to Joab, and sent it by the hand of Uriah. In the letter he wrote, "Set Uriah in the forefront of the hardest fighting, and then draw back from him, so that he may be struck down and die."

The Response   **Psalm 14**

Psalm 14   *Dixit insipiens*

1   The fool has said in his heart, "There is no God." *
        All are corrupt and commit abominable acts;
        there is none who does any good.

2   The LORD looks down from heaven upon us all, *
        to see if there is any who is wise,
        . if there is one who seeks after God.

3   Every one has proved faithless;
     all alike have turned bad; *
        there is none who does good; no, not one.

4   Have they no knowledge, all those evildoers *
        who eat up my people like bread
        and do not call upon the LORD?

5   See how they tremble with fear, *
        because God is in the company of the righteous.

6   Their aim is to confound the plans of the afflicted, *
        but the LORD is their refuge.

7   Oh, that Israel's deliverance would come out of Zion! *
        when the LORD restores the fortunes of his people,
        Jacob will rejoice and Israel be glad.

or, ✠ The Lesson   2 Kings 4:42-44

A man came from Baal-shalishah, bringing food from the first fruits to the
man of God: twenty loaves of barley and fresh ears of grain in his sack. Elisha
said, "Give it to the people and let them eat." But his servant said, "How can I
set this before a hundred people?" So he repeated, "Give it to the people and
let them eat, for thus says the LORD, 'They shall eat and have some left.' " He
set it before them, they ate, and had some left, according to the word of the
LORD.

✠ The Response   Psalm 145:10-19

Psalm 145:10-19   *Exaltabo te, Deus*

10   All your works praise you, O LORD, *
        and your faithful servants bless you.
11   They make known the glory of your kingdom *
        and speak of your power;
12   That the peoples may know of your power *
        and the glorious splendor of your kingdom.
13   Your kingdom is an everlasting kingdom; *
        your dominion endures throughout all ages.
14   The LORD is faithful in all his words *
        and merciful in all his deeds.
15   The LORD upholds all those who fall; *
        he lifts up those who are bowed down.
16   The eyes of all wait upon you, O LORD, *
        and you give them their food in due season.
17   You open wide your hand *
        and satisfy the needs of every living creature.
18   The LORD is righteous in all his ways *
        and loving in all his works.
19   The LORD is near to those who call upon him, *
        to all who call upon him faithfully.

The Epistle   Ephesians 3:14-21

I bow my knees before the Father, from whom every family in heaven and on
earth takes its name. I pray that, according to the riches of his glory, he may
grant that you may be strengthened in your inner being with power through his
Spirit, and that Christ may dwell in your hearts through faith, as you are

being rooted and grounded in love. I pray that you may have the power to comprehend, with all the saints, what is the breadth and length and height and depth, and to know the love of Christ that surpasses knowledge, so that you may be filled with all the fullness of God. Now to him who by the power at work within us is able to accomplish abundantly far more than all we can ask or imagine, to him be glory in the church and in Christ Jesus to all generations, forever and ever. Amen.

The Gospel   John 6:1-21

Jesus went to the other side of the Sea of Galilee, also called the Sea of Tiberias. A large crowd kept following him, because they saw the signs that he was doing for the sick. Jesus went up the mountain and sat down there with his disciples. Now the Passover, the festival of the Jews, was near. When he looked up and saw a large crowd coming toward him, Jesus said to Philip, "Where are we to buy bread for these people to eat?" He said this to test him, for he himself knew what he was going to do. Philip answered him, "Six months' wages would not buy enough bread for each of them to get a little." One of his disciples, Andrew, Simon Peter's brother, said to him, "There is a boy here who has five barley loaves and two fish. But what are they among so many people?" Jesus said, "Make the people sit down." Now there was a great deal of grass in the place; so they sat down, about five thousand in all. Then Jesus took the loaves, and when he had given thanks, he distributed them to those who were seated; so also the fish, as much as they wanted. When they were satisfied, he told his disciples, "Gather up the fragments left over, so that nothing may be lost." So they gathered them up, and from the fragments of the five barley loaves, left by those who had eaten, they filled twelve baskets. When the people saw the sign that he had done, they began to say, "This is indeed the prophet who is to come into the world." When Jesus realized that they were about to come and take him by force to make him king, he withdrew again to the mountain by himself. When evening came, his disciples went down to the sea, got into a boat, and started across the sea to Capernaum. It was now dark, and Jesus had not yet come to them. The sea became rough because a strong wind was blowing. When they had rowed about three or four miles, they saw Jesus walking on the sea and coming near the boat, and they were terrified. But he said to them, "It is I; do not be afraid." Then they wanted to take him into the boat, and immediately the boat reached the land toward which they were going.

Hosea 1:2-10   **or**   ✠ *Genesis 18:20-32*

Psalm 85   ✠ *Psalm 138*

Colossians 2:6-15, (16-19)

Luke 11:1-13

The Lesson   Hosea 1:2-10

When the LORD first spoke through Hosea, the LORD said to Hosea, "Go, take for yourself a wife of whoredom and have children of whoredom, for the land commits great whoredom by forsaking the LORD." So he went and took Gomer daughter of Diblaim, and she conceived and bore him a son. And the LORD said to him, "Name him Jezreel; for in a little while I will punish the house of Jehu for the blood of Jezreel, and I will put an end to the kingdom of the house of Israel. On that day I will break the bow of Israel in the valley of Jezreel." She conceived again and bore a daughter. Then the LORD said to him, "Name her Lo-ruhamah, for I will no longer have pity on the house of Israel or forgive them. But I will have pity on the house of Judah, and I will save them by the LORD their God; I will not save them by bow, or by sword, or by war, or by horses, or by horsemen." When she had weaned Lo-ruhamah, she conceived and bore a son. Then the LORD said, "Name him Lo-ammi, for you are not my people and I am not your God." Yet the number of the people of Israel shall be like the sand of the sea, which can be neither measured nor numbered; and in the place where it was said to them, "You are not my people," it shall be said to them, "Children of the living God."

The Response   Psalm 85

Psalm 85   *Benedixisti, Domine*

1   You have been gracious to your land, O LORD, *
      you have restored the good fortune of Jacob.

2   You have forgiven the iniquity of your people *
      and blotted out all their sins.

3   You have withdrawn all your fury *
      and turned yourself from your wrathful indignation.

4   Restore us then, O God our Savior; *
      let your anger depart from us.

5   Will you be displeased with us for ever? *
      will you prolong your anger from age to age?

6   Will you not give us life again, *
      that your people may rejoice in you?

7   Show us your mercy, O LORD, *
      and grant us your salvation.

8 I will listen to what the LORD God is saying, *
      for he is speaking peace to his faithful people
      and to those who turn their hearts to him.

9 Truly, his salvation is very near to those who fear him, *
      that his glory may dwell in our land.

10 Mercy and truth have met together; *
      righteousness and peace have kissed each other.

11 Truth shall spring up from the earth, *
      and righteousness shall look down from heaven.

12 The LORD will indeed grant prosperity, *
      and our land will yield its increase.

13 Righteousness shall go before him, *
      and peace shall be a pathway for his feet.

or, ✟ **The Lesson**   **Genesis 18:20-32**

The LORD said, "How great is the outcry against Sodom and Gomorrah and
how very grave their sin! I must go down and see whether they have done
altogether according to the outcry that has come to me; and if not, I will
know." So the men turned from there, and went toward Sodom, while
Abraham remained standing before the LORD. Then Abraham came near and
said, "Will you indeed sweep away the righteous with the wicked? Suppose
there are fifty righteous within the city; will you then sweep away the place
and not forgive it for the fifty righteous who are in it? Far be it from you to do
such a thing, to slay the righteous with the wicked, so that the righteous fare
as the wicked! Far be that from you! Shall not the Judge of all the earth do
what is just?" And the LORD said, "If I find at Sodom fifty righteous in the
city, I will forgive the whole place for their sake." Abraham answered, "Let
me take it upon myself to speak to the LORD, I who am but dust and ashes.
Suppose five of the fifty righteous are lacking? Will you destroy the whole
city for lack of five?" And he said, "I will not destroy it if I find forty-five
there." Again he spoke to him, "Suppose forty are found there." He answered,
"For the sake of forty I will not do it." Then he said, "Oh do not let the LORD
be angry if I speak. Suppose thirty are found there." He answered, "I will not
do it, if I find thirty there." He said, "Let me take it upon myself to speak to
the LORD. Suppose twenty are found there." He answered, "For the sake of
twenty I will not destroy it." Then he said, "Oh do not let the LORD be angry if
I speak just once more. Suppose ten are found there." He answered, "For the
sake of ten I will not destroy it." And the LORD went his way, when he had
finished speaking to Abraham; and Abraham returned to his place.

✛ **The Response**   **Psalm 138**

Psalm 138   *Confitebor tibi*

1   I will give thanks to you, O LORD, with my whole heart; *
      before the gods I will sing your praise.

2   I will bow down toward your holy temple
      and praise your Name, *
      because of your love and faithfulness;

3   For you have glorified your Name *
      and your word above all things.

4   When I called, you answered me; *
      you increased my strength within me.

5   All the kings of the earth will praise you, O LORD, *
      when they have heard the words of your mouth.

6   They will sing of the ways of the LORD, *
      that great is the glory of the LORD.

7   Though the LORD be high, he cares for the lowly; *
      he perceives the haughty from afar.

8   Though I walk in the midst of trouble, you keep me safe; *
      you stretch forth your hand against the fury of my enemies;
      your right hand shall save me.

9   The LORD will make good his purpose for me; *
      O LORD, your love endures for ever;
      do not abandon the works of your hands.

The Epistle   **Colossians 2:6-15 (16-19)**

Colossians 2:6-15

As you therefore have received Christ Jesus the Lord, continue to live your lives in him, rooted and built up in him and established in the faith, just as you were taught, abounding in thanksgiving. See to it that no one takes you captive through philosophy and empty deceit, according to human tradition, according to the elemental spirits of the universe, and not according to Christ. For in him the whole fullness of deity dwells bodily, and you have come to fullness in him, who is the head of every ruler and authority. In him also you were circumcised with a spiritual circumcision, by putting off the body of the flesh in the circumcision of Christ; when you were buried with him in baptism, you were also raised with him through faith in the power of God, who raised him from the dead. And when you were dead in trespasses and the uncircumcision of your flesh, God made you alive together with him, when he forgave us all our trespasses, erasing the record that stood against us with its legal demands. He set this aside, nailing it to the cross. He disarmed the rulers and authorities and made a public example of them, triumphing over them in it.

Colossians 2:(16-19) [Therefore do not let anyone condemn you in matters of food and drink or of observing festivals, new moons, or sabbaths. These are only a shadow of what is to come, but the substance belongs to Christ. Do not let anyone disqualify you, insisting on self-abasement and worship of angels, dwelling on visions, puffed up without cause by a human way of thinking, and not holding fast to the head, from whom the whole body, nourished and held together by its ligaments and sinews, grows with a growth that is from God.]

The Gospel   Luke 11:1-13

Jesus was praying in a certain place, and after he had finished, one of his disciples said to him, "Lord, teach us to pray, as John taught his disciples." He said to them, "When you pray, say: Father, hallowed be your name. Your kingdom come. Give us each day our daily bread. And forgive us our sins, for we ourselves forgive everyone indebted to us. And do not bring us to the time of trial." And he said to them, "Suppose one of you has a friend, and you go to him at midnight and say to him, 'Friend, lend me three loaves of bread; for a friend of mine has arrived, and I have nothing to set before him.' And he answers from within, 'Do not bother me; the door has already been locked, and my children are with me in bed; I cannot get up and give you anything.' I tell you, even though he will not get up and give him anything because he is his friend, at least because of his persistence he will get up and give him whatever he needs. So I say to you, Ask, and it will be given you; search, and you will find; knock, and the door will be opened for you. For everyone who asks receives, and everyone who searches finds, and for everyone who knocks, the door will be opened. Is there anyone among you who, if your child asks for a fish, will give a snake instead of a fish? Or if the child asks for an egg, will give a scorpion? If you then, who are evil, know how to give good gifts to your children, how much more will the heavenly Father give the Holy Spirit to those who ask him!"

PROPER 13

Sunday between July 31 and August 6 inclusive

The Collect

Let your continual mercy, O Lord, cleanse and defend your Church; and, because it cannot continue in safety without your help, protect and govern it always by your goodness; through Jesus Christ our Lord, who lives and reigns with you and the Holy Spirit, one God, for ever and ever. *Amen.*

Year A

Genesis 32:22-31	**or**	✠ *Isaiah 55:1-5*
Psalm 17:1-7, 16		✠ *Psalm 145:8-9, 15-22*

Romans 9:1-5
Matthew 14:13-21

The Lesson   **Genesis 32:22-31**

The same night Jacob got up and took his two wives, his two maids, and his eleven children, and crossed the ford of the Jabbok. He took them and sent them across the stream, and likewise everything that he had. Jacob was left alone; and a man wrestled with him until daybreak. When the man saw that he did not prevail against Jacob, he struck him on the hip socket; and Jacob's hip was put out of joint as he wrestled with him. Then he said, "Let me go, for the day is breaking." But Jacob said, "I will not let you go, unless you bless me." So he said to him, "What is your name?" And he said, "Jacob." Then the man said, "You shall no longer be called Jacob, but Israel, for you have striven with God and with humans, and have prevailed." Then Jacob asked him, "Please tell me your name." But he said, "Why is it that you ask my name?" And there he blessed him. So Jacob called the place Peniel, saying, "For I have seen God face to face, and yet my life is preserved." The sun rose upon him as he passed Penuel, limping because of his hip.

The Response   **Psalm 17:1-7, 16**

Psalm 17:1-7, 16   *Exaudi, Domine*

1   Hear my plea of innocence, O LORD;
        give heed to my cry; *
            listen to my prayer, which does not come from lying lips.

2   Let my vindication come forth from your presence; *
        let your eyes be fixed on justice.

3   Weigh my heart, summon me by night, *
        melt me down; you will find no impurity in me.

4   I give no offense with my mouth as others do; *
        I have heeded the words of your lips.

5   My footsteps hold fast to the ways of your law; *
        in your paths my feet shall not stumble.

6   I call upon you, O God, for you will answer me; *
        incline your ear to me and hear my words.

7   Show me your marvelous loving-kindness, *
        O Savior of those who take refuge at your right hand
            from those who rise up against them.

16 But at my vindication I shall see your face; *
        when I awake, I shall be satisfied, beholding
            your likeness.

or, ✝ **The Lesson**   **Isaiah 55:1-5**

Ho, everyone who thirsts, come to the waters; and you that have no money, come, buy and eat! Come, buy wine and milk without money and without price. Why do you spend your money for that which is not bread, and your labor for that which does not satisfy? Listen carefully to me, and eat what is good, and delight yourselves in rich food. Incline your ear, and come to me; listen, so that you may live. I will make with you an everlasting covenant, my steadfast, sure love for David. See, I made him a witness to the peoples, a leader and commander for the peoples. See, you shall call nations that you do not know, and nations that do not know you shall run to you, because of the LORD your God, the Holy One of Israel, for he has glorified you.

☩ The Response   Psalm 145:8-9, 15-22

Psalm 145:8-9, 15-22   *Exaltabo te, Deus*

8   The LORD is gracious and full of compassion, *
          slow to anger and of great kindness.
9   The LORD is loving to everyone *
          and his compassion is over all his works.
15   The LORD upholds all those who fall; *
          he lifts up those who are bowed down.
16   The eyes of all wait upon you, O LORD, *
          and you give them their food in due season.
17   You open wide your hand *
          and satisfy the needs of every living creature.
18   The LORD is righteous in all his ways *
          and loving in all his works.
19   The LORD is near to those who call upon him, *
          to all who call upon him faithfully.
20   He fulfills the desire of those who fear him; *
          he hears their cry and helps them.
21   The LORD preserves all those who love him, *
          but he destroys all the wicked.
22   My mouth shall speak the praise of the LORD; *
          let all flesh bless his holy Name for ever and ever.

The Epistle   Romans 9:1-5

I am speaking the truth in Christ—I am not lying; my conscience confirms it by the Holy Spirit—I have great sorrow and unceasing anguish in my heart. For I could wish that I myself were accursed and cut off from Christ for the sake of my own people, my kindred according to the flesh. They are Israelites, and to them belong the adoption, the glory, the covenants, the giving of the law, the worship, and the promises; to them belong the patriarchs, and from them, according to the flesh, comes the Messiah, who is over all, God blessed forever. Amen.

The Gospel   Matthew 14:13-21

Jesus withdrew in a boat to a deserted place by himself. But when the crowds heard it, they followed him on foot from the towns. When he went ashore, he saw a great crowd; and he had compassion for them and cured their sick. When it was evening, the disciples came to him and said, "This is a deserted place, and the hour is now late; send the crowds away so that they may go into the villages and buy food for themselves." Jesus said to them, "They need not go away; you give them something to eat." They replied, "We have nothing here but five loaves and two fish." And he said, "Bring them here to me." Then he ordered the crowds to sit down on the grass. Taking the five loaves and the two fish, he looked up to heaven, and blessed and broke the loaves, and gave them to the disciples, and the disciples gave them to the crowds. And all ate and were filled; and they took up what was left over of the broken pieces, twelve baskets full. And those who ate were about five thousand men, besides women and children.

Year B

2 Samuel 11:26—12:13a	**or**	✠ *Exodus 16:2-4, 9-15*
Psalm 51:1-13		✠ *Psalm 78:23-29*

Ephesians 4:1-16
John 6:24-35

The Lesson   2 Samuel 11:26—12:13*a*

When the wife of Uriah heard that her husband was dead, she made lamentation for him. When the mourning was over, David sent and brought her to his house, and she became his wife, and bore him a son. But the thing that David had done displeased the LORD, and the LORD sent Nathan to David. He came to him, and said to him, "There were two men in a certain city, the one rich and the other poor. The rich man had very many flocks and herds; but the poor man had nothing but one little ewe lamb, which he had bought. He brought it up, and it grew up with him and with his children; it used to eat of his meager fare, and drink from his cup, and lie in his bosom, and it was like a daughter to him. Now there came a traveler to the rich man, and he was loath to take one of his own flock or herd to prepare for the wayfarer who had come to him, but he took the poor man's lamb, and prepared that for the guest who had come to him." Then David's anger was greatly kindled against the man. He said to Nathan, "As the LORD lives, the man who has done this deserves to die; he shall restore the lamb fourfold, because he did this thing, and because he had no pity." Nathan said to David, "You are the man! Thus says the LORD, the God of Israel: I anointed you king over Israel, and I rescued you from the hand of Saul; I gave you your master's house, and your master's wives into your bosom, and gave you the house of Israel and of Judah; and if that had been too little, I would have added as much more. Why have you despised the word of the LORD, to do what is evil in his sight? You have struck down Uriah the Hittite with the sword, and have taken his wife to be your wife, and have killed him with the sword of the Ammonites. Now therefore the sword shall never depart from your house, for you have despised me, and have taken the wife of Uriah the Hittite to be your wife. Thus says the LORD: I will raise up trouble against you from within your own house; and I will take your wives before your eyes, and give them to your neighbor, and he shall lie with your wives in the sight of this very sun. For you did it secretly; but I will do this thing before all Israel, and before the sun." David said to Nathan, "I have sinned against the LORD."

The Response   Psalm 51:1-13

Psalm 51:1-13   *Miserere mei, Deus*

1   Have mercy on me, O God, according to your
        loving-kindness; *
     in your great compassion blot out my offenses.
2   Wash me through and through from my wickedness *
     and cleanse me from my sin.
3   For I know my transgressions, *
     and my sin is ever before me.
4   Against you only have I sinned *
     and done what is evil in your sight.
5   And so you are justified when you speak *
     and upright in your judgment.
6   Indeed, I have been wicked from my birth, *
     a sinner from my mother's womb.
7   For behold, you look for truth deep within me, *
     and will make me understand wisdom secretly.
8   Purge me from my sin, and I shall be pure; *
     wash me, and I shall be clean indeed.
9   Make me hear of joy and gladness, *
     that the body you have broken may rejoice.
10 Hide your face from my sins *
     and blot out all my iniquities.
11 Create in me a clean heart, O God, *
     and renew a right spirit within me.
12 Cast me not away from your presence *
     and take not your holy Spirit from me.
13 Give me the joy of your saving help again *
     and sustain me with your bountiful Spirit.

or, ✠ **The Lesson**   **Exodus 16:2-4, 9-15**

The whole congregation of the Israelites complained against Moses and Aaron in the wilderness. The Israelites said to them, "If only we had died by the hand of the LORD in the land of Egypt, when we sat by the fleshpots and ate our fill of bread; for you have brought us out into this wilderness to kill this whole assembly with hunger." Then the LORD said to Moses, "I am going to rain bread from heaven for you, and each day the people shall go out and gather enough for that day. In that way I will test them, whether they will follow my instruction or not." Then Moses said to Aaron, "Say to the whole congregation of the Israelites, 'Draw near to the LORD, for he has heard your complaining.' " And as Aaron spoke to the whole congregation of the Israelites, they looked toward the wilderness, and the glory of the LORD appeared in the cloud. The LORD spoke to Moses and said, "I have heard the complaining of the Israelites; say to them, 'At twilight you shall eat meat, and in the morning you shall have your fill of bread; then you shall know that I am the LORD your God.' " In the evening quails came up and covered the camp; and in the morning there was a layer of dew around the camp. When the layer of dew lifted, there on the surface of the wilderness was a fine flaky substance, as fine as frost on the ground. When the Israelites saw it, they said to one another, "What is it?" For they did not know what it was. Moses said to them, "It is the bread that the LORD has given you to eat."

✠ **The Response**   **Psalm 78:23-29**

Psalm 78:23-29   *Attendite, popule*

23   So he commanded the clouds above *
     and opened the doors of heaven.
24   He rained down manna upon them to eat *
     and gave them grain from heaven.
25   So mortals ate the bread of angels; *
     he provided for them food enough.
26   He caused the east wind to blow in the heavens *
     and led out the south wind by his might.
27   He rained down flesh upon them like dust *
     and wingèd birds like the sand of the sea.
28   He let it fall in the midst of their camp *
     and round about their dwellings.
29   So they ate and were well filled, *
     for he gave them what they craved.

The Epistle   Ephesians 4:1-16

I therefore, the prisoner in the Lord, beg you to lead a life worthy of the calling to which you have been called, with all humility and gentleness, with patience, bearing with one another in love, making every effort to maintain the unity of the Spirit in the bond of peace. There is one body and one Spirit, just as you were called to the one hope of your calling, one Lord, one faith, one baptism, one God and Father of all, who is above all and through all and in all. But each of us was given grace according to the measure of Christ's gift. Therefore it is said, "When he ascended on high he made captivity itself a captive; he gave gifts to his people." (When it says, "He ascended," what does it mean but that he had also descended into the lower parts of the earth? He who descended is the same one who ascended far above all the heavens, so that he might fill all things.) The gifts he gave were that some would be apostles, some prophets, some evangelists, some pastors and teachers, to equip the saints for the work of ministry, for building up the body of Christ, until all of us come to the unity of the faith and of the knowledge of the Son of God, to maturity, to the measure of the full stature of Christ. We must no longer be children, tossed to and fro and blown about by every wind of doctrine, by people's trickery, by their craftiness in deceitful scheming. But speaking the truth in love, we must grow up in every way into him who is the head, into Christ, from whom the whole body, joined and knit together by every ligament with which it is equipped, as each part is working properly, promotes the body's growth in building itself up in love.

The Gospel   John 6:24-35

The next day, when the people who remained after the feeding of the five thousand saw that neither Jesus nor his disciples were there, they themselves got into the boats and went to Capernaum looking for Jesus. When they found him on the other side of the sea, they said to him, "Rabbi, when did you come here?" Jesus answered them, "Very truly, I tell you, you are looking for me, not because you saw signs, but because you ate your fill of the loaves. Do not work for the food that perishes, but for the food that endures for eternal life, which the Son of Man will give you. For it is on him that God the Father has set his seal." Then they said to him, "What must we do to perform the works of God?" Jesus answered them, "This is the work of God, that you believe in him whom he has sent." So they said to him, "What sign are you going to give us then, so that we may see it and believe you? What work are you perform-ing? Our ancestors ate the manna in the wilderness; as it is written, 'He gave them bread from heaven to eat.' " Then Jesus said to them, "Very truly, I tell you, it was not Moses who gave you the bread from heaven, but it is my Father who gives you the true bread from heaven. For the bread of God is that which comes down from heaven and gives life to the world." They said to him, "Sir, give us this bread always." Jesus said to them, "I am the bread of life. Whoever comes to me will never be hungry, and whoever believes in me will never be thirsty."

Year C

Hosea 11:1-11	**or**	✝ *Ecclesiastes 1:2, 12-14;*
Psalm 107:1-9, 43		*2:18-23*
		✝ *Psalm 49:1-11*

Colossians 3:1-11
Luke 12:13-21

The Lesson   Hosea 11:1-11

When Israel was a child, I loved him, and out of Egypt I called my son. The more I called them, the more they went from me; they kept sacrificing to the Baals, and offering incense to idols. Yet it was I who taught Ephraim to walk, I took them up in my arms; but they did not know that I healed them. I led them with cords of human kindness, with bands of love. I was to them like those who lift infants to their cheeks. I bent down to them and fed them. They shall return to the land of Egypt, and Assyria shall be their king, because they have refused to return to me. The sword rages in their cities, it consumes their oracle-priests, and devours because of their schemes. My people are bent on turning away from me. To the Most High they call, but he does not raise them up at all. How can I give you up, Ephraim? How can I hand you over, O Israel? How can I make you like Admah? How can I treat you like Zeboiim? My heart recoils within me; my compassion grows warm and tender. I will not execute my fierce anger; I will not again destroy Ephraim; for I am God and no mortal, the Holy One in your midst, and I will not come in wrath. They shall go after the LORD, who roars like a lion; when he roars, his children shall come trembling from the west. They shall come trembling like birds from Egypt, and like doves from the land of Assyria; and I will return them to their homes, says the LORD.

The Response   Psalm 107:1-9, 43

Psalm 107:1-9, 43   *Confitemini Domino*

1   Give thanks to the LORD, for he is good, *
    and his mercy endures for ever.
2   Let all those whom the LORD has redeemed proclaim *
    that he redeemed them from the hand of the foe.
3   He gathered them out of the lands; *
    from the east and from the west,
    from the north and from the south.

4   Some wandered in desert wastes; *
       they found no way to a city where they might dwell.

5   They were hungry and thirsty; *
       their spirits languished within them.

6   Then they cried to the LORD in their trouble, *
       and he delivered them from their distress.

7   He put their feet on a straight path *
       to go to a city where they might dwell.

8   Let them give thanks to the LORD for his mercy *
       and the wonders he does for his children.

9   For he satisfies the thirsty *
       and fills the hungry with good things.

43   Whoever is wise will ponder these things, *
       and consider well the mercies of the LORD.

or, ✝ **The Lesson**   **Ecclesiastes 1:2, 12-14; 2:18-23**

Vanity of vanities, says the Teacher, vanity of vanities! All is vanity. I, the Teacher, when king over Israel in Jerusalem, applied my mind to seek and to search out by wisdom all that is done under heaven; it is an unhappy business that God has given to human beings to be busy with. I saw all the deeds that are done under the sun; and see, all is vanity and a chasing after wind. I hated all my toil in which I had toiled under the sun, seeing that I must leave it to those who come after me — and who knows whether they will be wise or foolish? Yet they will be master of all for which I toiled and used my wisdom under the sun. This also is vanity. So I turned and gave my heart up to despair concerning all the toil of my labors under the sun, because sometimes one who has toiled with wisdom and knowledge and skill must leave all to be enjoyed by another who did not toil for it. This also is vanity and a great evil. What do mortals get from all the toil and strain with which they toil under the sun? For all their days are full of pain, and their work is a vexation; even at night their minds do not rest. This also is vanity.

✝ **The Response**   **Psalm 49:1-11**

Psalm 49:1-11   *Audite haec, omnes*

1   Hear this, all you peoples;
       hearken, all you who dwell in the world, *
          you of high degree and low, rich and poor together.

2   My mouth shall speak of wisdom, *
       and my heart shall meditate on understanding.

3   I will incline my ear to a proverb *
       and set forth my riddle upon the harp.

4   Why should I be afraid in evil days, *
        when the wickedness of those at my heels surrounds me,
5   The wickedness of those who put their trust in their goods, *
        and boast of their great riches?
6   We can never ransom ourselves, *
        or deliver to God the price of our life;
7   For the ransom of our life is so great, *
        that we should never have enough to pay it,
8   In order to live for ever and ever, *
        and never see the grave.
9   For we see that the wise die also;
    like the dull and stupid they perish *
        and leave their wealth to those who come after them.
10 Their graves shall be their homes for ever,
    their dwelling places from generation to generation, *
        though they call the lands after their own names.
11 Even though honored, they cannot live for ever; *
        they are like the beasts that perish.

The Epistle   Colossians 3:1-11

If you have been raised with Christ, seek the things that are above, where
Christ is, seated at the right hand of God. Set your minds on things that are
above, not on things that are on earth, for you have died, and your life is
hidden with Christ in God. When Christ who is your life is revealed, then you
also will be revealed with him in glory. Put to death, therefore, whatever in
you is earthly: fornication, impurity, passion, evil desire, and greed (which is
idolatry). On account of these the wrath of God is coming on those who are
disobedient. These are the ways you also once followed, when you were living
that life. But now you must get rid of all such things — anger, wrath, malice,
slander, and abusive language from your mouth. Do not lie to one another,
seeing that you have stripped off the old self with its practices and have
clothed yourselves with the new self, which is being renewed in knowledge
according to the image of its creator. In that renewal there is no longer Greek
and Jew, circumcised and uncircumcised, barbarian, Scythian, slave and free;
but Christ is all and in all!

The Gospel   Luke 12:13-21

Someone in the crowd said to Jesus, "Teacher, tell my brother to divide the
family inheritance with me." But he said to him, "Friend, who set me to be a
judge or arbitrator over you?" And he said to them, "Take care! Be on your
guard against all kinds of greed; for one's life does not consist in the abundance of possessions." Then he told them a parable: "The land of a rich man

produced abundantly. And he thought to himself, 'What should I do, for I have no place to store my crops?' Then he said, 'I will do this: I will pull down my barns and build larger ones, and there I will store all my grain and my goods.' And I will say to my soul, 'Soul, you have ample goods laid up for many years; relax, eat, drink, be merry.' But God said to him, 'You fool! This very night your life is being demanded of you. And the things you have prepared, whose will they be?' So it is with those who store up treasures for themselves but are not rich toward God."

PROPER 14

Sunday between August 7 and August 13 inclusive

The Collect

Grant to us, Lord, we pray, the spirit to think and do always those things that are right, that we, who cannot exist without you, may by you be enabled to live according to your will; through Jesus Christ our Lord, who lives and reigns with you and the Holy Spirit, one God, for ever and ever. *Amen.*

Year A

Genesis 37:1-4, 12-28	**or**	✛ *1 Kings 19:9-18*
*Psalm 105:1-6, 16-22, 45*b		✛ *Psalm 85:8-13*

Romans 10:5-15
Matthew 14:22-33

The Lesson   Genesis 37:1-4, 12-28

Jacob settled in the land where his father had lived as an alien, the land of Canaan. This is the story of the family of Jacob. Joseph, being seventeen years old, was shepherding the flock with his brothers; he was a helper to the sons of Bilhah and Zilpah, his father's wives; and Joseph brought a bad report of them to their father. Now Israel loved Joseph more than any other of his children, because he was the son of his old age; and he had made him a long robe with sleeves. But when his brothers saw that their father loved him more than all his brothers, they hated him, and could not speak peaceably to him. Now his brothers went to pasture their father's flock near Shechem. And Israel said to Joseph, "Are not your brothers pasturing the flock at Shechem? Come, I will send you to them." He answered, "Here I am." So he said to him, "Go now, see if it is well with your brothers and with the flock; and bring word back to me." So he sent him from the valley of Hebron. He came to Shechem, and a man found him wandering in the fields; the man asked him, "What are you seeking?" "I am seeking my brothers," he said; "tell me, please, where they are pasturing the flock." The man said, "They have gone away, for I heard them say, 'Let us go to Dothan.'" So Joseph went after his brothers, and found them at Dothan. They saw him from a distance, and before he came near to them, they conspired to kill him. They said to one another, "Here comes this dreamer. Come now, let us kill him and throw him into one of the pits; then we shall say that a wild animal has devoured him, and we shall see what will become of his dreams." But when Reuben heard it, he delivered him out of their hands, saying, "Let us not take his life." Reuben said to them, "Shed no blood; throw him into this pit here in the wilderness, but lay no hand on him" — that he might rescue him out of their hand and restore him to his father. So when Joseph came to his brothers, they stripped him of his robe, the long robe with sleeves that he wore; and they took him and threw him into a pit. The pit was empty; there was no water in it. Then they sat down to eat; and looking up they saw a caravan of Ishmaelites coming from Gilead, with their camels carrying gum, balm, and resin, on their way to carry it down to Egypt. Then Judah said to his brothers, "What profit is it if we kill our brother and conceal his blood? Come, let us sell him to the Ishmaelites, and not lay our hands on him, for he is our brother, our own flesh." And his brothers agreed. When some Midianite traders passed by, they drew Joseph up, lifting him out of the pit, and sold him to the Ishmaelites for twenty pieces of silver. And they took Joseph to Egypt.

The Response   **Psalm 105:1-6, 16-22, 45*b***
Psalm 105:1-6, 16-22, 45*b*   *Confitemini Domino*

1   Give thanks to the LORD and call upon his Name; *
        make known his deeds among the peoples.
2   Sing to him, sing praises to him, *
        and speak of all his marvelous works.
3   Glory in his holy Name; *
        let the hearts of those who seek the LORD rejoice.
4   Search for the LORD and his strength; *
        continually seek his face.
5   Remember the marvels he has done, *
        his wonders and the judgments of his mouth,
6   O offspring of Abraham his servant, *
        O children of Jacob his chosen.
16 Then he called for a famine in the land *
        and destroyed the supply of bread.
17 He sent a man before them, *
        Joseph, who was sold as a slave.
18 They bruised his feet in fetters; *
        his neck they put in an iron collar.
19 Until his prediction came to pass, *
        the word of the LORD tested him.

20   The king sent and released him; *
        the ruler of the peoples set him free.

21   He set him as a master over his household,
        as a ruler over all his possessions,

22   To instruct his princes according to his will
        and to teach his elders wisdom. Hallelujah!

or, ✠ The Lesson   1 Kings 19:9-18

At Horeb the mount of God, Elijah came to a cave, and spent the night there.
Then the word of the LORD came to him, saying, "What are you doing here,
Elijah?" He answered, "I have been very zealous for the LORD, the God of
hosts; for the Israelites have forsaken your covenant, thrown down your
altars, and killed your prophets with the sword. I alone am left, and they are
seeking my life, to take it away." He said, "Go out and stand on the mountain
before the LORD, for the LORD is about to pass by." Now there was a great
wind, so strong that it was splitting mountains and breaking rocks in pieces
before the LORD, but the LORD was not in the wind; and after the wind an
earthquake, but the LORD was not in the earthquake; and after the earthquake a
fire, but the LORD was not in the fire; and after the fire a sound of sheer
silence. When Elijah heard it, he wrapped his face in his mantle and went out
and stood at the entrance of the cave. Then there came a voice to him that
said, "What are you doing here, Elijah?" He answered, "I have been very
zealous for the LORD, the God of hosts; for the Israelites have forsaken your
covenant, thrown down your altars, and killed your prophets with the sword. I
alone am left, and they are seeking my life, to take it away." Then the LORD
said to him, "Go, return on your way to the wilderness of Damascus; when
you arrive, you shall anoint Hazael as king over Aram. Also you shall anoint
Jehu son of Nimshi as king over Israel; and you shall anoint Elisha son of
Shaphat of Abel-meholah as prophet in your place. Whoever escapes from the
sword of Hazael, Jehu shall kill; and whoever escapes from the sword of
Jehu, Elisha shall kill. Yet I will leave seven thousand in Israel, all the knees
that have not bowed to Baal, and every mouth that has not kissed him."

✠ The Response   Psalm 85:8-13

Psalm 85:8-13   *Benedixisti, Domine*

    8   I will listen to what the LORD God is saying, *
         for he is speaking peace to his faithful people
         and to those who turn their hearts to him.

    9   Truly, his salvation is very near to those who fear him, *
         that his glory may dwell in our land.

   10   Mercy and truth have met together; *
         righteousness and peace have kissed each other.

11 Truth shall spring up from the earth, *
    and righteousness shall look down from heaven.
12 The LORD will indeed grant prosperity, *
    and our land will yield its increase.
13 Righteousness shall go before him, *
    and peace shall be a pathway for his feet.

The Epistle   Romans 10:5-15

Moses writes concerning the righteousness that comes from the law, that "the person who does these things will live by them." But the righteousness that comes from faith says, "Do not say in your heart, 'Who will ascend into heaven?' " (that is, to bring Christ down) "or 'Who will descend into the abyss?' " (that is, to bring Christ up from the dead). But what does it say? "The word is near you, on your lips and in your heart" (that is, the word of faith that we proclaim); because if you confess with your lips that Jesus is Lord and believe in your heart that God raised him from the dead, you will be saved. For one believes with the heart and so is justified, and one confesses with the mouth and so is saved. The scripture says, "No one who believes in him will be put to shame." For there is no distinction between Jew and Greek; the same Lord is Lord of all and is generous to all who call on him. For, "Everyone who calls on the name of the Lord shall be saved." But how are they to call on one in whom they have not believed? And how are they to believe in one of whom they have never heard? And how are they to hear without someone to proclaim him? And how are they to proclaim him unless they are sent? As it is written, "How beautiful are the feet of those who bring good news!"

The Gospel   Matthew 14:22-33

Jesus made the disciples get into the boat and go on ahead to the other side, while he dismissed the crowds. And after he had dismissed the crowds, he went up the mountain by himself to pray. When evening came, he was there alone, but by this time the boat, battered by the waves, was far from the land, for the wind was against them. And early in the morning he came walking toward them on the sea. But when the disciples saw him walking on the sea, they were terrified, saying, "It is a ghost!" And they cried out in fear. But immediately Jesus spoke to them and said, "Take heart, it is I; do not be afraid." Peter answered him, "Lord, if it is you, command me to come to you on the water." He said, "Come." So Peter got out of the boat, started walking on the water, and came toward Jesus. But when he noticed the strong wind, he became frightened, and beginning to sink, he cried out, "Lord, save me!" Jesus immediately reached out his hand and caught him, saying to him, "You of little faith, why did you doubt?" When they got into the boat, the wind ceased. And those in the boat worshiped him, saying, "Truly you are the Son of God."

2 Samuel 18:5-9, 15, 31-33   **or**   ✛ *1 Kings 19:4-8*

Psalm 130   ✛ *Psalm 34:1-8*

Ephesians 4:25—5:2
John 6:35, 41-51

The Lesson   2 Samuel 18:5-9, 15, 31-33

David the king ordered Joab and Abishai and Ittai, saying, "Deal gently for my sake with the young man Absalom." And all the people heard when the king gave orders to all the commanders concerning Absalom. So the army went out into the field against Israel; and the battle was fought in the forest of Ephraim. The men of Israel were defeated there by the servants of David, and the slaughter there was great on that day, twenty thousand men. The battle spread over the face of all the country; and the forest claimed more victims that day than the sword. Absalom happened to meet the servants of David. Absalom was riding on his mule, and the mule went under the thick branches of a great oak. His head caught fast in the oak, and he was left hanging between heaven and earth, while the mule that was under him went on. And ten young men, Joab's armor-bearers, surrounded Absalom and struck him, and killed him. Then the Cushite came; and the Cushite said, "Good tidings for my lord the king! For the LORD has vindicated you this day, delivering you from the power of all who rose up against you." The king said to the Cushite, "Is it well with the young man Absalom?" The Cushite answered, "May the enemies of my lord the king, and all who rise up to do you harm, be like that young man." The king was deeply moved, and went up to the chamber over the gate, and wept; and as he went, he said, "O my son Absalom, my son, my son Absalom! Would I had died instead of you, O Absalom, my son, my son!"

The Response   Psalm 130

Psalm 130   *De profundis*

1   Out of the depths have I called to you, O LORD;
     LORD, hear my voice; *
         let your ears consider well the voice of my supplication.

2   If you, LORD, were to note what is done amiss, *
         O LORD, who could stand?

3   For there is forgiveness with you; *
         therefore you shall be feared.

4   I wait for the LORD; my soul waits for him; *
         in his word is my hope.

5   My soul waits for the LORD,
     more than watchmen for the morning, *
         more than watchmen for the morning.

6 O Israel, wait for the L<small>ORD</small>, *
    for with the L<small>ORD</small> there is mercy;
7 With him there is plenteous redemption, *
    and he shall redeem Israel from all their sins.

or, ✠ The Lesson   1 Kings 19:4-8

Elijah went a day's journey into the wilderness, and came and sat down under a solitary broom tree. He asked that he might die: "It is enough; now, O L<small>ORD</small>, take away my life, for I am no better than my ancestors." Then he lay down under the broom tree and fell asleep. Suddenly an angel touched him and said to him, "Get up and eat." He looked, and there at his head was a cake baked on hot stones, and a jar of water. He ate and drank, and lay down again. The angel of the L<small>ORD</small> came a second time, touched him, and said, "Get up and eat, otherwise the journey will be too much for you." He got up, and ate and drank; then he went in the strength of that food forty days and forty nights to Horeb the mount of God.

✠ The Response   Psalm 34:1-8

Psalm 34:1-8   *Benedicam Dominum*
1 I will bless the L<small>ORD</small> at all times; *
    his praise shall ever be in my mouth.
2 I will glory in the L<small>ORD</small>; *
    let the humble hear and rejoice.
3 Proclaim with me the greatness of the L<small>ORD</small>;
    let us exalt his Name together.
4 I sought the L<small>ORD</small>, and he answered me *
    and delivered me out of all my terror.
5 Look upon him and be radiant, *
    and let not your faces be ashamed.
6 I called in my affliction and the L<small>ORD</small> heard me *
    and saved me from all my troubles.
7 The angel of the L<small>ORD</small> encompasses those who fear him, *
    and he will deliver them.
8 Taste and see that the L<small>ORD</small> is good; *
    happy are they who trust in him!

The Epistle   Ephesians 4:25-5:2

Putting away falsehood, let all of us speak the truth to our neighbors, for we are members of one another. Be angry but do not sin; do not let the sun go down on your anger, and do not make room for the devil. Thieves must give up stealing; rather let them labor and work honestly with their own hands, so as to have something to share with the needy. Let no evil talk come out of your mouths, but only what is useful for building up, as there is need, so that your words may give grace to those who hear. And do not grieve the Holy Spirit of God, with which you were marked with a seal for the day of redemption. Put away from you all bitterness and wrath and anger and wrangling and slander, together with all malice, and be kind to one another, tenderhearted, forgiving one another, as God in Christ has forgiven you. Therefore be imitators of God, as beloved children, and live in love, as Christ loved us and gave himself up for us, a fragrant offering and sacrifice to God.

The Gospel   John 6:35, 41-51

Jesus said to them, "I am the bread of life. Whoever comes to me will never be hungry, and whoever believes in me will never be thirsty." Then the Jews began to complain about him because he said, "I am the bread that came down from heaven." They were saying, "Is not this Jesus, the son of Joseph, whose father and mother we know? How can he now say, 'I have come down from heaven'?" Jesus answered them, "Do not complain among yourselves. No one can come to me unless drawn by the Father who sent me; and I will raise that person up on the last day. It is written in the prophets, 'And they shall all be taught by God.' Everyone who has heard and learned from the Father comes to me. Not that anyone has seen the Father except the one who is from God; he has seen the Father. Very truly, I tell you, whoever believes has eternal life. I am the bread of life. Your ancestors ate the manna in the wilderness, and they died. This is the bread that comes down from heaven, so that one may eat of it and not die. I am the living bread that came down from heaven. Whoever eats of this bread will live forever; and the bread that I will give for the life of the world is my flesh."

Year C

Isaiah 1:1, 10-20	**or**	✝ *Genesis 15:1-6*
Psalm 50:1-8, 23-24		✝ *Psalm 33:12-22*

Hebrews 11:1-3, 8-16
Luke 12:32-40

The Lesson   Isaiah 1:1, 10-20

The vision of Isaiah son of Amoz, which he saw concerning Judah and Jerusalem in the days of Uzziah, Jotham, Ahaz, and Hezekiah, kings of Judah. Hear the word of the LORD, you rulers of Sodom! Listen to the teaching of our God, you people of Gomorrah! What to me is the multitude of your sacrifices? says the LORD; I have had enough of burnt offerings of rams and the fat of fed beasts; I do not delight in the blood of bulls, or of lambs, or of goats. When you come to appear before me, who asked this from your hand? Trample my courts no more; bringing offerings is futile; incense is an abomination to me.

New moon and sabbath and calling of convocation — I cannot endure solemn assemblies with iniquity. Your new moons and your appointed festivals my soul hates; they have become a burden to me, I am weary of bearing them. When you stretch out your hands, I will hide my eyes from you; even though you make many prayers, I will not listen; your hands are full of blood. Wash yourselves; make yourselves clean; remove the evil of your doings from before my eyes; cease to do evil, learn to do good; seek justice, rescue the oppressed, defend the orphan, plead for the widow. Come now, let us argue it out, says the LORD: though your sins are like scarlet, they shall be like snow; though they are red like crimson, they shall become like wool. If you are willing and obedient, you shall eat the good of the land; but if you refuse and rebel, you shall be devoured by the sword; for the mouth of the LORD has spoken.

The Response   Psalm 50:1-8, 23-24

Psalm 50:1-8, 23-24   *Deus deorum*

1 The LORD, the God of gods, has spoken; *
         he has called the earth from the rising of the sun to
                  its setting.
2 Out of Zion, perfect in its beauty, *
         God reveals himself in glory.
3 Our God will come and will not keep silence; *
         before him there is a consuming flame,
         and round about him a raging storm.
4 He calls the heavens and the earth from above *
         to witness the judgment of his people.
5 "Gather before me my loyal followers, *
         those who have made a covenant with me
         and sealed it with sacrifice."
6 Let the heavens declare the rightness of his cause; *
         for God himself is judge.
7 Hear, O my people, and I will speak:
   "O Israel, I will bear witness against you; *
         for I am God, your God.
8 I do not accuse you because of your sacrifices; *
         your offerings are always before me.
23 Consider this well, you who forget God, *
         lest I rend you and there be none to deliver you.
24 Whoever offers me the sacrifice of thanksgiving
                  honors me; *
         but to those who keep in my way will I show
                  the salvation of God."

or, ✠ **The Lesson**   **Genesis 15:1-6**

The word of the LORD came to Abram in a vision, "Do not be afraid, Abram, I am your shield; your reward shall be very great." But Abram said, "O Lord GOD, what will you give me, for I continue childless, and the heir of my house is Eliezer of Damascus?" And Abram said, "You have given me no offspring, and so a slave born in my house is to be my heir." But the word of the LORD came to him, "This man shall not be your heir; no one but your very own issue shall be your heir." He brought him outside and said, "Look toward heaven and count the stars, if you are able to count them." Then he said to him, "So shall your descendants be." And he believed the LORD; and the LORD reckoned it to him as righteousness.

✠ **The Response**   **Psalm 33:12-22**

Psalm 33:12-22   *Exultate, justi*

12   Happy is the nation whose God is the LORD! *
          happy the people he has chosen to be his own!

13   The LORD looks down from heaven, *
          and beholds all the people in the world.

14   From where he sits enthroned he turns his gaze *
          on all who dwell on the earth.

15   He fashions all the hearts of them *
          and understands all their works.

16   There is no king that can be saved by a mighty army; *
          a strong man is not delivered by his great strength.

17   The horse is a vain hope for deliverance; *
          for all its strength it cannot save.

18   Behold, the eye of the LORD is upon those who fear him, *
          on those who wait upon his love,

19   To pluck their lives from death, *
          and to feed them in time of famine.

20   Our soul waits for the LORD; *
          he is our help and our shield.

21   Indeed, our heart rejoices in him, *
          for in his holy Name we put our trust.

22   Let your loving-kindness, O LORD, be upon us, *
          as we have put our trust in you.

The Epistle   **Hebrews 11:1-3, 8-16**

Faith is the assurance of things hoped for, the conviction of things not seen. Indeed, by faith our ancestors received approval. By faith we understand that the worlds were prepared by the word of God, so that what is seen was made from things that are not visible. By faith Abraham obeyed when he was called to set out for a place that he was to receive as an inheritance; and he set out, not knowing where he was going. By faith he stayed for a time in the land he had been promised, as in a foreign land, living in tents, as did Isaac and Jacob, who were heirs with him of the same promise. For he looked forward to the city that has foundations, whose architect and builder is God. By faith he received power of procreation, even though he was too old — and Sarah herself was barren — because he considered him faithful who had promised. Therefore from one person, and this one as good as dead, descendants were born, "as many as the stars of heaven and as the innumerable grains of sand by the seashore." All of these died in faith without having received the promises, but from a distance they saw and greeted them. They confessed that they were strangers and foreigners on the earth, for people who speak in this way make it clear that they are seeking a homeland. If they had been thinking of the land that they had left behind, they would have had opportunity to return. But as it is, they desire a better country, that is, a heavenly one. Therefore God is not ashamed to be called their God; indeed, he has prepared a city for them.

The Gospel   Luke 12:32-40

Jesus said to his disciples, "Do not be afraid, little flock, for it is your Father's good pleasure to give you the kingdom. Sell your possessions, and give alms. Make purses for yourselves that do not wear out, an unfailing treasure in heaven, where no thief comes near and no moth destroys. For where your treasure is, there your heart will be also. Be dressed for action and have your lamps lit; be like those who are waiting for their master to return from the wedding banquet, so that they may open the door for him as soon as he comes and knocks. Blessed are those slaves whom the master finds alert when he comes; truly I tell you, he will fasten his belt and have them sit down to eat, and he will come and serve them. If he comes during the middle of the night, or near dawn, and finds them so, blessed are those slaves. But know this: if the owner of the house had known at what hour the thief was coming, he would not have let his house be broken into. You also must be ready, for the Son of Man is coming at an unexpected hour."

PROPER 15

Sunday between August 14 and August 20 inclusive

The Collect

Almighty God, you have given your only Son to be for us a sacrifice for sin, and also an example of godly life: Give us grace to receive thankfully the fruits of his redeeming work, and to follow daily in the blessed steps of his most holy life; through Jesus Christ your Son our Lord, who lives and reigns with you and the Holy Spirit, one God, now and for ever. *Amen.*

Year A

Genesis 45:1-15   **or**   ☩ *Isaiah 56:1, 6-8*

Psalm 133   ☩ *Psalm 67*

Romans 11:1-2a, 29-32

Matthew 15:(10-20), 21-28

The Lesson   **Genesis 45:1-15**

Joseph could no longer control himself before all those who stood by him, and he cried out, "Send everyone away from me." So no one stayed with him when Joseph made himself known to his brothers. And he wept so loudly that the Egyptians heard it, and the household of Pharaoh heard it. Joseph said to his brothers, "I am Joseph. Is my father still alive?" But his brothers could not answer him, so dismayed were they at his presence. Then Joseph said to his brothers, "Come closer to me." And they came closer. He said, "I am your brother, Joseph, whom you sold into Egypt. And now do not be distressed, or angry with yourselves, because you sold me here; for God sent me before you to preserve life. For the famine has been in the land these two years; and there are five more years in which there will be neither plowing nor harvest. God sent me before you to preserve for you a remnant on earth, and to keep alive for you many survivors. So it was not you who sent me here, but God; he has made me a father to Pharaoh, and lord of all his house and ruler over all the land of Egypt. Hurry and go up to my father and say to him, 'Thus says your son Joseph, God has made me lord of all Egypt; come down to me, do not delay. You shall settle in the land of Goshen, and you shall be near me, you and your children and your children's children, as well as your flocks, your herds, and all that you have. I will provide for you there — since there are five more years of famine to come — so that you and your household, and all that you have, will not come to poverty.' And now your eyes and the eyes of my brother Benjamin see that it is my own mouth that speaks to you. You must tell my father how greatly I am honored in Egypt, and all that you have seen. Hurry and bring my father down here." Then he fell upon his brother Benjamin's neck and wept, while Benjamin wept upon his neck. And he kissed all his brothers and wept upon them; and after that his brothers talked with him.

The Response   **Psalm 133**

Psalm 133   *Ecce, quam bonum!*

   1   Oh, how good and pleasant it is, *
           when brethren live together in unity!

   2   It is like fine oil upon the head *
           that runs down upon the beard,

3   Upon the beard of Aaron, *
        and runs down upon the collar of his robe.
4   It is like the dew of Hermon *
        that falls upon the hills of Zion.
5   For there the LORD has ordained the blessing: *
        life for evermore.

or, ✠ The Lesson   Isaiah 56:1, 6-8

Thus says the LORD: Maintain justice, and do what is right, for soon my
salvation will come, and my deliverance be revealed. And the foreigners who
join themselves to the LORD, to minister to him, to love the name of the LORD,
and to be his servants, all who keep the sabbath, and do not profane it, and
hold fast my covenant — these I will bring to my holy mountain, and make
them joyful in my house of prayer; their burnt offerings and their sacrifices
will be accepted on my altar; for my house shall be called a house of prayer
for all peoples. Thus says the Lord GOD, who gathers the outcasts of Israel, I
will gather others to them besides those already gathered.

✠ The Response   Psalm 67

Psalm 67   *Deus misereatur*
1   May God be merciful to us and bless us, *
        show us the light of his countenance and come to us.
2   Let your ways be known upon earth, *
        your saving health among all nations.
3   Let the peoples praise you, O God; *
        let all the peoples praise you.
4   Let the nations be glad and sing for joy, *
        for you judge the peoples with equity
        and guide all the nations upon earth.
5   Let the peoples praise you, O God; *
        let all the peoples praise you.
6   The earth has brought forth her increase; *
        may God, our own God, give us his blessing.
7   May God give us his blessing, *
        and may all the ends of the earth stand in awe of him.

The Epistle   Romans 11:1-2a, 29-32

I ask, then, has God rejected his people? By no means! I myself am an Israelite, a descendant of Abraham, a member of the tribe of Benjamin. God has not
rejected his people whom he foreknew. For the gifts and the calling of God are
irrevocable. Just as you were once disobedient to God but have now received
mercy because of their disobedience, so they have now been disobedient in

order that, by the mercy shown to you, they too may now receive mercy. For God has imprisoned all in disobedience so that he may be merciful to all.

The Gospel   **Matthew 15:(10-20), 21-28**

Matthew 15:(10-20) [Then Jesus called the crowd to him and said to them, "Listen and understand: it is not what goes into the mouth that defiles a person, but it is what comes out of the mouth that defiles." Then the disciples approached and said to him, "Do you know that the Pharisees took offense when they heard what you said?" He answered, "Every plant that my heavenly Father has not planted will be uprooted. Let them alone; they are blind guides of the blind. And if one blind person guides another, both will fall into a pit." But Peter said to him, "Explain this parable to us." Then he said, "Are you also still without understanding? Do you not see that whatever goes into the mouth enters the stomach, and goes out into the sewer? But what comes out of the mouth proceeds from the heart, and this is what defiles. For out of the heart come evil intentions, murder, adultery, fornication, theft, false witness, slander. These are what defile a person, but to eat with unwashed hands does not defile."]

Matthew 15:21-28 Jesus left that place and went away to the district of Tyre and Sidon. Just then a Canaanite woman from that region came out and started shouting, "Have mercy on me, Lord, Son of David; my daughter is tormented by a demon." But he did not answer her at all. And his disciples came and urged him, saying, "Send her away, for she keeps shouting after us." He answered, "I was sent only to the lost sheep of the house of Israel." But she came and knelt before him, saying, "Lord, help me." He answered, "It is not fair to take the children's food and throw it to the dogs." She said, "Yes, Lord, yet even the dogs eat the crumbs that fall from their masters' table." Then Jesus answered her, "Woman, great is your faith! Let it be done for you as you wish." And her daughter was healed instantly.

Year B

1 Kings 2:10-12; 3:3-14	**or**	✠ *Proverbs 9:1-6*
Psalm 111		✠ *Psalm 34:9-14*
	Ephesians 5:15-20	
	John 6:51-58	

The Lesson   **1 Kings 2:10-12; 3:3-14**

David slept with his ancestors, and was buried in the city of David. The time that David reigned over Israel was forty years; he reigned seven years in Hebron, and thirty-three years in Jerusalem. So Solomon sat on the throne of his father David; and his kingdom was firmly established. Solomon loved the LORD, walking in the statutes of his father David; only, he sacrificed and offered incense at the high places. The king went to Gibeon to sacrifice there, for that was the principal high place; Solomon used to offer a thousand burnt offerings on that altar. At Gibeon the LORD appeared to Solomon in a dream by night; and God said, "Ask what I should give you." And Solomon said, "You have shown great and steadfast love to your servant my father David, because he walked before you in faithfulness, in righteousness, and in upright- ness of heart toward you; and you have kept for him this great and steadfast love, and have given him a son to sit on his throne today. And now, O LORD my God, you have made your servant king in place of my father David, although I am only a little child; I do not know how to go out or come in. And your servant is in the midst of the people whom you have chosen, a great people, so numerous they cannot be numbered or counted. Give your servant therefore an understanding mind to govern your people, able to discern between good and evil; for who can govern this your great people?" It pleased the LORD that Solomon had asked this. God said to him, "Because you have asked this, and have not asked for yourself long life or riches, or for the life of your enemies, but have asked for yourself understanding to discern what is right, I now do according to your word. Indeed I give you a wise and discern- ing mind; no one like you has been before you and no one like you shall arise after you. I give you also what you have not asked, both riches and honor all your life; no other king shall compare with you. If you will walk in my ways, keeping my statutes and my commandments, as your father David walked, then I will lengthen your life."

The Response   Psalm 111

Psalm 111   *Confitebor tibi*

1   Hallelujah!
    I will give thanks to the LORD with my whole heart, *
        in the assembly of the upright, in the congregation.
2   Great are the deeds of the LORD! *
        they are studied by all who delight in them.
3   His work is full of majesty and splendor, *
        and his righteousness endures for ever.
4   He makes his marvelous works to be remembered; *
        the LORD is gracious and full of compassion.
5   He gives food to those who fear him; *
        he is ever mindful of his covenant.
6   He has shown his people the power of his works *
        in giving them the lands of the nations.

7   The works of his hands are faithfulness and justice; *
      all his commandments are sure.
8   They stand fast for ever and ever, *
      because they are done in truth and equity.
9   He sent redemption to his people;
      he commanded his covenant for ever; *
      holy and awesome is his Name.
10 The fear of the LORD is the beginning of wisdom; *
      those who act accordingly have a good understanding;
      his praise endures for ever.

or, ☩ **The Lesson**   **Proverbs 9:1-6**

Wisdom has built her house, she has hewn her seven pillars. She has slaughtered her animals, she has mixed her wine, she has also set her table. She has
sent out her servant girls, she calls from the highest places in the town, "You
that are simple, turn in here!" To those without sense she says, "Come, eat of
my bread and drink of the wine I have mixed. Lay aside immaturity, and live,
and walk in the way of insight."

☩ **The Response**   **Psalm 34:9-14**

Psalm 34:9-14   *Benedicam Dominum*
9   Fear the LORD, you that are his saints, *
      for those who fear him lack nothing.
10 The young lions lack and suffer hunger, *
      but those who seek the LORD lack nothing that is good.
11 Come, children, and listen to me; *
      I will teach you the fear of the LORD.
12 Who among you loves life *
      and desires long life to enjoy prosperity?
13 Keep your tongue from evil-speaking *
      and your lips from lying words.
14 Turn from evil and do good; *
      seek peace and pursue it.

The Epistle   **Ephesians 5:15-20**

Be careful then how you live, not as unwise people but as wise, making the
most of the time, because the days are evil. So do not be foolish, but understand what the will of the Lord is. Do not get drunk with wine, for that is
debauchery; but be filled with the Spirit, as you sing psalms and hymns and
spiritual songs among yourselves, singing and making melody to the Lord in
your hearts, giving thanks to God the Father at all times and for everything in
the name of our Lord Jesus Christ.

The Gospel   John 6:51-58

Jesus said, "I am the living bread that came down from heaven. Whoever eats of this bread will live forever; and the bread that I will give for the life of the world is my flesh." The Jews then disputed among themselves, saying, "How can this man give us his flesh to eat?" So Jesus said to them, "Very truly, I tell you, unless you eat the flesh of the Son of Man and drink his blood, you have no life in you. Those who eat my flesh and drink my blood have eternal life, and I will raise them up on the last day; for my flesh is true food and my blood is true drink. Those who eat my flesh and drink my blood abide in me, and I in them. Just as the living Father sent me, and I live because of the Father, so whoever eats me will live because of me. This is the bread that came down from heaven, not like that which your ancestors ate, and they died. But the one who eats this bread will live forever."

Year C

Isaiah 5:1-7   **or**   ✢ *Jeremiah 23:23-29*
Psalm 80:1-2, 8-18   ✢ *Psalm 82*

Hebrews 11:29—12:2
Luke 12:49-56

The Lesson   Isaiah 5:1-7

Let me sing for my beloved my love-song concerning his vineyard: My beloved had a vineyard on a very fertile hill. He dug it and cleared it of stones, and planted it with choice vines; he built a watchtower in the midst of it, and hewed out a wine vat in it; he expected it to yield grapes, but it yielded wild grapes. And now, inhabitants of Jerusalem and people of Judah, judge between me and my vineyard. What more was there to do for my vineyard that I have not done in it? When I expected it to yield grapes, why did it yield wild grapes? And now I will tell you what I will do to my vineyard. I will remove its hedge, and it shall be devoured; I will break down its wall, and it shall be trampled down. I will make it a waste; it shall not be pruned or hoed, and it shall be overgrown with briers and thorns; I will also command the clouds that they rain no rain upon it. For the vineyard of the LORD of hosts is the house of Israel, and the people of Judah are his pleasant planting; he expected justice, but saw bloodshed; righteousness, but heard a cry!

The Response   Psalm 80:1-2, 8-18

Psalm 80:1-2, 8-18   *Qui regis Israel*

1   Hear, O Shepherd of Israel, leading Joseph like a flock; *
        shine forth, you that are enthroned upon the cherubim.

2   In the presence of Ephraim, Benjamin, and Manasseh, *
        stir up your strength and come to help us.
8   You have brought a vine out of Egypt; *
        you cast out the nations and planted it.
9   You prepared the ground for it; *
        it took root and filled the land.
10 The mountains were covered by its shadow *
        and the towering cedar trees by its boughs.
11 You stretched out its tendrils to the Sea *
        and its branches to the River.
12 Why have you broken down its wall, *
        so that all who pass by pluck off its grapes?
13 The wild boar of the forest has ravaged it, *
        and the beasts of the field have grazed upon it.
14 Turn now, O God of hosts, look down from heaven;
    behold and tend this vine; *
        preserve what your right hand has planted.
15 They burn it with fire like rubbish; *
        at the rebuke of your countenance let them perish.
16 Let your hand be upon the man of your right hand, *
        the son of man you have made so strong for yourself.
17 And so will we never turn away from you; *
        give us life, that we may call upon your Name.
18 Restore us, O Lord God of hosts; *
        show the light of your countenance, and we shall be saved.

or, ✛ **The Lesson**   **Jeremiah 23:23-29**

Am I a God near by, says the Lord, and not a God far off? Who can hide in
secret places so that I cannot see them? says the Lord. Do I not fill heaven
and earth? says the Lord. I have heard what the prophets have said who
prophesy lies in my name, saying, "I have dreamed, I have dreamed!" How
long? Will the hearts of the prophets ever turn back — those who prophesy
lies, and who prophesy the deceit of their own heart? They plan to make my
people forget my name by their dreams that they tell one another, just as their
ancestors forgot my name for Baal. Let the prophet who has a dream tell the
dream, but let the one who has my word speak my word faithfully. What has
straw in common with wheat? says the Lord. Is not my word like fire, says
the Lord, and like a hammer that breaks a rock in pieces?

✛ **The Response**   **Psalm 82**

Psalm 82   *Deus stetit*
1   God takes his stand in the council of heaven; *
        he gives judgment in the midst of the gods:

2   "How long will you judge unjustly, *
        and show favor to the wicked?
3   Save the weak and the orphan; *
        defend the humble and needy;
4   Rescue the weak and the poor; *
        deliver them from the power of the wicked.
5   They do not know, neither do they understand;
        they go about in darkness; *
        all the foundations of the earth are shaken.
6   Now I say to you, 'You are gods, *
        and all of you children of the Most High;
7   Nevertheless, you shall die like mortals, *
        and fall like any prince.'"
8   Arise, O God, and rule the earth, *
        for you shall take all nations for your own.

The Epistle   Hebrews 11:29—12:2

By faith the people passed through the Red Sea as if it were dry land, but
when the Egyptians attempted to do so they were drowned. By faith the walls
of Jericho fell after they had been encircled for seven days. By faith Rahab the
prostitute did not perish with those who were disobedient, because she had
received the spies in peace. And what more should I say? For time would fail
me to tell of Gideon, Barak, Samson, Jephthah, of David and Samuel and the
prophets — who through faith conquered kingdoms, administered justice,
obtained promises, shut the mouths of lions, quenched raging fire, escaped the
edge of the sword, won strength out of weakness, became mighty in war, put
foreign armies to flight. Women received their dead by resurrection. Others
were tortured, refusing to accept release, in order to obtain a better resurrection. Others suffered mocking and flogging, and even chains and imprisonment. They were stoned to death, they were sawn in two, they were killed by
the sword; they went about in skins of sheep and goats, destitute, persecuted,
tormented — of whom the world was not worthy. They wandered in deserts
and mountains, and in caves and holes in the ground. Yet all these, though
they were commended for their faith, did not receive what was promised,
since God had provided something better so that they would not, apart from
us, be made perfect. Therefore, since we are surrounded by so great a cloud of
witnesses, let us also lay aside every weight and the sin that clings so closely,
and let us run with perseverance the race that is set before us, looking to Jesus
the pioneer and perfecter of our faith, who for the sake of the joy that was set
before him endured the cross, disregarding its shame, and has taken his seat at
the right hand of the throne of God.

The Gospel   **Luke 12:49-56**

Jesus said, "I came to bring fire to the earth, and how I wish it were already
kindled! I have a baptism with which to be baptized, and what stress I am
under until it is completed! Do you think that I have come to bring peace to
the earth? No, I tell you, but rather division! From now on five in one household will be divided, three against two and two against three; they will be
divided: father against son and son against father, mother against daughter and
daughter against mother, mother-in-law against her daughter-in-law and
daughter-in-law against mother-in-law." He also said to the crowds, "When
you see a cloud rising in the west, you immediately say, 'It is going to rain';
and so it happens. And when you see the south wind blowing, you say, 'There
will be scorching heat'; and it happens. You hypocrites! You know how to
interpret the appearance of earth and sky, but why do you not know how to
interpret the present time?"

PROPER 16

Sunday between August 21 and August 27 inclusive

The Collect

Grant, O merciful God, that your Church, being gathered together in unity by
your Holy Spirit, may show forth your power among all peoples, to the glory
of your Name; through Jesus Christ our Lord, who lives and reigns with you
and the Holy Spirit, one God, for ever and ever. *Amen.*

Year A

| *Exodus 1:8—2:10* | **or** | ✠ *Isaiah 51:1-6* |
| *Psalm 124* | | ✠ *Psalm 138* |

Romans 12:1-8
Matthew 16:13-20

The Lesson   **Exodus 1:8—2:10**

Now a new king arose over Egypt, who did not know Joseph. He said to his
people, "Look, the Israelite people are more numerous and more powerful
than we. Come, let us deal shrewdly with them, or they will increase and, in
the event of war, join our enemies and fight against us and escape from the
land." Therefore they set taskmasters over them to oppress them with forced
labor. They built supply cities, Pithom and Rameses, for Pharaoh. But the
more they were oppressed, the more they multiplied and spread, so that the
Egyptians came to dread the Israelites. The Egyptians became ruthless in
imposing tasks on the Israelites, and made their lives bitter with hard service
in mortar and brick and in every kind of field labor. They were ruthless in all
the tasks that they imposed on them. The king of Egypt said to the Hebrew
midwives, one of whom was named Shiphrah and the other Puah, "When you
act as midwives to the Hebrew women, and see them on the birthstool, if it is a

boy, kill him; but if it is a girl, she shall live." But the midwives feared God; they did not do as the king of Egypt commanded them, but they let the boys live. So the king of Egypt summoned the midwives and said to them, "Why have you done this, and allowed the boys to live?" The midwives said to Pharaoh, "Because the Hebrew women are not like the Egyptian women; for they are vigorous and give birth before the midwife comes to them." So God dealt well with the midwives; and the people multiplied and became very strong. And because the midwives feared God, he gave them families. Then Pharaoh commanded all his people, "Every boy that is born to the Hebrews you shall throw into the Nile, but you shall let every girl live." Now a man from the house of Levi went and married a Levite woman. The woman conceived and bore a son; and when she saw that he was a fine baby, she hid him three months. When she could hide him no longer she got a papyrus basket for him, and plastered it with bitumen and pitch; she put the child in it and placed it among the reeds on the bank of the river. His sister stood at a distance, to see what would happen to him. The daughter of Pharaoh came down to bathe at the river, while her attendants walked beside the river. She saw the basket among the reeds and sent her maid to bring it. When she opened it, she saw the child. He was crying, and she took pity on him, "This must be one of the Hebrews' children," she said. Then his sister said to Pharaoh's daughter, "Shall I go and get you a nurse from the Hebrew women to nurse the child for you?" Pharaoh's daughter said to her, "Yes." So the girl went and called the child's mother. Pharaoh's daughter said to her, "Take this child and nurse it for me, and I will give you your wages." So the woman took the child and nursed it. When the child grew up, she brought him to Pharaoh's daughter, and she took him as her son. She named him Moses, "because," she said, "I drew him out of the water."

The Response   Psalm 124

Psalm 124   *Nisi quia Dominus*

1   If the LORD had not been on our side, *
       let Israel now say;
2   If the LORD had not been on our side, *
       when enemies rose up against us;
3   Then would they have swallowed us up alive *
       in their fierce anger toward us;
4   Then would the waters have overwhelmed us *
       and the torrent gone over us;
5   Then would the raging waters *
       have gone right over us.
6   Blessed be the LORD! *
       he has not given us over to be a prey for their teeth.

7 We have escaped like a bird from the snare of the fowler; *
  the snare is broken, and we have escaped.

8 Our help is in the Name of the LORD, *
  the maker of heaven and earth.

or, ✠ The Lesson   Isaiah 51:1-6

Listen to me, you that pursue righteousness, you that seek the LORD. Look to
the rock from which you were hewn, and to the quarry from which you were
dug. Look to Abraham your father and to Sarah who bore you; for he was but
one when I called him, but I blessed him and made him many. For the LORD
will comfort Zion; he will comfort all her waste places, and will make her
wilderness like Eden, her desert like the garden of the LORD; joy and gladness
will be found in her, thanksgiving and the voice of song. Listen to me, my
people, and give heed to me, my nation; for a teaching will go out from me,
and my justice for a light to the peoples. I will bring near my deliverance
swiftly, my salvation has gone out and my arms will rule the peoples; the
coastlands wait for me, and for my arm they hope. Lift up your eyes to the
heavens, and look at the earth beneath; for the heavens will vanish like smoke,
the earth will wear out like a garment, and those who live on it will die like
gnats; but my salvation will be forever, and my deliverance will never be
ended.

✠ The Response   Psalm 138

Psalm 138 *Confitebor tibi*

1 I will give thanks to you, O LORD, with my whole heart; *
  before the gods I will sing your praise.

2 I will bow down toward your holy temple
  and praise your Name, *
  because of your love and faithfulness;

3 For you have glorified your Name *
  and your word above all things.

4 When I called, you answered me; *
  you increased my strength within me.

5 All the kings of the earth will praise you, O LORD, *
  when they have heard the words of your mouth.

6 They will sing of the ways of the LORD, *
  that great is the glory of the LORD.

7 Though the LORD be high, he cares for the lowly; *
  he perceives the haughty from afar.

8 Though I walk in the midst of trouble, you keep me safe; *
  you stretch forth your hand against the fury of my enemies;
  your right hand shall save me.

9   The LORD will make good his purpose for me; *
      O LORD, your love endures for ever;
      do not abandon the works of your hands.

The Epistle   Romans 12:1-8

I appeal to you therefore, brothers and sisters, by the mercies of God, to present your bodies as a living sacrifice, holy and acceptable to God, which is your spiritual worship. Do not be conformed to this world, but be transformed by the renewing of your minds, so that you may discern what is the will of God — what is good and acceptable and perfect. For by the grace given to me I say to everyone among you not to think of yourself more highly than you ought to think, but to think with sober judgment, each according to the measure of faith that God has assigned. For as in one body we have many members, and not all the members have the same function, so we, who are many, are one body in Christ, and individually we are members one of another. We have gifts that differ according to the grace given to us: prophecy, in proportion to faith; ministry, in ministering; the teacher, in teaching; the exhorter, in exhortation; the giver, in generosity; the leader, in diligence; the compassionate, in cheerfulness.

The Gospel   Matthew 16:13-20

When Jesus came into the district of Caesarea Philippi, he asked his disciples, "Who do people say that the Son of Man is?" And they said, "Some say John the Baptist, but others Elijah, and still others Jeremiah or one of the prophets." He said to them, "But who do you say that I am?" Simon Peter answered, "You are the Messiah, the Son of the living God." And Jesus answered him, "Blessed are you, Simon son of Jonah! For flesh and blood has not revealed this to you, but my Father in heaven. And I tell you, you are Peter, and on this rock I will build my church, and the gates of Hades will not prevail against it. I will give you the keys of the kingdom of heaven, and whatever you bind on earth will be bound in heaven, and whatever you loose on earth will be loosed in heaven." Then he sternly ordered the disciples not to tell anyone that he was the Messiah.

Year B

1 Kings 8:(1, 6, 10-11), 22-30,   **or**   ✣ *Joshua 24:1-2a, 14-18*
              41-43   ✣ *Psalm 34:15-22*
Psalm 84

Ephesians 6:10-20
John 6:56-69

The Lesson   **1 Kings 8:(1, 6, 10-11), 22-30, 41-43**
1 Kings 8:(1, 6, 10-11)

[Then Solomon assembled the elders of Israel and all the heads of the tribes,
the leaders of the ancestral houses of the Israelites, before King Solomon in
Jerusalem, to bring up the ark of the covenant of the LORD out of the city of
David, which is Zion. Then the priests brought the ark of the covenant of the
LORD to its place, in the inner sanctuary of the house, in the most holy place,
underneath the wings of the cherubim. And when the priests came out of the
holy place, a cloud filled the house of the LORD, so that the priests could not
stand to minister because of the cloud; for the glory of the LORD filled the
house of the LORD.]

1 Kings 8:22-30, 41-43 Then Solomon stood before the altar of the LORD in
the presence of all the assembly of Israel, and spread out his hands to heaven.
He said, "O LORD, God of Israel, there is no God like you in heaven above or
on earth beneath, keeping covenant and steadfast love for your servants who
walk before you with all their heart, the covenant that you kept for your
servant my father David as you declared to him; you promised with your
mouth and have this day fulfilled with your hand. Therefore, O LORD, God of
Israel, keep for your servant my father David that which you promised him,
saying, 'There shall never fail you a successor before me to sit on the throne
of Israel, if only your children look to their way, to walk before me as you
have walked before me.' Therefore, O God of Israel, let your word be
confirmed, which you promised to your servant my father David. But will
God indeed dwell on the earth? Even heaven and the highest heaven cannot
contain you, much less this house that I have built! Regard your servant's
prayer and his plea, O LORD my God, heeding the cry and the prayer that your
servant prays to you today; that your eyes may be open night and day toward
this house, the place of which you said, 'My name shall be there,' that you
may heed the prayer that your servant prays toward this place. Hear the plea
of your servant and of your people Israel when they pray toward this place; O
hear in heaven your dwelling place; heed and forgive. Likewise when a
foreigner, who is not of your people Israel, comes from a distant land because
of your name — for they shall hear of your great name, your mighty hand,
and your outstretched arm — when a foreigner comes and prays toward this
house, then hear in heaven your dwelling place, and do according to all that
the foreigner calls to you, so that all the peoples of the earth may know your
name and fear you, as do your people Israel, and so that they may know that
your name has been invoked on this house that I have built."

The Response   Psalm 84

Psalm 84   *Quam dilecta!*

1   How dear to me is your dwelling, O LORD of hosts! *
    My soul has a desire and longing for the courts of
        the LORD;
    my heart and my flesh rejoice in the living God.

2   The sparrow has found her a house
    and the swallow a nest where she may lay her young; *
    by the side of your altars, O LORD of hosts,
    my King and my God.

3   Happy are they who dwell in your house! *
    they will always be praising you.

4   Happy are the people whose strength is in you! *
    whose hearts are set on the pilgrims' way.

5   Those who go through the desolate valley will find
        it a place of springs, *
    for the early rains have covered it with pools of water.

6   They will climb from height to height, *
    and the God of gods will reveal himself in Zion.

7   LORD God of hosts, hear my prayer; *
    hearken, O God of Jacob.

8   Behold our defender, O God; *
    and look upon the face of your Anointed.

9   For one day in your courts is better than
    a thousand in my own room, *
    and to stand at the threshold of the house of my God
    than to dwell in the tents of the wicked.

10   For the LORD God is both sun and shield; *
    he will give grace and glory;

11   No good thing will the LORD withhold *
    from those who walk with integrity.

12   O LORD of hosts, *
    happy are they who put their trust in you!

or, ✠ **The Lesson**   **Joshua 24:1-2a, 14-18**

Joshua gathered all the tribes of Israel to Shechem, and summoned the elders, the heads, the judges, and the officers of Israel; and they presented themselves before God. And Joshua said to all the people, "Thus says the LORD, the God of Israel: Now therefore revere the LORD, and serve him in sincerity and in faithfulness; put away the gods that your ancestors served beyond the River and in Egypt, and serve the LORD. Now if you are unwilling to serve the LORD, choose this day whom you will serve, whether the gods your ancestors served in the region beyond the River or the gods of the Amorites in whose land you are living; but as for me and my household, we will serve the LORD." Then the people answered, "Far be it from us that we should forsake the LORD to serve other gods; for it is the LORD our God who brought us and our ancestors up from the land of Egypt, out of the house of slavery, and who did those great signs in our sight. He protected us along all the way that we went, and among all the peoples through whom we passed; and the LORD drove out before us all the peoples, the Amorites who lived in the land. Therefore we also will serve the LORD, for he is our God."

☩ The Response   Psalm 34:15-22

Psalm 34:15-22   *Benedicam Dominum*

15   The eyes of the LORD are upon the righteous, *
         and his ears are open to their cry.
16   The face of the LORD is against those who do evil, *
         to root out the remembrance of them from the earth.
17   The righteous cry, and the LORD hears them *
         and delivers them from all their troubles.
18   The LORD is near to the brokenhearted *
         and will save those whose spirits are crushed.
19   Many are the troubles of the righteous, *
         but the LORD will deliver him out of them all.
20   He will keep safe all his bones; *
         not one of them shall be broken.
21   Evil shall slay the wicked, *
         and those who hate the righteous will be punished.
22   The LORD ransoms the life of his servants, *
         and none will be punished who trust in him.

The Epistle   Ephesians 6:10-20

Finally, be strong in the Lord and in the strength of his power. Put on the whole armor of God, so that you may be able to stand against the wiles of the devil. For our struggle is not against enemies of blood and flesh, but against the rulers, against the authorities, against the cosmic powers of this present darkness, against the spiritual forces of evil in the heavenly places. Therefore take up the whole armor of God, so that you may be able to withstand on that evil day, and having done everything, to stand firm. Stand therefore, and fasten the belt of truth around your waist, and put on the breastplate of righteousness. As shoes for your feet put on whatever will make you ready to proclaim the gospel of peace. With all of these, take the shield of faith, with which you will be able to quench all the flaming arrows of the evil one. Take the helmet of salvation, and the sword of the Spirit, which is the word of God.

Pray in the Spirit at all times in every prayer and supplication. To that end keep alert and always persevere in supplication for all the saints. Pray also for me, so that when I speak, a message may be given to me to make known with boldness the mystery of the gospel, for which I am an ambassador in chains. Pray that I may declare it boldly, as I must speak.

The Gospel   John 6:56-69

Jesus said, "Those who eat my flesh and drink my blood abide in me, and I in them. Just as the living Father sent me, and I live because of the Father, so whoever eats me will live because of me. This is the bread that came down from heaven, not like that which your ancestors ate, and they died. But the one who eats this bread will live forever." He said these things while he was teaching in the synagogue at Capernaum. When many of his disciples heard this, they said, "This teaching is difficult; who can accept it?" But Jesus, being aware that his disciples were complaining about it, said to them, "Does this offend you? Then what if you were to see the Son of Man ascending to where he was before? It is the spirit that gives life; the flesh is useless. The words that I have spoken to you are spirit and life. But among you there are some who do not believe." For Jesus knew from the first who were the ones that did not believe, and who was the one that would betray him. And he said, "For this reason I have told you that no one can come to me unless it is granted by the Father." Because of this many of his disciples turned back and no longer went about with him. So Jesus asked the twelve, "Do you also wish to go away?" Simon Peter answered him, "Lord, to whom can we go? You have the words of eternal life. We have come to believe and know that you are the Holy One of God."

Year C

Jeremiah 1:4-10	**or**	✝ *Isaiah 58:9b-14*
Psalm 71:1-6		✝ *Psalm 103:1-8*
	Hebrews 12:18-29	
	Luke 13:10-17	

The Lesson   Jeremiah 1:4-10

The word of the LORD came to me saying, "Before I formed you in the womb I knew you, and before you were born I consecrated you; I appointed you a prophet to the nations." Then I said, "Ah, Lord GOD! Truly I do not know how to speak, for I am only a boy." But the LORD said to me, "Do not say, 'I am only a boy'; for you shall go to all to whom I send you, and you shall speak whatever I command you, Do not be afraid of them, for I am with you to deliver you, says the LORD." Then the LORD put out his hand and touched my mouth; and the LORD said to me, "Now I have put my words in your mouth. See, today I appoint you over nations and over kingdoms, to pluck up and to pull down, to destroy and to overthrow, to build and to plant."

The Response   Psalm 71:1-6

Psalm 71:1-6   *In te, Domine, speravi*
1   In you, O LORD, have I taken refuge; *
    let me never be ashamed.
2   In your righteousness, deliver me and set me free; *
    incline your ear to me and save me.
3   Be my strong rock, a castle to keep me safe; *
    you are my crag and my stronghold.
4   Deliver me, my God, from the hand of the wicked, *
    from the clutches of the evildoer and the oppressor.
5   For you are my hope, O LORD God, *
    my confidence since I was young.
6   I have been sustained by you ever since I was born;
    from my mother's womb you have been my strength; *
    my praise shall be always of you.

or, ☩ The Lesson   Isaiah 58:9*b*-14

If you remove the yoke from among you, the pointing of the finger, the speaking of evil, if you offer your food to the hungry and satisfy the needs of the afflicted, then your light shall rise in the darkness and your gloom be like the noonday. The LORD will guide you continually, and satisfy your needs in parched places, and make your bones strong; and you shall be like a watered garden, like a spring of water, whose waters never fail. Your ancient ruins shall be rebuilt; you shall raise up the foundations of many generations; you shall be called the repairer of the breach, the restorer of streets to live in. If you refrain from trampling the sabbath, from pursuing your own interests on my holy day; if you call the sabbath a delight and the holy day of the LORD honorable; if you honor it, not going your own ways, serving your own interests, or pursuing your own affairs; then you shall take delight in the LORD, and I will make you ride upon the heights of the earth; I will feed you with the heritage of your ancestor Jacob, for the mouth of the LORD has spoken.

☩ The Response   Psalm 103:1-8

Psalm 103:1-8   *Benedic, anima mea*
1   Bless the LORD, O my soul, *
    and all that is within me, bless his holy Name.

2 Bless the Lord, O my soul, *
    and forget not all his benefits.
3 He forgives all your sins *
    and heals all your infirmities;
4 He redeems your life from the grave *
    and crowns you with mercy and loving-kindness;
5 He satisfies you with good things, *
    and your youth is renewed like an eagle's.
6 The Lord executes righteousness *
    and judgment for all who are oppressed.
7 He made his ways known to Moses *
    and his works to the children of Israel.
8 The Lord is full of compassion and mercy, *
    slow to anger and of great kindness.

The Epistle   Hebrews 12:18-29

You have not come to something that can be touched, a blazing fire, and
darkness, and gloom, and a tempest, and the sound of a trumpet, and a voice
whose words made the hearers beg that not another word be spoken to them.
(For they could not endure the order that was given, "If even an animal
touches the mountain, it shall be stoned to death." Indeed, so terrifying was
the sight that Moses said, "I tremble with fear.") But you have come to Mount
Zion and to the city of the living God, the heavenly Jerusalem, and to innumerable angels in festal gathering, and to the assembly of the firstborn who
are enrolled in heaven, and to God the judge of all, and to the spirits of the
righteous made perfect, and to Jesus, the mediator of a new covenant, and to
the sprinkled blood that speaks a better word than the blood of Abel. See that
you do not refuse the one who is speaking; for if they did not escape when
they refused the one who warned them on earth, how much less will we escape
if we reject the one who warns from heaven! At that time his voice shook the
earth; but now he has promised, "Yet once more I will shake not only the earth
but also the heaven." This phrase, "Yet once more," indicates the removal of
what is shaken — that is, created things — so that what cannot be shaken
may remain. Therefore, since we are receiving a kingdom that cannot be
shaken, let us give thanks, by which we offer to God an acceptable worship
with reverence and awe; for indeed our God is a consuming fire.

The Gospel   Luke 13:10-17

Jesus was teaching in one of the synagogues on the sabbath. And just then
there appeared a woman with a spirit that had crippled her for eighteen years.
She was bent over and was quite unable to stand up straight. When Jesus saw
her, he called her over and said, "Woman, you are set free from your ailment."

When he laid his hands on her, immediately she stood up straight and began praising God. But the leader of the synagogue, indignant because Jesus had cured on the sabbath, kept saying to the crowd, "There are six days on which work ought to be done; come on those days and be cured, and not on the sabbath day." But the Lord answered him and said, "You hypocrites! Does not each of you on the sabbath untie his ox or his donkey from the manger, and lead it away to give it water? And ought not this woman, a daughter of Abraham whom Satan bound for eighteen long years, be set free from this bondage on the sabbath day?" When he said this, all his opponents were put to shame; and the entire crowd was rejoicing at all the wonderful things that he was doing.

PROPER 17

Sunday between August 28 and September 3 inclusive

The Collect

Lord of all power and might, the author and giver of all good things: Graft in our hearts the love of your Name; increase in us true religion; nourish us with all goodness; and bring forth in us the fruit of good works; through Jesus Christ our Lord, who lives and reigns with you and the Holy Spirit, one God for ever and ever. *Amen.*

Year A

Exodus 3:1-15	**or**	✛ *Jeremiah 15:15-21*
Psalm 105:1-6, 23-26, 45c		✛ *Psalm 26:1-8*

Romans 12:9-21
Matthew 16:21-28

The Lesson   Exodus 3:1-15

Moses was keeping the flock of his father-in-law Jethro, the priest of Midian; he led his flock beyond the wilderness, and came to Horeb, the mountain of God. There the angel of the LORD appeared to him in a flame of fire out of a bush; he looked, and the bush was blazing, yet it was not consumed. Then Moses said, "I must turn aside and look at this great sight, and see why the bush is not burned up." When the LORD saw that he had turned aside to see, God called to him out of the bush, "Moses, Moses!" And he said, "Here I am." Then he said, "Come no closer! Remove the sandals from your feet, for the place on which you are standing is holy ground." He said further, "I am the God of your father, the God of Abraham, the God of Isaac, and the God of Jacob." And Moses hid his face, for he was afraid to look at God. Then the LORD said, "I have observed the misery of my people who are in Egypt; I have heard their cry on account of their taskmasters. Indeed, I know their sufferings, and I have come down to deliver them from the Egyptians, and to bring them up out of that land to a good and broad land, a land flowing with milk and honey, to the country of the Canaanites, the Hittites, the Amorites, the Perizzites, the Hivites, and the Jebusites. The cry of the Israelites has now come to me; I have also seen how the Egyptians oppress them. So come, I will send you to Pharaoh to bring my people, the Israelites, out of Egypt." But Moses said to God, "Who am I that I should go to Pharaoh, and bring the Israelites out of Egypt?" He said, "I will be with you; and this shall be the sign for you that it is I who sent you: when you have brought the people out of Egypt, you shall worship God on this mountain." But Moses said to God, "If I come to the Israelites and say to them, 'The God of your ancestors has sent me to you,' and they ask me, 'What is his name?' what shall I say to them?" God said to Moses, "I AM WHO I AM." He said further, "Thus you shall say to the Israelites, 'I AM has sent me to you.'" God also said to Moses, "Thus you shall say to the Israelites, 'The LORD, the God of your ancestors, the God of Abraham, the God of Isaac, and the God of Jacob, has sent me to you': This is my name forever, and this my title for all generations."

The Response   Psalm 105:1-6, 23-26, 45c
Psalm 105:1-6, 23-26, 45c   *Confitemini Domino*

1   Give thanks to the LORD and call upon his Name; *
      make known his deeds among the peoples.
2   Sing to him, sing praises to him, *
      and speak of all his marvelous works.
3   Glory in his holy Name; *
      let the hearts of those who seek the LORD rejoice.
4   Search for the LORD and his strength; *
      continually seek his face.
5   Remember the marvels he has done, *
      his wonders and the judgments of his mouth,
6   O offspring of Abraham his servant, *
      O children of Jacob his chosen.
23 Israel came into Egypt, *
      and Jacob became a sojourner in the land of Ham.
24 The LORD made his people exceedingly fruitful; *
      he made them stronger than their enemies;
25 Whose heart he turned, so that they hated his people, *
      and dealt unjustly with his servants.
26 He sent Moses his servant, *
      and Aaron whom he had chosen. Hallelujah!

or, ✠ **The Lesson**   **Jeremiah 15:15-21**

O LORD, you know; remember me and visit me, and bring down retribution for me on my persecutors. In your forbearance do not take me away; know that on your account I suffer insult. Your words were found, and I ate them, and your words became to me a joy and the delight of my heart; for I am called by your name, O LORD, God of hosts. I did not sit in the company of merrymakers, nor did I rejoice; under the weight of your hand I sat alone, for you had filled me with indignation. Why is my pain unceasing, my wound incurable, refusing to be healed? Truly, you are to me like a deceitful brook, like waters that fail. Therefore thus says the LORD: If you turn back, I will take you back, and you shall stand before me. If you utter what is precious, and not what is worthless, you shall serve as my mouth. It is they who will turn to you, not you who will turn to them. And I will make you to this people a fortified wall of bronze; they will fight against you, but they shall not prevail over you, for I am with you to save you and deliver you, says the LORD. I will deliver you out of the hand of the wicked, and redeem you from the grasp of the ruthless.

✠ **The Response**   **Psalm 26:1-8**

Psalm 26:1-8   *Judica me, Domine*

1   Give judgment for me, O LORD,
    for I have lived with integrity; *
       I have trusted in the LORD and have not faltered.

2   Test me, O LORD, and try me; *
       examine my heart and my mind.

3   For your love is before my eyes; *
       I have walked faithfully with you.

4   I have not sat with the worthless, *
       nor do I consort with the deceitful.

5   I have hated the company of evildoers; *
       I will not sit down with the wicked.

6   I will wash my hands in innocence, O LORD, *
       that I may go in procession round your altar,

7   Singing aloud a song of thanksgiving *
       and recounting all your wonderful deeds.

8   LORD, I love the house in which you dwell *
       and the place where your glory abides.

The Epistle   **Romans 12:9-21**

Let love be genuine; hate what is evil, hold fast to what is good; love one another with mutual affection; outdo one another in showing honor. Do not lag in zeal, be ardent in spirit, serve the Lord. Rejoice in hope, be patient in suffering, persevere in prayer. Contribute to the needs of the saints; extend hospitality to strangers. Bless those who persecute you; bless and do not curse them. Rejoice with those who rejoice, weep with those who weep. Live in harmony with one another; do not be haughty, but associate with the lowly; do not claim to be wiser than you are. Do not repay anyone evil for evil, but take thought for what is noble in the sight of all. If it is possible, so far as it depends on you, live peaceably with all. Beloved, never avenge yourselves, but leave room for the wrath of God; for it is written, "Vengeance is mine, I will repay, says the Lord." No, "if your enemies are hungry, feed them; if they are thirsty, give them something to drink; for by doing this you will heap burning coals on their heads." Do not be overcome by evil, but overcome evil with good.

The Gospel   Matthew 16:21-28

Jesus began to show his disciples that he must go to Jerusalem and undergo great suffering at the hands of the elders and chief priests and scribes, and be killed, and on the third day be raised. And Peter took him aside and began to rebuke him, saying, "God forbid it, Lord! This must never happen to you." But he turned and said to Peter, "Get behind me, Satan! You are a stumbling block to me; for you are setting your mind not on divine things but on human things." Then Jesus told his disciples, "If any want to become my followers, let them deny themselves and take up their cross and follow me. For those who want to save their life will lose it, and those who lose their life for my sake will find it. For what will it profit them if they gain the whole world but forfeit their life? Or what will they give in return for their life? For the Son of Man is to come with his angels in the glory of his Father, and then he will repay everyone for what has been done. Truly I tell you, there are some standing here who will not taste death before they see the Son of Man coming in his kingdom."

Year B

Song of Solomon 2:8-13	**or**	✟ *Deuteronomy 4:1-2, 6-9*
Psalm 45:1-2, 7-10		✟ *Psalm 15*

James 1:17-27
Mark 7:1-8, 14-15, 21-23

The Lesson   Song of Solomon 2:8-13

The voice of my beloved! Look, he comes, leaping upon the mountains, bounding over the hills. My beloved is like a gazelle or a young stag. Look, there he stands behind our wall, gazing in at the windows, looking through the lattice. My beloved speaks and says to me: "Arise, my love, my fair one, and come away; for now the winter is past, the rain is over and gone. The flowers appear on the earth; the time of singing has come, and the voice of the turtle-dove is heard in our land. The fig tree puts forth its figs, and the vines are in blossom; they give forth fragrance. Arise, my love, my fair one, and come away.

The Response   Psalm 45:1-2, 7-10

Psalm 45:1-2, 7-10   *Eructavit cor meum*

1   My heart is stirring with a noble song;
        let me recite what I have fashioned for the king; *
            my tongue shall be the pen of a skilled writer.

2   You are the fairest of men; *
        grace flows from your lips,
        because God has blessed you for ever.

7   Your throne, O God, endures for ever and ever, *
        a scepter of righteousness is the scepter of your kingdom;
        you love righteousness and hate iniquity.

8   Therefore God, your God, has anointed you *
        with the oil of gladness above your fellows.

9   All your garments are fragrant with myrrh, aloes, and cassia, *
        and the music of strings from ivory palaces makes you glad.

10   Kings' daughters stand among the ladies of the court; *
        on your right hand is the queen,
        adorned with the gold of Ophir.

or, ✠ The Lesson   Deuteronomy 4:1-2, 6-9

Moses said: Israel, give heed to the statutes and ordinances that I am teaching you to observe, so that you may live to enter and occupy the land that the LORD, the God of your ancestors, is giving you. You must neither add anything to what I command you nor take away anything from it, but keep the commandments of the LORD your God with which I am charging you. You must observe them diligently, for this will show your wisdom and discernment to the peoples, who, when they hear all these statutes, will say, "Surely this great nation is a wise and discerning people!" For what other great nation has a god so near to it as the LORD our God is whenever we call to him? And what other great nation has statutes and ordinances as just as this entire law that I am setting before you today? But take care and watch yourselves closely, so as neither to forget the things that your eyes have seen nor to let them slip from your mind all the days of your life; make them known to your children and your children's children.

✣ The Response

Psalm 15   *Domine, quis habitabit?*

1   LORD, who may dwell in your tabernacle? *
      who may abide upon your holy hill?

2   Whoever leads a blameless life and does what is right, *
      who speaks the truth from his heart.

3   There is no guile upon his tongue;
    he does no evil to his friend; *
      he does not heap contempt upon his neighbor.

4   In his sight the wicked is rejected, *
      but he honors those who fear the LORD.

5   He has sworn to do no wrong *
      and does not take back his word.

6   He does not give his money in hope of gain, *
      nor does he take a bribe against the innocent.

7   Whoever does these things *
      shall never be overthrown.

The Epistle   James 1:17-27

Every generous act of giving, with every perfect gift, is from above, coming down from the Father of lights, with whom there is no variation or shadow due to change. In fulfillment of his own purpose he gave us birth by the word of truth, so that we would become a kind of first fruits of his creatures. You must understand this, my beloved: let everyone be quick to listen, slow to speak, slow to anger; for your anger does not produce God's righteousness. Therefore rid yourselves of all sordidness and rank growth of wickedness, and welcome with meekness the implanted word that has the power to save your souls. But be doers of the word, and not merely hearers who deceive themselves. For if any are hearers of the word and not doers, they are like those who look at themselves in a mirror; for they look at themselves and, on going away, immediately forget what they were like. But those who look into the perfect law, the law of liberty, and persevere, being not hearers who forget but doers who act — they will be blessed in their doing. If any think they are religious, and do not bridle their tongues but deceive their hearts, their religion is worthless. Religion that is pure and undefiled before God, the Father, is this: to care for orphans and widows in their distress, and to keep oneself unstained by the world.

The Gospel   Mark 7:1-8, 14-15, 21-23

Now when the Pharisees and some of the scribes who had come from Jerusalem gathered around Jesus, they noticed that some of his disciples were eating with defiled hands, that is, without washing them. (For the Pharisees, and all the Jews, do not eat unless they thoroughly wash their hands, thus observing the tradition of the elders; and they do not eat anything from the market unless they wash it; and there are also many other traditions that they observe, the washing of cups, pots, and bronze kettles.) So the Pharisees and the scribes asked him, "Why do your disciples not live according to the tradition of the elders, but eat with defiled hands?" He said to them, "Isaiah prophesied rightly about you hypocrites, as it is written, 'This people honors me with their lips, but their hearts are far from me; in vain do they worship me, teaching human precepts as doctrines.' You abandon the commandment of God and hold to human tradition." Then he called the crowd again and said to them, "Listen to me, all of you, and understand: there is nothing outside a person that by going in can defile, but the things that come out are what defile. For it is from within, from the human heart, that evil intentions come: fornication, theft, murder, adultery, avarice, wickedness, deceit, licentiousness, envy, slander, pride, folly. All these evil things come from within, and they defile a person."

Year C

Jeremiah 2:4-13   **or**   ✠ *Sirach 10:12-18*
Psalm 81:1, 10-16   or *Proverbs 25:6-7*
                                          ✠ *Psalm 112*

Hebrews 13:1-8, 15-16
Luke 14:1, 7-14

The Lesson   **Jeremiah 2:4-13**

Hear the word of the LORD, O house of Jacob, and all the families of the house of Israel. Thus says the LORD: What wrong did your ancestors find in me that they went far from me, and went after worthless things, and became worthless themselves? They did not say, "Where is the LORD who brought us up from the land of Egypt, who led us in the wilderness, in a land of deserts and pits, in a land of drought and deep darkness, in a land that no one passes through, where no one lives?" I brought you into a plentiful land to eat its fruits and its good things. But when you entered you defiled my land, and made my heritage an abomination. The priests did not say, "Where is the LORD?" Those who handle the law did not know me; the rulers transgressed against me; the prophets prophesied by Baal, and went after things that do not profit. Therefore once more I accuse you, says the LORD, and I accuse your children's children. Cross to the coasts of Cyprus and look, send to Kedar and examine with care; see if there has ever been such a thing. Has a nation changed its gods, even though they are no gods? But my people have changed their glory for something that does not profit. Be appalled, O heavens, at this, be shocked, be utterly desolate, says the LORD, for my people have committed two evils: they have forsaken me, the fountain of living water, and dug out cisterns for themselves, cracked cisterns that can hold no water.

The Response   **Psalm 81:1, 10-16**

Psalm 81:1, 10-16   *Exultate Deo*

1   Sing with joy to God our strength *
        and raise a loud shout to the God of Jacob.

10   I am the LORD your God,
        who brought you out of the land of Egypt and said, *
        "Open your mouth wide, and I will fill it."

11   And yet my people did not hear my voice, *
        and Israel would not obey me.

12   So I gave them over to the stubbornness of their hearts, *
        to follow their own devices.

13   Oh, that my people would listen to me! *
        that Israel would walk in my ways!

14   I should soon subdue their enemies *
        and turn my hand against their foes.

15   Those who hate the LORD would cringe before him, *
        and their punishment would last for ever.

16   But Israel would I feed with the finest wheat *
        and satisfy him with honey from the rock.

or, ✠ **The Lesson**   **Sirach 10:12-18** *or* **Proverbs 25:6-7**
Sirach 10:12-18

The beginning of human pride is to forsake the Lord; the heart has withdrawn from its Maker. For the beginning of pride is sin, and the one who clings to it pours out abominations. Therefore the Lord brings upon them unheard-of calamities, and destroys them completely. The Lord overthrows the thrones of rulers, and enthrones the lowly in their place. The Lord plucks up the roots of the nations and plants the humble in their place. The Lord lays waste the lands of the nations, and destroys them to the foundations of the earth. He removes some of them and destroys them, and erases the memory of them from the earth. Pride was not created for human beings, or violent anger for those born of women.

or, ✠ **Proverbs 25:6-7**

Do not put yourself forward in the king's presence or stand in the place of the great; for it is better to be told, "Come up here," than to be put lower in the presence of a noble.

✠ **The Response**   **Psalm 112**

Psalm 112   *Beatus vir*

1   Hallelujah!
        Happy are they who fear the LORD *
        and have great delight in his commandments!

2 Their descendants will be mighty in the land; *
    the generation of the upright will be blessed.

3 Wealth and riches will be in their house, *
    and their righteousness will last for ever.

4 Light shines in the darkness for the upright; *
    the righteous are merciful and full of compassion.

5 It is good for them to be generous in lending *
    and to manage their affairs with justice.

6 For they will never be shaken; *
    the righteous will be kept in everlasting remembrance.

7 They will not be afraid of any evil rumors; *
    their heart is right;
    they put their trust in the LORD.

8 Their heart is established and will not shrink, *
    until they see their desire upon their enemies.

9 They have given freely to the poor, *
    and their righteousness stands fast for ever;
    they will hold up their head with honor.

10 The wicked will see it and be angry;
    they will gnash their teeth and pine away; *
    the desires of the wicked will perish.

The Epistle   Hebrews 13:1-8, 15-16

Let mutual love continue. Do not neglect to show hospitality to strangers, for by doing that some have entertained angels without knowing it. Remember those who are in prison, as though you were in prison with them; those who are being tortured, as though you yourselves were being tortured. Let marriage be held in honor by all, and let the marriage bed be kept undefiled; for God will judge fornicators and adulterers. Keep your lives free from the love of money, and be content with what you have; for he has said, "I will never leave you or forsake you." So we can say with confidence, "The Lord is my helper; I will not be afraid. What can anyone do to me?" Remember your leaders, those who spoke the word of God to you; consider the outcome of their way of life, and imitate their faith. Jesus Christ is the same yesterday and today and forever. Through him, then, let us continually offer a sacrifice of praise to God, that is, the fruit of lips that confess his name. Do not neglect to do good and to share what you have, for such sacrifices are pleasing to God.

The Gospel   Luke 14:1, 7-14

On one occasion when Jesus was going to the house of a leader of the Pharisees to eat a meal on the sabbath, they were watching him closely. When he noticed how the guests chose the places of honor, he told them a parable.

"When you are invited by someone to a wedding banquet, do not sit down at the place of honor, in case someone more distinguished than you has been invited by your host; and the host who invited both of you may come and say to you, 'Give this person your place,' and then in disgrace you would start to take the lowest place. But when you are invited, go and sit down at the lowest place, so that when your host comes, he may say to you, 'Friend, move up higher'; then you will be honored in the presence of all who sit at the table with you. For all who exalt themselves will be humbled, and those who humble themselves will be exalted." He said also to the one who had invited him, "When you give a luncheon or a dinner, do not invite your friends or your brothers or your relatives or rich neighbors, in case they may invite you in return, and you would be repaid. But when you give a banquet, invite the poor, the crippled, the lame, and the blind. And you will be blessed, because they cannot repay you, for you will be repaid at the resurrection of the righteous."

PROPER 18

Sunday between September 4 and September 10 inclusive

The Collect

Grant us, O Lord, to trust in you with all our hearts; for, as you always resist the proud who confide in their own strength, so you never forsake those who make their boast of your mercy; through Jesus Christ our Lord, who lives and reigns with you and the Holy Spirit, one God, now and for ever. *Amen.*

Year A

Exodus 12:1-14	**or**	✠ *Ezekiel 33:7-11*
Psalm 149		✠ *Psalm 119:33-40*

Romans 13:8-14
Matthew 18:15-20

The Lesson   **Exodus 12:1-14**

The LORD said to Moses and Aaron in the land of Egypt: This month shall mark for you the beginning of months; it shall be the first month of the year for you. Tell the whole congregation of Israel that on the tenth of this month they are to take a lamb for each family, a lamb for each household. If a household is too small for a whole lamb, it shall join its closest neighbor in obtaining one; the lamb shall be divided in proportion to the number of people who eat of it. Your lamb shall be without blemish, a year-old male; you may take it from the sheep or from the goats. You shall keep it until the fourteenth day of this month; then the whole assembled congregation of Israel shall slaughter it at twilight. They shall take some of the blood and put it on the two doorposts and the lintel of the houses in which they eat it. They shall eat the lamb that same night; they shall eat it roasted over the fire with unleavened bread and bitter herbs. Do not eat any of it raw or boiled in water, but roasted over the fire, with its head, legs, and inner organs. You shall let none of it remain until the morning; anything that remains until the morning you shall burn. This is how you shall eat it: your loins girded, your sandals on your feet, and your staff in your hand; and you shall eat it hurriedly. It is the passover of the LORD. For I will pass through the land of Egypt that night, and I will strike down every firstborn in the land of Egypt, both human beings and animals; on all the gods of Egypt I will execute judgments: I am the LORD. The blood shall be a sign for you on the houses where you live: when I see the blood, I will pass over you, and no plague shall destroy you when I strike the land of Egypt. This day shall be a day of remembrance for you. You shall celebrate it as a festival to the LORD; throughout your generations you shall observe it as a perpetual ordinance.

The Response   **Psalm 149**

Psalm 149 *Cantate Domino*

1   Hallelujah!
        Sing to the LORD a new song; *
            sing his praise in the congregation of the faithful.
2   Let Israel rejoice in his Maker; *
            let the children of Zion be joyful in their King.
3   Let them praise his Name in the dance; *
            let them sing praise to him with timbrel and harp.
4   For the LORD takes pleasure in his people *
            and adorns the poor with victory.
5   Let the faithful rejoice in triumph; *
            let them be joyful on their beds.
6   Let the praises of God be in their throat *
            and a two-edged sword in their hand;
7   To wreak vengeance on the nations *
            and punishment on the peoples;
8   To bind their kings in chains *
            and their nobles with links of iron;
9   To inflict on them the judgment decreed; *
            this is glory for all his faithful people.
            Hallelujah!

or, ✠ **The Lesson**   **Ezekiel 33:7-11**

You, mortal, I have made a sentinel for the house of Israel; whenever you hear a word from my mouth, you shall give them warning from me. If I say to the wicked, "O wicked ones, you shall surely die," and you do not speak to warn the wicked to turn from their ways, the wicked shall die in their iniquity, but their blood I will require at your hand. But if you warn the wicked to turn from their ways, and they do not turn from their ways, the wicked shall die in their iniquity, but you will have saved your life. Now you, mortal, say to the house of Israel, Thus you have said: "Our transgressions and our sins weigh upon us, and we waste away because of them; how then can we live?" Say to them, As I live, says the Lord GOD, I have no pleasure in the death of the wicked, but that the wicked turn from their ways and live; turn back, turn back from your evil ways; for why will you die, O house of Israel?

✠ The Response   Psalm 119:33-40

Psalm 119:33-40   *Legem pone*

33 Teach me, O LORD, the way of your statutes, *
       and I shall keep it to the end.
34 Give me understanding, and I shall keep your law; *
       I shall keep it with all my heart.
35 Make me go in the path of your commandments, *
       for that is my desire.
36 Incline my heart to your decrees *
       and not to unjust gain.
37 Turn my eyes from watching what is worthless; *
       give me life in your ways.
38 Fulfill your promise to your servant, *
       which you make to those who fear you.
39 Turn away the reproach which I dread, *
       because your judgments are good.
40 Behold, I long for your commandments; *
       in your righteousness preserve my life.

The Epistle   Romans 13:8-14

Owe no one anything, except to love one another; for the one who loves another has fulfilled the law. The commandments, "You shall not commit adultery; You shall not murder; You shall not steal; You shall not covet"; and any other commandment, are summed up in this word, "Love your neighbor as yourself." Love does no wrong to a neighbor; therefore, love is the fulfilling of the law. Besides this, you know what time it is, how it is now the moment for you to wake from sleep. For salvation is nearer to us now than when we became believers; the night is far gone, the day is near. Let us then lay aside the works of darkness and put on the armor of light; let us live honorably as in the day, not in reveling and drunkenness, not in debauchery and licentiousness, not in quarreling and jealousy. Instead, put on the Lord Jesus Christ, and make no provision for the flesh, to gratify its desires.

The Gospel   **Matthew 18:15-20**

Jesus said to his disciples, "If another member of the church sins against you, go and point out the fault when the two of you are alone. If the member listens to you, you have regained that one. But if you are not listened to, take one or two others along with you, so that every word may be confirmed by the evidence of two or three witnesses. If the member refuses to listen to them, tell it to the church; and if the offender refuses to listen even to the church, let such a one be to you as a Gentile and a tax collector. Truly I tell you, whatever you bind on earth will be bound in heaven, and whatever you loose on earth will be loosed in heaven. Again, truly I tell you, if two of you agree on earth about anything you ask, it will be done for you by my Father in heaven. For where two or three are gathered in my name, I am there among them."

Year B

Proverbs 22:1-2, 8-9, 22-23   **or**   ✞ *Isaiah 35:4-7a*
Psalm 125   ✞ *Psalm 146*

James 2:1-10, (11-13), 14-17
Mark 7:24-37

The Lesson   **Proverbs 22:1-2, 8-9, 22-23**

A good name is to be chosen rather than great riches, and favor is better than silver or gold. The rich and the poor have this in common: the LORD is the maker of them all. Whoever sows injustice will reap calamity, and the rod of anger will fail. Those who are generous are blessed, for they share their bread with the poor. Do not rob the poor because they are poor, or crush the afflicted at the gate; for the LORD pleads their cause and despoils of life those who despoil them.

The Response   **Psalm 125**

Psalm 125   *Qui confidunt*

1   Those who trust in the LORD are like Mount Zion, *
        which cannot be moved, but stands fast for ever.
2   The hills stand about Jerusalem; *
        so does the LORD stand round about his people,
        from this time forth for evermore.
3   The scepter of the wicked shall not hold sway over the
            land allotted to the just, *
        so that the just shall not put their hands to evil.
4   Show your goodness, O LORD, to those who are good *
        and to those who are true of heart.

5   As for those who turn aside to crooked ways,
        the LORD will lead them away with the evildoers; *
            but peace be upon Israel.

or, ☩ **The Lesson**   **Isaiah 35:4-7*a***

Say to those who are of a fearful heart, "Be strong, do not fear! Here is your
God. He will come with vengeance, with terrible recompense. He will come
and save you." Then the eyes of the blind shall be opened, and the ears of the
deaf unstopped; then the lame shall leap like a deer, and the tongue of the
speechless sing for joy. For waters shall break forth in the wilderness, and
streams in the desert; the burning sand shall become a pool, and the thirsty
ground springs of water.

☩ **The Response**   **Psalm 146**

Psalm 146   *Lauda, anima mea*

1   Hallelujah!
        Praise the LORD, O my soul! *
            I will praise the LORD as long as I live;
            I will sing praises to my God while I have my being.
2   Put not your trust in rulers, nor in any child of earth, *
            for there is no help in them.
3   When they breathe their last, they return to earth, *
            and in that day their thoughts perish.
4   Happy are they who have the God of Jacob for their help! *
            whose hope is in the LORD their God;
5   Who made heaven and earth, the seas, and all that is in them; *
            who keeps his promise for ever;
6   Who gives justice to those who are oppressed, *
            and food to those who hunger.
7   The LORD sets the prisoners free;
        the LORD opens the eyes of the blind; *
            the LORD lifts up those who are bowed down;
8   The LORD loves the righteous;
        the LORD cares for the stranger; *
            he sustains the orphan and widow,
            but frustrates the way of the wicked.
9   The LORD shall reign for ever, *
            your God, O Zion, throughout all generations.
            Hallelujah!

The Epistle   James 2:1-10, (11-13), 14-17

James 2:1-10

My brothers and sisters, do you with your acts of favoritism really believe in our glorious Lord Jesus Christ? For if a person with gold rings and in fine clothes comes into your assembly, and if a poor person in dirty clothes also comes in, and if you take notice of the one wearing the fine clothes and say, "Have a seat here, please," while to the one who is poor you say, "Stand there," or, "Sit at my feet," have you not made distinctions among yourselves, and become judges with evil thoughts? Listen, my beloved brothers and sisters. Has not God chosen the poor in the world to be rich in faith and to be heirs of the kingdom that he has promised to those who love him? But you have dishonored the poor. Is it not the rich who oppress you? Is it not they who drag you into court? Is it not they who blaspheme the excellent name that was invoked over you? You do well if you really fulfill the royal law according to the scripture, "You shall love your neighbor as yourself." But if you show partiality, you commit sin and are convicted by the law as transgressors. For whoever keeps the whole law but fails in one point has become accountable for all of it.

James 2:(11-13) [For the one who said, "You shall not commit adultery," also said, "You shall not murder." Now if you do not commit adultery but if you murder, you have become a transgressor of the law. So speak and so act as those who are to be judged by the law of liberty. For judgment will be without mercy to anyone who has shown no mercy; mercy triumphs over judgment.]

James 2:14-17 What good is it, my brothers and sisters, if you say you have faith but do not have works? Can faith save you? If a brother or sister is naked and lacks daily food, and one of you says to them, "Go in peace; keep warm and eat your fill," and yet you do not supply their bodily needs, what is the good of that? So faith by itself, if it has no works, is dead.

The Gospel   Mark 7:24-37

Jesus set out and went away to the region of Tyre. He entered a house and did not want anyone to know he was there. Yet he could not escape notice, but a woman whose little daughter had an unclean spirit immediately heard about him, and she came and bowed down at his feet. Now the woman was a Gentile, of Syrophoenician origin. She begged him to cast the demon out of her daughter. He said to her, "Let the children be fed first, for it is not fair to take the children's food and throw it to the dogs." But she answered him, "Sir, even the dogs under the table eat the children's crumbs." Then he said to her, "For saying that, you may go — the demon has left your daughter." So she went home, found the child lying on the bed, and the demon gone. Jesus returned from the region of Tyre, and went by way of Sidon towards the Sea of Galilee, in the region of the Decapolis. They brought to him a deaf man who had an impediment in his speech; and they begged him to lay his hand on him. He took him aside in private, away from the crowd, and put his fingers into his ears, and he spat and touched his tongue. Then looking up to heaven, he sighed and said to him, "Ephphatha," that is, "Be opened." And immediately his ears were opened, his tongue was released, and he spoke plainly. Then Jesus ordered them to tell no one; but the more he ordered them, the more zealously they proclaimed it. They were astounded beyond measure, saying, "He has done everything well; he even makes the deaf to hear and the mute to speak."

Year C

Jeremiah 18:1-11	**or**	✝ *Deuteronomy 30:15-20*
Psalm 139:1-5, 13-17		✝ *Psalm 1*

Philemon 1-21
Luke 14:25-33

The Lesson   Jeremiah 18:1-11

The word that came to Jeremiah from the LORD: "Come, go down to the potter's house, and there I will let you hear my words." So I went down to the potter's house, and there he was working at his wheel. The vessel he was making of clay was spoiled in the potter's hand, and he reworked it into another vessel, as seemed good to him. Then the word of the LORD came to me: Can I not do with you, O house of Israel, just as this potter has done? says the LORD. Just like the clay in the potter's hand, so are you in my hand, O house of Israel. At one moment I may declare concerning a nation or a kingdom, that I will pluck up and break down and destroy it, but if that nation, concerning which I have spoken, turns from its evil, I will change my mind about the disaster that I intended to bring on it. And at another moment I may declare concerning a nation or a kingdom that I will build and plant it, but if it does evil in my sight, not listening to my voice, then I will change my mind about the good that I had intended to do to it. Now, therefore, say to the people of Judah and the inhabitants of Jerusalem: Thus says the LORD: Look, I am a potter shaping evil against you and devising a plan against you. Turn now, all of you from your evil way, and amend your ways and your doings.

The Response   Psalm 139:1-5, 13-17

Psalm 139:1-5, 13-17   *Domine, probasti*

1   LORD, you have searched me out and known me; *
        you know my sitting down and my rising up;
        you discern my thoughts from afar.
2   You trace my journeys and my resting-places *
        and are acquainted with all my ways.

3 Indeed, there is not a word on my lips, *
  but you, O Lord, know it altogether.
4 You press upon me behind and before *
  and lay your hand upon me.
5 Such knowledge is too wonderful for me; *
  it is so high that I cannot attain to it.
13 I will thank you because I am marvelously made; *
  your works are wonderful, and I know it well.
14 My body was not hidden from you, *
  while I was being made in secret
  and woven in the depths of the earth.
15 Your eyes beheld my limbs, yet unfinished in the womb;
  all of them were written in your book; *
  they were fashioned day by day,
  when as yet there was none of them.
16 How deep I find your thoughts, O God! *
  how great is the sum of them!
17 If I were to count them, they would be more in number
  than the sand; *
  to count them all, my life span would need to
  be like yours.

or, ☩ **The Lesson**   **Deuteronomy 30:15-20**

Moses said, See, I have set before you today life and prosperity, death and adversity. If you obey the commandments of the Lord your God that I am commanding you today, by loving the Lord your God, walking in his ways, and observing his commandments, decrees, and ordinances, then you shall live and become numerous, and the Lord your God will bless you in the land that you are entering to possess. But if your heart turns away and you do not hear, but are led astray to bow down to other gods and serve them, I declare to you today that you shall perish; you shall not live long in the land that you are crossing the Jordan to enter and possess. I call heaven and earth to witness against you today that I have set before you life and death, blessings and curses. Choose life so that you and your descendants may live, loving the Lord your God, obeying him, and holding fast to him; for that means life to you and length of days, so that you may live in the land that the Lord swore to give to your ancestors, to Abraham, to Isaac, and to Jacob.

☩ **The Response**   **Psalm 1**

Psalm 1 *Beatus vir qui non abiit*
  1 Happy are they who have not walked in the counsel of
    the wicked, *
    nor lingered in the way of sinners,
    nor sat in the seats of the scornful!

2 Their delight is in the law of the LORD, *
    and they meditate on his law day and night.
3 They are like trees planted by streams of water,
    bearing fruit in due season, with leaves that do not wither; *
    everything they do shall prosper.
4 It is not so with the wicked; *
    they are like chaff which the wind blows away.
5 Therefore the wicked shall not stand upright when
        judgment comes, *
    nor the sinner in the council of the righteous.
6 For the LORD knows the way of the righteous, *
    but the way of the wicked is doomed.

The Epistle   Philemon 1-21

Paul, a prisoner of Christ Jesus, and Timothy our brother, To Philemon our dear friend and co-worker, to Apphia our sister, to Archippus our fellow soldier, and to the church in your house: Grace to you and peace from God our Father and the Lord Jesus Christ. When I remember you in my prayers, I always thank my God because I hear of your love for all the saints and your faith toward the Lord Jesus. I pray that the sharing of your faith may become effective when you perceive all the good that we may do for Christ. I have indeed received much joy and encouragement from your love, because the hearts of the saints have been refreshed through you, my brother. For this reason, though I am bold enough in Christ to command you to do your duty, yet I would rather appeal to you on the basis of love — and I, Paul, do this as an old man, and now also as a prisoner of Christ Jesus. I am appealing to you for my child, Onesimus, whose father I have become during my imprisonment. Formerly he was useless to you, but now he is indeed useful both to you and to me. I am sending him, that is, my own heart, back to you. I wanted to keep him with me, so that he might be of service to me in your place during my imprisonment for the gospel; but I preferred to do nothing without your consent, in order that your good deed might be voluntary and not something forced. Perhaps this is the reason he was separated from you for a while, so that you might have him back forever, no longer as a slave but more than a slave, a beloved brother — especially to me but how much more to you, both in the flesh and in the Lord. So if you consider me your partner, welcome him as you would welcome me. If he has wronged you in any way, or owes you anything, charge that to my account. I, Paul, am writing this with my own hand: I will repay it. I say nothing about your owing me even your own self. Yes, brother, let me have this benefit from you in the Lord! Refresh my heart in Christ. Confident of your obedience, I am writing to you, knowing that you will do even more than I say.

The Gospel   Luke 14:25-33

Large crowds were traveling with Jesus; and he turned and said to them, "Whoever comes to me and does not hate father and mother, wife and children, brothers and sisters, yes, and even life itself, cannot be my disciple. Whoever does not carry the cross and follow me cannot be my disciple. For which of you, intending to build a tower, does not first sit down and estimate the cost, to see whether he has enough to complete it? Otherwise, when he has laid a foundation and is not able to finish, all who see it will begin to ridicule him, saying, 'This fellow began to build and was not able to finish.' Or what king, going out to wage war against another king, will not sit down first and consider whether he is able with ten thousand to oppose the one who comes against him with twenty thousand? If he cannot, then, while the other is still far away, he sends a delegation and asks for the terms of peace. So therefore, none of you can become my disciple if you do not give up all your possessions."

PROPER 19

Sunday between September 11 and September 17 inclusive

The Collect

O God, because without you we are not able to please you mercifully grant that your Holy Spirit may in all things direct and rule our hearts; through Jesus Christ our Lord, who lives and reigns with you and the Holy Spirit, one God, now and for ever. *Amen.*

Year A

Exodus 14:19-31	**or**	✝ *Genesis 50:15-21*
Psalm 114		✝ *Psalm 103:(1-7), 8-13*
or *Exodus 15:1b-11, 20-21*		

Romans 14:1-12
Matthew 18:21-35

The Lesson   Exodus 14:19-31

The angel of God who was going before the Israelite army moved and went behind them; and the pillar of cloud moved from in front of them and took its place behind them. It came between the army of Egypt and the army of Israel. And so the cloud was there with the darkness, and it lit up the night; one did not come near the other all night. Then Moses stretched out his hand over the sea. The LORD drove the sea back by a strong east wind all night, and turned the sea into dry land; and the waters were divided. The Israelites went into the sea on dry ground, the waters forming a wall for them on their right and on their left. The Egyptians pursued, and went into the sea after them, all of Pharaoh's horses, chariots, and chariot drivers. At the morning watch the

LORD in the pillar of fire and cloud looked down upon the Egyptian army, and threw the Egyptian army into panic. He clogged their chariot wheels so that they turned with difficulty. The Egyptians said, "Let us flee from the Israelites, for the LORD is fighting for them against Egypt." Then the LORD said to Moses, "Stretch out your hand over the sea, so that the water may come back upon the Egyptians, upon their chariots and chariot drivers." So Moses stretched out his hand over the sea, and at dawn the sea returned to its normal depth. As the Egyptians fled before it, the LORD tossed the Egyptians into the sea. The waters returned and covered the chariots and the chariot drivers, the entire army of Pharaoh that had followed them into the sea; not one of them remained. But the Israelites walked on dry ground through the sea, the waters forming a wall for them on their right and on their left. Thus the LORD saved Israel that day from the Egyptians; and Israel saw the Egyptians dead on the seashore. Israel saw the great work that the LORD did against the Egyptians. So the people feared the LORD and believed in the LORD and in his servant Moses.

The Response   Psalm 114 *or* Exodus 15:1*b*-11, 20-21
Psalm 114   *In exitu Israel*

1   Hallelujah!
    When Israel came out of Egypt, *
        the house of Jacob from a people of strange speech,
2   Judah became God's sanctuary *
        and Israel his dominion.
3   The sea beheld it and fled; *
        Jordan turned and went back.
4   The mountains skipped like rams, *
        and the little hills like young sheep.
5   What ailed you, O sea, that you fled? *
        O Jordan, that you turned back?
6   You mountains, that you skipped like rams? *
        you little hills like young sheep?
7   Tremble, O earth, at the presence of the LORD, *
        at the presence of the God of Jacob,
8   Who turned the hard rock into a pool of water *
        and flint-stone into a flowing spring.

or, Exodus 15:1*b*-11, 20-21

1*b*   "I will sing to the LORD, for he has triumphed gloriously;
       horse and rider he has thrown into the sea.
2   The LORD is my strength and my might,
       and he has become my salvation;

this is my God, and I will praise him, my father's God,
and I will exalt him.

3   The LORD is a warrior; the LORD is his name.

4   Pharaoh's chariots and his army he cast into the sea;
his picked officers were sunk in the Red Sea.

5   The floods covered them;
they went down into the depths like a stone.

6   Your right hand, O LORD, glorious in power —
your right hand, O LORD, shattered the enemy.

7   In the greatness of your majesty you overthrew your adversaries;
you sent out your fury, it consumed them like stubble.

8   At the blast of your nostrils the waters piled up,
the floods stood up in a heap;
the deeps congealed in the heart of the sea.

9   The enemy said, 'I will pursue, I will overtake, I will divide the
spoil, my desire shall have its fill of them.
I will draw my sword, my hand shall destroy them.'

10   You blew with your wind, the sea covered them;
they sank like lead in the mighty waters.

11   Who is like you, O LORD, among the gods?
Who is like you, majestic in holiness,
awesome in splendor, doing wonders?"

20   Then the prophet Miriam, Aaron's sister,
took a tambourine in her hand;
and all the women went out after her
with tambourines and with dancing.

21   And Miriam sang to them:
"Sing to the LORD, for he has triumphed gloriously;
horse and rider he has thrown into the sea."

or, ✝ **Genesis 50:15-21**

Realizing that their father was dead, Joseph's brothers said, "What if Joseph
still bears a grudge against us and pays us back in full for all the wrong that
we did to him?" So they approached Joseph, saying, "Your father gave this
instruction before he died, 'Say to Joseph: I beg you, forgive the crime of your
brothers and the wrong they did in harming you.' Now therefore please forgive
the crime of the servants of the God of your father." Joseph wept when they
spoke to him. Then his brothers also wept, fell down before him, and said,
"We are here as your slaves." But Joseph said to them, "Do not be afraid! Am
I in the place of God? Even though you intended to do harm to me, God
intended it for good, in order to preserve a numerous people, as he is doing
today. So have no fear; I myself will provide for you and your little ones." In
this way he reassured them, speaking kindly to them.

✝ **The Response**   **Psalm 103:(1-7), 8-13**

Psalm 103:(1-7), 8-13   *Benedic, anima mea*

[1   Bless the LORD, O my soul, *
       and all that is within me, bless his holy Name.

2   Bless the LORD, O my soul, *
       and forget not all his benefits.

3   He forgives all your sins *
       and heals all your infirmities;

4   He redeems your life from the grave *
       and crowns you with mercy and loving-kindness;

5   He satisfies you with good things, *
       and your youth is renewed like an eagle's.

6   The LORD executes righteousness *
       and judgment for all who are oppressed.

7   He made his ways known to Moses *
       and his works to the children of Israel.]

8   The LORD is full of compassion and mercy, *
       slow to anger and of great kindness.

9   He will not always accuse us, *
       nor will he keep his anger for ever.

10   He has not dealt with us according to our sins, *
       nor rewarded us according to our wickedness.

11   For as the heavens are high above the earth, *
       so is his mercy great upon those who fear him.

12   As far as the east is from the west, *
       so far has he removed our sins from us.

13   As a father cares for his children, *
       so does the LORD care for those who fear him.

The Epistle   **Romans 14:1-12**

Welcome those who are weak in faith, but not for the purpose of quarreling over opinions. Some believe in eating anything, while the weak eat only vegetables. Those who eat must not despise those who abstain, and those who abstain must not pass judgment on those who eat; for God has welcomed them. Who are you to pass judgment on servants of another? It is before their own lord that they stand or fall. And they will be upheld, for the Lord is able to make them stand. Some judge one day to be better than another, while others judge all days to be alike. Let all be fully convinced in their own minds. Those who observe the day, observe it in honor of the Lord. Also those who eat, eat in honor of the Lord, since they give thanks to God; while those who abstain, abstain in honor of the Lord and give thanks to God. We do not live to ourselves, and we do not die to ourselves. If we live, we live to the Lord, and if we die, we die to the Lord; so then, whether we live or whether we die, we are the Lord's. For to this end Christ died and lived again, so that he might be Lord of both the dead and the living. Why do you pass judgment on your brother or sister? Or you, why do you despise your brother or sister? For we will all stand before the judgment seat of God. For it is written, "As I live, says the Lord, every knee shall bow to me, and every tongue shall give praise to God." So then, each of us will be accountable to God.

The Gospel   Matthew 18:21-35

Peter came and said to Jesus, "Lord, if another member of the church sins against me, how often should I forgive? As many as seven times?" Jesus said to him, "Not seven times, but, I tell you, seventy-seven times. For this reason the kingdom of heaven may be compared to a king who wished to settle accounts with his slaves. When he began the reckoning, one who owed him ten thousand talents was brought to him; and, as he could not pay, his lord ordered him to be sold, together with his wife and children and all his posses-sions, and payment to be made. So the slave fell on his knees before him, saying, 'Have patience with me, and I will pay you everything.' And out of pity for him, the lord of that slave released him and forgave him the debt. But that same slave, as he went out, came upon one of his fellow slaves who owed him a hundred denarii; and seizing him by the throat, he said, 'Pay what you owe.' Then his fellow slave fell down and pleaded with him, 'Have patience with me, and I will pay you.' But he refused; then he went and threw him into prison until he would pay the debt. When his fellow slaves saw what had happened, they were greatly distressed, and they went and reported to their lord all that had taken place. Then his lord summoned him and said to him, 'You wicked slave! I forgave you all that debt because you pleaded with me. Should you not have had mercy on your fellow slave, as I had mercy on you?' And in anger his lord handed him over to be tortured until he would pay his entire debt. So my heavenly Father will also do to every one of you, if you do not forgive your brother or sister from your heart."

Year B

Proverbs 1:20-33   **or**   ✟ *Isaiah 50:4-9a*
Psalm 19   ✟ *Psalm 116:1-8*
   or *Wisdom of Solomon 7:26—8:1*
                              James 3:1-12
                              Mark 8:27-38

The Lesson   Proverbs 1:20-33

Wisdom cries out in the street; in the squares she raises her voice. At the busiest corner she cries out; at the entrance of the city gates she speaks: "How long, O simple ones, will you love being simple? How long will scoffers delight in their scoffing and fools hate knowledge? Give heed to my reproof; I will pour out my thoughts to you; I will make my words known to you. Because I have called and you refused, have stretched out my hand and no one heeded, and because you have ignored all my counsel and would have none of my reproof, I also will laugh at your calamity; I will mock when panic strikes you, when panic strikes you like a storm, and your calamity comes like a whirlwind, when distress and anguish come upon you. Then they will call upon me, but I will not answer; they will seek me diligently, but will not find me. Because they hated knowledge and did not choose the fear of the LORD, would have none of my counsel, and despised all my reproof, therefore they shall eat the fruit of their way and be sated with their own devices. For waywardness kills the simple, and the complacency of fools destroys them; but those who listen to me will be secure and will live at ease, without dread of disaster."

The Response   **Psalm 19** *or* **Wisdom of Solomon 7:26—8:1**
Psalm 19   *Caeli enarrant*

1   The heavens declare the glory of God, *
      and the firmament shows his handiwork.

2   One day tells its tale to another, *
      and one night imparts knowledge to another.

3   Although they have no words or language, *
      and their voices are not heard,

4   Their sound has gone out into all lands, *
      and their message to the ends of the world.

5   In the deep has he set a pavilion for the sun; *
      it comes forth like a bridegroom out of his chamber;
      it rejoices like a champion to run its course.

6   It goes forth from the uttermost edge of the heavens
      and runs about to the end of it again; *
      nothing is hidden from its burning heat.

7   The law of the LORD is perfect
      and revives the soul; *
      the testimony of the LORD is sure
      and gives wisdom to the innocent.

8   The statutes of the LORD are just
      and rejoice the heart; *
      the commandment of the LORD is clear
      and gives light to the eyes.

9   The fear of the LORD is clean
      and endures for ever; *
      the judgments of the LORD are true
      and righteous altogether.

10   More to be desired are they than gold,
          more than much fine gold, *
       sweeter far than honey,
          than honey in the comb.
11   By them also is your servant enlightened, *
       and in keeping them there is great reward.
12   Who can tell how often he offends? *
       cleanse me from my secret faults.
13   Above all, keep your servant from presumptuous sins;
       let them not get dominion over me; *
          then shall I be whole and sound,
          and innocent of a great offense.
14   Let the words of my mouth and the meditation of my
       heart be acceptable in your sight, *
          O LORD, my strength and my redeemer.

or, **Wisdom of Solomon 7:26—8:1**

26   For wisdom is a reflection of eternal light,
       a spotless mirror of the working of God,
       and an image of his goodness.
27   Although she is but one, she can do all things,
       and while remaining in herself, she renews all things;
       in every generation she passes into holy souls,
       and makes them friends of God, and prophets;
28   for God loves nothing so much
       as the person who lives with wisdom.
29   She is more beautiful than the sun,
       and excels every constellation of the stars.
       Compared with the light she is found to be superior,
30   for it is succeeded only the night,
       but against wisdom evil does not prevail.
8:1 She reaches mightily from one end of the earth to the other,
       and she orders all things well.

or, ☩ The Lesson   Isaiah 50:4-9*a*

The Lord GOD has given me the tongue of a teacher, that I may know how to
sustain the weary with a word. Morning by morning he wakens — wakens my
ear to listen as those who are taught. The Lord GOD has opened my ear, and I
was not rebellious, I did not turn backward. I gave my back to those who
struck me, and my cheeks to those who pulled out the beard; I did not hide my
face from insult and spitting. The Lord GOD helps me; therefore I have not
been disgraced; therefore I have set my face like flint, and I know that I shall

not be put to shame; he who vindicates me is near. Who will contend with me? Let us stand up together. Who are my adversaries? Let them confront me. It is the Lord GOD who helps me; who will declare me guilty?

☩ The Response   Psalm 116:1-8
Psalm 116:1-8   *Dilexi, quoniam*

1   I love the LORD, because he has heard the voice of my supplication, *
    because he has inclined his ear to me whenever
        I called upon him.

2   The cords of death entangled me;
    the grip of the grave took hold of me; *
        I came to grief and sorrow.

3   Then I called upon the Name of the LORD: *
    "O LORD, I pray you, save my life."

4   Gracious is the LORD and righteous; *
    our God is full of compassion.

5   The LORD watches over the innocent; *
    I was brought very low, and he helped me.

6   Turn again to your rest, O my soul, *
    for the LORD has treated you well.

7   For you have rescued my life from death, *
    my eyes from tears, and my feet from stumbling.

8   I will walk in the presence of the LORD *
    in the land of the living.

The Epistle   James 3:1-12
Not many of you should become teachers, my brothers and sisters, for you know that we who teach will be judged with greater strictness. For all of us make many mistakes. Anyone who makes no mistakes in speaking is perfect, able to keep the whole body in check with a bridle. If we put bits into the mouths of horses to make them obey us, we guide their whole bodies. Or look at ships: though they are so large that it takes strong winds to drive them, yet they are guided by a very small rudder wherever the will of the pilot directs. So also the tongue is a small member, yet it boasts of great exploits. How great a forest is set ablaze by a small fire! And the tongue is a fire. The tongue is placed among our members as a world of iniquity; it stains the whole body, sets on fire the cycle of nature, and is itself set on fire by hell. For every species of beast and bird, of reptile and sea creature, can be tamed and has been tamed by the human species, but no one can tame the tongue — a restless evil, full of deadly poison. With it we bless the Lord and Father, and with it we curse those who are made in the likeness of God. From the same mouth come blessing and cursing. My brothers and sisters, this ought not to

be so. Does a spring pour forth from the same opening both fresh and brackish water? Can a fig tree, my brothers and sisters, yield olives, or a grapevine figs? No more can salt water yield fresh.

The Gospel   **Mark 8:27-38**

Jesus went on with his disciples to the villages of Caesarea Philippi; and on the way he asked his disciples, "Who do people say that I am?" And they answered him, "John the Baptist; and others, Elijah; and still others, one of the prophets." He asked them, "But who do you say that I am?" Peter answered him, "You are the Messiah." And he sternly ordered them not to tell anyone about him. Then he began to teach them that the Son of Man must undergo great suffering, and be rejected by the elders, the chief priests, and the scribes, and be killed, and after three days rise again. He said all this quite openly. And Peter took him aside and began to rebuke him. But turning and looking at his disciples, he rebuked Peter and said, "Get behind me, Satan! For you are setting your mind not on divine things but on human things." He called the crowd with his disciples, and said to them, "If any want to become my followers, let them deny themselves and take up their cross and follow me. For those who want to save their life will lose it, and those who lose their life for my sake, and for the sake of the gospel will save it. For what will it profit them to gain the whole world and forfeit their life? Indeed, what can they give in return for their life? Those who are ashamed of me and of my words in this adulterous and sinful generation, of them the Son of Man will also be ashamed when he comes in the glory of his Father with the holy angels."

Year C

Jeremiah 4:11-12, 22-28	**or**	☩ *Exodus 32:7-14*
Psalm 14		☩ *Psalm 51:1-11*
	1 Timothy 1:12-17	
	Luke 15:1-10	

The Lesson   **Jeremiah 4:11-12, 22-28**

At that time it will be said to this people and to Jerusalem: A hot wind comes from me out of the bare heights in the desert toward my poor people, not to winnow or cleanse — a wind too strong for that. Now it is I who speak in judgment against them. "For my people are foolish, they do not know me; they are stupid children, they have no understanding. They are skilled in doing evil, but do not know how to do good." I looked on the earth, and lo, it was waste and void; and to the heavens, and they had no light. I looked on the mountains, and lo, they were quaking, and all the hills moved to and fro. I looked, and lo, there was no one at all, and all the birds of the air had fled. I looked, and lo, the fruitful land was a desert, and all its cities were laid in ruins before the

LORD, before his fierce anger. For thus says the LORD: The whole land shall be a desolation; yet I will not make a full end. Because of this the earth shall mourn, and the heavens above grow black; for I have spoken, I have purposed; I have not relented nor will I turn back.

The Response   Psalm 14

Psalm 14   *Dixit insipiens*

1   The fool has said in his heart, "There is no God." *
        All are corrupt and commit abominable acts;
        there is none who does any good.

2   The LORD looks down from heaven upon us all, *
        to see if there is any who is wise,
        if there is one who seeks after God.

3   Every one has proved faithless;
    all alike have turned bad; *
        there is none who does good; no, not one.

4   Have they no knowledge, all those evildoers *
        who eat up my people like bread
        and do not call upon the LORD?

5   See how they tremble with fear, *
        because God is in the company of the righteous.

6   Their aim is to confound the plans of the afflicted, *
        but the LORD is their refuge.

7   Oh, that Israel's deliverance would come out of Zion! *
        when the LORD restores the fortunes of his people,
        Jacob will rejoice and Israel be glad.

or, ✙ The Lesson   Exodus 32:7-14

The LORD said to Moses, "Go down at once! Your people, whom you brought up out of the land of Egypt, have acted perversely; they have been quick to turn aside from the way that I commanded them; they have cast for themselves an image of a calf, and have worshiped it and sacrificed to it, and said, 'These are your gods, O Israel, who brought you up out of the land of Egypt!' " The LORD said to Moses, "I have seen this people, how stiff-necked they are. Now let me alone, so that my wrath may burn hot against them and I may consume them; and of you I will make a great nation." But Moses implored the LORD his God, and said, "O LORD, why does your wrath burn hot against your people, whom you brought out of the land of Egypt with great power and with a mighty hand? Why should the Egyptians say, 'It was with evil intent that he brought them out to kill them in the mountains, and to consume them from the face of the earth?' Turn from your fierce wrath; change your mind and do not bring disaster on your people. Remember Abraham, Isaac, and Israel, your servants, how you swore to them by your own self, saying to them, 'I will multiply your descendants like the stars of heaven, and all this land that I have promised I will give to your descendants, and they shall inherit it forever.' " And the LORD changed his mind about the disaster that he planned to bring on his people.

✝ The Response   Psalm 51:1-11

Psalm 51:1-11   *Miserere mei, Deus*

1   Have mercy on me, O God, according to your
            loving-kindness; *
        in your great compassion blot out my offenses.
2   Wash me through and through from my wickedness *
        and cleanse me from my sin.
3   For I know my transgressions, *
        and my sin is ever before me.
4   Against you only have I sinned *
        and done what is evil in your sight.
5   And so you are justified when you speak *
        and upright in your judgment.
6   Indeed, I have been wicked from my birth, *
        a sinner from my mother's womb.
7   For behold, you look for truth deep within me, *
        and will make me understand wisdom secretly.
8   Purge me from my sin, and I shall be pure; *
        wash me, and I shall be clean indeed.
9   Make me hear of joy and gladness, *
        that the body you have broken may rejoice.
10   Hide your face from my sins *
        and blot out all my iniquities.
11   Create in me a clean heart, O God, *
        and renew a right spirit within me.

The Epistle   1 Timothy 1:12-17

I am grateful to Christ Jesus our Lord, who has strengthened me, because he judged me faithful and appointed me to his service, even though I was formerly a blasphemer, a persecutor, and a man of violence. But I received mercy because I had acted ignorantly in unbelief, and the grace of our Lord overflowed for me with the faith and love that are in Christ Jesus. The saying is sure and worthy of full acceptance, that Christ Jesus came into the world to save sinners — of whom I am the foremost. But for that very reason I received mercy, so that in me, as the foremost, Jesus Christ might display the utmost patience, making me an example to those who would come to believe in him for eternal life. To the King of the ages, immortal, invisible, the only God, be honor and glory forever and ever. Amen.

The Gospel   Luke 15:1-10

Now all the tax collectors and sinners were coming near to listen to Jesus. And the Pharisees and the scribes were grumbling and saying, "This fellow welcomes sinners and eats with them." So he told them this parable: "Which one of you, having a hundred sheep and losing one of them, does not leave the ninety-nine in the wilderness and go after the one that is lost until he finds it? When he has found it, he lays it on his shoulders and rejoices. And when he comes home, he calls together his friends and neighbors, saying to them, 'Rejoice with me, for I have found my sheep that was lost.' Just so, I tell you, there will be more joy in heaven over one sinner who repents than over ninety-nine righteous persons who need no repentance. Or what woman having ten silver coins, if she loses one of them, does not light a lamp, sweep the house, and search carefully until she finds it? When she has found it, she calls together her friends and neighbors, saying, 'Rejoice with me, for I have found the coin that I had lost.' Just so, I tell you, there is joy in the presence of the angels of God over one sinner who repents."

PROPER 20

Sunday between September 18 and September 24 inclusive

The Collect

Grant us, Lord, not to be anxious about earthly things, but to love things heavenly; and even now, while we are placed among things that are passing away, to hold fast to those that shall endure; through Jesus Christ our Lord, who lives and reigns with you and the Holy Spirit, one God, for ever and ever. *Amen.*

Year A

Exodus 16:2-15	**or**	✠ *Jonah 3:10—4:11*
Psalm 105:1-6, 37-45		✠ *Psalm 145:1-8*
	Philippians 1:21-30	
	Matthew 20:1-16	

The Lesson   Exodus 16:2-15

The whole congregation of the Israelites complained against Moses and Aaron in the wilderness. The Israelites said to them, "If only we had died by the hand of the LORD in the land of Egypt, when we sat by the fleshpots and ate our fill of bread; for you have brought us out into this wilderness to kill this whole assembly with hunger." Then the LORD said to Moses, "I am going to rain bread from heaven for you, and each day the people shall go out and gather enough for that day. In that way I will test them, whether they will follow my instruction or not. On the sixth day, when they prepare what they bring in, it will be twice as much as they gather on other days." So Moses and Aaron said to all the Israelites, "In the evening you shall know that it was the LORD who brought you out of the land of Egypt, and in the morning you shall see the glory of the LORD, because he has heard your complaining against the LORD. For what are we, that you complain against us?" And Moses said, "When the LORD gives you meat to eat in the evening and your fill of bread in the morning, because the LORD has heard the complaining that you utter against him — what are we? Your complaining is not against us but against the LORD." Then Moses said to Aaron, "Say to the whole congregation of the Israelites, 'Draw near to the LORD, for he has heard your complaining.' " And as Aaron spoke to the whole congregation of the Israelites, they looked toward the wilderness, and the glory of the LORD appeared in the cloud. The LORD spoke to Moses and said, "I have heard the complaining of the Israelites; say to them, 'At twilight you shall eat meat, and in the morning you shall have your fill of bread; then you shall know that I am the LORD your God.'" In the evening quails came up and covered the camp; and in the morning there was a layer of dew around the camp. When the layer of dew lifted, there on the surface of the wilderness was a fine flaky substance, as fine as frost on the ground. When the Israelites saw it, they said to one another, "What is it?" For they did not know what it was. Moses said to them, "It is the bread that the LORD has given you to eat."

The Response   **Psalm 105:1-6, 37-45**

Psalm 105:1-6, 37-45   *Confitemini Domino*

  1   Give thanks to the LORD and call upon his Name; *
       make known his deeds among the peoples.

  2   Sing to him, sing praises to him, *
       and speak of all his marvelous works.

  3   Glory in his holy Name; *
       let the hearts of those who seek the LORD rejoice.

  4   Search for the LORD and his strength; *
       continually seek his face.

  5   Remember the marvels he has done, *
       his wonders and the judgments of his mouth,

  6   O offspring of Abraham his servant, *
       O children of Jacob his chosen.

 37   He led out his people with silver and gold; *
       in all their tribes there was not one that stumbled.

38   Egypt was glad of their going, *
      because they were afraid of them.

39   He spread out a cloud for a covering *
      and a fire to give light in the night season.

40   They asked, and quails appeared, *
      and he satisfied them with bread from heaven.

41   He opened the rock, and water flowed, *
      so the river ran in the dry places.

42   For God remembered his holy word *
      and Abraham his servant.

43   So he led forth his people with gladness, *
      his chosen with shouts of joy.

44   He gave his people the lands of the nations, *
      and they took the fruit of others' toil,

45   That they might keep his statutes *
      and observe his laws.
      Hallelujah!

or, ✠ The Lesson   Jonah 3:10—4:11

When God saw what the Ninevites did, how they turned from their evil ways, God changed his mind about the calamity that he had said he would bring upon them; and he did not do it. But this was very displeasing to Jonah, and he became angry. He prayed to the LORD and said, "O LORD! Is not this what I said while I was still in my own country? That is why I fled to Tarshish at the beginning; for I knew that you are a gracious God and merciful, slow to anger, and abounding in steadfast love, and ready to relent from punishing. And now, O LORD, please take my life from me, for it is better for me to die than to live." And the LORD said, "Is it right for you to be angry?" Then Jonah went out of the city and sat down east of the city, and made a booth for himself there. He sat under it in the shade, waiting to see what would become of the city. The LORD God appointed a bush, and made it come up over Jonah, to give shade over his head, to save him from his discomfort; so Jonah was very happy about the bush. But when dawn came up the next day, God appointed a worm that attacked the bush, so that it withered. When the sun rose, God prepared a sultry east wind, and the sun beat down on the head of Jonah so that he was faint and asked that he might die. He said, "It is better for me to die than to live." But God said to Jonah, "Is it right for you to be angry about the bush?" And he said, "Yes, angry enough to die." Then the LORD said, "You are concerned about the bush, for which you did not labor and which you did not grow; it came into being in a night and perished in a night. And should I not be concerned about Nineveh, that great city, in which there are more than a hundred and twenty thousand persons who do not know their right hand from their left, and also many animals?"

☩ The Response   Psalm 145:1-8

Psalm 145:1-8 *Exaltabo te, Deus*

1 I will exalt you, O God my King, *
       and bless your Name for ever and ever.
2 Every day will I bless you *
       and praise your Name for ever and ever.
3 Great is the LORD and greatly to be praised; *
       there is no end to his greatness.
4 One generation shall praise your works to another *
       and shall declare your power.
5 I will ponder the glorious splendor of your majesty *
       and all your marvelous works.
6 They shall speak of the might of your wondrous acts, *
       and I will tell of your greatness.
7 They shall publish the remembrance of your great goodness; *
       they shall sing of your righteous deeds.
8 The LORD is gracious and full of compassion, *
       slow to anger and of great kindness.

The Epistle   Philippians 1:21-30

For to me, living is Christ and dying is gain. If I am to live in the flesh, that
means fruitful labor for me; and I do not know which I prefer. I am hard
pressed between the two: my desire is to depart and be with Christ, for that is
far better; but to remain in the flesh is more necessary for you. Since I am
convinced of this, I know that I will remain and continue with all of you for
your progress and joy in faith, so that I may share abundantly in your boasting in Christ Jesus when I come to you again. Only, live your life in a manner
worthy of the gospel of Christ, so that, whether I come and see you or am
absent and hear about you, I will know that you are standing firm in one
spirit, striving side by side with one mind for the faith of the gospel, and are in
no way intimidated by your opponents. For them this is evidence of their
destruction, but of your salvation. And this is God's doing. For he has graciously granted you the privilege not only of believing in Christ, but of
suffering for him as well — since you are having the same struggle that you
saw I had and now hear that I still have.

The Gospel   Matthew 20:1-16

Jesus said, "For the kingdom of heaven is like a landowner who went out early
in the morning to hire laborers for his vineyard. After agreeing with the
laborers for the usual daily wage, he sent them into his vineyard. When he
went out about nine o'clock, he saw others standing idle in the marketplace;
and he said to them, 'You also go into the vineyard, and I will pay you what-

ever is right.' So they went. When he went out again about noon and about three o'clock, he did the same. And about five o'clock he went out and found others standing around; and he said to them, 'Why are you standing here idle all day?' They said to him, 'Because no one has hired us.' He said to them, 'You also go into the vineyard.' When evening came, the owner of the vineyard said to his manager, 'Call the laborers and give them their pay, beginning with the last and then going to the first.' When those hired about five o'clock came, each of them received the usual daily wage. Now when the first came, they thought they would receive more; but each of them also received the usual daily wage. And when they received it, they grumbled against the landowner, saying, 'These last worked only one hour, and you have made them equal to us who have borne the burden of the day and the scorching heat.' But he replied to one of them, 'Friend, I am doing you no wrong; did you not agree with me for the usual daily wage? Take what belongs to you and go; I choose to give to this last the same as I give to you. Am I not allowed to do what I choose with what belongs to me? Or are you envious because I am generous?' So the last will be first, and the first will be last."

Year B

Proverbs 31:10-31	**or**	✢ *Wisdom of Solomon 1:16—2:1, 12-22*
Psalm 1		or *Jeremiah 11:18-20*
		✢ *Psalm 54*

James 3:13—4:3, 7-8a
Mark 9:30-37

The Lesson   Proverbs 31:10-31

A capable wife who can find? She is far more precious than jewels. The heart of her husband trusts in her, and he will have no lack of gain. She does him good, and not harm, all the days of her life. She seeks wool and flax, and works with willing hands. She is like the ships of the merchant, she brings her food from far away. She rises while it is still night and provides food for her household and tasks for her servant girls. She considers a field and buys it; with the fruit of her hands she plants a vineyard. She girds herself with strength, and makes her arms strong. She perceives that her merchandise is profitable. Her lamp does not go out at night. She puts her hands to the distaff, and her hands hold the spindle. She opens her hand to the poor, and reaches out her hands to the needy. She is not afraid for her household when it snows, for all her household are clothed in crimson. She makes herself coverings; her clothing is fine linen and purple. Her husband is known in the city gates, taking his seat among the elders of the land. She makes linen garments and sells them; she supplies the merchant with sashes. Strength and dignity are her clothing, and she laughs at the time to come. She opens her mouth with wisdom, and the teaching of kindness is on her tongue. She looks well to the ways of her household, and does not eat the bread of idleness. Her children rise up and call her happy; her husband too, and he praises her: "Many women have done excellently, but you surpass them all." Charm is deceitful, and beauty is vain, but a woman who fears the LORD is to be praised. Give her a share in the fruit of her hands, and let her works praise her in the city gates.

The Response   Psalm 1

Psalm 1   *Beatus vir qui non abiit*

1   Happy are they who have not walked in the counsel of
              the wicked, *
         nor lingered in the way of sinners,
         nor sat in the seats of the scornful!
2   Their delight is in the law of the LORD, *
         and they meditate on his law day and night.
3   They are like trees planted by streams of water,
         bearing fruit in due season, with leaves that do not wither; *
         everything they do shall prosper.
4   It is not so with the wicked; *
         they are like chaff which the wind blows away.
5   Therefore the wicked shall not stand upright when
              judgment comes, *
         nor the sinner in the council of the righteous.
6   For the LORD knows the way of the righteous, *
         but the way of the wicked is doomed.

or, ✝ **The Lesson**   **Wisdom of Solomon 1:16—2:1, 12-22**
                                       or ✝ **Jeremiah 11:18-20**

Wisdom of Solomon 1:16—2:1, 12-22

The ungodly by their words and deeds summoned death; considering him a friend, they pined away and made a covenant with him, because they are fit to belong to his company. For they reasoned unsoundly, saying to themselves, "Short and sorrowful is our life, and there is no remedy when a life comes to its end, and no one has been known to return from Hades. Let us lie in wait for the righteous man, because he is inconvenient to us and opposes our actions; he reproaches us for sins against the law, and accuses us of sins against our training. He professes to have knowledge of God, and calls himself a child of the Lord. He became to us a reproof of our thoughts; the very sight of him is a burden to us, because his manner of life is unlike that of others, and his ways are strange. We are considered by him as something base, and he avoids our ways as unclean; he calls the last end of the righteous happy, and boasts that God is his father. Let us see if his words are true, and let us test what will happen at the end of his life; for if the righteous man is

God's child, he will help him, and will deliver him from the hand of his adversaries. Let us test him with insult and torture, so that we may find out how gentle he is, and make trial of his forbearance. Let us condemn him to a shameful death, for, according to what he says, he will be protected." Thus they reasoned, but they were led astray, for their wickedness blinded them, and they did not know the secret purposes of God, nor hoped for the wages of holiness, nor discerned the prize for blameless souls.

or, ✠ Jeremiah 11:18-20

It was the LORD who made it known to me, and I knew; then you showed me their evil deeds. But I was like a gentle lamb led to the slaughter. And I did not know it was against me that they devised schemes, saying, "Let us destroy the tree with its fruit, let us cut him off from the land of the living, so that his name will no longer be remembered!" But you, O LORD of hosts, who judge righteously, who try the heart and the mind, let me see your retribution upon them, for to you I have committed my cause.

✠ The Response   Psalm 54

Psalm 54   *Deus, in nomine*

1   Save me, O God, by your Name; *
    in your might, defend my cause.
2   Hear my prayer, O God; *
    give ear to the words of my mouth.
3   For the arrogant have risen up against me,
  and the ruthless have sought my life, *
    those who have no regard for God.
4   Behold, God is my helper; *
    it is the LORD who sustains my life.
5   Render evil to those who spy on me; *
    in your faithfulness, destroy them.
6   I will offer you a freewill sacrifice *
    and praise your Name, O LORD, for it is good.
7   For you have rescued me from every trouble, *
    and my eye has seen the ruin of my foes.

The Epistle   James 3:13—4:3, 7-8*a*

Who is wise and understanding among you? Show by your good life that your works are done with gentleness born of wisdom. But if you have bitter envy and selfish ambition in your hearts, do not be boastful and false to the truth. Such wisdom does not come down from above, but is earthly, unspiritual, devilish. For where there is envy and selfish ambition, there will also be disorder and wickedness of every kind. But the wisdom from above is first pure, then peaceable, gentle, willing to yield, full of mercy and good fruits, without a trace of partiality or hypocrisy. And a harvest of righteousness is sown in peace for those who make peace. Those conflicts and disputes among you, where do they come from? Do they not come from your cravings that are at war within you? You want something and do not have it; so you commit murder. And you covet something and cannot obtain it; so you engage in disputes and conflicts. You do not have, because you do not ask. You ask and do not receive, because you ask wrongly, in order to spend what you get on your pleasures. Submit yourselves therefore to God. Resist the devil, and he will flee from you. Draw near to God, and he will draw near to you.

The Gospel   Mark 9:30-37

Jesus and his disciples went on from there and passed through Galilee. He did not want anyone to know it; for he was teaching his disciples, saying to them, "The Son of Man is to be betrayed into human hands, and they will kill him, and three days after being killed, he will rise again." But they did not understand what he was saying and were afraid to ask him. Then they came to Capernaum; and when he was in the house he asked them, "What were you arguing about on the way?" But they were silent, for on the way they had argued with one another who was the greatest. He sat down, called the twelve, and said to them, "Whoever wants to be first must be last of all and servant of all." Then he took a little child and put it among them; and taking it in his arms, he said to them, "Whoever welcomes one such child in my name welcomes me, and whoever welcomes me welcomes not me but the one who sent me."

Year C

Jeremiah 8:18—9:1	**or**	✝ *Amos 8:4-7*
Psalm 79:1-9		✝ *Psalm 113*

1 Timothy 2:1-7
Luke 16:1-13

The Lesson   Jeremiah 8:18—9:1

My joy is gone, grief is upon me, my heart is sick. Hark, the cry of my poor people from far and wide in the land: "Is the LORD not in Zion? Is her King not in her?" ("Why have they provoked me to anger with their images, with their foreign idols?") "The harvest is past, the summer is ended, and we are not saved." For the hurt of my poor people I am hurt, I mourn, and dismay has taken hold of me. Is there no balm in Gilead? Is there no physician there? Why then has the health of my poor people not been restored? O that my head were a spring of water, and my eyes a fountain of tears, so that I might weep day and night for the slain of my poor people!

The Response

Psalm 79:1-9

Psalm 79:1-9 *Deus, venerunt*

1 O God, the heathen have come into your inheritance;
they have profaned your holy temple; *
they have made Jerusalem a heap of rubble.

2 They have given the bodies of your servants as food for the
birds of the air, *
and the flesh of your faithful ones to the beasts of the field.

3 They have shed their blood like water on every side
of Jerusalem, *
and there was no one to bury them.

4 We have become a reproach to our neighbors, *
an object of scorn and derision to those around us.

5 How long will you be angry, O Lord? *
will your fury blaze like fire for ever?

6 Pour out your wrath upon the heathen who have not
known you *
and upon the kingdoms that have not called upon
your Name.

7 For they have devoured Jacob *
and made his dwelling a ruin.

8 Remember not our past sins;
let your compassion be swift to meet us; *
for we have been brought very low.

9 Help us, O God our Savior, for the glory of your Name; *
deliver us and forgive us our sins, for your Name's sake.

or, ✠ The Lesson

Amos 8:4-7

Hear this, you that trample on the needy, and bring to ruin the poor of the land, saying, "When will the new moon be over so that we may sell grain; and the sabbath, so that we may offer wheat for sale? We will make the ephah small and the shekel great, and practice deceit with false balances, buying the poor for silver and the needy for a pair of sandals, and selling the sweepings of the wheat." The Lord has sworn by the pride of Jacob: Surely I will never forget any of their deeds.

✠ The Response

Psalm 113

Psalm 113 *Laudate, pueri*

1 Hallelujah!
Give praise, you servants of the Lord; *
praise the Name of the Lord.

2   Let the Name of the LORD be blessed, *
        from this time forth for evermore.

3   From the rising of the sun to its going down *
        let the Name of the LORD be praised.

4   The LORD is high above all nations, *
        and his glory above the heavens.

5   Who is like the LORD our God, who sits enthroned on high *
        but stoops to behold the heavens and the earth?

6   He takes up the weak out of the dust *
        and lifts up the poor from the ashes.

7   He sets them with the princes, *
        with the princes of his people.

8   He makes the woman of a childless house *
        to be a joyful mother of children.

The Epistle   1 Timothy 2:1-7

First of all, then, I urge that supplications, prayers, intercessions, and thanksgivings be made for everyone, for kings and all who are in high positions, so
that we may lead a quiet and peaceable life in all godliness and dignity. This is
right and is acceptable in the sight of God our Savior, who desires everyone to
be saved and to come to the knowledge of the truth. For there is one God;
there is also one mediator between God and humankind, Christ Jesus, himself
human, who gave himself a ransom for all — this was attested at the right
time. For this I was appointed a herald and an apostle (I am telling the truth, I
am not lying), a teacher of the Gentiles in faith and truth.

The Gospel   Luke 16:1-13

Jesus said to the disciples, "There was a rich man who had a manager, and
charges were brought to him that this man was squandering his property. So
he summoned him and said to him, 'What is this that I hear about you? Give
me an accounting of your management, because you cannot be my manager
any longer.' Then the manager said to himself, 'What will I do, now that my
master is taking the position away from me? I am not strong enough to dig,
and I am ashamed to beg. I have decided what to do so that, when I am
dismissed as manager, people may welcome me into their homes.' So, summoning his master's debtors one by one, he asked the first, 'How much do you
owe my master?' He answered, 'A hundred jugs of olive oil.' He said to him,
'Take your bill, sit down quickly, and make it fifty.' Then he asked another,
'And how much do you owe?' He replied, 'A hundred containers of wheat.'
He said to him, 'Take your bill and make it eighty.' And his master commended the dishonest manager because he had acted shrewdly; for the children
of this age are more shrewd in dealing with their own generation than are the

children of light. And I tell you, make friends for yourselves by means of dishonest wealth so that when it is gone, they may welcome you into the eternal homes. Whoever is faithful in a very little is faithful also in much; and whoever is dishonest in a very little is dishonest also in much. If then you have not been faithful with the dishonest wealth, who will entrust to you the true riches? And if you have not been faithful with what belongs to another, who will give you what is your own? No slave can serve two masters; for a slave will either hate the one and love the other, or be devoted to the one and despise the other. You cannot serve God and wealth."

PROPER 21

Sunday between September 25 and October 1 inclusive

The Collect

O God, you declare your almighty power chiefly in showing mercy and pity: Grant us the fullness of your grace, that we, running to obtain your promises, may become partakers of your heavenly treasure; through Jesus Christ our Lord, who lives and reigns with you and the Holy Spirit, one God, for ever and ever. *Amen.*

Year A

Exodus 17:1-7	**or**	✛ *Ezekiel 18:1-4, 25-32*
Psalm 78:1-4, 12-16		✛ *Psalm 25:1-8*

Philippians 2:1-13
Matthew 21:23-32

The Lesson   Exodus 17:1-7

From the wilderness of Sin the whole congregation of the Israelites journeyed by stages, as the LORD commanded. They camped at Rephidim, but there was no water for the people to drink. The people quarreled with Moses, and said, "Give us water to drink." Moses said to them, "Why do you quarrel with me? Why do you test the LORD?" But the people thirsted there for water; and the people complained against Moses and said, "Why did you bring us out of Egypt, to kill us and our children and livestock with thirst?" So Moses cried out to the LORD, "What shall I do with this people? They are almost ready to stone me." The LORD said to Moses, "Go on ahead of the people, and take some of the elders of Israel with you; take in your hand the staff with which you struck the Nile, and go. I will be standing there in front of you on the rock at Horeb. Strike the rock, and water will come out of it, so that the people may drink." Moses did so, in the sight of the elders of Israel. He called the place Massah and Meribah, because the Israelites quarreled and tested the LORD, saying, "Is the LORD among us or not?"

The Response   **Psalm 78:1-4, 12-16**

Psalm 78:1-4, 12-16   *Attendite, popule*

1   Hear my teaching, O my people; *
        incline your ears to the words of my mouth.

2   I will open my mouth in a parable; *
        I will declare the mysteries of ancient times.

3   That which we have heard and known,
        and what our forefathers have told us, *
        we will not hide from their children.

4   We will recount to generations to come
        the praiseworthy deeds and the power of the LORD, *
        and the wonderful works he has done.

12   He worked marvels in the sight of their forefathers, *
        in the land of Egypt, in the field of Zoan.

13   He split open the sea and let them pass through; *
        he made the waters stand up like walls.

14   He led them with a cloud by day, *
        and all the night through with a glow of fire.

15   He split the hard rocks in the wilderness *
        and gave them drink as from the great deep.

16   He brought streams out of the cliff, *
        and the waters gushed out like rivers.

---

or, ✠ **The Lesson**   **Ezekiel 18:1-4, 25-32**

The word of the LORD came to me: What do you mean by repeating this
proverb concerning the land of Israel, "The parents have eaten sour grapes,
and the children's teeth are set on edge"? As I live, says the LORD God, this
proverb shall no more be used by you in Israel. Know that all lives are mine;
the life of the parent as well as the life of the child is mine: it is only the
person who sins that shall die. Yet you say, "The way of the LORD is unfair."
Hear now, O house of Israel: Is my way unfair? Is it not your ways that are
unfair? When the righteous turn away from their righteousness and commit
iniquity, they shall die for it; for the iniquity that they have committed they
shall die. Again, when the wicked turn away from the wickedness they have
committed and do what is lawful and right, they shall save their life. Because
they considered and turned away from all the transgressions that they had
committed, they shall surely live; they shall not die. Yet the house of Israel
says, "The way of the LORD is unfair." O house of Israel, are my ways unfair?
Is it not your ways that are unfair? Therefore I will judge you, O house of
Israel, all of you according to your ways, says the Lord GOD. Repent and turn
from all your transgressions; otherwise iniquity will be your ruin. Cast away
from you all the transgressions that you have committed against me, and get
yourselves a new heart and a new spirit! Why will you die, O house of Israel?

For I have no pleasure in the death of anyone, says the Lord GOD. Turn, then, and live.

✠ The Response
Psalm 25:1-8

Psalm 25:1-8   *Ad te, Domine, levavi*

1   To you, O LORD, I lift up my soul;
    my God, I put my trust in you; *
        let me not be humiliated,
        nor let my enemies triumph over me.
2   Let none who look to you be put to shame; *
        let the treacherous be disappointed in their schemes.
3   Show me your ways, O LORD, *
        and teach me your paths.
4   Lead me in your truth and teach me, *
        for you are the God of my salvation;
        in you have I trusted all the day long.
5   Remember, O LORD, your compassion and love, *
        for they are from everlasting.
6   Remember not the sins of my youth and my transgressions; *
        remember me according to your love
        and for the sake of your goodness, O LORD.
7   Gracious and upright is the LORD; *
        therefore he teaches sinners in his way.
8   He guides the humble in doing right *
        and teaches his way to the lowly.

The Epistle
Philippians 2:1-13

If there is any encouragement in Christ, any consolation from love, any sharing in the Spirit, any compassion and sympathy, make my joy complete: be of the same mind, having the same love, being in full accord and of one mind. Do nothing from selfish ambition or conceit, but in humility regard others as better than yourselves. Let each of you look not to your own interests, but to the interests of others. Let the same mind be in you that was in Christ Jesus, who, though he was in the form of God, did not regard equality with God as something to be exploited, but emptied himself, taking the form of a slave, being born in human likeness. And being found in human form, he humbled himself and became obedient to the point of death — even death on a cross. Therefore God also highly exalted him and gave him the name that is above every name, so that at the name of Jesus every knee should bend, in heaven and on earth and under the earth, and every tongue should confess that Jesus Christ is Lord, to the glory of God the Father. Therefore, my beloved, just as you have always obeyed me, not only in my presence, but much more now in my absence, work out your own salvation with fear and trembling; for it is God who is at work in you, enabling you both to will and to work for his good pleasure.

The Gospel   Matthew 21:23-32

When Jesus entered the temple, the chief priests and the elders of the people came to him as he was teaching, and said, "By what authority are you doing these things, and who gave you this authority?" Jesus said to them, "I will also ask you one question; if you tell me the answer, then I will also tell you by what authority I do these things. Did the baptism of John come from heaven, or was it of human origin?" And they argued with one another, "If we say, 'From heaven,' he will say to us, 'Why then did you not believe him?' But if we say, 'Of human origin,' we are afraid of the crowd; for all regard John as a prophet." So they answered Jesus, "We do not know." And he said to them, "Neither will I tell you by what authority I am doing these things. What do you think? A man had two sons; he went to the first and said, 'Son, go and work in the vineyard today.' He answered, 'I will not'; but later he changed his mind and went. The father went to the second and said the same; and he answered, 'I go, sir'; but he did not go. Which of the two did the will of his father?" They said, "The first." Jesus said to them, "Truly I tell you, the tax collectors and the prostitutes are going into the kingdom of God ahead of you. For John came to you in the way of righteousness and you did not believe him, but the tax collectors and the prostitutes believed him; and even after you saw it, you did not change your minds and believe him."

Year B

Esther 7:1-6, 9-10; 9:20-22   **or**   ✠ *Numbers 11:4-6, 10-16, 24-29*
Psalm 124   ✠ *Psalm 19:7-14*
James 5:13-20
Mark 9:38-50

The Lesson   Esther 7:1-6, 9-10; 9:20-22

The king and Haman went in to feast with Queen Esther. On the second day, as they were drinking wine, the king again said to Esther, "What is your petition, Queen Esther? It shall be granted you. And what is your request? Even to the half of my kingdom, it shall be fulfilled." Then Queen Esther answered, "If I have won your favor, O king, and if it pleases the king, let my life be given me — that is my petition — and the lives of my people — that is my request. For we have been sold, I and my people, to be destroyed, to be killed, and to be annihilated. If we had been sold merely as slaves, men and women, I would have held my peace; but no enemy can compensate for this damage to the king." Then King Ahasuerus said to Queen Esther, "Who is he, and where is he, who has presumed to do this?" Esther said, "A foe and enemy, this wicked Haman!" Then Haman was terrified before the king and the queen. Then Harbona, one of the eunuchs in attendance on the king, said, "Look, the very gallows that Haman has prepared for Mordecai, whose word saved the king, stands at Haman's house, fifty cubits high." And the king said, "Hang him on that." So they hanged Haman on the gallows that he had prepared for Mordecai. Then the anger of the king abated. Mordecai recorded these things, and sent letters to all the Jews who were in all the provinces of King Ahasuerus, both near and far, enjoining them that they should keep the fourteenth day of the month Adar and also the fifteenth day of the same month, year by year, as the days on which the Jews gained relief from their enemies, and as the month that had been turned for them from sorrow into gladness and from mourning into a holiday; that they should make them days of feasting and gladness, days for sending gifts of food to one another and presents to the poor.

The Response   Psalm 124

Psalm 124 *Nisi quia Dominus*

1   If the LORD had not been on our side, *
        let Israel now say;
2   If the LORD had not been on our side, *
        when enemies rose up against us;
3   Then would they have swallowed us up alive *
        in their fierce anger toward us;
4   Then would the waters have overwhelmed us *
        and the torrent gone over us;
5   Then would the raging waters *
        have gone right over us.
6   Blessed be the LORD! *
        he has not given us over to be a prey for their teeth.
7   We have escaped like a bird from the snare of the fowler; *
        the snare is broken, and we have escaped.
8   Our help is in the Name of the LORD, *
        the maker of heaven and earth.

or, ✠ Numbers 11:4-6, 10-16, 24-29

The rabble among them had a strong craving; and the Israelites also wept again, and said, "If only we had meat to eat! We remember the fish we used to eat in Egypt for nothing, the cucumbers, the melons, the leeks, the onions, and the garlic; but now our strength is dried up, and there is nothing at all but this manna to look at." Moses heard the people weeping throughout their families, all at the entrances of their tents. Then the LORD became very angry, and Moses was displeased. So Moses said to the LORD, "Why have you treated your servant so badly? Why have I not found favor in your sight, that you lay the burden of all this people on me? Did I conceive all this people? Did I give birth to them, that you should say to me, 'Carry them in your bosom, as a nurse carries a sucking child,' to the land that you promised on oath to their ancestors? Where am I to get meat to give to all this people? For they come weeping to me and say, 'Give us meat to eat!' I am not able to carry all this people alone, for they are too heavy for me. If this is the way you are going to treat me, put me to death at once — if I have found favor in your sight - and do not let me see my misery." So the LORD said to Moses, "Gather for me seventy of the elders of Israel, whom you know to be the elders of the people and officers over them; bring them to the tent of meeting, and have them take their place there with you." So Moses went out and told the people the words of the LORD; and he gathered seventy elders of the people, and placed them all around the tent. Then the LORD came down in the cloud and spoke to him, and took some of the spirit that was on him and put it on the seventy elders; and when the spirit rested upon them, they prophesied. But they did not do so again. Two men remained in the camp, one named Eldad, and the other named Medad, and the spirit rested on them; they were among those registered, but they had not gone out to the tent, and so they prophesied in the camp. And a young man ran and told Moses, "Eldad and Medad are prophesying in the camp." And Joshua son of Nun, the assistant of Moses, one of his chosen men, said, "My lord Moses, stop them!" But Moses said to him, "Are you jealous for my sake? Would that all the LORD's people were prophets, and that the LORD would put his spirit on them!"

☩ The Response   Psalm 19:7-14

Psalm 19:7-14   *Caeli enarrant*

7   The law of the LORD is perfect
                and revives the soul; *
        the testimony of the LORD is sure
                and gives wisdom to the innocent.
8   The statutes of the LORD are just
                and rejoice the heart; *
        the commandment of the LORD is clear
                and gives light to the eyes.
9   The fear of the LORD is clean
                and endures for ever; *
        the judgments of the LORD are true
                and righteous altogether.
10 More to be desired are they than gold,
                more than much fine gold, *

sweeter far than honey,
than honey in the comb.
11 By them also is your servant enlightened, *
and in keeping them there is great reward.
12 Who can tell how often he offends? *
cleanse me from my secret faults.
13 Above all, keep your servant from presumptuous sins;
let them not get dominion over me; *
then shall I be whole and sound,
and innocent of a great offense.
14 Let the words of my mouth and the meditation of my
heart be acceptable in your sight, *
O LORD, my strength and my redeemer.

The Epistle   James 5:13-20

Are any among you suffering? They should pray. Are any cheerful? They should sing songs of praise. Are any among you sick? They should call for the elders of the church and have them pray over them, anointing them with oil in the name of the Lord. The prayer of faith will save the sick, and the Lord will raise them up; and anyone who has committed sins will be forgiven. Therefore confess your sins to one another, and pray for one another, so that you may be healed. The prayer of the righteous is powerful and effective. Elijah was a human being like us, and he prayed fervently that it might not rain, and for three years and six months it did not rain on the earth. Then he prayed again, and the heaven gave rain and the earth yielded its harvest. My brothers and sisters, if anyone among you wanders from the truth and is brought back by another, you should know that whoever brings back a sinner from wandering will save the sinner's soul from death and will cover a multitude of sins.

The Gospel   Mark 9:38-50

John said to Jesus, "Teacher, we saw someone casting out demons in your name, and we tried to stop him, because he was not following us." But Jesus said, "Do not stop him; for no one who does a deed of power in my name will be able soon afterward to speak evil of me. Whoever is not against us is for us. For truly I tell you, whoever gives you a cup of water to drink because you bear the name of Christ will by no means lose the reward. If any of you put a stumbling block before one of these little ones who believe in me, it would be better for you if a great millstone were hung around your neck and you were thrown into the sea. If your hand causes you to stumble, cut it off; it is better for you to enter life maimed than to have two hands and to go to hell, to the unquenchable fire. And if your foot causes you to stumble, cut it off; it is better for you to enter life lame than to have two feet and to be thrown into hell. And if your eye causes you to stumble, tear it out; it is better for you to enter the kingdom of God with one eye than to have two eyes and to be thrown into hell, where their worm never dies, and the fire is never quenched. For everyone will be salted with fire. Salt is good; but if salt has lost its saltiness, how can you season it? Have salt in yourselves, and be at peace with one another."

Year C

Jeremiah 32:1-3a, 6-15	**or**	✠ *Amos 6:1a, 4-7*
Psalm 91:1-6, 14-16		✠ *Psalm 146*
	1 Timothy 6:6-19	
	Luke 16:19-31	

The Lesson   Jeremiah 32:1-3*a*, 6-15

The word that came to Jeremiah from the LORD in the tenth year of King Zedekiah of Judah, which was the eighteenth year of Nebuchadrezzar. At that time the army of the king of Babylon was besieging Jerusalem, and the prophet Jeremiah was confined in the court of the guard that was in the palace of the king of Judah, where King Zedekiah of Judah had confined him. Jeremiah said, The word of the LORD came to me: Hanamel son of your uncle Shallum is going to come to you and say, "Buy my field that is at Anathoth, for the right of redemption by purchase is yours." Then my cousin Hanamel came to me in the court of the guard, in accordance with the word of the LORD, and said to me, "Buy my field that is at Anathoth in the land of Benjamin, for the right of possession and redemption is yours; buy it for yourself." Then I knew that this was the word of the LORD. And I bought the field at Anathoth from my cousin Hanamel, and weighed out the money to him, seventeen shekels of silver. I signed the deed, sealed it, got witnesses, and weighed the money on scales. Then I took the sealed deed of purchase, containing the terms and conditions, and the open copy; and I gave the deed of purchase to Baruch son of Neriah son of Mahseiah, in the presence of my cousin Hanamel, in the presence of the witnesses who signed the deed of purchase, and in the presence of all the Judeans who were sitting in the court of the guard. In their presence I charged Baruch, saying, Thus says the LORD of hosts, the God of Israel: Take these deeds, both this sealed deed of purchase and this open deed, and put them in an earthenware jar, in order that they may last for a long time. For thus says the LORD of hosts, the God of Israel: Houses and fields and vineyards shall again be bought in this land.

The Response   Psalm 91:1-6, 14-16

Psalm 91:1-6, 14-16   *Qui habitat*

1   He who dwells in the shelter of the Most High, *
         abides under the shadow of the Almighty.
2   He shall say to the LORD,
         "You are my refuge and my stronghold, *
         my God in whom I put my trust."
3   He shall deliver you from the snare of the hunter *
         and from the deadly pestilence.
4   He shall cover you with his pinions,
         and you shall find refuge under his wings; *
         his faithfulness shall be a shield and buckler.
5   You shall not be afraid of any terror by night, *
         nor of the arrow that flies by day;
6   Of the plague that stalks in the darkness, *
         nor of the sickness that lays waste at mid-day.
14   Because he is bound to me in love,
         therefore will I deliver him; *
         I will protect him, because he knows my Name.
15   He shall call upon me, and I will answer him; *
         I am with him in trouble;
         I will rescue him and bring him to honor.
16   With long life will I satisfy him, *
         and show him my salvation.

or, ✠ The Lesson   Amos 6:1*a*, 4-7

Alas for those who are at ease in Zion, and for those who feel secure on
Mount Samaria, alas for those who lie on beds of ivory, and lounge on their
couches, and eat lambs from the flock, and calves from the stall; who sing idle
songs to the sound of the harp, and like David improvise on instruments of
music; who drink wine from bowls, and anoint themselves with the finest oils,
but are not grieved over the ruin of Joseph! Therefore they shall now be the
first to go into exile, and the revelry of the loungers shall pass away.

✠ The Response   Psalm 146

Psalm 146   *Lauda, anima mea*

1   Hallelujah!
     Praise the LORD, O my soul! *
         I will praise the LORD as long as I live;
         I will sing praises to my God while I have my being.
2   Put not your trust in rulers, nor in any child of earth, *
         for there is no help in them.

3   When they breathe their last, they return to earth, *
      and in that day their thoughts perish.

4   Happy are they who have the God of Jacob for their help! *
      whose hope is in the LORD their God;

5   Who made heaven and earth, the seas, and all that is in them; *
      who keeps his promise for ever;

6   Who gives justice to those who are oppressed, *
      and food to those who hunger.

7   The LORD sets the prisoners free;
    the LORD opens the eyes of the blind; *
      the LORD lifts up those who are bowed down;

8   The LORD loves the righteous;
    the LORD cares for the stranger; *
      he sustains the orphan and widow,
      but frustrates the way of the wicked.

9   The LORD shall reign for ever, *
      your God, O Zion, throughout all generations.
      Hallelujah!

The Epistle   1 Timothy 6:6-19

There is great gain in godliness combined with contentment; for we brought nothing into the world, so that we can take nothing out of it; but if we have food and clothing, we will be content with these. But those who want to be rich fall into temptation and are trapped by many senseless and harmful desires that plunge people into ruin and destruction. For the love of money is a root of all kinds of evil, and in their eagerness to be rich some have wandered away from the faith and pierced themselves with many pains. As for you, man of God, shun all this; pursue righteousness, godliness, faith, love, endurance, gentleness. Fight the good fight of the faith; take hold of the eternal life, to which you were called and for which you made the good confession in the presence of many witnesses. In the presence of God, who gives life to all things, and of Christ Jesus, who in his testimony before Pontius Pilate made the good confession, I charge you to keep the commandment without spot or blame until the manifestation of our Lord Jesus Christ, which he will bring about at the right time — he who is the blessed and only Sovereign, the King of kings and Lord of lords. It is he alone who has immortality and dwells in unapproachable light, whom no one has ever seen or can see; to him be honor and eternal dominion. Amen. As for those who in the present age are rich, command them not to be haughty, or to set their hopes on the uncertainty of riches, but rather on God who richly provides us with everything for our enjoyment. They are to do good, to be rich in good works, generous, and ready to share, thus storing up for themselves the treasure of a good foundation for the future, so that they may take hold of the life that really is life.

The Gospel   Luke 16:19-31

Jesus said to the Pharisees, "There was a rich man who was dressed in purple and fine linen and who feasted sumptuously every day. And at his gate lay a poor man named Lazarus, covered with sores, who longed to satisfy his hunger with what fell from the rich man's table; even the dogs would come and lick his sores. The poor man died and was carried away by the angels to be with Abraham. The rich man also died and was buried. In Hades, where he was being tormented, he looked up and saw Abraham far away with Lazarus by his side. He called out, 'Father Abraham, have mercy on me, and send Lazarus to dip the tip of his finger in water and cool my tongue; for I am in agony in these flames.' But Abraham said, 'Child, remember that during your lifetime you received your good things, and Lazarus in like manner evil things; but now he is comforted here, and you are in agony. Besides all this, between you and us a great chasm has been fixed, so that those who might want to pass from here to you cannot do so, and no one can cross from there to us.' He said, 'Then, father, I beg you to send him to my father's house — for I have five brothers — that he may warn them, so that they will not also come into this place of torment.' Abraham replied, 'They have Moses and the prophets; they should listen to them.' He said, 'No, father Abraham; but if someone goes to them from the dead, they will repent.' He said to him, 'If they do not listen to Moses and the prophets, neither will they be convinced even if someone rises from the dead.' "

PROPER 22

Sunday between October 2 and October 8 inclusive

The Collect

Almighty and everlasting God, you are always more ready to hear than we to pray, and to give more than we either desire or deserve: Pour upon us the abundance of your mercy, forgiving us those things of which our conscience is afraid, and giving us those good things for which we are not worthy to ask, except through the merits and mediation of Jesus Christ our Savior; who lives and reigns with you and the Holy Spirit, one God, for ever and ever. *Amen.*

Year A

Exodus 20:1-4, 7-9, 12-20	**or**	✛ *Isaiah 5:1-7*
Psalm 19		✛ *Psalm 80:7-14*

Philippians 3:4b-14
Matthew 21:33-46

The Lesson   **Exodus 20:1-4, 7-9, 12-20**

Then God spoke all these words: I am the LORD your God, who brought you
out of the land of Egypt, out of the house of slavery; you shall have no other
gods before me. You shall not make for yourself an idol, whether in the form
of anything that is in heaven above, or that is on the earth beneath, or that is in
the water under the earth. You shall not make wrongful use of the name of the
LORD your God, for the LORD will not acquit anyone who misuses his name.
Remember the sabbath day, and keep it holy. Six days you shall labor and do
all your work. Honor your father and your mother, so that your days may be
long in the land that the LORD your God is giving you. You shall not murder.
You shall not commit adultery. You shall not steal. You shall not bear false
witness against your neighbor. You shall not covet your neighbor's house; you
shall not covet your neighbor's wife, or male or female slave, or ox, or
donkey, or anything that belongs to your neighbor. When all the people
witnessed the thunder and lightning, the sound of the trumpet, and the mountain smoking, they were afraid and trembled and stood at a distance, and said
to Moses, "You speak to us, and we will listen; but do not let God speak to us,
or we will die." Moses said to the people, "Do not be afraid; for God has
come only to test you and to put the fear of him upon you so that you do not
sin."

The Response   **Psalm 19**

Psalm 19 *Caeli enarrant*
  1   The heavens declare the glory of God, *
          and the firmament shows his handiwork.
  2   One day tells its tale to another, *
          and one night imparts knowledge to another.
  3   Although they have no words or language, *
          and their voices are not heard,
  4   Their sound has gone out into all lands, *
          and their message to the ends of the world.
  5   In the deep has he set a pavilion for the sun; *
          it comes forth like a bridegroom out of his chamber;
          it rejoices like a champion to run its course.
  6   It goes forth from the uttermost edge of the heavens
          and runs about to the end of it again; *
          nothing is hidden from its burning heat.
  7   The law of the LORD is perfect
          and revives the soul; *
          the testimony of the LORD is sure
          and gives wisdom to the innocent.

8   The statutes of the LORD are just
     and rejoice the heart; *
          the commandment of the LORD is clear
          and gives light to the eyes.
9   The fear of the LORD is clean
     and endures for ever; *
          the judgments of the LORD are true
          and righteous altogether.
10   More to be desired are they than gold,
     more than much fine gold, *
          sweeter far than honey,
          than honey in the comb.
11   By them also is your servant enlightened, *
          and in keeping them there is great reward.
12   Who can tell how often he offends? *
          cleanse me from my secret faults.
13   Above all, keep your servant from presumptuous sins;
     let them not get dominion over me; *
          then shall I be whole and sound,
          and innocent of a great offense.
14   Let the words of my mouth and the meditation of my
     heart be acceptable in your sight, *
          O LORD, my strength and my redeemer.

or, ✝ The Lesson   Isaiah 5:1-7

Let me sing for my beloved my love-song concerning his vineyard: My
beloved had a vineyard on a very fertile hill. He dug it and cleared it of stones,
and planted it with choice vines; he built a watchtower in the midst of it, and
hewed out a wine vat in it; he expected it to yield grapes, but it yielded wild
grapes. And now, inhabitants of Jerusalem and people of Judah, judge between
me and my vineyard. What more was there to do for my vineyard that I have
not done in it? When I expected it to yield grapes, why did it yield wild
grapes? And now I will tell you what I will do to my vineyard. I will remove
its hedge, and it shall be devoured; I will break down its wall, and it shall be
trampled down. I will make it a waste; it shall not be pruned or hoed, and it
shall be overgrown with briers and thorns; I will also command the clouds that
they rain no rain upon it. For the vineyard of the LORD of hosts is the house of
Israel, and the people of Judah are his pleasant planting; he expected justice,
but saw bloodshed; righteousness, but heard a cry!

Psalm 80:7-14   *Qui regis Israel*

7   Restore us, O God of hosts; *
        show the light of your countenance, and we shall be saved.

8   You have brought a vine out of Egypt; *
        you cast out the nations and planted it.

9   You prepared the ground for it; *
        it took root and filled the land.

10   The mountains were covered by its shadow *
        and the towering cedar trees by its boughs.

11   You stretched out its tendrils to the Sea *
        and its branches to the River.

12   Why have you broken down its wall, *
        so that all who pass by pluck off its grapes?

13   The wild boar of the forest has ravaged it, *
        and the beasts of the field have grazed upon it.

14   Turn now, O God of hosts, look down from heaven;
        behold and tend this vine; *
        preserve what your right hand has planted.

The Epistle   **Philippians 3:4*b*-14**

If anyone else has reason to be confident in the flesh, I have more: circumcised
on the eighth day, a member of the people of Israel, of the tribe of Benjamin, a
Hebrew born of Hebrews; as to the law, a Pharisee; as to zeal, a persecutor of
the church; as to righteousness under the law, blameless. Yet whatever gains I
had, these I have come to regard as loss because of Christ. More than that, I
regard everything as loss because of the surpassing value of knowing Christ
Jesus my Lord. For his sake I have suffered the loss of all things, and I regard
them as rubbish, in order that I may gain Christ and be found in him, not
having a righteousness of my own that comes from the law, but one that
comes through faith in Christ, the righteousness from God based on faith. I
want to know Christ and the power of his resurrection and the sharing of his
sufferings by becoming like him in his death, if somehow I may attain the
resurrection from the dead. Not that I have already obtained this or have
already reached the goal; but I press on to make it my own, because Christ
Jesus has made me his own. Beloved, I do not consider that I have made it my
own; but this one thing I do: forgetting what lies behind and straining forward
to what lies ahead, I press on toward the goal for the prize of the heavenly call
of God in Christ Jesus.

The Gospel   Matthew 21:33-46

Jesus said, "Listen to another parable. There was a landowner who planted a vineyard, put a fence around it, dug a wine press in it, and built a watchtower. Then he leased it to tenants and went to another country. When the harvest time had come, he sent his slaves to the tenants to collect his produce. But the tenants seized his slaves and beat one, killed another, and stoned another. Again he sent other slaves, more than the first; and they treated them in the same way. Finally he sent his son to them, saying, 'They will respect my son.' But when the tenants saw the son, they said to themselves, 'This is the heir; come, let us kill him and get his inheritance.' So they seized him, threw him out of the vineyard, and killed him. Now when the owner of the vineyard comes, what will he do to those tenants?" They said to him, "He will put those wretches to a miserable death, and lease the vineyard to other tenants who will give him the produce at the harvest time." Jesus said to them, "Have you never read in the scriptures: 'The stone that the builders rejected has become the cornerstone; this was the Lord's doing, and it is amazing in our eyes'? Therefore I tell you, the kingdom of God will be taken away from you and given to a people that produces the fruits of the kingdom. The one who falls on this stone will be broken to pieces; and it will crush anyone on whom it falls." When the chief priests and the Pharisees heard his parables, they realized that he was speaking about them. They wanted to arrest him, but they feared the crowds, because they regarded him as a prophet.

Year B

Job 1:1; 2:1-10	**or**	☩ *Genesis 2:18-24*
Psalm 26		☩ *Psalm 8*

Hebrews 1:1-4; 2:5-12
Mark 10:2-16

The Lesson   Job 1:1; 2:1-10

There was once a man in the land of Uz whose name was Job. That man was blameless and upright, one who feared God and turned away from evil. One day the heavenly beings came to present themselves before the LORD, and Satan also came among them to present himself before the LORD. The LORD said to Satan, "Where have you come from?" Satan answered the LORD, "From going to and fro on the earth, and from walking up and down on it." The LORD said to Satan, "Have you considered my servant Job? There is no one like him on the earth, a blameless and upright man who fears God and turns away from evil. He still persists in his integrity, although you incited me against him, to destroy him for no reason." Then Satan answered the LORD, "Skin for skin! All that people have they will give to save their lives. But stretch out your hand now and touch his bone and his flesh, and he will curse you to your face." The LORD said to Satan, "Very well, he is in your power; only spare his life." So Satan went out from the presence of the LORD, and inflicted loathsome sores on Job from the sole of his foot to the crown of his head. Job took a potsherd with which to scrape himself, and sat among the ashes. Then his wife said to him, "Do you still persist in your integrity? Curse God, and die." But he said to her, "You speak as any foolish woman would speak. Shall we receive the good at the hand of God, and not receive the bad?" In all this Job did not sin with his lips.

The Response   Psalm 26

Psalm 26 *Judica me, Domine*

1   Give judgment for me, O LORD,
        for I have lived with integrity; *
            I have trusted in the LORD and have not faltered.

2   Test me, O LORD, and try me; *
        examine my heart and my mind.

3   For your love is before my eyes; *
        I have walked faithfully with you.

4   I have not sat with the worthless, *
        nor do I consort with the deceitful.

5   I have hated the company of evildoers; *
        I will not sit down with the wicked.

6   I will wash my hands in innocence, O LORD, *
        that I may go in procession round your altar,

7   Singing aloud a song of thanksgiving *
        and recounting all your wonderful deeds.

8   LORD, I love the house in which you dwell *
        and the place where your glory abides.

9   Do not sweep me away with sinners, *
        nor my life with those who thirst for blood,

10   Whose hands are full of evil plots, *
        and their right hand full of bribes.

11   As for me, I will live with integrity; *
        redeem me, O LORD, and have pity on me.

12   My foot stands on level ground; *
        in the full assembly I will bless the LORD.

or, ☩ The Lesson   Genesis 2:18-24

The LORD God said, "It is not good that the man should be alone; I will make him a helper as his partner." So out of the ground the LORD God formed every animal of the field and every bird of the air, and brought them to the man to see what he would call them; and whatever the man called every living creature, that was its name. The man gave names to all cattle, and to the birds of the air, and to every animal of the field; but for the man there was not found a helper as his partner. So the LORD God caused a deep sleep to fall upon the man, and he slept; then he took one of his ribs and closed up its place with flesh. And the rib that the LORD God had taken from the man he made into a woman and brought her to the man. Then the man said, "This at last is bone of my bones and flesh of my flesh; this one shall be called Woman, for out of Man this one was taken." Therefore a man leaves his father and his mother and clings to his wife, and they become one flesh.

☩ The Response   Psalm 8

Psalm 8   *Domine, Dominus noster*

1   O LORD our Governor, *
        how exalted is your Name in all the world!
2   Out of the mouths of infants and children *
        your majesty is praised above the heavens.
3   You have set up a stronghold against your adversaries, *
        to quell the enemy and the avenger.
4   When I consider your heavens, the work of your fingers, *
        the moon and the stars you have set in their courses,
5   What is man that you should be mindful of him? *
        the son of man that you should seek him out?
6   You have made him but little lower than the angels; *
        you adorn him with glory and honor;
7   You give him mastery over the works of your hands; *
        you put all things under his feet:
8   All sheep and oxen, *
        even the wild beasts of the field,
9   The birds of the air, the fish of the sea, *
        and whatsoever walks in the paths of the sea.
10 O LORD our Governor, *
        how exalted is your Name in all the world!

The Epistle   Hebrews 1:1-4; 2:5-12

Long ago God spoke to our ancestors in many and various ways by the prophets, but in these last days he has spoken to us by a Son, whom he appointed heir of all things, through whom he also created the worlds. He is the reflection of God's glory and the exact imprint of God's very being, and he sustains all things by his powerful word. When he had made purification for sins, he sat down at the right hand of the Majesty on high, having become as much superior to angels as the name he has inherited is more excellent than theirs. Now God did not subject the coming world, about which we are speaking, to angels. But someone has testified somewhere, "What are human beings that you are mindful of them, or mortals, that you care for them? You have made them for a little while lower than the angels; you have crowned them with glory and honor, subjecting all things under their feet." Now in subjecting all things to them, God left nothing outside their control. As it is, we do not yet see everything in subjection to them, but we do see Jesus, who for a little while was made lower than the angels, now crowned with glory and honor because of the suffering of death, so that by the grace of God he might taste death for everyone. It was fitting that God, for whom and through whom all things exist, in bringing many children to glory, should make the pioneer of their salvation perfect through sufferings. For the one who sanctifies and those who are sanctified all have one Father. For this reason Jesus is not ashamed to call them brothers and sisters, saying, "I will proclaim your name to my brothers and sisters, in the midst of the congregation I will praise you."

The Gospel   Mark 10:2-16

Some Pharisees came, and to test Jesus they asked, "Is it lawful for a man to divorce his wife?" He answered them, "What did Moses command you?" They said, "Moses allowed a man to write a certificate of dismissal and to divorce her." But Jesus said to them, "Because of your hardness of heart he wrote this commandment for you. But from the beginning of creation, 'God made them male and female.' 'For this reason a man shall leave his father and mother and be joined to his wife, and the two shall become one flesh.' So they are no longer two, but one flesh. Therefore what God has joined together, let no one separate." Then in the house the disciples asked him again about this matter. He said to them, "Whoever divorces his wife and marries another commits adultery against her; and if she divorces her husband and marries another, she commits adultery." People were bringing little children to him in order that he might touch them; and the disciples spoke sternly to them. But when Jesus saw this, he was indignant and said to them, "Let the little children come to me; do not stop them; for it is to such as these that the kingdom of God belongs. Truly I tell you, whoever does not receive the kingdom of God as a little child will never enter it." And he took them up in his arms, laid his hands on them, and blessed them.

Year C

Lamentations 1:1-6   **or**   ✟ *Habakkuk 1:1-4; 2:1-4*
Lamentations 3:19-26   ✟ *Psalm 37:1-10*
  or *Psalm 137*

2 Timothy 1:1-14
Luke 17:5-10

The Lesson   **Lamentations 1:1-6**

How lonely sits the city that once was full of people! How like a widow she
has become, she that was great among the nations! She that was a princess
among the provinces has become a vassal. She weeps bitterly in the night,
with tears on her cheeks; among all her lovers she has no one to comfort her;
all her friends have dealt treacherously with her, they have become her enemies. Judah has gone into exile with suffering and hard servitude; she lives
now among the nations, and finds no resting place; her pursuers have all
overtaken her in the midst of her distress. The roads to Zion mourn, for no one
comes to the festivals; all her gates are desolate, her priests groan; her young
girls grieve, and her lot is bitter. Her foes have become the masters, her
enemies prosper, because the LORD has made her suffer for the multitude of
her transgressions; her children have gone away, captives before the foe. From
daughter Zion has departed all her majesty. Her princes have become like
stags that find no pasture; they fled without strength before the pursuer.

The Response   **Lamentations 3:19-26** *or* **Psalm 137**
Lamentations 3:19-26

19   The thought of my affliction and homelessness
         is wormwood and gall!
20   My soul continually thinks of it
         and is bowed down within me.
21   But this I call to mind,
         and therefore I have hope:
22   The steadfast love of the LORD never ceases,
         his mercies never come to an end;
23   they are new every morning:
         great is your faithfulness.
24   "The LORD is my portion," says my soul,
         "therefore I will hope in him."
25   The LORD is good to those who wait for him,
         to the soul that seeks him.
26   It is good that one should wait quietly
         for the salvation of the LORD.

or, **Psalm 137**   *Super flumina*

1   By the waters of Babylon we sat down and wept, *
         when we remembered you, O Zion.
2   As for our harps, we hung them up *
         on the trees in the midst of that land.
3   For those who led us away captive asked us for a song,
        and our oppressors called for mirth: *
         "Sing us one of the songs of Zion."

4   How shall we sing the LORD's song *
        upon an alien soil?
5   If I forget you, O Jerusalem, *
        let my right hand forget its skill.
6   Let my tongue cleave to the roof of my mouth
     if I do not remember you, *
            if I do not set Jerusalem above my highest joy.
7   Remember the day of Jerusalem, O LORD,
     against the people of Edom, *
            who said, "Down with it! down with it!
            even to the ground!"
8   O Daughter of Babylon, doomed to destruction, *
        happy the one who pays you back
        for what you have done to us!
9   Happy shall he be who takes your little ones, *
        and dashes them against the rock!

or, ✛ The Lesson   Habakkuk 1:1-4; 2:1-4

The oracle that the prophet Habakkuk saw. O LORD, how long shall I cry for
help, and you will not listen? Or cry to you "Violence!" and you will not save?
Why do you make me see wrongdoing and look at trouble? Destruction and
violence are before me; strife and contention arise. So the law becomes slack
and justice never prevails. The wicked surround the righteous — therefore
judgment comes forth perverted. I will stand at my watchpost, and station
myself on the rampart; I will keep watch to see what he will say to me, and
what he will answer concerning my complaint. Then the LORD answered me
and said: Write the vision; make it plain on tablets, so that a runner may read
it. For there is still a vision for the appointed time; it speaks of the end, and
does not lie. If it seems to tarry, wait for it; it will surely come, it will not
delay. Look at the proud! Their spirit is not right in them, but the righteous
live by their faith.

✛ The Response   Psalm 37:1-10

Psalm 37:1-10   *Noli aemulari*
1   Do not fret yourself because of evildoers; *
        do not be jealous of those who do wrong.
2   For they shall soon wither like the grass, *
        and like the green grass fade away.
3   Put your trust in the LORD and do good; *
        dwell in the land and feed on its riches.
4   Take delight in the LORD, *
        and he shall give you your heart's desire.

5   Commit your way to the Lord and put your trust in him, *
       and he will bring it to pass.

6   He will make your righteousness as clear as the light *
       and your just dealing as the noonday.

7   Be still before the Lord *
       and wait patiently for him.

8   Do not fret yourself over the one who prospers, *
       the one who succeeds in evil schemes.

9   Refrain from anger, leave rage alone; *
       do not fret yourself; it leads only to evil.

10   For evildoers shall be cut off, *
       but those who wait upon the Lord shall possess the land.

The Epistle   2 Timothy 1:1-14

Paul, an apostle of Christ Jesus by the will of God, for the sake of the promise of life that is in Christ Jesus, To Timothy, my beloved child: Grace, mercy, and peace from God the Father and Christ Jesus our Lord. I am grateful to God — whom I worship with a clear conscience, as my ancestors did — when I remember you constantly in my prayers night and day. Recalling your tears, I long to see you so that I may be filled with joy. I am reminded of your sincere faith, a faith that lived first in your grandmother Lois and your mother Eunice and now, I am sure, lives in you. For this reason I remind you to rekindle the gift of God that is within you through the laying on of my hands; for God did not give us a spirit of cowardice, but rather a spirit of power and of love and of self-discipline. Do not be ashamed, then, of the testimony about our Lord or of me his prisoner, but join with me in suffering for the gospel, relying on the power of God, who saved us and called us with a holy calling, not according to our works but according to his own purpose and grace. This grace was given to us in Christ Jesus before the ages began, but it has now been revealed through the appearing of our Savior Christ Jesus, who abolished death and brought life and immortality to light through the gospel. For this gospel I was appointed a herald and an apostle and a teacher, and for this reason I suffer as I do. But I am not ashamed, for I know the one in whom I have put my trust, and I am sure that he is able to guard until that day what I have entrusted to him. Hold to the standard of sound teaching that you have heard from me, in the faith and love that are in Christ Jesus. Guard the good treasure entrusted to you, with the help of the Holy Spirit living in us.

The Gospel   Luke 17:5-10

The apostles said to the Lord, "Increase our faith!" The Lord replied, "If you had faith the size of a mustard seed, you could say to this mulberry tree, 'Be uprooted and planted in the sea,' and it would obey you. Who among you would say to your slave who has just come in from plowing or tending sheep in the field, 'Come here at once and take your place at the table'? Would you not rather say to him, 'Prepare supper for me, put on your apron and serve me while I eat and drink; later you may eat and drink'? Do you thank the slave for doing what was commanded? So you also, when you have done all that you were ordered to do, say, 'We are worthless slaves; we have done only what we ought to have done!' "

PROPER 23

Sunday between October 9 and October 15 inclusive

The Collect

Lord, we pray that your grace may always precede and follow us, that we may continually be given to good works; through Jesus Christ our Lord, who lives and reigns with you and the Holy Spirit, one God, now and for ever. *Amen.*

Year A

Exodus 32:1-14	**or**	✝ *Isaiah 25:1-9*
Psalm 106:1-6, 19-23		✝ *Psalm 23*
	Philippians 4:1-9	
	Matthew 22:1-14	

The Lesson   Exodus 32:1-14

When the people saw that Moses delayed to come down from the mountain, the people gathered around Aaron, and said to him, "Come, make gods for us, who shall go before us; as for this Moses, the man who brought us up out of the land of Egypt, we do not know what has become of him." Aaron said to them, "Take off the gold rings that are on the ears of your wives, your sons, and your daughters, and bring them to me." So all the people took off the gold rings from their ears, and brought them to Aaron. He took the gold from them, formed it in a mold, and cast an image of a calf; and they said, "These are your gods, O Israel, who brought you up out of the land of Egypt!" When Aaron saw this, he built an altar before it; and Aaron made proclamation and said, "Tomorrow shall be a festival to the LORD." They rose early the next day, and offered burnt offerings and brought sacrifices of well-being; and the people sat down to eat and drink, and rose up to revel. The LORD said to Moses, "Go down at once! Your people, whom you brought up out of the land of Egypt, have acted perversely; they have been quick to turn aside from the way that I commanded them; they have cast for themselves an image of a calf, and have worshiped it and sacrificed to it, and said, 'These are your gods, O Israel, who brought you up out of the land of Egypt!' " The LORD said to Moses, "I have seen this people, how stiff-necked they are. Now let me alone, so that my wrath may burn hot against them and I may consume them; and of you I will make a great nation." But Moses implored the LORD his God, and said, "O LORD, why does your wrath burn hot against your people, whom you brought out of the land of Egypt with great power and with a mighty hand? Why should the Egyptians say, 'It was with evil intent that he brought them out to kill them in the mountains, and to consume them from the face of the earth'? Turn from your fierce wrath; change your mind and do not bring disaster on your people. Remember Abraham, Isaac, and Israel, your servants, how you swore to them by your own self, saying to them, 'I will multiply your descendants like the stars of heaven, and all this land that I have promised I will give to your descendants, and they shall inherit it forever.'" And the LORD changed his mind about the disaster that he planned to bring on his people.

The Response   **Psalm 106:1-6, 19-23**

Psalm 106:1-6, 19-23   *Confitemini Domino*

1   Hallelujah!
    Give thanks to the LORD, for he is good, *
        for his mercy endures for ever.
2   Who can declare the mighty acts of the LORD *
        or show forth all his praise?
3   Happy are those who act with justice *
        and always do what is right!
4   Remember me, O LORD, with the favor you have
                for your people, *
        and visit me with your saving help;
5   That I may see the prosperity of your elect
    and be glad with the gladness of your people, *
        that I may glory with your inheritance.
6   We have sinned as our forebears did; *
        we have done wrong and dealt wickedly.
19 Israel made a bull-calf at Horeb *
        and worshiped a molten image;
20 And so they exchanged their Glory *
        for the image of an ox that feeds on grass.
21 They forgot God their Savior, *
        who had done great things in Egypt,
22 Wonderful deeds in the land of Ham, *
        and fearful things at the Red Sea.
23 So he would have destroyed them,
    had not Moses his chosen stood before him in the breach, *
        to turn away his wrath from consuming them.

or, ✣ **The Lesson**   **Isaiah 25:1-9**

O LORD, you are my God; I will exalt you, I will praise your name; for you have done wonderful things, plans formed of old, faithful and sure. For you have made the city a heap, the fortified city a ruin; the palace of aliens is a city no more, it will never be rebuilt. Therefore strong peoples will glorify you; cities of ruthless nations will fear you. For you have been a refuge to the poor, a refuge to the needy in their distress, a shelter from the rainstorm and a shade from the heat. When the blast of the ruthless was like a winter rainstorm, the noise of aliens like heat in a dry place, you subdued the heat with the shade of clouds; the song of the ruthless was stilled. On this mountain the LORD of hosts will make for all peoples a feast of rich food, a feast of well-aged wines, of rich food filled with marrow, of well-aged wines strained clear. And he will destroy on this mountain the shroud that is cast over all peoples, the sheet that is spread over all nations; he will swallow up death forever. Then the Lord GOD will wipe away the tears from all faces, and the disgrace of his people he will take away from all the earth, for the LORD has spoken. It will be said on that day, Lo, this is our God; we have waited for him, so that he might save us. This is the LORD for whom we have waited; let us be glad and rejoice in his salvation.

☩ The Response   Psalm 23

Psalm 23 *Dominus regit me*

1   The LORD is my shepherd; *
        I shall not be in want.
2   He makes me lie down in green pastures *
        and leads me beside still waters.
3   He revives my soul *
        and guides me along right pathways for his Name's sake.
4   Though I walk through the valley of the shadow of death,
    I shall fear no evil; *
        for you are with me;
        your rod and your staff, they comfort me.
5   You spread a table before me in the presence of those
                        who trouble me; *
        you have anointed my head with oil,
        and my cup is running over.
6   Surely your goodness and mercy shall follow me all the days
                        of my life, *
        and I will dwell in the house of the LORD for ever.

The Epistle   Philippians 4:1-9

My brothers and sisters, whom I love and long for, my joy and crown, stand firm in the Lord in this way, my beloved. I urge Euodia and I urge Syntyche to be of the same mind in the Lord. Yes, and I ask you also, my loyal companion, help these women, for they have struggled beside me in the work of the gospel, together with Clement and the rest of my co-workers, whose names are in the book of life. Rejoice in the Lord always; again I will say, Rejoice. Let your gentleness be known to everyone. The Lord is near. Do not worry about anything, but in everything by prayer and supplication with thanksgiving let your requests be made known to God. And the peace of God, which surpasses all understanding, will guard your hearts and your minds in Christ Jesus. Finally, beloved, whatever is true, whatever is honorable, whatever is just, whatever is pure, whatever is pleasing, whatever is commendable, if there is any excellence and if there is anything worthy of praise, think about these things. Keep on doing the things that you have learned and received and heard and seen in me, and the God of peace will be with you.

The Gospel   Matthew 22:1-14

Jesus spoke to them in parables, saying: "The kingdom of heaven may be compared to a king who gave a wedding banquet for his son. He sent his slaves to call those who had been invited to the wedding banquet, but they would not come. Again he sent other slaves, saying, 'Tell those who have been invited: Look, I have prepared my dinner, my oxen and my fat calves have been slaughtered, and everything is ready; come to the wedding banquet.' But they made light of it and went away, one to his farm, another to his business, while the rest seized his slaves, mistreated them, and killed them. The king was enraged. He sent his troops, destroyed those murderers, and burned their city. Then he said to his slaves, 'The wedding is ready, but those invited were not worthy. Go therefore into the main streets, and invite everyone you find to the wedding banquet.' Those slaves went out into the streets and gathered all whom they found, both good and bad; so the wedding hall was filled with guests. But when the king came in to see the guests, he noticed a man there who was not wearing a wedding robe, and he said to him, 'Friend, how did you get in here without a wedding robe?' And he was speechless. Then the king said to the attendants, 'Bind him hand and foot, and throw him into the outer darkness, where there will be weeping and gnashing of teeth.' For many are called, but few are chosen."

Year B

Job 23:1-9, 16-17	**or**	✛ Amos 5:6-7, 10-15
Psalm 22:1-15		✛ Psalm 90:12-17
	Hebrews 4:12-16	
	Mark 10:17-31	

The Lesson   Job 23:1-9, 16-17

Then Job answered: "Today also my complaint is bitter; his hand is heavy despite my groaning. Oh, that I knew where I might find him, that I might come even to his dwelling! I would lay my case before him, and fill my mouth with arguments. I would learn what he would answer me, and understand what he would say to me. Would he contend with me in the greatness of his power? No; but he would give heed to me. There an upright person could reason with him, and I should be acquitted forever by my judge. "If I go forward, he is not there; or backward, I cannot perceive him; on the left he hides, and I cannot behold him; I turn to the right, but I cannot see him. God has made my heart faint; the Almighty has terrified me; If only I could vanish in darkness, and thick darkness would cover my face!"

The Response   **Psalm 22:1-15**

Psalm 22:1-15   *Deus, Deus meus*

1   My God, my God, why have you forsaken me? *
         and are so far from my cry
         and from the words of my distress?

2   O my God, I cry in the daytime, but you do not answer; *
         by night as well, but I find no rest.

3   Yet you are the Holy One, *
         enthroned upon the praises of Israel.

4   Our forefathers put their trust in you; *
         they trusted, and you delivered them.

5   They cried out to you and were delivered; *
         they trusted in you and were not put to shame.

6   But as for me, I am a worm and no man, *
         scorned by all and despised by the people.

7   All who see me laugh me to scorn; *
         they curl their lips and wag their heads, saying,

8   "He trusted in the LORD; let him deliver him; *
         let him rescue him, if he delights in him."

9   Yet you are he who took me out of the womb, *
         and kept me safe upon my mother's breast.

10   I have been entrusted to you ever since I was born; *
         you were my God when I was still in my
                 mother's womb.

11   Be not far from me, for trouble is near, *
         and there is none to help.

12   Many young bulls encircle me; *
         strong bulls of Bashan surround me.

13   They open wide their jaws at me, *
         like a ravening and a roaring lion.

14   I am poured out like water;
          all my bones are out of joint; *
              my heart within my breast is melting wax.
15   My mouth is dried out like a pot-sherd;
          my tongue sticks to the roof of my mouth; *
              and you have laid me in the dust of the grave.

or, ✠ **The Lesson**   Amos 5:6-7, 10-15

Seek the LORD and live, or he will break out against the house of Joseph like
fire, and it will devour Bethel, with no one to quench it. Ah, you that turn
justice to wormwood, and bring righteousness to the ground! They hate the
one who reproves in the gate, and they abhor the one who speaks the truth.
Therefore because you trample on the poor and take from them levies of grain,
you have built houses of hewn stone, but you shall not live in them; you have
planted pleasant vineyards, but you shall not drink their wine. For I know how
many are your transgressions, and how great are your sins — you who afflict
the righteous, who take a bribe, and push aside the needy in the gate. Therefore the prudent will keep silent in such a time; for it is an evil time. Seek
good and not evil, that you may live; and so the LORD, the God of hosts, will
be with you, just as you have said. Hate evil and love good, and establish
justice in the gate; it may be that the LORD, the God of hosts, will be gracious
to the remnant of Joseph.

✠ **The Response**   Psalm 90:12-17

Psalm 90:12-17   *Domine, refugium*
12   So teach us to number our days *
          that we may apply our hearts to wisdom.
13   Return, O LORD; how long will you tarry? *
          be gracious to your servants.
14   Satisfy us by your loving-kindness in the morning; *
          so shall we rejoice and be glad all the days of our life.
15   Make us glad by the measure of the days that you afflicted us *
          and the years in which we suffered adversity.
16   Show your servants your works *
          and your splendor to their children.
17   May the graciousness of the LORD our God be upon us; *
          prosper the work of our hands;
          prosper our handiwork.

The Epistle   Hebrews 4:12-16

Indeed, the word of God is living and active, sharper than any two-edged
sword, piercing until it divides soul from spirit, joints from marrow; it is able
to judge the thoughts and intentions of the heart. And before him no creature

is hidden, but all are naked and laid bare to the eyes of the one to whom we must render an account. Since, then, we have a great high priest who has passed through the heavens, Jesus, the Son of God, let us hold fast to our confession. For we do not have a high priest who is unable to sympathize with our weaknesses, but we have one who in every respect has been tested as we are, yet without sin. Let us therefore approach the throne of grace with boldness, so that we may receive mercy and find grace to help in time of need.

The Gospel   Mark 10:17-31

As Jesus was setting out on a journey, a man ran up and knelt before him, and asked him, "Good Teacher, what must I do to inherit eternal life?" Jesus said to him, "Why do you call me good? No one is good but God alone. You know the commandments: 'You shall not murder; You shall not commit adultery; You shall not steal; You shall not bear false witness; You shall not defraud; Honor your father and mother.'" He said to him, "Teacher, I have kept all these since my youth." Jesus, looking at him, loved him and said, "You lack one thing; go, sell what you own, and give the money to the poor, and you will have treasure in heaven; then come, follow me." When he heard this, he was shocked and went away grieving, for he had many possessions. Then Jesus looked around and said to his disciples, "How hard it will be for those who have wealth to enter the kingdom of God!" And the disciples were perplexed at these words. But Jesus said to them again, "Children, how hard it is to enter the kingdom of God! It is easier for a camel to go through the eye of a needle than for someone who is rich to enter the kingdom of God." They were greatly astounded and said to one another, "Then who can be saved?" Jesus looked at them and said, "For mortals it is impossible, but not for God; for God all things are possible." Peter began to say to him, "Look, we have left everything and followed you." Jesus said, "Truly I tell you, there is no one who has left house or brothers or sisters or mother or father or children or fields, for my sake and for the sake of the good news, who will not receive a hundredfold now in this age — houses, brothers and sisters, mothers and children, and fields with persecutions — and in the age to come eternal life. But many who are first will be last, and the last will be first."

Year C
or

Jeremiah 29:1, 4-7
Psalm 66:1-11

✝ *2 Kings 5:1-3, 7-15c*
✝ *Psalm 111*

2 Timothy 2:8-15
Luke 17:11-19

The Lesson **Jeremiah 29:1, 4-7**

These are the words of the letter that the prophet Jeremiah sent from Jerusalem to the remaining elders among the exiles, and to the priests, the prophets, and all the people, whom Nebuchadnezzar had taken into exile from Jerusalem to Babylon. Thus says the LORD of hosts, the God of Israel, to all the exiles whom I have sent into exile from Jerusalem to Babylon: Build houses and live in them; plant gardens and eat what they produce. Take wives and have sons and daughters; take wives for your sons, and give your daughters in marriage, that they may bear sons and daughters; multiply there, and do not decrease. But seek the welfare of the city where I have sent you into exile, and pray to the LORD on its behalf, for in its welfare you will find your welfare.

The Response **Psalm 66:1-11**

Psalm 66:1-11   *Jubilate Deo*

1   Be joyful in God, all you lands; *
    sing the glory of his Name;
    sing the glory of his praise.
2   Say to God, "How awesome are your deeds! *
    because of your great strength your enemies
        cringe before you.
3   All the earth bows down before you, *
    sings to you, sings out your Name."
4   Come now and see the works of God, *
    how wonderful he is in his doing toward all people.
5   He turned the sea into dry land,
    so that they went through the water on foot, *
        and there we rejoiced in him.
6   In his might he rules for ever;
    his eyes keep watch over the nations; *
        let no rebel rise up against him.
7   Bless our God, you peoples; *
    make the voice of his praise to be heard;
8   Who holds our souls in life, *
    and will not allow our feet to slip.
9   For you, O God, have proved us; *
    you have tried us just as silver is tried.
10   You brought us into the snare; *
    you laid heavy burdens upon our backs.
11   You let enemies ride over our heads; *
    we went through fire and water; *
        but you brought us out into a place of refreshment.

or, ✠ **The Lesson**   **2 Kings 5:1-3, 7-15c**

Naaman, commander of the army of the king of Aram, was a great man and in
high favor with his master, because by him the LORD had given victory to
Aram. The man, though a mighty warrior, suffered from leprosy. Now the
Arameans on one of their raids had taken a young girl captive from the land of
Israel, and she served Naaman's wife. She said to her mistress, "If only my
lord were with the prophet who is in Samaria! He would cure him of his
leprosy." When the king of Israel read the letter, he tore his clothes and said,
"Am I God, to give death or life, that this man sends word to me to cure a
man of his leprosy? Just look and see how he is trying to pick a quarrel with
me." But when Elisha the man of God heard that the king of Israel had torn
his clothes, he sent a message to the king, "Why have you torn your clothes?
Let him come to me, that he may learn that there is a prophet in Israel." So
Naaman came with his horses and chariots, and halted at the entrance of
Elisha's house. Elisha sent a messenger to him, saying, "Go, wash in the
Jordan seven times, and your flesh shall be restored and you shall be clean."
But Naaman became angry and went away, saying, "I thought that for me he
would surely come out, and stand and call on the name of the LORD his God,
and would wave his hand over the spot, and cure the leprosy! Are not Abana
and Pharpar, the rivers of Damascus, better than all the waters of Israel?
Could I not wash in them, and be clean?" He turned and went away in a rage.
But his servants approached and said to him, "Father, if the prophet had
commanded you to do something difficult, would you not have done it? How
much more, when all he said to you was, 'Wash, and be clean'?" So he went
down and immersed himself seven times in the Jordan, according to the word
of the man of God; his flesh was restored like the flesh of a young boy, and he
was clean. Then he returned to the man of God, he and all his company; he
came and stood before him.

✠ **The Response**   **Psalm 111**

Psalm 111   *Confitebor tibi*

1   Hallelujah!
      I will give thanks to the LORD with my whole heart, *
         in the assembly of the upright, in the congregation.
2   Great are the deeds of the LORD! *
         they are studied by all who delight in them.
3   His work is full of majesty and splendor, *
         and his righteousness endures for ever.
4   He makes his marvelous works to be remembered; *
         the LORD is gracious and full of compassion.
5   He gives food to those who fear him; *
         he is ever mindful of his covenant.

6   He has shown his people the power of his works *
     in giving them the lands of the nations.
7   The works of his hands are faithfulness and justice; *
     all his commandments are sure.
8   They stand fast for ever and ever, *
     because they are done in truth and equity.
9   He sent redemption to his people;
     he commanded his covenant for ever; *
     holy and awesome is his Name.
10   The fear of the LORD is the beginning of wisdom; *
     those who act accordingly have a good understanding;
     his praise endures for ever.

The Epistle   2 Timothy 2:8-15

Remember Jesus Christ, raised from the dead, a descendant of David — that is my gospel, for which I suffer hardship, even to the point of being chained like a criminal. But the word of God is not chained. Therefore I endure everything for the sake of the elect, so that they may also obtain the salvation that is in Christ Jesus, with eternal glory. The saying is sure: If we have died with him, we will also live with him; if we endure, we will also reign with him; if we deny him, he will also deny us; if we are faithless, he remains faithful — for he cannot deny himself. Remind them of this, and warn them before God that they are to avoid wrangling over words, which does no good but only ruins those who are listening. Do your best to present yourself to God as one approved by him, a worker who has no need to be ashamed, rightly explaining the word of truth.

The Gospel   Luke 17:11-19

On the way to Jerusalem Jesus was going through the region between Samaria and Galilee. As he entered a village, ten lepers approached him. Keeping their distance, they called out, saying, "Jesus, Master, have mercy on us!" When he saw them, he said to them, "Go and show yourselves to the priests." And as they went, they were made clean. Then one of them, when he saw that he was healed, turned back, praising God with a loud voice. He prostrated himself at Jesus' feet and thanked him. And he was a Samaritan. Then Jesus asked, "Were not ten made clean? But the other nine, where are they? Was none of them found to return and give praise to God except this foreigner?" Then he said to him, "Get up and go on your way; your faith has made you well."

PROPER 24

Sunday between October 16 and October 22 inclusive

The Collect

Almighty and everlasting God, in Christ you have revealed your glory among
the nations: Preserve the works of your mercy, that your Church throughout
the world may persevere with steadfast faith in the confession of your Name;
through Jesus Christ our Lord, who lives and reigns with you and the Holy
Spirit, one God, for ever and ever. *Amen.*

Year A

Exodus 33:12-23	**or**	✛ *Isaiah 45:1-7*
Psalm 99		✛ *Psalm 96:1-9, (10-13)*

1 Thessalonians 1:1-10
Matthew 22:15-22

The Lesson   Exodus 33:12-23

Moses said to the LORD, "See, you have said to me, 'Bring up this people'; but
you have not let me know whom you will send with me. Yet you have said, 'I
know you by name, and you have also found favor in my sight.' Now if I have
found favor in your sight, show me your ways, so that I may know you and
find favor in your sight. Consider too that this nation is your people." He said,
"My presence will go with you, and I will give you rest." And he said to him,
"If your presence will not go, do not carry us up from here. For how shall it
be known that I have found favor in your sight, I and your people, unless you
go with us? In this way, we shall be distinct, I and your people, from every
people on the face of the earth." The LORD said to Moses, "I will do the very
thing that you have asked; for you have found favor in my sight, and I know
you by name." Moses said, "Show me your glory, I pray." And he said, "I will
make all my goodness pass before you, and will proclaim before you the
name, 'The LORD'; and I will be gracious to whom I will be gracious, and will
show mercy on whom I will show mercy. But," he said, "you cannot see my
face; for no one shall see me and live." And the LORD continued, "See, there is
a place by me where you shall stand on the rock; and while my glory passes
by I will put you in a cleft of the rock, and I will cover you with my hand until
I have passed by; then I will take away my hand, and you shall see my back;
but my face shall not be seen."

The Response   Psalm 99

Psalm 99   *Dominus regnavit*

1   The LORD is King;
        let the people tremble; *
            he is enthroned upon the cherubim;
            let the earth shake.

2 The Lord is great in Zion; *
    he is high above all peoples.

3 Let them confess his Name, which is great and awesome; *
    he is the Holy One.

4 "O mighty King, lover of justice,
    you have established equity; *
        you have executed justice and righteousness in Jacob."

5 Proclaim the greatness of the Lord our God
    and fall down before his footstool; *
        he is the Holy One.

6 Moses and Aaron among his priests,
    and Samuel among those who call upon his Name, *
        they called upon the Lord, and he answered them.

7 He spoke to them out of the pillar of cloud; *
    they kept his testimonies and the decree that he gave them.

8 "O Lord our God, you answered them indeed; *
    you were a God who forgave them,
        yet punished them for their evil deeds."

9 Proclaim the greatness of the Lord our God
    and worship him upon his holy hill; *
        for the Lord our God is the Holy One.

or, ✠ The Lesson   Isaiah 45:1-7

Thus says the Lord to his anointed, to Cyrus, whose right hand I have grasped to subdue nations before him and strip kings of their robes, to open doors before him — and the gates shall not be closed: I will go before you and level the mountains, I will break in pieces the doors of bronze and cut through the bars of iron, I will give you the treasures of darkness and riches hidden in secret places, so that you may know that it is I, the Lord, the God of Israel, who call you by your name. For the sake of my servant Jacob, and Israel my chosen, I call you by your name, I surname you, though you do not know me. I am the Lord, and there is no other; besides me there is no god. I arm you, though you do not know me, so that they may know, from the rising of the sun and from the west, that there is no one besides me; I am the Lord, and there is no other. I form light and create darkness, I make weal and create woe; I the Lord do all these things.

✠ The Response   Psalm 96:1-9, (10-13)

Psalm 96:1-9, (10-13)   *Cantate Domino*

1 Sing to the Lord a new song; *
    sing to the Lord, all the whole earth.

2   Sing to the Lord and bless his Name; *
        proclaim the good news of his salvation from day to day.

3   Declare his glory among the nations *
        and his wonders among all peoples.

4   For great is the Lord and greatly to be praised; *
        he is more to be feared than all gods.

5   As for all the gods of the nations, they are but idols; *
        but it is the Lord who made the heavens.

6   Oh, the majesty and magnificence of his presence! *
        Oh, the power and the splendor of his sanctuary!

7   Ascribe to the Lord, you families of the peoples; *
        ascribe to the Lord honor and power.

8   Ascribe to the Lord the honor due his Name; *
        bring offerings and come into his courts.

9   Worship the Lord in the beauty of holiness; *
        let the whole earth tremble before him.

[10 Tell it out among the nations: "The Lord is King! *
        he has made the world so firm that it cannot be moved;
        he will judge the peoples with equity."

11 Let the heavens rejoice, and let the earth be glad;
        let the sea thunder and all that is in it; *
        let the field be joyful and all that is therein.

12 Then shall all the trees of the wood shout for joy
        before the Lord when he comes, *
        when he comes to judge the earth.

13 He will judge the world with righteousness *
        and the peoples with his truth.]

The Epistle   1 Thessalonians 1:1-10

Paul, Silvanus, and Timothy, To the church of the Thessalonians in God the
Father and the Lord Jesus Christ: Grace to you and peace. We always give
thanks to God for all of you and mention you in our prayers, constantly
remembering before our God and Father your work of faith and labor of love
and steadfastness of hope in our Lord Jesus Christ. For we know, brothers and
sisters beloved by God, that he has chosen you, because our message of the
gospel came to you not in word only, but also in power and in the Holy Spirit
and with full conviction; just as you know what kind of persons we proved to
be among you for your sake. And you became imitators of us and of the Lord,
for in spite of persecution you received the word with joy inspired by the Holy
Spirit, so that you became an example to all the believers in Macedonia and in
Achaia. For the word of the Lord has sounded forth from you not only in
Macedonia and Achaia, but in every place your faith in God has become

known, so that we have no need to speak about it. For the people of those regions report about us what kind of welcome we had among you, and how you turned to God from idols, to serve a living and true God, and to wait for his Son from heaven, whom he raised from the dead — Jesus, who rescues us from the wrath that is coming.

The Gospel   Matthew 22:15-22

The Pharisees went and plotted to entrap Jesus in what he said. So they sent their disciples to him, along with the Herodians, saying, "Teacher, we know that you are sincere, and teach the way of God in accordance with truth, and show deference to no one; for you do not regard people with partiality. Tell us, then, what you think. Is it lawful to pay taxes to the emperor, or not?" But Jesus, aware of their malice, said, "Why are you putting me to the test, you hypocrites? Show me the coin used for the tax." And they brought him a denarius. Then he said to them, "Whose head is this, and whose title?" They answered, "The emperor's." Then he said to them, "Give therefore to the emperor the things that are the emperor's, and to God the things that are God's." When they heard this, they were amazed; and they left him and went away.

Year B

Job 38:1-7, (34-41)	**or**	✠ *Isaiah 53:4-12*
Psalm 104:1-9, 25, 37c		✠ *Psalm 91:9-16*
	Hebrews 5:1-10	
	Mark 10:35-45	

The Lesson   Job 38:1-7 (34-41)
Job 38:1-7

The LORD answered Job out of the whirlwind: "Who is this that darkens counsel by words without knowledge? Gird up your loins like a man, I will question you, and you shall declare to me. "Where were you when I laid the foundation of the earth? Tell me, if you have understanding. Who determined its measurements — surely you know! Or who stretched the line upon it? On what were its bases sunk, or who laid its cornerstone when the morning stars sang together and all the heavenly beings shouted for joy?

Job 38:(34-41) [Can you lift up your voice to the clouds, so that a flood of waters may cover you? Can you send forth lightnings, so that they may go and say to you, 'Here we are'? Who has put wisdom in the inward parts, or given understanding to the mind? Who has the wisdom to number the clouds? Or who can tilt the waterskins of the heavens, when the dust runs into a mass and the clods cling together? Can you hunt the prey for the lion, or satisfy the appetite of the young lions, when they crouch in their dens, or lie in wait in their covert? Who provides for the raven its prey, when its young ones cry to God, and wander about for lack of food?"]

The Response   Psalm 104:1-9, 25, 37c

Psalm 104:1-9, 25, 37c   *Benedic, anima mea*

1   Bless the LORD, O my soul; *
       O LORD my God, how excellent is your greatness!
       you are clothed with majesty and splendor.

2   You wrap yourself with light as with a cloak *
       and spread out the heavens like a curtain.

3   You lay the beams of your chambers in the waters above; *
       you make the clouds your chariot;
       you ride on the wings of the wind.

4   You make the winds your messengers *
       and flames of fire your servants.

5   You have set the earth upon its foundations, *
       so that it never shall move at any time.

6   You covered it with the Deep as with a mantle; *
       the waters stood higher than the mountains.

7   At your rebuke they fled; *
       at the voice of your thunder they hastened away.

8   They went up into the hills and down to the valleys beneath, *
       to the places you had appointed for them.

9   You set the limits that they should not pass; *
       they shall not again cover the earth.

25 O LORD, how manifold are your works! *
       in wisdom you have made them all;
       the earth is full of your creatures. Hallelujah!

or, ✠ **The Lesson**   **Isaiah 53:4-12**

Surely God's servant has borne our infirmities and carried our diseases; yet we accounted him stricken, struck down by God, and afflicted. But he was wounded for our transgressions, crushed for our iniquities; upon him was the punishment that made us whole, and by his bruises we are healed. All we like sheep have gone astray; we have all turned to our own way, and the LORD has laid on him the iniquity of us all. He was oppressed, and he was afflicted, yet he did not open his mouth; like a lamb that is led to the slaughter, and like a sheep that before its shearers is silent, so he did not open his mouth. By a perversion of justice he was taken away. Who could have imagined his future?

For he was cut off from the land of the living, stricken for the transgression of my people. They made his grave with the wicked and his tomb with the rich, although he had done no violence, and there was no deceit in his mouth. Yet it was the will of the LORD to crush him with pain. When you make his life an offering for sin, he shall see his offspring, and shall prolong his days; through him the will of the LORD shall prosper. Out of his anguish he shall see light; he shall find satisfaction through his knowledge. The righteous one, my servant, shall make many righteous, and he shall bear their iniquities. Therefore I will allot him a portion with the great, and he shall divide the spoil with the strong; because he poured out himself to death, and was numbered with the transgressors; yet he bore the sin of many, and made intercession for the transgressors.

✛ The Response   Psalm 91:9-16

Psalm 91:9-16   *Qui habitat*

9   Because you have made the LORD your refuge, *
    and the Most High your habitation,

10   There shall no evil happen to you, *
    neither shall any plague come near your dwelling.

11   For he shall give his angels charge over you, *
    to keep you in all your ways.

12   They shall bear you in their hands, *
    lest you dash your foot against a stone.

13   You shall tread upon the lion and adder; *
    you shall trample the young lion and the serpent under your feet.

14   Because he is bound to me in love,
therefore will I deliver him; *
    I will protect him, because he knows my Name.

15   He shall call upon me, and I will answer him; *
    I am with him in trouble;
    I will rescue him and bring him to honor.

16   With long life will I satisfy him, *
    and show him my salvation.

The Epistle   Hebrews 5:1-10

Every high priest chosen from among mortals is put in charge of things pertaining to God on their behalf, to offer gifts and sacrifices for sins. He is able to deal gently with the ignorant and wayward, since he himself is subject to weakness; and because of this he must offer sacrifice for his own sins as well as for those of the people. And one does not presume to take this honor, but takes it only when called by God, just as Aaron was. So also Christ did not glorify himself in becoming a high priest, but was appointed by the one who said to him, "You are my Son, today I have begotten you"; as he says also in another place, "You are a priest forever, according to the order of

Melchizedek." In the days of his flesh, Jesus offered up prayers and supplications, with loud cries and tears, to the one who was able to save him from death, and he was heard because of his reverent submission. Although he was a Son, he learned obedience through what he suffered; and having been made perfect, he became the source of eternal salvation for all who obey him, having been designated by God a high priest according to the order of Melchizedek.

The Gospel   Mark 10:35-45

James and John, the sons of Zebedee, came forward to Jesus and said to him, "Teacher, we want you to do for us whatever we ask of you." And he said to them, "What is it you want me to do for you?" And they said to him, "Grant us to sit, one at your right hand and one at your left, in your glory." But Jesus said to them, "You do not know what you are asking. Are you able to drink the cup that I drink, or be baptized with the baptism that I am baptized with?" They replied, "We are able." Then Jesus said to them, "The cup that I drink you will drink; and with the baptism with which I am baptized, you will be baptized; but to sit at my right hand or at my left is not mine to grant, but it is for those for whom it has been prepared." When the ten heard this, they began to be angry with James and John. So Jesus called them and said to them, "You know that among the Gentiles those whom they recognize as their rulers lord it over them, and their great ones are tyrants over them. But it is not so among you; but whoever wishes to become great among you must be your servant, and whoever wishes to be first among you must be slave of all. For the Son of Man came not to be served but to serve, and to give his life a ransom for many."

Year C

Jeremiah 31:27-34	**or**	✝ *Genesis 32:22-31*
Psalm 119:97-104		✝ *Psalm 121*

2 Timothy 3:14—4:5
Luke 18:1-8

The Lesson   Jeremiah 31:27-34

The days are surely coming, says the LORD, when I will sow the house of Israel and the house of Judah with the seed of humans and the seed of animals. And just as I have watched over them to pluck up and break down, to overthrow, destroy, and bring evil, so I will watch over them to build and to plant, says the LORD. In those days they shall no longer say: "The parents have eaten sour grapes, and the children's teeth are set on edge." But all shall die for their own sins; the teeth of everyone who eats sour grapes shall be set on edge. The days are surely coming, says the LORD, when I will make a new covenant with the house of Israel and the house of Judah. It will not be like the covenant that I made with their ancestors when I took them by the hand to bring them out of the land of Egypt — a covenant that they broke, though I was their husband, says the LORD. But this is the covenant that I will make with the house of Israel after those days, says the LORD: I will put my law within them, and I will write it on their hearts; and I will be their God, and they shall be my people. No longer shall they teach one another, or say to each other, "Know the LORD," for they shall all know me, from the least of them to the greatest, says the LORD; for I will forgive their iniquity, and remember their sin no more.

The Response   Psalm 119:97-104

Psalm 119:97-104   *Quomodo dilexi!*

97   Oh, how I love your law! *
           all the day long it is in my mind.
98   Your commandment has made me wiser than my enemies, *
           and it is always with me.
99   I have more understanding than all my teachers, *
           for your decrees are my study.
100   I am wiser than the elders, *
           because I observe your commandments.
101   I restrain my feet from every evil way, *
           that I may keep your word.
102   I do not shrink from your judgments, *
           because you yourself have taught me.
103   How sweet are your words to my taste! *
           they are sweeter than honey to my mouth.
104   Through your commandments I gain understanding; *
           therefore I hate every lying way.

or, ✛ The Lesson   Genesis 32:22-31

The same night Jacob got up and took his two wives, his two maids, and his eleven children, and crossed the ford of the Jabbok. He took them and sent them across the stream, and likewise everything that he had. Jacob was left alone; and a man wrestled with him until daybreak. When the man saw that he did not prevail against Jacob, he struck him on the hip socket; and Jacob's hip was put out of joint as he wrestled with him. Then he said, "Let me go, for the day is breaking." But Jacob said, "I will not let you go, unless you bless me." So he said to him, "What is your name?" And he said, "Jacob." Then the man said, "You shall no longer be called Jacob, but Israel, for you have striven with God and with humans, and have prevailed." Then Jacob asked him, "Please tell me your name?" But he said, "Why is it that you ask my name?" And there he blessed him. So Jacob called the place Peniel, saying, "For I have seen God face to face, and yet my life is preserved." The sun rose upon him as he passed Penuel, limping because of his hip.

Psalm 121   *Levavi oculos*

1   I lift up my eyes to the hills; *
        from where is my help to come?

2   My help comes from the LORD, *
        the maker of heaven and earth.

3   He will not let your foot be moved *
        and he who watches over you will not fall asleep.

4   Behold, he who keeps watch over Israel *
        shall neither slumber nor sleep;

5   The LORD himself watches over you; *
        the LORD is your shade at your right hand,

6   So that the sun shall not strike you by day, *
        nor the moon by night.

7   The LORD shall preserve you from all evil; *
        it is he who shall keep you safe.

8   The LORD shall watch over your going out and your coming in, *
        from this time forth for evermore.

The Epistle   2 Timothy 3:14—4:5

As for you, continue in what you have learned and firmly believed, knowing
from whom you learned it, and how from childhood you have known the
sacred writings that are able to instruct you for salvation through faith in
Christ Jesus. All scripture is inspired by God and is useful for teaching, for
reproof, for correction, and for training in righteousness, so that everyone who
belongs to God may be proficient, equipped for every good work. In the
presence of God and of Christ Jesus, who is to judge the living and the dead,
and in view of his appearing and his kingdom, I solemnly urge you: proclaim
the message; be persistent whether the time is favorable or unfavorable;
convince, rebuke, and encourage, with the utmost patience in teaching. For the
time is coming when people will not put up with sound doctrine, but having
itching ears, they will accumulate for themselves teachers to suit their own
desires, and will turn away from listening to the truth and wander away to
myths. As for you, always be sober, endure suffering, do the work of an
evangelist, carry out your ministry fully.

The Gospel   Luke 18:1-8

Jesus told the disciples a parable about their need to pray always and not to
lose heart. He said, "In a certain city there was a judge who neither feared
God nor had respect for people. In that city there was a widow who kept
coming to him and saying, 'Grant me justice against my opponent.' For a
while he refused; but later he said to himself, 'Though I have no fear of God

and no respect for anyone, yet because this widow keeps bothering me, I will grant her justice, so that she may not wear me out by continually coming.' " And the Lord said, "Listen to what the unjust judge says. And will not God grant justice to his chosen ones who cry to him day and night? Will he delay long in helping them? I tell you, he will quickly grant justice to them. And yet, when the Son of Man comes, will he find faith on earth?"

PROPER 25

Sunday between October 23 and October 29 inclusive

The Collect

Almighty and everlasting God, increase in us the gifts of faith, hope, and charity; and, that we may obtain what you promise, make us love what you command; through Jesus Christ our Lord, who lives and reigns with you and the Holy Spirit, one God, for ever and ever. *Amen.*

Year A

Deuteronomy 34:1-12	**or**	✝ *Leviticus 19:1-2, 15-18*
Psalm 90:1-6, 13-17		✝ *Psalm 1*

1 Thessalonians 2:1-8
Matthew 22:34-46

The Lesson   Deuteronomy 34:1-12

Moses went up from the plains of Moab to Mount Nebo, to the top of Pisgah, which is opposite Jericho, and the LORD showed him the whole land: Gilead as far as Dan, all Naphtali, the land of Ephraim and Manasseh, all the land of Judah as far as the Western Sea, the Negeb, and the Plain — that is, the valley of Jericho, the city of palm trees — as far as Zoar. The LORD said to him, "This is the land of which I swore to Abraham, to Isaac, and to Jacob, saying, 'I will give it to your descendants'; I have let you see it with your eyes, but you shall not cross over there." Then Moses, the servant of the LORD, died there in the land of Moab, at the Lord's command. He was buried in a valley in the land of Moab, opposite Beth-peor, but no one knows his burial place to this day. Moses was one hundred twenty years old when he died; his sight was unimpaired and his vigor had not abated. The Israelites wept for Moses in the plains of Moab thirty days; then the period of mourning for Moses was ended. Joshua son of Nun was full of the spirit of wisdom, because Moses had laid his hands on him; and the Israelites obeyed him, doing as the LORD had commanded Moses. Never since has there arisen a prophet in Israel like Moses, whom the LORD knew face to face. He was unequaled for all the signs and wonders that the LORD sent him to perform in the land of Egypt, against Pharaoh and all his servants and his entire land, and for all the mighty deeds and all the terrifying displays of power that Moses performed in the sight of all Israel.

The Response   **Psalm 90:1-6, 13-17**

Psalm 90:1-6, 13-17   *Domine, refugium*

1   LORD, you have been our refuge *
    from one generation to another.

2   Before the mountains were brought forth,
    or the land and the earth were born, *
    from age to age you are God.

3   You turn us back to the dust and say, *
    "Go back, O child of earth."

4   For a thousand years in your sight are like yesterday when it is past *
    and like a watch in the night.

5   You sweep us away like a dream; *
    we fade away suddenly like the grass.

6   In the morning it is green and flourishes; *
    in the evening it is dried up and withered.

13   Return, O LORD; how long will you tarry? *
    be gracious to your servants.

14   Satisfy us by your loving-kindness in the morning; *
    so shall we rejoice and be glad all the days of our life.

15   Make us glad by the measure of the days that you afflicted us *
    and the years in which we suffered adversity.

16   Show your servants your works *
    and your splendor to their children.

17   May the graciousness of the LORD our God be upon us; *
    prosper the work of our hands;
    prosper our handiwork.

or, ✙ **The Lesson**   **Leviticus 19:1-2, 15-18**

The LORD spoke to Moses, saying: Speak to all the congregation of the people of Israel and say to them: You shall be holy, for I the LORD your God am holy. You shall not render an unjust judgment; you shall not be partial to the poor or defer to the great: with justice you shall judge your neighbor. You shall not go around as a slanderer among your people, and you shall not profit by the blood of your neighbor: I am the LORD. You shall not hate in your heart anyone of your kin; you shall reprove your neighbor, or you will incur guilt yourself. You shall not take vengeance or bear a grudge against any of your people, but you shall love your neighbor as yourself: I am the LORD.

✙ **The Response**   **Psalm 1**

Psalm 1   *Beatus vir qui non abiit*

1   Happy are they who have not walked in the counsel of the wicked, *
      nor lingered in the way of sinners,
      nor sat in the seats of the scornful!

2 Their delight is in the law of the Lord, *
and they meditate on his law day and night.
3 They are like trees planted by streams of water,
bearing fruit in due season, with leaves that do not wither; *
everything they do shall prosper.
4 It is not so with the wicked; *
they are like chaff which the wind blows away.
5 Therefore the wicked shall not stand upright when judgment comes, *
nor the sinner in the council of the righteous.
6 For the Lord knows the way of the righteous, *
but the way of the wicked is doomed.

The Epistle   1 Thessalonians 2:1-8

You yourselves know, brothers and sisters, that our coming to you was not in
vain, but though we had already suffered and been shamefully mistreated at
Philippi, as you know, we had courage in our God to declare to you the gospel
of God in spite of great opposition. For our appeal does not spring from deceit
or impure motives or trickery, but just as we have been approved by God to be
entrusted with the message of the gospel, even so we speak, not to please
mortals, but to please God who tests our hearts. As you know and as God is
our witness, we never came with words of flattery or with a pretext for greed;
nor did we seek praise from mortals, whether from you or from others, though
we might have made demands as apostles of Christ. But we were gentle
among you, like a nurse tenderly caring for her own children. So deeply do we
care for you that we are determined to share with you not only the gospel of
God but also our own selves, because you have become very dear to us.

The Gospel   Matthew 22:34-46

When the Pharisees heard that Jesus had silenced the Sadducees, they gathered
together, and one of them, a lawyer, asked him a question to test him.
"Teacher, which commandment in the law is the greatest?" He said to him,
" 'You shall love the Lord your God with all your heart, and with all your
soul, and with all your mind.' This is the greatest and first commandment.
And a second is like it: 'You shall love your neighbor as yourself.' On these
two commandments hang all the law and the prophets." Now while the
Pharisees were gathered together, Jesus asked them this question: "What do
you think of the Messiah? Whose son is he?" They said to him, "The son of
David." He said to them, "How is it then that David by the Spirit calls him
Lord, saying, 'The Lord said to my Lord, "Sit at my right hand, until I put
your enemies under your feet' "? If David thus calls him Lord, how can he be
his son?" No one was able to give him an answer, nor from that day did
anyone dare to ask him any more questions.

Year B

Job 42:1-6, 10-17   **or**   ✠ *Jeremiah 31:7-9*
Psalm 34:1-8, (19-22)   ✠ *Psalm 126*

Hebrews 7:23-28
Mark 10:46-52

The Lesson   Job 42:1-6, 10-17

Job answered the LORD: "I know that you can do all things, and that no
purpose of yours can be thwarted. 'Who is this that hides counsel without
knowledge?' Therefore I have uttered what I did not understand, things too
wonderful for me, which I did not know. 'Hear, and I will speak; I will
question you, and you declare to me.' I had heard of you by the hearing of the
ear, but now my eye sees you; therefore I despise myself, and repent in dust
and ashes." And the LORD restored the fortunes of Job when he had prayed for
his friends; and the LORD gave Job twice as much as he had before. Then there
came to him all his brothers and sisters and all who had known him before,
and they ate bread with him in his house; they showed him sympathy and
comforted him for all the evil that the LORD had brought upon him; and each
of them gave him a piece of money and a gold ring. The LORD blessed the
latter days of Job more than his beginning; and he had fourteen thousand
sheep, six thousand camels, a thousand yoke of oxen, and a thousand donkeys.
He also had seven sons and three daughters. He named the first Jemimah, the
second Keziah, and the third Keren-happuch. In all the land there were no
women so beautiful as Job's daughters; and their father gave them an inheritance along with their brothers. After this Job lived one hundred and forty
years, and saw his children, and his children's children, four generations. And
Job died, old and full of days.

The Response   Psalm 34:1-8, (19-22)

Psalm 34:1-8, (19-22)   *Benedicam Dominum*
1   I will bless the LORD at all times; *
        his praise shall ever be in my mouth.
2   I will glory in the LORD; *
        let the humble hear and rejoice.
3   Proclaim with me the greatness of the LORD; *
        let us exalt his Name together.
4   I sought the LORD, and he answered me *
        and delivered me out of all my terror.
5   Look upon him and be radiant, *
        and let not your faces be ashamed.
6   I called in my affliction and the LORD heard me *
        and saved me from all my troubles.

7   The angel of the LORD encompasses those who fear him, *
    and he will deliver them.

8   Taste and see that the LORD is good; *
    happy are they who trust in him!

[19   Many are the troubles of the righteous, *
    but the LORD will deliver him out of them all.

20   He will keep safe all his bones; *
    not one of them shall be broken.

21   Evil shall slay the wicked, *
    and those who hate the righteous will be punished.

22   The LORD ransoms the life of his servants, *
    and none will be punished who trust in him.]

or, ✠ **The Lesson**   Jeremiah 31:7-9

Thus says the LORD: Sing aloud with gladness for Jacob, and raise shouts for the chief of the nations; proclaim, give praise, and say, "Save, O LORD, your people, the remnant of Israel." See, I am going to bring them from the land of the north, and gather them from the farthest parts of the earth, among them the blind and the lame, those with child and those in labor, together; a great company, they shall return here. With weeping they shall come, and with consolations I will lead them back, I will let them walk by brooks of water, in a straight path in which they shall not stumble; for I have become a father to Israel, and Ephraim is my firstborn.

✠ **The Response**   Psalm 126

Psalm 126   *In convertendo*

1   When the LORD restored the fortunes of Zion, *
    then were we like those who dream.

2   Then was our mouth filled with laughter, *
    and our tongue with shouts of joy.

3   Then they said among the nations, *
    "The LORD has done great things for them."

4   The LORD has done great things for us, *
    and we are glad indeed.

5   Restore our fortunes, O LORD, *
    like the watercourses of the Negev.

6   Those who sowed with tears *
    will reap with songs of joy.

7   Those who go out weeping, carrying the seed, *
    will come again with joy, shouldering their sheaves.

The Epistle   **Hebrews 7:23-28**

The former priests were many in number, because they were prevented by death from continuing in office; but he holds his priesthood permanently, because he continues forever. Consequently he is able for all time to save those who approach God through him, since he always lives to make intercession for them. For it was fitting that we should have such a high priest, holy, blameless, undefiled, separated from sinners, and exalted above the heavens. Unlike the other high priests, he has no need to offer sacrifices day after day, first for his own sins, and then for those of the people; this he did once for all when he offered himself. For the law appoints as high priests those who are subject to weakness, but the word of the oath, which came later than the law, appoints a Son who has been made perfect forever.

The Gospel   **Mark 10:46-52**

Jesus and his disciples came to Jericho. As he and his disciples and a large crowd were leaving Jericho, Bartimaeus son of Timaeus, a blind beggar, was sitting by the roadside. When he heard that it was Jesus of Nazareth, he began to shout out and say, "Jesus, Son of David, have mercy on me!" Many sternly ordered him to be quiet, but he cried out even more loudly, "Son of David, have mercy on me!" Jesus stood still and said, "Call him here." And they called the blind man, saying to him, "Take heart; get up, he is calling you." So throwing off his cloak, he sprang up and came to Jesus. Then Jesus said to him, "What do you want me to do for you?" The blind man said to him, "My teacher, let me see again." Jesus said to him, "Go; your faith has made you well." Immediately he regained his sight and followed him on the way.

Year C

Joel 2:23-32   **or**   ✛ *Sirach 35:12-17*
Psalm 65   or *Jeremiah 14:7-10, 19-22*
                                              ✛ *Psalm 84:1-6*

2 Timothy 4:6-8, 16-18
Luke 18:9-14

The Lesson   **Joel 2:23-32**

O children of Zion, be glad and rejoice in the LORD your God; for he has given the early rain for your vindication, he has poured down for you abundant rain, the early and the later rain, as before. The threshing floors shall be full of grain, the vats shall overflow with wine and oil. I will repay you for the years that the swarming locust has eaten, the hopper, the destroyer, and the cutter, my great army, which I sent against you. You shall eat in plenty and be satisfied, and praise the name of the LORD your God, who has dealt wondrously with you. And my people shall never again be put to shame. You shall know that I am in the midst of Israel, and that I, the LORD, am your God and there is no other. And my people shall never again be put to shame. Then afterward I will pour out my spirit on all flesh; your sons and your daughters shall prophesy, your old men shall dream dreams, and your young men shall see visions. Even on the male and female slaves, in those days, I will pour out my spirit. I will show portents in the heavens and on the earth, blood and fire and columns of smoke. The sun shall be turned to darkness, and the moon to blood, before the great and terrible day of the LORD comes. Then everyone who calls on the name of the LORD shall be saved; for in Mount Zion and in Jerusalem there shall be those who escape, as the LORD has said, and among the survivors shall be those whom the LORD calls.

The Response   Psalm 65

Psalm 65   *Te decet hymnus*

1   You are to be praised, O God, in Zion; *
        to you shall vows be performed in Jerusalem.
2   To you that hear prayer shall all flesh come, *
        because of their transgressions.
3   Our sins are stronger than we are, *
        but you will blot them out.
4   Happy are they whom you choose
     and draw to your courts to dwell there! *
        they will be satisfied by the beauty of your house,
        by the holiness of your temple.
5   Awesome things will you show us in your righteousness,
     O God of our salvation, *
        O Hope of all the ends of the earth
        and of the seas that are far away.
6   You make fast the mountains by your power; *
        they are girded about with might.
7   You still the roaring of the seas, *
        the roaring of their waves,
        and the clamor of the peoples.
8   Those who dwell at the ends of the earth will tremble at your
                            marvelous signs; *
        you make the dawn and the dusk to sing for joy.
9   You visit the earth and water it abundantly;
     you make it very plenteous; *
        the river of God is full of water.
10   You prepare the grain, *
        for so you provide for the earth.
11   You drench the furrows and smooth out the ridges; *
        with heavy rain you soften the ground and bless its increase.
12   You crown the year with your goodness, *
        and your paths overflow with plenty.

13   May the fields of the wilderness be rich for grazing, *
     and the hills be clothed with joy.
14   May the meadows cover themselves with flocks,
    and the valleys cloak themselves with grain; *
     let them shout for joy and sing.

or, ✣ The Lesson   Sirach 35:12-17 *or* Jeremiah 14:7-10, 19-22
Sirach 35:12-17

Give to the Most High as he has given to you, and as generously as you can afford. For the Lord is the one who repays, and he will repay you sevenfold. Do not offer him a bribe, for he will not accept it; and do not rely on a dishonest sacrifice; for the Lord is the judge, and with him there is no partiality. He will not show partiality to the poor; but he will listen to the prayer of one who is wronged. He will not ignore the supplication of the orphan, or the widow when she pours out her complaint.

or, ✣ Jeremiah 14:7-10, 19-22

Although our iniquities testify against us, act, O Lord, for your name's sake; our apostasies indeed are many, and we have sinned against you. O hope of Israel, its savior in time of trouble, why should you be like a stranger in the land, like a traveler turning aside for the night? Why should you be like someone confused, like a mighty warrior who cannot give help? Yet you, O Lord, are in the midst of us, and we are called by your name; do not forsake us! Thus says the Lord concerning this people: Truly they have loved to wander, they have not restrained their feet; therefore the Lord does not accept them, now he will remember their iniquity and punish their sins. Have you completely rejected Judah? Does your heart loathe Zion? Why have you struck us down so that there is no healing for us? We look for peace, but find no good; for a time of healing, but there is terror instead. We acknowledge our wickedness, O Lord, the iniquity of our ancestors, for we have sinned against you. Do not spurn us, for your name' s sake; do not dishonor your glorious throne; remember and do not break your covenant with us. Can any idols of the nations bring rain? Or can the heavens give showers? Is it not you, O Lord our God? We set our hope on you, for it is you who do all this.

✣ The Response   Psalm 84:1-6

Psalm 84:1-6   *Quam dilecta!*
1   How dear to me is your dwelling, O Lord of hosts! *
     My soul has a desire and longing for the courts of
       the Lord;
     my heart and my flesh rejoice in the living God.

2   The sparrow has found her a house
     and the swallow a nest where she may lay her young; *
          by the side of your altars, O LORD of hosts,
          my King and my God.
3   Happy are they who dwell in your house! *
          they will always be praising you.
4   Happy are the people whose strength is in you! *
          whose hearts are set on the pilgrims' way.
5   Those who go through the desolate valley will find
               it a place of springs, *
          for the early rains have covered it with pools of water.
6   They will climb from height to height, *
          and the God of gods will reveal himself in Zion.

The Epistle   2 Timothy 4:6-8, 16-18

As for me, I am already being poured out as a libation, and the time of my
departure has come. I have fought the good fight, I have finished the race, I
have kept the faith. From now on there is reserved for me the crown of
righteousness, which the Lord, the righteous judge, will give me on that day,
and not only to me but also to all who have longed for his appearing. At my
first defense no one came to my support, but all deserted me. May it not be
counted against them! But the Lord stood by me and gave me strength, so that
through me the message might be fully proclaimed and all the Gentiles might
hear it. So I was rescued from the lion's mouth. The Lord will rescue me from
every evil attack and save me for his heavenly kingdom. To him be the glory
forever and ever. Amen.

The Gospel   Luke 18:9-14

Jesus also told this parable to some who trusted in themselves that they were
righteous and regarded others with contempt: "Two men went up to the temple
to pray, one a Pharisee and the other a tax collector. The Pharisee, standing by
himself, was praying thus, 'God, I thank you that I am not like other people:
thieves, rogues, adulterers, or even like this tax collector. I fast twice a week; I
give a tenth of all my income.' But the tax collector, standing far off, would
not even look up to heaven, but was beating his breast and saying, 'God, be
merciful to me, a sinner!' I tell you, this man went down to his home justified
rather than the other; for all who exalt themselves will be humbled, but all
who humble themselves will be exalted."

PROPER 26

Sunday between October 30 and November 5 inclusive

The Collect

Almighty and merciful God, it is only by your gift that your faithful people offer you true and laudable service: Grant that we may run without stumbling to obtain your heavenly promises; through Jesus Christ our Lord, who lives and reigns with you and the Holy Spirit, one God, now and for ever. *Amen.*

Year A

Joshua 3:7-17	**or**	☩ *Micah 3:5-12*
Psalm 107:1-7, 33-37		☩ *Psalm 43*

1 Thessalonians 2:9-13
Matthew 23:1-12

The Lesson   Joshua 3:7-17

The LORD said to Joshua, "This day I will begin to exalt you in the sight of all Israel, so that they may know that I will be with you as I was with Moses. You are the one who shall command the priests who bear the ark of the covenant, 'When you come to the edge of the waters of the Jordan, you shall stand still in the Jordan.' " Joshua then said to the Israelites, "Draw near and hear the words of the LORD your God." Joshua said, "By this you shall know that among you is the living God who without fail will drive out from before you the Canaanites, Hittites, Hivites, Perizzites, Girgashites, Amorites, and Jebusites: the ark of the covenant of the Lord of all the earth is going to pass before you into the Jordan. So now select twelve men from the tribes of Israel, one from each tribe. When the soles of the feet of the priests who bear the ark of the LORD, the Lord of all the earth, rest in the waters of the Jordan, the waters of the Jordan flowing from above shall be cut off; they shall stand in a single heap." When the people set out from their tents to cross over the Jordan, the priests bearing the ark of the covenant were in front of the people. Now the Jordan overflows all its banks throughout the time of harvest. So when those who bore the ark had come to the Jordan, and the feet of the priests bearing the ark were dipped in the edge of the water, the waters flowing from above stood still, rising up in a single heap far off at Adam, the city that is beside Zarethan, while those flowing toward the sea of the Arabah, the Dead Sea, were wholly cut off. Then the people crossed over opposite Jericho. While all Israel were crossing over on dry ground, the priests who bore the ark of the covenant of the LORD stood on dry ground in the middle of the Jordan, until the entire nation finished crossing over the Jordan.

The Response   **Psalm 107:1-7, 33-37**

Psalm 107:1-7, 33-37   *Confitemini Domino*

1   Give thanks to the LORD, for he is good, *
        and his mercy endures for ever.
2   Let all those whom the LORD has redeemed proclaim *
        that he redeemed them from the hand of the foe.
3   He gathered them out of the lands; *
        from the east and from the west,
        from the north and from the south.
4   Some wandered in desert wastes; *
        they found no way to a city where they might dwell.
5   They were hungry and thirsty; *
        their spirits languished within them.
6   Then they cried to the LORD in their trouble, *
        and he delivered them from their distress.
7   He put their feet on a straight path *
        to go to a city where they might dwell.
33 The LORD changed rivers into deserts, *
        and water-springs into thirsty ground,
34 A fruitful land into salt flats, *
        because of the wickedness of those who dwell there.
35 He changed deserts into pools of water *
        and dry land into water-springs.
36 He settled the hungry there, *
        and they founded a city to dwell in.
37 They sowed fields, and planted vineyards, *
        and brought in a fruitful harvest.

or, ✠ **The Lesson**   **Micah 3:5-12**

Thus says the Lord concerning the prophets who lead my people astray, who
cry "Peace" when they have something to eat, but declare war against those
who put nothing into their mouths. Therefore it shall be night to you, without
vision, and darkness to you, without revelation. The sun shall go down upon
the prophets, and the day shall be black over them; the seers shall be disgraced, and the diviners put to shame; they shall all cover their lips, for there
is no answer from God. But as for me, I am filled with power, with the spirit
of the Lord, and with justice and might, to declare to Jacob his transgression
and to Israel his sin. Hear this, you rulers of the house of Jacob and chiefs of
the house of Israel, who abhor justice and pervert all equity, who build Zion
with blood and Jerusalem with wrong! Its rulers give judgment for a bribe, its
priests teach for a price, its prophets give oracles for money; yet they lean
upon the Lord and say, "Surely the Lord is with us! No harm shall come upon

us." Therefore because of you Zion shall be plowed as a field; Jerusalem shall become a heap of ruins, and the mountain of the house a wooded height.

✟ The Response   Psalm 43

Psalm 43   *Judica me, Deus*

1   Give judgment for me, O God,
       and defend my cause against an ungodly people; *
          deliver me from the deceitful and the wicked.

2   For you are the God of my strength;
       why have you put me from you? *
          and why do I go so heavily while the enemy   oppresses me?

3   Send out your light and your truth, that they may lead me, *
          and bring me to your holy hill
          and to your dwelling;

4   That I may go to the altar of God,
       to the God of my joy and gladness; *
          and on the harp I will give thanks to you, O God my God.

5   Why are you so full of heaviness, O my soul? *
          and why are you so disquieted within me?

6   Put your trust in God; *
          for I will yet give thanks to him,
          who is the help of my countenance, and my God.

The Epistle   1 Thessalonians 2:9-13

You remember our labor and toil, brothers and sisters; we worked night and day, so that we might not burden any of you while we proclaimed to you the gospel of God. You are witnesses, and God also, how pure, upright, and blameless our conduct was toward you believers. As you know, we dealt with each one of you like a father with his children, urging and encouraging you and pleading that you lead a life worthy of God, who calls you into his own kingdom and glory. We also constantly give thanks to God for this, that when you received the word of God that you heard from us, you accepted it not as a human word but as what it really is, God's word, which is also at work in you believers.

The Gospel   Matthew 23:1-12

Jesus said to the crowds and to his disciples, "The scribes and the Pharisees sit on Moses' seat; therefore, do whatever they teach you and follow it; but do not do as they do, for they do not practice what they teach. They tie up heavy burdens, hard to bear, and lay them on the shoulders of others; but they themselves are unwilling to lift a finger to move them. They do all their deeds to be seen by others; for they make their phylacteries broad and their fringes long. They love to have the place of honor at banquets and the best seats in the synagogues, and to be greeted with respect in the marketplaces, and to have people call them rabbi. But you are not to be called rabbi, for you have one teacher, and you are all students. And call no one your father on earth, for you have one Father — the one in heaven. Nor are you to be called instructors, for you have one instructor, the Messiah. The greatest among you will be your servant. All who exalt themselves will be humbled, and all who humble themselves will be exalted."

Year B

Ruth 1:1-18	**or**	✛ *Deuteronomy 6:1-9*
Psalm 146		✛ *Psalm 119:1-8*
	Hebrews 9:11-14	
	Mark 12:28-34	

The Lesson   **Ruth 1:1-18**

In the days when the judges ruled, there was a famine in the land, and a certain man of Bethlehem in Judah went to live in the country of Moab, he and his wife and two sons. The name of the man was Elimelech and the name of his wife Naomi, and the names of his two sons were Mahlon and Chilion; they were Ephrathites from Bethlehem in Judah. They went into the country of Moab and remained there. But Elimelech, the husband of Naomi, died, and she was left with her two sons. These took Moabite wives; the name of the one was Orpah and the name of the other Ruth. When they had lived there about ten years, both Mahlon and Chilion also died, so that the woman was left without her two sons and her husband. Then she started to return with her daughters-in-law from the country of Moab, for she had heard in the country of Moab that the LORD had considered his people and given them food. So she set out from the place where she had been living, she and her two daughters-in-law, and they went on their way to go back to the land of Judah. But Naomi said to her two daughters-in-law, "Go back each of you to your mother's house. May the LORD deal kindly with you, as you have dealt with the dead and with me. The LORD grant that you may find security, each of you in the house of your husband." Then she kissed them, and they wept aloud. They said to her, "No, we will return with you to your people." But Naomi said, "Turn back, my daughters, why will you go with me? Do I still have sons in my womb that they may become your husbands? Turn back, my daughters, go your way, for I am too old to have a husband. Even if I thought there was hope for me, even if I should have a husband tonight and bear sons, would you then wait until they were grown? Would you then refrain from marrying? No, my daughters, it has been far more bitter for me than for you, because the hand of the LORD has turned against me." Then they wept aloud again. Orpah kissed her mother-in-law, but Ruth clung to her. So she said, "See, your sister-in-law has gone back to her people and to her gods; return after your sister-in-law." But Ruth said, "Do not press me to leave you or to turn back from following you! Where you go, I will go; where you lodge, I will lodge; your people shall be my people, and your God my God. Where you die, I will die — there will I be buried. May the LORD do thus and so to me, and more as well, if even death parts me from you!" When Naomi saw that she was determined to go with her, she said no more to her.

The Response   Psalm 146

Psalm 146   *Lauda, anima mea*
1   Hallelujah!
     Praise the LORD, O my soul! *
          I will praise the LORD as long as I live;
          I will sing praises to my God while I have my being.
2   Put not your trust in rulers, nor in any child of earth, *
          for there is no help in them.
3   When they breathe their last, they return to earth, *
          and in that day their thoughts perish.
4   Happy are they who have the God of Jacob for their help! *
          whose hope is in the LORD their God;
5   Who made heaven and earth, the seas, and all that is in them; *
          who keeps his promise for ever;
6   Who gives justice to those who are oppressed, *
          and food to those who hunger.
7   The LORD sets the prisoners free;
     the LORD opens the eyes of the blind; *
          the LORD lifts up those who are bowed down;
8   The LORD loves the righteous;
     the LORD cares for the stranger; *
          he sustains the orphan and widow,
          but frustrates the way of the wicked.
9   The LORD shall reign for ever, *
          your God, O Zion, throughout all generations.
          Hallelujah!

or, ✠ The Lesson   Deuteronomy 6:1-9

Moses said, "Now this is the commandment — the statutes and the ordinances — that the LORD your God charged me to teach you to observe in the land that you are about to cross into and occupy, so that you and your children and your children's children, may fear the LORD your God all the days of your life, and keep all his decrees and his commandments that I am commanding you, so that your days may be long. Hear therefore, O Israel, and observe them diligently, so that it may go well with you, and so that you may multiply greatly in a land flowing with milk and honey, as the LORD, the God of your ancestors, has promised you. Hear, O Israel: The LORD is our God, the LORD alone. You shall love the LORD your God with all your heart, and with all your soul, and with all your might. Keep these words that I am commanding you today in your heart. Recite them to your children and talk about them when you are at home and when you are away, when you lie down and when you rise. Bind them as a sign on your hand, fix them as an emblem on your forehead, and write them on the doorposts of your house and on your gates."

☩ The Response   Psalm 119:1-8

Psalm 119:1-8   *Beati immaculati*

1   Happy are they whose way is blameless, *
        who walk in the law of the LORD!
2   Happy are they who observe his decrees *
        and seek him with all their hearts!
3   Who never do any wrong, *
        but always walk in his ways.
4   You laid down your commandments, *
        that we should fully keep them.
5   Oh, that my ways were made so direct *
        that I might keep your statutes!
6   Then I should not be put to shame, *
        when I regard all your commandments.
7   I will thank you with an unfeigned heart, *
        when I have learned your righteous judgments.
8   I will keep your statutes; *
        do not utterly forsake me.

The Epistle   Hebrews 9:11-14

When Christ came as a high priest of the good things that have come, then through the greater and perfect tent (not made with hands, that is, not of this creation), he entered once for all into the Holy Place, not with the blood of goats and calves, but with his own blood, thus obtaining eternal redemption. For if the blood of goats and bulls, with the sprinkling of the ashes of a heifer, sanctifies those who have been defiled so that their flesh is purified, how much more will the blood of Christ, who through the eternal Spirit offered himself without blemish to God, purify our conscience from dead works to worship the living God!

The Gospel   Mark 12:28-34

One of the scribes came near and heard the Sadducees disputing with one another, and seeing that Jesus answered them well, he asked him, "Which commandment is the first of all?" Jesus answered, "The first is 'Hear, O Israel: the Lord our God, the Lord is one; you shall love the Lord your God with all your heart, and with all your soul, and with all your mind, and with all your strength.' The second is this, 'You shall love your neighbor as yourself.' There is no other commandment greater than these." Then the scribe said to him, "You are right, Teacher; you have truly said that 'he is one, and besides him there is no other'; and 'to love him with all the heart, and with all the understanding, and with all the strength', and 'to love one's neighbor as oneself,' — this is much more important than all whole burnt offerings and sacrifices." When Jesus saw that he answered wisely, he said to him, "You are not far from the kingdom of God." After that no one dared to ask him any question.

Year C

Habakkuk 1:1-4; 2:1-4   **or**   ✠ *Isaiah 1:10-18*
Psalm 119:137-144   ✠ *Psalm 32:1-7*
2 Thessalonians 1:1-4, 11-12
Luke 19:1-10

The Lesson   Habakkuk 1:1-4; 2:1-4

The oracle that the prophet Habakkuk saw. O LORD, how long shall I cry for help, and you will not listen? Or cry to you "Violence!" and you will not save? Why do you make me see wrong-doing and look at trouble? Destruction and violence are before me; strife and contention arise. So the law becomes slack and justice never prevails. The wicked surround the righteous — therefore judgment comes forth perverted. I will stand at my watchpost, and station myself on the rampart; I will keep watch to see what he will say to me, and what he will answer concerning my complaint. Then the LORD answered me and said: Write the vision; make it plain on tablets, so that a runner may read it. For there is still a vision for the appointed time; it speaks of the end, and does not lie. If it seems to tarry, wait for it; it will surely come, it will not delay. Look at the proud! Their spirit is not right in them, but the righteous live by their faith.

The Response   Psalm 119:137-144

Psalm 119:137-144   *Justus es, Domine*
  137   You are righteous, O LORD, *
          and upright are your judgments.

138   You have issued your decrees *
       with justice and in perfect faithfulness.
139   My indignation has consumed me, *
       because my enemies forget your words.
140   Your word has been tested to the uttermost, *
       and your servant holds it dear.
141   I am small and of little account, *
       yet I do not forget your commandments.
142   Your justice is an everlasting justice *
       and your law is the truth.
143   Trouble and distress have come upon me, *
       yet your commandments are my delight.
144   The righteousness of your decrees is everlasting; *
       grant me understanding, that I may live.

or, ✠ The Lesson   Isaiah 1:10-18

Hear the word of the LORD, you rulers of Sodom! Listen to the teaching of our God, you people of Gomorrah! What to me is the multitude of your sacrifices? says the LORD; I have had enough of burnt offerings of rams and the fat of fed beasts; I do not delight in the blood of bulls, or of lambs, or of goats. When you come to appear before me, who asked this from your hand? Trample my courts no more; bringing offerings is futile; incense is an abomination to me. New moon and sabbath and calling of convocation — I cannot endure solemn assemblies with iniquity. Your new moons and your appointed festivals my soul hates; they have become a burden to me, I am weary of bearing them. When you stretch out your hands, I will hide my eyes from you; even though you make many prayers, I will not listen; your hands are full of blood. Wash yourselves; make yourselves clean; remove the evil of your doings from before my eyes; cease to do evil, learn to do good; seek justice, rescue the oppressed, defend the orphan, plead for the widow. Come now, let us argue it out, says the LORD: though your sins are like scarlet, they shall be like snow; though they are red like crimson, they shall become like wool.

✠ The Response   Psalm 32:1-7

Psalm 32:1-7   *Beati quorum*

1   Happy are they whose transgressions are forgiven, *
      and whose sin is put away!
2   Happy are they to whom the LORD imputes no guilt, *
      and in whose spirit there is no guile!
3   While I held my tongue, my bones withered away, *
      because of my groaning all day long.

4   For your hand was heavy upon me day and night; *
            my moisture was dried up as in the heat of summer.

5   Then I acknowledged my sin to you, *
            and did not conceal my guilt.

6   I said, "I will confess my transgressions to the LORD." *
            Then you forgave me the guilt of my sin.

7   Therefore all the faithful will make their prayers to you in
                    time of trouble; *
            when the great waters overflow, they shall not reach them.

The Epistle   2 Thessalonians 1:1-4, 11-12

Paul, Silvanus, and Timothy, To the church of the Thessalonians in God our
Father and the Lord Jesus Christ: Grace to you and peace from God our
Father and the Lord Jesus Christ. We must always give thanks to God for you,
brothers and sisters, as is right, because your faith is growing abundantly, and
the love of everyone of you for one another is increasing. Therefore we
ourselves boast of you among the churches of God for your steadfastness and
faith during all your persecutions and the afflictions that you are enduring. To
this end we always pray for you, asking that our God will make you worthy of
his call and will fulfill by his power every good resolve and work of faith, so
that the name of our Lord Jesus may be glorified in you, and you in him,
according to the grace of our God and the Lord Jesus Christ.

The Gospel   Luke 19:1-10

Jesus entered Jericho and was passing through it. A man was there named
Zacchaeus; he was a chief tax collector and was rich. He was trying to see
who Jesus was, but on account of the crowd he could not, because he was
short in stature. So he ran ahead and climbed a sycamore tree to see him,
because he was going to pass that way. When Jesus came to the place, he
looked up and said to him, "Zacchaeus, hurry and come down; for I must stay
at your house today." So he hurried down and was happy to welcome him. All
who saw it began to grumble and said, "He has gone to be the guest of one
who is a sinner." Zacchaeus stood there and said to the Lord, "Look, half of
my possessions, Lord, I will give to the poor; and if I have defrauded anyone
of anything, I will pay back four times as much." Then Jesus said to him,
"Today salvation has come to this house, because he too is a son of Abraham.
For the Son of Man came to seek out and to save the lost."

PROPER 27

Sunday between November 6 and November 12 inclusive

The Collect

O God, whose blessed Son came into the world that he might destroy the works of the devil and make us children of God and heirs of eternal life: Grant that, having this hope, we may purify ourselves as he is pure; that, when he comes again with power and great glory, we may be made like him in his eternal and glorious kingdom; where he lives and reigns with you and the Holy Spirit, one God, for ever and ever. *Amen.*

Year A

Joshua 24:1-3a, 14-25   **or**   ✠ *Wisdom of Solomon 6:12-16*
Psalm 78:1-7   **or** *Amos 5:18-24*
                              ✠ *Wisdom of Solomon 6:17-20*
                                        or *Psalm 70*

1 Thessalonians 4:13-18
Matthew 25:1-13

The Lesson   Joshua 24:1-3*a*, 14-25

Joshua gathered all the tribes of Israel to Shechem, and summoned the elders, the heads, the judges, and the officers of Israel; and they presented themselves before God. And Joshua said to all the people, "Thus says the LORD, the God of Israel: Long ago your ancestors — Terah and his sons Abraham and Nahor — lived beyond the Euphrates and served other gods. Then I took your father Abraham from beyond the River and led him through all the land of Canaan and made his offspring many. "Now therefore revere the LORD, and serve him in sincerity and in faithfulness; put away the gods that your ancestors served beyond the River and in Egypt, and serve the LORD. Now if you are unwilling to serve the LORD, choose this day whom you will serve, whether the gods your ancestors served in the region beyond the River or the gods of the Amorites in whose land you are living; but as for me and my household, we will serve the LORD." Then the people answered, "Far be it from us that we should forsake the LORD to serve other gods; for it is the LORD our God who brought us and our ancestors up from the land of Egypt, out of the house of slavery, and who did those great signs in our sight. He protected us along all the way that we went, and among all the peoples through whom we passed; and the LORD drove out before us all the peoples, the Amorites who lived in the land. Therefore we also will serve the LORD, for he is our God." But Joshua said to the people, "You cannot serve the LORD, for he is a holy God. He is a jealous God; he will not forgive your transgressions or your sins. If you forsake the LORD and serve foreign gods, then he will turn and do you harm, and consume you, after having done you good." And the people said to Joshua, "No, we will serve the LORD!" Then Joshua said to the people, "You are witnesses against yourselves that you have chosen the LORD, to serve him." And they said, "We are witnesses." He said, "Then put away the foreign gods that are among you, and incline your hearts to the LORD, the God of Israel." The people said to Joshua, "The LORD our God we will serve, and him we will obey." So Joshua made a covenant with the people that day, and made statutes and ordinances for them at Shechem.

The Response   Psalm 78:1-7

Psalm 78   *Attendite, popule*

1   Hear my teaching, O my people; *
         incline your ears to the words of my mouth.
2   I will open my mouth in a parable; *
         I will declare the mysteries of ancient times.
3   That which we have heard and known,
     and what our forefathers have told us, *
         we will not hide from their children.
4   We will recount to generations to come
     the praiseworthy deeds and the power of the LORD, *
         and the wonderful works he has done.
5   He gave his decrees to Jacob
     and established a law for Israel, *
         which he commanded them to teach their children;
6   That the generations to come might know,
     and the children yet unborn; *
         that they in their turn might tell it to their children;
7   So that they might put their trust in God, *
         and not forget the deeds of God,
         but keep his commandments;

or, ✛ **The Lesson   Wisdom of Solomon 6:12-16** *or* **Amos 5:18-24**
Wisdom of Solomon 6:12-16
Wisdom is radiant and unfading, and she is easily discerned by those who love her, and is found by those who seek her. She hastens to make herself known to those who desire her. One who rises early to seek her will have no difficulty, for she will be found sitting at the gate. To fix one's thought on her is perfect understanding, and one who is vigilant on her account will soon be free from care, because she goes about seeking those worthy of her, and she graciously appears to them in their paths, and meets them in every thought.

or, ✛ **Amos 5:18-24**

Alas for you who desire the day of the LORD! Why do you want the day of the LORD? It is darkness, not light; as if someone fled from a lion, and was met by a bear; or went into the house and rested a hand against the wall, and was bitten by a snake. Is not the day of the LORD darkness, not light, and gloom with no brightness in it? I hate, I despise your festivals, and I take no delight in your solemn assemblies. Even though you offer me your burnt offerings and grain offerings, I will not accept them; and the offerings of well-being of your fatted animals I will not look upon. Take away from me the noise of your songs; I will not listen to the melody of your harps. But let justice roll down like waters, and righteousness like an everflowing stream.

✛ **The Response**   **Wisdom of Solomon 6:17-20** *or* **Psalm 70**

Wisdom of Solomon 6:17-20

17   The beginning of wisdom is the most sincere desire for instruction,
       and concern for instruction is love of her,
18   and love of her is the keeping of her laws,
       and giving heed to her laws is assurance of immortality,
19   and immortality brings one near to God;
20   so the desire for wisdom leads to a kingdom.

or, ✛ **Psalm 70**

Psalm 70   *Deus, in adjutorium*

1   Be pleased, O God, to deliver me; *
       O LORD, make haste to help me.
2   Let those who seek my life be ashamed
     and altogether dismayed; *
       let those who take pleasure in my misfortune
       draw back and be disgraced.
3   Let those who say to me "Aha!" and gloat over me turn back, *
       because they are ashamed.
4   Let all who seek you rejoice and be glad in you; *
       let those who love your salvation say for ever,
       "Great is the LORD!"
5   But as for me, I am poor and needy; *
       come to me speedily, O God.
6   You are my helper and my deliverer; *
       O LORD, do not tarry.

The Epistle   **1 Thessalonians 4:13-18**

We do not want you to be uninformed, brothers and sisters, about those who have died, so that you may not grieve as others do who have no hope. For since we believe that Jesus died and rose again, even so, through Jesus, God will bring with him those who have died. For this we declare to you by the word of the Lord, that we who are alive, who are left until the coming of the Lord, will by no means precede those who have died. For the Lord himself, with a cry of command, with the archangel's call and with the sound of God's trumpet, will descend from heaven, and the dead in Christ will rise first. Then we who are alive, who are left, will be caught up in the clouds together with them to meet the Lord in the air; and so we will be with the Lord forever. Therefore encourage one another with these words.

The Gospel   Matthew 25:1-13

Jesus said, "The kingdom of heaven will be like this. Ten bridesmaids took their lamps and went to meet the bridegroom. Five of them were foolish, and five were wise. When the foolish took their lamps, they took no oil with them; but the wise took flasks of oil with their lamps. As the bridegroom was delayed, all of them became drowsy and slept. But at midnight there was a shout, 'Look! Here is the bridegroom! Come out to meet him.' Then all those bridesmaids got up and trimmed their lamps. The foolish said to the wise, 'Give us some of your oil, for our lamps are going out.' But the wise replied, 'No! there will not be enough for you and for us; you had better go to the dealers and buy some for yourselves.' And while they went to buy it, the bridegroom came, and those who were ready went with him into the wedding banquet; and the door was shut. Later the other bridesmaids came also, saying, 'Lord, lord, open to us.' But he replied, 'Truly I tell you, I do not know you.' Keep awake therefore, for you know neither the day nor the hour."

Year B

Ruth 3:1-5; 4:13-17	**or**	✝ *1 Kings 17:8-16*
Psalm 127		✝ *Psalm 146*

Hebrews 9:24-28
Mark 12:38-44

The Lesson   Ruth 3:1-5; 4:13-17

Naomi, Ruth's mother-in-law, said to her, "My daughter, I need to seek some security for you, so that it may be well with you. Now here is our kinsman Boaz, with whose young women you have been working. See, he is winnowing barley tonight at the threshing floor. Now wash and anoint yourself, and put on your best clothes and go down to the threshing floor; but do not make yourself known to the man until he has finished eating and drinking. When he lies down, observe the place where he lies; then, go and uncover his feet and lie down; and he will tell you what to do." She said to her, "All that you tell me I will do." So Boaz took Ruth and she became his wife. When they came together, the LORD made her conceive, and she bore a son. Then the women said to Naomi, "Blessed be the LORD, who has not left you this day without next-of-kin; and may his name be renowned in Israel! He shall be to you a restorer of life and a nourisher of your old age; for your daughter-in-law who loves you, who is more to you than seven sons, has borne him." Then Naomi took the child and laid him in her bosom, and became his nurse. The women of the neighborhood gave him a name, saying, "A son has been born to Naomi." They named him Obed; he became the father of Jesse, the father of David.

The Response   Psalm 127

Psalm 127   *Nisi Dominus*

1   Unless the LORD builds the house, *
        their labor is in vain who build it.
2   Unless the LORD watches over the city, *
        in vain the watchman keeps his vigil.
3   It is in vain that you rise so early and go to bed so late; *
        vain, too, to eat the bread of toil,
        for he gives to his beloved sleep.
4   Children are a heritage from the LORD, *
        and the fruit of the womb is a gift.
5   Like arrows in the hand of a warrior *
        are the children of one's youth.
6   Happy is the man who has his quiver full of them! *
        he shall not be put to shame
        when he contends with his enemies in the gate.

or, ✠ The Lesson   1 Kings 17:8-16

The word of the LORD came to Elijah, saying, "Go now to Zarephath, which belongs to Sidon, and live there; for I have commanded a widow there to feed you." So he set out and went to Zarephath. When he came to the gate of the town, a widow was there gathering sticks; he called to her and said, "Bring me a little water in a vessel, so that I may drink." As she was going to bring it, he called to her and said, "Bring me a morsel of bread in your hand." But she said, "As the LORD your God lives, I have nothing baked, only a handful of meal in a jar, and a little oil in a jug; I am now gathering a couple of sticks, so that I may go home and prepare it for myself and my son, that we may eat it, and die." Elijah said to her, "Do not be afraid; go and do as you have said; but first make me a little cake of it and bring it to me, and afterwards make something for yourself and your son. For thus says the LORD the God of Israel: The jar of meal will not be emptied, and the jug of oil will not fail until the day that the LORD sends rain on the earth." She went and did as Elijah said, so that she as well as he and her household ate for many days. The jar of meal was not emptied, neither did the jug of oil fail, according to the word of the LORD that he spoke by Elijah.

✠ The Response   Psalm 146

Psalm 146   *Lauda, anima mea*

1   Hallelujah!
    Praise the LORD, O my soul! *
        I will praise the LORD as long as I live;
        I will sing praises to my God while I have my being.
2   Put not your trust in rulers, nor in any child of earth, *
        for there is no help in them.
3   When they breathe their last, they return to earth, *
        and in that day their thoughts perish.
4   Happy are they who have the God of Jacob for their help! *
        whose hope is in the LORD their God;
5   Who made heaven and earth, the seas, and all that is in them; *
        who keeps his promise for ever;
6   Who gives justice to those who are oppressed, *
        and food to those who hunger.
7   The LORD sets the prisoners free;
    the LORD opens the eyes of the blind; *
        the LORD lifts up those who are bowed down;
8   The LORD loves the righteous;
    the LORD cares for the stranger; *
        he sustains the orphan and widow,
        but frustrates the way of the wicked.
9   The LORD shall reign for ever, *
        your God, O Zion, throughout all generations.
        Hallelujah!

The Epistle   Hebrews 9:24-28

Christ did not enter a sanctuary made by human hands, a mere copy of the true one, but he entered into heaven itself, now to appear in the presence of God on our behalf. Nor was it to offer himself again and again, as the high priest enters the Holy Place year after year with blood that is not his own; for then he would have had to suffer again and again since the foundation of the world. But as it is, he has appeared once for all at the end of the age to remove sin by the sacrifice of himself. And just as it is appointed for mortals to die once, and after that the judgment, so Christ, having been offered once to bear the sins of many will appear a second time, not to deal with sin, but to save those who are eagerly waiting for him.

The Gospel
Mark 12:38-44

Teaching in the temple, Jesus said, "Beware of the scribes, who like to walk around in long robes, and to be greeted with respect in the marketplaces, and to have the best seats in the synagogues and places of honor at banquets! They devour widows' houses and for the sake of appearance say long prayers. They will receive the greater condemnation." He sat down opposite the treasury, and watched the crowd putting money into the treasury. Many rich people put in large sums. A poor widow came and put in two small copper coins, which are worth a penny. Then he called his disciples and said to them, "Truly I tell you, this poor widow has put in more than all those who are contributing to the treasury. For all of them have contributed out of their abundance; but she out of her poverty has put in everything she had, all she had to live on."

Year C

Haggai 1:15b—2:9   **or**   ✛ *Job 19:23-27a*
Psalm 145:1-5, 18-22   ✛ *Psalm 17:1-9*
   or *Psalm 98*

2 Thessalonians 2:1-5, 13-17
Luke 20:27-38

The Lesson
Haggai 1:15b—2:9

In the second year of King Darius, in the seventh month, on the twenty-first day of the month, the word of the LORD came by the prophet Haggai, saying: Speak now to Zerubbabel son of Shealtiel, governor of Judah, and to Joshua son of Jehozadak, the high priest, and to the remnant of the people, and say, Who is left among you that saw this house in its former glory? How does it look to you now? Is it not in your sight as nothing? Yet now take courage, O Zerubbabel, says the LORD; take courage, O Joshua, son of Jehozadak, the high priest; take courage, all you people of the land, says the LORD; work, for I am with you, says the LORD of hosts, according to the promise that I made you when you came out of Egypt. My spirit abides among you; do not fear. For thus says the LORD of hosts: Once again, in a little while, I will shake the heavens and the earth and the sea and the dry land; and I will shake all the nations, so that the treasure of all nations shall come, and I will fill this house with splendor, says the LORD of hosts. The silver is mine, and the gold is mine, says the LORD of hosts. The latter splendor of this house shall be greater than the former, says the LORD of hosts; and in this place I will give prosperity, says the LORD of hosts.

The Response   **Psalm 145:1-5, 18-22** *or* **Psalm 98**

Psalm 145:1-5, 18-22   *Exaltabo te, Deus*

1   I will exalt you, O God my King, *
        and bless your Name for ever and ever.
2   Every day will I bless you *
        and praise your Name for ever and ever.
3   Great is the LORD and greatly to be praised; *
        there is no end to his greatness.
4   One generation shall praise your works to another *
        and shall declare your power.
5   I will ponder the glorious splendor of your majesty *
        and all your marvelous works.
18   The LORD is righteous in all his ways *
        and loving in all his works.
19   The LORD is near to those who call upon him, *
        to all who call upon him faithfully.
20   He fulfills the desire of those who fear him; *
        he hears their cry and helps them.
21   The LORD preserves all those who love him, *
        but he destroys all the wicked.
22   My mouth shall speak the praise of the LORD; *
        let all flesh bless his holy Name for ever and ever.

or, **Psalm 98**   *Cantate Domino*

1   Sing to the LORD a new song, *
        for he has done marvelous things.
2   With his right hand and his holy arm *
        has he won for himself the victory.
3   The LORD has made known his victory; *
        his righteousness has he openly shown in
                the sight of the nations.
4   He remembers his mercy and faithfulness to
                the house of Israel, *
        and all the ends of the earth have seen the
                victory of our God.
5   Shout with joy to the LORD, all you lands; *
        lift up your voice, rejoice, and sing.
6   Sing to the LORD with the harp, *
        with the harp and the voice of song.
7   With trumpets and the sound of the horn *
        shout with joy before the King, the LORD.

8   Let the sea make a noise and all that is in it, *
        the lands and those who dwell therein.
9   Let the rivers clap their hands, *
        and let the hills ring out with joy before the LORD,
        when he comes to judge the earth.
10 In righteousness shall he judge the world *
        and the peoples with equity.

or, ✠ **The Lesson**   **Job 19:23-27a**

Job said, "O that my words were written down! O that they were inscribed in
a book! O that with an iron pen and with lead they were engraved on a rock
forever! For I know that my Redeemer lives, and that at the last he will stand
upon the earth; and after my skin has been thus destroyed, then in my flesh I
shall see God, whom I shall see on my side, and my eyes shall behold, and not
another.

✠ **The Response**   **Psalm 17:1-9**

Psalm 17:1-9 *Exaudi, Domine*
1   Hear my plea of innocence, O LORD;
        give heed to my cry; *
            listen to my prayer, which does not come from lying lips.
2   Let my vindication come forth from your presence; *
        let your eyes be fixed on justice.
3   Weigh my heart, summon me by night, *
        melt me down; you will find no impurity in me.
4   I give no offense with my mouth as others do; *
        I have heeded the words of your lips.
5   My footsteps hold fast to the ways of your law; *
        in your paths my feet shall not stumble.
6   I call upon you, O God, for you will answer me; *
        incline your ear to me and hear my words.
7   Show me your marvelous loving-kindness, *
        O Savior of those who take refuge at your right hand
        from those who rise up against them.
8   Keep me as the apple of your eye; *
        hide me under the shadow of your wings,
9   From the wicked who assault me, *
        from my deadly enemies who surround me.

The Epistle   2 Thessalonians 2:1-5, 13-17

As to the coming of our Lord Jesus Christ and our being gathered together to him, we beg you, brothers and sisters, not to be quickly shaken in mind or alarmed, either by spirit or by word or by letter, as though from us, to the effect that the day of the Lord is already here. Let no one deceive you in any way; for that day will not come unless the rebellion comes first and the lawless one is revealed, the one destined for destruction. He opposes and exalts himself above every so-called god or object of worship, so that he takes his seat in the temple of God, declaring himself to be God. Do you not remember that I told you these things when I was still with you? But we must always give thanks to God for you, brothers and sisters beloved by the Lord, because God chose you as the first fruits for salvation through sanctification by the Spirit and through belief in the truth. For this purpose he called you through our proclamation of the good news, so that you may obtain the glory of our Lord Jesus Christ. So then, brothers and sisters, stand firm and hold fast to the traditions that you were taught by us, either by word of mouth or by our letter. Now may our Lord Jesus Christ himself and God our Father, who loved us and through grace gave us eternal comfort and good hope, comfort your hearts and strengthen them in every good work and word.

The Gospel   Luke 20:27-38

Some Sadducees, those who say there is no resurrection, came to Jesus and asked him a question, "Teacher, Moses wrote for us that if a man's brother dies, leaving a wife but no children, the man shall marry the widow and raise up children for his brother. Now there were seven brothers; the first married, and died childless; then the second and the third married her, and so in the same way all seven died childless. Finally the woman also died. In the resurrection, therefore, whose wife will the woman be? For the seven had married her." Jesus said to them, "Those who belong to this age marry and are given in marriage; but those who are considered worthy of a place in that age and in the resurrection from the dead neither marry nor are given in marriage. Indeed they cannot die anymore, because they are like angels and are children of God, being children of the resurrection. And the fact that the dead are raised Moses himself showed, in the story about the bush, where he speaks of the Lord as the God of Abraham, the God of Isaac, and the God of Jacob. Now he is God not of the dead, but of the living; for to him all of them are alive."

PROPER 28

Sunday between November 13 and November 19 inclusive

The Collect

Blessed Lord, who caused all holy Scriptures to be written for our learning: Grant us so to hear them, read, mark, learn, and inwardly digest them, that we may embrace and ever hold fast the blessed hope of everlasting life, which you have given us in our Savior Jesus Christ; who lives and reigns with you and the Holy Spirit, one God, for ever and ever. *Amen.*

Year A

Judges 4:1-7   **or**   ✛ *Zephaniah 1:7, 12-18*
Psalm 123   ✛ *Psalm 90:1-8, (9-11), 12*
                    1 Thessalonians 5:1-11
                    Matthew 25:14-30

The Lesson   Judges 4:1-7

The Israelites again did what was evil in the sight of the LORD, after Ehud died. So the LORD sold them into the hand of King Jabin of Canaan, who reigned in Hazor; the commander of his army was Sisera, who lived in Harosheth-ha-goiim. Then the Israelites cried out to the LORD for help; for he had nine hundred chariots of iron, and had oppressed the Israelites cruelly twenty years. At that time Deborah, a prophetess, wife of Lappidoth, was judging Israel. She used to sit under the palm of Deborah between Ramah and Bethel in the hill country of Ephraim; and the Israelites came up to her for judgment. She sent and summoned Barak son of Abinoam from Kedesh in Naphtali, and said to him, "The LORD, the God of Israel, commands you, 'Go, take position at Mount Tabor, bringing ten thousand from the tribe of Naphtali and the tribe of Zebulun. I will draw out Sisera, the general of Jabin's army, to meet you by the Wadi Kishon with his chariots and his troops; and I will give him into your hand.' "

The Response   Psalm 123

Psalm 123   *Ad te levavi oculos meos*
  1   To you I lift up my eyes, *
          to you enthroned in the heavens.
  2   As the eyes of servants look to the hand of their masters, *
          and the eyes of a maid to the hand of her mistress,
  3   So our eyes look to the LORD our God, *
          until he show us his mercy.
  4   Have mercy upon us, O LORD, have mercy, *
          for we have had more than enough of contempt,
  5   Too much of the scorn of the indolent rich, *
          and of the derision of the proud.

or, ✠ **The Lesson**   **Zephaniah 1:7, 12-18**

Be silent before the Lord God! For the day of the Lord is at hand; the Lord has prepared a sacrifice, he has consecrated his guests. At that time, says the Lord, I will search Jerusalem with lamps, and I will punish the people who rest complacently on their dregs, those who say in their hearts, "The Lord will not do good, nor will he do harm." Their wealth shall be plundered, and their houses laid waste. Though they build houses, they shall not inhabit them; though they plant vineyards, they shall not drink wine from them. The great day of the Lord is near, near and hastening fast; the sound of the day of the Lord is bitter, the warrior cries aloud there. That day will be a day of wrath, a day of distress and anguish, a day of ruin and devastation, a day of darkness and gloom, a day of clouds and thick darkness, a day of trumpet blast and battle cry against the fortified cities and against the lofty battlements. I will bring such distress upon people that they shall walk like the blind; because they have sinned against the Lord, their blood shall be poured out like dust, and their flesh like dung. Neither their silver nor their gold will be able to save them on the day of the Lord's wrath; in the fire of his passion the whole earth shall be consumed; for a full, a terrible end he will make of all the inhabitants of the earth.

✠ **The Response**   **Psalm 90:1-8, (9-11), 12**

Psalm 90:1-8, (9-11), 12   *Domine, refugium*

1   Lord, you have been our refuge *
        from one generation to another.

2   Before the mountains were brought forth,
        or the land and the earth were born, *
        from age to age you are God.

3   You turn us back to the dust and say, *
        "Go back, O child of earth."

4   For a thousand years in your sight are like yesterday
               when it is past *
        and like a watch in the night.

5   You sweep us away like a dream; *
        we fade away suddenly like the grass.

6   In the morning it is green and flourishes; *
        in the evening it is dried up and withered.

7   For we consume away in your displeasure; *
        we are afraid because of your wrathful indignation.

8   Our iniquities you have set before you, *
        and our secret sins in the light of your countenance.

[9   When you are angry, all our days are gone; *
     we bring our years to an end like a sigh.
10   The span of our life is seventy years,
     perhaps in strength even eighty; *
         yet the sum of them is but labor and sorrow,
         for they pass away quickly and we are gone.
11   Who regards the power of your wrath? *
     who rightly fears your indignation?]

12   So teach us to number our days *
     that we may apply our hearts to wisdom.

The Epistle   1 Thessalonians 5:1-11

Concerning the times and the seasons, brothers and sisters, you do not need to
have anything written to you. For you yourselves know very well that the day
of the Lord will come like a thief in the night. When they say, "There is peace
and security," then sudden destruction will come upon them, as labor pains
come upon a pregnant woman, and there will be no escape! But you, beloved,
are not in darkness, for that day to surprise you like a thief; for you are all
children of light and children of the day; we are not of the night or of darkness. So then let us not fall asleep as others do, but let us keep awake and be
sober; for those who sleep, sleep at night and those who are drunk get drunk at
night. But since we belong to the day, let us be sober, and put on the breastplate of faith and love, and for a helmet the hope of salvation. For God has
destined us not for wrath but for obtaining salvation through our Lord Jesus
Christ, who died for us, so that whether we are awake or asleep we may live
with him. Therefore encourage one another and build up each other, as indeed
you are doing.

The Gospel   Matthew 25:14-30

Jesus said, "For it is as if a man, going on a journey, summoned his slaves and
entrusted his property to them; to one he gave five talents, to another two, to
another one, to each according to his ability. Then he went away. The one who
had received the five talents went off at once and traded with them, and made
five more talents. In the same way, the one who had the two talents made two
more talents. But the one who had received the one talent went off and dug a
hole in the ground and hid his master's money. After a long time the master of
those slaves came and settled accounts with them. Then the one who had
received the five talents came forward, bringing five more talents, saying,
'Master, you handed over to me five talents; see, I have made five more
talents.' His master said to him, 'Well done, good and trustworthy slave; you
have been trustworthy in a few things, I will put you in charge of many things;

enter into the joy of your master.' And the one with the two talents also came forward, saying, 'Master, you handed over to me two talents; see, I have made two more talents.' His master said to him, 'Well done, good and trustworthy slave; you have been trustworthy in a few things, I will put you in charge of many things; enter into the joy of your master.' Then the one who had received the one talent also came forward, saying, 'Master, I knew that you were a harsh man, reaping where you did not sow, and gathering where you did not scatter seed; so I was afraid, and I went and hid your talent in the ground. Here you have what is yours.' But his master replied, 'You wicked and lazy slave! You knew, did you, that I reap where I did not sow, and gather where I did not scatter? Then you ought to have invested my money with the bankers, and on my return I would have received what was my own with interest. So take the talent from him, and give it to the one with the ten talents. For to all those who have, more will be given, and they will have an abundance; but from those who have nothing, even what they have will be taken away. As for this worthless slave, throw him into the outer darkness, where there will be weeping and gnashing of teeth.' "

Year B

1 Samuel 1:4-20	**or**	✠ *Daniel 12:1-3*
1 Samuel 2:1-10		✠ *Psalm 16*

Hebrews 10:11-14, (15-18), 19-25
Mark 13:1-8

The Lesson   **1 Samuel 1:4-20**

On the day when Elkanah sacrificed, he would give portions to his wife Peninnah and to all her sons and daughters; but to Hannah he gave a double portion, because he loved her, though the LORD had closed her womb. Her rival used to provoke her severely, to irritate her, because the LORD had closed her womb. So it went on year by year; as often as she went up to the house of the LORD, she used to provoke her. Therefore Hannah wept and would not eat. Her husband Elkanah said to her, "Hannah, why do you weep? Why do you not eat? Why is your heart sad? Am I not more to you than ten sons?" After they had eaten and drunk at Shiloh, Hannah rose and presented herself before the LORD. Now Eli the priest was sitting on the seat beside the doorpost of the temple of the LORD. She was deeply distressed and prayed to the LORD, and wept bitterly. She made this vow: "O LORD of hosts, if only you will look on the misery of your servant, and remember me, and not forget your servant, but will give to your servant a male child, then I will set him before you as a nazirite until the day of his death. He shall drink neither wine nor intoxicants, and no razor shall touch his head." As she continued praying before the LORD, Eli observed her mouth. Hannah was praying silently; only her lips moved, but her voice was not heard; therefore Eli thought she was drunk. So Eli said to her, "How long will you make a drunken spectacle of yourself? Put away your wine." But Hannah answered, "No, my lord, I am a woman deeply troubled; I have drunk neither wine nor strong drink, but I have been pouring out my soul before the LORD. Do not regard your servant as a worthless woman, for I have been speaking out of my great anxiety and vexation all this time." Then Eli answered, "Go in peace; the God of Israel grant the petition you have made to him." And she said, "Let your servant find favor in your sight." Then the woman went to her quarters, ate and drank with her husband, and her countenance was sad no longer. They rose early in the morning and worshiped before the LORD; then they went back to their house at Ramah. Elkanah knew his wife Hannah, and the LORD remembered her. In due time Hannah conceived and bore a son. She named him Samuel, for she said, "I have asked him of the LORD."

The Response   1 Samuel 2:1-10

1   Hannah prayed and said, "My heart exults in the LORD;
    my strength is exalted in my God.
    My mouth derides my enemies, because I rejoice in my victory.
2   There is no Holy One like the LORD,
    no one besides you; there is no Rock like our God.
3   Talk no more so very proudly,
    let not arrogance come from your mouth;
    for the LORD is a God of knowledge,
    and by him actions are weighed.
4   The bows of the mighty are broken,
    but the feeble gird on strength.
5   Those who were full have hired themselves out for bread,
    but those who were hungry are fat with spoil.
    The barren has borne seven,
    but she who has many children is forlorn.
6   The LORD kills and brings to life;
    he brings down to Sheol and raises up.
7   The LORD makes poor and makes rich;
    he brings low, he also exalts.
8   He raises up the poor from the dust;
    he lifts the needy from the ash heap,
    to make them sit with princes and inherit a seat of honor.
    For the pillars of the earth are the LORD'S,
    and on them he has set the world.
9   He will guard the feet of his faithful ones,
    but the wicked shall be cut off in darkness;
    for not by might does one prevail.

10   The LORD! His adversaries shall be shattered;
      the Most High will thunder in heaven.
      The LORD will judge the ends of the earth;
      he will give strength to his king,
      and exalt the power of his anointed."

or, ☩ The Lesson   Daniel 12:1-3

The Lord spoke to Daniel saying, "At that time Michael, the great prince, the
protector of your people, shall arise. There shall be a time of anguish, such as
has never occurred since nations first came into existence. But at that time
your people shall be delivered, everyone who is found written in the book.
Many of those who sleep in the dust of the earth shall awake, some to everlasting life, and some to shame and everlasting contempt. Those who are wise
shall shine like the brightness of the sky, and those who lead many to
righteousness, like the stars forever and ever.

☩ The Response   Psalm 16

Psalm 16   *Conserva me, Domine*
  1   Protect me, O God, for I take refuge in you; *
         I have said to the LORD, "You are my LORD,
         my good above all other."
  2   All my delight is upon the godly that are in the land, *
         upon those who are noble among the people.
  3   But those who run after other gods *
         shall have their troubles multiplied.
  4   Their libations of blood I will not offer, *
         nor take the names of their gods upon my lips.
  5   O LORD, you are my portion and my cup; *
         it is you who uphold my lot.
  6   My boundaries enclose a pleasant land; *
         indeed, I have a goodly heritage.
  7   I will bless the LORD who gives me counsel; *
         my heart teaches me, night after night.
  8   I have set the LORD always before me; *
         because he is at my right hand I shall not fall.
  9   My heart, therefore, is glad, and my spirit rejoices; *
         my body also shall rest in hope.
 10   For you will not abandon me to the grave, *
         nor let your holy one see the Pit.
 11   You will show me the path of life; *
         in your presence there is fullness of joy,
         and in your right hand are pleasures for evermore.

The Epistle   **Hebrews 10:11-14, (15-18), 19-25**
Hebrews 10:11-14

Every priest stands day after day at his service, offering again and again the same sacrifices that can never take away sins. But when Christ had offered for all time a single sacrifice for sins, "he sat down at the right hand of God," and since then has been waiting "until his enemies would be made a footstool for his feet." For by a single offering he has perfected for all time those who are sanctified.

Hebrews 10:(15-18) [And the Holy Spirit also testifies to us, for after saying, "This is the covenant that I will make with them after those days, says the Lord: I will put my laws in their hearts, and I will write them on their minds," he also adds, "I will remember their sins and their lawless deeds no more." Where there is forgiveness of these, there is no longer any offering for sin.]

Hebrews 10:19-25 Therefore, my friends, since we have confidence to enter the sanctuary by the blood of Jesus, by the new and living way that he opened for us through the curtain (that is, through his flesh), and since we have a great priest over the house of God, let us approach with a true heart in full assurance of faith, with our hearts sprinkled clean from an evil conscience and our bodies washed with pure water. Let us hold fast to the confession of our hope without wavering, for he who has promised is faithful. And let us consider how to provoke one another to love and good deeds, not neglecting to meet together, as is the habit of some, but encouraging one another, and all the more as you see the Day approaching.

The Gospel   **Mark 13:1-8**

As Jesus came out of the temple, one of his disciples said to him, "Look, Teacher, what large stones and what large buildings!" Then Jesus asked him, "Do you see these great buildings? Not one stone will be left here upon another; all will be thrown down." When he was sitting on the Mount of Olives opposite the temple, Peter, James, John, and Andrew asked him privately, "Tell us, when will this be, and what will be the sign that all these things are about to be accomplished?" Then Jesus began to say to them, "Beware that no one leads you astray. Many will come in my name and say, 'I am he!' and they will lead many astray. When you hear of wars and rumors of wars, do not be alarmed; this must take place, but the end is still to come. For nation will rise against nation, and kingdom against kingdom; there will be earthquakes in various places; there will be famines. This is but the beginning of the birth pangs.

Year C

Isaiah 65:17-25   **or**   ☩ *Malachi 4:1-2a*

Canticle 9   ☩ *Psalm 98*

2 Thessalonians 3:6-13

Luke 21:5-19

The Lesson   **Isaiah 65:17-25**

Thus says the Lord GOD: For I am about to create new heavens and a new earth; the former things shall not be remembered or come to mind. But be glad and rejoice forever in what I am creating; for I am about to create Jerusalem as a joy, and its people as a delight. I will rejoice in Jerusalem, and delight in my people; no more shall the sound of weeping be heard in it, or the cry of distress. No more shall there be in it an infant that lives but a few days, or an old person who does not live out a lifetime; for one who dies at a hundred years will be considered a youth, and one who falls short of a hundred will be considered accursed. They shall build houses and inhabit them; they shall plant vineyards and eat their fruit. They shall not build and another inhabit; they shall not plant and another eat; for like the days of a tree shall the days of my people be, and my chosen shall long enjoy the work of their hands. They shall not labor in vain, or bear children for calamity; for they shall be off-spring blessed by the LORD — and their descendants as well. Before they call I will answer, while they are yet speaking I will hear. The wolf and the lamb shall feed together, the lion shall eat straw like the ox; but the serpent — its food shall be dust! They shall not hurt or destroy on all my holy mountain, says the LORD.

The Response   **Canticle 9**

Canticle 9   **The First Song of Isaiah**   *Ecce, Deus*

         Isaiah 12:2-6

Surely, it is God who saves me; *

    I will trust in him and not be afraid.

For the Lord is my stronghold and my sure defense, *

    and he will be my Savior.

Therefore you shall draw water with rejoicing *

    from the springs of salvation.

And on that day you shall say, *

    Give thanks to the Lord and call upon his Name;

Make his deeds known among the peoples; *

    see that they remember that his Name is exalted.

Sing the praises of the Lord, for he has done great things, *

    and this is known in all the world.

Cry aloud, inhabitants of Zion, ring out your joy, *
    for the great one in the midst of you is the Holy One of Israel.

or, ✟ **The Lesson**   **Malachi 4:1-2***a*

See, the day is coming, burning like an oven, when all the arrogant and all evildoers will be stubble; the day that comes shall burn them up, says the LORD of hosts, so that it will leave them neither root nor branch. But for you who revere my name the sun of righteousness shall rise, with healing in its wings.

✟ **The Response**   **Psalm 98**

Psalm 98   *Cantate Domino*

1   Sing to the LORD a new song, *
        for he has done marvelous things.

2   With his right hand and his holy arm *
        has he won for himself the victory.

3   The LORD has made known his victory; *
        his righteousness has he openly shown in
                the sight of the nations.

4   He remembers his mercy and faithfulness to
                the house of Israel, *
        and all the ends of the earth have seen the
                victory of our God.

5   Shout with joy to the LORD, all you lands; *
        lift up your voice, rejoice, and sing.

6   Sing to the LORD with the harp, *
        with the harp and the voice of song.

7   With trumpets and the sound of the horn *
        shout with joy before the King, the LORD.

8   Let the sea make a noise and all that is in it, *
        the lands and those who dwell therein.

9   Let the rivers clap their hands, *
        and let the hills ring out with joy before the LORD,
        when he comes to judge the earth.

10   In righteousness shall he judge the world *
        and the peoples with equity.

The Epistle   **2 Thessalonians 3:6-13**

Now we command you, beloved, in the name of our lord Jesus Christ, to keep away from believers who are living in idleness and not according to the tradition that they received from us. For you yourselves know how you ought to imitate us; we were not idle when we were with you, and we did not eat anyone's bread without paying for it; but with toil and labor we worked night and day, so that we might not burden any of you. This was not because we do not have that right, but in order to give you an example to imitate. For even when we were with you, we gave you this command: Anyone unwilling to work should not eat. For we hear that some of you are living in idleness, mere busybodies, not doing any work. Now such persons we command and exhort in the Lord Jesus Christ to do their work quietly and to earn their own living. Brothers and sisters, do not be weary in doing what is right.

The Gospel   Luke 21:5-19

When some were speaking about the temple, how it was adorned with beautiful stones and gifts dedicated to God, Jesus said, "As for these things that you see, the days will come when not one stone will be left upon another; all will be thrown down." They asked him, "Teacher, when will this be, and what will be the sign that this is about to take place?" And he said, "Beware that you are not led astray; for many will come in my name and say, 'I am he!' and, 'The time is near!' Do not go after them. When you hear of wars and insurrections, do not be terrified; for these things must take place first, but the end will not follow immediately." Then he said to them, "Nation will rise against nation, and kingdom against kingdom; there will be great earthquakes, and in various places famines and plagues; and there will be dreadful portents and great signs from heaven. But before all this occurs, they will arrest you and persecute you; they will hand you over to synagogues and prisons, and you will be brought before kings and governors because of my name. This will give you an opportunity to testify. So make up your minds not to prepare your defense in advance; for I will give you words and a wisdom that none of your opponents will be able to withstand or contradict. You will be betrayed even by parents and brothers, by relatives and friends; and they will put some of you to death. You will be hated by all because of my name. But not a hair of your head will perish. By your endurance you will gain your souls."

PROPER 29 (The Reign of Christ or Christ the King)
Sunday between November 20 and November 26 inclusive

The Collect

Almighty and everlasting God, whose will it is to restore all things in your well-beloved Son, the King of kings and Lord of lords: Mercifully grant that the peoples of the earth, divided and enslaved by sin, may be freed and brought together under his most gracious rule; who lives and reigns with you and the Holy Spirit, one God, now and for ever. *Amen.*

Year A

Ezekiel 34:11-16, 20-24   **or**   ✠ Ezekiel 34:11-16, 20-24
Psalm 100   ✠ Psalm 95:1-7a
                    Ephesians 1:15-23
                    Matthew 25:31-46

The Lesson   Ezekiel 34:11-16, 20-24

Thus says the Lord GOD: I myself will search for my sheep, and will seek
them out. As shepherds seek out their flocks when they are among their
scattered sheep, so I will seek out my sheep. I will rescue them from all the
places to which they have been scattered on a day of clouds and thick darkness. I will bring them out from the peoples and gather them from the countries, and will bring them into their own land; and I will feed them on the
mountains of Israel, by the watercourses, and in all the inhabited parts of the
land. I will feed them with good pasture, and the mountain heights of Israel
shall be their pasture; there they shall lie down in good grazing land, and they
shall feed on rich pasture on the mountains of Israel. I myself will be the
shepherd of my sheep, and I will make them lie down, says the Lord GOD. I
will seek the lost, and I will bring back the strayed, and I will bind up the
injured, and I will strengthen the weak, but the fat and the strong I will
destroy. I will feed them with justice. Therefore, thus says the Lord GOD to
them: I myself will judge between the fat sheep and the lean sheep. Because
you pushed with flank and shoulder, and butted at all the weak animals with
your horns until you scattered them far and wide, I will save my flock, and
they shall no longer be ravaged; and I will judge between sheep and sheep. I
will set up over them one shepherd, my servant David, and he shall feed them:
he shall feed them and be their shepherd. And I, the LORD, will be their God,
and my servant David shall be prince among them; I, the LORD, have spoken.

The Response   Psalm 100

Psalm 100   *Jubilate Deo*

   1   Be joyful in the LORD, all you lands; *
         serve the LORD with gladness
         and come before his presence with a song.
   2   Know this: The LORD himself is God; *
         he himself has made us, and we are his;
         we are his people and the sheep of his pasture.
   3   Enter his gates with thanksgiving;
         go into his courts with praise; *
         give thanks to him and call upon his Name.
   4   For the LORD is good;
         his mercy is everlasting; *
         and his faithfulness endures from age to age.

PROPER 29 - *November 20 - November 26 — Year A*   **551**

or, ✠ **The Lesson**   **Ezekiel 34:11-16, 20-24**

Thus says the Lord GOD: I myself will search for my sheep, and will seek them out. As shepherds seek out their flocks when they are among their scattered sheep, so I will seek out my sheep. I will rescue them from all the places to which they have been scattered on a day of clouds and thick darkness. I will bring them out from the peoples and gather them from the countries, and will bring them into their own land; and I will feed them on the mountains of Israel, by the watercourses, and in all the inhabited parts of the land. I will feed them with good pasture, and the mountain heights of Israel shall be their pasture; there they shall lie down in good grazing land, and they shall feed on rich pasture on the mountains of Israel. I myself will be the shepherd of my sheep, and I will make them lie down, says the Lord GOD. I will seek the lost, and I will bring back the strayed, and I will bind up the injured, and I will strengthen the weak, but the fat and the strong I will destroy. I will feed them with justice. Therefore, thus says the Lord GOD to them: I myself will judge between the fat sheep and the lean sheep. Because you pushed with flank and shoulder, and butted at all the weak animals with your horns until you scattered them far and wide, I will save my flock, and they shall no longer be ravaged; and I will judge between sheep and sheep. I will set up over them one shepherd, my servant David, and he shall feed them: he shall feed them and be their shepherd. And I, the LORD, will be their God, and my servant David shall be prince among them; I, the LORD, have spoken.

✠ **The Response**   **Psalm 95:1-7a**

Psalm 95:1-7a   *Venite, exultemus*

1   Come, let us sing to the LORD; *
        let us shout for joy to the Rock of our salvation.
2   Let us come before his presence with thanksgiving *
        and raise a loud shout to him with psalms.
3   For the LORD is a great God, *
        and a great King above all gods.
4   In his hand are the caverns of the earth, *
        and the heights of the hills are his also.
5   The sea is his, for he made it, *
        and his hands have molded the dry land.
6   Come, let us bow down, and bend the knee, *
        and kneel before the LORD our Maker.
7   For he is our God,
        and we are the people of his pasture and the sheep of his hand. *

The Epistle   Ephesians 1:15-23

I have heard of your faith in the Lord Jesus and your love toward all the
saints, and for this reason I do not cease to give thanks for you as I remember
you in my prayers. I pray that the God of our Lord Jesus Christ, the Father of
glory, may give you a spirit of wisdom and revelation as you come to know
him, so that, with the eyes of your heart enlightened, you may know what is
the hope to which he has called you, what are the riches of his glorious
inheritance among the saints, and what is the immeasurable greatness of his
power for us who believe, according to the working of his great power. God
put this power to work in Christ when he raised him from the dead and seated
him at his right hand in the heavenly places, far above all rule and authority
and power and dominion, and above every name that is named, not only in this
age but also in the age to come. And he has put all things under his feet and
has made him the head over all things for the church, which is his body, the
fullness of him who fills all in all.

The Gospel   Matthew 25:31-46

Jesus said, "When the Son of Man comes in his glory, and all the angels with
him, then he will sit on the throne of his glory. All the nations will be gathered
before him, and he will separate people one from another as a shepherd
separates the sheep from the goats, and he will put the sheep at his right hand
and the goats at the left. Then the king will say to those at his right hand,
'Come, you that are blessed by my Father, inherit the kingdom prepared for
you from the foundation of the world; for I was hungry and you gave me food,
I was thirsty and you gave me something to drink, I was a stranger and you
welcomed me, I was naked and you gave me clothing, I was sick and you took
care of me, I was in prison and you visited me.' Then the righteous will
answer him, 'Lord, when was it that we saw you hungry and gave you food,
or thirsty and gave you something to drink? And when was it that we saw you
a stranger and welcomed you, or naked and gave you clothing? And when
was it that we saw you sick or in prison and visited you?' And the king will
answer them, 'Truly I tell you, just as you did it to one of the least of these
who are members of my family, you did it to me.' Then he will say to those at
his left hand, 'You that are accursed, depart from me into the eternal fire
prepared for the devil and his angels; for I was hungry and you gave me no
food, I was thirsty and you gave me nothing to drink, I was a stranger and you
did not welcome me, naked and you did not give me clothing, sick and in
prison and you did not visit me.' Then they also will answer, 'Lord, when was
it that we saw you hungry or thirsty or a stranger or naked or sick or in
prison, and did not take care of you?' Then he will answer them, 'Truly I tell
you, just as you did not do it to one of the least of these, you did not do it to
me.' And these will go away into eternal punishment, but the righteous into
eternal life."

Year B

2 Samuel 23:1-7   **or**   ✠ *Daniel 7:9-10, 13-14*

Psalm 132:1-13, (14-19)   ✠ *Psalm 93*

Revelation 1:4b-8

John 18:33-37

The Lesson   2 Samuel 23:1-7

Now these are the last words of David: The oracle of David, son of Jesse, the oracle of the man whom God exalted, the anointed of the God of Jacob, the favorite of the Strong One of Israel: The spirit of the LORD speaks through me, his word is upon my tongue. The God of Israel has spoken, the Rock of Israel has said to me: One who rules over people justly, ruling in the fear of God, is like the light of morning, like the sun rising on a cloudless morning, gleaming from the rain on the grassy land. Is not my house like this with God? For he has made with me an everlasting covenant, ordered in all things and secure. Will he not cause to prosper all my help and my desire? But the godless are all like thorns that are thrown away; for they cannot be picked up with the hand; to touch them one uses an iron bar or the shaft of a spear. And they are entirely consumed in fire on the spot.

The Response   Psalm 132:1-13, (14-19)

Psalm 132:1-13, (14-19)   *Memento, Domine*

1   LORD, remember David, *
      and all the hardships he endured;

2   How he swore an oath to the LORD *
      and vowed a vow to the Mighty One of Jacob:

3   "I will not come under the roof of my house," *
      nor climb up into my bed;

4   I will not allow my eyes to sleep, *
      nor let my eyelids slumber;

5   Until I find a place for the LORD, *
      a dwelling for the Mighty One of Jacob."

6   "The ark! We heard it was in Ephrathah; *
      we found it in the fields of Jearim.

7   Let us go to God's dwelling place; *
      let us fall upon our knees before his footstool."

8   Arise, O LORD, into your resting-place, *
      you and the ark of your strength.

9   Let your priests be clothed with righteousness; *
      let your faithful people sing with joy.

10   For your servant David's sake, *
      do not turn away the face of your Anointed.

11   The Lord has sworn an oath to David; *
        in truth, he will not break it:
12   "A son, the fruit of your body *
        will I set upon your throne.
13   If your children keep my covenant
        and my testimonies that I shall teach them, *
        their children will sit upon your throne for evermore."

[14 For the Lord has chosen Zion; *
        he has desired her for his habitation:
15   "This shall be my resting-place for ever; *
        here will I dwell, for I delight in her.
16   I will surely bless her provisions, *
        and satisfy her poor with bread.
17   I will clothe her priests with salvation, *
        and her faithful people will rejoice and sing.
18   There will I make the horn of David flourish; *
        I have prepared a lamp for my Anointed.
19   As for his enemies, I will clothe them with shame; *
        but as for him, his crown will shine."]

or, ✛ The Lesson   Daniel 7:9-10, 13-14

As I (Daniel) watched, thrones were set in place, and an Ancient One took his
throne, his clothing was white as snow, and the hair of his head like pure
wool; his throne was fiery flames, and its wheels were burning fire. A stream
of fire issued and flowed out from his presence. A thousand thousands served
him, and ten thousand times ten thousand stood attending him. The court sat
in judgment, and the books were opened. As I watched in the night visions, I
saw one like a human being coming with the clouds of heaven. And he came to
the Ancient One and was presented before him. To him was given dominion
and glory and kingship, that all peoples, nations, and languages should serve
him. His dominion is an everlasting dominion that shall not pass away, and his
kingship is one that shall never be destroyed.

✛ The Response   Psalm 93

Psalm 93   *Dominus regnavit*
1   The Lord is King;
        he has put on splendid apparel; *
        the Lord has put on his apparel
        and girded himself with strength.
2   He has made the whole world so sure *
        that it cannot be moved;

3   Ever since the world began, your throne has been established; *
        you are from everlasting.
4   The waters have lifted up, O LORD,
        the waters have lifted up their voice; *
            the waters have lifted up their pounding waves.
5   Mightier than the sound of many waters,
        mightier than the breakers of the sea, *
            mightier is the LORD who dwells on high.
6   Your testimonies are very sure, *
        and holiness adorns your house, O LORD,
            for ever and for evermore.

The Epistle   Revelation 1:4*b*-8

Grace to you and peace from him who is and who was and who is to come,
and from the seven spirits who are before his throne, and from Jesus Christ,
the faithful witness, the firstborn of the dead, and the ruler of the kings of the
earth. To him who loves us and freed us from our sins by his blood, and made
us to be a kingdom, priests serving his God and Father, to him be glory and
dominion forever and ever. Amen. Look! He is coming with the clouds; every
eye will see him, even those who pierced him; and on his account all the tribes
of the earth will wail. So it is to be. Amen. "I am the Alpha and the Omega,"
says the Lord God, who is and who was and who is to come, the Almighty.

The Gospel   John 18:33-37

Pilate entered the headquarters again, summoned Jesus, and asked him, "Are
you the King of the Jews?" Jesus answered, "Do you ask this on your own, or
did others tell you about me?" Pilate replied, "I am not a Jew, am I? Your own
nation and the chief priests have handed you over to me. What have you
done?" Jesus answered, "My kingdom is not from this world. If my kingdom
were from this world, my followers would be fighting to keep me from being
handed over to the Jews. But as it is, my kingdom is not from here." Pilate
asked him, "So you are a king?" Jesus answered, "You say that I am a king.
For this I was born, and for this I came into the world, to testify to the truth.
Everyone who belongs to the truth listens to my voice."

Year C

Jeremiah 23:1-6	**or**	✠ *Jeremiah 23:1-6*
Canticle 4 or 16		✠ *Psalm 46*

Colossians 1:11-20
Luke 23:33-43

The Lesson   Jeremiah 23:1-6

Woe to the shepherds who destroy and scatter the sheep of my pasture! says
the LORD. Therefore thus says the LORD, the God of Israel, concerning the
shepherds who shepherd my people: It is you who have scattered my flock,
and have driven them away, and you have not attended to them. So I will
attend to you for your evil doings, says the LORD. Then I myself will gather
the remnant of my flock out of all the lands where I have driven them, and I
will bring them back to their fold, and they shall be fruitful and multiply. I
will raise up shepherds over them who will shepherd them, and they shall not
fear any longer, or be dismayed, nor shall any be missing, says the LORD. The
days are surely coming, says the LORD, when I will raise up for David a
righteous Branch, and he shall reign as king and deal wisely, and shall execute
justice and righteousness in the land. In his days Judah will be saved and
Israel will live in safety. And this is the name by which he will be called: "The
LORD is our righteousness."

The Response   Canticle 4 *or* 16
Canticle 4 *(Page 50 BCP)*

or, **Canticle 16   The Song of Zechariah** *Benedictus Dominus Deus*
             Luke 1:68-79

Blessed be the Lord, the God of Israel; *
    he has come to his people and set them free.
He has raised up for us a mighty savior, *
    born of the house of his servant David.
Through his holy prophets he promised of old,
that he would save us from our enemies, *
    from the hands of all who hate us.
He promised to show mercy to our fathers *
    and to remember his holy covenant.
This was the oath he swore to our father Abraham, *
    to set us free from the hands of our enemies,
Free to worship him without fear, *
    holy and righteous in his sight
    all the days of our life.
You, my child, shall be called the prophet of the Most High, *
    for you will go before the Lord to prepare his way,
To give his people knowledge of salvation *
    by the forgiveness of their sins.
In the tender compassion of our God *
    the dawn from on high shall break upon us,

To shine on those who dwell in darkness and the
shadow of death, *
and to guide our feet into the way of peace.

or, ✛ **The Lesson**   **Jeremiah 23:1-6**

Woe to the shepherds who destroy and scatter the sheep of my pasture! says
the LORD. Therefore thus says the LORD, the God of Israel, concerning the
shepherds who shepherd my people: It is you who have scattered my flock,
and have driven them away, and you have not attended to them. So I will
attend to you for your evil doings, says the LORD. Then I myself will gather
the remnant of my flock out of all the lands where I have driven them, and I
will bring them back to their fold, and they shall be fruitful and multiply. I
will raise up shepherds over them who will shepherd them, and they shall not
fear any longer, or be dismayed, nor shall any be missing, says the LORD. The
days are surely coming, says the LORD, when I will raise up for David a
righteous Branch, and he shall reign as king and deal wisely, and shall execute
justice and righteousness in the land. In his days Judah will be saved and
Israel will live in safety. And this is the name by which he will be called: "The
LORD is our righteousness."

✛ **The Response**   **Psalm 46**

Psalm 46   *Deus noster refugium*

1   God is our refuge and strength, *
        a very present help in trouble.

2   Therefore we will not fear, though the earth be moved, *
        and though the mountains be toppled into the
                depths of the sea;

3   Though its waters rage and foam, *
        and though the mountains tremble at its tumult.

4   The LORD of hosts is with us; *
        the God of Jacob is our stronghold.

5   There is a river whose streams make glad the city of God, *
        the holy habitation of the Most High.

6   God is in the midst of her;
        she shall not be overthrown; *
        God shall help her at the break of day.

7   The nations make much ado, and the kingdoms are shaken; *
        God has spoken, and the earth shall melt away.

8   The LORD of hosts is with us; *
        the God of Jacob is our stronghold.

9   Come now and look upon the works of the LORD, *
        what awesome things he has done on earth.

10	It is he who makes war to cease in all the world; *
	he breaks the bow, and shatters the spear,
	and burns the shields with fire.
11	"Be still, then, and know that I am God; *
	I will be exalted among the nations;
	I will be exalted in the earth."
12	The LORD of hosts is with us; *
	the God of Jacob is our stronghold.

The Epistle   Colossians 1:11-20

May you be made strong with all the strength that comes from his glorious power, and may you be prepared to endure everything with patience, while joyfully giving thanks to the Father, who has enabled you to share in the inheritance of the saints in the light. He has rescued us from the power of darkness and transferred us into the kingdom of his beloved Son, in whom we have redemption, the forgiveness of sins. He is the image of the invisible God, the firstborn of all creation; for in him all things in heaven and on earth were created, things visible and invisible, whether thrones or dominions or rulers or powers — all things have been created through him and for him. He himself is before all things, and in him all things hold together. He is the head of the body, the church; he is the beginning, the firstborn from the dead, so that he might come to have first place in everything. For in him all the fullness of God was pleased to dwell, and through him God was pleased to reconcile to himself all things, whether on earth or in heaven, by making peace through the blood of his cross.

The Gospel   Luke 23:33-43

When they came to the place that is called The Skull, they crucified Jesus there with the criminals, one on his right and one on his left. Then Jesus said, "Father, forgive them; for they do not know what they are doing." And they cast lots to divide his clothing. The people stood by, watching Jesus on the cross; but the leaders scoffed at him, saying, "He saved others; let him save himself if he is the Messiah of God, his chosen one!" The soldiers also mocked him, coming up and offering him sour wine, and saying, "If you are the King of the Jews, save yourself!" There was also an inscription over him, "This is the King of the Jews." One of the criminals who were hanged there kept deriding him and saying, "Are you not the Messiah? Save yourself and us!" But the other rebuked him, saying, "Do you not fear God, since you are under the same sentence of condemnation? And we indeed have been condemned justly, for we are getting what we deserve for our deeds, but this man has done nothing wrong." Then he said, "Jesus, remember me when you come into your kingdom." He replied, "Truly I tell you, today you will be with me in Paradise."

HOLY DAYS

HOLY DAYS

SAINT ANDREW - *November 30*

The Collect

Almighty God, who gave such grace to your apostle Andrew that he readily obeyed the call of your Son Jesus Christ, and brought his brother with him: Give us, who are called by your Holy Word, grace to follow him without delay, and to bring those near to us into his gracious presence; who lives and reigns with you and the Holy Spirit, one God, now and for ever. *Amen.*

Deuteronomy 30:11-14
Psalm 19 or 19:1-6
Romans 10:8b-18
Matthew 4:18-22

The Lesson   Deuteronomy 30:11-14

Moses said to the people of Israel, "Surely, this commandment that I am commanding you today is not too hard for you, nor is it too far away. It is not in heaven, that you should say, 'Who will go up to heaven for us, and get it for us so that we may hear it and observe it?' Neither is it beyond the sea, that you should say, "Who will cross to the other side of the sea for us, and get it for us so that we may hear it and observe it?" No, the word is very near to you; it is in your mouth and in your heart for you to observe."

The Response   Psalm 19:1-6, (7-14)

Psalm 19 *Caeli enarrant*

1   The heavens declare the glory of God, *
       and the firmament shows his handiwork.
2   One day tells its tale to another, *
       and one night imparts knowledge to another.
3   Although they have no words or language, *
       and their voices are not heard,
4   Their sound has gone out into all lands, *
       and their message to the ends of the world.
5   In the deep has he set a pavilion for the sun; *
       it comes forth like a bridegroom out of his chamber;
       it rejoices like a champion to run its course.
6   It goes forth from the uttermost edge of the heavens
    and runs about to the end of it again; *
       nothing is hidden from its burning heat.

[7 The law of the LORD is perfect and revives the soul; *
   the testimony of the LORD is sure
          and gives wisdom to the innocent.
8 The statutes of the LORD are just and rejoice the heart; *
   the commandment of the LORD is clear
          and gives light to the eyes.
9 The fear of the LORD is clean and endures for ever; *
   the judgments of the LORD are true
          and righteous altogether.
10 More to be desired are they than gold,
          more than much fine gold, *
   sweeter far than honey, than honey in the comb.
11 By them also is your servant enlightened, *
   and in keeping them there is great reward.
12 Who can tell how often he offends? *
   cleanse me from my secret faults.
13 Above all, keep your servant from presumptuous sins;
   let them not get dominion over me; *
          then shall I be whole and sound,
          and innocent of a great offense.
14 Let the words of my mouth and the meditation of my
          heart be acceptable in your sight, *
   O LORD, my strength and my redeemer.]

The Epistle   Romans 10:8b-18

"The word is near you, on your lips and in your heart" (that is, the word of faith that we proclaim); because if you confess with your lips that Jesus is Lord and believe in your heart that God raised him from the dead, you will be saved. For one believes with the heart and so is justified, and one confesses with the mouth and so is saved. The scripture says, "No one who believes in him will be put to shame." For there is no distinction between Jew and Greek; the same Lord is Lord of all and is generous to all who call on him. For, "Everyone who calls on the name of the Lord shall be saved." But how are they to call on one in whom they have not believed? And how are they to believe in one of whom they have never heard? And how are they to hear without someone to proclaim him? And how are they to proclaim him unless they are sent? As it is written, "How beautiful are the feet of those who bring good news!" But not all have obeyed the good news; for Isaiah says, "Lord, who has believed our message?" So faith comes from what is heard, and what is heard comes through the word of Christ. But I ask, have they not heard? Indeed they have; for "Their voice has gone out to all the earth, and their words to the ends of the world."

The Gospel   **Matthew 4:18-22**

As Jesus walked by the Sea of Galilee, he saw two brothers, Simon, who is
called Peter, and Andrew his brother, casting a net into the sea — for they
were fishermen. And he said to them, "Follow me, and I will make you fish
for people." Immediately they left their nets and followed him. As he went
from there, he saw two other brothers, James son of Zebedee and his brother
John, in the boat with their father Zebedee, mending their nets, and he called
them. Immediately they left the boat and their father, and followed him.

SAINT THOMAS - *December 21*

The Collect

Everliving God, who strengthened your apostle Thomas with firm and certain
faith in your Son's resurrection: Grant us so perfectly and without doubt to
believe in Jesus Christ, our Lord and our God, that our faith may never be
found wanting in your sight; through him who lives and reigns with you and
the Holy Spirit, one God, now and for ever. *Amen.*

> *Habakkuk 2:1-4*
> *Psalm 126*
> *Hebrews 10:35—11:1*
> *John 20:24-29*

The Lesson   **Habakkuk 2:1-4**

I will stand at my watchpost, and station myself on the rampart; I will keep
watch to see what he will say to me, and what he will answer concerning my
complaint. Then the Lord answered me and said: Write the vision; make it
plain on tablets, so that a runner may read it. For there is still a vision for the
appointed time; it speaks of the end, and does not lie. If it seems to tarry, wait
for it; it will surely come, it will not delay. Look at the proud! Their spirit is
not right in them, but the righteous live by their faith.

The Response   **Psalm 126**

Psalm 126   *In convertendo*

1   When the LORD restored the fortunes of Zion, *
        then were we like those who dream.
2   Then was our mouth filled with laughter, *
        and our tongue with shouts of joy.
3   Then they said among the nations, *
        "The LORD has done great things for them."
4   The LORD has done great things for us, *
        and we are glad indeed.

5   Restore our fortunes, O LORD, *
       like the watercourses of the Negev.
6   Those who sowed with tears *
       will reap with songs of joy.
7   Those who go out weeping, carrying the seed, *
       will come again with joy, shouldering their sheaves.

The Epistle   **Hebrews 10:35—11:1**

Do not, therefore, abandon that confidence of yours; it brings a great reward. For you need endurance, so that when you have done the will of God, you may receive what was promised. For yet "in a very little while, the one who is coming will come and will not delay; but my righteous one will live by faith. My soul takes no pleasure in anyone who shrinks back." But we are not among those who shrink back and so are lost, but among those who have faith and so are saved. Now faith is the assurance of things hoped for, the conviction of things not seen.

The Gospel   **John 20:24-29**

Thomas (who was called the Twin), one of the twelve, was not with them when Jesus came. So the other disciples told him, "We have seen the Lord." But he said to them, "Unless I see the mark of the nails in his hands, and put my finger in the mark of the nails and my hand in his side, I will not believe." A week later his disciples were again in the house, and Thomas was with them. Although the doors were shut, Jesus came and stood among them and said, "Peace be with you." Then he said to Thomas, "Put your finger here and see my hands. Reach out your hand and put it in my side. Do not doubt but believe." Thomas answered him, "My Lord and my God!" Jesus said to him, "Have you believed because you have seen me? Blessed are those who have not seen and yet have come to believe."

SAINT STEPHEN - *December 26*

The Collect

We give you thanks, O Lord of glory, for the example of the first martyr Stephen, who looked up to heaven and prayed for his persecutors to your Son Jesus Christ, who stands at your right hand; where he lives and reigns with you and the Holy Spirit, one God, in glory everlasting. *Amen.*

Jeremiah 26:1-9, 12-15
Psalm 31 or 31:1-5
Acts 6:8—7:2a, 51c-60
Matthew 23:34-39

The Lesson   Jeremiah 26:1-9, 12-15

At the beginning of the reign of King Jehoiakim son of Josiah of Judah, this word came from the Lord: Thus says the Lord: Stand in the court of the Lord's house, and speak to all the cities of Judah that come to worship in the house of the Lord; speak to them all the words that I command you; do not hold back a word. It may be that they will listen, all of them, and will turn from their evil way, that I may change my mind about the disaster that I intend to bring on them because of their evil doings. You shall say to them: Thus says the Lord: If you will not listen to me, to walk in my law that I have set before you, and to heed the words of my servants the prophets whom I send to you urgently — though you have not heeded — then I will make this house like Shiloh, and I will make this city a curse for all the nations of the earth. The priests and the prophets and all the people heard Jeremiah speaking these words in the house of the Lord. And when Jeremiah had finished speaking all that the Lord had commanded him to speak to all the people, then the priests and the prophets and all the people laid hold of him, saying, "You shall die! Why have you prophesied in the name of the Lord, saying, 'This house shall be like Shiloh, and this city shall be desolate, without inhabitant'?" And all the people gathered around Jeremiah in the house of the Lord. Then Jeremiah spoke to all the officials and all the people, saying, "It is the Lord who sent me to prophesy against this house and this city all the words you have heard. Now therefore amend your ways and your doings, and obey the voice of the Lord your God, and the Lord will change his mind about the disaster that he has pronounced against you. But as for me, here I am in your hands. Do with me as seems good and right to you. Only know for certain that if you put me to death, you will be bring innocent blood upon yourselves and upon this city and its inhabitants, for in truth the Lord sent me to you to speak all these words in your ears."

Psalm 31   *In te, Domine, speravi*

1   In you, O LORD, have I taken refuge;
     let me never be put to shame; *
         deliver me in your righteousness.

2   Incline your ear to me; *
         make haste to deliver me.

3   Be my strong rock, a castle to keep me safe,
     for you are my crag and my stronghold; *
         for the sake of your Name, lead me and guide me.

4   Take me out of the net that they have secretly set for me, *
         for you are my tower of strength.

5   Into your hands I commend my spirit, *
         for you have redeemed me,
         O LORD, O God of truth.

[6   I hate those who cling to worthless idols, *
         and I put my trust in the LORD.

7   I will rejoice and be glad because of your mercy; *
         for you have seen my affliction;
         you know my distress.

8   You have not shut me up in the power of the enemy; *
         you have set my feet in an open place.

9   Have mercy on me, O LORD, for I am in trouble; *
         my eye is consumed with sorrow,
         and also my throat and my belly.

10   For my life is wasted with grief,
     and my years with sighing; *
         my strength fails me because of affliction,
         and my bones are consumed.

11   I have become a reproach to all my enemies and
                   even to my neighbors,
     a dismay to those of my acquaintance; *
         when they see me in the street they avoid me.

12   I am forgotten like a dead man, out of mind; *
         I am as useless as a broken pot.

13   For I have heard the whispering of the crowd;
     fear is all around; *
         they put their heads together against me;
         they plot to take my life.

14 But as for me, I have trusted in you, O LORD. *
     I have said, "You are my God.

15 My times are in your hand; *
     rescue me from the hand of my enemies,
     and from those who persecute me.

16 Make your face to shine upon your servant, *
     and in your loving-kindness save me."

17 LORD, let me not be ashamed for having called upon you; *
     rather, let the wicked be put to shame;
     let them be silent in the grave.

18 Let the lying lips be silenced which speak against the righteous, *
     haughtily, disdainfully, and with contempt.

19 How great is your goodness, O LORD!
   which you have laid up for those who fear you; *
     which you have done in the sight of all
     for those who put their trust in you.

20 You hide them in the covert of your presence from those
               who slander them; *
     you keep them in your shelter from the strife of tongues.

21 Blessed be the LORD! *
     for he has shown me the wonders of his love in a
               besieged city.

22 Yet I said in my alarm,
   "I have been cut off from the sight of your eyes." *
     Nevertheless, you heard the sound of my entreaty
     when I cried out to you.

23 Love the LORD, all you who worship him; *
     the LORD protects the faithful,
     but repays to the full those who act haughtily.

24 Be strong and let your heart take courage, *
     all you who wait for the LORD.]

The Epistle   Acts 6:8—7:2a, 51c-60

Stephen, full of grace and power, did great wonders and signs among the
people. Then some of those who belonged to the synagogue of the Freedmen
(as it was called), Cyrenians, Alexandrians, and others of those from Cilicia
and Asia, stood up and argued with Stephen. But they could not withstand the
wisdom and the Spirit with which he spoke. Then they secretly instigated
some men to say, "We have heard him speak blasphemous words against
Moses and God." They stirred up the people as well as the elders and the
scribes; then they suddenly confronted him, seized him, and brought him
before the council. They set up false witnesses who said, "This man never

stops saying things against this holy place and the law; for we have heard him say that this Jesus of Nazareth will destroy this place and will change the customs that Moses handed on to us." And all who sat in the council looked intently at him, and they saw that his face was like the face of an angel. Then the high priest asked him, "Are these things so?" And Stephen replied: "Brothers and fathers, listen to me. You are forever opposing the Holy Spirit, just as your ancestors used to do. Which of the prophets did your ancestors not persecute? They killed those who foretold the coming of the Righteous One, and now you have become his betrayers and murderers. You are the ones that received the law as ordained by angels, and yet you have not kept it." When they heard these things, they became enraged and ground their teeth at Stephen. But filled with the Holy Spirit, he gazed into heaven and saw the glory of God and Jesus standing at the right hand of God. "Look," he said, "I see the heavens opened and the Son of Man standing at the right hand of God!" But they covered their ears, and with a loud shout all rushed together against him. Then they dragged him out of the city and began to stone him; and the witnesses laid their coats at the feet of a young man named Saul. While they were stoning Stephen, he prayed, "Lord Jesus, receive my spirit." Then he knelt down and cried out in a loud voice, "Lord, do not hold this sin against them." When he had said this, he died.

The Gospel   Matthew 23:34-39

Jesus said, "Therefore I send you prophets, sages, and scribes, some of whom you will kill and crucify, and some you will flog in your synagogues and pursue from town to town, so that upon you may come all the righteous blood shed on earth, from the blood of righteous Abel to the blood of Zechariah son of Barachiah, whom you murdered between the sanctuary and the altar. Truly I tell you, all this will come upon this generation. "Jerusalem, Jerusalem, the city that kills the prophets and stones those who are sent to it! How often have I desired to gather your children together as a hen gathers her brood under her wings, and you were not willing! See, you house is left to you, desolate. For I tell you, you will not see me again until you say, 'Blessed is the one who comes in the name of the Lord.' "

SAINT JOHN - *December 27*

The Collect

Shed upon your Church, O Lord, the brightness of your light, that we, being illumined by the teaching of your apostle and evangelist John, may so walk in the light of your truth, that at length we may attain to the fullness of eternal life; through Jesus Christ our Lord, who lives and reigns with you and the Holy Spirit, one God, for ever and ever. *Amen.*

Exodus 33:18-23
Psalm 92: or 92:1-4, 11-14
1 John 1:1-9
*John 21:19*b*-24*

The Lesson   Exodus 33:18-23

Moses said, "Show me your glory, I pray." And he said, "I will make all my goodness pass before you, and will proclaim before you the name, 'The Lord'; and I will be gracious to whom I will be gracious, and will show mercy on whom I will show mercy. But," he said, "you cannot see my face; for no one shall see me and live." And the Lord continued, "See, there is a place by me where you shall stand on the rock; and while my glory passes by I will put you in a cleft of the rock, and I will cover you with my hand until I have passed by; then I will take away my hand, and you shall see my back; but my face shall not be seen."

The Response   Psalm 92:1-4, (5-10), 11-14

Psalm 92   *Bonum est confiteri*

1   It is a good thing to give thanks to the LORD, *
    and to sing praises to your Name, O Most High;

2   To tell of your loving-kindness early in the morning *
    and of your faithfulness in the night season;

3   On the psaltery, and on the lyre, *
    and to the melody of the harp.

4   For you have made me glad by your acts, O LORD; *
    and I shout for joy because of the works of your hands.]

[5   LORD, how great are your works! *
    your thoughts are very deep.

6   The dullard does not know,
    nor does the fool understand, *
        that though the wicked grow like weeds,
        and all the workers of iniquity flourish,

7　They flourish only to be destroyed for ever; *
　　but you, O Lord, are exalted for evermore.
8　For lo, your enemies, O Lord,
　　lo, your enemies shall perish, *
　　and all the workers of iniquity shall be scattered.
9　But my horn you have exalted like the horns of wild bulls; *
　　I am anointed with fresh oil.
10　My eyes also gloat over my enemies, *
　　and my ears rejoice to hear the doom of the wicked who
　　　　rise up against me.]

11　The righteous shall flourish like a palm tree, *
　　and shall spread abroad like a cedar of Lebanon.
12　Those who are planted in the house of the Lord *
　　shall flourish in the courts of our God;
13　They shall still bear fruit in old age; *
　　they shall be green and succulent;
14　That they may show how upright the Lord is, *
　　my Rock, in whom there is no fault.

The Epistle   1 John 1:1-9

We declare to you what was from the beginning, what we have heard, what we
have seen with our eyes, what we have looked at and touched with our hands,
concerning the word of life - this life was revealed, and we have seen it and
testify to it, and declare to you the eternal life that was with the Father and
was revealed to us - we declare to you what we have seen and heard so that
you also may have fellowship with us; and truly our fellowship is with the
Father and with his Son Jesus Christ. We are writing these things so that our
joy may be complete. This is the message we have heard from him and
proclaim to you, that God is light and in him there is no darkness at all. If we
say that we have fellowship with him while we are walking in darkness, we lie
and do not do what is true; but if we walk in the light as he himself is in the
light, we have fellowship with one another, and the blood of Jesus his Son
cleanses us from all sin. If we say that we have no sin, we deceive ourselves,
and the truth is not in us. If we confess our sins, he who is faithful and just
will forgive us our sins and cleanse us from all unrighteousness.

The Gospel   John 21:19b-24

Jesus said to Peter, "Follow me." Peter turned and saw the disciple whom
Jesus loved following them; he was the one who had reclined next to Jesus at
the supper and had said, "Lord, who is it that is going to betray you?" When
Peter saw him, he said to Jesus, "Lord, what about him?" Jesus said to him,

"If it is my will that he remain until I come, what is that to you ? Follow me!" So the rumor spread in the community that this disciple would not die. Yet Jesus did not say to him that he would not die, but, "If it is my will that he remain until I come, what is that to you?" This is the disciple who is testifying to these things and has written them, and we know that his testimony is true.

HOLY INNOCENTS - *December 28*

The Collect

We remember today, O God, the slaughter of the holy innocents of Bethlehem by King Herod. Receive, we pray, into the arms of your mercy all innocent victims; and by your great might frustrate the designs of evil tyrants and establish your rule of justice, love, and peace; through Jesus Christ our Lord, who lives and reigns with you, in the unity of the Holy Spirit, one God, for ever and ever. *Amen.*

Jeremiah 31:15-17
Psalm 124
Revelation 21:1-7
Matthew 2:13-18

The Lesson   Jeremiah 31:15-17

Thus says the Lord: A voice is heard in Ramah, lamentation and bitter weeping. Rachel is weeping for her children; she refuses to be comforted for her children, because they are no more. Thus says the Lord: Keep your voice from weeping, and your eyes from tears; for there is a reward for your work, says the Lord: they shall come back from the land of the enemy; there is hope for your future, says the Lord: your children shall come back to their own country.

The Response   Psalm 124

Psalm 124 *Nisi quia Dominus*

1   If the LORD had not been on our side, *
        let Israel now say;
2   If the LORD had not been on our side, *
        when enemies rose up against us;
3   Then would they have swallowed us up alive *
        in their fierce anger toward us;
4   Then would the waters have overwhelmed us *
        and the torrent gone over us;
5   Then would the raging waters *
        have gone right over us.

6   Blessed be the LORD! *
>> he has not given us over to be a prey for their teeth.
7   We have escaped like a bird from the snare of the fowler; *
>> the snare is broken, and we have escaped.
8   Our help is in the Name of the LORD, *
>> the maker of heaven and earth.

The Epistle   Revelation 21:1-7

Then I (John) saw a new heaven and a new earth; for the first heaven and the first earth had passed away, and the sea was no more. And I saw the holy city, the new Jerusalem, coming down out of heaven from God, prepared as a bride adorned for her husband. And I heard a loud voice from the throne saying, "See, the home of God is among mortals. He will dwell with them as their God; they will be his peoples, and God himself will be with them; he will wipe every tear from their eyes. Death will be no more; mourning and crying and pain will be no more, for the first things have passed away." And the one who was seated on the throne said, "See, I am making all things new." Also he said, "Write this, for these words are trustworthy and true." Then he said to me, "It is done! I am the Alpha and the Omega, the beginning and the end. To the thirsty I will give water as a gift from the spring of the water of life. Those who conquer will inherit these things, and I will be their God and they will be my children."

The Gospel   Matthew 2:13-18

After the wise men had left, an angel of the Lord appeared to Joseph in a dream and said, "Get up, take the child and his mother, and flee to Egypt, and remain there until I tell you; for Herod is about to search for the child, to destroy him." Then Joseph got up, took the child and his mother by night, and went to Egypt, and remained there until the death of Herod. This was to fulfill what had been spoken by the Lord through the prophet, "Out of Egypt I have called my son." When Herod saw that he had been tricked by the wise men, he was infuriated, and he sent and killed all the children in and around Bethlehem who were two years old or under, according to the time that he had learned from the wise men. Then was fulfilled what had been spoken through the prophet Jeremiah: "A voice was heard in Ramah, wailing and loud lamentation, Rachel weeping for her children; she refused to be consoled, because they are no more."

CONFESSION OF SAINT PETER - *January 18*

The Collect

Almighty Father, who inspired Simon Peter, first among the apostles, to confess Jesus as Messiah and Son of the living God: Keep your Church steadfast upon the rock of this faith, so that in unity and peace we may proclaim the one truth and follow the one Lord, our Savior Jesus Christ; who lives and reigns with you and the Holy Spirit, one God, now and for ever. *Amen.*

Acts 4:8-13
Psalm 23
1 Peter 5:1-4
Matthew 16:13-19

The Lesson   Acts 4:8-13

Peter, filled with the Holy Spirit, said to them, "Rulers of the people and elders, if we are questioned today because of a good deed done to someone who was sick and are asked how this man has been healed, let it be known to all of you, and to all the people of Israel, that this man is standing before you in good health by the name of Jesus Christ of Nazareth, whom you crucified, whom God raised from the dead. This Jesus is 'the stone that was rejected by you, the builders; it has become the cornerstone.' There is salvation in no one else, for there is no other name under heaven given among mortals by which we must be saved." Now when they saw the boldness of Peter and John and realized that they were uneducated and ordinary men, they were amazed and recognized them as companions of Jesus.

The Response   Psalm 23

Psalm 23   *Dominus regit me*

1   The LORD is my shepherd; *
        I shall not be in want.
2   He makes me lie down in green pastures *
        and leads me beside still waters.
3   He revives my soul *
        and guides me along right pathways for his Name's sake.
4   Though I walk through the valley of the shadow of death,
    I shall fear no evil; *
        for you are with me;
        your rod and your staff, they comfort me.
5   You spread a table before me in the presence of those
                who trouble me; *

you have anointed my head with oil,
    and my cup is running over.
6   Surely your goodness and mercy shall follow me all the days
            of my life, *
    and I will dwell in the house of the LORD for ever.

The Epistle   1 Peter 5:1-4

As an elder myself and a witness of the sufferings of Christ, as well as one
who shares in the glory to be revealed, I exhort the elders among you to tend
the flock of God that is in your charge, exercising the oversight, not under
compulsion but willingly, as God would have you do it — not for sordid gain
but eagerly. Do not lord it over those in your charge, but be examples to the
flock. And when the chief shepherd appears, you will win the crown of glory
that never fades away.

The Gospel   Matthew 16:13-19

When Jesus came into the district of Caesarea Philippi, he asked his disciples,
"Who do people say that the Son of Man is?" And they said, "Some say John
the Baptist, but others Elijah, and still others Jeremiah or one of the prophets."
He said to them, "But who do you say that I am?" Simon Peter answered,
"You are the Messiah, the Son of the living God." And Jesus answered him,
"Blessed are you, Simon son of Jonah! For flesh and blood has not revealed
this to you, but my Father in heaven. And I tell you, you are Peter, and on this
rock I will build my church, and the gates of Hades will not prevail against it.
I will give you the keys of the kingdom of heaven, and whatever you bind on
earth will be bound in heaven, and whatever you loose on earth will be loosed
in heaven."

CONVERSION OF SAINT PAUL - *January 25*
The Collect

O God, by the preaching of your apostle Paul you have caused the light of the
Gospel to shine throughout the world: Grant, we pray, that we, having his
wonderful conversion in remembrance, may show ourselves thankful to you
by following his holy teaching; through Jesus Christ our Lord, who lives and
reigns with you, in the unity of the Holy Spirit, one God, now and for ever.
Amen.

Acts 26:9-21
Psalm 67
Galatians 1:11-24
Matthew 10:16-22

The Lesson

Paul said to King Agrippa, "Indeed, I myself was convinced that I ought to do many things against the name of Jesus of Nazareth. And that is what I did in Jerusalem; with authority received from the chief priests, I not only locked up many of the saints in prison, but I also cast my vote against them when they were being condemned to death. By punishing them often in all the synagogues I tried to force them to blaspheme; and since I was so furiously enraged at them, I pursued them even to foreign cities. With this in mind, I was traveling to Damascus with the authority and commission of the chief priests, when at midday along the road, your Excellency, I saw a light from heaven, brighter than the sun, shining around me and my companions. When we had all fallen to the ground, I heard a voice saying to me in the Hebrew language, 'Saul, Saul, why are you persecuting me? It hurts you to kick against the goads.' I asked, 'Who are you, Lord?' The Lord answered, 'I am Jesus whom you are persecuting. But get up and stand on your feet; for I have appeared to you for this purpose, to appoint you to serve and testify to the things in which you have seen me and to those in which I will appear to you. I will rescue you from your people and from the Gentiles — to whom I am sending you to open their eyes so that they may turn from darkness to light and from the power of Satan to God, so that they may receive forgiveness of sins and a place among those who are sanctified by faith in me.' After that, King Agrippa, I was not disobedient to the heavenly vision, but declared first to those in Damascus, then in Jerusalem and throughout the countryside of Judea, and also to the Gentiles, that they should repent and turn to God and do deeds consistent with repentance. For this reason the Jews seized me in the temple and tried to kill me."

The Response

Psalm 67 *Deus misereatur*

1 May God be merciful to us and bless us, *
     show us the light of his countenance and come to us.

2 Let your ways be known upon earth, *
     your saving health among all nations.

3 Let the peoples praise you, O God; *
     let all the peoples praise you.

4 Let the nations be glad and sing for joy, *
     for you judge the peoples with equity
     and guide all the nations upon earth.

5 Let the peoples praise you, O God; *
     let all the peoples praise you.

6   The earth has brought forth her increase; *
    may God, our own God, give us his blessing.
7   May God give us his blessing, *
    and may all the ends of the earth stand in awe of him.

The Epistle   Galatians 1:11-24

I want you to know, brother and sisters, that the gospel that was proclaimed by me is not of human origin; for I did not receive it from a human source, nor was I taught it, but I received it through a revelation of Jesus Christ. You have heard, no doubt, of my earlier life in Judaism. I was violently persecuting the church of God and was trying to destroy it. I advanced in Judaism beyond many among my people of the same age, for I was far more zealous for the traditions of my ancestors. But when God, who had set me apart before I was born and called me through his grace, was pleased to reveal his Son to me, so that I might proclaim him among the Gentiles, I did not confer with any human being, nor did I go up to Jerusalem to those who were already apostles before me, but I went away at once into Arabia, and afterwards I returned to Damascus. Then after three years I did go up to Jerusalem to visit Cephas and stayed with him fifteen days; but I did not see any other apostle except James the Lord's brother. In what I am writing to you, before God, I do not lie! Then I went into the regions of Syria and Cilicia, and I was still unknown by sight to the churches of Judea that are in Christ; they only heard it said, "The one who formerly was persecuting us is now proclaiming the faith he once tried to destroy." And they glorified God because of me.

The Gospel   Matthew 10:16-22

Jesus said to the twelve, "See, I am sending you out like sheep into the midst of wolves; so be wise as serpents and innocent as doves. Beware of them, for they will hand you over to councils and flog you in their synagogues; and you will be dragged before governors and kings because of me, as a testimony to them and the Gentiles. When they hand you over, do not worry about how you are to speak or what you are to say; for what you are to say will be given to you at that time; for it is not you who speak, but the Spirit of your Father speaking through you. Brother will betray brother to death, and a father his child, and children will rise against parents and have them put to death; and you will be hated by all because of my name. But the one who endures to the end will be saved."

THE PRESENTATION - *February 2*

The Collect

Almighty and everliving God, we humbly pray that, as your only-begotten Son was this day presented in the temple, so we may be presented to you with pure and clean hearts by Jesus Christ our Lord; who lives and reigns with you and the Holy Spirit, one God, now and for ever. *Amen.*

Malachi 3:1-4
Psalm 84 or Psalm 24:7-10
Hebrews 2:14-18
Luke 2:22-40

The Lesson   **Malachi 3:1-4**

See, I am sending my messenger to prepare the way before me, and the Lord whom you seek will suddenly come to his temple. The messenger of the covenant in whom you delight — indeed, he is coming, says the Lord of hosts. But who can endure the day of his coming, and who can stand when he appears? For he is like a refiner's fire and like fullers' soap; he will sit as a refiner and purifier of silver, and he will purify the descendants of Levi and refine them like gold and silver, until they present offerings to the Lord in righteousness. Then the offering of Judah and Jerusalem will be pleasing to the Lord as in the days of old and as in former years.

The Response   **Psalm 84** *or* **Psalm 24:7-10**

Psalm 84   *Quam dilecta!*

1   How dear to me is your dwelling, O LORD of hosts! *
     My soul has a desire and longing for the courts of the LORD;
     my heart and my flesh rejoice in the living God.

2   The sparrow has found her a house
   and the swallow a nest where she may lay her young; *
     by the side of your altars, O LORD of hosts,
     my King and my God.

3   Happy are they who dwell in your house! *
     they will always be praising you.

4   Happy are the people whose strength is in you! *
     whose hearts are set on the pilgrims' way.

5   Those who go through the desolate valley will find
       it a place of springs, *
     for the early rains have covered it with pools of water.

6 They will climb from height to height, *
    and the God of gods will reveal himself in Zion.

7 LORD God of hosts, hear my prayer; *
    hearken, O God of Jacob.

8 Behold our defender, O God; *
    and look upon the face of your Anointed.

9 For one day in your courts is better than
          a thousand in my own room, *
    and to stand at the threshold of the house of my God
    than to dwell in the tents of the wicked.

10 For the LORD God is both sun and shield; *
    he will give grace and glory;

11 No good thing will the LORD withhold *
    from those who walk with integrity.

12 O LORD of hosts, *
    happy are they who put their trust in you!

or, **Psalm 24:7-10**   *Domini est terra*

7 Lift up your heads, O gates;
    lift them high, O everlasting doors; *
      and the King of glory shall come in.

8 "Who is this King of glory?" *
    "The LORD, strong and mighty,
    the LORD, mighty in battle."

9 Lift up your heads, O gates;
    lift them high, O everlasting doors; *
      and the King of glory shall come in.

10 "Who is he, this King of glory?"*
    "The LORD of hosts,
    he is the King of glory."

The Epistle   Hebrews 2:14-18

Since the children share flesh and blood, he himself likewise shared the same things, so that through death he might destroy the one who has the power of death, that is, the devil, and free those who all their lives were held in slavery by the fear of death. For it is clear that he did not come to help angels, but the descendants of Abraham. Therefore he had to become like his brothers and sisters in every respect, so that he might be a merciful and faithful high priest in the service of God, to make a sacrifice of atonement for the sins of the people. Because he himself was tested by what he suffered, he is able to help those who are being tested.

The Gospel   Luke 2:22-40

When the time came for their purification according to the law of Moses, the parents of Jesus brought him up to Jerusalem to present him to the Lord (as it is written in the law of the Lord, "Every firstborn male shall be designated as holy to the Lord"), and they offered a sacrifice according to what is stated in the law of the Lord, "a pair of turtledoves or two young pigeons." Now there was a man in Jerusalem whose name was Simeon; this man was righteous and devout, looking forward to the consolation of Israel, and the Holy Spirit rested on him. It had been revealed to him by the Holy Spirit that he would not see death before he had seen the Lord's Messiah. Guided by the Spirit, Simeon came into the temple; and when the parents brought in the child Jesus, to do for him what was customary under the law, Simeon took him in his arms and praised God, saying, "Master, now you are dismissing your servant in peace, according to your word; for my eyes have seen your salvation, which you have prepared in the presence of all peoples, a light for revelation to the Gentiles and for glory to your people Israel." And the child's father and mother were amazed at what was being said about him. Then Simeon blessed them and said to his mother Mary, "This child is destined for the falling and the rising of many in Israel, and to be a sign that will be opposed so that the inner thoughts of many will be revealed — and a sword will pierce your own soul too." There was also a prophet, Anna the daughter of Phanuel, of the tribe of Asher. She was of a great age, having lived with her husband seven years after her marriage, then as a widow to the age of eighty-four. She never left the temple but worshiped there with fasting and prayer night and day. At that moment she came, and began to praise God and to speak about the child to all who were looking for the redemption of Jerusalem. When they had finished everything required by the law of the Lord, they returned to Galilee, to their own town of Nazareth. The child grew and became strong, filled with wisdom; and the favor of God was upon him.

SAINT MATTHIAS - *February 24*

The Collect

Almighty God, who in the place of Judas chose your faithful servant Matthias to be numbered among the Twelve: Grant that your Church, being delivered from false apostles, may always be guided and governed by faithful and true pastors; through Jesus Christ our Lord, who lives and reigns with you, in the unity of the Holy Spirit, one God, now and for ever. *Amen.*

Acts 1:15-16
Psalm 15
Philippians 3:13-21
John 15:1, 6-16

The Lesson   Acts 1:15-26

In those days Peter stood up among the believers (together the crowd numbered about one hundred twenty persons) and said, "Friends, the scripture had to be fulfilled, which the Holy Spirit through David foretold concerning Judas, who became a guide for those who arrested Jesus - for he was numbered among us and was allotted his share in this ministry." (Now this man acquired a field with the reward of his wickedness; and falling headlong, he burst open in the middle and all his bowels gushed out. This became known to all the residents of Jerusalem, so that the field was called in their language Hakeldama, that is, Field of Blood.) "For it is written in the book of Psalms, 'Let his homestead become desolate, and let there be no one to live in it'; and 'Let another take his position of overseer.' So one of the men who have accompanied us during all the time that the Lord Jesus went in and out among us, beginning from the baptism of John until the day when he was taken up from us — one of these must become a witness with us to his resurrection." So they proposed two, Joseph called Barsabbas, who was also known as Justus, and Matthias. Then they prayed and said, "Lord, you know everyone's heart. Show us which one of these two you have chosen to take the place in this ministry and apostleship from which Judas turned aside to go to his own place." And they cast lots for them, and the lot fell on Matthias; and he was added to the eleven apostles.

The Response   **Psalm 15**

Psalm 15   *Domine, quis habitabit?*

1   LORD, who may dwell in your tabernacle? *
    who may abide upon your holy hill?

2   Whoever leads a blameless life and does what is right, *
    who speaks the truth from his heart.

3   There is no guile upon his tongue;
    he does no evil to his friend; *
    he does not heap contempt upon his neighbor.

4   In his sight the wicked is rejected, *
    but he honors those who fear the LORD.

5   He has sworn to do no wrong *
    and does not take back his word.

6   He does not give his money in hope of gain, *
    nor does he take a bribe against the innocent.

7   Whoever does these things *
    shall never be overthrown.

The Epistle   **Philippians 3:13-21**

Beloved, I do not consider that I have made it my own; but this one thing I do: forgetting what lies behind and straining forward to what lies ahead, I press on toward the goal for the prize of the heavenly call of God in Christ Jesus. Let those of us then who are mature be of the same mind; and if you think differently about anything, this too God will reveal to you. Only let us hold fast to what we have attained. Brothers and sisters, join in imitating me, and observe those who live according to the example you have in us. For many live as enemies of the cross of Christ; I have often told you of them, and now I tell you even with tears. Their end is destruction; their god is the belly; and their glory is in their shame; their minds are set on earthly things. But our citizenship is in heaven, and it is from there that we are expecting a Savior, the Lord Jesus Christ. He will transform the body of our humiliation that it may be conformed to the body of his glory, by the power that also enables him to make all things subject to himself.

The Gospel   John 15:1, 6-16

Jesus said, "I am the true vine, and my Father is the vinegrower. Whoever does not abide in me is thrown away like a branch and withers; such branches are gathered, thrown into the fire, and burned. If you abide in me, and my words abide in you, ask for whatever you wish, and it will be done for you. My Father is glorified by this, that you bear much fruit and become my disciples. As the Father has loved me, so I have loved you; abide in my love. If you keep my commandments, you will abide in my love, just as I have kept my Father's commandments and abide in his love. I have said these things to you so that my joy may be in you, and that your joy may be complete. This is my commandment, that you love one another as I have loved you. No one has greater love than this, to lay down one's life for one's friends. You are my friends if you do what I command you. I do not call you servants any longer, because the servant does not know what the master is doing; but I have called you friends, because I have made known to you everything that I have heard from my Father. You did not choose me but I chose you. And I appointed you to go and bear fruit, fruit that will last, so that the Father will give you whatever you ask him in my name."

SAINT JOSEPH - *March 19*

The Collect

O God, who from the family of your servant David raised up Joseph to be the guardian of your incarnate Son and the spouse of his virgin mother: Give us grace to imitate his uprightness of life and his obedience to your commands; through Jesus Christ our Lord, who lives and reigns with you and the Holy Spirit, one God, for ever and ever. *Amen.*

2 Samuel 7:4, 8-16
Psalm 89:1-29 or *Psalm 89:1-4, 26-29*
Romans 4:13-18
Luke 2:41-52

The Lesson   2 Samuel 7:4, 8-16

The word of the Lord came to Nathan: Now therefore thus you shall say to my
servant David: Thus says the Lord of hosts: I took you from the pasture, from
following the sheep to be prince over my people Israel; and I have been with
you wherever you went, and have cut off all your enemies from before you;
and I will make for you a great name, like the name of the great ones of the
earth. And I will appoint a place for my people Israel and will plant them, so
that they may live in their own place, and be disturbed no more; and evildoers
shall afflict them no more, as formerly, from the time that I appointed judges
over my people Israel; and I will give you rest from all your enemies. Moreover the Lord declares to you that the Lord will make you a house. When your
days are fulfilled and you lie down with your ancestors, I will raise up your
offspring after you, who shall come forth from your body, and I will establish
his kingdom. He shall build a house for my name, and I will establish the
throne of his kingdom forever. I will be a father to him, and he shall be a son
to me. When he commits iniquity, I will punish him with a rod such as mortals
use, with blows inflicted by human beings. But I will not take my steadfast
love from him, as I took it from Saul, whom I put away from before you. Your
house and your kingdom shall be made sure forever before me; your throne
shall be established forever.

The Response   Psalm 89:1-4, (5-25), 26-29
Psalm 89:1-29 *Misericordias Domini*
    1   Your love, O LORD, for ever will I sing; *
          from age to age my mouth will proclaim your faithfulness.
    2   For I am persuaded that your love is established for ever; *
          you have set your faithfulness firmly in the heavens.
    3   "I have made a covenant with my chosen one; *
          I have sworn an oath to David my servant:
    4   'I will establish your line for ever, *
          and preserve your throne for all generations.' "

  [5   The heavens bear witness to your wonders, O LORD, *
          and to your faithfulness in the assembly of the holy ones;
    6   For who in the skies can be compared to the LORD? *
          who is like the LORD among the gods?

7   God is much to be feared in the council of the holy ones, *
    great and terrible to all those round about him.

8   Who is like you, LORD God of hosts? *
    O mighty LORD, your faithfulness is all around you.

9   You rule the raging of the sea *
    and still the surging of its waves.

10 You have crushed Rahab of the deep with a deadly wound; *
    you have scattered your enemies with your mighty arm.

11 Yours are the heavens; the earth also is yours; *
    you laid the foundations of the world and all that is in it.

12 You have made the north and the south; *
    Tabor and Hermon rejoice in your Name.

13 You have a mighty arm; *
    strong is your hand and high is your right hand.

14 Righteousness and justice are the foundations of your throne; *
    love and truth go before your face.

15 Happy are the people who know the festal shout! *
    they walk, O LORD, in the light of your presence.

16 They rejoice daily in your Name; *
    they are jubilant in your righteousness.

17 For you are the glory of their strength, *
    and by your favor our might is exalted.

18 Truly, the LORD is our ruler; *
    the Holy One of Israel is our King.

19 You spoke once in a vision and said to your faithful people: *
    "I have set the crown upon a warrior
    and have exalted one chosen out of the people.

20 I have found David my servant; *
    with my holy oil have I anointed him.

21 My hand will hold him fast *
    and my arm will make him strong.

22 No enemy shall deceive him, *
    nor any wicked man bring him down.

23 I will crush his foes before him *
    and strike down those who hate him.

24 My faithfulness and love shall be with him, *
    and he shall be victorious through my Name.

25 I shall make his dominion extend *
    from the Great Sea to the River.]

26 He will say to me, 'You are my Father, *
    my God, and the rock of my salvation.'

27 I will make him my firstborn *
      and higher than the kings of the earth.
28 I will keep my love for him for ever, *
      and my covenant will stand firm for him.
29 I will establish his line for ever *
      and his throne as the days of heaven."

The Epistle   Romans 4:13-18

The promise that he would inherit the world did not come to Abraham or to
his descendants through the law but through the righteousness of faith. If it is
the adherents of the law who are to be the heirs, faith is null and the promise
is void. For the law brings wrath; but where there is no law, neither is there
violation. For this reason it depends on faith, in order that the promise may
rest on grace and be guaranteed to all his descendants, not only to the adherents of the law but also to those who share the faith of Abraham (for he is the
father of all of us, as it is written, "I have made you the father of many
nations") in the presence of the God in whom he believed, who gives life to the
dead and calls into existence the things that do not exist. Hoping against hope,
he believed that he would become "the father of many nations," according to
what was said, "So numerous shall your descendants be."

The Gospel   Luke 2:41-52

Every year Jesus' parents went to Jerusalem for the festival of the Passover.
And when he was twelve years old, they went up as usual for the festival.
When the festival was ended and they started to return, the boy Jesus stayed
behind in Jerusalem, but his parents did not know it. Assuming that he was in
the group of travelers, they went a day's journey. Then they started to look for
him among their relatives and friends. When they did not find him, they
returned to Jerusalem to search for him. After three days they found him in the
temple, sitting among the teachers, listening to them and asking them questions. And all who heard him were amazed at his understanding and his
answers. When his parents saw him they were astonished; and his mother said
to him, "Child, why have you treated us like this? Look, your father and I
have been searching for you in great anxiety." He said to them, "Why were
you searching for me? Did you not know that I must be in my Father's
house?" But they did not understand what he said to them. Then he went down
with them and came to Nazareth, and was obedient to them. His mother
treasured all these things in her heart. And Jesus increased in wisdom and in
years, and in divine and human favor.

THE ANNUNCIATION - *March 25*

The Collect

Pour your grace into our hearts, O Lord, that we who have known the incarnation of your Son Jesus Christ, announced by an angel to the Virgin Mary, may by his cross and passion be brought to the glory of his resurrection; who lives and reigns with you, in the unity of the Holy Spirit, one God, now and for ever. *Amen.*

Isaiah 7:10-14
Psalm 45 or *Psalm 40:5-11* or *Canticle 3* or *15*
Hebrews 10:4-10
Luke 1:26-38

The Lesson   Isaiah 7:10-14

The Lord spoke to Ahaz, saying, Ask a sign of the Lord your God; let it be deep as Sheol or high as heaven. But Ahaz said, I will not ask, and I will not put the Lord to the test. Then Isaiah said: "Hear then, O house of David! Is it too little for you to weary mortals, that you weary my God also? Therefore the Lord himself will give you a sign. Look, the young woman is with child and shall bear a son, and shall name him Immanuel."

The Response   Psalm 45 *or* Psalm 40:5-11 *or* Canticle 3 *or* 15

Psalm 45   *Eructavit cor meum*

1   My heart is stirring with a noble song;
        let me recite what I have fashioned for the king; *
            my tongue shall be the pen of a skilled writer.

2   You are the fairest of men; *
        grace flows from your lips,
        because God has blessed you for ever.

3   Strap your sword upon your thigh, O mighty warrior, *
        in your pride and in your majesty.

4   Ride out and conquer in the cause of truth *
        and for the sake of justice.

5   Your right hand will show you marvelous things; *
        your arrows are very sharp, O mighty warrior.

6   The peoples are falling at your feet, *
        and the king's enemies are losing heart.

7   Your throne, O God, endures for ever and ever, *
        a scepter of righteousness is the scepter of your kingdom;
        you love righteousness and hate iniquity.

8   Therefore God, your God, has anointed you *
        with the oil of gladness above your fellows.

9   All your garments are fragrant with myrrh, aloes, and cassia, *
        and the music of strings from ivory palaces makes you glad.
10   Kings' daughters stand among the ladies of the court; *
        on your right hand is the queen,
        adorned with the gold of Ophir.
11   "Hear, O daughter; consider and listen closely; *
        forget your people and your father's house.
12   The king will have pleasure in your beauty; *
        he is your master; therefore do him honor.
13   The people of Tyre are here with a gift; *
        the rich among the people seek your favor."
14   All glorious is the princess as she enters; *
        her gown is cloth-of-gold.
15   In embroidered apparel she is brought to the king; *
        after her the bridesmaids follow in procession.
16   With joy and gladness they are brought, *
        and enter into the palace of the king.
17   "In place of fathers, O king, you shall have sons; *
        you shall make them princes over all the earth.
18   I will make your name to be remembered
     from one generation to another; *
        therefore nations will praise you for ever and ever."

or, **Psalm 40:5-11** *Expectans, expectavi*
5   Great things are they that you have done, O LORD my God!
     how great your wonders and your plans for us! *
        there is none who can be compared with you.
6   Oh, that I could make them known and tell them! *
        but they are more than I can count.
7   In sacrifice and offering you take no pleasure *
        (you have given me ears to hear you);
8   Burnt-offering and sin-offering you have not required, *
        and so I said, "Behold, I come.
9   In the roll of the book it is written concerning me: *
        'I love to do your will, O my God;
        your law is deep in my heart.' "
10   I proclaimed righteousness in the great congregation; *
        behold, I did not restrain my lips;
        and that, O LORD, you know.
11   Your righteousness have I not hidden in my heart;
     I have spoken of your faithfulness and your deliverance;*
        I have not concealed your love and faithfulness from the
        great congregation.

or, **Canticle 3**   *(Page 50 BCP)*

or, **Canticle 15**   **The Song of Mary**   *Magnificat*
                        Luke 1:46-55

My soul proclaims the greatness of the Lord,
my spirit rejoices in God my Savior;*
> for he has looked with favor on his lowly servant.

From this day all generations will call me blessed:*
> the Almighty has done great things for me,
> and holy is his Name.

He has mercy on those who fear him*
> in every generation.

He has shown the strength of his arm,*
> he has scattered the proud in their conceit.

He has cast down the mighty from their thrones,*
> and has lifted up the lowly.

He has filled the hungry with good things,*
> and the rich he has sent away empty.

He has come to the help of his servant Israel,*
> for he has remembered his promise of mercy,

The promise he made to our fathers,*
> to Abraham and his children for ever.

The Epistle   Hebrews 10:4-10

It is impossible for the blood of bulls and goats to take away sins. Consequently, when Christ came into the world, he said, "Sacrifices and offerings
you have not desired, but a body you have prepared for me; in burnt offerings
and sin offerings you have taken no pleasure. Then I said, 'See, God, I have
come to do your will, O God' (in the scroll of the book it is written of me)."
When he said above, "You have neither desired nor taken pleasure in sacrifices and offerings and burnt offerings and sin offerings" (these are offered
according to the law), then he added, "See, I have come to do your will." He
abolishes the first in order to establish the second. And it is by God's will that
we have been sanctified through the offering of the body of Jesus Christ once
for all.

The Gospel   Luke 1:26-38

In the sixth month the angel Gabriel was sent by God to a town in Galilee
called Nazareth, to a virgin engaged to a man whose name was Joseph, of the
house of David. The virgin's name was Mary. And he came to her and said,
"Greetings, favored one! The Lord is with you." But she was much perplexed
by his words and pondered what sort of greeting this might be. The angel said
to her, "Do not be afraid, Mary, for you have found favor with God. And now,

you will conceive in your womb and bear a son, and you will name him Jesus. He will be great, and will be called the Son of the Most High, and the Lord God will give to him the throne of his ancestor David. He will reign over the house of Jacob forever, and of his kingdom there will be no end." Mary said to the angel, "How can this be, since I am a virgin?" The angel said to her, "The Holy Spirit will come upon you, and the power of the Most High will over-shadow you; therefore the child to be born will be holy; he will be called Son of God. And now, your relative Elizabeth in her old age has also conceived a son; and this is the sixth month for her who was said to be barren. For nothing will be impossible with God." Then Mary said, "Here am I, the servant of the Lord; let it be with me according to your word." Then the angel departed from her.

SAINT MARK - *April 25*

The Collect

Almighty God, by the hand of Mark the evangelist you have given to your Church the Gospel of Jesus Christ the Son of God: We thank you for this witness, and pray that we may be firmly grounded in its truth; through Jesus Christ our Lord, who lives and reigns with you and the Holy Spirit, one God, for ever and ever. *Amen.*

Isaiah 52:7-10
Psalm 2 or 2:7-10
Ephesians 4:7-8, 11-16
Mark 1:1-15 or Mark 16:15-20

The Lesson   Isaiah 52:7-10

How beautiful upon the mountains are the feet of the messenger who an-nounces peace, who brings good news, who announces salvation, who says to Zion, "Your God reigns." Listen! Your sentinels lift up their voices, together they sing for joy; for in plain sight they see the return of the Lord to Zion. Break forth together into singing, you ruins of Jerusalem; for the Lord has comforted his people, he has redeemed Jerusalem. The Lord has bared his holy arm before the eyes of all the nations; and all the ends of the earth shall see the salvation of our God.

The Response   Psalm 2:(1-6), 7-10, (11-12)

Psalm 2   *Quare fremuerunt gentes?*

[1   Why are the nations in an uproar? *
        Why do the peoples mutter empty threats?

2   Why do the kings of the earth rise up in revolt,
        and the princes plot together, *
            against the LORD and against his Anointed?

3   "Let us break their yoke," they say; *
      "let us cast off their bonds from us."
4   He whose throne is in heaven is laughing; *
      the LORD has them in derision.
5   Then he speaks to them in his wrath, *
      and his rage fills them with terror.
6   "I myself have set my king *
      upon my holy hill of Zion."]

7   Let me announce the decree of the LORD: *
      he said to me, "You are my Son;
      this day have I begotten you.
8   Ask of me, and I will give you the nations for your inheritance *
      and the ends of the earth for your possession.
9   You shall crush them with an iron rod *
      and shatter them like a piece of pottery."
10 And now, you kings, be wise; *
      be warned, you rulers of the earth.

[11 Submit to the LORD with fear, *
      and with trembling bow before him;
12 Lest he be angry and you perish; *
      for his wrath is quickly kindled.
13 Happy are they all *
      who take refuge in him!]

The Epistle   Ephesians 4:7-8, 11-16

Each of us was given grace according to the measure of Christ's gift. Therefore it is said, "When he ascended on high he made captivity itself a captive;
he gave gifts to his people." The gifts he gave were that some would be
apostles, some prophets, some evangelists, some pastors and teachers, to
equip the saints for the work of ministry, for building up the body of Christ,
until all of us come to the unity of the faith and of the knowledge of the Son of
God, to maturity, to the measure of the full stature of Christ. We must no
longer be children, tossed to and fro and blown about by every wind of
doctrine, by people's trickery, by their craftiness in deceitful scheming. But
speaking the truth in love, we must grow up in every way into him who is the
head, into Christ, from whom the whole body, joined and knit together by
every ligament with which it is equipped, as each part is working properly,
promotes the body's growth in building itself up in love.

The Gospel   **Mark 1:1-15 or Mark 16:15-20**
Mark 1:1-15

The beginning of the good news of Jesus Christ, the Son of God. As it is written in the prophet Isaiah, "See, I am sending my messenger ahead of you, who will prepare your way; the voice of one crying out in the wilderness: 'Prepare the way of the Lord, make his paths straight,'" John the baptizer appeared in the wilderness, proclaiming a baptism of repentance for the forgiveness of sins. And people from the whole Judean countryside and all the people of Jerusalem were going out to him, and were baptized by him in the river Jordan, confessing their sins. Now John was clothed with camel's hair, with a leather belt around his waist, and he ate locusts and wild honey. He proclaimed, "The one who is more powerful than I is coming after me; I am not worthy to stoop down and untie the thong of his sandals. I have baptized you with water; but he will baptize you with the Holy Spirit." In those days Jesus came from Nazareth of Galilee and was baptized by John in the Jordan. And just as he was coming up out of the water, he saw the heavens torn apart and the Spirit descending like a dove on him. And a voice came from heaven, "You are my Son, the Beloved; with you I am well pleased." And the Spirit immediately drove him out into the wilderness. He was in the wilderness forty days, tempted by Satan; and he was with the wild beasts; and the angels waited on him. Now after John was arrested, Jesus came to Galilee, proclaiming the good news of God, and saying, "The time is fulfilled, and the kingdom of God has come near; repent, and believe in the good news."

or, **Mark 16:15-20**

Jesus said to the apostles, "Go into all the world and proclaim the good news to the whole creation. The one who believes and is baptized will be saved; but the one who does not believe will be condemned. And these signs will accompany those who believe: by using my name they will cast out demons; they will speak in new tongues; they will pick up snakes in their hands, and if they drink any deadly thing, it will not hurt them; they will lay their hands on the sick, and they will recover." So then the Lord Jesus, after he had spoken to them, was taken up into heaven and sat down at the right hand of God. And they went out and proclaimed the good news everywhere, while the Lord worked with them and confirmed the message by the signs that accompanied it.

SAINT PHILIP & SAINT JAMES - *May 1*

The Collect

Almighty God, who gave to your apostles Philip and James grace and strength to bear witness to the truth: Grant that we, being mindful of their victory of faith, may glorify in life and death the Name of our Lord Jesus Christ; who lives and reigns with you and the Holy Spirit, one God, now and for ever. *Amen.*

Isaiah 30:18-21
Psalm 119:33-40
2 Corinthians 4:1-6
John 14:6-14

The Lesson   Isaiah 30:18-21

The Lord waits to be gracious to you; therefore he will rise up to show mercy to you. For the Lord is a God of justice; blessed are all those who wait for him. Truly, O people in Zion, inhabitants of Jerusalem, you shall weep no more. He will surely be gracious to you at the sound of your cry; when he hears it, he will answer you. Though the Lord may give you the bread of adversity and the water of affliction, yet your Teacher will not hide himself any more, but your eyes shall see your Teacher. And when you turn to the right or when you turn to the left, your ears shall hear a word behind you, saying, "This is the way; walk in it."

The Response   Psalm 119:33-40

Psalm 119:33-40   *Legem pone*

33   Teach me, O LORD, the way of your statutes, *
    and I shall keep it to the end.

34   Give me understanding, and I shall keep your law; *
    I shall keep it with all my heart.

35   Make me go in the path of your commandments, *
    for that is my desire.

36   Incline my heart to your decrees *
    and not to unjust gain.

37   Turn my eyes from watching what is worthless; *
    give me life in your ways.

38   Fulfill your promise to your servant, *
    which you make to those who fear you.

39   Turn away the reproach which I dread, *
    because your judgments are good.

40   Behold, I long for your commandments; *
    in your righteousness preserve my life.

The Epistle

The Epistle   **2 Corinthians 4:1-6**

Since it is by God's mercy that we are engaged in this ministry, we do not lose heart. We have renounced the shameful things that one hides; we refuse to practice cunning or falsify God's word; but by the open statement of the truth we commend ourselves to the conscience of everyone in the sight of God. And even if our gospel is veiled, it is veiled to those who are perishing. In their case the god of this world has blinded the minds of the unbelievers, to keep them from seeing the light of the gospel of the glory of Christ, who is the image of God. For we do not proclaim ourselves; we proclaim Jesus Christ as Lord and ourselves as your slaves for Jesus' sake. For it is the God who said, "Let light shine out of darkness," who has shone in our hearts to give the light of the knowledge of the glory of God in the face of Jesus Christ.

The Gospel   **John 14:6-14**

Jesus said to Thomas, "I am the way, and the truth, and the life. No one comes to the Father except through me. If you know me, you will know my Father also. From now on you do know him and have seen him." Philip said to him, "Lord, show us the Father, and we will be satisfied." Jesus said to him, "Have I been with you all this time, Philip, and you still do not know me? Whoever has seen me has seen the Father. How can you say, 'Show us the Father'? Do you not believe that I am in the Father and the Father is in me? The words that I say to you I do not speak on my own; but the Father who dwells in me does his works. Believe me that I am in the Father and the Father is in me; but if you do not, then believe me because of the works themselves. Very truly, I tell you, the one who believes in me will also do the works that I do and, in fact, will do greater works than these, because I am going to the Father. I will do whatever you ask in my name, so that the Father may be glorified in the Son. If in my name you ask me for anything I will do it."

THE VISITATION - *May 31*

The Collect

Father in heaven, by your grace the virgin mother of your incarnate Son was blessed in bearing him, but still more blessed in keeping your word: Grant us who honor the exaltation of her lowliness to follow the example of her devotion to your will; through Jesus Christ our Lord, who lives and reigns with you and the Holy Spirit, one God, for ever and ever. *Amen.*

*Zephaniah 3:14-18*a
Psalm 113 or *Canticle 9*
Colossians 3:12-17
Luke 1:39-57

The Lesson   **Zephaniah 3:14-18***a*

Sing aloud, O daughter Zion; shout, O Israel! Rejoice and exult with all your
heart, O daughter Jerusalem! The Lord has taken away the judgments against
you, he has turned away your enemies. The king of Israel, the Lord, is in your
midst; you shall fear disaster no more. On that day it shall be said to Jerusalem: Do not fear, O Zion; do not let your hands grow weak. The Lord, your
God, is in your midst, a warrior who gives victory; he will rejoice over you
with gladness, he will renew you in his love; he will exult over you with loud
singing as on a day of festival.

The Response   **Psalm 113**

Psalm 113   *Laudate, pueri*

   1   Hallelujah!
          Give praise, you servants of the LORD; *
               praise the Name of the LORD.
   2   Let the Name of the LORD be blessed, *
               from this time forth for evermore.
   3   From the rising of the sun to its going down *
               let the Name of the LORD be praised.
   4   The LORD is high above all nations, *
               and his glory above the heavens.
   5   Who is like the LORD our God, who sits enthroned on high *
               but stoops to behold the heavens and the earth?
   6   He takes up the weak out of the dust *
               and lifts up the poor from the ashes.
   7   He sets them with the princes, *
               with the princes of his people.
   8   He makes the woman of a childless house *
               to be a joyful mother of children.

or, **Canticle 9   The First Song of Isaiah**   *Ecce, Deus*
                    Isaiah 12:2-6

          Surely, it is God who saves me;*
               I will trust in him and not be afraid.
          For the Lord is my stronghold and my sure defense,*
               and he will be my Savior.
          Therefore you shall draw water with rejoicing*
               from the springs of salvation.
          And on that day you shall say,*
               Give thanks to the Lord and call upon his Name;

Make his deeds known among the peoples;*
    see that they remember that his Name is exalted.
Sing the praises of the Lord, for he has done great things,*
    and this is known in all the world.
Cry aloud, inhabitants of Zion, ring out your joy,*
    for the great one in the midst of you is the Holy One of Israel.

The Epistle   Colossians 3:12-17

As God's chosen ones, holy and beloved, clothe yourselves with compassion, kindness, humility, meekness, and patience. Bear with one another and, if anyone has a complaint against another, forgive each other; just as the Lord has forgiven you, so you also must forgive. Above all, clothe yourselves with love, which binds everything together in perfect harmony. And let the peace of Christ rule in your hearts, to which indeed you were called in the one body. And be thankful. Let the word of Christ dwell in you richly; teach and admonish one another in all wisdom; and with gratitude in your hearts sing psalms, hymns, and spiritual songs to God. And whatever you do, in word or deed, do everything in the name of the Lord Jesus, giving thanks to God the Father through him.

The Gospel   Luke 1:39-57

Mary set out and went with haste to a Judean town in the hill country, where she entered the house of Zechariah and greeted Elizabeth. When Elizabeth heard Mary's greeting, the child leaped in her womb. And Elizabeth was filled with the Holy Spirit and exclaimed with a loud cry, "Blessed are you among women, and blessed is the fruit of your womb. And why has this happened to me, that the mother of my Lord comes to me? For as soon as I heard the sound of your greeting, the child in my womb leaped for joy. And blessed is she who believed that there would be a fulfillment of what was spoken to her by the Lord." And Mary said, "My soul magnifies the Lord, and my spirit rejoices in God my Savior, for he has looked with favor on the lowliness of his servant. Surely, from now on all generations will call me blessed; for the Mighty One has done great things for me, and holy is his name. His mercy is for those who fear him from generation to generation. He has shown strength with his arm; he has scattered the proud in the thoughts of their hearts. He has brought down the powerful from their thrones, and lifted up the lowly; he has filled the hungry with good things, and sent the rich away empty. He has helped his servant Israel, in remembrance of his mercy, according to the promise he made to our ancestors, to Abraham and to his descendants forever." And Mary remained with her about three months and then returned to her home. Now the time came for Elizabeth to give birth, and she bore a son.

SAINT BARNABAS - *June 11*

The Collect

Grant, O God, that we may follow the example of your faithful servant Barnabas, who, seeking not his own renown but the well-being of your Church, gave generously of his life and substance for the relief of the poor and the spread of the Gospel; through Jesus Christ our Lord, who lives and reigns with you and the Holy Spirit, one God, for ever and ever. *Amen.*

Isaiah 42:5-12
Psalm 112
Acts 11:19-30; 13:1-3
Matthew 10:7-16

The Lesson   Isaiah 42:5-12

Thus says God, the Lord, who created the heavens and stretched them out, who spread out the earth and what comes from it, who gives breath to the people upon it and spirit to those who walk in it: I am the Lord, I have called you in righteousness, I have taken you by the hand and kept you; I have given you as a covenant to the people, a light to the nations, to open the eyes that are blind, to bring out the prisoners from the dungeon, from the prison those who sit in darkness. I am the Lord, that is my name; my glory I give to no other, nor my praise to idols. See, the former things have come to pass, and new things I now declare; before they spring forth, I tell you of them. Sing to the Lord a new song, his praise from the end of the earth! Let the sea roar and all that fills it, the coastlands and their inhabitants. Let the desert and its towns lift up their voice, the villages that Kedar inhabits; let the inhabitants of Sela sing for joy, let them shout from the tops of the mountains. Let them give glory to the Lord, and declare his praise in the coastlands.

The Response   Psalm 112

Psalm 112   *Beatus vir*

1   Hallelujah!
    Happy are they who fear the LORD *
        and have great delight in his commandments!

2   Their descendants will be mighty in the land; *
        the generation of the upright will be blessed.

3   Wealth and riches will be in their house, *
        and their righteousness will last for ever.

4   Light shines in the darkness for the upright; *
        the righteous are merciful and full of compassion.

5   It is good for them to be generous in lending *
        and to manage their affairs with justice.

6   For they will never be shaken; *
      the righteous will be kept in everlasting remembrance.
7   They will not be afraid of any evil rumors; *
      their heart is right;
      they put their trust in the LORD.
8   Their heart is established and will not shrink, *
      until they see their desire upon their enemies.
9   They have given freely to the poor, *
      and their righteousness stands fast for ever;
      they will hold up their head with honor.
10   The wicked will see it and be angry;
      they will gnash their teeth and pine away; *
      the desires of the wicked will perish.

The Epistle   Acts 11:19-30, 13:1-3

Those believers who were scattered because of the persecution that took place
over Stephen traveled as far as Phoenicia, Cyprus, and Antioch, and they
spoke the word to no one except Jews. But among them were some men of
Cyprus and Cyrene who, on coming to Antioch, spoke to the Hellenists also,
proclaiming the Lord Jesus. The hand of the Lord was with them, and a great
number became believers and turned to the Lord. News of this came to the
ears of the church in Jerusalem, and they sent Barnabas to Antioch. When he
came and saw the grace of God, he rejoiced, and he exhorted them all to
remain faithful to the Lord with steadfast devotion; for he was a good man,
full of the Holy Spirit and of faith. And a great many people were brought to
the Lord. Then Barnabas went to Tarsus to look for Saul, and when he had
found him, he brought him to Antioch. So it was that for an entire year they
met with the church and taught a great many people, and it was in Antioch
that the disciples were first called "Christians." At that time prophets came
down from Jerusalem to Antioch. One of them named Agabus stood up and
predicted by the Spirit that there would be a severe famine over all the world;
and this took place during the reign of Claudius. The disciples determined that
according to their ability, each would send relief to the believers living in
Judea; this they did, sending it to the elders by Barnabas and Saul. Now in the
church at Antioch there were prophets and teachers: Barnabas, Simeon who
was called Niger, Lucius of Cyrene, Manaen a member of the court of Herod
the ruler, and Saul. While they were worshiping the Lord and fasting, the Holy
Spirit said, "Set apart for me Barnabas and Saul for the work to which I have
called them." Then after fasting and praying they laid their hands on them and
sent them off.

The Gospel **Matthew 10:7-16**

Jesus said to the twelve, "As you go, proclaim the good news, 'The kingdom of heaven has come near.' Cure the sick, raise the dead, cleanse the lepers, cast out demons. You received without payment; give without payment. Take no gold, or silver, or copper in your belts, no bag for your journey, or two tunics, or sandals, or a staff; for laborers deserve their food. Whatever town or village you enter, find out who in it is worthy, and stay there until you leave. As you enter the house, greet it. If the house is worthy, let your peace come upon it; but if it is not worthy, let your peace return to you. If anyone will not welcome you or listen to your words, shake off the dust from your feet as you leave that house or town. Truly I tell you, it will be more tolerable for the land of Sodom and Gomorrah on the day of judgment than for that town. See, I am sending you out like sheep into the midst of wolves; so be wise as serpents and innocent as doves."

NATIVITY OF SAINT JOHN THE BAPTIST - *June 24*
The Collect

Almighty God, by whose providence your servant John the Baptist was wonderfully born, and sent to prepare the way of your Son our Savior by preaching repentance: Make us so to follow his teaching and holy life, that we may truly repent according to his preaching; and, following his example, constantly speak the truth, boldly rebuke vice, and patiently suffer for the truth's sake; through Jesus Christ your Son our Lord, who lives and reigns with you and the Holy Spirit, one God, for ever and ever. *Amen.*

Isaiah 40:1-11
Psalm 85 or 85:7-13
Acts 13:14b-26
Luke 1:57-80

The Lesson **Isaiah 40:1-11**

Comfort, O comfort my people, says your God. Speak tenderly to Jerusalem, and cry to her that she has served her term, that her penalty is paid, that she has received from the Lord's hand double for all her sins. A voice cries out: "In the wilderness prepare the way of the Lord, make straight in the desert a highway for our God. Every valley shall be lifted up, and every mountain and hill be made low; the uneven ground shall become level, and the rough places a plain. Then the glory of the Lord shall be revealed, and all people shall see it together, for the mouth of the Lord has spoken." A voice says, "Cry out!" And I said, "What shall I cry?" All people are grass, their constancy is like the flower of the field. The grass withers, the flower fades, when the breath of the Lord blows upon it; surely the people are grass. The grass withers, the flower fades; but the word of our God will stand forever. Get you up to a high mountain, O Zion, herald of good tidings; lift up your voice with strength, O Jerusalem, herald of good tidings, lift it up, do not fear; say to the cities of Judah, "Here is your God!" See, the Lord God comes with might, and his arm rules for him; his reward is with him, and his recompense before him. He will feed his flock like a shepherd; he will gather the lambs in his arms, and carry them in his bosom, and gently lead the mother sheep.

The Response   Psalm 85:(1-6), 7-13

Psalm 85   *Benedixisti, Domine*

  [1   You have been gracious to your land, O LORD, *
         you have restored the good fortune of Jacob.

  2   You have forgiven the iniquity of your people *
         and blotted out all their sins.

  3   You have withdrawn all your fury *
         and turned yourself from your wrathful indignation.

  4   Restore us then, O God our Savior; *
         let your anger depart from us.

  5   Will you be displeased with us for ever? *
         will you prolong your anger from age to age?

  6   Will you not give us life again, *
         that your people may rejoice in you?]

  7   Show us your mercy, O LORD, *
         and grant us your salvation.

  8   I will listen to what the LORD God is saying, *
         for he is speaking peace to his faithful people
         and to those who turn their hearts to him.

  9   Truly, his salvation is very near to those who fear him, *
         that his glory may dwell in our land.

10   Mercy and truth have met together; *
         righteousness and peace have kissed each other.

11   Truth shall spring up from the earth, *
         and righteousness shall look down from heaven.

12   The LORD will indeed grant prosperity, *
         and our land will yield its increase.

13   Righteousness shall go before him, *
         and peace shall be a pathway for his feet.

The Epistle   Acts 13:14*b*-26

On the sabbath day Paul and his companions went into the synagogue and sat down. After the reading of the law and the prophets, the officials of the synagogue sent them a message, saying, "Brothers, if you have any word of exhortation for the people, give it." So Paul stood up and with a gesture began to speak: "You Israelites, and others who fear God, listen. The God of this people Israel chose our ancestors and made the people great during their stay in the land of Egypt, and with uplifted arm he led them out of it. For about forty years he put up with them in the wilderness. After he had destroyed seven nations in the land of Canaan, he gave them their land as an inheritance for about four hundred fifty years. After that he gave them judges until the time of the prophet Samuel. Then they asked for a king; and God gave them Saul son of Kish, a man of the tribe of Benjamin, who reigned for forty years. When he had removed him, he made David their king. In his testimony about him he said, 'I have found David, son of Jesse, to be a man after my heart, who will carry out all my wishes.' Of this man's posterity God has brought to Israel a Savior, Jesus, as he promised; before his coming John had already proclaimed a baptism of repentance to all the people of Israel. And as John was finishing his work, he said, 'What do you suppose that I am? I am not he. No, but one is coming after me; I am not worthy to untie the thong of the sandals on his feet.' My brothers, you descendants of Abraham's family, and others who fear God, to us the message of this salvation has been sent."

The Gospel   Luke 1:57-80

The time came for Elizabeth to give birth, and she bore a son. Her neighbors and relatives heard that the Lord had shown his great mercy to her, and they rejoiced with her. On the eighth day they came to circumcise the child, and they were going to name him Zechariah after his father. But his mother said, "No; he is to be called John." They said to her, "None of your relatives has this name." Then they began motioning to his father to find out what name he wanted to give him. He asked for a writing tablet and wrote, "His name is John." And all of them were amazed. Immediately his mouth was opened and his tongue freed, and he began to speak, praising God. Fear came over all their neighbors, and all these things were talked about throughout the entire hill country of Judea. All who heard them pondered them and said, "What then will this child become?" For, indeed, the hand of the Lord was with him. Then his father Zechariah was filled with the Holy Spirit and spoke this prophecy: "Blessed be the Lord God of Israel, for he has looked favorably on his people and redeemed them. He has raised up a mighty savior for us in the house of his servant David, as he spoke through the mouth of his holy prophets from of old, that we would be saved from our enemies and from the hand of all who hate us. Thus he has shown the mercy promised to our ancestors, and has remembered his holy covenant, the oath that he swore to our ancestor Abraham, to grant us that we, being rescued from the hands of our enemies, might serve him without fear, in holiness and righteousness before him all our days. And you, child, will be called the prophet of the Most High; for you will go before the Lord to prepare his ways, to give knowledge of salvation to his people by the forgiveness of their sins. By the tender mercy of our God, the dawn from on high will break upon us, to give light to those who sit in darkness and in the shadow of death, to guide our feet into the way of peace." The child grew and became strong in spirit, and he was in the wilderness until the day he appeared publicly to Israel.

SAINT PETER & SAINT PAUL - *June 29*
The Collect
Almighty God, whose blessed apostles Peter and Paul glorified you by their martyrdom: Grant that your Church, instructed by their teaching and example, and knit together in unity by your Spirit, may ever stand firm upon the one foundation, which is Jesus Christ our Lord; who lives and reigns with you, in the unity of the Holy Spirit, one God, now and for ever. *Amen.*

Ezekiel 34:11-16
Psalm 87
2 Timothy 4:1-8
John 21:15-19

The Lesson   Ezekiel 34:11-16
Thus says the Lord God: I myself will search for my sheep, and will seek them out. As shepherds seek out their flocks when they are among their scattered sheep, so I will seek out my sheep. I will rescue them from all the places to which they have been scattered on a day of clouds and thick darkness. I will bring them out from the peoples and gather them from the countries, and will bring them into their own land; and I will feed them on the mountains of Israel, by the watercourses, and in all the inhabited parts of the land. I will feed them with good pasture, and the mountain heights of Israel shall be their pasture; there they shall lie down in good grazing land, and they shall feed on rich pasture on the mountains of Israel. I myself will be the shepherd of my sheep, and I will make them lie down, says the Lord God. I will seek the lost, and I will bring back the strayed, and I will bind up the injured, and I will strengthen the weak, but the fat and the strong I will destroy. I will feed them with justice.

The Response   Psalm 87
Psalm 87   *Fundamenta ejus*
1   On the holy mountain stands the city he has founded; *
    the LORD loves the gates of Zion
    more than all the dwellings of Jacob.
2   Glorious things are spoken of you, *
    O city of our God.

3   I count Egypt and Babylon among those who know me; *
        behold Philistia, Tyre, and Ethiopia:
        in Zion were they born.

4   Of Zion it shall be said, "Everyone was born in her, *
        and the Most High himself shall sustain her."

5   The LORD will record as he enrolls the peoples, *
        "These also were born there."

6   The singers and the dancers will say, *
        "All my fresh springs are in you."

The Epistle   2 Timothy 4:1-8

In the presence of God and of Christ Jesus, who is to judge the living and the
dead, and in view of his appearing and his kingdom, I solemnly urge you:
proclaim the message; be persistent whether the time is favorable or unfavorable; convince, rebuke, and encourage, with the utmost patience in teaching.
For the time is coming when people will not put up with sound doctrine, but
having itching ears, they will accumulate for themselves teachers to suit their
own desires, and will turn away from listening to the truth and wander away
to myths. As for you, always be sober, endure suffering, do the work of an
evangelist, carry out your ministry fully. As for me, I am already being poured
out as a libation, and the time of my departure has come. I have fought the
good fight, I have finished the race, I have kept the faith. From now on there is
reserved for me the crown of righteousness, which the Lord, the righteous
judge, will give me on that day, and not only to me but also to all who have
longed for his appearing.

The Gospel   John 21:15-19

When they had finished breakfast, Jesus said to Simon Peter, "Simon son of
John, do you love me more than these?" He said to him, "Yes, Lord; you know
that I love you." Jesus said to him, "Feed my lambs." A second time he said to
him, "Simon son of John, do you love me?" He said to him, "Yes, Lord; you
know that I love you." Jesus said to him, "Tend my sheep." He said to him the
third time, "Simon son of John, do you love me?" Peter felt hurt because he
said to him the third time, "Do you love me?" And he said to him, "Lord, you
know everything; you know that I love you." Jesus said to him, "Feed my
sheep. Very truly, I tell you, when you were younger, you used to fasten your
own belt and to go wherever you wished. But when you grow old, you will
stretch out your hands, and someone else will fasten a belt around you and
take you where you do not wish to go." (He said this to indicate the kind of
death by which he would glorify God.) After this he said to him, "Follow me."

INDEPENDENCE DAY - *July 4*

The Collect
Lord God Almighty, in whose Name the founders of this country won liberty
for themselves and for us, and lit the torch of freedom for nations then unborn:
Grant that we and all the people of this land may have grace to maintain our
liberties in righteousness and peace; through Jesus Christ our Lord, who lives
and reigns with you and the Holy Spirit, one God, for ever and ever. *Amen.*

Deuteronomy 10:17-21
Psalm 145 or 145:1-9
Hebrews 11:8-16
Matthew 5:43-48

The Lesson   Deuteronomy 10:17-21
Moses said to Israel, For the Lord your God is God of gods and Lord of lords,
the great God, mighty and awesome, who is not partial and takes no bribe,
who executes justice for the orphan and the widow, and who loves the strangers, providing them food and clothing. You shall also love the stranger, for you
were strangers in the land of Egypt. You shall fear the Lord your God; him
alone you shall worship; to him you shall hold fast, and by his name you shall
swear. He is your praise; he is your God, who has done for you these great
and awesome things that your own eyes have seen.

The Response   Psalm 145:1-9, (10-22)
Psalm 145   *Exaltabo te, Deus*
   1   I will exalt you, O God my King, *
           and bless your Name for ever and ever.
   2   Every day will I bless you *
           and praise your Name for ever and ever.
   3   Great is the LORD and greatly to be praised; *
           there is no end to his greatness.
   4   One generation shall praise your works to another *
           and shall declare your power.
   5   I will ponder the glorious splendor of your majesty *
           and all your marvelous works.
   6   They shall speak of the might of your wondrous acts, *
           and I will tell of your greatness.
   7   They shall publish the remembrance of your great goodness; *
           they shall sing of your righteous deeds.
   8   The LORD is gracious and full of compassion, *
           slow to anger and of great kindness.

9   The LORD is loving to everyone *
        and his compassion is over all his works.

[10   All your works praise you, O LORD, *
        and your faithful servants bless you.
11   They make known the glory of your kingdom *
        and speak of your power;
12   That the peoples may know of your power *
        and the glorious splendor of your kingdom.
13   Your kingdom is an everlasting kingdom; *
        your dominion endures throughout all ages.
14   The LORD is faithful in all his words *
        and merciful in all his deeds.
15   The LORD upholds all those who fall; *
        he lifts up those who are bowed down.
16   The eyes of all wait upon you, O LORD, *
        and you give them their food in due season.
17   You open wide your hand *
        and satisfy the needs of every living creature.
18   The LORD is righteous in all his ways *
        and loving in all his works.
19   The LORD is near to those who call upon him, *
        to all who call upon him faithfully.
20   He fulfills the desire of those who fear him; *
        he hears their cry and helps them.
21   The LORD preserves all those who love him, *
        but he destroys all the wicked.
22   My mouth shall speak the praise of the LORD; *
        let all flesh bless his holy Name for ever and ever.]

The Epistle   Hebrews 11:8-16

By faith Abraham obeyed when he was called to set out for a place that he was to receive as an inheritance; and he set out, not knowing where he was going. By faith he stayed for a time in the land he had been promised, as in a foreign land, living in tents, as did Isaac and Jacob, who were heirs with him of the same promise. For he looked forward to the city that has foundations, whose architect and builder is God. By faith he received power of procreation, even though he was too old — and Sarah herself was barren — because he considered him faithful who had promised. Therefore from one person, and this one as good as dead, descendants were born, "as many as the stars of heaven and as the innumerable grains of sand by the seashore." All of these died in faith without having received the promises, but from a distance they saw and greeted them. They confessed that they were strangers and foreigners on the earth, for people who speak in this way make it clear that they are seeking a homeland. If they had been thinking of the land that they had left behind, they would have had opportunity to return. But as it is, they desire a better country, that is, a heavenly one. Therefore God is not ashamed to be called their God; indeed, he has prepared a city for them.

The Gospel   Matthew 5:43-48

Jesus said to the disciples, "You have heard that it was said, 'You shall love your neighbor and hate your enemy.' But I say to you, Love your enemies and pray for those who persecute you, so that you may be children of your Father in heaven; for he makes his sun rise on the evil and on the good, and sends rain on the righteous and on the unrighteous. For if you love those who love you, what reward do you have? Do not even the tax collectors do the same? And if you greet only your brothers and sisters, what more are you doing than others? Do not even the Gentiles do the same? Be perfect, therefore, as your heavenly Father is perfect."

SAINT MARY MAGDALENE - *July 22*

The Collect

Almighty God, whose blessed Son restored Mary Magdalene to health of body and of mind, and called her to be a witness of his resurrection: Mercifully grant that by your grace we may be healed from all our infirmities and know you in the power of his unending life; who with you and the Holy Spirit lives and reigns, one God, now and for ever. *Amen.*

Judith 9:1, 11-14
Psalm 42:1-7
2 Corinthians 5:14-18
John 20:11-18

The Lesson   Judith 9:1, 11-14

Judith prostrated herself, put ashes on her head, and uncovered the sackcloth she was wearing. At the very time when the evening incense was being offered in the house of God in Jerusalem, Judith cried out to the Lord with a loud voice, and said, "For your strength does not depend on numbers, nor your might on the powerful. But you are the God of the lowly, helper of the oppressed, upholder of the weak, protector of the forsaken, savior of those without hope. Please, please, God of my father, God of the heritage of Israel, Lord of heaven and earth, Creator of the waters, King of all your creation, hear my prayer! Make my deceitful words bring wound and bruise on those who have planned cruel things against your covenant, and against your sacred house, and against Mount Zion, and against the house your children possess.

Let your whole nation and every tribe know and understand that you are God, the God of all power and might, and that there is no other who protects the people of Israel but you alone!"

The Response   Psalm 42:1-7

Psalm 42:1-7   *Quemadmodum*

1   As the deer longs for the water-brooks, *
        so longs my soul for you, O God.
2   My soul is athirst for God, athirst for the living God; *
        when shall I come to appear before the presence of God?
3   My tears have been my food day and night, *
        while all day long they say to me,
        "Where now is your God?"
4   I pour out my soul when I think on these things: *
        how I went with the multitude and led them into the
                house of God,
5   With the voice of praise and thanksgiving, *
        among those who keep holy-day.
6   Why are you so full of heaviness, O my soul? *
        and why are you so disquieted within me?
7   Put your trust in God; *
        for I will yet give thanks to him,
        who is the help of my countenance, and my God.

The Epistle   2 Corinthians 5:14-18

The love of Christ urges us on, because we are convinced that one has died for all; therefore all have died. And he died for all, so that those who live might live no longer for themselves, but for him who died and was raised for them. From now on, therefore, we regard no one from a human point of view; even though we once knew Christ from a human point of view, we know him no longer in that way. So if anyone is in Christ, there is a new creation: everything old has passed away; see, everything has become new! All this is from God, who reconciled us to himself through Christ, and has given us the ministry of reconciliation.

The Gospel   John 20:11-18

Mary stood weeping outside the tomb. As she wept, she bent over to look into the tomb; and she saw two angels in white, sitting where the body of Jesus had been lying, one at the head and the other at the feet. They said to her, "Woman, why are you weeping?" She said to them, "They have taken away my Lord, and I do not know where they have laid him." When she had said this, she turned around and saw Jesus standing there, but she did not know that it was Jesus. Jesus said to her, "Woman, why are you weeping? Whom are you looking for?" Supposing him to be the gardener, she said to him, "Sir, if you have carried him away, tell me where you have laid him, and I will take him away." Jesus said to her, "Mary!" She turned and said to him in Hebrew, "Rabbouni!" (which means Teacher). Jesus said to her, "Do not hold on to me, because I have not yet ascended to the Father. But go to my brothers and say to them, 'I am ascending to my Father and your Father, to my God and your God.'" Mary Magdalene went and announced to the disciples, "I have seen the Lord"; and she told them that he had said these things to her.

SAINT JAMES - *July 25*

The Collect

O gracious God, we remember before you today your servant and apostle James, first among the Twelve to suffer martyrdom for the Name of Jesus Christ; and we pray that you will pour out upon the leaders of your Church that spirit of self-denying service by which alone they may have true authority among your people; through Jesus Christ our Lord, who lives and reigns with you and the Holy Spirit, one God, now and for ever. *Amen.*

Jeremiah 45:1-5
Psalm 7:1-10
Acts 11:27—12:3
Matthew 20:20-28

The Lesson   Jeremiah 45:1-5

The word that the prophet Jeremiah spoke to Baruch son of Neriah, when he wrote these words in a scroll at the dictation of Jeremiah, in the fourth year of King Hehoiakim son of Josiah of Judah: Thus says the Lord, the God of Israel, to you, O Baruch: You said, "Woe is me! The Lord has added sorrow to my pain; I am weary with my groaning, and I find no rest." Thus you shall say to him, "Thus says the Lord: I am going to break down what I have built, and pluck up what I have planted — that is, the whole land. And you, do you seek great things for yourself? Do not seek them; for I am going to bring disaster upon all flesh, says the Lord; but I will give you your life as a prize of war in every place to which you may go."

The Response   Psalm 7:1-10

Psalm 7:1-10   *Domine, Deus meus*

1   O Lord my God, I take refuge in you; *
         save and deliver me from all who pursue me;
2   Lest like a lion they tear me in pieces *
         and snatch me away with none to deliver me.

3   O Lord my God, if I have done these things: *
        if there is any wickedness in my hands,
4   If I have repaid my friend with evil, *
        or plundered him who without cause is my enemy;
5   Then let my enemy pursue and overtake me, *
        trample my life into the ground,
        and lay my honor in the dust.
6   Stand up, O Lord, in your wrath; *
        rise up against the fury of my enemies.
7   Awake, O my God, decree justice; *
        let the assembly of the peoples gather round you.
8   Be seated on your lofty throne, O Most High; *
        O Lord, judge the nations.
9   Give judgment for me according to my
                        righteousness, O Lord, *
        and according to my innocence, O Most High.
10 Let the malice of the wicked come to an end,
    but establish the righteous; *
        for you test the mind and heart, O righteous God.

The Epistle   Acts 11:27—12:3

At that time prophets came down from Jerusalem to Antioch. One of them
named Agabus stood up and predicted by the Spirit that there would be a
severe famine over all the world; and this took place during the reign of
Claudius. The disciples determined that according to their ability, each would
send relief to the believers living in Judea; this they did, sending it to the elders
by Barnabas and Saul. About that time King Herod laid violent hands upon
some who belonged to the church. He had James, the brother of John, killed
with the sword. After he saw that it pleased the Jews, he proceeded to arrest
Peter also. (This was during the festival of Unleavened Bread.)

The Gospel   Matthew 20:20-28

The mother of the sons of Zebedee came to Jesus with her sons, and kneeling
before him, she asked a favor of him. And he said to her, "What do you
want?" She said to him, "Declare that these two sons of mine will sit, one at
your right hand and one at your left, in your kingdom." But Jesus answered,
"You do not know what you are asking. Are you able to drink the cup that I
am about to drink?" They said to him, "We are able." He said to them, "You
will indeed drink my cup, but to sit at my right hand and at my left, this is not
mine to grant, but it is for those for whom it has been prepared by my Father."
When the ten heard it, they were angry with the two brothers. But Jesus called
them to him and said, "You know that the rulers of the Gentiles lord it over
them, and their great ones are tyrants over them. It will not be so among you;

but whoever wishes to be great among you must be your servant, and whoever wishes to be first among you must be your slave; just as the Son of Man came not to be served but to serve, and to give his life a ransom for many."

THE TRANSFIGURATION - *August 6*

The Collect

O God, who on the holy mount revealed to chosen witnesses your well-beloved Son, wonderfully transfigured, in raiment white and glistening: Mercifully grant that we, being delivered from the disquietude of this world, may by faith behold the King in his beauty; who with you, O Father, and you, O Holy Spirit, lives and reigns, one God, for ever and ever. *Amen.*

Exodus 34:29-35
Psalm 99 or 99:5-9
2 Peter 1:13-21
Luke 9:28-36

The Lesson   **Exodus 34:29-35**

Moses came down from Mount Sinai. As he came down from the mountain with the two tablets of the covenant in his hand, Moses did not know that the skin of his face shone because he had been talking with God. When Aaron and all the Israelites saw Moses, the skin of his face was shining, and they were afraid to come near him. But Moses called to them; and Aaron and all the leaders of the congregation returned to him, and Moses spoke with them. Afterward all the Israelites came near, and he gave them in commandment all that the Lord had spoken with him on Mount Sinai. When Moses had finished speaking with them, he put a veil on his face; but whenever Moses went in before the Lord to speak with him, he would take the veil off, until he came out; and when he came out, and told the Israelites what he had been commanded, the Israelites would see the face of Moses, that the skin of his face was shining; and Moses would put the veil on his face again, until he went in to speak with him.

The Response   **Psalm 99:(1-4), 5-9**

Psalm 99 *Dominus regnavit*

[1   The LORD is King;
        let the people tremble; *
                he is enthroned upon the cherubim;
                let the earth shake.

2   The LORD is great in Zion; *
                he is high above all peoples.

3   Let them confess his Name, which is great and awesome; *
        he is the Holy One.
4   "O mighty King, lover of justice,
        you have established equity; *
            you have executed justice and righteousness in Jacob."]

5   Proclaim the greatness of the Lord our God
        and fall down before his footstool; *
            he is the Holy One.
6   Moses and Aaron among his priests,
        and Samuel among those who call upon his Name, *
            they called upon the Lord, and he answered them.
7   He spoke to them out of the pillar of cloud; *
        they kept his testimonies and the decree that he gave them.
8   "O Lord our God, you answered them indeed; *
        you were a God who forgave them,
            yet punished them for their evil deeds."
9   Proclaim the greatness of the Lord our God
        and worship him upon his holy hill; *
            for the Lord our God is the Holy One.

The Epistle   2 Peter 1:13-21

I think it right, as long as I am in this body, to refresh your memory, since I
know that my death will come soon, as indeed our Lord Jesus Christ has made
clear to me. And I will make every effort so that after my departure you may
be able at any time to recall these things. For we did not follow cleverly
devised myths when we made known to you the power and coming of our
Lord Jesus Christ, but we had been eyewitnesses of his majesty. For he
received honor and glory from God the Father when that voice was conveyed
to him by the Majestic Glory, saying, "This is my Son, my Beloved, with
whom I am well pleased." We ourselves heard this voice come from heaven,
while we were with him on the holy mountain. So we have the prophetic
message more fully confirmed. You will do well to be attentive to this as to a
lamp shining in a dark place, until the day dawns and the morning star rises in
your hearts. First of all you must understand this, that no prophecy of scripture is a matter of one's own interpretation, because no prophecy ever came
by human will, but men and women moved by the Holy Spirit spoke from
God.

The Gospel   Luke 9:28-36

Now about eight days after Jesus had foretold his death and resurrection,
Jesus took with him Peter and John and James, and went up on the mountain

to pray. And while he was praying, the appearance of his face changed, and his clothes became dazzling white. Suddenly they saw two men, Moses and Elijah, talking to him. They appeared in glory and were speaking of his departure, which he was about to accomplish at Jerusalem. Now Peter and his companions were weighed down with sleep; but since they had stayed awake, they saw his glory and the two men who stood with him. Just as they were leaving him, Peter said to Jesus, "Master, it is good for us to be here; let us make three dwellings, one for you, one for Moses, and one for Elijah" — not knowing what he said. While he was saying this, a cloud came and overshadowed them; and they were terrified as they entered the cloud. Then from the cloud came a voice that said, "This is my Son, my Chosen; listen to him!" When the voice had spoken, Jesus was found alone. And they kept silent and in those days told no one any of the things they had seen.

SAINT MARY THE VIRGIN - *August 15*

The Collect

O God, you have taken to yourself the blessed Virgin Mary, mother of your incarnate Son: Grant that we, who have been redeemed by his blood, may share with her the glory of your eternal kingdom; through Jesus Christ our Lord, who lives and reigns with you, in the unity of the Holy Spirit, one God, now and for ever. *Amen.*

Isaiah 61:10-11
Psalm 34 or 34:1-9
Galatians 4:4-7
Luke 1:46-55

The Lesson   Isaiah 61:10-11

I will greatly rejoice in the Lord, my whole being shall exult in my God; for he has clothed me with the garments of salvation, he has covered me with the robe of righteousness, as a bridegroom decks himself with a garland, and as a bride adorns herself with her jewels. For as the earth brings forth its shoots, and as a garden causes what is sown in it to spring up, so the Lord God will cause righteousness and praise to spring up before all the nations.

The Response   Psalm 34:1-9, (10-22)

Psalm 34   *Benedicam Dominum*

1   I will bless the Lord at all times;*
        his praise shall ever be in my mouth.
2   I will glory in the Lord;*
        let the humble hear and rejoice.

3   Proclaim with me the greatness of the Lord;*
      let us exalt his Name together.
4   I sought the Lord, and he answered me*
      and delivered me out of all my terror.
5   Look upon him and be radiant,*
      and let not your faces be ashamed.
6   I called in my affliction and the Lord heard me*
      and saved me from all my troubles.
7   The angel of the Lord encompasses those who fear him,*
      and he will deliver them.
8   Taste and see that the Lord is good;*
      happy are they who trust in him!
9   Fear the Lord, you that are his saints,*
      for those who fear him lack nothing.

[10   The young lions lack and suffer hunger,*
      but those who seek the Lord lack nothing that is good.
11   Come, children, and listen to me;*
      I will teach you the fear of the Lord.
12   Who among you loves life*
      and desire long life to enjoy prosperity?
13   Keep your tongue from evil-speaking*
      and your lips from lying words.
14   Turn from evil and do good;*
      seek peace and pursue it.
15   The eyes of the Lord are upon the righteous,*
      and his ears are open to their cry.
16   The face of the Lord is against those who do evil,*
      to root out the remembrance of them from the earth.
17   The righteous cry, and the Lord hears them*
      and delivers them from all their troubles.
18   The Lord is near to the brokenhearted*
      and will save those whose spirits are crushed.
19   Many are the troubles of the righteous,*
      but the Lord will deliver him out of them all.
20   He will keep safe all his bones;*
      not one of them shall be broken.
21   Evil shall slay the wicked,*
      and those who hate the righteous will be punished.
22   The Lord ransoms the life of his servants,*
      and none will be punished who trust in him.]

The Epistle   **Galatians 4:4-7**

When the fullness of time had come, God sent his Son, born of a woman, born under the law, in order to redeem those who were under the law, so that we might receive adoption as children. And because you are children, God has sent the Spirit of his Son into our hearts, crying, "Abba! Father!" So you are no longer a slave but a child, and if a child then also an heir, through God.

The Gospel   **Luke 1:46-55**

Mary said, "My soul magnifies the Lord, and my spirit rejoices in God my Savior, for he has looked with favor on the lowliness of his servant. Surely, from now on all generations will call me blessed; for the Mighty One has done great things for me, and holy is his name. His mercy is for those who fear him from generation to generation. He has shown strength with his arm; he has scattered the proud in the thoughts of their hearts. He has brought down the powerful from their thrones, and lifted up the lowly; he has filled the hungry with good things, and sent the rich away empty. He has helped his servant Israel, in remembrance of his mercy, according to the promise he made to our ancestors, to Abraham and to his descendants forever."

SAINT BARTHOLOMEW - *August 24*

The Collect

Almighty and everlasting God, who gave to your apostle Bartholomew grace truly to believe and to preach your Word: Grant that your Church may love what he believed and preach what he taught; through Jesus Christ our Lord, who lives and reigns with you and the Holy Spirit, one God, for ever and ever. *Amen.*

Deuteronomy 18:15-18
Psalm 91 or *91:1-4*
1 Corinthians 4:9-15
Luke 22:24-30

The Lesson   **Deuteronomy 18:15-18**

Moses said to the Israelites, "The Lord your God will raise up for you a prophet like me from among your own people; you shall heed such a prophet. This is what you requested of the Lord you God at Horeb on the day of the assembly when you said: 'If I hear the voice of the Lord my God any more, or ever again see this great fire, I will die.' Then the Lord replied to me: 'They are right in what they have said. I will raise up for them a prophet like you from among their own people; I will put my words in the mouth of the prophet, who shall speak to them everything that I command.'"

The Response   **Psalm 91:1-4, (5-16)**

Psalm 91   *Qui habitat*

1   He who dwells in the shelter of the Most High, *
        abides under the shadow of the Almighty.

2   He shall say to the LORD,
    "You are my refuge and my stronghold, *
        my God in whom I put my trust."

3   He shall deliver you from the snare of the hunter *
        and from the deadly pestilence.

4   He shall cover you with his pinions,
    and you shall find refuge under his wings; *
        his faithfulness shall be a shield and buckler.

[5   You shall not be afraid of any terror by night, *
        nor of the arrow that flies by day;

6   Of the plague that stalks in the darkness, *
        nor of the sickness that lays waste at mid-day.

7   A thousand shall fall at your side
    and ten thousand at your right hand, *
        but it shall not come near you.

8   Your eyes have only to behold *
        to see the reward of the wicked.

9   Because you have made the LORD your refuge, *
        and the Most High your habitation,

10 There shall no evil happen to you, *
        neither shall any plague come near your dwelling.

11 For he shall give his angels charge over you, *
        to keep you in all your ways.

12 They shall bear you in their hands, *
        lest you dash your foot against a stone.

13 You shall tread upon the lion and adder; *
        you shall trample the young lion and the serpent
                        under your feet.

14 Because he is bound to me in love,
    therefore will I deliver him; *
        I will protect him, because he knows my Name.

15 He shall call upon me, and I will answer him; *
        I am with him in trouble;
        I will rescue him and bring him to honor.

16 With long life will I satisfy him, *
        and show him my salvation.]

The Epistle   1 Corinthians 4:9-15

I think that God has exhibited us apostles as last of all, as though sentenced to death, because we have become a spectacle to the world, to angels and mortals. We are fools for the sake of Christ, but you are wise in Christ. We are weak, but you are strong. You are held in honor, but we in disrepute. To the present hour we are hungry and thirsty, we are poorly clothed and beaten and homeless, and we grow weary from the work of our own hands. When reviled, we bless; when persecuted, we endure; when slandered, we speak kindly. We have become like the rubbish of the world, the dregs of all things, to this very day. I am not writing this to make you ashamed, but to admonish you as my beloved children. For though you might have ten thousand guardians in Christ, you do not have many fathers. Indeed, in Christ Jesus I became your father through the gospel.

The Gospel   Luke 22:24-30

A dispute arose among the disciples as to which one of them was to be regarded as the greatest. But Jesus said to them, "The kings of the Gentiles lord it over them; and those in authority over them are called benefactors. But not so with you; rather the greatest among you must become like the youngest, and the leader like one who serves. For who is greater, the one who is at the table or the one who serves? Is it not the one at the table? But I am among you as one who serves. You are those who have stood by me in my trials; and I confer on you, just as my Father has conferred on me, a kingdom, so that you may eat and drink at my table in my kingdom, and you will sit on thrones judging the twelve tribes of Israel."

HOLY CROSS DAY - *September 14*

The Collect

Almighty God, whose Son our Savior Jesus Christ was lifted high upon the cross that he might draw the whole world to himself: Mercifully grant that we, who glory in the mystery of our redemption, may have grace to take up our cross and follow him; who lives and reigns with you and the Holy Spirit, one God, in glory everlasting. *Amen.*

Isaiah 45:21-25
Psalm 98 or 98:1-4
Philippians 2:5-11 or Galatians 6:14-18
John 12:31-36a

The Lesson   Isaiah 45:21-25

Thus says the Lord, Declare and present your case; let them take counsel together! Who told this long ago? Who declared it of old? Was it not I, the Lord? There is no other god besides me, a righteous God and a Savior; there is no one besides me. Turn to me and be saved, all the ends of the earth! For I am God, and there is no other. By myself I have sworn, from my mouth has gone forth in righteousness a word that shall not return: "To me every knee shall bow, every tongue shall swear." Only in the Lord, it shall be said of me, are righteousness and strength; all who were incensed against him shall come to him and be ashamed. In the Lord all the offspring of Israel shall triumph and glory.

The Response   **Psalm 98:1-4, (5-10)**
Psalm 98   *Cantate Domino*
   1   Sing to the LORD a new song, *
             for he has done marvelous things.
   2   With his right hand and his holy arm *
             has he won for himself the victory.
   3   The LORD has made known his victory; *
             his righteousness has he openly shown in
                         the sight of the nations.
   4   He remembers his mercy and faithfulness to
       the house of Israel, *
             and all the ends of the earth have seen the
                         victory of our God.

   [5   Shout with joy to the LORD, all you lands; *
             lift up your voice, rejoice, and sing.
   6   Sing to the LORD with the harp, *
             with the harp and the voice of song.
   7   With trumpets and the sound of the horn *
             shout with joy before the King, the LORD.
   8   Let the sea make a noise and all that is in it, *
             the lands and those who dwell therein.
   9   Let the rivers clap their hands, *
             and let the hills ring out with joy before the LORD,
             when he comes to judge the earth.
   10   In righteousness shall he judge the world *
             and the peoples with equity.]

The Epistle   **Philippians 2:5-11** *or* **Galatians 6:14-18**
Philippians 2:5-11
Let the same mind be in you that was in Christ Jesus, who, though he was in the form of God, did not regard equality with God as something to be exploited, but emptied himself, taking the form of a slave, being born in human likeness. And being found in human form, he humbled himself and became

obedient to the point of death — even death on a cross. Therefore God also highly exalted him and gave him the name that is above every name, so that at the name of Jesus every knee should bend, in heaven and on earth and under the earth, and every tongue should confess that Jesus Christ is Lord, to the glory of God the Father.

or, Galatians 6:14-18

May I never boast of anything except the cross of our Lord Jesus Christ, by which the world has been crucified to me, and I to the world. For neither circumcision nor uncircumcision is anything; but a new creation is everything! As for those who will follow this rule — peace be upon them, and mercy, and upon the Israel of God. From now on, let no one make trouble for me; for I carry the marks of Jesus branded on my body. May the grace of our Lord Jesus Christ be with your spirit, brothers and sisters. Amen.

The Gospel   John 12:31-36*a*

Jesus said, "Now is the judgment of this world; now the ruler of this world will be driven out. And I, when I am lifted up from the earth, will draw all people to myself." He said this to indicate the kind of death he was to die. The crowd answered him, "We have heard from the law that the Messiah remains forever. How can you say that the Son of Man must be lifted up? Who is this Son of Man?" Jesus said to them, "The light is with you for a little longer. Walk while you have the light, so that the darkness may not overtake you. If you walk in the darkness, you do not know where you are going. While you have the light, believe in the light, so that you may become children of light."

SAINT MATTHEW - *September 21*

The Collect

We thank you, heavenly Father, for the witness of your apostle and evangelist Matthew to the Gospel of your Son our Savior; and we pray that, after his example, we may with ready wills and hearts obey the calling of our Lord to follow him; through Jesus Christ our Lord, who lives and reigns with you and the Holy Spirit, one God, now and for ever. *Amen.*

Proverbs 3:1-6
Psalm 119:33-40
2 Timothy 3:14-17
Matthew 9:9-13

The Lesson   Proverbs 3:1-6

My child, do not forget my teaching, but let your heart keep my command-ments; for length of days and years of life and abundant welfare they will give you. Do not let loyalty and faithfulness forsake you; bind them around your neck, write them on the tablet of your heart. So you will find favor and good repute in the sight of God and of people. Trust in the Lord with all your heart, and do not rely on your own insight. In all your ways acknowledge him, and he will make straight your paths.

The Response   Psalm 119:33-40

Psalm 119:33-40   *Legem pone*

33   Teach me, O LORD, the way of your statutes, *
    and I shall keep it to the end.
34   Give me understanding, and I shall keep your law; *
    I shall keep it with all my heart.
35   Make me go in the path of your commandments, *
    for that is my desire.
36   Incline my heart to your decrees *
    and not to unjust gain.
37   Turn my eyes from watching what is worthless; *
    give me life in your ways.
38   Fulfill your promise to your servant, *
    which you make to those who fear you.
39   Turn away the reproach which I dread, *
    because your judgments are good.
40   Behold, I long for your commandments; *
    in your righteousness preserve my life.

The Epistle   2 Timothy 3:14-17

As for you, continue in what you have learned and firmly believed, knowing from whom you learned it, and how from childhood you have known the sacred writings that are able to instruct you for salvation through faith in Christ Jesus. All scripture is inspired by God and is useful for teaching, for reproof, for correction, and for training in righteousness, so that everyone who belongs to God may be proficient, equipped for every good work.

The Gospel   Matthew 9:9-13

As Jesus was walking along, he saw a man called Matthew sitting at the tax booth; and he said to him, "Follow me." And he got up and followed him. And as he sat at dinner in the house, many tax collectors and sinners came and were sitting with him and his disciples. When the Pharisees saw this, they said to his disciples, "Why does your teacher eat with tax collectors and sinners?" But when he heard this, he said, "Those who are well have no need of a physician, but those who are sick. Go and learn what this means, 'I desire mercy, not sacrifice.' For I have come to call not the righteous but sinners."

SAINT MICHAEL & ALL ANGELS - *September 29*

The Collect

Everlasting God, you have ordained and constituted in a wonderful order the ministries of angels and mortals: Mercifully grant that, as your holy angels always serve and worship you in heaven, so by your appointment they may help and defend us here on earth; through Jesus Christ our Lord, who lives and reigns with you and the Holy Spirit, one God, for ever and ever. *Amen.*

Genesis 28:10-17
Psalm 103 or 103:19-22
Revelation 12:7-12
John 1:47-51

The Lesson   Genesis 28:10-17

Jacob left Beer-sheba and went toward Haran. He came to a certain place and stayed there for the night, because the sun had set. Taking one of the stones of the place, he put it under his head and lay down in that place. And he dreamed that there was a ladder set up on the earth, the top of it reaching to heaven; and the angels of God were ascending and descending on it. And the Lord stood beside him and said, "I am the Lord, the God of Abraham your father and the God of Isaac; the land on which you lie I will give to you and to your offspring; and your offspring shall be like the dust of the earth, and you shall spread abroad to the west and to the east and to the north and to the south; and all the families of the earth shall be blessed in you and in your offspring. Know that I am with you and will keep you wherever you go, and will bring you back to this land; for I will not leave you until I have done what I have promised you." Then Jacob woke from his sleep and said, "Surely the Lord is in this place — and I did not know it!" And he was afraid, and said, "How awesome is this place! This is none other than the house of God, and this is the gate of heaven."

The Response   Psalm 103:(1-18), 19-22

Psalm 103 *Benedic, anima mea*

[1 Bless the LORD, O my soul, *
    and all that is within me, bless his holy Name.

2 Bless the LORD, O my soul, *
    and forget not all his benefits.

3 He forgives all your sins *
    and heals all your infirmities;

4 He redeems your life from the grave *
    and crowns you with mercy and loving-kindness;

5 He satisfies you with good things, *
    and your youth is renewed like an eagle's.

6 The Lord executes righteousness *
   and judgment for all who are oppressed.
7 He made his ways known to Moses *
   and his works to the children of Israel.
8 The Lord is full of compassion and mercy, *
   slow to anger and of great kindness.
9 He will not always accuse us, *
   nor will he keep his anger for ever.
10 He has not dealt with us according to our sins, *
   nor rewarded us according to our wickedness.
11 For as the heavens are high above the earth, *
   so is his mercy great upon those who fear him.
12 As far as the east is from the west, *
   so far has he removed our sins from us.
13 As a father cares for his children, *
   so does the Lord care for those who fear him.
14 For he himself knows whereof we are made; *
   he remembers that we are but dust.
15 Our days are like the grass; *
   we flourish like a flower of the field;
16 When the wind goes over it, it is gone, *
   and its place shall know it no more.
17 But the merciful goodness of the Lord endures for ever
                     on those who fear him, *
   and his righteousness on children's children;
18 On those who keep his covenant *
   and remember his commandments and do them.]

19 The Lord has set his throne in heaven, *
   and his kingship has dominion over all.
20 Bless the Lord, you angels of his,
   you mighty ones who do his bidding, *
   and hearken to the voice of his word.
21 Bless the Lord, all you his hosts, *
   you ministers of his who do his will.
22 Bless the Lord, all you works of his,
   in all places of his dominion; *
   bless the Lord, O my soul.

The Epistle   **Revelation 12:7-12**

War broke out in heaven; Michael and his angels fought against the dragon.
The dragon and his angels fought back, but they were defeated, and there was

no longer any place for them in heaven. The great dragon was thrown down, that ancient serpent, who is called the Devil and Satan, the deceiver of the whole world — he was thrown down to the earth, and his angels were thrown down with him. Then I heard a loud voice in heaven, proclaiming, "Now have come the salvation and the power and the kingdom of our God and the authority of his Messiah, for the accuser of our comrades has been thrown down, who accuses them day and night before our God. But they have conquered him by the blood of the Lamb and by the word of their testimony, for they did not cling to life even in the face of death. Rejoice then, you heavens and those who dwell in them! But woe to the earth and the sea, for the devil has come down to you with great wrath, because he knows that his time is short!"

The Gospel   John 1:47-51

When Jesus saw Nathanael coming toward him, he said of him, "Here is truly an Israelite in whom there is no deceit!" Nathanael asked him, "Where did you get to know me?" Jesus answered, "I saw you under the fig tree before Philip called you." Nathanael replied, "Rabbi, you are the Son of God! You are the King of Israel!" Jesus answered, "Do you believe because I told you that I saw you under the fig tree? You will see greater things than these." And he said to him, "Very truly, I tell you, you will see heaven opened and the angels of God ascending and descending upon the Son of Man."

SAINT LUKE - *October 18*

The Collect

Almighty God, who inspired your servant Luke the physician to set forth in the Gospel the love and healing power of your Son: Graciously continue in your Church this love and power to heal, to the praise and glory of your Name; through Jesus Christ our Lord, who lives and reigns with you, in the unity of the Holy Spirit, one God, now and for ever. *Amen.*

Sirach 38:1-4, 6-10, 12-14
Psalm 147 or 147:1-7
2 Timothy 4:5-13
Luke 4:14-21

The Lesson   Sirach 38:1-4, 6-10, 12-14

Honor physicians for their services, for the Lord created them; for their gift of healing come from the Most High, and they are rewarded by the king. The skill of physicians makes them distinguished, and in the presence of the great they are admired. The Lord created medicines out of the earth, and the sensible will not despise them. And he gave skill to human beings that he might be glorified in his marvelous works. By them the physician heals and takes away pain; the pharmacist makes a mixture from them. God's works will never be finished; and from him health spreads over all the earth. My child, when you are ill, do not delay, but pray to the Lord, and he will heal you. Give up your faults and direct your hands rightly, and cleanse your heart from all sin. Then give the physician his place, for the Lord created him; do not let him leave you, for you need him. There may come a time when recovery lies in the hands of physicians, for they too pray to the Lord that he grant them success in diagnosis and in healing, for the sake of preserving life.

The Response   Psalm 147:1-7, (8-21)
Psalm 147 *Laudate Dominum*

1   Hallelujah!
    How good it is to sing praises to our God! *
        how pleasant it is to honor him with praise!
2   The LORD rebuilds Jerusalem; *
        he gathers the exiles of Israel.
3   He heals the brokenhearted *
        and binds up their wounds.
4   He counts the number of the stars *
        and calls them all by their names.
5   Great is our LORD and mighty in power; *
        there is no limit to his wisdom.
6   The LORD lifts up the lowly, *
        but casts the wicked to the ground.
7   Sing to the LORD with thanksgiving; *
        make music to our God upon the harp.

[8 He covers the heavens with clouds *
        and prepares rain for the earth;
9   He makes grass to grow upon the mountains *
        and green plants to serve mankind.
10 He provides food for flocks and herds *
        and for the young ravens when they cry.
11 He is not impressed by the might of a horse; *
        he has no pleasure in the strength of a man;
12 But the LORD has pleasure in those who fear him, *
        in those who await his gracious favor.
13 Worship the LORD, O Jerusalem; *
        praise your God, O Zion;
14 For he has strengthened the bars of your gates; *
        he has blessed your children within you.
15 He has established peace on your borders; *
        he satisfies you with the finest wheat.

16 He sends out his command to the earth, *
    and his word runs very swiftly.
17 He gives snow like wool; *
    he scatters hoarfrost like ashes.
18 He scatters his hail like bread crumbs; *
    who can stand against his cold?
19 He sends forth his word and melts them; *
    he blows with his wind, and the waters flow.
20 He declares his word to Jacob, *
    his statutes and his judgments to Israel.
21 He has not done so to any other nation; *
    to them he has not revealed his judgments.
    Hallelujah!]

The Epistle   2 Timothy 4:5-13

As for you, always be sober, endure suffering, do the work of an evangelist,
carry out your ministry fully. As for me, I am already being poured out as a
libation, and the time of my departure has come. I have fought the good fight,
I have finished the race, I have kept the faith. From now on there is reserved
for me the crown of righteousness, which the Lord, the righteous judge, will
give me on that day, and not only to me but also to all who have longed for his
appearing. Do your best to come to me soon, for Demas, in love with this
present world, has deserted me and gone to Thessalonica; Crescens has gone
to Galatia, Titus to Dalmatia. Only Luke is with me. Get Mark and bring him
with you, for he is useful in my ministry. I have sent Tychicus to Ephesus.
When you come, bring the cloak that I left with Carpus at Troas, also the
books, and above all the parchments.

The Gospel   Luke 4:14-21

Jesus, filled with the power of the Spirit, returned to Galilee, and a report
about him spread through all the surrounding country. He began to teach in
their synagogues and was praised by everyone. When he came to Nazareth,
where he had been brought up, he went to the synagogue on the sabbath day,
as was his custom. He stood up to read, and the scroll of the prophet Isaiah
was given to him. He unrolled the scroll and found the place where it was
written: "The Spirit of the Lord is upon me, because he has anointed me to
bring good news to the poor. He has sent me to proclaim release to the captives and recovery of sight to the blind, to let the oppressed go free, to proclaim the year of the Lord's favor." And he rolled up the scroll, gave it back to
the attendant, and sat down. The eyes of all in the synagogue were fixed on
him. Then he began to say to them, "Today this scripture has been fulfilled in
your hearing."

SAINT JAMES OF JERUSALEM - *October 23*

The Collect

Grant, O God, that, following the example of your servant James the Just, brother of our Lord, your Church may give itself continually to prayer and to the reconciliation of all who are at variance and enmity; through Jesus Christ our Lord, who lives and reigns with you and the Holy Spirit, one God, now and for ever. *Amen.*

Acts 15:12-22a

Psalm 1

1 Corinthians 15:1-11

Matthew 13:54-58

The Lesson   Acts 15:12-22*a*

The whole assembly kept silence, and listened to Barnabas and Paul as they told of all the signs and wonders that God had done through them among the Gentiles. After they finished speaking, James replied, "My brothers, listen to me. Simeon has related how God first looked favorably on the Gentiles, to take from among them a people for his name. This agrees with the words of the prophets, as it is written, 'After this I will return, and I will rebuild the dwelling of David, which has fallen; from its ruins I will rebuild it, and I will set it up, so that all other peoples may seek the Lord — even all the Gentiles over whom my name has been called. Thus says the Lord, who has been making these things known from long ago.' Therefore I have reached the decision that we should not trouble those Gentiles who are turning to God, but we should write to them to abstain only from things polluted by idols and from fornication and from whatever has been strangled and from blood. For in every city, for generations past, Moses has had those who proclaim him, for he has been read aloud every sabbath in the synagogues." Then the apostles and the elders, with the consent of the whole church, decided to choose men from among their members and to send them to Antioch with Paul and Barnabas.

The Response   Psalm 1

Psalm 1   *Beatus vir qui non abiit*

 1   Happy are they who have not walked in the counsel of
              the wicked, *
          nor lingered in the way of sinners,
          nor sat in the seats of the scornful!
 2   Their delight is in the law of the LORD, *
          and they meditate on his law day and night.

3   They are like trees planted by streams of water,
        bearing fruit in due season, with leaves that do not wither; *
            everything they do shall prosper.
4   It is not so with the wicked; *
        they are like chaff which the wind blows away.
5   Therefore the wicked shall not stand upright when
                judgment comes, *
        nor the sinner in the council of the righteous.
6   For the LORD knows the way of the righteous, *
        but the way of the wicked is doomed.

The Epistle   1 Corinthians 15:1-11

Now I would remind you, brothers and sisters, of the good news that I proclaimed to you, which you in turn received, in which also you stand, through
which also you are being saved, if you hold firmly to the message that I
proclaimed to you — unless you have come to believe in vain. For I handed on
to you as of first importance what I in turn had received: that Christ died for
our sins in accordance with the scriptures, and that he was buried, and that he
was raised on the third day in accordance with the scriptures, and that he
appeared to Cephas, then to the twelve. Then he appeared to more than five
hundred brothers and sisters at one time, most of whom are still alive, though
some have died. Then he appeared to James, then to all the apostles. Last of
all, as to one untimely born, he appeared also to me. For I am the least of the
apostles, unfit to be called an apostle, because I persecuted the church of God.
But by the grace of God I am what I am, and his grace toward me has not
been in vain. On the contrary, I worked harder than any of them — though it
was not I, but the grace of God that is with me. Whether then it was I or they,
so we proclaim and so you have come to believe.

The Gospel   Matthew 13:54-58

Jesus came to his hometown and began to teach the people in their synagogue,
so that they were astounded and said, "Where did this man get this wisdom
and these deeds of power? Is not this the carpenter's son? Is not his mother
called Mary? And are not his brothers James and Joseph and Simon and
Judas? And are not all his sisters with us? Where then did this man get all
this?" And they took offense at him. But Jesus said to them, "Prophets are not
without honor except in their own country and in their own house." And he
did not do many deeds of power there, because of their unbelief.

SAINT SIMON & SAINT JUDE - *October 28*

The Collect

O God, we thank you for the glorious company of the apostles, and especially on this day for Simon and Jude; and we pray that, as they were faithful and zealous in their mission, so we may with ardent devotion make known the love and mercy of our Lord and Savior Jesus Christ; who lives and reigns with you and the Holy Spirit, one God, for ever and ever. *Amen.*

Deuteronomy 32:1-4
Psalm 119:89-96
Ephesians 2:13-22
John 15:17-27

The Lesson   Deuteronomy 32:1-4

Moses spoke these words to the whole assembly of Israel; "Give ear, O heavens, and I will speak; let the earth hear the words of my mouth. May my teaching drop like the rain, my speech condense like the dew; like gentle rain on grass, like showers on new growth. For I will proclaim the name of the Lord; ascribe greatness to our God! The Rock, his work is perfect, and all his ways are just. A faithful God, without deceit, just and upright is he."

The Response   Psalm 119:89-96

Psalm 119:89-96   *In aeternum, Domine*

89   O LORD, your word is everlasting; *
        it stands firm in the heavens.
90   Your faithfulness remains from one generation to another; *
        you established the earth, and it abides.
91   By your decree these continue to this day, *
        for all things are your servants.
92   If my delight had not been in your law, *
        I should have perished in my affliction.
93   I will never forget your commandments, *
        because by them you give me life.
94   I am yours; oh, that you would save me! *
        for I study your commandments.
95   Though the wicked lie in wait for me to destroy me, *
        I will apply my mind to your decrees.
96   I see that all things come to an end, *
        but your commandment has no bounds.

The Epistle   **Ephesians 2:13-22**

In Christ Jesus you who once were far off have been brought near by the blood of Christ. For he is our peace; in his flesh he has made both groups into one and has broken down the dividing wall, that is, the hostility between us. He has abolished the law with its commandments and ordinances, that he might create in himself one new humanity in place of the two, thus making peace, and might reconcile both groups to God in one body through the cross, thus putting to death that hostility through it. So he came and proclaimed peace to you who were far off and peace to those who were near; for through him both of us have access in one Spirit to the Father. So then you are no longer strangers and aliens, but you are citizens with the saints and also members of the household of God, built upon the foundation of the apostles and prophets, with Christ Jesus himself as the cornerstone. In him the whole structure is joined together and grows into a holy temple in the Lord; in whom you also are built together spiritually into a dwelling place for God.

The Gospel   **John 15:17-27**

Jesus said to the disciples, "I am giving you these commands so that you may love one another. If the world hates you, be aware that it hated me before it hated you. If you belonged to the world, the world would love you as its own. Because you do not belong to the world, but I have chosen you out of the world — therefore the world hates you. Remember the word that I said to you, 'Servants are not greater than their master.' If they persecuted me, they will persecute you; if they kept my word, they will keep yours also. But they will do all these things to you on account of my name, because they do not know him who sent me. If I had not come and spoken to them, they would not have sin; but now they have no excuse for their sin. Whoever hates me hates my Father also. If I had not done among them the works that no one else did, they would not have sin. But now they have seen and hated both me and my father. It was to fulfill the word that is written in their law, 'They hated me without a cause.' When the Advocate comes, whom I will send to you from the Father, the Spirit of truth who comes from the Father, he will testify on my behalf. You also are to testify because you have been with me from the beginning."

ALL SAINTS' DAY - *November 1*

The Collect

Almighty God, you have knit together your elect in one communion and fellowship in the mystical body of your Son Christ our Lord: Give us grace so to follow your blessed saints in all virtuous and godly living, that we may come to those ineffable joys that you have prepared for those who truly love you; through Jesus Christ our Lord, who with you and the Holy Spirit lives and reigns, one God, in glory everlasting. *Amen.*

Year A
Revelation 7:9-17
Psalm 34:1-10, 22
1 John 3:1-3
Matthew 5:1-12

The Lesson   **Revelation 7:9-17**

After this I (John) looked, and there was a great multitude that no one could count, from every nation, from all tribes and peoples and languages, standing before the throne and before the Lamb, robed in white, with palm branches in their hands. They cried out in a loud voice, saying, "Salvation belongs to our God who is seated on the throne, and to the Lamb!" And all the angels stood around the throne and around the elders and the four living creatures, and they fell on their faces before the throne and worshiped God, singing, "Amen! Blessing and glory and wisdom and thanksgiving and honor and power and might be to our God forever and ever! Amen." Then one of the elders addressed me, saying, "Who are these, robed in white, and where have they come from?" I said to him, "Sir, you are the one that knows." Then he said to me, "These are they who have come out of the great ordeal; they have washed their robes and made them white in the blood of the Lamb. For this reason they are before the throne of God, and worship him day and night within his temple, and the one who is seated on the throne will shelter them. They will hunger no more, and thirst no more; the sun will not strike them, nor any scorching heat; for the Lamb at the center of the throne will be their shepherd, and he will guide them to springs of the water of life, and God will wipe away every tear from their eyes."

The Response   **Psalm 34:1-10, 22**

Psalm 34:1-10, 22   *Benedicam Dominum*

1   I will bless the LORD at all times; *
       his praise shall ever be in my mouth.
2   I will glory in the LORD; *
       let the humble hear and rejoice.
3   Proclaim with me the greatness of the LORD;
       let us exalt his Name together.
4   I sought the LORD, and he answered me *
       and delivered me out of all my terror.
5   Look upon him and be radiant, *
       and let not your faces be ashamed.
6   I called in my affliction and the LORD heard me *
       and saved me from all my troubles.
7   The angel of the LORD encompasses those who fear him, *
       and he will deliver them.

8   Taste and see that the Lord is good; *
      happy are they who trust in him!
9   Fear the Lord, you that are his saints, *
      for those who fear him lack nothing.
10   The young lions lack and suffer hunger, *
      but those who seek the Lord lack nothing that is good.
22   The Lord ransoms the life of his servants, *
      and none will be punished who trust in him.

The Epistle   1 John 3:1-3

See what love the Father has given us, that we should be called children of God; and that is what we are. The reason the world does not know us is that it did not know him. Beloved, we are God's children now; what we will be has not yet been revealed. What we do know is this: when he is revealed, we will be like him, for we will see him as he is. And all who have this hope in him purify themselves, just as he is pure.

The Gospel   Matthew 5:1-12

When Jesus saw the crowds, he went up the mountain; and after he sat down, his disciples came to him. Then he began to speak, and taught them, saying: "Blessed are the poor in spirit, for theirs is the kingdom of heaven. Blessed are those who mourn, for they will be comforted. Blessed are the meek, for they will inherit the earth. Blessed are those who hunger and thirst for righteousness, for they will be filled. Blessed are the merciful, for they will receive mercy. Blessed are the pure in heart, for they will see God. Blessed are the peacemakers, for they will be called children of God. Blessed are those who are persecuted for righteousness' sake, for theirs is the kingdom of heaven. Blessed are you when people revile you and persecute you and utter all kinds of evil against you falsely on my account. Rejoice and be glad, for your reward is great in heaven, for in the same way they persecuted the prophets who were before you."

Year B

Wisdom of Solomon 3:1-9 or *Isaiah 25:6-9*
Psalm 24
Revelation 21:1-6a
John 11:32-44

The Lesson   Wisdom of Solomon 3:1-9 *or* Isaiah 25:6-9
Wisdom of Solomon 3:1-9

The souls of the righteous are in the hand of God, and no torment will ever touch them. In the eyes of the foolish they seemed to have died, and their departure was thought to be a disaster, and their going from us to be their destruction; but they are at peace. For though in the sight of others they were punished, their hope is full of immortality. Having been disciplined a little, they will receive great good, because God tested them and found them worthy of himself; like gold in the furnace he tried them, and like a sacrificial burnt offering he accepted them. In the time of their visitation they will shine forth, and will run like sparks through the stubble. They will govern nations and rule over peoples, and the Lord will reign over them forever. Those who trust in him will understand truth, and the faithful will abide with him in love, because grace and mercy are upon his holy ones, and he watches over his elect.

or, Isaiah 25:6-9

On this mountain the Lord of hosts will make for all peoples a feast of rich food, a feast of well-aged wines, of rich food filled with marrow, of well-aged wines strained clear. And he will destroy on this mountain the shroud that is cast over all peoples, the sheet that is spread over all nations; he will swallow up death forever. Then the Lord God will wipe away the tears from all faces, and the disgrace of his people he will take away from all the earth, for the Lord has spoken. It will be said on that day, Lo, this is our God; we have waited for him, so that he might save us. This is the Lord for whom we have waited; let us be glad and rejoice in his salvation.

The Response   Psalm 24

Psalm 24 *Domini est terra*

1 The earth is the Lord's and all that is in it, *
    the world and all who dwell therein.
2 For it is he who founded it upon the seas *
    and made it firm upon the rivers of the deep.
3 "Who can ascend the hill of the Lord? *
    and who can stand in his holy place?"
4 "Those who have clean hands and a pure heart, *
    who have not pledged themselves to falsehood,
    nor sworn by what is a fraud.
5 They shall receive a blessing from the Lord *
    and a just reward from the God of their salvation."
6 Such is the generation of those who seek him, *
    of those who seek your face, O God of Jacob.
7 Lift up your heads, O gates;
  lift them high, O everlasting doors; *
    and the King of glory shall come in.
8 "Who is this King of glory?" *
    "The Lord, strong and mighty,
    the Lord, mighty in battle."

9   Lift up your heads, O gates;
     lift them high, O everlasting doors; *
          and the King of glory shall come in.
10   "Who is he, this King of glory?" *
          "The LORD of hosts,
          he is the King of glory."

The Epistle   Revelation 21:1-6*a*

Then I (John) saw a new heaven and a new earth; for the first heaven and the
first earth had passed away, and the sea was no more. And I saw the holy city,
the new Jerusalem, coming down out of heaven from God, prepared as a bride
adorned for her husband. And I heard a loud voice from the throne saying,
"See, the home of God is among mortals. He will dwell with them as their
God; they will be his peoples, and God himself will be with them; he will wipe
every tear from their eyes. Death will be no more; mourning and crying and
pain will be no more, for the first things have passed away." And the one who
was seated on the throne said, "See, I am making all things new." Also he
said, "Write this, for these words are trustworthy and true." Then he said to
me, "It is done! I am the Alpha and the Omega, the beginning and the end. To
the thirsty I will give water as a gift from the spring of the water of life."

The Gospel   John 11:32-44

When Mary came where Jesus was and saw him, she knelt at his feet and said
to him, "Lord, if you had been here, my brother would not have died." When
Jesus saw her weeping, and the Jews who came with her also weeping, he was
greatly disturbed in spirit and deeply moved. He said, "Where have you laid
him?" They said to him, "Lord, come and see." Jesus began to weep. So the
Jews said, "See how he loved him!" But some of them said, "Could not he
who opened the eyes of the blind man have kept this man from dying?" Then
Jesus, again greatly disturbed, came to the tomb. It was a cave, and a stone
was lying against it. Jesus said, "Take away the stone." Martha, the sister of
the dead man, said to him, "Lord, already there is a stench because he has
been dead four days." Jesus said to her, "Did I not tell you that if you believed, you would see the glory of God?" So they took away the stone. And
Jesus looked upward and said, "Father, I thank you for having heard me. I
knew that you always hear me, but I have said this for the sake of the crowd
standing here, so that they may believe that you sent me." When he had said
this, he cried with a loud voice, "Lazarus, come out!" The dead man came
out, his hands and feet bound with strips of cloth, and his face wrapped in a
cloth. Jesus said to them, "Unbind him, and let him go."

Daniel 7:1-3, 15-18
Psalm 149
Ephesians 1:11-23
Luke 6:20-31

The Lesson   **Daniel 7:1-3, 15-18**

In the first year of King Belshazzar of Babylon, Daniel had a dream and visions of his head as he lay in bed. Then he wrote down the dream: I, Daniel, saw in my vision by night the four winds of heaven stirring up the great sea, and four great beasts came up out of the sea, different from one another. As for me, Daniel, my spirit was troubled within me, and the visions of my head terrified me. I approached one of the attendants to ask him the truth concerning all this. So he said that he would disclose to me the interpretation of the matter: "As for these four great beasts, four kings shall arise out o the earth. But the holy ones of the Most High shall receive the kingdom and possess the kingdom forever — forever and ever.

The Response   **Psalm 149**

Psalm 149 *Cantate Domino*

  1 Hallelujah!
      Sing to the LORD a new song; *
         sing his praise in the congregation of the faithful.
  2 Let Israel rejoice in his Maker; *
         let the children of Zion be joyful in their King.
  3 Let them praise his Name in the dance; *
         let them sing praise to him with timbrel and harp.
  4 For the LORD takes pleasure in his people *
         and adorns the poor with victory.
  5 Let the faithful rejoice in triumph; *
         let them be joyful on their beds.
  6 Let the praises of God be in their throat *
         and a two-edged sword in their hand;
  7 To wreak vengeance on the nations *
         and punishment on the peoples;
  8 To bind their kings in chains *
         and their nobles with links of iron;
  9 To inflict on them the judgment decreed; *
         this is glory for all his faithful people.
         Hallelujah!

The Epistle   **Ephesians 1:11-23**

In Christ we have also obtained an inheritance, having been destined according to the purpose of him who accomplishes all things according to his counsel and will, so that we, who were the first to set our hope on Christ, might live for the praise of his glory. In him you also, when you had heard the word of truth, the gospel of your salvation, and had believed in him, were marked with the seal of the promised Holy Spirit; this is the pledge of our inheritance toward redemption as God's own people, to the praise of his glory. I have heard of your faith in the Lord Jesus and your love toward all the saints, and for this reason I do not cease to give thanks for you as I remember you in my prayers. I pray that the God of our Lord Jesus Christ, the Father of glory, may give you a spirit of wisdom and revelation as you come to know him, so that, with the eyes of your heart enlightened, you may know what is the hope to which he has called you, what are the riches of his glorious inheritance among the saints, and what is the immeasurable greatness of his power for us who believe, according to the working of his great power. God put this power to work in Christ when he raised him from the dead and seated him at his right hand in the heavenly places, far above all rule and authority and power and dominion, and above every name that is named, not only in this age but also in the age to come. And he has put all things under his feet and has made him the head over all things for the church, which is his body, the fullness of him who fills all in all.

The Gospel   **Luke 6:20-31**

Then Jesus looked up at his disciples and said: "Blessed are you who are poor, for yours is the kingdom of God. Blessed are you who are hungry now, for you will be filled. Blessed are you who weep now, for you will laugh. Blessed are you when people hate you, and when they exclude you, revile you, and defame you on account of the Son of Man. Rejoice in that day and leap for joy, for surely your reward is great in heaven; for that is what their ancestors did to the prophets. But woe to you who are rich, for you have received your consolation. Woe to you who are full now, for you will be hungry. Woe to you who are laughing now, for you will mourn and weep. Woe to you when all speak well of you, for that is what their ancestors did to the false prophets. But I say to you that listen, Love your enemies, do good to those who hate you, bless those who curse you, pray for those who abuse you. If anyone strikes you on the cheek, offer the other also; and from anyone who takes away your coat do not withhold even your shirt. Give to everyone who begs from you; and if anyone takes away your goods, do not ask for them again. Do to others as you would have them do to you."

THANKSGIVING DAY

The Collect

Almighty and gracious Father, we give you thanks for the fruits of the earth in their season and for the labors of those who harvest them. Make us, we pray, faithful stewards of your great bounty, for the provision of our necessities and the relief of all who are in need, to the glory of your Name; through Jesus Christ our Lord, who lives and reigns with you and the Holy Spirit, one God, now and for ever. *Amen.*

Year A
Deuteronomy 8:7-18
Psalm 65
2 Corinthians 9:6-15
Luke 17:11-19

The Lesson   **Deuteronomy 8:7-18**

Moses said: For the LORD your God is bringing you into a good land, a land with flowing streams, with springs and underground waters welling up in valleys and hills, a land of wheat and barley, of vines and fig trees and pomegranates, a land of olive trees and honey, a land where you may eat bread without scarcity, where you will lack nothing, a land whose stones are iron and from whose hills you may mine copper. You shall eat your fill and bless the LORD your God for the good land that he has given you. Take care that you do not forget the LORD your God, by failing to keep his commandments, his ordinances, and his statutes, which I am commanding you today. When you have eaten your fill and have built fine houses and live in them, and when your herds and flocks have multiplied, and your silver and gold is multiplied, and all that you have is multiplied, then do not exalt yourself, forgetting the LORD your God, who brought you out of the land of Egypt, out of the house of slavery, who led you through the great and terrible wilderness, an arid wasteland with poisonous snakes and scorpions. He made water flow for you from flint rock, and fed you in the wilderness with manna that your ancestors did not know, to humble you and to test you, and in the end to do you good. Do not say to yourself, "My power and the might of my own hand have gotten me this wealth." But remember the LORD your God, for it is he who gives you power to get wealth, so that he may confirm his covenant that he swore to your ancestors, as he is doing today.

The Response   Psalm 65

Psalm 65   *Te decet hymnus*

1 You are to be praised, O God, in Zion; *
    to you shall vows be performed in Jerusalem.

2 To you that hear prayer shall all flesh come, *
    because of their transgressions.

3 Our sins are stronger than we are, *
    but you will blot them out.

4 Happy are they whom you choose
and draw to your courts to dwell there! *
    they will be satisfied by the beauty of your house,
    by the holiness of your temple.

5 Awesome things will you show us in your righteousness,
O God of our salvation, *
    O Hope of all the ends of the earth
    and of the seas that are far away.

6 You make fast the mountains by your power; *
    they are girded about with might.

7 You still the roaring of the seas, *
    the roaring of their waves,
    and the clamor of the peoples.

8 Those who dwell at the ends of the earth will tremble at your
              marvelous signs; *
    you make the dawn and the dusk to sing for joy.

9 You visit the earth and water it abundantly;
you make it very plenteous; *
    the river of God is full of water.

10 You prepare the grain, *
    for so you provide for the earth.

11 You drench the furrows and smooth out the ridges; *
    with heavy rain you soften the ground and bless its increase.

12 You crown the year with your goodness, *
    and your paths overflow with plenty.

13 May the fields of the wilderness be rich for grazing, *
    and the hills be clothed with joy.

14 May the meadows cover themselves with flocks,
and the valleys cloak themselves with grain; *
    let them shout for joy and sing.

The Epistle   2 Corinthians 9:6-15

The point is this: the one who sows sparingly will also reap sparingly, and the one who sows bountifully will also reap bountifully. Each of you must give as you have made up your mind, not reluctantly or under compulsion, for God loves a cheerful giver. And God is able to provide you with every blessing in abundance, so that by always having enough of everything, you may share abundantly in every good work. As it is written, "He scatters abroad, he gives to the poor; his righteousness endures forever." He who supplies seed to the sower and bread for food will supply and multiply your seed for sowing and increase the harvest of your righteousness. You will be enriched in every way for your great generosity, which will produce thanksgiving to God through us; for the rendering of this ministry not only supplies the needs of the saints but also overflows with many thanksgivings to God. Through the testing of this ministry you glorify God by your obedience to the confession of the gospel of Christ and by the generosity of your sharing with them and with all others, while they long for you and pray for you because of the surpassing grace of God that he has given you. Thanks be to God for his indescribable gift!

The Gospel   Luke 17:11-19
On the way to Jerusalem Jesus was going through the region between Samaria and Galilee. As he entered a village, ten lepers approached him. Keeping their distance, they called out, saying, "Jesus, Master, have mercy on us!" When he saw them, he said to them, "Go and show yourselves to the priests." And as they went, they were made clean. Then one of them, when he saw that he was healed, turned back, praising God with a loud voice. He prostrated himself at Jesus' feet and thanked him. And he was a Samaritan. Then Jesus asked, "Were not ten made clean? But the other nine, where are they? Was none of them found to return and give praise to God except this foreigner?" Then he said to him, "Get up and go on your way; your faith has made you well."

Year B
Joel 2:21-27
Psalm 126
1 Timothy 2:1-7
Matthew 6:25-33

The Lesson   Joel 2:21-27
Do not fear, O soil; be glad and rejoice, for the Lord has done great things! Do not fear, you animals of the field, for the pastures of the wilderness are green; the tree bears its fruit, the fig tree and vine give their full yield. O children of Zion, be glad and rejoice in the Lord your God; for he has given the early rain for your vindication, he has poured down for you abundant rain, the early and the later rain, as before. The threshing floors shall be full of grain, the vats shall overflow with wine and oil. I will repay you for the years that the swarming locust has eaten, the hopper, the destroyer, and the cutter, my great army, which I sent against you. You shall eat in plenty and be

satisfied, and praise the name of the LORD your God, who has dealt wondrously with you. And my people shall never again be put to shame. You shall know that I am in the midst of Israel, and that I, the LORD, am your God and there is no other. And my people shall never again be put to shame.

The Response   Psalm 126

Psalm 126 *In convertendo*

1   When the LORD restored the fortunes of Zion, *
        then were we like those who dream.
2   Then was our mouth filled with laughter, *
        and our tongue with shouts of joy.
3   Then they said among the nations, *
        "The LORD has done great things for them."
4   The LORD has done great things for us, *
        and we are glad indeed.
5   Restore our fortunes, O LORD, *
        like the watercourses of the Negev.
6   Those who sowed with tears *
        will reap with songs of joy.
7   Those who go out weeping, carrying the seed, *
        will come again with joy, shouldering their sheaves.

The Epistle   1 Timothy 2:1-7

First of all, then, I urge that supplications, prayers, intercessions, and thanksgivings be made for everyone, for kings and all who are in high positions, so that we may lead a quiet and peaceable life in all godliness and dignity. This is right and is acceptable in the sight of God our Savior, who desires everyone to be saved and to come to the knowledge of the truth. For there is one God; there is also one mediator between God and humankind, Christ Jesus, himself human, who gave himself a ransom for all — this was attested at the right time. For this I was appointed a herald and an apostle (I am telling the truth, I am not lying), a teacher of the Gentiles in faith and truth.

The Gospel   Matthew 6:25-33

Jesus said, "Therefore I tell you, do not worry about your life, what you will eat or what you will drink, or about your body, what you will wear. Is not life more than food, and the body more than clothing? Look at the birds of the air; they neither sow nor reap nor gather into barns, and yet your heavenly Father feeds them. Are you not of more value than they? And can any of you by worrying add a single hour to your span of life? And why do you worry about clothing? Consider the lilies of the field, how they grow; they neither toil nor spin, yet I tell you, even Solomon in all his glory was not clothed like one of these. But if God so clothes the grass of the field, which is alive today and tomorrow is thrown into the oven, will he not much more clothe you — you of little faith? Therefore do not worry, saying, 'What will we eat?' or 'What will we drink?' or 'What will we wear?' For it is the Gentiles who strive for all these things; and indeed your heavenly Father knows that you need all these things. But strive first for the kingdom of God and his righteousness, and all these things will be given to you as well.

Year C
Deuteronomy 26:1-11
Psalm 100
Philippians 4:4-9
John 6:25-35

The Lesson   **Deuteronomy 26:1-11**

Moses said: When you have come into the land that the LORD your God is giving you as an inheritance to possess, and you possess it, and settle in it, you shall take some of the first of all the fruit of the ground, which you harvest from the land that the LORD your God is giving you, and you shall put it in a basket and go to the place that the LORD your God will choose as a dwelling for his name. You shall go to the priest who is in office at that time, and say to him, "Today I declare to the LORD your God that I have come into the land that the LORD swore to our ancestors to give us." When the priest takes the basket from your hand and sets it down before the altar of the LORD your God, you shall make this response before the LORD your God: "A wandering Aramean was my ancestor; he went down into Egypt and lived there as an alien, few in number, and there he became a great nation, mighty and populous. When the Egyptians treated us harshly and afflicted us, by imposing hard labor on us, we cried to the LORD, the God of our ancestors; the LORD heard our voice and saw our affliction, our toil, and our oppression. The LORD brought us out of Egypt with a mighty hand and an outstretched arm, with a terrifying display of power, and with signs and wonders; and he brought us into this place and gave us this land, a land flowing with milk and honey. So now I bring the first of the fruit of the ground that you, O LORD, have given me." You shall set it down before the LORD your God and bow down before the LORD your God. Then you, together with the Levites and the aliens who reside among you, shall celebrate with all the bounty that the LORD your God has given to you and to your house.

The Response   **Psalm 100**

Psalm 100 *Jubilate Deo*

1   Be joyful in the LORD, all you lands; *
          serve the LORD with gladness
          and come before his presence with a song.

2 Know this: The LORD himself is God; *
    he himself has made us, and we are his;
        we are his people and the sheep of his pasture.

3 Enter his gates with thanksgiving;
    go into his courts with praise; *
        give thanks to him and call upon his Name.

4 For the LORD is good;
    his mercy is everlasting; *
        and his faithfulness endures from age to age.

The Epistle   Philippians 4:4-9

Rejoice in the Lord always; again I will say, Rejoice. Let your gentleness be known to everyone. The Lord is near. Do not worry about anything, but in everything by prayer and supplication with thanksgiving let your requests be made known to God. And the peace of God, which surpasses all understanding, will guard your hearts and your minds in Christ Jesus. Finally, beloved, whatever is true, whatever is honorable, whatever is just, whatever is pure, whatever is pleasing, whatever is commendable, if there is any excellence and if there is anything worthy of praise, think about these things. Keep on doing the things that you have learned and received and heard and seen in me, and the God of peace will be with you.

The Gospel   John 6:25-35

When the crowd found Jesus on the other side of the sea, they said to him, "Rabbi, when did you come here?" Jesus answered them, "Very truly, I tell you, you are looking for me, not because you saw signs, but because you ate your fill of the loaves. Do not work for the food that perishes, but for the food that endures for eternal life, which the Son of Man will give you. For it is on him that God the Father has set his seal." Then they said to him, "What must we do to perform the works of God?" Jesus answered them, "This is the work of God, that you believe in him whom he has sent." So they said to him, "What sign are you going to give us then, so that we may see it and believe you? What work are you performing? Our ancestors ate the manna in the wilderness; as it is written, 'He gave them bread from heaven to eat.' " Then Jesus said to them, "Very truly, I tell you, it was not Moses who gave you the bread from heaven, but it is my Father who gives you the true bread from heaven. For the bread of God is that which comes down from heaven and gives life to the world." They said to him, "Sir, give us this bread always." Jesus said to them, "I am the bread of life. Whoever comes to me will never be hungry, and whoever believes in me will never be thirsty."

INDEX

Old Testament

Apocrypha

New Testament